SEVENTH EDITION

THE
UNITED STATES
Becoming a World Power

Volume II

Leon F. Litwack
University of California, Berkeley

Winthrop D. Jordan
University of Mississippi

Prentice Hall, Englewood Cliffs, New Jersey 07632

Library of Congress Cataloging-in-Publication Data

Jordan, Winthrop D.
      The United States/Winthrop D. Jordan, Leon F. Litwack.— 7th
ed.
          p.   cm.
      Updated ed. of: The United States/Winthrop D. Jordan . . . [et
al.].
      Issued also in 1 v.
      Includes bibliographical references and index.
      Contents: v. 1. Conquering a continent — v. 2. Becoming a world
power.
      ISBN 0-13-933516-1 (v. 1). — ISBN 0-13-933490-4 (v. 2)
      -1. United States — History. I. Litwack, Leon F. II. United
States. III. Title.
E178.1.J8 1991
973 — dc20

Editorial/production supervision: *Kathleen Schiaparelli*
Interior design: *Judith A. Matz-Coniglio*
Manufacturing buyers: *Debbie Kesar and Mary Ann Gloriande*
Cover photo: *"Sixth Avenue Elevated at Third Street" (1928) by John Sloan. Oil on
    canvas, 30 × 40". Collection of Whitney Museum of American Art. Purchase 36.154.*
Cover designer: *CIRCA 86, Inc.*
Photo editor: *Lorinda Morris-Nantz*
Photo research: *Barbara Schultz*

© 1991, 1987, 1982, 1976, 1972, 1967, 1957 by Prentice-Hall, Inc.
A Division of Simon & Schuster
Englewood Cliffs, New Jersey 07632

Printed in the United States of America

10 9 8 7 6 5 4 3 2

ISBN 0-13-933490-4

Prentice-Hall International (UK) Limited, *London*
Prentice-Hall of Australia Pty. Limited, *Sydney*
Prentice-Hall Canada Inc., *Toronto*
Prentice-Hall Hispanoamericana, S.A., *Mexico*
Prentice-Hall of India Private Limited, *New Delhi*
Prentice-Hall of Japan, Inc., *Tokyo*
Simon & Schuster Asia Pte. Ltd., *Singapore*
Editora Prentice-Hall do Brasil, Ltda., *Rio de Janeiro*

CONTENTS

CHAPTER 19

THE LAST AMERICAN WEST 419

CHAPTER 20

THE NEW INDUSTRIAL SOCIETY 439

CHAPTER 21

PARTIES, POLITICS, AND REFORM 469

CHAPTER 22

THE EMERGENCE OF URBAN AMERICA   497

CHAPTER 23

CULTURE AND THOUGHT   521

CHAPTER 24

THE AMERICAN EMPIRE   545

CHAPTER 25

PEOPLE AND POLITICS: THE PROGRESSIVE ERA   569

CHAPTER 26

WORLD WAR AND WORLD REVOLUTION   605

CHAPTER 27

THE TWENTIES: BUSINESS AND CULTURE   625

CHAPTER 28

THE GREAT DEPRESSION AND THE NEW DEAL   663

CHAPTER 29

THE AGE OF VIOLENCE: WORLD WAR II   695

CHAPTER 30

THE SEARCH FOR SECURITY 729

CHAPTER 31

SUPERPOWERS IN THE MISSILE AGE 765

CHAPTER 32

CRUMBLING CONSENSUS 795

CHAPTER 33

THE POLITICS OF RIGHTEOUSNESS: NIXON AND CARTER   831

CHAPTER 34

TOWARD A NEW CENTURY: AMERICA IN THE '80S AND '90S   863

APPENDIX   897

INDEX   909

PHOTO ESSAYS

MAPS AND CHARTS

WORDS AND NAMES
IN AMERICAN HISTORY

A NOTE
OF INTRODUCTION

A word about history. The word *history* has a double meaning. It refers to what did in fact take place in the past. It also refers to our study and understanding of those events and how we talk and write about them.

These two meanings are often confused. We all have met such expressions as "history tells us . . .," "history shows . . .," and "the lessons of history are. . . ." These expressions assume that the actual events of the past can themselves teach us about the present and perhaps even the future. However, past events cannot themselves speak, let alone teach. But we can and do learn from what has been said and written about them. We learn from what other people today are saying about what went on in the past, as well as from what people in *our* past said about *their* past.

Here things get tricky, simply because historians are people. No two historians look at past events in exactly the same manner. They draw differing conclusions about the meaning of what went on and sometimes about what actually did go on. They also disagree about what was important enough to bother discussing. For example, historians still disagree as to exactly when President Woodrow Wilson suffered his first stroke. At a different level of inquiry, they disagree about the causes and consequences of the American Civil War and the Cold War. Today, much more than they used to, historians are learning and writing about the lives of ordinary men and women. Whether Joe and Josephine Smith went to the supermarket on October 4, 1958, is in itself obviously not of great importance, but the fact that millions of Americans were getting their food in

such a manner obviously is, especially since we know that the Smiths' parents could not have fed themselves or their families in that manner.

Why bother with the past in any form? The most basic answer is that we cannot do without it. As individuals, we use it all the time. Each of us lives in the present, but our immediate experiences, thoughts, and perceptions are shaped by our previous ones. We are what we have been—and what we think we have been. An important part of our present is our awareness of our past. Similarly, an entire society is shaped by its past and by its consciousness of that past. As individuals and as a nation, we cannot tell where we are (much less where we are going) without knowing where we have been. And because the United States is a vast and profoundly complex entity, including over the years more than half a billion individual lives and millions of group, the task of understanding this nation is not an easy one. But it can be very rewarding and even fun.

This book has a number of thematic chapters, such as those dealing with important intellectual and literary developments. Nonetheless we have adhered to a fundamentally chronological structure, an approach that is dictated by the unfolding of events. We are convinced that anyone who thinks that the U.S. Constitution was adopted before the American Revolution is not going to be able to understand either of those two major developments. The same may be said of the Vietnam War and World War II, or of the invention of the atomic bomb and creation of the steam engine.

A few words about this substantially revised

edition of *The United States*. We have tried to convey both the personalities and importance of such public leaders as George Whitefield, John Calhoun, and Dorothea Dix; of Franklin Roosevelt, Martin Luther King, Jr., and Ronald Reagan. We have also emphasized the history of less powerful people. The ordinary folk who have made up the great bulk of American society expressed themselves in various ways in the past, as they still do today. We have stressed their experiences and their voices—the lives of Indians, blacks, Hispanic Americans, and dozens of immigrant groups from Europe and Asia, as well as working people in the fields, boats, shops, factories, mines, and homes of the nation.

This edition has much more about women because a solid body of scholarship in women's history has emerged in very recent years. We have dealt with women in such various roles as young daughters and child laborers, mothers and grandmothers, factory and office workers, farmers and westward pioneers, reformers, intellectuals, professionals, and politicians. As we have with ethnic, racial, and religious groups, we have dealt with the record of women's achievements and with the record of the obstacles and defeats that barred their way.

This edition also includes a unique feature—a series of boxes entitled "Words and Names in American History." These are miniature essays about the specifically American background of words that are in common use today, or were until quite recently. Some are political, such as *lobby, logrolling, gerrymander,* and *platform;* others are geographical, such as *Mississippi, Wall Street,* and the *Mason-Dixon line;* still others defy classification, such as *Uncle Sam, cafeteria, deadline, lynch,* and *hazing.* All of them cast small shafts of light on the American past.

Finally, we have tried to set American history into the context of global history, to convey American developments as they related to the ongoing development of the rapidly modernizing society in which the inhabitants of the entire world are participants, whether they wish to be or not.

This book derives from one first published in 1957 by Richard Hofstadter. William Miller, and Daniel Aaron. Since then it has been successively revised, after 1976 by the present two authors. As with the previous edition, the text of the chapters through the Civil War is by Winthrop Jordan; those from Reconstruction and Restoration to the present, by Leon Litwack.

Both of us hope that readers of this book will gain more than a formal knowledge of American history. We hope they will also gain an appreciation of the richness and diversity of American cultural expression, and a deeper, more subtle sense of what it means to live in this somewhat ambiguous, ever-changing nation.

A number of teaching and learning aids are available with the text. These include a **Two-Volume Study Guide,** prepared by Elizabeth Neumeyer of Kellogg Community College, Battle Creek, Michigan. An **Instructor's Manual,** authored by Robert Tomes of St. John's University, Staten Island New York and a **Test Item File** by Paul Harvey of the University of California at Berkeley provide, respectively, teaching suggestions, chapter outlines, and film lists, and over one thousand objective-test and essay questions. The material in the Test Item File is also available on **Floppy Disk** for the IBM and compatible computers, or the instructor may make use of Prentice-Hall's **Telephone Test Preparation Service. Full-color Transparencies** of over eighty maps are available on adoption, as are **Free Videos and Films** of high quality, award-winning documentaries, and docudramas.

Many instructors read the manuscript of the text and offered helpful suggestions for improvement. They include William C. Hine, South Carolina State College; Roger L. Nichols, University of Arizona; George H. Skau, Bergen Community College; Alwyn Barr, Texas Tech University; Robert Haws, University of Mississippi; Robert D. Cross, University of Virginia; Leonard L. Richards, University of Massachusetts; Peyton McCrary, University of South Alabama; Richard Wightman Fox, Yale University; Robert G. Pope, State University of New York at Buffalo; Joseph C. Morton, Northeastern Illinois University; Thomas A. Drueger, University of Illinois at Urbana; John Mayfield, University of Kentucky; Linda Dudik Guerrero, Palomar College; Bradley R. Rice, Clayton Junior College; David C. Hammack, Princeton University; Alasdair Macphail, Connecticut College; Harvey H. Jackson, Clayton Junior College; Jerry Rodnitzky, University of Texas at Arlington; Michael L. Lanza, University of New Orleans; Clarence F. Walker, University of California at Davis; and Ray White, Ball State University. We would especially like to thank our editors at Prentice Hall—Kathleen Schiaparelli, Steve Dalphin, and our copy editor, Bruce Fulton—as well as the many others whose hard work is reflected in this new edition.

Winthrop D. Jordan

Leon F. Litwack

THE
UNITED STATES
Becoming a World Power

FROM THE PLANTATION TO THE SENATE.

CHAPTER 18

AFTER THE WAR: RECONSTRUCTION AND RESTORATION

After four years of warfare, the Union had withstood its most serious challenge. Measured in physical devastation and human lives, the Civil War remains the costliest war in the experience of the American people. When it ended, in April 1865, 620,000 men (in a nation of 35 million) had been killed, at least that many more had been wounded, and portions of the Confederacy lay in ruins. Two questions were firmly settled: the right of a state to secede and the right to own slaves. But new problems soon surfaced that would plunge the nation into still another period of turmoil and uncertainty.

Having won the war, the victors had no rules to guide them in how to reconstruct the South and ensure its future loyalty. Under what conditions should the former Confederate states be permitted to return? What if any punishment should be meted out to those southerners who had led their states out of the Union? Were the nearly 4 million freed slaves entitled to the same rights as white citizens? Finally, where did the responsibility lie for resolving these difficult questions—with the president or with Congress?

Lincoln's view of reconstruction was consistent with his theory of secession and rebellion. He held from the outset that states could not break away from the Union. The Civil War, then, had been an illegal rebellion waged by disloyal men. Now that the rebellion was over, the task of reconstruction consisted simply of restoring loyal governments to the former Confederate states. The rebels themselves could be quickly reinstated as citizens by presidential pardon, and they could then take part in the establishment of the new governments. Although this became known as the "moderate" approach to reconstruction, stressing the president's generous spirit and statesmanship, the meaning of Lincoln's "moderation" should be clearly understood: After agreeing to repudiate secession and to recognize the abolition of slavery, the newly restored southern states would retain the same powers of decision enjoyed by all states, including the right to determine the status of their black residents.

The Radical Republicans, a faction within the party, believed Lincoln's program would hamper their objective; they wanted to rebuild southern society around the equality of newly freed slaves and whites. The rebel states, they argued, had been reduced to the status of territories because of their "rebellion." In seeking statehood once again, they came under the jurisdiction not of the president but of Congress, which governed territorial affairs. This was not simply an argument over the respective powers of the legislative and executive branches of government; it was a battle over the very objectives and content of southern reconstruction.

By his policy, President Lincoln hoped to build a Republican party in the South based on the votes of white men and on the leadership of those who had initially opposed secession. His successor, Andrew Johnson, also advocated a "moderate" approach, based on his strict reading of the Constitution and on his belief in white supremacy. The Radicals, on the other hand, viewed the southern black vote as the only means of winning that section of the country for the Republicans and ensuring the party's national strength. Lincoln and Johnson were willing to entrust the fate of the newly freed slaves to the defeated whites. The Radicals tried to develop a program of civil rights and education that would protect the freed blacks from the defeated whites.

Despite the war and emancipation, the white South's attitude toward blacks remained the same. The "corner-stone" of the Confederacy, Vice-President Alexander Stephens had declared in 1861, "rests upon the great truth, that the negro is not equal to the white man; that slavery— subordination to the superior race—is his natural and normal condition." Even as they acknowledged emancipation, few whites surrendered their justifications for having held black men and women as slaves. A planter in South Carolina gave voice to that sentiment in the questions he asked after the war: "Can not freedmen be organized and disciplined as well as slaves? Is not the dollar as potent as the lash? The belly as tender as the back?"

Neither military defeat nor the collapse of slavery suggested to whites the need to reexamine their racial relationships or assumptions. If anything, the need to maintain white supremacy took on an even greater urgency now that the slaves had been freed. The repression of the newly freed slaves made a shambles of "moderate" or presidential Reconstruction. By refusing to grant blacks minimal civil rights and educational opportunities, the white South succeeded only in alienating northern public opinion, strengthening the Radical position, and helping to make possible Radical or congressional Reconstruction.

Radical rule in the South ended in 1877 (much sooner in most states), having failed to achieve the objective of a democratic, biracial society. That failure does not mean Lincoln's or Johnson's programs would have worked any better. Whatever its shortcomings, Radical Reconstruction transformed the lives of southern blacks and raised black expectations and aspirations. This remarkable but brief experiment in biracial government enabled blacks to gain political experience as voters and officeholders, it brought badly needed reforms to southern society, and it laid the legal foundations for a "second reconstruction" in the 1950s and 1960s, when black leaders and movements would seek to complete the work of emancipation.

THE DEFEATED SOUTH

The Civil War took a heavy toll of families in the North as well as the South, among both whites and blacks. But the physical devastation was largely limited to the South, where almost all the fighting had taken place. Large sections of Richmond, Charleston, Atlanta, Mobile, and Vicksburg had burned to the ground. The countryside through which the armies had passed was littered with gutted plantation houses and barns, burned bridges, and uprooted railroad lines. Many crops had been destroyed or confiscated, and much of the livestock had been slain. To rebuild the devastated areas and to restore agricultural production required outlays of capital and labor that were not readily available.

In the North, the $4 billion in direct wartime expenditures had provided huge profits. But only a few southerners managed to accumulate capital during the war—some by running cotton through the northern blockade; others by demanding gold or goods instead of Confederate paper money in payment for food, clothing, and farm supplies. Most southerners were now poor.

The planters' land, worth $1.5 billion in 1860, was evaluated at half that amount ten years later. The South's $1 billion in banking capital had been wiped out, and its credit system was paralyzed. The money invested in Confederate bonds and currency was lost. Finally, and most critically, the planters' $2.5 billion investment in slaves had vanished, along with many of the slaves.

Aftermath of Slavery

After Appomattox, most planters assembled what blacks were left, acknowledged their freedom, and asked them to work for wages or shares of the crop. Having lived for years in close daily contact with the "white folks," and facing an uncertain future with a vaguely defined freedom, the emancipated slaves had to make some difficult decisions. If they remained on the farms and plantations, what relations would they now have with those who had once owned them? How adequately would they be paid for their labor? If they left, where would they go, and how would they support themselves?

For some, the first need was to take some kind of action to prove to themselves that they were really free. The quickest and most direct test was to leave the plantation. As one newly freed slave explained to his former master, "I must go, for if I stay here I'll never know I am free." By leaving, many expected to improve their economic prospects; others hoped to locate family members from whom they had been separated during slavery; and some expected greater freedom by settling in the nearest town.

To throw off a lifetime of bondage, black men and women adopted different priorities, ranging from dramatic breaks with the past to subtle though no less significant changes in demeanor and behavior. Many did not move at all, at least not in the first postwar year, choosing to remain in familiar surroundings and to find ways of exercising their freedom even as they worked in the same fields and kitchens. "Henney is still with me," a South Carolina white woman said of her former slave, "but she is not the same person that she was."

Family members who had been sold away during slavery sought each other out after emancipation—an effort that spanned several decades for some and ended for many in failure, tragedy, and disappointment. New emotional ties had sometimes replaced the old; husbands and wives who had given up any hope of seeing each other again had remarried, and children sold away from their parents had been raised by other black women or by the white mistress, creating complications. The question facing some freedmen and freedwomen was not whether to formalize their slave marriages, as so many did in the postwar years, but which marriage should take precedence. And that often proved to be a difficult and agonizing decision.

After emancipation, many black women opted to stop working in the fields and kitchens in order to spend more time tending to their own households and children. If the women themselves did not initiate such moves, the men sometimes insisted, as a way of reinforcing their position as head of the family. "When I married my wife," a

WORDS AND NAMES IN AMERICAN HISTORY

The word *miscegenation* refers to interracial sexual contact, with or without resulting children. It was made by combining the Latin *miscere*—to mix—and *genus*—race, people, or even species. The word was minted in 1863, during the Civil War, by two New York newspapermen, David Croly and George Wakeman, who were both antiblack and antiabolitionist. They raised the matter of interracial sex in order to appeal to widely held prejudices against it. Their purposes were primarily political, yet the term has endured, superseding the more common word then in use, *amalgamation*. Perhaps because the word is long and so many Americans feel so awkward about the matter, *miscegenation* is commonly mispronounced: the accents are on the first and fourth syllables.

THE LEGACY OF SLAVERY

Several years after their forced separation during slavery, the husband of Laura Spicer remarried in the belief that his wife had died. When he learned after the war that she was still alive, the news stung him. He dictated a letter to her:

I want to see you and I don't want to see you. I love you just as well as I did the last day I saw you, and it will not do for you and I to meet. I am married, and my wife have two children. . . . You know it never was our wishes to be separated from each other, and it never was our fault. Oh, I can see you so plain, at any-time. I had rather anything to had happened to me most that ever have been parted from you and the children. As I am, I do not know

which I love best, you or Anna. If I was to die, today or tomorrow, I do not think I would die satisfied till you tell me you will try and marry some good, smart man that will take good care of you and the children; and do it because you love me; and not because I think more of the wife I have got than I do of you. The woman is not born that feels as near to me as you do. Tell them [the children] they must remember they have a good father and one that cares for them and one that thinks about them every day.

Source: Henry L. Swint (ed.) *Dear Ones at Home: Letters from Contraband Camps* (Nashville: Vanderbilt University Press, 1966), pp. 242–43. Photograph courtesy of the Cook Collection, Valentine Museum, Richmond.

Tennessee freedman told his employer, in rejecting his request for her services, "I married her to wait on me and she has got all she can do right here for me and the children." But not all black women agreed to such a narrow definition of their roles. And even if they wanted to leave the labor force, they could seldom afford to do so. Many continued to work in the fields alongside their men, in the white family's kitchen, and at other tasks that would supplement the family income. "They do double duty," a black Mississippi woman observed—"a man's share in the field, and a woman's part at home. They do any kind of field work, even ploughing, and at home the cooking, washing, milking and gardening."

That many freedmen and freedwomen changed their lives, displayed feelings of independence, deserted their former owners, seized the land of absentee owners, engaged in work stoppages, sat where they pleased in public places and vehicles, and no longer felt the need to humble themselves

in the presence of whites should not obscure the extent to which life went on very much as it had before the war. As long as whites had political and economic dominance, they were in a position to control the very content of black freedom. "The Master he say we are all free," a former South Carolina slave recalled, "but it don't mean we is white. And it don't mean we is equal. Just equal for to work and earn our living and not depend on him for no more meats and clothes."

During the war, various plans were advanced to help blacks who sought shelter and freedom behind Union lines. With federal approval, blacks in portions of the occupied South—as on the Sea Islands along the South Carolina coast and on the land in Mississippi that had belonged to Jefferson Davis and his brother—were permitted to work on the plantations with the expectation of dividing the crops and carving out plots of land for themselves. Some abandoned lands were offered on easy terms to former slaves, and many of them on easy terms to former slaves, and many of them did well as independent farmers. But most of the land was ultimately returned to its original owners, and the freedmen's goal of becoming landowning farmers remained unrealized.

To ease the transition from slavery to freedom, Congress in March 1865 created the Freedmen's Bureau. It was authorized to furnish food, clothing, and transportation to refugees and freed blacks, to oversee labor contracts, and to settle freedmen on abandoned or confiscated lands. Although the bureau provided relief, tried to ensure the fairness of labor contracts, and helped to maintain schools for black children, it never fulfilled its promise or potential.

Oliver Otis Howard, the bureau's commissioner and a founder of Howard University, was well meaning and sympathetic, as were a number of the field agents. But many of the regional and local officers were more concerned with gaining the approval of the white communities in which they worked. Too often, bureau officers thought their main responsibility was to get the ex-slaves to accept contracts with their former masters and to prevent them from drifting into the towns. Some of the more dedicated officers who identified with the freed blacks' cause found themselves quickly removed under President Johnson.

With capital and even food in short supply, white farmers and planters often did little better than the blacks. Famine struck many parts of the South in the middle of the war. Afterward, wartime systems of relief collapsed in the general ruin of the Confederacy. In the first four years after the war, the Freedmen's Bureau fed thousands of starving whites as well as blacks. In several instances, the ex-slaves themselves came to the assistance of their former masters and mistresses, some by making small contributions for their welfare, others by agreeing to stay with those who seemed incapable of running the plantations without them.

Perhaps the heaviest blow to the white South was the moral and psychic cost of war and defeat. Purpose, morale, and aspiration declined. The losses in youth and talent hurt beyond measure. And it had all been in vain—the suffering, the self-sacrifice, the devastation. That was the most difficult fact to accept. "Now we belong to Negroes and Yankees," a South Carolina woman cried in despair. Emancipation, moreover, forcibly reminded former slaveholding families of how dependent they remained on their black laborers, of how helpless they were. "They need us all the time," a black domestic recalled.

They don't want no food unless a nigger cooks it. They want niggers to do all their washing and ironing. They want niggers to do their sweeping and cleaning and everything around their houses. The niggers handle everything they wears and hands them everything they eat and drink. Ain't nobody can get closer to a white person than a colored person. If we'd a wanted to kill 'em, they'd all done been dead.

With equal frankness, a Virginia planter conceded his dependence on black labor: "I must have niggers to work for me. I can't do nothin' on my place without 'em. If they send all the niggers to Africa, I'll have to go thar, too."

The former slaveholding class seemed less equipped, mentally and physically, to make the transition from slave to free labor than their former slaves. No matter how hard a few of them tried, they seemed incapable of learning new ways and shaking off old attitudes. That failure was demonstrated during presidential Reconstruction, when the white South was given the opportunity to reconstruct itself with a minimum of federal interference.

Lincoln's Plan

The Civil War began as a war with limited objectives. The Crittenden Resolution, adopted by the House of Representatives on July 22, 1861, with only two dissenting votes, made those objectives abundantly clear:

This war is not waged . . . for any purpose . . . but to defend and maintain the supremacy of the Constitution and to preserve the Union, with all the dignity, equality, and rights of the several States unimpaired; and . . . as soon as these objects are accomplished the war ought to cease.

Three days later, the Senate adopted an almost identical resolution. Although the Emancipation Proclamation broadened the objectives of the war, President Lincoln remained faithful to the spirit of the resolution.

When in 1862 much of Tennessee, Louisiana, and North Carolina had fallen, Lincoln appointed military governors to bring these states into conformity with the Constitution. On December 8, 1863, with still other rebel states on the verge of surrender, the president issued his Proclamation of Amnesty and Reconstruction, which became known as the "10 percent plan" and set forth the terms by which the southern states would be restored to the Union.

Except for high military and civil officers of the

Confederacy, any southern citizen would be granted amnesty by the president after taking an oath of loyalty to the Constitution and the laws of the Union. Confiscated property other than slaves would be restored. As soon as 10 percent of those who had voted in the presidential election of 1860 had taken the oath and sworn allegiance to the Union, that state could proceed to write a new constitution, elect new state officers, and send members to the United States Congress. The House and Senate, of course, retained their constitutional privilege of seating or rejecting such members.

The president failed to confront the social realities of emancipation. Lincoln assured the states to which his proclamation applied that he would not object to "any provision" they might wish to make regarding the freed slaves "which may yet be consistent with their present condition as a laboring, landless, and homeless class." This was nothing short of an invitation to the former Confederate states to adopt the inflammatory Black Codes they enacted in 1865 and 1866.

Until late in the war, Lincoln still held that the best way to deal with "the Negro problem" was to persuade blacks to leave the country. "There is an unwillingness on the part of our people, harsh as it may be, for you free colored people to remain with us," he told a black delegation in August 1862. "It is better for us both, therefore, to be separated." But black leaders rejected Lincoln's colonization scheme, even as Radical Republicans would reject his "moderate" reconstruction program. In his last public address, on April 11, 1865, Lincoln made no mention of colonizing freed blacks. In defending his reconstruction plan, he suggested that the states might wish to extend the suffrage to "the very intelligent" blacks and to "those who serve our cause as soldiers." That was for the states to decide, however, and it soon became apparent that none of them thought the president's suggestion worthy of serious consideration.

The Radical Plan

In treating the former Confederate states, Lincoln had urged a minimum of federal interference. The Radical Republicans called for a more thorough reconstruction of southern society. Under their program, the power of the old planter class would be destroyed, and the freedom of the emancipated blacks fully protected. Thaddeus Stevens of Pennsylvania, a Radical leader in the House, stated this

position most forcefully. To make the Confederacy "a safe republic," he insisted, "the whole fabric of southern society must be changed."

To Stevens, this meant the confiscation of the estates of the southern ruling class and their distribution to the very people who had made the land productive—the freed slaves. In the Senate, Charles Sumner added his voice to that of Stevens; to preserve the gains of the war, the Union must extend the vote to blacks, he insisted.

Practical political considerations also encouraged Republicans to favor a tougher program. With the abolition of slavery, all freedmen (rather than three-fifths of them) would be counted for purposes of representation. And the reconstructed South would regain its seats in Congress, even if it denied the vote to blacks. That latter fact won over many conservative Republicans, who feared that northern and southern Democrats would again close ranks and overturn Republican economic legislation.

The Wade-Davis bill, adopted by Congress a few days before it adjourned in July 1864, set forth the first Radical response to Lincoln's program. It required a majority of the citizens of a state, not just 10 percent, to swear loyalty to the Union before a provisional governor could call an election for a state constitutional convention. Only those southerners able to swear that they had *always* been loyal to the Union and had not "voluntarily borne arms against the United States" were entitled to vote for delegates to the constitutional conventions. The bill also prescribed that new state constitutions in the South must abolish slavery, repudiate state debts, and deprive former Confederate leaders of the right to vote.

Radical strategists hoped to commit the Republican party to their program in the 1864 presidential campaign. Lincoln attempted to stop them by permitting the Wade-Davis bill to die by a pocket veto. Defending his action, Lincoln said rebel states might follow the Wade-Davis provisions if they wished, but he refused to make them mandatory. Most Radical leaders supported Lincoln in the 1864 campaign because they did not want to disrupt the party and endanger the war effort.

Once the election was over, the Radicals pressed again for their program. In January 1865 they adopted the Thirteenth Amendment, passed by Congress and submitted to the states, which would abolish slavery throughout the United States. (It was ratified in December of that year by the required three-fourths of the states, including eight formerly of the Confederacy, which Congress for other purposes did not even recognize as states.) In February, Congress refused to admit members from Louisiana, which Lincoln had declared "reconstructed" under the 10 percent plan. In March, Congress created the Freedmen's Bureau. With these measures, Congress adjourned. When it reconvened, in December, it would have to deal with a new president and with a South that had been "reconstructed" under the president's plan.

Johnsonian Restoration

When Lincoln died on April 15, 1865, the victim of an assassin's bullet, Andrew Johnson of Tennessee became president. Like Lincoln, he was born in poverty. Uneducated, he was ultimately taught to read by his wife. Unlike Lincoln, he was tactless and inflexible, possessing neither humility nor the capacity for compromise. He rose to political power in nonslaveholding eastern Tennessee. When he told poor farmers of his dislike for rich cotton planters, they rallied to his support. But even though Johnson delighted his constituents with attacks on special privilege and the planter aristocracy, he never became a vocal opponent of slavery, and he held traditional southern views on race relations. "I wish to God," he said on one occasion, "every head of a family in the United States had one slave to take the drudgery and menial service off his family."

He refused, however, to give up his seat in the Senate after Tennessee left the Union. In 1864, as a demonstration of wartime unity, the Republican party nominated Johnson for the vice-presidency even though he had been a Democrat all his life. During the campaign, Johnson made himself attractive to Radicals by his fierce denunciations of rebel leaders as "traitors." But the enthusiasm with which Johnson appeared to have embraced the Radical cause proved to be short-lived.

With Congress still in recess, the new president set out to complete Lincoln's restoration of the South to the Union. Early in May 1865, he recognized Lincoln's "10 percent" governments in Louisiana, Tennessee, Arkansas, and Virginia. He next appointed military governors in the seven states that had not yet complied. On May 29 he offered executive amnesty to all citizens of these states except high Confederate military and civil officers and others owning more than $20,000 worth of property. These people had to apply for amnesty to the president.

The "whitewashed" electorate—that is, those who benefited by the amnesty offer—was then to elect members to a constitutional convention in each state. They were to abolish slavery, rescind the state's secession ordinance, adopt the Thir-

While Thaddeus Stevens (left), House leader of the Radical Republicans, sought to alter "the whole fabric of southern society" and provide a legal and economic underpinning for black freedom, President Johnson (right) proceeded with a restoration of the former Confederate states to the Union that would have permitted southern whites to determine the status of blacks. *(Library of Congress)*

teenth Amendment, repudiate the war debt, and call an election for a new state government. The suffrage for this election was to be determined by each state rather than by Congress, and that clearly meant blacks would be denied participation in southern political life.

By the winter of 1865, all the seceding states but Texas had complied with Johnson's terms. Given the opportunity to reconstruct themselves, the former Confederate states moved quickly to restore the old planter class to political power. The president cooperated in this move. For all his dislike of the southern Old Guard, Johnson's personal grants of amnesty exceeded all bounds. He pardoned the heroes of the "Lost Cause," whom the whitewashed voters proceeded to elect to national, state, and local offices. None other than Alexander Stephens, for example, the former vice-president of the Confederacy, became Georgia's duly elected United States senator.

The spirit that dominated the former Confederate states was apparent not only in the individuals elected to office, but in the decisions made by the new governments. Widespread reluctance to renounce the war debt was accompanied in some states by determination to resist taxation for redemption of the Union debt. That was bound to provoke northern public opinion, as was the legislation adopted to deal with the emancipated slaves.

While ratifying the Thirteenth Amendment as required, the reconstructed states, almost as a unit, warned Congress to leave the status of the freedmen to those who knew them best—the white southerners. And when the new governments confronted the question of what to do with the former slaves, they used the old slave codes and their previous experience with free blacks.

In the Black Codes adopted in 1865 and 1866, the new southern governments recognized the fact of emancipation in some of the rights accorded to blacks for the first time. Although still universally forbidden to serve on juries, even in cases involving blacks, freedmen could now swear out affidavits in criminal cases, sue and be sued in civil actions, appear as witnesses, and otherwise give testimony. Marriages between blacks were to be sanctified under law, but interracial marriages carried sentences of up to life imprisonment for both parties. Blacks could make wills and pass on personal property. Their children could go to school and were to be protected from abuse if they were apprenticed.

But nowhere could blacks bear arms, vote, hold public office, or assemble freely. In some states they could work at any jobs and quit jobs freely. Most states, however, forbade them to leave their jobs except under stated conditions. Nor in some states could they work as artisans, mechanics, or in other capacities in which they competed with white labor. The Mississippi code forbade freedmen to rent or lease land or houses.

The idea behind these codes was that blacks would not work except under compulsion and proper supervision, and with the vigorous enforcement of contracts and vagrancy laws. The vagrancy provisions were the worst. In Georgia, for example, the law said that "all persons wandering or strolling about in idleness, who are able to work and who have no property to support them," could be picked up and tried. If convicted, they could be set to work on state chain gangs or contracted out to planters and other employers who would pay their fines and their upkeep for a stated period.

The Johnson governments confirmed the worst fears and predictions of the Radicals and shocked many moderates. The rapid return to power of the Confederate leadership suggested an unwillingness by the South to accept defeat. By defining the freedman's role in a way that was bound to keep him propertyless and voteless, the Black Codes attempted to deny the fact of black freedom. In the North, the conviction grew that the white South was preparing to regain what it had lost on the battlefield. By their actions, the South and President Johnson had set the stage for Congress to act.

THE RADICAL CONGRESS

When Congress met in December 1865, it was faced with Johnson's actions and the South's responses. As their first countermove, Radicals set up the Joint Committee of Fifteen—six senators and nine representatives—to review the work of presidential reconstruction and the qualifications of those elected by the southern states to serve in Congress. Exercising its constitutional power, Congress refused to seat the southerners. Early in 1866, it enacted a bill continuing the Freedmen's Bureau; Johnson vetoed the bill because he believed that care and protection of the freedmen should be left to the states.

In March 1866 Johnson also vetoed a civil rights bill that forbade states to discriminate among citizens on the basis of color or race, as they had in the Black Codes. By now a sufficient number of conservative senators were ready to join the Radicals in defense of congressional power, if not of Radical principles, and both houses overrode the president. A few months later, in July 1866, Radicals pushed through a second Freedmen's Bureau bill over Johnson's veto.

Even if many Republicans, like their constituents, remained divided over the proper place of blacks in American society, they could agree that the newly freed slaves should be protected in their basic rights and given the opportunity to advance themselves economically. The actions of the southern governments and the president's vetoes undermined those possibilities. With growing unanimity, Republicans now moved to provide a constitutional basis for black freedom.

The Fourteenth Amendment

When Radicals introduced the Fourteenth Amendment in June 1866, they were concerned about the constitutionality of the Civil Rights Act and the danger that another Congress might repeal it. A civil rights amendment would end the constitutional issue and make repeal more difficult. It was perhaps the most far-reaching amendment ever added to the Constitution, but its importance rested largely on how it was later interpreted.

The Fourteenth Amendment, for the first time, defined citizenship in the United States as distinct from citizenship in a state. By identifying as citizens "all persons born or naturalized in the United States," it automatically extended citizenship to American-born blacks. It also forbade any state to abridge "the privileges and immunities" of United States citizens, to "deprive any person of life, liberty, or property, without due process of law," and to "deny to any person within its jurisdiction the equal protection of the laws."

The second section of the amendment did not give blacks the vote, as many Radicals hoped it would, but penalized any state for withholding it. (The penalty was never imposed and was replaced by the Fifteenth Amendment.) The third section disqualified from federal or state office all Confederates who before the war had taken a federal oath of office, unless Congress specifically lifted the disqualification by a two-thirds vote. Finally, the amendment guaranteed the Union debt but outlawed redemption of the Confederate debt and any claims for compensation for loss of slaves.

The Fourteenth Amendment had a stormy history before it was finally ratified in July 1868.

Many years later, the use of the word "person" in the first section of the amendment was interpreted by the federal courts as applying to "legal persons" such as business corporations as well as to blacks, who were the only persons the framers of the amendment had in mind. It thus supplied legal grounds for the courts to declare unconstitutional state regulation of railroads and trusts. Still later, the phrase in Section 1 prohibiting the denial of "equal protection of the laws" supplied legal grounds for the Supreme Court's school desegregation decision in 1954.

As far-reaching as it would become through subsequent interpretation, the Fourteenth Amendment failed to satisfy the Radicals as a final condition for the reconstruction of the southern states. They thought it too full of compromises, and hoped in time to stiffen its provisions. Dissatisfaction with the amendment was also voiced by Susan B. Anthony, Elizabeth Cady Stanton, and other agitators for women's suffrage who had hoped to win the franchise because of women's contributions to victory in the Civil War. They fought to delete the word *male* from the voting provisions of the Fourteenth Amendment and later to add the word *sex* to "race, color, or previous condition of servitude" in the Fifteenth Amendment. But Radical leaders and black activists believed that merging women's rights with blacks' rights would imperil passage of both amendments. Although an abolitionist and an advocate of civil rights, Stanton became so furious over the failure of women to win the vote that she denounced poor, uneducated blacks as a "liability to the electorate and a danger to women."

Radicals demanded that the southern states ratify the Fourteenth Amendment as a condition for regaining representation in Congress. Johnson advised them not to. By mid-February 1867, all but Tennessee—that is, ten of the eleven former Confederate states—had followed his advice. Without the required three-fourths majority of the states, the amendment was dead. But the rejection of the amendment, along with the president's defiance, only reinforced in the minds of Republicans—Radicals and moderates alike—the need to take over southern reconstruction.

The Reconstruction Acts and Impeachment

The Fourteenth Amendment had drawn the issue clearly between president and Congress. In the congressional campaign of 1866, Johnson visited

395

key cities on behalf of candidates who favored his policy. The more the president talked, however, the more he antagonized northern voters. At the same time, racial clashes in New Orleans and Memphis appeared to confirm Radical warnings about the consequences of Johnson's southern policy.

The Democrats tried to exploit northern fears of racial equality, warning that Republican rule would not only Africanize the nation but encourage cheap black labor from the South to compete with northern workers. The Republicans responded with their own appeal, called "waving the bloody shirt," which exploited wartime passions and identified the Democrats with treason. "In short," cried Oliver P. Morton, the Radical governor of Indiana, "the Democratic party may be described as a common sewer and loathsome receptacle, into which is emptied every element of inhumanity and barbarism which has dishonored the age." The strategy worked, and the Radicals won a sweeping electoral victory. With a two-thirds majority in Congress, they would be able to impose even sterner measures and carry them over presidential vetoes.

The Radicals began with the First Reconstruction Act, passed over Johnson's veto on March 2, 1867. Tennessee had been accepted back into the Union in 1866, but all other southern state governments were declared illegal. The South was organized into five military districts, each under a general to be named by the president. The general's main task was to call a new constitutional convention in each state, its delegates to be elected by universal adult male suffrage, black and white, excluding those deprived of the vote under the proposed Fourteenth Amendment. The new conventions would establish state governments in which blacks could vote and hold office. These governments were to ratify the Fourteenth Amendment as a condition for their return to the Union and the acceptance of their representatives by Congress.

By June 1868 all but three states—Mississippi, Texas, and Virginia—had complied with these requirements, and in July the ratification of the Fourteenth Amendment was completed. The three reluctant states were readmitted in 1870, as was Georgia, whose earlier readmittance had been suspended because of the expulsion of black members from its legislature.

The Radicals' next step was to protect their program from the Supreme Court. In the case of *ex parte Milligan* (1866), which arose over Lincoln's suspension of habeas corpus in Indiana during the war, the Supreme Court had held that any military rule persisting after the regular courts were reinstated would constitute "a gross usurpation of power." That is exactly what happened when the First Reconstruction Act was passed. Southern courts were open, but by establishing military rule, the act usurped their power.

The constitutionality of the act was challenged in *ex parte McCardle*, but the Supreme Court yielded to Radical pressure and elected not to hear the case. The First Reconstruction Act survived.

Having checked the Supreme Court, the Radicals next set about defending their program from presidential sabotage. The Tenure of Office Act, passed along with the First Reconstruction Act, declared that the president could not remove federal officers who had been appointed with the consent of the Senate unless the Senate agreed. The second, the Command of the Army Act, forbade the president to issue orders to the army except through the General of the Army (Ulysses S. Grant). These measures were designed to prevent the president from using patronage or control of the army to undermine the Radical program.

The conflict between Congress and Johnson ended in a move to impeach the president. Radicals held that as long as he remained in office, their reconstruction program could never be fully or fairly implemented. Although Johnson had no real choice but to enforce the acts of Congress, he had used his executive powers to weaken them. As commander in chief, for example, he had removed district commanders who were overly sympathetic to Radical policies and to the cause of the freedmen. He had also helped to restore the vote to southerners of doubtful loyalty. But there was no evidence directly implicating the president in any "high crimes and misdemeanors"—the only constitutional grounds for impeachment.

After almost a year of investigation, the House Judiciary Committee in 1867 voted by a narrow majority to recommend that the president be impeached. It charged him with attempting to reconstruct the former Confederate states "in accordance with his own will, in the interests of the great criminals who carried them into rebellion." This charge proved too vague for the whole House to accept, and it rejected the recommendation. But by attempting to remove Secretary of War Stanton, the remaining Radical in his cabinet, in apparent violation of the Tenure of Office Act, Johnson provided new grounds for impeachment. On February 21, 1868, Stanton was formally removed. Three days later, a new impeachment resolution came before the House. This time the House voted for impeachment 126 to 47. All but one of the charges ("particular articles") referred to the Tenure of Office Act. (Johnson's lawyers would contend that the Tenure of Office Act was unconstitutional and that it could not be applied to Stanton in any case, since he was a Lincoln appointee.) The tenth article charged that Johnson had been "unmindful of the high duties of his office" and had attempted to bring Congress into "disgrace, ridicule, hatred, contempt and reproach." This proved to be the major thrust of the impeachment move.

To convict Johnson, two-thirds of the Senate would have to be convinced that the charges against him amounted to "high crimes and misdemeanors" or that impeachment could be broadened to include political conduct that rendered a president unfit to hold office. But seven Republicans could not be persuaded, and that was enough. By the barest possible margin—only one vote—the Senate refused to remove the president.

The Election of 1868: Grant

Although they had done everything possible to block the president before the election of 1868, the Radicals were determined to secure the office for themselves that year. Their choice was General Grant, who had no known political allegiances—or, for that matter, any known political ambitions. He had served the Radicals in the controversy over Stanton's removal, and his war record appeared to make him a certain winner. At the Republican convention, Grant was nominated on the first ballot. Johnson sought the Democratic nomination. But after twenty-two ballots, the Democratic convention chose former New York governor Horatio Seymour.

In the campaign, the Democrats sought to divert attention from their reconstruction record by making an issue of cheap money. In 1866 Congress had passed a measure providing for the gradual retirement of the wartime greenbacks, whose dollar value had always remained below that of gold. In the next two years, almost $100 million worth were withdrawn from circulation, much to the disappointment of businessmen as well as farmers.

Western farmers, although emotionally attached to the Republican party for its liberal land policy, wanted cheap money to meet mortgage obligations and other debts. The Democrats' platform made a bid for their support by advocating the reissue of greenbacks to retire war bonds that did not specifically require repayment in gold. The leading proponent of this "soft money" plank was an early aspirant for the 1868 Democratic nomination, George H. Pendleton of Ohio. The plank became the Ohio Idea.

The Republicans had another idea. War bonds, they said, should be redeemed in gold; anything else would be a repudiation of a sacred debt. At the same time, they promised businessmen they would extend redemption "over a fair period," so as not to disturb the credit structure. When the time came, all bondholders would be paid in gold.

The Radicals kept the main political issue before the voters—Radical Reconstruction versus Democratic dishonor. The "bloody shirt," which had done such service in the 1866 campaign, was waved again. The Democratic party, cried Republicans, was the standard-bearer of rebellion, repression of blacks, and financial repudiation.

But the campaign did not overwhelm the opposition. In 1868, against a weak opponent, Grant was elected with a popular plurality of only 310,000 (about 52.7 percent of the popular vote). If not for the seven reconstructed southern states and the black vote, he might have lost.

The part blacks played in winning the election—or rather the fact that blacks in states such as Louisiana and Georgia had been prevented from casting what might have been much-needed Republican votes—led Radicals to attempt to strengthen the Fourteenth Amendment's protection of black suffrage. When Congress convened early in 1869, it promptly passed the Fifteenth Amendment: "The right of citizens of the United States to vote shall not be denied or abridged by the United States or by any State on account of race, color, or previous condition of servitude." This amendment was ratified in March 1870. By then, blacks had already made their influence known in the newly established southern governments.

RADICAL RECONSTRUCTION: LEGEND AND REALITY

With the passage of the First Reconstruction Act in 1867, Congress began a new era in southern political history. The new state governments were the first to be organized on the basis of universal male suffrage and to operate on the premise that

"Yes, yes, we are ignorant. We know it. I am ignorant for one, and they say all niggers is. They say we don't know what the word constitution means. But if we don't know enough to know what the Constitution is, we know enough to know what Justice is. I can see for myself down at my own court-house. If they makes a white man pay five dollars for doing something today, and makes a nigger pay ten dollars for doing that thing tomorrow, don't I know that ain't justice? They've got a figure of a woman with a sword hung up thar, sir; Mr. President, I don't know what you call it—

["Justice," "Justice," several delegates shouted]—well, she's got a handkercher over her eyes, and the sword is in one hand and a pair o' scales in the other. When a white man and a nigger gets into the scales, don't I know the nigger is always mighty light? Don't we all see it? Ain't it so at your court-house, Mr. President?" (Delegate to a freedmen's convention, Raleigh, North Carolina, 1865)

Source: John R. Dennett, *The South as It Is,* 1865–1866, ed. Henry M. Christman (New York: Viking, 1965), pp. 150–51. Illustration from the Library of Congress.

all men, white and black, were entitled to equal legal protection. For whites, as well as for the blacks themselves, this proved to be an extraordinary experience—black voters, black officeholders, black jurors, black sheriffs, black militias. Here was a society, remarked one observer, "suddenly turned bottom-side up." That statement captured the spirit of Radical rule in several of the states, even though it exaggerated black strength and influence in most of them.

Contrary to legend, blacks did not dominate any of the new governments; federal military occupation was never extensive; and only in South Carolina, Florida, and Louisiana did Radical rule last as long as eight years. The impressions that survived Reconstruction, however, impressions that generations of Americans would believe, added up to a "tragic era" in which corrupt carpetbaggers, poor white scalawags, and illiterate blacks ran wild in an unprecedented and

outrageous orgy of misrule. The historians later supplied the footnotes, the novelists embroidered the plots, and finally the motion picture industry (in films such as *The Birth of a Nation* and *Gone with the Wind*) depicted this version of Reconstruction for millions of believing spectators. For nearly a century, this distorted image of Reconstruction helped to freeze the white southern mind in opposition to any challenge to the racial status quo.

Few periods of American history have produced a worse collection of villains—white and black. The very names by which the white South came to know them suggested deceit, treachery, and alien rule. The carpetbaggers were "those Yankees who came South like buzzards after the surrender with all their worldly possessions in one carpetbag." The scalawags were "southerners who had turned Republican very profitably" and in doing so betrayed their own people. And the misled former slaves, as Woodrow Wilson would later write of them, had been nothing more than "a host of dusky children untimely put out of school."

Like most stereotypes, this picture is simplified, distorted, and falsified. The carpetbaggers were northerners who moved to the South after the Civil War and supported or participated in the Radical state governments. Their reasons for settling in the South were as varied as their personal character. For some, legitimate business opportunities and the availability of land and natural resources provided the incentive. Others were Union veterans who had found the South an attractive place in which to live. Still others were teachers, clergy, and agents of charitable societies who had committed themselves to the tasks of educating and converting the former slaves. Finally, there were political adventurers, but their numbers were small. To the white South, however, the fact that some carpetbaggers aided black voting and officeholding was enough to make the rest guilty by association.

Like the carpetbaggers, the scalawags—native white Republicans who supported Radical rule—were a varied lot. In no state were they a majority of southern whites. They were not necessarily poor whites, nor did they all welcome or support black participation in political life. To those who had been Whigs before the war, the Republican party appeared to offer the best hope for promoting the industrial and economic interests of a new South. To those who had opposed secession, the Radical program was a way to neutralize the dominant planters and gain political power. And some felt it important to participate in order to retain some control.

But whatever their individual motives, the scalawags faced ostracism in their communities. Some found it impossible to withstand the pressure, and few had any enthusiasm for racial equality. When blacks demanded a more substantial share of political power, many whites deserted the party.

Although carpetbaggers and scalawags aroused white hatred, black voters and officeholders symbolized the changes in postwar southern society far more dramatically. To find black men, many of them only recently slaves, now voting and holding public office was a change so drastic and so fearful in its implications that few white southerners could accept it; "If the negro is fit to make laws for the control of our conduct and property," a southern educator warned, "he is certainly fit to eat with us at our tables, to sleep in our beds, to be invited into our parlors, and to do all acts and things which a white man may do."

No matter how competently carpetbaggers, scalawags, and blacks might have carried out their political responsibilities, they would have been denounced by a majority of white southerners. Their very presence in the government and their commitment to black voting and officeholding was enough to condemn them.

Radical Rule in the South

Although blacks voted in large numbers, they did not in fact dominate any of the southern states. At the beginning of Radical Reconstruction, of the 1.35 million citizens qualified to vote in the former Confederate states, about half were black. In Alabama, Florida, Louisiana, Mississippi, and South Carolina, black voters were a majority. Only in South Carolina, however, did black legislators outnumber whites (eighty-eight to sixty-seven). In other state legislatures, blacks made up sizable minorities. But in no state did blacks control the executive mansion.

There were black lieutenant governors, secretaries of state, state treasurers, speakers of the house, and superintendents of education. Fourteen blacks were elected to the United States House of Representatives between 1869 and 1877, and two (Hiram Revels and Blanche K.

Hiram R. Revels of Mississippi, the first black senator in the United States (seated at far left), was elected to Jefferson Davis's seat in 1870. The first black representatives, elected in the Forty-first and Forty-second Congresses, were (seated) Benjamin S. Turner, Alabama; Josiah T. Walls, Florida; and Joseph H. Rainey and Robert Brown Elliott, South Carolina; and (standing) Robert C. Delarge, South Carolina; and Jefferson H. Long, Georgia. *(Granger Collection)*

Robert Smalls (left), South Carolina legislator and U.S. congressman, and John R. Lynch (right), Speaker of the Mississippi House of Representatives and U.S. congressman. *(Library of Congress)*

Bruce of Mississippi) to the United States Senate. The majority of black officeholders had local positions, such as justice of the peace, sheriff, and county supervisor, which were important at a time of much local decision-making.

Most were young men, generally in their twenties and thirties at the outset of Reconstruction. Some were illiterate, some were self-educated, and a few were graduates of northern colleges. Many were ministers, teachers, artisans, and farmers who had managed to accumulate small landholdings. Before the war, a number of them had been members of the class of free blacks in the South. Still others, either northern-born or self-imposed "exiles" from their homeland, had resided in the North. Most impressive, however, were those who had only recently been slaves. The skills they had gained from learning how to survive as slaves may explain why many of them proved to be successful politicians.

The Radical governments operated on the principle that all men, black and white, were entitled to equal political and civil liberties. Both races, in fact, made impressive political and social advances. Many of the gains grew out of the new state constitutions, written by conventions in which blacks and whites participated. These constitutions eliminated property qualifications for voting and holding office, for whites as well as

blacks. They apportioned representation in state legislatures and in Congress more fairly. Judicial systems were revised, and juries were opened to blacks. Imprisonment for debt was abolished, along with other archaic social legislation. Above all, for the first time in many southern states, the constitutions provided for public schools for whites and blacks.

Next to giving blacks the vote, nothing offended the white South more than Radical efforts to give blacks schooling at public expense. Even the segregation of black and white pupils did not satisfy critics. It had long been an article of faith among white southerners that education spoiled blacks as laborers, developing in them wants that could never be satisfied and expectations that could never be realized. Invariably, then, an educated black person could be expected to be discontented, frustrated, and troublesome. That was reason enough for whites to burn black schools and to threaten and harass teachers and students. Yet blacks persisted in their quest for education, and by 1877 southern schools had enrolled 600,000 blacks.

Several colleges and universities, including Fisk, Howard, Atlanta, and the Hampton Institute in Virginia, had been established by the Freedmen's Bureau and northern philanthropic agencies. Night schools for adults flourished. But

P. B. S. Pinchback (left), president pro tempore of the Louisiana State Senate and later acting governor of that state, and Blanche K. Bruce (right), assessor and sheriff of Bolivar County, Mississippi, elected in 1874 to the U.S. Senate. *(Library of Congress)*

despite the commitment of the Radical governments to education, the financial resources of the states were often not sufficient to support a dual school system. It was the private efforts of various northern groups, such as the American Missionary Association, that enabled many blacks to obtain an education.

The Radical governments displayed restraint when dealing with economic matters. Even black legislators refused to interfere with the rights of private property, though land ownership remained the principal goal of their black constituents. Rather than experiment with land redistribution, most black leaders urged the familiar mid-nineteenth-century self-help creed: be thrifty and industrious and buy property. (These leaders assumed that whites would welcome evidence of black economic success and independence—a mistaken assumption.) Like their white colleagues, most black legislators accepted the idea of individual responsibility for one's own material well-being. In their overriding concern for realizing the same rights to life, liberty, and property enjoyed by whites, black leaders did not wish to undermine their own position by advocating anything as un-American as confiscation. Nor did they want to alienate native whites, with whom they expected to share political power.

Black sharecroppers and tenants knew only too well, however, that legal equality and the vote could not feed hungry mouths or end economic hardship. They needed land of their own and the means to farm that land. "Give us our own land," said one freedman, "and we take care of ourselves; but widout land, de ole massas can hire or starve us, as dey please." But neither the Radical legislatures nor Congress, even while giving liberally to railroads, were willing to make that kind of commitment to the former slaves—even as a token payment for years of unpaid labor.

The black officeholder gained experience in governing during an era in which corruption marked much of American political life. Although corruption in the Radical governments was not as bad as painted, there was enough to tarnish them and to confirm the skepticism in the North about the entire experiment. Between 1868 and 1874, the bonded debt of the eleven ex-Confederate states grew by over $100 million. This enormous sum was not itself evidence of corruption. To raise money, the southern states had to sell bonds in the North, where southern credit was so poor that investors often demanded a 75 percent discount from a bond's face value. Thus, for every $100 worth of bonds sold, a southern state might actually realize only $25.

Many of the social and humanitarian reforms of the Reconstruction legislatures were costly, as was the relief extended to the starving and homeless of both races. Taxes to pay for such expenditures, including new "luxuries" such as public schools, fell heavily on the planters, who before the war had been able to pass taxes on to other groups.

Still, much of the debt was incurred corruptly, though carpetbaggers, scalawags, and blacks were not necessarily the principal beneficiaries. Like the rest of the nation, the South suffered at the hands of railroad interests, business speculators, and contractors who sought legislative favors and were willing to pay for them. Corruption in the South, as elsewhere, tended to be bipartisan, involving men of both races and all classes, and it included some of the most distinguished names of the South. It had been under way before Radical rule, and it lasted long after the overthrow of Reconstruction.

A black legislator might quickly learn from white colleagues of both parties that payoffs were a natural part of the political process and often a necessary supplement to an otherwise meager income. After accepting a bribe, one black legislator, a former slave, offered this perspective: "I've been sold in my life eleven times. And this is the first time I ever got the money." For most black leaders, however, political participation entailed personal sacrifice rather than financial gain. Henry Johnson of South Carolina, for example, was a former slave, a bricklayer and plasterer by trade, and an active participant in Republican politics. "I always had plenty of work before I went into politics," he noted, "but I have never got a job since. I suppose they do it merely because they think they will break me down and keep me from interfering with politics." Jefferson Long, a Macon tailor elected to Congress, found that his political position "ruined his business with the whites who had been his patrons chiefly." But black leaders faced more serious dangers than the loss of business—and that was the loss of their lives.

The ability of black officeholders varied considerably; most important, blacks were learning the uses of political power and gaining confidence in their ability to rule. As they did, and as they began to demand political power on a par with their electoral strength, the shaky alliance on which Radical rule rested began to fall apart. When blacks made startling gains in Mississippi and South Carolina in the early 1870s, for example, they vividly demonstrated their new independence and self-confidence. At the same time, they may have sealed their own doom.

The idea of black success, independence, and power drove numerous whites out of the party, accelerated internal divisions, and gave the Democrats the opportunity for which they had carefully prepared. If anything about "black reconstruction" truly alarmed the white South, it was not so much the evidence of corruption, but the very real possibility that this unique experiment in biracial government might succeed! As W. E. B. Du Bois wrote: "There was one thing that the white South feared more than negro dishonesty, ignorance, and incompetency, and that was negro honesty, knowledge, and efficiency."

The End of Reconstruction: The Shotgun Policy

From the beginning of Radical rule, before any evidence of corruption had come to light, the white South was determined to use every method at its disposal to maintain control of black labor and black lives. To overthrow Radical rule and the black vote on which it rested, thousands of even the most respectable people in the South banded together in the Ku Klux Klan, the Knights of the White Camellia, and other secret groups. Between 1867 and 1879, hooded or otherwise disguised, they roamed the land, shot, flogged, and terrorized blacks and their supporters, burned homes and public buildings, and assaulted Reconstruction officials. To suppress this violence, Congress responded with the Force Act of 1870 and the Ku Klux Klan Act of 1871. These laws imposed heavy fines and jail sentences for offenses under the Fourteenth and Fifteenth amendments and gave Republican-controlled federal courts, rather than southern state courts, jurisdiction in all cases arising under the amendments or out of conspiracies or terrorism against freedmen. The president was empowered to suspend habeas corpus in any terrorized community, to declare martial law, and to send troops to maintain order. In October 1871, President Grant invoked that authority in nine South Carolina counties where the Klan was especially active.

Federal intervention in South Carolina marked the peak of forceful repression of southern violence. Except for the passage of the Civil Rights Act of 1875—a seldom-enforced law that guaranteed blacks equal access to public accommodations—the Republican party began to retreat from its commitment to civil rights and black voting. In May 1872 Congress passed an Amnesty Act that restored voting and officeholding privileges to all white southerners except a few hundred of the

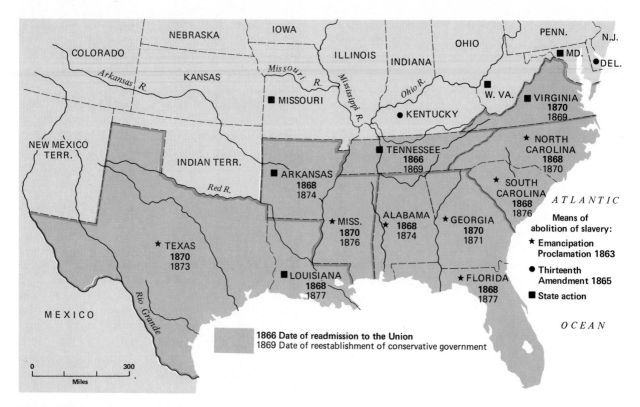

Reconstruction

highest Confederate dignitaries. In that same year, the Freedmen's Bureau was permitted to expire. By 1877 white terrorism, economic coercion, federal indifference, and factionalism in the Radical governments had brought Radical Reconstruction to an end.

The Mississippi Plan (sometimes called the "shotgun policy"), by which Democrats regained power in that state in 1875, proved to be a model of repression. It consisted of organized violence and threats, the systematic breakup of Republican gatherings, and the incitement of riots. Its aim was to force all whites into the Democratic party, and at the same time to eliminate black leadership and political participation. "Carry the election peaceably if we can, forcibly if we must," was the way one newspaper described the objective.

In communities where blacks were a majority or nearly so, the plan was carried out with full white support. Where persuasion failed, violence and terrorism were used by well-armed paramilitary units called Rifle Clubs, White Leagues, or Red Shirts. White Republicans who resisted were driven from their homes and their communities. Defiant black sharecroppers were denied credit by southern merchants; they were evicted from the land, denied other employment, assaulted, and murdered.

Even when the governor of Mississippi ap-

pealed to President Grant for assistance, claiming he had exhausted all local resources, the president refused to call upon the army to support troubled Republican regimes. Encouraged by Grant's turnabout, southern leaders in states still under Radical rule became more determined than ever to "redeem" their states through their own efforts.

The federal government's refusal to act reflected the North's growing disillusion with the reconstruction experiment. Northern whites were busy with their own economic problems. Traditional racist views persisted, and neither northern whites nor the Republicans were prepared to undertake the massive intervention and federal force necessary to sustain this unique experiment in biracial government. Northern businessmen concluded that only southern Democrats could establish the kind of stability necessary for economic advancement and investment. Alarmed over the persistent turmoil and unwilling to allow federal power to sustain the Reconstruction governments, northerners chose to permit the white South to work out its own solution to "the race problem."

The white southern response to Reconstruction is hardly surprising. Even honest and capable carpetbaggers came to symbolize alien rule, and even if corruption was fashionable, Radical corruption was not. Most important, if blacks were to succeed, politically or economically, they would no longer be content with a lower place in southern society. That was a difficult proposition for whites to accept. Whites wanted a docile, dependent, and productive black laboring class. Blacks acquiring and working their own land posed dangers as great as those of blacks voting or legislating. "The Nigger, when poverty stricken, will work well for you," a Georgia farmer observed, "but as soon as he begins to be prosperous, he becomes impudent and unmanageable." For many in the white South, that observation became an article of faith.

While maintaining that blacks were incapable of becoming their political, social, or economic equals, many whites betrayed the fear that they might. The black person as a buffoon, a menial, a servant was perfectly acceptable; indeed, many whites assumed that irresponsibility, ignorance, and submissiveness were black traits. Consequently, those blacks who failed to fit the stereotype seemed somehow abnormal, even dangerous. "The Negro as a poor ignorant creature," Frederick Douglass observed, "does not contradict the race pride of the white race. He is more a source of amusement to that race than an object of resentment. . . . It is only when he acquires education, property, and influence, only when he attempts to rise and be a man among men that he invites repression." For blacks who aspired to improve themselves, this posed an obvious dilemma.

Within ten years, then, Reconstruction was over. Although the Fourteenth and Fifteenth amendments eventually helped to make a "second reconstruction" possible in the 1950s and 1960s, that may not be enough to judge Radical Reconstruction a success. But what blacks demonstrated in that brief period, even if imperfectly, has too often been ignored. Despite their shortcomings, inexperience, and failure to resolve the most pressing problems of their people, black leaders exercised political responsibility with reasonable competence and gave every indication of learning from their errors. This achievement and the potential it suggested prompted W. E. B. Du Bois to write in *Black Reconstruction* (1935): "The attempt to make black men American citizens was in a certain sense all a failure, but a splendid failure. It did not fail where it was expected to fail."[*]

---

[*]W. E. B. Du Bois, *Black Reconstruction in America 1860–1880* (New York: Russell & Russell, 1956) p. 708. Copyright 1962, 1935 by W. E. B. Du Bois.

The tragedy of Radical Reconstruction is that it failed to reconstruct southern white racial attitudes. From the very outset, this unique experiment in biracial government rested on a weak base. The commitment of the federal government was limited, and even Republicans did not seek any long-term federal intervention in southern affairs. The commitment of blacks was limited by their economic weakness and dependence. If many of them chose to withdraw from political activism altogether, they did so as a result not only of white intimidation, but of the recognition that politics had not significantly altered the quality of their day-to-day lives.

The end of Reconstruction solidified white supremacy. But this victory entailed serious costs for the South: the corruption of public discourse, political and economic backwardness, high rates of illiteracy and poverty, and continuing racial tension. For blacks, Reconstruction, though short-lived, had been a moment of promise and excitement, a time when they had envisioned a biracial democracy that would revolutionize white–black relations and give substance to abstract notions of freedom. The expectations raised by this promise made the final outcome all the more tragic. The range of choices open to blacks narrowed considerably. The political violence devastated an emerging black leadership class, claiming the lives of many black officeholders and political organizers and driving even more into exile. Nearly a century would pass before southern blacks would be so fully mobilized for political purposes.

THE GRANT PRESIDENCY

When Ulysses S. Grant became president in 1869, the American people expected him to exercise the same qualities of leadership he had shown in the Civil War. He would, many believed, organize a strong government staffed by able aides, much as he had mobilized a victorious army. But the problems Grant faced as president—turmoil in the South, the tariff, falling farm prices, and business speculation—were far different from those he had confronted on the battlefield.

He entered the White House with no political experience and few political convictions; he expected Congress to represent the will of the people and to act on that basis. A failure in business, Grant admired those who had succeeded, accepted their gracious hospitality, and tried to satisfy their needs. Moving in circles far different

The Ku Klux Klan: plan of the contemplated murder of John Campbell, on August 10, 1871, in Moore County, North Carolina. (*Library of Congress*)

from those he had known, he turned for advice to people with whom he felt most comfortable. The White House staff—his "kitchen cabinet"—consisted largely of wartime friends. The regular cabinet, with few exceptions, was made up of obscure men.

The First Term: The Great Barbecue

Although personally honest, Grant permitted himself and his office to be used by self-seeking politicians and businessmen. He found it difficult to believe that many of those who befriended him were interested only in personal profit. During his administration, his secretary of war, his private secretary, and officials in the Treasury and navy departments used their positions and influence to enhance their incomes. Even as a disbelieving Grant learned of the scandals, he seemed more disturbed by those who made the charges than by the revelations themselves.

Grant, no doubt, was victimized by men whose honesty and loyalty he had never thought to question. If he appointed some of his wealthy friends to cabinet posts, he did so in the conviction that these men had operated in the national interest. Many had made fortunes on war contracts, but in Grant's eyes they had also contributed to winning the war. Some of them were now

sustaining the postwar boom. Positions in government were simply a recognition of their achievement and patriotism. To those who expressed alarm over the scandals, moreover, Grant could reply that he had inherited a government already far gone in corruption. The competition for war contracts and the battles for other wartime legislation covering protective tariffs, land grants, and the money system had made lobbying a full-time occupation. After the war, lobbyists often prowled the floors of the House and Senate to keep their legislators in line.

Few political plums were more valuable than the tariff, which by 1870 had added to the profits of eastern manufacturing and industrial interests. But railroads also shared handsomely in congressional handouts. The last federal land grant for railroad building was made in 1871. By that time, the total distributed to the roads directly or through the states had reached 160 million acres, valued conservatively at $335 million. The railroads also received lavish government loans. Each year after the Union Pacific and Central Pacific railroads obtained their loans, Congress debated legislation that would have provided for repayment. But the railroad owners fought these measures stubbornly and successfully, often distributing company shares among the legislators "where they will do us the most good."

The Union Pacific, for example, was built by the Crédit Mobilier of America, a construction company owned largely by Union Pacific promoters. By awarding themselves large contracts on the most favorable terms, these men were able to realize huge profits. Faced with a congressional inquiry in 1868, the company directors, through Massachusetts congressman Oakes Ames, himself a stockholder in both companies, distributed stock among key members of Congress and government officials. The scandal destroyed some political reputations, including that of Vice-President Schuyler Colfax, but only Representative Ames was censured.

Northern financiers also joined in the Great Barbecue, as Grant's regime has been called. In March 1869, fulfilling campaign promises made the year before, both houses of Congress adopted a resolution pledging the government to redeem the entire war debt in gold or in new gold bonds. This pledge, and the laws soon passed to carry it out, sent the value of war bonds soaring and brought substantial profits to speculators. These laws were also good for the government's credit. Forced during the war to offer interest as high as

6 percent, the victorious national government was soon able to borrow for as little as 2.5 percent.

Grant's Second Term: Disenchantment

In the 1872 presidential campaign, Carl Schurz of Missouri, alienated by Grant's appointments and policies, led a Liberal Republican movement. With a platform stressing civil service reform, the Liberals tried to attract candidates of "superior intelligence and superior virtue." Unfortunately, they were joined by victims of the Radical grafters, political hacks who had lost patronage, and others who were out for revenge. Many northern Democrats also joined the movement, hoping to get rid of the treasonous label of their party and win back power.

At the Liberal convention, the differences among them forced the delegates to name a less-than-inspiring compromise candidate, Horace Greeley, editor for more than thirty years of the *New York Tribune*. The Democrats, seeking to regain national power, gave their support to Greeley. But Grant easily won reelection, carrying all but six states.

The Democrats' hopes were by no means shattered. The scandals of the Grant administration increased public disillusion with the Republican party and those who profited by its corrupt dealings and control of patronage. The first major Grant scandal, the Crédit Mobilier affair, broke while the 1872 campaign was in progress. After the business crash of 1873, each new revelation struck with added force, and once the Democrats captured the House in 1874, the revelations and prosecutions snowballed.

Two scandals hit Grant personally. One was the uncovering in St. Louis of the Whiskey Ring, which had defrauded the government of millions of dollars in internal revenue charges. Deeply involved in this, as in other frauds, was Grant's private secretary, Orville Babcock, whom the president saved from imprisonment only by interfering in his trial. The second affair led to the impeachment of Grant's third secretary of war, W. W. Belknap. Since his appointment in 1870, Belknap had been "kept" by traders in the Indian Territory, which his department administered. When his impeachment appeared imminent, Belknap offered his resignation to the president. Grant, with characteristic loyalty, accepted "with great regret."

Grant deserved a better fate. He had been a great military leader. But he showed little aptitude for the complex machinery of government, politics, and party. His personal honesty, trust, and naiveté made him an easy victim of interests that even the wisest politician found difficult to control. "It was the age of the audacious confidence man," Edmund Wilson has written, "and Grant was the incurable sucker. He easily fell victim to their trickery and allowed them to betray him into compromising his office because he could not believe that such people existed."

The Election of 1876: Hayes

As convention time approached in 1876, Democrats were making an issue of corruption, and Republicans were deeply divided on the best way to answer them. The Grand Old Party, as Republicans were calling themselves, separated into Stalwarts and Half-Breeds. Stalwarts were the hard-core political professionals who put politics first; if business wanted favors, let them pay up. Half-Breeds were Republican reformers who had not deserted to the Liberal Republicans in 1872.

Stalwarts, closest to Grant, wanted him to run for a third term. Half-Breeds lined up behind Congressman James G. Blaine of Maine, despite the dramatic disclosure of his shady relations with the Union Pacific Railroad while serving as Speaker of the House. When the movement to renominate Grant failed to materialize, the nomination went to Rutherford B. Hayes, the reform governor of Ohio.

The Democratic surge in the South, meanwhile, and the vicious repression on which it was based, accented sectional differences in that party on every issue. Hunger for the presidency, long denied them, led the Democrats to close ranks behind Samuel J. Tilden, a rich corporation lawyer and hard-money man who had won a national reputation as a reform governor of New York.

The presidential scandals, the severity of the economic depression of the mid-1870s, and the rising demand for reform all seemed to work to the Democrats' advantage. The campaign they waged stressed the need to end misrule in the South and to weed out corruption in the federal government. On economic issues, little differentiated Tilden from Hayes; both were conservatives who proclaimed their belief in "sound money" and limited government.

First reports of the election results suggested a

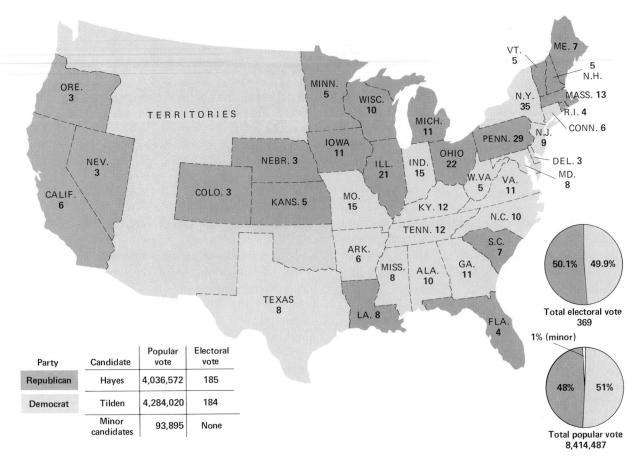

Party	Candidate	Popular vote	Electoral vote
Republican	Hayes	4,036,572	185
Democrat	Tilden	4,284,020	184
	Minor candidates	93,895	None

The election of 1876.

Democratic victory. Tilden had a plurality of 250,000 votes, and the press proclaimed him the new president. But Republican strategists suddenly awoke to the fact that returns from Louisiana, Florida, and South Carolina, three states still under Radical control, had not yet come in because of election irregularities. Tilden needed only one electoral vote from these states to win; Hayes needed every one. Any accurate count in the disputed states was complicated by the threats, violence, and fraud used by Democrats to keep blacks from voting. Both parties claimed to have won. Congress would have to determine which of the double sets of returns from the three states should be accepted, the Democratic count or the Republican.

The two parties agreed to the extraordinary device of deciding the election by turning the problem over to a commission of five representatives, five senators, and five Supreme Court justices. One of the justices, David Davis, presumably was independent in politics. The remaining fourteen members of the commission were equally divided between Democrats and Republicans. Unfortunately for Tilden, Davis quit the

commission before it met and was replaced by a Republican justice. The Republican majority of eight then voted unanimously for Hayes. The Compromise of 1877, by which the South conceded Hayes's election, rested largely on Republican assurances that Hayes "would deal justly and generously with the South." That was understood to mean the withdrawal of the remaining federal troops and no more interference in the restoration of white political supremacy.

In his inaugural speech, Hayes spoke out clearly on the need for a permanent federal civil service beyond the reach of politics and patronage. To show that he meant business, he succeeded in getting rid of some of the party faithful from the New York Customs House, although not for long. In his southern strategy, Hayes chose David M. Key of Tennessee, a high-ranking former Confederate officer and a Democrat, as postmaster general. By the end of April 1877 he had withdrawn the last federal troops from the South; with their departure, the last Radical state governments collapsed.

That autumn he set forth on a good-will tour of the South. He was joined by former Confederate general Wade Hampton, whom "straight-out" Democrats had just elected governor of South Carolina, chiefly by suppressing the black vote. At an enthusiastic meeting in Atlanta, Hayes assured the blacks in the audience that their "rights and interests would be safer if this great mass of intelligent white men were let alone by the general government." On his return to Washington, the president observed of his journey: "Received everywhere heartily. The country is again one and united."

The real losers in the election of 1876 were not the Democrats, but black southerners. Between 1879 and 1881, nearly 50,000 blacks, mostly from rural Texas, Louisiana, Mississippi, and Tennessee, left for Kansas, another 5000 for Iowa and Nebraska. The spirit that pervaded the "great exodus" was largely that of desperation, and the Exodusters, as they were called, appeared to be more refugees than migrants, fleeing from oppression and violence that had become intolerable. A newspaper reporter in Mississippi, observing the daily departures, described families "who seem to think anywhere is better than here." The Exodusters voted with their feet, but another quarter of a century would pass before that vote became overwhelming. Until the early twentieth century, some 90 percent of black Americans spent their whole lives in the South.

THE NEW SOUTH

With the collapse of the remaining Radical governments, politics in the South came to be dominated by a new class of men—industrialists, merchants, bankers, and railroad promoters. Calling themselves Redeemers, for having "redeemed" their states from "carpetbag rule," they envisioned a New South devoted to material progress and based on the profitable use of the region's natural resources and abundant labor supply. The old planter class found its prewar power diminished; the heavy voting strength it commanded in the rural sections, however, particularly the Black Belt, enabled it to exert considerable influence. These two classes were generally able to resolve their differences, ruling by coalition if necessary, and thus maintaining the supremacy of their values.

The new state governments set out to cut spending. The principal victims were the public schools and other state-supported services left over from the Radical years. But the same governments that cut taxes and made a virtue of

economy proved to be most generous in their encouragement of economic enterprises, bestowing on them liberal charters and tax exemptions. Corruption was no less widespread under the Redeemer governments than under the previous Radical regimes, but somehow it seemed less offensive when committed by whites.

Although blacks continued to vote, they were able to exert little if any political influence. The race relations of the New South were based on the suppression of black hopes—political, economic, and social. Not even the occasional challenges to Redeemer rule altered that fact of southern life. For most blacks, politics became less important in their daily lives. The need to survive—to grow a crop and to pay their debts—took precedence over a politics that offered them no real choices.

The Economics of Dependency: Agriculture

Even before the overthrow of Radical rule in the South, blacks were economically dependent on whites. Radicals had tried to reconstruct the Union by giving the freed slaves the vote, but political privileges were not backed by economic gains. During their brief hours of joy over freedom, the former slaves had talked about owning their own farms and living like "white folks." With few exceptions, however, it never worked out that way. Denied land, dependent on and in debt to the landlord and the merchant (often the same person), who held claims on their unharvested crops, few blacks could achieve the economic independence they coveted. As one former slave recalled:

We thought we was going to be richer than the white folks, 'cause we was stronger and knowed how to work, and the whites didn't, and they didn't have us to work for them any more. But it didn't turn out that way. We soon found out that freedom could make folks proud, but it didn't make 'em rich.

If there was any consolation for the blacks, it would have to be the knowledge that many whites were far from being as independent as they seemed. Before the war, most large southern plantations had been heavily mortgaged. Afterward, hard-pressed creditors began demanding payment of interest and principal. Some southern planters sold off part of their land in order to finance cultivation of the rest. Others leased acreage for money rents. But obviously there was not money enough available to keep this up very long. The result was a continuation of the familiar

LABOR RELATIONS IN THE NEW SOUTH

In my condition, and the way I see it for everybody, if you don't make enough to have some left you ain't done nothin, except given the other fellow your labor. . . . Now it's right for me to pay you for usin' what's yours—your land, stock, plow tools, fertilizer. But how much should I pay? The answer ought to be closely seeked. How much is a man due to pay out? Half his crop? A third part of his crop? And how much is he due to keep for hisself? You got a right to your part—rent; and I got a right to mine. But who's the man ought to decide how much? The one that owns the property or the one that works it? (Ned Cobb, black cotton farmer, born in Alabama in 1885)

Source: Theodore Rosengarten, *All God's Dangers: The Life of Nate Shaw* (New York: Knopf, 1974), p. 108. Photograph courtesy of the Cook Collection, Valentine Museum, Richmond.

routine of the prewar South: Planters paid no wages for labor, and their workers paid no rent for land. Instead, each was to share in the forthcoming crop.

In order to get this crop into the ground, both parties had to borrow. Since they had no other security, they had to borrow against the crop they hoped to produce. Only then would the merchants advance the required seed, fertilizer, and equipment, as well as food and clothing. For his own stock, the local merchant had to seek credit from northern suppliers. Risks in the South were so great that these suppliers demanded high prices for the goods and high interest for credit. In addition, oppressive fees were charged for transportation, insurance, and other commercial ser-

vices. The merchant passed all these charges on to the landlords and sharecroppers. The merchant also added his own profit, and perhaps took a little more to reward himself for his literacy, at the expense of borrowers who could not read his account books. The South became more firmly chained to northern creditors, while the sharecropper was enslaved to the merchant.

The South drifted more and more deeply into sharecropping and crop debts because they offered a solution to the problems of labor and capital. Immediately after the war, many planters had tried to keep their newly freed workers by offering them cash wages. A typical contract stipulated that the planter pay wages of ten to twelve dollars a month, less the cost, determined by the planter, of "quarters, fuel, healthy and substantial rations." In exchange, the freedman agreed to labor faithfully "in the usual way before the War." The wage system failed because there was too little money. Few laborers received the pay they had been promised, and the freedman found little reason to trust his former master.

Sharecropping gradually stabilized labor relations in the cash-poor South. It also helped preserve the plantation system. The plantation was divided into small plots, which the landowner rented to blacks. Typically, the freedman agreed to pay a share of the forthcoming crop, usually one-third, for his use of the land, and still another share, again about one-third, for the necessary tools, seed, and work animals. Once he realized the government was not about to grant him any land, sharecropping seemed better than working in gangs under an overseer or foreman.

But if sharecropping seemed to give blacks some economic independence and the hope of eventually buying the land on which they worked, the financial realities of the postwar South soon turned the arrangement into a form of economic bondage. The sharecropper had to borrow continually on future crops to pay his debts to the planter and supply merchant. He was caught in a web of debt from which there was seldom any escape. Under the sharecropping system, moreover, with its emphasis on the single cash crop, overproduction soon caused cotton prices to fall.

If black southerners sensed an unfairness in their economic lives, it rested in the perception that they worked largely to enrich others—an all too familiar pattern.

> *The old bee makes de honey-comb*
> *The young bee makes de honey.*
> *Colored folks plant de cotton and corn*
> *And de white folks gits de money.*

The devastation of the war also caught up with the small white farmer. He too needed credit from the local merchants to get his land back into production and his home and barns repaired. And as in the case of the sharecroppers, the merchants dictated that the whites grow little but cotton. At first, the white farmer might give the merchant a lien on forthcoming crops. As debts mounted, the merchant demanded a mortgage on the land as well. And as the cotton market deteriorated, the merchant foreclosed. Some white farmers managed to beat the trend and became substantial landowners, even merchants. But by the 1880s, most of them had gone under and become sharecroppers or were left with the poorest land.

The Economics of Dependency: Industry

After the white South had been "redeemed," many people expected it to share in the industrialization that was booming in the North. To achieve self-respect as a region, some argued, the South would need to demonstrate material and financial strength. The idea of a New South was based on industrial development like that of the North, with comparable business institutions and captains of industry, and an end to the dependency that had until now characterized North-South relationships.

The movement to create a New South through industry became a crusade. After 1880, white professionals and retired generals and colonels gave their names and reputations, their energy and their capital, to the mission. The textile industry, already restored, continued to grow rapidly. During the depression of the mid-1880s, southern iron began to compete successfully with Pittsburgh's. The North Carolina tobacco industry responded to the new fad of cigarette smoking, and a bit later the cottonseed-oil industry spurted upward.

Another and more important goal of the crusade was to draw northern capital southward. It was to this goal that Henry Grady, publisher of the powerful *Atlanta Constitution,* devoted the most attention. Invading the North to recruit capital, Grady told a New York audience: "We have sowed towns and cities in the place of theories, and put business in place of politics. We have challenged

Workers in a North Carolina cotton mill, 1895. *(Brown Brothers)*

your spinners in Massachusetts and your iron-makers in Pennsylvania. . . . We have fallen in love with work."

In the 1880s, northern capital had good reason to look hopefully to the South. The availability of natural resources and abundant waterpower should have been enough. But there was more: the promise of low taxes, legislative favors, and a cheap labor force said to be immune to trade unions and strikes. As late as 1900, however, the so-called industrialized New South actually produced a smaller proportion of American manufactures than had the Old South in 1860. Fewer than 4 percent of the people in the important textile state of South Carolina were engaged in manufacturing, while 70 percent remained in agriculture. The ratios in the rest of the South were the same. Where new industries had established themselves, they had done so largely as branches of northern-owned enterprises.

The social price exacted from the southern people proved to be considerable. Champions of the New South expected black laborers to "keep their place," growing staples in the hot sun, while whites found employment in the mills and factories. Industry would redeem the South, and the cotton mills would be the salvation of the poor whites. But when the white farmer gave up his struggle with the land to accept work in the mills, he found that little had changed. He lived in villages that resembled the old slave quarters. He now owed his allegiance to the company store, the company landlord, and the company church. He labored long hours, rarely saw sunlight or breathed fresh air, and fell victim to a variety of diseases. "The harvest was soon at hand," Wilbur Cash writes in *The Mind of the South*.

By 1900 the cotton-mill worker was a pretty distinct type in the South. . . . A dead-white skin, a sunken chest, and stooping shoulders were the earmarks of the breed. Chinless faces, microcephalic foreheads, rabbit teeth, goggling dead-fish eyes, rickety limbs, and stunted bodies abounded—over and beyond the limit of their prevalence in the countryside. The women were characteristically stringy-haired and limp of breast at twenty, and shrunken hags at thirty or forty.

The wages paid to adult male workers varied from forty to fifty cents a day; women and children worked for still lower pay to supplement a meager family income. But there was one compensation: The mill villages were the exclusive domain of whites. And that, said the industrial promoters, lent dignity to their labor. For whites, moreover, the consciousness of race superiority assumed even greater importance and intensity in the late

nineteenth century as the South moved systematically to repress the last vestiges of civil rights.

A Closed Society: Disfranchisement, Jim Crow, and Repression

Although Radical Reconstruction ended in 1877 and white violence at the polls persisted, black voting had not been altogether eliminated. Most blacks remained loyal to the Republicans. But the Redeemers—or Conservatives, as southern Democrats often called themselves—became adept in some regions at making political arrangements with local black leaders whenever black votes were needed to win local elections. And any time the black vote posed a threat, reviving the specter of "Negro domination," whites returned to the tactics of repression, ranging from crude election frauds to threats of loss of land, credit, or jobs. These same tactics might also be employed by the ruling Conservative regimes to thwart the challenge of white independents.

Forced to make political choices that had little or nothing to do with their immediate needs and problems, growing numbers of blacks withdrew from politics altogether or permitted their votes to be bought. What difference did it make who carried the election? "This is a white man's country and government," said one disillusioned black, "and he is proving it North, South, East, and West, democrats and republicans. For my part, I am tired of both parties; the Negro's back is sleek where they have rode him so much."

Despite their traditional allegiance to the Republicans as "the party of emancipation," some blacks were critical of the minimal role they were permitted to play in party affairs and disappointed by the party's failure to represent the needs of common people. "The colored people are consumers," the chairman of a black meeting in Richmond declared. "The Republicans have deserted them and undertaken to protect the capitalist and manufacturer of the North."

In the late 1880s and early 1890s, agricultural hard times prompted discontented staple farmers to organize in the Populist movement. In some states, it even seemed possible that depressed white and black farmers might be able to challenge the entrenched Conservative regimes. Populist leaders such as Thomas E. Watson of Georgia preached a degree of cooperation among black and white farmers and sharecroppers on the grounds that their economic grievances crossed racial lines. He asked them to recognize their

THE LEGACY OF THE NEW SOUTH

*When I was a little boy I watched em disfranchise
the Negro from votin. . . . Never did hear my daddy
say nothin bout losin the vote. But I believe with all
my heart he knowed what it meant. . . . the way he
handled hisself in this votin business and other
colored handled themselves, they had to come under
these southern rulins. They thought they did, and
the white man said they did, and that's all there was
to it. . . . Who was behind it? I felt to an extent it
was the rich white man and the poor white man,
both of em, workin to take the vote away from the
nigger—the big man and a heap of the little ones.
The little ones thought they had a voice, but they
only had a voice to this extent: they could speak
against the nigger and the big man was happy for
em to do it. But they didn't have no more voice than
a cat against the big man of their own color.* (Ned
Cobb, black cotton farmer, born in Alabama in 1885)

Source: Theodore Rosengarten, *All God's Dangers: The Life of
Nate Shaw* (New York: Knopf, 1974), pp 34–35.

Unidentified man, 1890s. *(Library of Congress)*

---

common plight and to subordinate race consciousness to class consciousness. At the same
time, Watson made it clear that he did not believe
in race mixing, nor would he tolerate "Negro
domination." But why should white supremacy be
jeopardized by simply telling the black sharecropper that he was "in the same boat as the white
tenant; the colored laborer with the white laborer. . . . Why cannot the cause of one be made
the cause of both?"

In several states, the Populists openly courted
the black vote, entered into political coalitions
with blacks, and named some blacks to party
posts. But the degree of Populist commitment
varied considerably, many Populists refused to
compromise on white supremacy, and blacks
themselves remained skeptical about the motives
of white farmers who had been their traditional
enemies. Although Populists coveted the votes of
blacks, in the end they proved no more committed
to equality for blacks than most other southern
white men. Only in North Carolina were the
Populists able, by joining with the Republicans, to
defeat the Conservative Democrats. The triumph
proved to be short-lived, however. The Democratic return to power in North Carolina was
followed by a race riot in 1898 in the town of
Wilmington and by 1900 the Populists were ready
to accept an amendment to the North Carolina
Constitution eliminating black participation in

politics. When Populists succumbed to the ram-
pant racism of this period, they often did so with
frightening enthusiasm. Few would be more
virulent than Tom Watson himself, who would
write of the "hideous, ominous, national menace"
of black domination, advocate depriving blacks of
the vote, and condone lynching.

Between 1890 and 1915, the white South
moved to disfranchise blacks. The issue was not
black political power, which no longer posed a
serious threat, but how to reconcile racial coexistence with white supremacy. This took on additional urgency as a new generation of blacks—
one that had never known the discipline of
slavery—reached maturity. In the white southern
mind, black political participation remained
linked with social equality. Therefore, if blacks
could be made to give up their political aspirations, they would abandon any hope of achieving
social equality. And the new generation would
learn that there were substantial restraints on
their freedom and clear limits to their ambitions.

Mississippi had set the pattern in 1890. Some
twenty years later, through such devices as the
poll tax, residence requirements, and literacy
tests, black voting in the South virtually ceased. In
Louisiana, for example, as late as 1896 some
130,000 blacks registered to vote; eight years later
only 1342 did so. Because the new laws "did not
on their face discriminate between the races," as

they were forbidden to do by the Fifteenth Amendment, the Supreme Court, in the case of *Williams v. Mississippi* in 1898, upheld the Mississippi scheme.

Various loopholes were provided for prospective white voters, and Democratic registration boards and "discreet" election officials could make certain that the right people qualified. The effect of the new suffrage laws, however, was to reduce white voting, too. Property qualifications were uniformly high. Poll taxes could be a financial barrier, and literacy clauses could be enforced strictly enough to discourage white illiterates from exposing their limitations.

Throughout the South, small Democratic oligarchies or machines maintained control of politics. The occasional challengers who won office by inflating the racial and class hatreds of the poor whites, "rednecks," and "wool-hat boys" more often than not ended up constructing their own political machines and serving the same business interests they had challenged.

Where southern custom and etiquette had previously set the races apart, in the 1890s and early 1900s the Jim Crow laws made segregation even more systematic and extensive. Few places where the two races might come into social contact were unaffected. When the Supreme Court in 1883 declared the Civil Rights Act of 1875 unconstitutional, it ruled that the federal government had no jurisdiction over discrimination practiced by private persons or organizations. Later on, the Court sanctioned state segregation laws requiring separate public facilities for whites and blacks. In *Plessy v. Ferguson* in 1896, the Court decided that blacks' equal rights under the Fourteenth Amendment were not violated if the separate facilities on railroads (and by implication, in schools and other public places) were equal. In *Cumming v. County Board of Education* in 1899, the Court formally extended the philosophy of "separate but equal" to schools.

Against this background of growing repression, what remained of black leadership in the 1890s found little comfort in any political party—or in politics. Disillusioned with the failure of black expectations, and fearing still more repressive measures, Bishop Henry M. Turner of the African Methodist Episcopal church, a former black reconstruction leader in Georgia, came to advocate emigration to Africa. Like Marcus Garvey, who would launch a similar movement in the 1920s, Turner urged his people to think differently about themselves, to cease to despise themselves. Rather than "doing nothing day and night but cry: Glory, honor, dominion and greatness to White," the black man must look to himself, for "a man must believe he is somebody before he is acknowledged to be somebody. . . . Neither [the] Republican nor Democratic party can do for the colored race what [it] can do for [itself]. Respect Black!"

Unlike Garvey, Turner never had a mass following; nor did he have any illusions about the realization of his African dream. Some day, though, he felt that his people would realize the true nature of their plight in white America. "They are now sullen, despondent and discontented and sooner or later these feelings will lead to trouble. The Southern whites rely upon the strong arm of power to produce submission, but they are resting

WORDS AND NAMES IN AMERICAN HISTORY

Originally, *Jim Crow* was the name of a song and dance done on the stage. During the 1820s, a growing number of white performers began blackening their faces and hands with burnt cork and offering to their audiences, mostly in northern cities, versions of what they fancied to be Negro songs and dances. These were the first blackface minstrel shows. One of these popular entertainers, T. D. Rice, copied a routine he had seen done by a crippled old black man. The song went, along with a deliberately awkward dance: "Weel about and turn about and do jus so; Ebery time I weel about, I jump Jim Crow." The word *crow* probably came from the supposed similarity of the bird's and the black man's color. Soon, however, *Jim Crow* took on a broader and more ominous meaning. It became a shorthand phrase for discrimination against and especially segregation of black people. This latter meaning was first applied to railroad cars in Massachusetts in 1841, where blacks were prohibited from sitting in the same sections with whites. Gradually *Jim Crow* came to include all the ways and places that blacks were excluded from public facilities and confined to separate, inferior accommodations throughout the country. It became, for blacks and even for whites, a code word for the entire system of humiliating racial segregation, in public transportation, in schools, in offices of the federal government, in the armed forces, in private industry, and at restaurants, movie theaters, public toilets, and water fountains. By the 1890s Jim Crow in the southern states was rapidly becoming more rigidly applied to all public situations where the two races might come in contact. It was becoming central to the southern way of life.

upon a slumbering volcano, which sooner or later will cause a fearful eruption."

In 1900 that "fearful eruption" was still more than half a century away. The pattern of race relations established in the aftermath of Reconstruction, reinforced by the triumph of Jim Crow and disfranchisement, persisted until the 1950s and 1960s. The concept of a New South proclaimed by industrialists, promoters, and editors had little meaning for the great mass of southerners—white or black. Sunk in poverty, debt, and ignorance, ravaged by various diseases, many resigned themselves to a dreary and hopeless way of life. The southern white's fear of black domination effectively stifled dissent, class consciousness was subordinated to race consciousness, the Democrats established virtual one-party rule, and race baiting remained a necessary vehicle for every aspiring southern politician. Such was the legacy of the New South.

SUMMARY

The Civil War settled two important questions—secession and slavery—but it raised a great many new ones. What was to happen to the South? How were freed blacks to be treated? And who would decide: the president or Congress?

Lincoln's policy of presidential Reconstruction, based on the idea that the southern states had rebelled and now should be restored to the Union, free again to govern themselves like all other states, was one solution. In Congress, Radical Republicans proposed quite another. They considered the South a conquered territory under the jurisdiction of Congress and wanted to create a new southern society based on the equality of blacks and whites.

The South over which the advocates of these policies contended was a ruined land. Its people, both black and white, lacked food and clothing. Buildings, farms, factories were gone. Blacks had the additional problem of learning to deal with their new freedom. Some left to find a new life, but most stayed where they were. And life was much the same, for defeat had in no way changed the beliefs or attitudes of white southerners.

Presidential Reconstruction failed, and not only because of Lincoln's assassination. The new president, Andrew Johnson, believed in white supremacy and followed policies designed to restore the old planter class to power. His liberal pardon policy, plus the sanctioning of Black Codes that kept the freed slaves from participating in economic and political life, brought northern public opinion and the Radicals in Congress to a boil. The war seemed to have been fought for nothing.

By December 1865, the Radicals had begun a legislative counterattack. A bill continuing the Freedmen's Bureau was pushed through Congress over Johnson's veto, and the Fourteenth Amendment was introduced in June 1866. When it was finally ratified in July 1868, the question of civil rights was legally settled, even though it would be another century before its provisions were enforced. The Radical program was written into a series of laws. The First Reconstruction Act was passed over the president's veto in March 1867. It divided the South into five military districts, put each under a general to be named by the president, and directed the generals to call a constitutional convention in each former state. Delegates were to be elected by universal adult male suffrage, black and white, and the conventions were to set up new state governments in which blacks could vote and hold office. Ratification of the Fourteenth Amendment was necessary for readmittance to the Union and acceptance of representatives by Congress.

By 1870, reconstruction under this plan was complete. It was protected by other laws, designed to neutralize the Supreme Court and the president. Johnson had survived an attempt to impeach him, but had lost his bid for renomination. In 1868 Ulysses Grant, Civil War hero, had become the new Republican president, thanks in large part to the black vote.

In the South, Radical Reconstruction, with its carpetbaggers and scalawags, brought blacks into government for the first time and gave them valuable experience. But it also brought corruption, white backlash, and repression—fueled by fear that blacks, given education and opportunity, might actually become equal to whites. The "shotgun policy"—terror and violence—brought Radical Reconstruction to an end. By 1877, the federal government had retreated from its commitment to civil rights, and the Republican party in the South was almost destroyed.

The scandals of Grant's presidency had not helped the Republicans. Though a successful general, Grant was a naive and trusting politician and a failure as a businessman. He was reelected in 1872, but the great Crédit Mobilier scandal that broke during the campaign, followed by the crash of 1873 and more revelations of wrongdoing in high places, diminished Republican strength and led to the disputed election of 1876. In return for southern support, the new Republican president, Rutherford B. Hayes, promised to leave the South alone.

The New South that emerged after 1877 was marked by characteristics that have only recently begun to change: white supremacy and repression of blacks; one-party rule; a small and wealthy ruling class holding both blacks and poor whites in economic bondage; and a weak industrial base very much dependent on northern capital.

TIME LINE

1865 Civil War ends
Lincoln assassinated; Johnson becomes president
Johnsonian (Presidential) Reconstruction begins
Black Codes
Congress refuses to seat newly elected southern representatives
Thirteenth Amendment ratified

1866 Freedmen's Bureau extension and Civil Rights Act passed over Johnson's veto
Congress approves Fourteenth Amendment (ratified in 1868)
Race riots in New Orleans and Memphis
Republicans win sweeping victory in Congressional elections

1867 Congress passes Reconstruction acts
Constitutional conventions convene in the South, launching Radical Reconstruction

1868 House votes to impeach Johnson; Senate fails to convict him
Most southern states comply with reconstruction requirements and are readmitted
Ulysses S. Grant elected president

1869 Congress approves Fifteenth Amendment (ratified in 1870)

1870–1871 Force Act and Ku Klux Klan Act

1872 Amnesty Act
Grant reelected president

1875 Civil Rights Act (overturned by Supreme Court in 1883)
Mississippi election returns Democrats to power

1876 Hayes-Tilden election

1877 Federal troops withdrawn from the South; last Radical state governments collapse

1879–1881 Black "exodusters" migrate to Kansas

1890s Legal disfranchisement and segregation (Jim Crow) inaugurate new era in race relations in the South, lasting until the 1950s

1896 *Plessy* v. *Ferguson*

Suggested Readings

The best introductions to the Reconstruction period are K. M. Stampp, *The Era of Reconstruction 1865–1877* (1965), and E. Foner, *Reconstruction: America's Unfinished Revolution 1863–1877* (1988). W. E. B. Du Bois, *Black Reconstruction in America 1860–1880* (1935), although ignored by historians when it first appeared, remains a classic by a leading black intellectual. K. M. Stampp and L. F. Litwack (eds.), *Reconstruction* (1969), is a collection of revisionist historical interpretations. D. Sterling (ed.), *The Trouble They Seen* (1976), is a collection of black testimony on Reconstruction. For insights into postwar southern white life and attitudes, see R. M. Myers (ed.), *The Children of Pride* (1971).

W. J. Cash, *The Mind of the South* (1941), and B. Wyatt-Brown, *Southern Honor* (1982), are stimulating studies of ethics and behavior in the Old and New South. H. M. Hyman, *A More Perfect Union* (1973), examines legal and constitutional issues during the Civil War and Reconstruction. For a broad and thoughtful examination of white racial attitudes, North and South, see G. M. Fredrickson, *The Black Image in the White Mind* (1971).

The reaction of the former slaves to freedom, in their own words, is exhaustively documented in G. P. Rawick (ed.), *The American Slave: A Composite Autobiography* (41 vols., 1972–79), and in an ongoing documentary history of emancipation edited by I. Berlin and others, *Freedom* (1982–). The transition from slavery to freedom is described in E. Foner, *Nothing but Freedom* (1983), and in L. F. Litwack, *Been in the Storm So Long* (1979). For regional studies, see B. J. Fields on Maryland, *Slavery and Freedom on the Middle Ground* (1985), and C. L. Mohr on Georgia, *On the Threshold of Freedom* (1986). W. S. McFeely, *Yankee Stepfather: General O. O. Howard and the Freedmen* (1968), is a critical study of the Freedmen's Bureau. J. W. De Forest, *A Union Officer in the Reconstruction* (1948), is the personal account of a Freedmen's Bureau agent.

The evolution of Lincoln's commitment to a planter-dominated Reconstruction is examined in P. McCrary, *Abraham Lincoln and Reconstruction: The Louisiana Experiment* (1978). E. L. McKitrick, *Andrew Johnson and Reconstruction* (1960), is highly critical of Johnson. L. Cox and J. H. Cox, *Politics, Principle and Prejudice 1865–1866* (1963), emphasizes Johnson's racial attitudes and his efforts to restore the Democratic party in the North. D. Carter, *When the War Was Over* (1985), assesses the failure of presidential Reconstruction. M. Perman, in *Reunion without Compromise* (1973) and *The Road to Redemption* (1984), examines postwar southern politics in depth.

The Radical Republicans have usually fared badly at the hands of historians. The traditional view is presented in T. H. Williams, *Lincoln and the Radicals* (1941). A sympathetic treatment may be found in H. L. Trefousse, *The Radical Republicans: Lincoln's Vanguard for Radical Justice* (1969). On the economics of Republican rule, see M. W. Summers, *Railroads, Reconstruction, and the Gospel of Prosperity* (1984). J. M. McPherson, in *The Struggle for Equality* (1964) and *The Abolitionist Legacy* (1976), explores the ongoing abolitionist commitment to equal rights. Among the important biographical studies of the Radicals are F. M. Brodie, *Thaddeus Stevens* (1959); D. Donald, *Charles Sumner and the Rights of Man* (1970); and B. P. Thomas and H. M. Hyman, *Stanton* (1962). R. N. Current, *Three Carpetbag Governors* (1967), and O. H. Olsen, *Carpetbaggers' Crusade: The Life of Albion Winegar Tourgee* (1965), examine an equally maligned group.

The best study of Ulysses S. Grant and his presidency is W. S. McFeely, *Grant* (1981). On the abandonment of Radical goals, see R. W. Logan, *The Negro in American Life and Thought: The Nadir 1877–1901* (1954), which focuses on the presidents and their southern strategies.

Two pioneers in exploring the neglected black role in Reconstruction were W. E. B. Du Bois and A. A. Taylor. More recent state studies with the same focus are V. L. Wharton, *The Negro in Mississippi 1865–1890* (1947); J. Williamson, *After Slavery: The Negro in South Carolina during Reconstruction, 1861–1877* (1965); J. M. Richardson, *The Negro in the Reconstruction of Florida, 1865–1877* (1965); E. L. Drago, *Black Politicians and Reconstruction in Georgia: A Splendid Failure* (1982); and T. Tunnell, *Crucible of Reconstruction: War, Radicalism and Race in Louisiana 1862–1877* (1984). Two important local studies are W. M. Evans, *Ballots and Fence Rails: Reconstruction on the Lower Cape Fear* (1966), and O. B. Burton, *In My Father's House Are Many Mansions: Family and Community in Edgefield, South Carolina* (1985). Studies of black leadership include T. Holt, *Black over White: Negro Political Leadership in South Carolina during Reconstruction* (1978); J. H. Franklin (ed.), *Reminiscences of an Active Life: The Autobiography of John Roy Lynch* (1970); H. N. Rabinowitz (ed.), *Southern Black Leaders of the Reconstruction Era* (1982); and W. E. Martin, Jr., *The Mind of Frederick Douglass* (1984).

The violent overthrow of Radical rule is described in A. W. Trelease, *White Terror: The Ku Klux Klan Conspiracy and Southern Reconstruction* (1971). The classic study of the post-Reconstruction South remains C. V. Woodward, *Origins of the New South 1877–1913* (1951). The spirit of the New South is examined in P. Gaston, *The New South Creed: A Study in Southern Mythmaking* (1970). On black labor in the New South, see G. D. Jaynes, *Branches without Roots: Genesis of the Black Working Class in the American South, 1862–1882* (1986). On southern agrarian protest, see C. V. Woodward, *Tom Watson: Agrarian Rebel* (1938); L. Goodwyn, *Democratic Promise: The Populist Movement in America* (1976); S. Hahn, *The Roots of Southern Populism: Yeoman Farmers and the Transformation of the Georgia Upcountry, 1850–1890* (1983); W. I. Hair, *Bourbonism and Agrarian Protest: Louisiana Politics 1877–1900* (1969); and B. C. Shaw, *Wool-Hat Boys: Georgia's Populist Party* (1984).

The most ambitious and far-reaching reinterpretation of race relations in the South since emancipation is J. Williamson, *The Crucible of Race* (1984), which focuses on the post-Reconstruction period. A. Meier, *Negro Thought in America 1880–1915* (1963), and G. B. Tindall, *South Carolina Negroes 1877–1900* (1952), are able examinations of black organization and ideology in the post-Reconstruction South. On the disfranchisement of blacks and poor whites, see J. M. Kousser, *The Shaping of Southern Politics* (1974). On crime and punishment in the New South, see E. L. Ayers, *Vengeance and Justice* (1984). On race relations and the more rigid forms of segregation imposed after 1890, see C. V. Woodward, *The Strange Career of Jim Crow* (1974 ed.); H. N. Rabinowitz, *Race Relations in the Urban South, 1865–1890* (1978); G. M. Fredrickson, *White Supremacy* (1981); J. W. Cell, *The Highest Stage of White Supremacy* (1982); and an outstanding state study by N. R. McMillen, *Dark Journey: Black Mississippians in the Age of Jim Crow* (1989).

How blacks responded to the deterioration of race relations is examined in two works on migration movements: N. I. Painter, *Exodusters: Black Migration to Kansas after Reconstruction* (1977), and E. S. Redkey, *Black Exodus: Black Nationalist and Back-to-Africa Movements, 1890–1910* (1969). See also J. Dittmer, *Black Georgia in the Progressive Era, 1900–1920* (1977), W. I. Hair, *Carnival of Fury: Robert Charles and the New Orleans Race Riot of 1900* (1976), and L. F. Litwack and A. Meier (eds.), *Black Leaders of the Nineteenth Century* (1988). In *Black Culture and Black Consciousness* (1977), a pathbreaking study employing the folklore, music, and humor of Afro-Americans, L. W. Levine illuminates how black southerners perceived themselves, their place in American society, and their relations with whites. Among the most compelling accounts of black life in the South is Theodore Rosengarten, *All God's Dangers: The Life of Nate Shaw* (1974), in which an eighty-five-year-old Alabama cotton farmer recounts his life.

CHAPTER 19

THE LAST AMERICAN WEST

Since the first settlements on the Atlantic coast, Americans had learned to conquer new frontiers. They had moved westward, carving out of forest and plain new towns, plantations, and farm sites. By the 1840s, this movement had reached the Missouri River. From there, until they reached the West Coast, pioneers had to cross plains, mountains, and deserts. Many found other ways to reach California and Oregon: some went by clipper ship around the Horn; others sailed to Panama, made the portage across the Isthmus, and sailed up the Pacific coast. The plains themselves were strewn with the wrecks of wagons, the bones of cows and oxen, and the graves of the unlucky.

After 1820, the western plains, which extended well into Mexico and Canada, appeared on most maps as the Great American Desert. There were few trees for fuel, houses, fences, or shade. Nor was there much rain, although the weather was violent. Hailstorms and heavy snows, gale winds and tornados were common, as were extremes of heat and cold. There was little to attract those used to the forests, rivers,

and rolling hills of Europe and the East. As late as 1860, except for Texas, not a single state had been set up between the Missouri River and the Rocky Mountains. Farther west, in the mountain country of the Rockies and the Sierra Nevada and in the Great Basin between these two ranges, settlement was still sparse.

On the eve of the Civil War, about 175,000 whites and a sprinkling of blacks were in the future Dakota country: Montana, Idaho, Wyoming, Colorado, New Mexico, Arizona, Utah, and Nevada. Except for the 25,000 Mormons who settled in Utah, almost all of them kept on the move, like most of the Indian inhabitants. They prospected for precious metals, hunted buffalo, trapped marten and beaver, drove cattle and sheep, guided trains bound for California and Oregon, scouted for the army, hauled overland freight and mail, and traded and fought with the Indians.

The real invasion came after the war. Miners, cattlemen, farmers, land speculators, railroad men, businessmen were drawn by newly perceived opportunities in the region. By 1890, all of the Wild West except the area that was to become Utah, Arizona, New Mexico, and Oklahoma had been cut up into states. Railroads spanned the continent and opened connecting lines to the mines,

Henry F. Farny, *The Song of the Talking Wire,* 1904. (detail) Oil on canvas, 22¹/₁₆ × 40″. The Taft Museum, Cincinnati, Ohio. Bequest of Mr. and Mrs. Charles Phelps Taft.

ranches, and farms that great corporations now controlled. The Indian wars were over. The army had been withdrawn from the western forts, and the Indian nations had been reduced, dispersed, and humbled. The frontier was officially closed. The Wild West had become part of the American myth; Sitting Bull and William F. (Buffalo Bill) Cody now played starring roles in a Wild West Show.

THE INDIANS: CONCENTRATION AND REPRESSION

Just before the Civil War, about 225,000 Indians shared the plains and mountains with the buffalo, the wild horse, the jackrabbit, and the coyote. But they would soon be overwhelmed as white Americans moved in at a breathtaking pace. The speed with which prospectors, ranchers, and farmers conquered the last frontier was made possible by the transcontinental railroads. They crisscrossed the region, transporting people and supplies and providing access to outside markets. Eager to attract settlers, the railroads made land available at low prices. The federal government also played a critical role. It proved to be as liberal in giving away land to corporations and prospective farmers as it was thorough and ruthless in moving the Indians to the less desirable places. At the same time, its policies undermined Indian culture and made Native Americans the wards of government bureaucrats.

The Plains Indians

When Columbus discovered America, far more than a million people lived on the continent north of Mexico. They were grouped in more than 600 distinct tribes, few of which numbered more than 2000 persons. By the Civil War, only about 300,000 "Indians" remained in the United States, more than two-thirds of them on the Great Plains. To the north—in southwestern Canada, the Dakotas, Montana, Minnesota, and Wyoming—the major tribes included the Blackfoot, Sioux, Crow, Cheyenne, and Arapaho. A little to the south—in Nebraska, Kansas, and Oklahoma—were the Osage, Kiowa, Iowa, Omaha, Pawnee, and Comanche. In the Southwest, on the desert of Arizona and New Mexico, rode the Navajo and Apache. Although differing in languages and customs, the Plains Indians tended to share a common culture. Most were nomadic and nonagricultural, and all depended for survival on hunting the bison, or buffalo.

Great buffalo herds, estimated at 12 to 15 million in the 1850s and 1860s, provided food, clothing, and shelter. Daily life revolved around the buffalo hunt, as did much ritual and worship. For centuries, the Plains Indians had hunted the buffalo on foot. In the sixteenth century Spaniards brought the horse to the American continent. The mounted Indian, now a more efficient hunter, steadily reduced the herds. As time went on, wars over the buffalo became more frequent and bloody. To survive, the Indians grew more nomadic and violent and more hostile to trespassers. For 250 years their pride and their skill as horsemen and warriors had been enough to hold their lands. Armed with a short bow superbly adapted to shooting from horseback, the Plains Indians were a match for cavalrymen armed with carbines and revolvers.

Not all Indians of the West were as fierce as the fighting tribes of the plains and the desert. In the naturally protected areas of the Colorado Plateau and the southern Great Basin, agricultural tribes such as the Hopi and Zuni built their homes, called *pueblos*, into cliffs. They cultivated fields sometimes as far as twenty miles from their homes. To the north and west, in the upper regions of the Great Basin and on the Columbia Plateau, lived the Ute, Bannock, and Snake, whose diet consisted of bear and elk, reptiles, vermin, and grasshoppers. Still farther west lived the California Indians, whose diet was acorns, tubers, and seeds dug out of the earth. Though numerous, they were too scattered to offer resistance to the gold prospectors and other whites, who waged a brutal campaign of extermination. Completing the Indian population were the sad remnants of the Five Civilized Tribes of the East (the Cherokee, Chickasaw, Choctaw, Creek, and Seminole), now in the Oklahoma country. There were also other "woods Indians" who had been driven west.

These groups found no welcome among the Plains tribes and got little help from the government. When Americans had deemed the Great American Desert uninhabitable and economically useless, the Plains Indians had been left relatively free to roam in the vast area west of the Missouri

A Sioux encampment near Pine Ridge, South Dakota, in 1891. *(Library of Congress)*

River. And then whites came. The migration to Oregon in the 1840s, the surveys for transcontinental railroads starting in 1853, the organization and settlement of the Kansas-Nebraska region in 1854, and the Colorado gold rush of 1859 all convinced the western Indians that their world was ending. If further evidence was needed, the attitudes and actions of the United States government furnished it.

The Indian Wars

In the 1840s and 1850s, when traders, travelers, and explorers demanded protection against Indians, the army established a line of forts on the plains. But even before the Civil War, the advance of the mining and agricultural frontier forced the federal government to reconsider the policy of maintaining "one big reservation." Determined to restrict if not destroy the Indians altogether, the government adopted a policy of "concentration." Individual tribes would be confined to smaller reserves, and the government would deal with each tribe separately.

The Indians also had to deal with officials of the Indian Bureau of the Department of the Interior, many of whom made fortunes by supplying reservation Indians with inferior goods, by cheating them of their lands, and by selling them forbidden liquor. Caught among dishonest and incompetent administrators, greedy prospectors and hunters, and touchy soldiers, the Indians were either starved on the reservations or killed in the open country. In the 1850s, one western soldier wrote:

It was customary to speak of the Indian man as a Buck; of the woman as a squaw. . . . By a very natural and easy transition, from being spoken of as brutes, they came to be thought of as game to be shot, or a vermin to be destroyed.

Such attitudes made for a long and brutal conflict between advancing white settlers and Indians determined to hold their lands.

The treaties of 1851 and after, which permitted the government to build roads and railroads across Indian lands, were often made only with "leaders" and small groups; most Indians were never consulted. But it was one thing to set aside reservations, another to force the Indians onto them and keep them there. In 1862, when regular army units were recalled for Civil War service and replaced by new recruits, the first of the Indian wars broke out. A small band of Sioux youths murdered five whites near a reservation in the vicinity of New Ulm, Minnesota. To forestall retaliation, a larger force under Little Crow, took to the warpath. They killed hundreds of settlers and burned their farmhouses. The militia finally caught them, and thirty-eight Indians were hanged in a public ceremony. Fights between the eastern Sioux and the army continued until later in 1863, the year of Little Crow's death. Sioux lands in Minnesota were then confiscated, and what was left of the tribe moved elsewhere.

Two years later, in an attempt to satisfy the miners' demands for access to supplies and civili-

Indian relations beyond the Mississippi, 1850–1890.

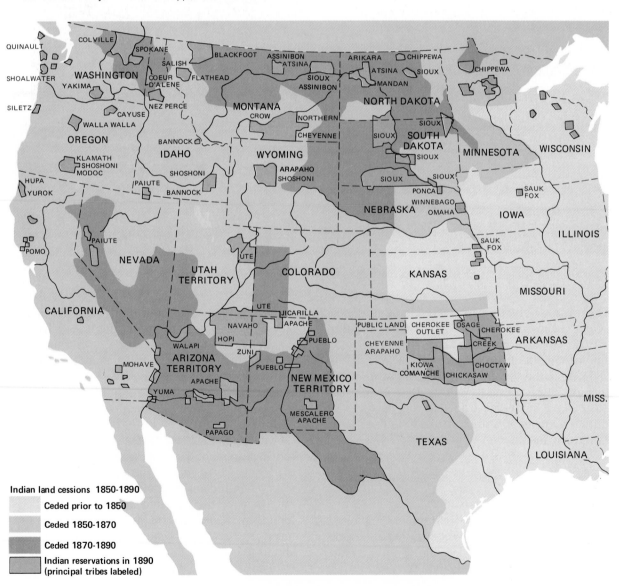

Indian land cessions 1850-1890

Ceded prior to 1850

Ceded 1850-1870

Ceded 1870-1890

Indian reservations in 1890 (principal tribes labeled)

CUSTER'S LAST STAND

More than half a century after the Battle of the Little Big Horn (June 25, 1876), historian Stanley Vestal visited the Cheyenne River Sioux Reservation and spoke with Chief White Bull, who as a twenty-six-year-old warrior had killed a white man he later learned was General George Armstrong Custer.

I charged in. A tall, well-built soldier with yellow hair and mustache saw me coming and tried to bluff me. . . . But when I rushed him, he threw his rifle at me without shooting. I dodged it. We grabbed each other and wrestled there in the dust and smoke. . . . This soldier was very strong and brave. He tried to wrench my rifle from me. I lashed him across the face with my quirt, striking the coup. He let go, then grabbed my gun with both hands until I struck him again.

But the tall soldier fought hard. He was desperate. He hit me with his fists on the jaw and shoulders, then grabbed my long braids with both hands, pulled my face close and tried to bite my nose off. . . . I thought that soldier would kill me. . . .

Finally I broke free. He drew his pistol. I wrenched it out of his hand and struck him with it three or four times on the head, knocked him over, shot him in the head, and fired at his heart. . . .

Source: Stanley Vestal, *The Man Who Killed Custer* (Norman: University of Oklahoma Press, 1957).

General George A. Custer. *(National Archives)*

zation, the government tried to build a good wagon road along the Bozeman Trail from Fort Laramie, in what is now Wyoming, north to isolated Bozeman and Helena in present-day Montana. The road would have cut across the best hunting grounds of the western Sioux. Red Cloud, chief of the western tribes, led his warriors in a campaign to stop the work. They raided the wagon trains bringing in supplies and attacked every woodcutting party. To protect the workers, the army ordered a small force under Captain W. J. Fetterman to the scene. Red Cloud's braves ambushed and massacred all eighty-two men, including Fetterman. Encouraged by their success, the Sioux increased the frequency and violence of their attacks. The project was abandoned.

To the south, warfare with the Cheyenne and Arapaho had been raging since 1861, when miners claimed lands that only ten years earlier the government had guaranteed to the Indians. This phase of the Indian wars came to a climax in 1864, when a force under Colonel John M. Chivington butchered about 450 unsuspecting men, women, and children in a Cheyenne encampment at Sand Creek. The Indians, under Chief Black Kettle, had tried to surrender peacefully, by raising first an American flag and then the traditional white flag. But Chivington was "following orders" in committing these atrocities.

General S. R. Curtis, United States Army commander in the West, had said: "I want no peace till the Indians suffer more." Such savagery fed upon itself, and Indian–army warfare in the Southwest grew more and more brutal. In 1868, at Washita in the Oklahoma country, an army group under Colonel George A. Custer defeated a band of Cheyenne and Arapaho warriors. The objective of the troops, as Custer recalled, was "to conquer or kill the warriors of an entire village." Black Kettle was killed here, and his braves were forced to give up their land claims and move into a restricted area.

Many other battles took place between the army and the Indians and between the Indians and white civilians. But the Sioux and Cheyenne wars convinced Congress that the cost of controlling the Indians was too great and progress too slow. To carry the "concentration" policy one step further, peace commissioners were sent in 1867

I WILL FIGHT NO MORE FOREVER

I am tired of fighting. Looking Glass is dead. Too-hul-hul-sote is dead. The old men are all dead. It is the young men who say yes or no. He who led on the young men is dead. It is cold and we have no blankets. The little children are freezing to death. My people, some of them, have run away to the hills, and have no blankets, no food; no one knows where they are—perhaps freezing to death. I want to have time to look for my children and see how many of them I can find. Maybe I shall find them among the dead. Hear me, my chiefs. I am tired; my heart is sick and sad. From where the sun now stands I will fight no more forever. (Chief Joseph of the Nez Percé)

Chief Joseph of the Nez Percé. *(Smithsonian Institution, National Anthropological Archives)*

Source: Mark H. Brown, *The Flight of the Nez Percé* (New York: Putnam's, 1967), p. 407.

---

to convince the tribes to move to selected reservations. One was in the Black Hills of Dakota; the other was in present-day Oklahoma. By 1868, treaties to this effect were forced on the Indians. Not only were they given inferior land, but they were told to submit to white rule and to give up many of their traditions.

The government had made a mistake. The Indians had no intention of keeping pledges they had no reason to believe the whites themselves would honor. They refused to give up their way of life, and the conflict became constant. Between 1869 and 1875, over two hundred pitched battles were fought between the army and the Indians. On the reservations, a new civilian Board of Indian Commissioners, created in 1869, tried to break down the tribal structure and convert the Indians to agriculture. But the land was poor, and the Indians were put on welfare; unable to support themselves, they were made to depend on the government.

In the 1870s, the Indians were kept on the new reservations with great difficulty; the whites, with equal difficulty, were kept off them. Moldy flour, spoiled beef, and moth-eaten blankets were typical of the supplies the Indians received. The Sioux in Dakota were further enraged by Northern Pacific Railroad crews intruding on their reservation and by the gold prospectors in the Black Hills in 1874.

Warfare broke out again in 1876. During this conflict, Custer made his famous last stand against Crazy Horse and Sitting Bull at the Battle of the Little Big Horn on June 25, 1876. The Sioux killed Custer and 264 men of his Seventh Cavalry. Had Custer survived, he no doubt would have faced a court-martial for his recklessness and his incompetent leadership. But his death sealed his martyrdom, the battle came to be known as a "massacre," and Custer's place in the mythology of the West had been secured. As for the Sioux, shortages of ammunition and food forced them to scatter, and eventually they were captured.

In Oregon, the Nez Percé, whose religious leaders urged them to drive out the whites, took to the warpath in 1877 rather than be placed on a smaller reservation. Until they gave up because of starvation and disease, the Nez Percé under Chief Joseph led five thousand government troops on a wild chase through the Idaho and Montana territories. For almost three decades, the Apache resisted. In the 1880s they made a desperate stand in present-day Arizona and New Mexico until their chief, Geronimo, was captured in 1886.

The end of the buffalo herds finished the Plains Indians. In the late 1860s the building of the Union Pacific left the animals at the mercy of every railroad worker, miner, adventurer, and traveler. Since a stampeding herd could overturn a train, buffalo hunting became a part of railroad building. Buffalo Bill Cody made his reputation by killing some four thousand buffalo in eighteen months as a hunter for the Kansas Pacific Railroad. In 1871, a Pennsylvania tannery discovered it could process buffalo skins into commercial leather. Between 1872 and 1874, 3 million head a year were killed; by 1878, the southern herd had been wiped out.

"I saw buffalos lying dead on the prairie so thick that one could hardly see the ground," a hunter declared in the winter of 1881–1882. "A man could have walked for twenty miles upon their carcasses." In 1886, when the National Museum wanted to mount some buffalo, it found only about six hundred of the northern herd left, deep in the Canadian woods.

Fearful that the Indians' religion contributed to the constant warfare, the government in 1884 prohibited many practices, among them the Sun Dance. The government hoped to prevent the surviving Indian bands from joining together even for ceremonies. But in 1890, a Paiute religious prophet named Wovoka attracted many Plains Indians to a faith that featured a ceremonial rite known to whites as the Ghost Dance. Although Wovoka preached love and nonviolence, the new faith promised a time in which the dead would be revived and the earth would be returned to the Indians. When the Sioux adopted this faith, alarmed officials urged military intervention.

Confronted with heavily armed cavalry, the Indians fled. The troops followed and, in December 1890, in the "battle" of Wounded Knee, they massacred the half-starved remnants of the tribe, leaving behind a two-mile trail strewn with the butchered bodies of women and children who had tried to run. "My father ran and fell down and the blood came out of his mouth," the son of Yellow Bird, the medicine man, recalled, "and then a soldier put his gun up to my pony's nose and shot him, and then I ran and a policeman got me."

The Wounded Knee massacre was a final and tragic chapter in the military conquest of the American Indians. Whatever the pride, the military prowess, and the horsemanship of the Plains Indians, whatever their willingness to defend their land, families, and traditions, in the end the army's superior firepower and technology ensured the triumph of the white man on the Great Plains.

The Dawes Act and After

In 1887, three years before Wounded Knee, Congress had passed the Dawes Act, which

Geronimo, Apache chief. *(Library of Congress)*

defined the federal government's Indian policy until 1934. The act broke up the tribe as a basic unit of Indian society: Reservation land was divided, and each family head was given 160 acres to cultivate. After a probation period of twenty-five years, he was to be granted full rights of ownership and citizenship in the United States. In 1924, the United States granted citizenship to all the Indians.

The Dawes Act was the result of growing opposition to the policy of the army and the Interior Department. The alternative was forcing the Indians to become settled farmers and to adapt themselves to white ways. But the Dawes Act did the Indians little good. In dividing the land, the government usually gave them the poorest; the best was sold to white settlers. Even when an Indian obtained good land, inexperience in legal matters left him open to the same kind of cheating that had marked the making of the tribal treaties.

Again and again, Indians were tricked into selling their best holdings to white speculators. Worse still, they lacked the cultural tradition, the necessary training, and the competitive incentive to cultivate the land they kept. Deprived of the

By the 1890s the Wild West existed largely in the national imagination, made vivid in pulp literature and in Buffalo Bill's Wild West Exhibition, featuring Sitting Bull, a Sioux medicine man, and William F. (Buffalo Bill) Cody, a scout and buffalo hunter. *(Library of Congress)*

kind of support the tribe had once provided, most became paupers. Some found outlets in alcohol or petty crime. The year the Dawes Act passed, the Indian tribes still had title to about 138 million acres of land. By 1932, some 90 million acres had found their way into white ownership.

THE GREAT AMERICAN WEST: MINERS, RANCHERS, FARMERS

With a thoroughness equaled only by their extermination of the buffalo and the Indians, Americans after the Civil War exploited the natural wealth of the West. The plains and mountains, it was discovered, were rich in agricultural and mineral wealth. The most productive of the earth's wheat lands stretched across the Dakotas and eastern Montana. In large areas of Wyoming, Colorado, and Texas, and even in sections of Nevada, Utah, and Arizona, there were grazing lands for cattle and sheep that would supply much of the world's beef, mutton, hides, and wool. Other parts of the plains and mountains held some of the world's largest and purest veins of copper and iron ore, some of the world's greatest deposits of lead and zinc, valuable seams of coal, and gold and silver. Beneath the earth in Texas (and elsewhere in the West) lay incredible reserves of crude petroleum and natural gas.

For generations Americans had had even less use for these resources than the Indians who roamed the western lands. But the demands of the booming cities and expanding industry in the postwar years changed the western landscape. Within a generation, this vast area was providing essential raw materials, meat, and grain for eastern and midwestern markets. By 1890, many individual enterprises had been replaced by corporations, frontier boom camps converted into company towns, and prospectors and small businessmen reduced to wage laborers.

The Mining Frontier

Although gold had brought miners to the West in the 1840s, the era of the prospector was actually short, from the mid-1850s to the mid-1870s. But during those twenty years, speculation was wild. The mining frontier changed with every new rumor of a strike; as soon as one boom ended, another developed. Towns sprang up overnight, and many of them disappeared soon after the prospectors rushed off to still another find.

By the late 1850s, the fabulous discoveries in California—at Sutter's Fort and elsewhere in the San Joaquin and Sacramento valleys—were staked out and some of the best locations had begun to run thin. In a single decade, miners had extracted hundreds of millions in gold from the hills and streams, much of it by the crudest methods. Plenty of gold remained, but it was buried in hills that had to be blasted away and worked with costly equipment by teams of miners. The operations required more capital and business ability than most of the prospectors had. When surface gold ran out, a few took up more stable occupations. Some became miners for corporations, others even became farmers. But tens of thousands made "prospectin' " a way of life and quickly headed for the next strike.

On their way to California in 1848, Captain John Beck of the Oklahoma country and W. Green Russell of Georgia had seen signs of gold around the South Platte River in the northeastern part of

THE LAST STAND

Black Elk, a holy man of the Oglala Sioux, was present at the "battle" of Wounded Knee. Forty years later, he would recall its impact:

And so it was all over.

I did not know then how much was ended. When I look back now from this high hill of my old age, I can still see the butchered women and children lying heaped and scattered all along the crooked gulch as plain as when I saw them with eyes still young. And I can see that something else died there in the bloody mud, and was buried in the blizzard. A people's dream died there. It was a beautiful dream.

And I, to whom so great a vision was given in my youth—you see me now a pitiful old man who has done nothing, for the nation's hoop is broken and scattered. There is no center any longer, and the sacred tree is dead.

Source: John G. Neihardt, *Black Elk Speaks* (Lincoln: University of Nebraska Press, 1961), p. 276.

what is today Colorado. In 1858, having sold out in California, they decided to go back and check into Colorado's possibilities. That July they staked out the first claim in the Pike's Peak region, near present-day Denver. Soon eastern newspapers were full of news of other Colorado strikes. By the end of 1858, "Pike's Peak or Bust" had become a national slogan. By June 1859, over 100,000 had made the trek to Colorado, some from California, but many from the East and the Mississippi Valley.

Tall stories kept them coming, but the truth

Main Street, Helena, Montana, which was originally a mining town known as Last Chance Gulch, 1872. *(Denver Public Library, Western History Collection)*

soon became known: there was gold around Pike's Peak, but very little. When the trek home began, the wagons carried the complaint "Pike's Peak and Busted." Some prospectors stayed on to try their hand at farming and grazing and to lay the foundations for Colorado's economy. In the early 1870s, rich beds of silver were worked near Leadville, and gold was found later in the region of Cripple Creek. Such discoveries, together with the growth of Denver as a commercial center, made statehood certain. In 1876 Colorado was admitted to the Union as the Centennial State.

Before the Colorado boom ended, news out of western Nevada in the spring of 1859 sent prospectors swarming into that area. By summer twenty thousand men were seeking their fortunes, this time in silver, at the fabulous Comstock Lode on Mount Davidson. By 1877, Comstock miners had taken $306 million worth of silver. This strike helped to make the remarkable career of Virginia City, which overnight became a camp town and a legend. The discovery of the Comstock Lode set others looking for deposits nearby.

By 1861 Nevada had a population larger perhaps than it has ever had since. Organized as a territory in that year, Nevada became a state in 1864. Its admittance was designed to secure its vote to ratify the Thirteenth Amendment and to help reelect Lincoln. Mining booms also helped the organization of Idaho (1863), Arizona (1863), and Montana (1864) as territories.

The era of the prospectors was drawing to a close when, in 1874, rumors of gold on the Sioux reservation in the Black Hills of southwestern Dakota Territory were confirmed. The area had been made unapproachable by the Sioux, who were anxious to retain their lands. The United States Army was as determined to keep the Sioux on the reservation as it was to keep out white intruders. But stories kept the lure of the Hills alive: Indians with bags of nuggets, army officers concealing their knowledge of outcroppings so troops would not desert, and a few desperate men who worked a stake and ran.

By October 1876 the army could no longer keep the prospectors out, and the reservation was opened to anyone who wanted to come. Fifteen thousand prospectors poured in almost at once, and the army did what it could to protect them. In the winter of 1876, the richest veins were discovered around Deadwood Gulch. The nearby supply center of Deadwood, South Dakota, an overnight migrant city of some 25,000, soon outdid Tombstone, Arizona, as the toughest of the "badman"

towns. All told, the Black Hills mines yielded ore worth $287 million. But the life of the strike was short, and the town of Deadwood quickly passed into legend too.

The first copper seam was discovered in 1881 in Butte, Montana. By the end of the decade, Montana was the leading mining state, with an annual output worth $41 million. Annual national copper production passed that of gold in value; by 1900, it was nearing that of gold and silver combined. Most of the copper went into the miles and miles of electric wiring that were lighting cities and powering factories. Lead production increased with the growing use of electric storage batteries. Missouri remained the main source of lead. After 1880, sizable quantities from the Leadville district of Colorado and the Coeur d'Alene district of Idaho became available. In 1901, in time for the coming of the automobile, Black Gold roared onto the western scene from the gushers of the Spindletop fields in Texas, establishing the oil industry of that state.

By 1880, big business had moved in to dominate the development of the West. Exploitation of

The James gang: Jesse James is seated left, with Frank James seated right; standing are Cole Younger (left) and Bob Younger (right). The Youngers were captured in 1876 and sentenced to life imprisonment. "We were drove to it, sir," Cole Younger told the judge. "Circumstances sometimes makes men what they are." Six years later Jesse James was shot in the head by a fellow gang member for a $10,000 reward. *(Library of Congress)*

the new metals and minerals required heavy investment in plants, machinery, and hired workers. It was not long before financiers such as Henry H. Rogers and the Rockefellers of New York, the Guggenheims of Philadelphia, and the Mellons of Pittsburgh dominated the economy of the West. And with their arrival, the mining frontier of the prospector came to a close.

Before that frontier closed, however, it had had an extraordinary life of its own. The wide-open mining towns exemplified the boisterous and optimistic spirit of the last American West. The inhabitants were mostly recent arrivals, and all of them, it seemed, were on the make, sustained by the stories of instant success. The people who filled these towns gave them their unique character: desperadoes, deserters, prostitutes, confidence men, and gamblers preyed on the prospectors and on one another. Places such as Virginia City, with its own opera house, elaborate homes, and newspaper (on which Samuel Clemens worked as "Mark Twain"), aspired to better status,

but they were still largely towns of saloons, gambling houses, brothels, and dance halls.

Although the mining country attracted an assortment of refugees from society, it soon developed a legal code. This code applied not only to personal crimes but also to such matters as claims, assays, and water rights. Enforcement, however, was usually an individual matter. In 1866, Congress simply declared that the mining country was free to all, "subject to local customs or rules of miners in the several mining districts." But when lawbreaking grew intolerable, "law and order" citizens imposed vigilante justice, at least until the settlement of the West brought formal government agencies and stable local authorities.

The Cattle Frontier

Even as prospectors were seeking their fortunes in precious metals, cattlemen were moving into the Great Plains, turning the vast open ranges of

The mining bonanza and the Cattle Kingdom.

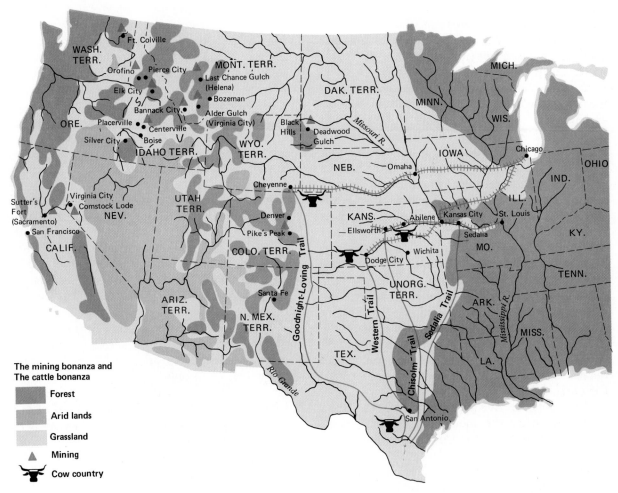

The mining bonanza and
The cattle bonanza

- Forest
- Arid lands
- Grassland
- ▲ Mining
- 🐂 Cow country

unclaimed grassland into grazing lands for increasingly valuable herds. Before the Civil War, the number of Texas cattle alone was estimated at nearly 5 million. The incentives for reaching northern markets with these cattle multiplied along with the rapid growth of the population and the fantastic prices offered for steers. The fortunes that could be made equaled those of many of the more successful prospectors.

Western-style ranching and cowpunching came into American life with the annexation of Texas in 1845. Long before, Mexicans had designed the bit, bridle, saddle, and spurs, the lariat, chaps, and five-gallon hat of the traditional cowboy. For centuries they had broken broncos, grazed calves, and roped steers. But they did not use the branding iron.

When Americans from Missouri, Mississippi, Alabama, and Tennessee began to trickle into Texas in the 1820s, many of them simply put their brands on what they called wild herds and set themselves up as cattle kings. Other Americans grabbed horses and cattle that had broken away from Mexican herds. In this way, the range cattle industry of Kansas and Nebraska began. The northern ranchers supplied beef and fresh horses to people going west and to mining camps and railroad crews. Compared with those of Texas, however, the northern herds were tiny.

In the 1850s, some Texas ranchers tried to drive their cattle west to the Colorado and California markets or north to Illinois. But herds and herders fell easy prey to the Indians, and the surviving steers reached their destination too thin and tough to bring a good price. The ranchers waited out the Civil War, then began looking again for markets. When they learned that Texas steers worth three or four dollars would bring as much as forty dollars a head in the North, they decided to try the cross-country drive once more. The risk seemed less because of the westward extension of the railroads.

The year 1866 marked the first of the "long drives" to a railroad town—Sedalia, Missouri, on the Missouri Pacific. Sedalia had just been connected with Kansas City, and Kansas City with St. Louis; these thriving Missouri cities would serve as markets and distribution points for other metropolitan markets.

By the fall of that year, some 260,000 Texas steers were on the move. But the trail went through forests, which made the longhorns of the open range stampede. It also crossed over new Missouri farmland, where settlers came rushing out with guns to protect their crops. Cattle rustlers raided the herds. And the Indians, though supposedly confined to the reservations, still roamed the plains. In the end, only a few steers ever reached Sedalia. Those that did, however, brought thirty-five dollars a head, a price that led many ranchers to try again the next year or to find some other route.

By then a smart Illinois meat dealer, Joseph G. McCoy, realized he could make a fortune if he could set up a convenient meeting point for northern buyers and western breeders. McCoy chose Abilene, Kansas, on the Kansas Pacific, which (with the Hannibal and St. Jo Railroad and other lines) connected Abilene with Chicago. At Abilene, McCoy built a hotel, barns, stables, pens, and loading chutes. In 1868, Abilene received 75,000 head of cattle. Within three years this number had grown nearly ten times, and Abilene became the capital of the cattle frontier. It was the legendary cow town where Wild Bill Hickok made his reputation as a straight shooter and federal marshal.

As the railroads extended westward and southward, new trails and new railroad towns nearer the cattle range were developed. Ellsworth, Kansas, received over a million head between 1872 and 1879. On the Union Pacific route, first Cheyenne and then Laramie became important cattle railheads. And Dodge City, Kansas, the "Cowboy's Capital," rivaled Tombstone, Deadwood, and Abilene. But since the drive to even the nearest railhead was not good for steers ready for market, in the 1870s ranchers began to drive Texas yearlings to the northern range—western Kansas, Nebraska, Colorado, Wyoming, Montana, the Dakotas.

Northern "feeders" bought the young cattle and fattened them free on public lands until they were ready for market. The best cows and bulls were taken from the herds, and breeds were constantly improved. The open-range cattle industry came into its own after 1878, when the business depression of the mid-1870s had ended and beef prices had revived.

Although a romantic chapter in the history of the West, the "long drive" held little glamour for the participants, the much-celebrated cowboys. Equipped with only cow ponies, lassos, and six-shooters, for two months they tried to keep safe and under control a thousand head of hungry, thirsty, touchy steers. P. A. Rollins, a veteran of the drive, wrote: "It was tiresome, grimy business for the attendant punchers, who travelled ever in a cloud of dust, and heard little but the constant chorus from the crackling of hoofs and of ankle joints, from the bellows, lows, and bleats of the trudging animals."[*]

With his picturesque outfits and reputation for daring, the cowboy captured the eastern imagination. But in actuality he was little more than a hired hand who led a lonely existence and worked long hours for low wages.

Like the isolated mining centers, the range too developed its own laws. Here the vital need was for water, and "range rights" along a stream became the most precious part of any ranch. Local regulations had the force of law in determining the extent of each individual's or company's "range rights," but claims often had to be backed up with a gun. Even when the ranchers respected one another's territory, the cattle did not. Here again, rules had to be established for recording brands and for disposing of unbranded cattle.

Ranches that covered as many as thirty or forty square miles could not be policed efficiently, and rustling became common. With so much invested in their herds, ranchers needed to find ways to protect themselves. The enforcement of rude justice was one of the main objectives of the numerous stockgrowers' associations organized in the 1870s. Eventually, these groups developed hidden governments in their territories. One of their more important business objectives was to prevent competition by making it difficult for newcomers to become members and dangerous for them to operate without joining up. The ranchers were aware of the speed with which the range, endless though it seemed, could be overstocked.

But in spite of all their efforts, news soon leaked out about how five-dollar steers could be transformed into property worth forty-five to sixty dollars a head with a mere investment of four years of free grazing. New ranchers flocked to the range like prospectors to the mines. When great profits materialized, large investors set up corporations. By 1885 the range had finally grown overcrowded, and the disastrous winter of 1885–1886, followed by a blistering summer, destroyed most of the feed and cattle. The steers that found their way to market were of such poor quality that beef prices crashed despite the shortage.

It was at this time too that sheepherders began to cross the range in large numbers. Their flocks, which spoiled the water, ate not only the grass but the roots as well, leaving in their wake barren range. To add to the stockgrowers' misery, farmers began homesteading in larger numbers and fencing in the open range. Many farmers kept herds of their own in fenced fields, where they could control breeding more carefully and regulate feed. The beef they produced was superior to that grown on the open range. In 1882, range beef sold for $9.35 per hundred pounds in Chicago; by 1887, the price had fallen to $1.90. The end of the open range hastened the end of the last frontier.

The Agricultural Frontier

Although the farmers' frontier had been steadily moving westward, the expansion of agriculture in the post–Civil War decades was extraordinary. The revolution in farm machinery, transportation, and marketing was a factor as was immigration from abroad. Between 1870 and 1900, American farmers more than doubled their landholdings—from 407 to 841 million acres—and placed more new land under cultivation than had been farmed in the entire country since 1607.

Much of the new acreage lay in the Great Plains, which tens of thousands of homesteaders were helping to convert to an agricultural economy. But not all farmers were wealthy and comfortable. This was particularly true in the plains country. Because they had to adapt to semiarid land, harsh weather, grasshopper plagues, and isolation, the plains settlers lived hard lives.

The Homestead Act of 1862 opened public lands in the West to free settlement by American citizens or those who declared their intention to become citizens. Much of the best land found its way into the hands of large landholders and speculators. And although adequate for the Mississippi Valley and lavish compared with New England (the two regions from which most of the supporters of the law came), the quarter-section (160 acres) offered by the Homestead Act was either too large or too small for the dry, treeless plains. It was too small for cattle or grain production and too large for irrigated farming. Prospective settlers faced high costs in transporting their families and possessions to the land and in preparing enough of the 160 acres to get a paying crop. In addition, there was the expense of irrigation, buildings, equipment, taxes, and hired help. For the large farmer or farming corporation willing to use the costly new machinery, a quarter-section was hardly worth the investment.

Recognition of these problems prompted new

[*]From Philip Ashton Rollins, *The Cowboys* (New York: Charles Scribner's Sons, 1936). Copyright 1922, 1936; copyrights renewed. Reprinted with the permission of Charles Scribner's Sons.

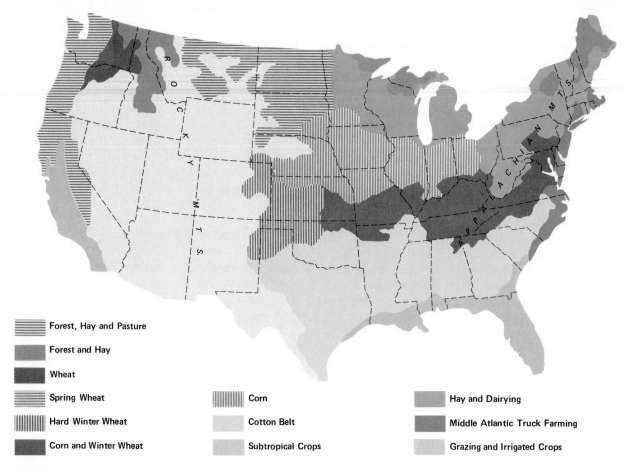

Forest, Hay and Pasture

Forest and Hay

Wheat

Spring Wheat

Hard Winter Wheat

Corn and Winter Wheat

Corn

Cotton Belt

Subtropical Crops

Hay and Dairying

Middle Atlantic Truck Farming

Grazing and Irrigated Crops

Agricultural regions of the United States.

congressional legislation designed to stimulate settlement and to deal with the shortage of water and timber. The Timber Culture Act of 1873 offered an additional quarter-section to the settler who would put at least 40 acres of it into forest. But the act encouraged fraudulent claims, and before its repeal in 1891 fewer than 25 percent of those who took advantage of its provisions obtained final title to the land. Two other laws passed to stimulate settlement by farmers actually worked to keep them out. The Desert Land Act of 1877 allowed a settler to occupy 640 acres by paying $1.25 an acre. The settler could win clear title to the land in three years for an additional payment of $1 an acre, provided he could prove he had irrigated the plot. Thousands of farmers agreed to try to irrigate the land, but the job proved too difficult, and most of them quickly abandoned the effort. Cattle ranchers, however, used the act to get title to grazing range; they registered thousands of acres in the names of cowboys who then signed over the land to them. Some 2.6 million acres were taken up under the act, and an estimated 95 percent of the claims were fraudulent. Nor did settlers gain anything

from the Timber and Stone Act of 1878, which operated to benefit lumber companies seeking a share of public lands. This act offered a maximum of 160 acres of rich timberland—land "unfit for cultivation"—in California, Nevada, Oregon, and Washington Territory, at $2.50 an acre. With the lumber companies paying handsome bonuses to those who registered claims and then signed over the land, the act amounted to a giant giveaway of natural resources.

Between 1862 and 1900, 80 million acres were registered under the Homestead Act, a figure that includes many dummy registrations used by speculators to accumulate large holdings. During the same period, railroads, land companies, and states receiving grants of federal land for educational purposes under the Morrill Act of 1862 sold at least five or six times as much land. These sellers charged from two to ten dollars an acre, a fair enough price for the best sites near transportation and markets. Railroads and land companies often gave mortgages on the land and extended credit for equipment to develop it.

In 1868, when the Union Pacific Railroad was nearly ready for passengers, it advertised its land in Kansas and other states on the edge of the frontier. Every land-grant railroad opened a land department and a bureau of immigration. In the 1870s, the Union Pacific and the Burlington railroads each spent over $1 million for advertising abroad. Other railroads and land companies opened London offices with agents who searched Europe for settlers. Western states with land to sell and steamship companies carrying immigrants to the New World also looked for settlers abroad.

These campaigns were remarkably successful. According to the 1880 census, 73 percent of Wisconsin's population was of foreign parentage, 71 percent of Minnesota's, 66 percent of the Dakotas', and 44 percent of Nebraska's. In the following two years, "American fever" swept western and central Europe. In 1882 alone, the record year for immigration to the United States in the nineteenth century, almost 650,000 foreigners arrived in American ports.

Large numbers remained in the coastal cities, and many others got no farther west than Pittsburgh and Cleveland. But hundreds of thousands went to the farmlands of the plains. After the war,

thousands of Cotton Belt blacks from northern Louisiana and neighboring southern states joined the move to the plains areas. At first the Exodusters were welcome (they would be Republican voters). But as more and more came, Kansas officials began to send agents south to stop the flow. Most of those who did complete the journey failed to get land. Lacking the money to set up farms, some eventually found jobs laboring on the railroads or mining coal; women took in washing or became domestics. Others drifted farther west.

The obstacles confronting those who came to the plains were immense. To make a living was a family enterprise in which men and women worked equally hard. For the women, in addition to helping with the crops and feeding the livestock, there were household tasks made even more difficult on the prairie: keeping a dirt house clean, washing clothes with water that defied attempts to soften it, making soap and candles, undergoing childbirth with no help, and raising the children. For most women, as for most men, the loneliness of prairie life was the worst problem. In the Texas panhandle, this sign was found on an empty cabin in 1886: "250 miles to the

Homesteaders rest by their covered wagons in Colorado in the 1870s. *(Denver Public Library, Western History Collection)*

nearest post office; 100 miles to wood; 20 miles to water; 6 inches to hell. God bless our home! Gone to live with wife's folks."

Before the new settlers could transform the country into farmland, they had to deal with the problems of shelter and water. Not even log cabins could be built on the treeless plains; the first shelters were sod huts. Lack of wood made these dwellings difficult to heat in a region that covered some of the coldest parts of the United States. The first settlers burned dried buffalo dung. They next turned to hay, burned in special stoves designed to consume it slowly. But nothing really worked until the railroads brought in coal.

The lack of water, which increased as one moved west, made for even greater difficulties. By 1880, mechanical well-digging equipment was in use, but even when wells could be dug to the necessary depth of two or three hundred feet, there remained the problem of getting the water to the surface. Windmills that harnessed the power of the strong prevailing winds promised an answer. But before windmills became cheap enough for the average farmer, the water problem had been solved in other ways. One was *dry farming*. Under this system, a field was plowed after each rainfall in order to slow down evaporation. The turned-over mud formed a mulch that stored water on which roots continued to feed long after the rain had ended.

The tough sod of the plains, like the tough sod of the prairie, resisted the eastern plow. In a region blasted by hailstorms, windstorms, and sudden frosts, production was limited not by how much farmers could plant, but by how much they could harvest. With the mechanization of farming and the inventions of the 1870s and 1880s, two men and a team of horses could harvest 20 acres of wheat a day. Eastern farmers dared not plant more than 8 acres of wheat a *season*. At the end of the century, one plains farmer with a cord binder

could count on harvesting 135 acres. In 1879, Illinois, the leading wheat state for twenty years, still held first place; by 1899 it had fallen out of the first ten, which were now led by Minnesota, the Dakotas, Kansas, California, and Nebraska.

During the 1870s, plains farmers began to insist that ranchers fence in their cattle. The ranchers, in turn, urged the "nesters" to move away or else buy fences to keep the range cattle out. Hostility between the two groups led to gunfights, but cheap fencing, not guns, eventually won the plains for the farmers. Materials for the wood and stone fences used by farmers were lacking on the plains, and neither would have been an effective barrier to cattle. But then in 1874 barbed wire was patented. Available in large quantities at low cost, barbed-wire fencing provided farmers with the means to enclose and protect their lands. By 1890, much of the farmland had been fenced.

When a disastrous series of grasshopper invasions ended early in the 1870s, everything worked in favor of the new wheat country. After 1875, Europe suffered one crop failure after another. The Russo-Turkish War of 1877–1878 closed Russia's ports and cut off Europe's main source of grain. All the improvements in American farm technology coincided with the new needs of the European market. This market continued to expand as western Europe turned from farming to industry. The future of wheat growing on the plains appeared brighter because for eight consecutive years after 1877 the region enjoyed such good rainfall that many people believed the climate had changed.

While production soared, demand kept prices high. Good prices encouraged expansion, mainly by farmers mortgaging their land to the limit in order to raise money to acquire more land before the next person claimed it. The banks encouraged this practice. "Most of us," said a Kansas official,

WORDS AND NAMES IN AMERICAN HISTORY

In an increasingly technological world, Americans' everyday language has been affected by technological developments. Some such words have become so common that most people today are unaware of their technological origin. Take the perfectly ordinary word *sidetrack*. To be *sidetracked* is to be taken away from one's main line of activity. A bill in Congress can be *sidetracked* by a vote to send it back for further consideration by a committee. Few people associate the word with railroads, but that's where it originated, in the 1880s, nearly fifty years after the first railroads were built in the United States. As more and more trains began running on the single tracks, it became necessary to build "sidetracks"— short tracks beside the main line where one train could wait while another train moved by in the opposite direction.

RURAL LIFE IN THE 1880S

Born on a farm in Wisconsin in 1860, Hamlin Garland accompanied his family as they migrated to Iowa and Dakota Territory. In 1884 he left for the East, seeking the life of a writer and teacher. Three years later, he returned for a visit to Osage, Iowa, where he had spent much of his youth.

Every house I visited had its individual message of sordid struggle and half-hidden despair. Agnes had married and moved away to Dakota, and Bess had taken upon her girlish shoulders the burdens of wifehood and motherhood almost before her girlhood had reached its first period of bloom. In addition to the work of being cook and scrubwoman, she was now a mother and nurse. As I looked around upon her worn chairs, faded rag carpets and sagging sofas—the bare walls of her pitiful little house seemed a prison. I thought of her as she was in the days of her radiant girlhood and my throat filled with rebellious pain.

All the gilding of farm life melted away. The hard and bitter realities came back upon me in a flood. Nature was as beautiful as ever . . . but no splendor of cloud, no grace of sunset could conceal the poverty of these people; on the contrary they brought out, with a more intolerable poignancy, the gracelessness of these homes, and the sordid quality of the mechanical daily routine of these lives.

I perceived beautiful youth becoming bowed and bent. I saw lovely girlhood wasting away into thin and hopeless age. Some of the women I had known had withered into querulous and complaining spinsterhood, and I heard ambitious youth cursing the bondage of the farm. . . .

Source: Hamlin Garland, "A Visit to the West," *A Son of the Middle Border* (New York: Macmillan Co., 1962), p. 309. © The Macmillan Company 1962; Copyright by Hamlin Garland 1917; Copyright renewed 1945 by Mary I. Lord and Constance G. Williams. Photograph by G. J. Van Schaick, State Historical Society of Wisconsin.

"crossed the Mississippi or Missouri with no money but with a vast wealth of hope and courage. Haste to get rich has made us borrowers, and the borrower has made booms, and booms made men wild, and Kansas became a vast insane asylum covering 80,000 square miles."

Just as buffalo had drawn the Indian to the West, gold the prospector, and grass the rancher, so wheat had drawn the farmer. But the agricul-tural West was riding for a fall. Overproduction in the United States by the mid-1880s, the entry of India and Australia into the world wheat market, the revival of Russian wheat exports—all were bad signs. In the 1870s, the commercial farmers of the plains country, like farmers elsewhere, found their freedom declining, almost in proportion to their increasing dependence on impersonal forces (markets, railroads, and middlemen) over which they had no control. For the plains farmers, that development only sharpened the isolation and grimness of the environment that drained much of the pleasure from their lives. For many of their sons and daughters, the rewards would be too meager, economically and psychologically, to sustain that kind of existence. They would seek their fortunes elsewhere—in the industrial and urban East.

SUMMARY

After the Civil War, Americans began to move in earnest into the Great Plains and to settle the land between the Mississippi and the Rockies. As they did so, they displaced and overwhelmed the Indian tribes whose home it was. But this time the Indians did not go peaceably—perhaps because there was nowhere to go. The Plains Indians were hunters and fighters, and for twenty years they battled settlers, prospectors, miners, and the United States Cavalry to keep their home.

The reservation system was no solution, for the lands given to the Indians were the poorest and most barren, and could not support a population. Eventually, by the late 1880s, the Indians were crushed; those who remained became wards of the federal government and a forgotten part of American society. What the army had not been able to do by force, government bureaucrats did by regulations and policies that systematically stripped the Indians of their culture, their self-respect, and their independence. These were policies so cruel and so brutal that it was another half-century before most Americans even knew of the suffering that expansionism had caused.

As the Indians were killed or driven onto barren reservations, white settlers poured in to exploit the resources of the West. Mines yielded great quantities of copper, iron, lead, zinc, gold, and silver. The rush of prospectors to areas where ore had been found created boomtowns overnight—and the raw, rough culture of legend.

The building of a cattle empire on the plains did the same for other areas. Growing markets for meat in the booming cities of the East made ranching profitable, and the railroad made a western cattle industry possible. Towns such as Abilene, Dodge City, Tombstone, and Deadwood, where cattle were driven to be shipped to market, roared to life and contributed to the legend that was the Wild West.

Law and order was a problem in the mining and cattle areas, as was the regulation of competition. Much of the policing was done by private groups who provided their own rough justice. All this changed when the secret of farming the plains successfully was discovered. The open range was fenced in, and the Great Plains became one of the greatest grain-producing areas in the world. Farming brought stability, government, and eventually statehood, despite the great obstacles settlers had to overcome. The climate was awful, there was not even enough wood to build houses, manufactured goods were scarce, and success demanded long hours of labor and great isolation and loneliness.

But new farming techniques and technology, the availability of land through such government programs as the Homestead Act, and the growing flood of European immigrants willing to work hard for a better life signaled the end of the last frontier. By the 1880s the settlement boom and the Wild West were over. Mining, cattle ranching, and farming were now businesses that entailed the risk of failure when prices dropped during swings of the business cycle. For the newer immigrants and for the children of the Plains settlers, the cities and the industrialized East seemed to offer new and easier opportunities for a good life.

TIME LINE

1862	Homestead Act
	Morrill Land Grant Act
1866	Cattle drives from Texas begin
1869	Transcontinental railroad completed
1870s	Destruction of the buffalo herds
1874	Barbed-wire patented
1876	Battle of Little Big Horn (Custer's Last Stand)
	Colorado granted statehood

1877	Desert Land Act
1878	Timber and Stone Act
1887	Dawes Act
1880s	Last stand of the Apache Indians; Geronimo captured in 1886
1890	Indian massacre at Wounded Knee, South Dakota

Suggested Readings

R. A. Billington, *Westward Expansion* (1967), R. Bartlett, *The New Country: A Social History of the American Frontier* (1974) and R. H. Hine, *The American West* (2nd ed. 1984) are informative surveys. Bernard De Voto, *Across the Wide Missouri* (1947), provides illuminating background material and is engrossing reading. W. P. Webb, *The Great Plains* (1931), and J. C. Malin, *The Grassland of North America* (1948), are classic studies of the relationship between the natural environment and social life. H. N. Smith, *Virgin Land: The American West as Symbol and Myth* (1950), is a good study of the impact of the West on American literature and thought. On the far reaching impact of the frontier myth, see R. Slotkin, *The Fatal Environment: The Myth of the Frontier in the Age of Industrialization, 1800–1890* (1985). Regional studies include O. O. Winther, *The Great Northwest* (1950); H. R. Lamar, *The Far Southwest 1846–1912* (1966); J. C. Caughey, *History of the Pacific Coast* (1933); and H. E. Briggs, *Frontiers of the Northwest: A History of the Upper Missouri Valley* (1940). The lure of California is imaginatively told in Kevin Starr, *Americans and the California Dream 1850–1915* (1973). Sexual imbalance on the frontier was less than many popular accounts have suggested, argues J. R. Jeffrey in her study of a much neglected subject, *Frontier Women: The Trans-Mississippi West 1840–1880* (1979).

W. E. Washburn, *The Indian in America* (1975), is an authoritative history. The plight of individual tribes is chronicled in M. H. Brown, *The Flight of the Nez Percé* (1967); Robert Utley, *Last Days of the Sioux Nation* (1963); and S. L. Marshall, *Crimsoned Prairie: The War between the United States and the Plains Indians* (1972). F. G. Roe, *The Indian and the Horse* (1955), is an important study. Wayne Gard, *The Great Buffalo Hunt* (1959), and Mari Sandoz, *The Buffalo Hunters* (1954), describe the destruction of the herds. C. C. Rister, *Border Command: General Phil Sheridan in the West* (1944), and R. G. Athearn, *William Tecumseh Sherman and the Settlement of the West* (1956), examine the army's role in the Indian wars. H. H. Jackson, *A Century of Dishonor* (1881), is a classic indictment of federal Indian policy. On the relations between the federal government and the Indians, see F. P. Prucha, *The Great Father* (2 vols., 1984); L. C. Priest, *Uncle Sam's Stepchildren: The Reformation of United States Indian Policy 1865–1887* (1942); C. Bolt, *American Indian Policy and American Reform* (1987); and H. E. Fritz, *The Movement for Indian Assimilation 1860–1890* (1963).

Modern studies of the mining country include R. W. Paul, *Mining Frontiers of the Far West 1848–1880* (1963), and W. S. Greever, *The Bonanza West: The Story of the Western Mining Rushes 1848–1900* (1963). R. H. Peterson, *The Bonanza Kings* (1977), examines the social origins and business behavior of the western mining entrepreneurs. C. H. Shinn, *Mining Camps: A Study in American Frontier Government* (1885), is based on personal experience. Mark Twain, *Roughing It* (1872), is a stirring account of the writer's Nevada days.

On the Cattle Kingdom, see Lewis Atherton, *The Cattle Kings* (1961); R. R. Dykstra, *The Cattle Towns* (1970); E. S. Osgood, *The Day of the Cattleman* (1929); E. E. Dale, *The Range Cattle Industry* (1930); and Louis Pelzer, *The Cattleman's Frontier* (1936). On the cowboy, see Andy Adams, *The Log of a Cowboy* (1927); J. F. Dobie (ed.), *A Texas Cowboy* (1950); Philip Durham and E. L. Jones, *The Negro Cowboys* (1965); and J. B. Frantz and J. E. Choate, *The American Cowboy: The Myth and the Reality* (1955). On the badmen and the coming of law and order to the West, see Wayne Gard, *Frontier Justice* (1949).

F. A. Shannon, *The Farmer's Last Frontier: Agriculture 1860–1897* (1945); G. C. Fite, *The Farmer's Frontier 1865–1900* (1966); and A. G. Bogue, *From Prairie to Cornbelt: Farming on the Illinois and Iowa Prairies in the Nineteenth Century* (1963), are important scholarly studies. R. M. Robbins, *Our Landed Heritage* (1942), and P. W. Gates, *History of Public Land Development* (1968), examine the distribution and sale of the western domain. H. R. Lamar, *Dakota Territory 1861–1889* (1956), is a model study of statehood politics. On pioneer farm life, Everett Dick, *The Sod-House Frontier 1854–1890* (1937), and Mari Sandoz, *Old Jules* (1935), present detailed and dramatic stories. Equally revealing are the novels of Ole Rolvaag, especially *Giants in the Earth* (1929); Willa Cather's *O Pioneers!* (1913) and *My Antonia* (1918); and Hamlin Garland's autobiographical accounts.

CHAPTER 20

THE NEW INDUSTRIAL SOCIETY

With the closing of the land frontier, Americans crossed new frontiers in science, technology, and business management. The American people were to make their abundant resources—iron, coal, oil, lumber, and waterpower—yield wealth and riches far beyond the dreams of even the most optimistic prospectors and promoters of the past. By the turn of the century, the nation had undergone a massive economic transformation.

The population increased 132 percent between 1870 and 1910. The proportion of Americans living in rural and urban areas, like the proportion engaged in agriculture and industry, shifted. Tens of thousands of farm youths joined equal numbers of European immigrants in urban and industrial centers. And with rapidly expanding markets, improved transportation, new technological breakthroughs, a large and willing labor force, and a responsive federal government, the productivity of American industry seemed limitless—as did its profits.

But even as the conquests on the new frontiers pushed the United States to world industrial supremacy, Americans began to assess the price they had paid for success. The low wages paid workers, the long hours and unsafe conditions they were forced to endure, the poor structures that housed them, and the employment of women and children attested to glaring inequalities in wealth. The American labor force did not share equally in the benefits of technological advances and increased productivity. Nor could workers easily improve their lot when they had to face industries that were rapidly being dominated by monopolies, trusts, and financial mergers. The history of industrialization in the last decades of the nineteenth century yields impressive statistics of manufacturing growth. But the personal ordeals and dislocations that made that growth possible defy easy measurement. For scores of American workers, the dream of economic success gave way to a concern for day-to-day survival.

Currier and Ives, *The Ladder of Fortune,* 1875. Museum of the City of New York.

THE GOSPEL OF SUCCESS

After the Civil War, succeeding by making money became more important than ever. "What is the chief end of man?" Mark Twain asked in 1871. "To get rich. In what way? Dishonestly if he can; honestly if he must. Who is God, the one and only true? Money is God." But most Americans took a more positive view of personal gain. The dominant economic, political, and educational institutions embraced a gospel of success that justified the accumulation of wealth, equated economic success with virtue, and excused the human costs of industrialization. To succeed was to develop those qualities of character suited to increasing profits and acquiring material goods. "Abhor one hour of idleness as you would be ashamed of one hour of drunkenness," a father instructed his son at Harvard. No less infused with the new morality, Andrew Carnegie, the millionaire steel magnate, advised aspiring young men: "Aim High. Do not rest content as head clerk, or foreman, or general manager in any concern, no matter how extensive. Say to yourself, 'My place is at the top.' Be King in your dreams."

If businessmen needed to defend their careers and operations, they could turn to a sociological interpretation in Charles Darwin's law of evolution. Herbert Spencer, an English philosopher, attracted attention in the United States by arguing that Darwin's biological theories, particularly the concept of natural selection, were relevant for human society. This interpretation found favor in intellectual circles, and its popularization by writers and lecturers soon made it an article of faith for many Americans.

The social Darwinists, as Spencer's followers became known, contended that human society too evolved by the survival of the fittest, and they applied Darwin's "struggle for life" to the system of unregulated business competition. If industrialists such as John D. Rockefeller and Andrew Carnegie overcame their competitors, if their companies swallowed up smaller and weaker businesses, they had simply proved themselves the fittest to enjoy wealth and power. The progress of society demanded that business be left free to operate, just as nature was in selecting and "rejecting" species. Government intervention in economic affairs, such as the regulation of business or social legislation to assist the weak and less fortunate, only interfered with this natural process.

When Andrew Carnegie first read Spencer, he recalled in his *Autobiography,* "light came as in a flood and all was clear." Once he discovered "the truth of evolution," he had no more doubts about the pursuit of wealth. He could now comfort himself with the thought that what he did in his business operations ultimately benefited society: " 'All is well since all grows better,' became my motto, my source of comfort." But few American capitalists experienced such inspirational moments of truth, and still fewer read Spencer. Like most Americans, they had been raised in the spirit of the Protestant ethic to think of worldly success as a sign of God's favor, as outward evidence of inward moral and religious character.

AN OLD MAN AT THIRTY–FOUR

Whatever the moral virtues imparted by school readers and success manuals, many Americans came to learn that hard work, sacrifice, frugality, and punctuality did not necessarily ensure success in a rapidly industrializing society. Florence Kelley, as state inspector of factories and workshops for Illinois, found that in the garment trades, for example, long hours at low wages under unhealthy conditions inevitably took a toll among the "sweaters" who worked there.

A typical example is the experience of a cloakmaker who began work at his machine in this ward at the age of fourteen years, and was found, after twenty years of temperate life and faithful work, living in a rear basement, with four of his children apparently dying of pneumonia, at the close of a winter during *which they had had, for weeks together, no food but bread and water, and had been four days without bread. The visiting nurse had two of the children removed to a hospital, and nursed the other two safely through their illness, feeding the entire family nearly four months. Place after place was found for the father; but he was too feeble to be of value to any sweater, and was constantly told that he was not worth the room he took up. A place being found for him in charge of an elevator, he could not stand; and two competent physicians, after a careful examination, agreed that he was suffering from old age. Twenty years at a machine had made him an old man at thirty-four.*

Source: Florence Kelley, "The Sweating-System," in *Hull-House Maps and Papers* (New York: Thomas Y. Crowell, 1895), pp. 31, 37.

And they had been taught at school and at home, as were at least three generations of Americans, the simple moral code set forth in *McGuffey's Reader*. For many a successful businessmen, as for Henry Ford, who left school at the age of fifteen, the *Reader* was his alma mater. The qualities of character and the moral virtues stressed in these widely read textbooks were precisely those to which the average businessman attributed his success—frugality, sobriety, industry, and piety. Applied to an industrializing society, both the Protestant ethic and *McGuffey's Reader* taught that to accumulate wealth was natural, Christian, and progressive. Those who succeeded proved that they deserved a high place in this life and salvation in the next.

The gospel of success taught still another important lesson: the individual was ultimately responsible for his or her economic condition. Those who succeeded had taken full advantage of the opportunities available to them. Those who fell by the wayside, whatever the circumstances, had failed to make the most of their opportunities. The failure lay in themselves, in their own weaknesses, not in any defects in the economic system. The poor were poor because they had proved themselves less fit. That they must live in slums and in poverty was unfortunate but unavoidable. In seeking to help them, labor unions and proponents of social legislation interfered with the workings of the laws of nature.

The philosophy of success hid the realities of a stratified economic society. Rags-to-riches success stories helped to sustain the idea of upward mobility and an essentially good social system. But these stories were exceptional experiences. The vast majority of the most successful Americans came from families of wealth, privilege, and social position. A study of 190 of the topmost American business leaders in the first decade of the twentieth century revealed that poor immigrant and poor farm boys together made up no more than 3 percent of them; the other 97 percent were white, Anglo-Saxon, Protestant men who came from high-status families. Nor has the log cabin myth—the common notion that most American presidents rose from humble backgrounds—withstood critical scrutiny: only seven of America's first thirty-five presidents came from the lower middle class or below.

The experiences of tens of thousands of Americans in the late nineteenth and early twentieth century contradicted the gospel of success. No matter how hard these people practiced all the necessary moral virtues, their success was by no means ensured. What their experiences dramatized was a basic conflict between the value of economic growth and the human cost of such growth. In nearly every phase of American industrial life, that conflict would become strikingly clear.

THE RAILROAD: MASS TRANSPORTATION AND BIG MONEY

Few enterprises were more important to American industrial development and expansion than the railroad. The United States would be joined together as never before: distant markets would be tapped, vast new regions would be opened for settlement and exploitation, mass production and mass consumption would be stimulated, and efficient distribution of goods would affect every sector of the economy. For many industries, the railroad was the key to development. For many towns and cities, the railroad was the critical factor in growth or decline.

Because of the power they had, railroad executives enjoyed an authority and influence seldom

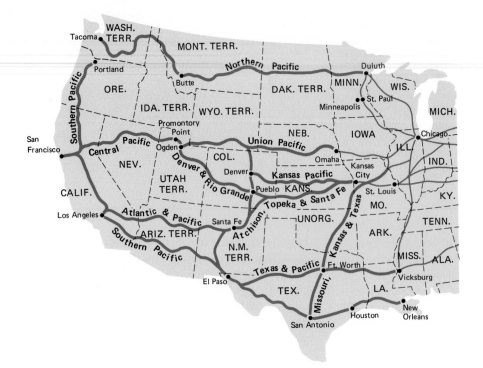

The railroad network, 1885.

possessed by political leaders. "When the master of one of the great Western lines travels towards the Pacific on his palace car," an English writer observed in the 1880s, "his journey is like a royal progress. Governors of States and Territories bow before him; legislatures receive him in solemn session; cities and towns seek to propitiate him, for has he not the means of making or marring a city's fortune?"

In 1865 approximately 35,000 miles of railroad track served the country. By the time of the panic of 1873, this figure had been doubled. About 5000 miles of new track had been laid in the South. Most of the remainder was in the East and the Old Northwest, where trunk lines were being extended to the Mississippi Valley and a network of feeder lines was opened up. Almost all the new construction was privately financed through security issues sold to individuals and banks. None of it enjoyed land-grant benefits, and little of it received any other kind of governmental assistance.

Whatever the ultimate benefits of the growth of the railroad lines, most of them were constructed for profit rather than for society's needs. The financial stakes were high. By clever financing and by using their control of strategic routes, individuals could make fortunes. Competition among the railroad promoters was fierce and ruthless. The reputations of the railroad barons (Jay Gould, Jim Fisk, and Daniel Drew were the best-known examples) were well deserved; they made fortunes largely through speculation and stock manipulation. Like feudal chieftains, they fought for control of territories, leaving behind them a trail of ruined competitors, bribed public officials, mortgaged cities and towns, and heavily indebted and poorly constructed railroads.

The Battle for the East

As important as the new roads and routes was the consolidation of independent lines into several large companies, which proceeded to gain control of vast areas. Cornelius Vanderbilt, the shipping magnate who began investing in railroads in 1862, became one of the principal operators of the postwar period. By 1869, through a series of stock manipulations, he had secured control of the New York Central and connecting lines, a network that gave him a direct route from New York City to Buffalo. Through a series of acquisitions and agreements with other roads, Vanderbilt subsequently extended the railroad into Chicago and beyond, all the way to Omaha, Nebraska. In 1871 Vanderbilt opened the first Grand Central Terminal in New York City, from which passenger trains made the 965-mile run to Chicago in the incredible time of twenty-four hours.

In the 1870s the Pennsylvania Railroad, guided by its vice-president, Thomas A. Scott, built and bought up lines to gain wholly owned routes from Philadelphia to Chicago and St. Louis. In 1871 the Pennsylvania at last gained access to New York City, and it soon would reach Baltimore and Washington. In the cutthroat competition of the postwar decades, Chicago, Cleveland, New York, and other cities that were served by rival railroads enjoyed low rates and fine service. To attract freight, competing lines often made special concessions to large shippers in the form of *rebates* (secret deductions from the published rates). But where one railroad had a monopoly of the traffic, as in Pittsburgh, cities were treated with contempt. The lines felt free to charge what the traffic would bear, and shippers had little choice but to pay.

After northern railroad building passed its peak in the 1880s, capital from that section and abroad turned to the South; between 1880 and 1890 nearly 25,000 miles of track were laid, a rate of growth almost twice that of the country as a whole. At the same time, the southern lines adopted the standard gauge, making it possible for railroad cars to move freely from one system to another throughout the country. In the South, too, consolidation accompanied expansion, and it was not long before a few northern capitalists controlled most of the lines.

The Transcontinental Railroads

Much more spectacular than railroad building in the older sections was the construction of the first transcontinental roads, which Congress chartered during the Civil War. The Union Pacific was to build westward from Omaha, and the Central Pacific eastward from Sacramento. Both companies received huge land grants and generous loans from Congress.

The Union Pacific and the Central Pacific were not built by the railroad corporations, but by

The Union Pacific Railroad joins with the Central Pacific, May 10, 1869, at Promontory Point, Utah. *(Library of Congress)*

separate construction companies. These companies were handsomely paid by the railroads. And since they were largely owned by the directors of the railroads they served, it was through construction rather than rail service that the promoters made their fortunes. Parts of these fortunes also found their way into the pockets of congressmen and senators who looked after the railroads' legislative business.

The engineering problems of this construction had been at least as difficult as the financial ones. Although both roads had to be almost completely rebuilt some years later, the feat of crossing the broad plains and the forbidding mountain ranges remains one of the great engineering accomplishments in history.

All told, the Union Pacific construction company laid 1086 miles of track, most of it the work of Civil War veterans and Irish immigrants. The Central Pacific, its construction crews made up largely of Chinese, laid 689 miles. With both companies competing for government subsidies (granted according to each mile of track laid), speed outweighed all other considerations. In the spring of 1869 the two lines approached each other, and on May 10 they were joined by golden spikes at Promontory Point, near Ogden, Utah. In the fanfare that greeted the linking by rail of the Atlantic and Pacific coasts, few people looked at the quality of the construction or the debt that resulted.

Before the panic of 1873, three other transcontinentals were chartered by the federal government—the Northern Pacific in 1864, the Atlantic and Pacific in 1866, and the Texas and Pacific in 1871. Of the three, only the Northern Pacific eventually reached the coast. The other two, along with their land grants, were controlled by the Central Pacific's Big Four—Charles Crocker, Leland Stanford, Collis P. Huntington, and Mark Hopkins. In an effort to dominate all California railroading, this group also acquired the Southern Pacific Railroad, a company that had been chartered in California in 1865 to connect the ports of San Francisco and San Diego. After 1876, they began pushing the Southern Pacific eastward.

The Battle for the West

The Big Four were not alone. Enriched by his dealings in the stock market and in railroad financing, Jay Gould plunged into the struggle for control of the West. By 1881 Gould had pieced together a series of lines in the Southwest which

so menaced the Southern Pacific that Collis Huntington, the leader of the California group, felt obliged to make a traffic-sharing and rate-fixing agreement with him. By 1890 Gould controlled nearly half the railroad mileage of the Southwest. The shippers of the area were at his mercy.

Huntington and Gould came to consider the entire West Coast, if not the entire West, as their private empire. In the North, however, they were confronted with vast transcontinental enterprises they could not quite control. One of these was the Northern Pacific, which in 1864 received the biggest of all federal land grants, some 40 million acres. German-born Henry Villard, a former journalist, took it over in 1881 and extended its operations to Portland, Oregon, and Tacoma, Washington. Meanwhile, James J. Hill had his own ideas about the Pacific Northwest and how to build and run railroads. With the support of Canadian financiers, he acquired the St. Paul and Pacific. In 1889 that line took the name Great Northern. By then, with very little government assistance, Hill and his backers had pushed construction 2775 miles west through Minnesota, North Dakota, and Montana and north to Winnipeg, Canada. In 1893 the Great Northern, on a route north of Villard's line, reached Puget Sound.

From the start, Hill insisted on constructing Great Northern track and roadbed with the best materials. He also chose to build around mountains rather than over them. Not only did this approach greatly reduce construction costs, but it also reduced operating costs once the road was built. The Great Northern's long trains and heavy loads, which the track for the mountainous routes of the other western roads could not carry, became the wonder of the railroad world. The proof of Hill's policies came in 1893, when only the Great Northern among the transcontinentals survived the business crash of that year.

During the next decade, Hill acquired the Northern Pacific, which had been financially reorganized with the aid of J. P. Morgan and Company in 1898. In 1901, with Morgan's help, Hill also won control of the Chicago, Burlington & Quincy, the best entry to Chicago from the west, and began a bitter fight with Edward H. Harriman. The year before, Collis Huntington had died and Harriman had acquired 45 percent of Southern Pacific's stock. (Gould was already dead.) Harriman's backer, Jacob H. Schiff, was head of Kuhn, Loeb and Company, Morgan's main banking rival. Harriman also enjoyed the financial confidence of the Rockefeller Standard Oil group, always on the lookout for a place to put their millions.

Thus the stage was set and the parts assigned for one of the great financial contests of the twentieth century: Harriman, Rockefeller, the National City Bank, and Kuhn, Loeb versus Hill, the First National Bank, and Morgan. Control of the western—and the national—railroad network was the prize.

After a titanic Wall Street battle that ruined many investors but settled nothing, the antagonists, in November 1901, finally decided to merge their interests. For this purpose they formed the Northern Securities Company. In 1904 this company was broken up by a Supreme Court decision that was one of the highlights of Theodore Roosevelt's administration. The contestants quickly made new financial arrangements to keep from killing one another off.

By the turn of the century, the American railroad network of about 200,000 miles had been virtually completed. There was nothing like it anywhere else in the world. Technological advances—steel rails, heavier and faster locomotives, larger freight and passenger cars, and the double tracking and quadruple tracking of thousands of miles of routes in the West and in the East—also ensured safer and more efficient rail service. Even so, Americans were angry with railroad management. In the 1870s and 1880s, management abuses such as discriminatory carrying charges and rebates to powerful shippers, together with the corruption of public officials, had brought a strong movement for reform and regulation (see Chapter 21). Many of these abuses lasted into the new century, as did the reform efforts. But even as Americans continued to argue over them, few questioned the influence the railroads had had on industrial development.

THE AGE OF ENTERPRISE: HEAVY INDUSTRY

Railroad expansion and improvement had a great deal to do with the growth of northern industry after the war. New construction had expanded the market for all kinds of goods, from iron and steel for rails to meat and blankets for construction crews. Railroad financing attracted large amounts of foreign capital to America and helped make the public familiar with investment procedures that corporations could use to sell securities in the growing money markets of the country. Industrialists Carnegie, Rockefeller, and meat-packing

baron Philip D. Armour could use their profits to expand their own businesses and to exploit profitable by-products; others would supply the carriers to haul raw materials to their factories and manufactured products to market.

Railroad development added to the spirit of optimism that dominated the northern economy after the war. With the opening of the industrial frontier, new men emerged to vie for economic leadership. Most were possessed by ambition; they were aggressive, confident, and ruthless, willing to manipulate anyone who stood in their way. But they were at the same time imaginative and talented. They crushed their competitors, used the government, and ignored the human cost of their operations. But they were conscious of themselves as industrial pioneers conquering new frontiers.

Few showed these qualities more vividly than John D. Rockefeller and Andrew Carnegie. And the enterprises they directed—Standard Oil and Carnegie Steel—became models for the new wave of economic organization and consolidation.

Petroleum: Rockefeller and Standard Oil

In the 1850s, whale oil, then the world's chief commercial lighting source, had become so scarce that its price was almost two dollars a gallon. Seepages of surface petroleum had been detected in many parts of the world for centuries. As "rock oil" it had gradually gained a reputation as a medical cure-all. Some chemical pioneers had also begun to refine petroleum into kerosene, to design lamps for burning it conveniently, and to promote it as a cheap source of lighting.

What no one knew was how to find enough petroleum to meet the rising demand. Then, in 1857, a young New York lawyer, George H. Bissell, and his associates sent Edwin L. Drake to Titusville, Pennsylvania, to make the first real attempt to drill for oil. Two years later "Drake's Folly" gushed in. By 1872, oilfields covered 2000 square miles in Pennsylvania, West Virginia, and Ohio, and annual production had soared to 40 million barrels. Of this total, John D. Rockefeller's Standard Oil Company was already refining no less than one-fifth.

Born in 1839 in Richford, New York, Rockefeller had by 1865 already made a wartime fortune in a grain and meat partnership in Cleveland. Two years earlier he had invested in a small Cleveland oil refinery, to which he was ready now

John D. Rockefeller. *(Brown Brothers)*

to devote all his time. In 1870, Rockefeller organized the Standard Oil Company, using its capital of $1 million for an all-out attack on the competition, which was located mainly in the oil region and in Cleveland, Pittsburgh, and New York.

First, Rockefeller spent heavily to make his plants the most efficient in the country, so that he could undersell competitors and still make a profit. He would often sell his products well below cost in selected markets to ruin a competitor—a practice known as *cutthroat competition*. To make up his losses, he would charge more than ever once he had the market to himself.

With his volume of business soaring, Rockefeller then demanded that the railroads grant him lower freight rates than his competitors. Railroad rates were required by law to be public and equal, so Rockefeller devised a system of rebates. Standard Oil would pay the regular charges "on the books" and then get money back secretly. Since Cleveland was a city where competition was intense, the railroads had to agree in order to keep his business.

Having eliminated almost all his competition in Cleveland, Rockefeller applied similar techniques—rebates and discriminatory freight rates on oil shipments—to railroads in other areas and enlarged his industrial empire. By 1879, Rockefeller held about 95 percent of the country's refining capacity and had captured almost the entire world market for his products. But by then the oil pipeline was well on the way to replacing

the railroad tank car as the major oil carrier. Before long, Standard Oil had used its power to gain a monopoly of pipeline transportation. Consolidating his control of the industry, Rockefeller divided the country into sales districts and sent out executives and agents to sell the products of Standard Oil.

In establishing centralized management and monopoly control, Rockefeller stabilized an industry that had once been marked by many small producers and changing prices and profits. He got rid of wasteful practices, established sound financing, and provided an efficient system of distribution. In Rockefeller's mind, that was reason enough for the methods he employed. "The day of combination is here to stay. Individualism has gone, never to return," Rockefeller observed—no doubt convinced that it was all in the national interest, as well as his own.

Steel: Andrew Carnegie

Before the Civil War, steel had been a rare and costly metal that could be made only in quantities of twenty-five to fifty pounds by processes that took weeks. In 1847, William Kelly of Kentucky discovered a simple method by which tons of steel could be produced in a matter of minutes. Nothing much was heard of his discovery until ten years later, when Kelly contested the application of an Englishman, Henry Bessemer, for an American patent on a process similar to his own and on an efficient "converter." The patent dispute was soon straightened out, but it was not until the early 1870s that what has since become known as

Andrew Carnegie. *(Culver Pictures, Inc.)*

Bessemer steel began to be produced in quantity in the United States.

In 1872, with long experience in railroading and the building of steel railroad bridges, Andrew Carnegie entered the steelmaking industry. He put off adopting the Bessemer process, but a trip to England the next year convinced him to use the new method. He came back and built the biggest steel mill in the world near Pittsburgh.

By 1879 American steel production had risen to 930,000 tons, three-fourths of it in the form of steel rails, almost all manufactured by the Carnegie company. By 1890 American steel production had taken another spectacular leap, to an annual figure of over 4 million tons. Carnegie's success came in part from his ability as a salesman. But he also had a far better grasp of management than his competitors. Other steel men often used their profits to live in the grand style; Carnegie, like Rockefeller, plowed back his own and the company's earnings, expanding, integrating, and modernizing.

Before he retired in 1901, Carnegie had acquired immense holdings in the fabulous Mesabi ore lands in Minnesota, from which as much as 85 percent of America's iron ore in the first half of the twentieth century was to come. He also bought up Pennsylvania coal fields, some limestone quarries, and the coke business of Henry Clay Frick, who became his partner. Ore, coal, limestone, and coke are the basic raw materials for the manufacture of steel; to ensure their regular delivery to his plants, Carnegie also invested heavily in ships and railroad cars.

From the mines to the market, Carnegie controlled every phase in the processing of steel. That was the meaning of integration and modernization. By 1890, although three other giant steel enterprises had grown up in the South and the West, the Pittsburgh district continued to lead the industry. Carnegie maintained control until he sold out in 1901 to the newly formed United States Steel Corporation, financed by J. P. Morgan; with the Carnegie empire as its base, it became the world's leading steel producer. It controlled 70 percent of the steel business and was capitalized at nearly $1.5 billion dollars.

What made the Rockefeller and Carnegie enterprises unique was not just the scale of their operations and the monopolies they enjoyed, but the enormous profits they made. Rockefeller and Carnegie competed in giving funds to foundations, churches, and colleges. The idea was that by sharing their wealth, they helped to justify the means they had used to acquire it. A New York newspaper that kept track of their philanthropic gifts estimated Carnegie's at $332 million, Rockefeller's at $175 million. But while they competed freely in philanthropy, the techniques of monopoly control they had pioneered came to dominate American industry.

The New Technology: The Telephone, the Telegraph, and Electric Light

Among the many new management problems in the giant enterprises emerging after the Civil War were mechanical ones, such as communication and record keeping. Simple mechanical devices— the typewriter, first used in business in 1867, and the adding machine, made practical by 1888—set in motion the mechanization of the office. Now record keeping could keep up with the flow of products and the volume of sales.

Two other advances were the electric telegraph and the telephone. In 1876, Alexander Graham Bell patented the telephone he had invented the year before. The next year, Western Union, which already controlled most of the telegraph business, entered the telephone field. But Bell sued for patent infringement and won, and during the 1880s the Bell Company bought out its remaining rivals. Thereafter, patented improvements kept the company protected from competition.

To expand long-distance telephone service, which was developed in 1884, the Bell directors set up a new corporation, the American Telephone and Telegraph Company. In 1900, AT&T became the overall holding company of the entire Bell system, with a capitalization of $250 million. In that year, 1.35 million Bell telephones were in use in the United States. It cost New Yorkers $240 a year for a private phone, and AT&T's profits became the envy of the industry.

While Bell and others were improving the telephone, Thomas A. Edison was experimenting with electric lighting. In 1879 he perfected a reasonably priced incandescent bulb. Three years later, in New York City, he built the first central power station, from which he distributed *direct current* to eighty-five buildings. But direct current could be transmitted great distances only at great cost. With the use of transformers, *alternating current* could take direct current from a power plant, increase the voltage for distant transmission, and then lower it again for ordinary purposes. George Westinghouse and William Stanley developed the first generators and transformers for alternating current, and in 1893 Westinghouse made alternating current famous by using it to light the Chicago World's Fair. The great era of electricity, however, was yet to come. Until then, the United States, as well as the rest of the world, looked to water and steam for power.

With the move toward consolidation in public utilities as well as in steel and petroleum, the American economy changed. Now fewer and fewer industrial and financial organizations had greater and greater influence and power. In one industry after another, small enterprises disappeared. By the turn of the century, it was not uncommon for only one enterprise to control more than 50 percent of the total product of an industry. The concentration of so much economic power in the hands of so few was bound to have an effect on a society that believed in free competition and the idea that anyone who was willing to work hard could succeed.

PANICS, TRUSTS, AND THE BANKS: CONGLOMERATION

By 1860, $1 billion had been invested in American industry, and in that year the factories and shops that made up the industrial community produced goods valued at about $1.8 billion. By 1890, investment had soared to $6.5 billion and annual output was approaching $10 billion in value. These are crude indicators of the transformation of the United States in only thirty years from a nation of farmers to one of the leading industrial powers of the world. In refining crude oil, making steel and lumber, packing meat, and extracting gold, silver, coal, and iron, the United States had passed all its rivals. In specialties such as hardware, machine tools, and small arms and ammunition, it retained the leadership it had assumed before the Civil War. In addition, American pianos as well as locomotives ranked with the world's best.

In any age, this would have been a towering performance. In an age that worshiped bigness, it meant the achievement of the ideal. Despite frequent complaints of hard times, very few Americans blamed business or questioned "the system." Boom and depression were assumed to be natural. In the nineteenth century, and even up to the crash of 1929, depressions continued to be seen simply as the results of errors in judgment, to be followed soon by recovery.

Instead of destroying hope, depressions paid dividends for faith. They presented opportunities to expand and modernize plants at low cost, to corner raw materials at bottom prices, to capture customers by offering attractive schedules, rates, and deliveries. It was during the depression of the 1870s that Rockefeller organized his oil monopoly, Carnegie built his first great steel plant, Armour and Morris built their meat-packing empires, the Comstock Lode was exploited, and Boston capitalists began to finance Bell's telephone.

The Panic of 1873

Signs of trouble during the postwar boom had become apparent as early as 1871, when the number of business failures reached 3000. By 1872, more than 4000 more firms had collapsed. A clue to the problem may be found in the fact that during the boom period from 1868 to 1873, the volume of bank loans had grown seven times as fast as the amount of deposits. The panic of 1873 began on September 8, when the New York Warehouse and Securities Company went into bankruptcy, carrying many of its creditors down with it. The greatest shock came ten days later with the failure of Jay Cooke and Company, the most famous banking house in the country.

On September 20, the New York Stock Exchange, "to save Wall Street from utter ruin," suspended all trading for ten days. Shock then gave way to depression: railroads halted construction, mills closed down, and trade suffered. As late as 1877, over 18,000 business firms failed.

WORDS AND NAMES IN AMERICAN HISTORY

The first *iceboxes* were sometimes called *refrigerators*. The Latin roots of the latter term meant simply "to make cold." The earliest versions were large chests with a drain hole to let the ice water run out. The ice came from frozen ponds during northern winters; it was packed in sawdust in icehouses, and occasionally shipped as a luxury item to the West Indies and the South after about 1800. After about 1900, electric models came into use, though as late as the 1930s commercial ice companies were still delivering fifty-pound blocks of ice for nonelectric models throughout many American cities.

What this meant for ordinary people was unemployment, poverty, and labor violence. With large numbers of Americans dependent on factory payrolls, unemployment could quickly use up the savings of even the most frugal families. But the industrial giants did well; they had the resources to ride out any storm. "So many of my friends needed money," Carnegie explained later, "that they begged me to repay them. I did so and bought out 5 or 6 of them. That was what gave me my leading interest in this steel business."

Trusts and Pools

Once the depression of the 1870s had run its course, production boomed again and prices fell rapidly. These changes called for greater industrial efficiency. To keep production costs down, manufacturers were forced to use the most efficient machinery in the most efficient way. Engineers branched into a new field, the factory assembly line. Even before the Civil War, firearms and farm machinery companies had speeded up production by using interchangeable parts. Meatpackers had also begun to use continuous-flow methods. In the 1870s and after, the use of interchangeable parts and their assembly along a continuous line became common in many new industries.

By mechanizing factories and simplifying workers' tasks, the new techniques made it possible for business to reduce production costs. Yet there was a catch. The machinery cost so much that the reduction in the cost of individual items was possible only when plants operated at or near full capacity. If plants produced fewer items than they were geared for, the cost of each item rose remarkably; if plants ran at capacity, so much was produced that markets were flooded and prices sank.

Each new avenue of hope for bigger markets in the postwar era—the opening of a new railroad line, a boom in immigration, a burst of exports, a rise in the tariff—promoted expansion and mechanization. But each new development soon ran its course and left behind idle plants and equipment—usually purchased with borrowed money on which interest still had to be paid. One outcome of this competitive struggle was that many family firms and independent companies were forced to shut down. A second was the move toward industrial pools and trusts. This was an effort to bring order out of the chaos of competition and to ensure profits.

Pools were essentially secret agreements among competitors to restrict output, maintain prices, and divide up markets. Pools were usually created in emergencies, and they quickly collapsed when the crisis was over. Far more permanent—and also far more secure—was the *trust.* The first trust, which became a model for all the others, was organized by Rockefeller in 1879 and reorganized in 1882.

A trust is formed when the stock of the companies involved is turned over to a group of trustees chosen by the combining firms. Trustee certificates are issued in exchange for stock, which remains in the original hands. Management of the enterprises is concentrated in the hands of a single board of trustees. After the Standard Oil trust came the cottonseed oil trust, the salt trust, the whiskey trust, the sugar trust, and others. Not all were actually trusts, but the label was given to any large combination whose purpose was to restrain competition.

The power of a trust was enormous. It could shut down every one of its plants at will, or close some and keep others open. It could cut purchases of raw material, artificially limit production, raise prices to enrich itself at the public expense, and lower prices to get rid of a competitor. For business, the trust was an attractive solution. For the economy, however, it could be a problem.

The Panic of 1893: Banker Control

Pools and trusts seemed to be the answer abroad as well as in the United States. In Germany in particular, the *cartel,* a large pooling arrangement with powerful control, became the accepted means of regulating production, marketing, and prices. In Europe, these arrangements usually had the open approval of the government. In the United States, free competition was the ideal and the only politically acceptable position. For a long time, the government did nothing about the consolidations and the tendency toward monopoly.

The Sherman Anti-Trust Act of 1890, the first attempt at federal control, was the result of growing public anger at the artificially raised prices and artificially closed opportunities the trusts brought about. Competition, however, grew more intense than ever after the passage of the Sherman Act and especially after the panic of 1893, when once again thousands of industrial firms failed, banks closed, and one railroad out of

John Pierpont Morgan. *(National Portrait Gallery, Smithsonian Institution.)*

every six fell into the hands of court-appointed receivers, who tried to keep the bankrupt roads from going out of business altogether.

This panic began in February 1893, when the Philadelphia & Reading Railroad—with negotiable assets of $100,000 and short-term debts of $18 million—was forced into bankruptcy. As the business collapse snowballed and unemployment soared, the federal government was bombarded with demands for relief. Pressure on the government intensified because even the nation's most conservative leaders now feared revolution. "It is probably safe to say," a leading industrial journal observed, "that in no civilized country in this century, not actually in the throes of war or open insurrection, has society been so disorganized as it was in the United States during the first half of 1894; never was human life held so cheap; never did the constituted authorities appear so incompetent to enforce respect for the law."

At the same time, just as the panic of 1873 had given Carnegie and Rockefeller opportunities for expansion at bargain rates, the panic of 1893 gave Morgan and a few other investment bankers their opportunity. Their first objective was to bring order out of chaos in railroad finance. By 1904, they had consolidated 1040 railroad lines into six huge combinations with an aggregate capital of $10 billion. Each in turn was allied to either the Morgan or the Kuhn, Loeb interests. After this success, investment bankers moved into manufacturing and public utilities.

The return of prosperity in 1898 made it even easier to market the securities of new combines. Many combinations were formed, in fact, just so their directors could make banking profits from the issuing of new stocks and bonds. The strong movement toward consolidation following the panic of 1873 had produced in twenty years only twelve great industrial trusts, with an aggregate capital of under $1 billion. By contrast, Morgan's United States Steel Corporation alone had a capitalization of almost $1.5 billion.

In 1904, John Moody, in his classic study *The Truth about the Trusts,* listed no less than 318 new industrial combinations, with an aggregate capital of $7.25 billion. They controlled 5288 separate plants. Moody also listed 111 public utility combinations, all but 14 of them organized after 1893. They controlled 1336 plants, with an aggregate capital of $3.7 billion.

The power of the investment bankers came from their ability to supply the capital for growing companies. Having gotten the money from investors who gave it largely because of confidence in the bankers themselves, the bankers felt it necessary to place their own men on the companies' boards of directors and to take a hand in management. In this way, the bankers' economic power, and Morgan's especially, spread from the financial community to the heart of the big business system. By 1913 the Morgan-Rockefeller interests alone held 341 directorships in 112 corporations whose worth was estimated at more than $22 billion.

A second feature of the Morgan method was the bankers' control of, or close alliance with, other sources of capital, such as commercial banks, trust companies that administered large estates and other properties, and huge life insurance companies that collected payments from millions of small policyholders. The bankers' influence thus eventually extended over almost the entire population.

With the control it exercised over railroad lines, banks, and life insurance, steel, electrical, and shipping companies, the Morgan empire was an awesome concentration of economic power—in many ways the supreme monopoly, or *conglomerate.* Although the public might appreciate the order and efficiency Morgan and others introduced into the companies they controlled or influenced, it still had reason to feel uneasy. The sheer size and impersonality of the economic structure invited suspicion. It was as though Americans were losing control over their lives and destinies. For hundreds of thousands of workers, that realization had already become a reality. It was reflected in the changing nature of their work, hopes, and organizations.

THE WORKERS

The impact of industrialization on American life is clearly shown in the 300 percent rise in nonagricultural employment in the decades after the Civil War, compared with a rise of only 50 percent in the number of persons working on farms. By 1890, more than 4.6 million Americans were working in factories, and another 3 million were divided equally between construction industries and transportation. The 10 million immigrants who poured into the United States between 1870 and 1900 added to the rapidly growing labor force. But these statistics only begin to suggest what industrialization meant. Even though many workers still aspired to middle-class status and managerial positions, the facts of industrial capitalism resulted in a loss of personal autonomy, new work patterns, and a new lifestyle to fit the new surroundings and conditions of labor.

The tension between the demands of industrial capitalism and traditional work habits and rhythms grew rapidly and sometimes erupted into open warfare. Few modern industrial nations experienced such intensive labor conflict. The battlefields on which these skirmishes were fought—Homestead, Pullman, Cripple Creek, Lawrence, Paterson, McKees Rock, and "Bloody" Ludlow—came to occupy an important place in the history of the American working class. Out of these conflicts emerged an acute awareness among workers of the meaning of industrialization for their own lives, an awareness based on their perception of class relations in the factory world. Trade unions emerged from a need to deal with these conditions. But in the last decades of the nineteenth century, workers were not sure what form their response should take.

In some industries, periodic unemployment was certain because factories worked long hours when demand was high and laid off workers when demand fell off. Work weeks ranging from sixty to over eighty hours were common; the seven-day week was the rule in steel and paper mills, oil refineries, and other mechanized plants. Advances in technology speeded up the pace of production, and the worker was expected to keep up. Fast machines greatly increased the physical danger of factory work; long hours and fatigue increased accidents, injuries, and deaths.

Another result of technology was that the machines did more and more of the skilled work, draining much of the personal satisfaction from labor. Proud craftsmen were reduced to the status and pay of menials. "When I first went to learn the trade," a twenty-three-year-old worker testified in 1883, "a machinist considered himself more than the average workingman; in fact he did not like to be called a workingman. He liked to be called a mechanic . . . and felt he belonged in the middle class; but today he recognizes the fact that he is simply the same as any other ordinary laborer, no more and no less."

This steady lowering of the skilled craftsman's position not only made it difficult for him to support his family, but forced him to change many work habits. The informality of the old work establishments was replaced by rigid discipline. "During working hours," a Massachusetts leatherworker declared, "the men are not allowed to speak to each other, though working close together, on pain of instant discharge. Men are hired to watch and patrol the shop." To this worker, the new conditions of labor demanded a response. But like many others, he was not sure what they could or should do. "The workers of Massachusetts have always been law and order men," he concluded. "We loved the country, and respected the laws. For the last five years [1874–1879] the times have been growing worse every year, until we have been brought down so far that we have not much farther to go. What do the mechanics of Massachusetts say to each other? I

Percentage of farm and nonfarm workers, 1840–1920. *(Reprinted by permission from* Promise of America: Breaking and Building *by Larry Cuban and Philip Roden; copyright © 1975, 1971 Scott, Foresman and Company.)*

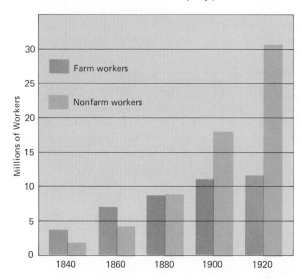

Only a Miner

Sung in various versions from 1888 to 1961 in coal, gold, silver, copper, and lead mining regions, "Only a Miner" became known as the American miner's national anthem:

The hard-working miners, their dangers are great
Many while mining have met their sad fate,
While doing their duties as miners all do,
Shut out from the daylight and their darling ones, too.

> He's only a miner been killed in the ground,
> Only a miner and one more is found,
> Killed by an accident, no one can tell,
> His mining's all over, poor miner farewell.

He leaves his dear wife and little ones, too,
To earn them a living as miners all do,
While he was working for those whom he loved,
He met a sad fate from a boulder above.

> *Chorus:*

With a heart full of sorrow we bid him farewell,
How soon we may follow there's no one can tell.
God pity the miners, protect them as well,
And shield them from danger while down in the ground.

> *Chorus:* (twice)

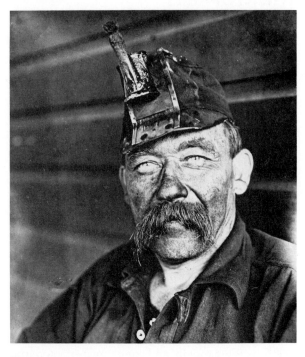

Pittsburgh coal miner, 1910. *(Lewis Hine, Library of Congress)*

In a garment sweatshop, a twelve-year-old boy pulls threads. *(Jacob A. Riis, the Jacob A. Riis Collection, Museum of the City of New York)*

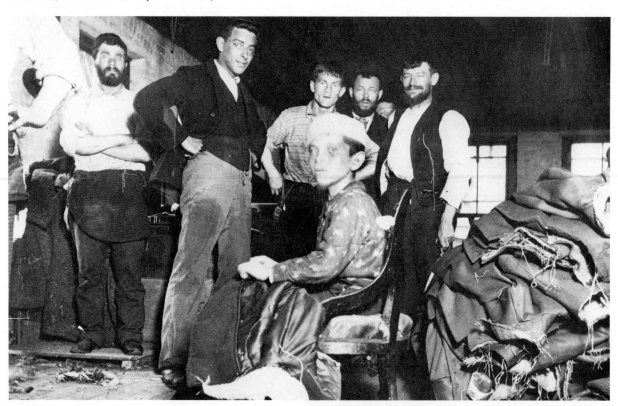

Girl in cotton mill. *(Lewis Hine, Library of Congress)*

The New Feudalism

We work in *his* mill. We live in *his* houses. Our children go to *his* schools. We go to *his* YMCA. We spend our leisure in *his* reading room. Our children play in *his* streets. We go to *his* hospital. We are arrested by *his* constable and tried by *his* magistrate. And when we die we are buried in *his* cemetery. (southern cotton mill worker, 1913)

Source: A. J. McKelway, "Child Wages in the Cotton Mill: Our Modern Feudalism," *Child Labor Bulletin*, 2 (1913), 7.

Steelworkers. *(Eastman House)*

Mighty Few Men Have Stood What I Have

Fifteen years after the Homestead strike, John Griswold, a Scotch-Irish worker at a Pittsburgh blast furnace, assessed the conditions in his plant and his future prospects:

Mighty few men have stood what I have, I can tell you. I've been twenty years at the furnaces and been workin' a twelve-hour day all that time, seven days in the week. We go to work at seven in the mornin' and we get through at night at six. We work that way for two weeks and then we work the long turn and change to the night shift of thirteen hours. The long turn is when we go on at seven Sunday mornin' and work through the whole twenty-four hours up to Monday mornin'. That puts us onto the night turn for the next two weeks, and the other crew onto the day. The next time they get the long turn and we get twenty-four hours off, but it don't do us much good. I get home at about half past seven Sunday mornin' and go to bed as soon as I've had breakfast. I get up about noon so as to get a bit o'Sunday to enjoy, but I'm tired and sleepy all the afternoon. . . .

Everybody says I'm a fool to stay here. I dunno, mebbe I am. It don't make so much difference though. I'm gettin' along, but I don't want the kids ever to work this way. I'm goin' to educate them so they won't have to work twelve hours.

Source: John A. Fitch, *The Steel Workers* (New York: Russell Sage Foundation, 1911), pp. 11–12.

A domestic worker. *(Courtesy of the Cook Collection, Valentine Museum, Richmond)*

The Autobiography of a Domestic

I am a negro woman, and I was born and reared in the South. I am now past forty years of age and am the mother of three children. My husband died nearly fifteen years ago. . . . For more than thirty years—or since I was ten years old—I have been a servant in one capacity or another in white families. . . .

I frequently work from fourteen to sixteen hours a day. I am compelled . . . to sleep in the house. I am allowed to go home to my own children, the oldest of whom is a girl of 18 years, only once in two weeks, every other Sunday afternoon—even then I'm not permitted to stay all night. . . . I don't know what it is to go to church; I don't know what it is to go to a lecture or entertainment or anything of the kind; I live a treadmill life. . . . You might as well say that I'm on duty all the time—from sunrise to sunrise, every day in the week. I am the slave, body and soul, of this family.

Another thing—it's a small indignity, it may be, but an indignity just the same. No white person, not even the little children just learning to talk . . . ever thinks of addressing any negro man or woman as *Mr.* or *Mrs.*, or *Miss.* The women are called, "Cook," or "Nurse," or "Mammy," or "Mary Jane," or "Lou," or "Dilcey," as the case might be. . . . In many cases our white employers refer to us, and in our presence, too, as their "niggers." No matter what they call us—no matter what they teach their children to call us—we must tamely submit, and answer when we are called; we must enter no protest; if we did object, we should be driven out . . . and, in applying for work at other places, we should find it very hard to procure another situation.

Source: "More Slavery at the South," *Independent,* 72 (January 25, 1912), 196–200.

A garment worker. *(Brown Brothers)*

Women at Work

From where I sat I could see the whole floor from end to end. I saw hundreds and hundreds of girls bending over sewing machines. The floor vibrated, beat steadily like a pulse, with the steam power. The air was filled with the whirr. I had to keep my head low to distinguish the noise of my own machine and we girls shouted and watched each other's lips when we talked. But we did not talk much! Right in front of me at a big table stood . . . the head forewoman. . . . There were also assistant forewomen and assistant foremen, and superintendents and assistant superintendents. They were all watching us.

Source: Rose Cohen, *Out of the Shadow* (New York: George H. Doran, 1918), pp. 000.

Factory workers. *(National Archives)*

will tell you: 'We must have a change. Any thing is better than this. We cannot be worse off, no matter what the change is.' "

Women and Work

The working class was by no means an exclusively male domain. The number of women wage workers in manufacturing increased from 226,000 in 1850 to 1,313,000 in 1900, by which time nearly one of every five workers was female. In such industries as textiles, shoes, and clothing, women might make up as much as 40 to 60 percent of the work force. Most women workers were young, single, and childless, or widows; 66 percent of unmarried immigrant women worked, as did nearly all unmarried black women. Nearly half of employed women worked in domestic service. By the late nineteenth century, however, domestic work had declined in status and become increasingly associated with groups viewed as socially inferior, such as blacks, Chinese, and recent immigrants. Clerical work was becoming increasingly available to white women, and in the first decade of the twentieth century, when women continued to swell the work force, they dominated such occupations as steam laundries, retail sales, food processing, and garment making. But differences in pay for men and women reflected persistent sexual biases as well as the concentration of women in the lowest-paying, lowest-status positions in the work force; one study in 1900 found women's wages to be, on the average, only 53 percent of men's.

The women's-garment industry, the nation's largest single employer of women, typified the exploitation of women workers in the early twentieth century. The industry was organized around a system that might include both factory and home labor. Firms often sent finishing work to individual subcontractors who parceled out the tasks to small workshops in tenement apartments—what came to be known as "sweatshops," because of their unsafe and unsanitary conditions. Laborers, particularly women, worked in these shops for very little pay. The women who worked in the regular factories, mostly immigrants, were no less exploited: they worked at least a ten-hour day and a half-day on Saturdays, they were forced to buy their own equipment, and their jobs paid less and carried less status than the work assumed by male workers in the same factories.

For the working-class women who remained at home, the daily tasks they confronted were as demanding as many industrial jobs. To maintain a household required a continual struggle with filth and disease. Since sewer systems, indoor plumbing, lighting, and decent water were rarely available in working-class neighborhoods, that struggle proved impossible to win. The task of hauling water from the backyard pump or nearby river or creek in order to wash clothes, dishes, bodies, and floors required considerable time and labor; one load of laundry, for example, demanded some fifty gallons of water—four hundred pounds. To make ends meet, moreover, many families took in boarders, and housewives cooked, shopped, and washed for them as well. In the late nineteenth century, between 25 and 50 percent of working-class families kept boarders, and most urban immigrants spent some portion of their lives as boarders.

When women applying for work at a Minnesota employment bureau in 1909 were asked what kind of job they preferred, many simply responded, "Anything but housework." Some twenty-five years later, that attitude had not essentially changed: a sociologist interviewing white North Carolina tenant-farm women found that many preferred worming tobacco plants or chopping cotton to doing household chores. "In the field," one of them observed, "there's just one thing and you can finish it up; but here in the house there's cooking, cleaning, washing, milking, churning, mending, sewing, canning—and always the children—and you don't know what to turn to next."

The middle-class ideals of home, family, and school had little relevance for working-class families. In 1910, a government commission reported that every one of the twelve basic industries paid the average head of a family $100 a year less than the minimum thought necessary for family subsistence ($800); two-thirds of these twelve basic industries paid the family head less than $500 a year. But not even better-paid workers could afford leisure pursuits, vacations, personal or family illness, or periodic layoffs. For tens of thousands of families, the spectacular industrial success enjoyed by the United States at the turn of the century exacted a heavy price in the quality of their working and home lives.

The Great Strike of 1877

Work in railroad transportation was freer of constant supervision than work in factories, but it

MAN AND MACHINE

Encouraged by the increased demand for shoes, mill owners during the Civil War had introduced automatic machinery. Workers became specialized in one simple operation among the hundred or so involved in the making of shoes. Horace M. Eaton, general secretary-treasurer of the Boot and Shoe Workers' Union, testified in 1899 before a congressional commission on the results.

q. *The workman only knows how to perform the labor of one department?*

a. *That is all, and he becomes a mere machine. . . . Now, take the proposition of a man operating a machine to nail on forty to sixty cases of heels in a day. That is 2,400 pairs, 4,800 shoes, in a day. One not accustomed to it would wonder how a man could pick up and lay down 4,800 shoes in a day, to say nothing of putting them on a jack into a machine and having them nailed on. That is the driving method of the manufacture of shoes under these minute subdivisions. . . .*

q. *Are there many workmen in the factory who can make a whole shoe?*

a. *No, the art of shoemaking, so far as the individual is concerned, has got to be a thing of the past. About all the actual shoemakers you can find today are located in small cobbling and custom shops—old-time workmen; and almost invariably you will find that they are old men. . . .*

q. *What effect, if any, has it had on the social habits of the workman?*

a. *I think it has had quite an effect. . . . In these old shops, years ago, one man owned the shop; he took in work and three, four, five, or six others, neighbors, came in there and sat down and made shoes right in their laps, and there was no machinery. Everybody was at liberty to talk; they were all politicians. . . . Of course, under these conditions, there was absolute freedom and exchange of ideas, they naturally would become more intelligent than shoe workers can at the present time, when they are driving each man to see how many shoes he can handle, and where he is surrounded by noisy machinery. And another thing, this nervous strain on a man doing just one thing over and over and over again must necessarily have a wearing effect on him; and his ideals, I believe, must be lowered.*

q. *What are the hours of labor?*

a. *Ten hours a day almost uniformly.*

Source: U. S. Congress, House, *Report of the Industrial Commission on the Relations and Conditions of Capital and Labor Employed in Manufactures and General Business*, 56th Cong., 2d Sess., House Doc. 495 (Washington: U.S. Government Printing Office, 1901), VII, 359, 361, 363.

took such a heavy toll in accidents that life insurance companies rejected railroad workers as bad risks. Soon after the Civil War, and principally to establish some means of protection for their families, railroad workers began to set up labor organizations. These were called "brotherhoods" and "orders," not unions. Their members paid "premiums," not dues. Their constitutions did not mention collective bargaining or working conditions. Their main goal, as the Brotherhood of Locomotive Engineers put it, was "postmortem" security.

Working conditions on the railroads grew so bad during the depression of the 1870s that spontaneous strikes spread across the country in 1877. The stage had been set by local railroad strikes earlier in the depression and by strikes in other industries. The Long Strike of 1875 by coal workers in Pennsylvania had been marked by the exceptional brutality of Pinkerton detectives hired by the coal operators. The six-month strike ended only when hunger forced the miners to give in and accept a 20 percent wage cut.

One of the railroad workers' major complaints by mid-1877 was the practice of blacklisting all who even dared join the brotherhoods and orders.

Another sore point was the high prices charged at the railroad hotels when the men worked away from home. Discontent deepened when the roads ordered greater numbers of "doubleheaders"— that is, trains of approximately twice the normal number of cars—without added workers. The last straw was the announcement of further wage cuts, late in the spring of 1877.

The leaderless revolt began on July 16, when firemen on the Baltimore and Ohio quit work. The *Baltimore Sun* commented:

There is no disguising the fact that the strikers in all their lawful acts have the fullest sympathy of the community. The 10 percent reduction after two previous reductions was ill advised. . . . The singular part of the disturbance is in the very active part taken by the women, who are the wives and mothers of the firemen. They look famished and wild, and declare for starvation rather than have their people work for reduced wages.

The strike soon spread to Pittsburgh. Although ordered out to break the strike, the local militia chose to side with the workers of the hated Pennsylvania Railroad. Philadelphia militiamen were then called in. They opened fire on the demonstrators, and an enraged crowd of 20,000 men and women attacked the soldiers and forced them to seek shelter. President Hayes finally had to send federal troops to restore order.

What they could not restore were two miles of Pennsylvania track strewn with the ruins of 104 locomotives and more than 2000 railroad cars. Meanwhile, the strike had spread from the Pennsylvania, along the Erie and New York Central, all the way to St. Louis. Coal miners, stevedores, farmers, small businessmen, and thousands of the unemployed joined in demonstrations to support the railroad workers' cause.

The president repeatedly had to order out federal troops when local militia units proved unreliable. "Many of us," an officer with the New York militia explained, "have reason to know what long hours and low pay mean, and any movement that aims at one or the other will have our sympathy and support. We may be militiamen, but we are workingmen first."

Within a year after its centennial celebration, then, the United States had experienced its first national strike—or rather, as a St. Louis newspaper observed, "a labor revolution." What made it so ominous was its rapid spread and its unplanned character. The workers lacked any real leadership or organization, and yet nothing like this had happened before: street fighting in Baltimore, Pittsburgh, and Chicago; widespread destruction of railroad equipment; the president of the United States meeting regularly with his cabinet over the crisis, sending federal troops, threatening to impose martial law, and taking precautions to safeguard public buildings in Washington, D.C. To many Americans, including those who shared the workers' grievances against the railroads, the very scale of the strike and the bitterness of the struggle raised serious concerns about the survival of society. Newspaper editors, clergymen, intellectuals, and politicians alike talked about impending disaster. Some of them attributed the unrest to newly arrived immigrants and to "the devilish spirit of communism."

By August 2, after hundreds of strikers and others had been killed and thousands injured, railroad service was forcibly restored on all lines. The *New York Times* called the outcome "a drawn battle," and there was considerable truth in this assessment. The workers had made their point. They had succeeded, with virtually no organization, in shutting down two-thirds of the nation's 75,000 miles of track. Some railroad managers wisely halted further wage cuts or took back those made earlier: "We have seen," said one railroad

president, "that a reduction of pay to employees may be as expensive to the company as an increase of the pay." Another director suggested a profit-sharing plan for employees.

At the same time, the employer class moved to firm up their defenses. Railroad leaders now demanded that National Guardsmen be trained specifically to combat "labor violence." Many states did, in fact, appropriate large sums for the expansion of their guards and for building and equipping new armories. The railroads and many other corporations also set up private armies of their own. Detectives were used to discover union members, who were promptly fired. New employees now had to sign *yellow-dog contracts,* which forced them not to engage in any union activity. But the workers also learned some valuable lessons. There was talk about an organization that would include all branches of railroad labor. Some railroad men left the brotherhoods to join the new national union, the Knights of Labor.

National Unions

After the Civil War, efforts were made to organize labor nationally. The National Labor Union, formed in Baltimore in 1866, drew delegates from many local organizations and from reform groups interested in laborer's welfare. In 1872, it was ambitious enough to form a Labor Reform party and to run a candidate in the presidential election. Most of its other efforts were as impractical as this one, however, and although at one time it claimed a membership of nearly 650,000, it failed to survive the panic of 1873.

The Noble Order of the Knights of Labor was organized in Philadelphia in 1869. It achieved little until Terence V. Powderly, a Scranton machinist, became grand master in 1878. The Knights' principal aim was to unite all those who worked (except for liquor dealers, lawyers, gamblers, and bankers) into one huge union that would produce and distribute goods on a cooperative basis. It opened its membership to women as well as to men (by 1885, 50,000 women were members), and it advocated equal pay for equal work and the abolition of labor by children under the age of fourteen. Powderly traveled all over the country, recruiting people and establishing more than thirty cooperative enterprises. Although Powderly opposed strikes and violence, his organization benefited from a successful strike against the Missouri Pacific Railroad in 1885. Certain unions affiliated with the Knights forced Jay

Samuel Gompers. *(AFL–CIO News)*

immediate economic gains. It accepted modern capitalism and the reality of a fixed working class. It proposed to protect workers from the worst abuses of the economic system, to sell their labor at the most favorable price, and to improve the standard of living of those who most likely would remain in the working class for the rest of their lives. The primary aim of the AFL, then, was to force employers to engage in collective bargaining with member unions on everyday issues such as wages, hours, and working conditions. An essential goal was the establishment of the *closed shop*—that is, a shop that would agree to employ only AFL members.

Between 1886 and 1892, the AFL gained the affiliation of unions with some 250,000 members. By 1910, 1.5 million workers belonged to the organization. But this impressive increase in membership needs to be measured against the far more rapid increase of the industrial work force. At Gompers's death in 1924, the AFL was the dominant workers' organization in the United States, but fewer than 10 percent of the nation's wage earners were organized into trade unions. Most wage earners, many of them women, worked in the new mass-production industries without protection of any kind. Long hours, low wages, and poor living conditions continued to take their toll.

Gould to restore a wage cut and rehire hundreds of union men he had fired. This victory so raised the Knights' standing that within a year membership had grown from about 100,000 to more than 700,000.

The American Federation of Labor, given its modern form in 1886 by the "business unionists," was a very different organization. Led by Samuel Gompers, its members were not individual workers, but national craft unions. The AFL imposed certain standards on its members. It insisted on regular dues to provide members and the federation (which took a share) with strike funds. It hired full-time organizers. It settled all issues of jurisdiction that arose when two or more member unions tried to organize workers in similar fields, and it sought to protect its members from raids by nonaffiliated rivals. Unlike the Knights, the AFL organized few women workers, for traditional biases and notions of women's work had combined to exclude women from most of the craft industries. "A machinist is born and not made," an official of the International Association of Machinists told a labor investigator. "One must have a feeling for machines and women haven't got that."

Avoiding politics and radical ideology, the AFL under Gompers appealed to the elite of the working class, the skilled workers, and focused on

The Black Worker

Although relatively few blacks had entered the industrial labor force during the early postwar decades, the race issue troubled the new unions and industrial workers generally. Should black workers be organized, or should they be left to become an industrial labor pool that would work for minimum wages and serve as strikebreakers? If organized, should black workers be invited to join with white workers, or should they be segregated in their own unions? The National Labor Union endorsed solidarity with black workers. "There is no concealing the fact," said one spokesman, "that the time will come when the Negro will take possession of the shops if we have not taken possession of the Negro." The leaders, however, had trouble with their followers, and no specific action was taken.

Meanwhile, under the leadership of Isaac Myers, a Baltimore ship caulker, blacks organized a National Colored Labor Union in 1869. But workers figured less prominently in the organization than black Republican politicans, ministers, and government clerks. Reflecting a middle-class orientation, the NCLU discouraged strikes and advised blacks to try to improve themselves by self-reliance, perseverance, and economy. When politicians such as Frederick Douglass replaced the union-oriented Myers, the organization became a part of the Republican party machinery and then disappeared.

At the peak of its strength, the Knights of Labor included some 70,000 blacks and organized black as well as mixed locals, in both the South and the North. Organizers in the South, however, were assaulted by vigilantes and lynch mobs, often with the assistance of law enforcement officers. The mobs usually had the law on their side, since most southern state governments had passed laws forbidding persons to join together to alter contracts—even oral contracts—between workers and employers.

Few blacks were admitted to the craft unions that made up the AFL; they were found mainly among the miners. Gompers's position was made clear in his annual report of 1890, when he repeated the "necessity of avoiding as far as possible all controversial questions." Certain questions did arise from time to time about AFL unions whose constitutions excluded blacks. These were handled by directives from the national leadership, which were ignored. The AFL simply went along with the practices of its members—practices that reflected the racial attitudes shared by most Americans.

Racism in the trade unions, as well as the willingness of employers to exploit racial and ethnic divisions in the working class, would doom the possibility of labor solidarity. Not until World War I and the Great Migration (see Chapter 27) did black workers become a major part of the industrial labor force. But even then, the advantages of union organization were extended only to black miners and longshoremen; other black workers had to wait a generation more.

Strikes and Confrontation: Haymarket, Homestead, Pullman

On May Day 1886, Knights of Labor unions and other groups sponsored a massive demonstration to promote the eight-hour day. In Chicago, where an independent strike against the McCormick Harvester Company was in progress, the Knights' demonstration was followed by outdoor meetings addressed by anarchists. At a meeting in Haymarket Square on May 4, a bomb thrown at the police killed an officer. Seven more officers and four civilians died in a riot that followed.

The bomb thrower never was found, but seven of the eight anarchists arrested and accused of murder were sentenced to death. Four of the seven were executed and one committed suicide. The sentence of the other two was changed to life imprisonment. Six years later, accusing the sentencing judge of "malicious ferocity," Governor John P. Altgeld courageously and unconditionally pardoned them.

The Haymarket riot outraged the general public, intensified fears of radicalism, and broke the back of the eight-hour-day movement. Although the Knights of Labor had nothing to do with the incident, newspapers and employers exploited Haymarket to ruin the entire labor movement. Within a few years, because of Haymarket and growing internal dissension, the Knights had just about disappeared.

Two massive confrontations between capital and labor in the 1890s—Homestead and Pullman—revived fears of revolution. Only two years after Gompers had negotiated a contract with the Carnegie Steel Company, the Homestead strike dealt a severe blow to the ironworkers and steelworkers. The strike was incited by the company itself. While Carnegie was in Europe, Henry Clay Frick tried to cut wages. The powerful Amalgamated Association of Iron and Steel Workers, an AFL affiliate, refused to accept.

On July 1, 1892, Frick closed down the huge Homestead plant and hired three hundred Pinkertons to protect it. When the Pinkertons arrived by barge several days later, they were met by an army of angry workers. Frick then requested the governor of Pennsylvania to call out the state militia. Only after five months did the workers begin to go back to their jobs on company terms. But by then they had lost more than the strike.

Public sympathy had been with them at first, but when Alexander Berkman, an anarchist who had nothing to do with the strike, tried to assassinate Frick, feelings changed. Fifteen years later, an investigation of conditions at Homestead revealed that wages remained low. Most of the men worked a twelve-hour day, with a twenty-four-hour stretch every two weeks when they changed day and night shifts.

The second great strike of the 1890s broke out at a Pullman company town near Chicago but soon spread to most of the western railroads. The control George Pullman had over the lives of the workers in his "model" town had been virtually complete. With the coming of the depression in

Eugene Debs of the American Railway Union recalled of his days of organizing activity: "My grip was always packed, to tramp through a railroad yard in the rain, snow, or sleet half the night. To be ordered out of the roundhouse for being an agitator or to be put off a train were all in the program." *(Brown Brothers)*

1893, the Pullman Company began laying off workers and cutting the pay of those who were kept on. When in May 1894 the workers asked for some reductions in rent and store prices, they were refused and their negotiators were fired. The workers then walked out and appealed for help from the American Railway Union, which many of them had joined. This was the union of all levels of railroad workers Eugene V. Debs had begun to organize in 1893, when he found the individual railroad craft unions could not fight the companies.

Late in June 1894, when Pullman refused to arbitrate with Debs, 120,000 railroad workers joined the Pullman strikers. The western roads were paralyzed. By July 1, Debs thought he had won. The railroads' "immediate resources were exhausted," he wrote, "and they were unable to operate their trains." All this was accomplished with "no sign of violence or disorder."

But that hopeful outlook soon changed. The General Managers Association, an employer orga-

nization representing all the railroads terminating in Chicago, had appealed to Attorney General Richard Olney for federal troops to get the trains rolling. Olney, a former railroad lawyer, was more than willing. Using the Sherman Anti-Trust Act, which forbade "combinations in restraint of trade," he obtained a series of orders in federal courts enjoining the union and "all other persons" to stop virtually every kind of activity impeding railroad operation, even "persuasion" of workers to quit their jobs. By July 3, Olney had gathered the first of thousands of federal marshals in the Chicago area to see that the injunctions were obeyed.

Somehow violence broke out. Using as his excuse the need to move the mail (railroad owners made a point of attaching Pullman cars to the mail trains), President Grover Cleveland ordered in federal troops, making a bad situation worse. Workers resisted military efforts to move the trains and had to be forcibly driven from the tracks. Angered by having federal troops in his state without his invitation, as the Constitution required, Governor Altgeld poured in his own militia. By July 10 there were 14,000 soldiers in Chicago and on the railroads' right of way. In twenty states the National Guard had been mobilized, and many American Railway Union members were arrested.

To obey the federal injunctions was to break the strike. Rather than do so, Debs and three other union officers allowed themselves to be arrested on charges of contempt of court. Harassment of union leaders soon disorganized the strikers. The American Railway Union itself disintegrated. Pullman workers who had not played an active role in the strike straggled back to work under the old conditions. In December, the United States Circuit Court convicted Debs of the contempt charge and sentenced him to six months in jail. The Supreme Court subsequently upheld the sentence.

The Court's decision had enormous consequences for organized labor. Employers now had a powerful weapon with which to fight strikes and boycotts, and they used it widely and effectively until such injunctions were outlawed by the Norris–La Guardia Act of 1932.

Despite the publicity given to labor warfare and organization, the vast majority of the work force remained unorganized. By 1898, there were more than 17 million factory workers, but only 500,000 belonged to unions. Even as the United States became the leading industrial power in the world, millions of workers did not share in its prosperity.

An investigator who spent ten months in the Pittsburgh district not long after the Homestead strike concluded that the men in the steel plants existed to work and worked to exist: "The years have done their work, and these men, with spirit dead, face a future in which they expect nothing and ask for nothing. They look dull-eyed on a world from which the brightness is gone."

The Industrial Workers of the World

In the entire history of the American labor movement, no organization provoked as much hostility, controversy, and commitment as the Industrial Workers of the World—the Wobblies—between 1905 and 1924. The kind of people it attracted suggested much about its appeal: disgruntled trade unionists such as Charles Moyer, president of the battle-scarred Western Federation of Miners, and radical intellectuals such as Daniel DeLeon of the Socialist Labor party. A Marxist priest, Father Thomas J. Hagerty, wrote the IWW Preamble, which began: "The working class and the employing class have nothing in common."

William (Big Bill) Haywood of the IWW. "I do not care a snap of my fingers whether or not the skilled workers join. We are going down in the gutter to get at the mass of workers and bring them up to a decent plane of living." *(Culver Pictures, Inc.)*

Among IWW revolutionaries were the almost legendary Mother Jones, seventy-five years old in 1905 and an organizer for the United Mine Workers, and the young Elizabeth Gurley Flynn, "the Rebel Girl." Another of its workers, Joel Ammanuel Haagland (alias Joe Hill), supplied the IWW with songs that survived both his execution by a Utah firing squad and the end of the IWW itself.

> There are women of many descriptions
> In this queer world, as everyone knows.
> Some are living in beautiful mansions,
> And are wearing the finest of clothes.
> There are blue-blooded queens and princesses,
> Who have charms made of diamond and pearl;
> But the only and thoroughbred lady
> Is the Rebel Girl.
>
> "The Rebel Girl" by Joe Hill

But the dominant personality proved to be William "Big Bill" Haywood, a former hard-rock miner with a massive physical presence. His experiences in the Colorado mining wars had made him bitter toward both the employer class and the conservative AFL. "This is not a rival of the American Federation of Labor," he told the IWW founding convention, "for the very simple reason that this is a labor organization, in contrast with the American Separation of Labor, which was neither American, nor a federation, nor of labor."

Unlike the AFL, the Wobblies appealed to the forgotten, unskilled, casual, and marginal laborers, including the most degraded segments of the working class: lumberjacks; western gold, lead, silver, and copper miners; construction, cannery, and dock workers; migratory field hands; and the "blanket stiffs" and "bindle bums" who rode the "rattlers" and lived in hobo jungles beside railroad embankments. The IWW organized black lumber workers in Louisiana and Texas as well as black dockworkers in Baltimore and Philadelphia.

Like the AFL, the Wobblies believed in direct economic action to improve workers' lives. But by direct action, the IWW meant not simply strikes, but massive work slowdowns ending in a general strike that would force the capitalist class to surrender its power and replace the state with an industrial syndicate directed by the workers. In the meantime, the IWW concentrated on improving the lives of workers. "The final aim is revolution," a Wobbly organizer explained. "But for the present let's see if we can get a bed to sleep in, water enough to take a bath and decent food to eat."

THE PREACHER AND THE SLAVE

Joe Hill, songwriter for the IWW, explained that he wanted to reach the great mass of workers "who are too unintelligent and too indifferent to read a pamphlet or an editorial on economic science." In "The Preacher and the Slave," Hill parodied the popular Salvation Army gospel hymn "In the Sweet Bye and Bye." The Salvation Army, according to this version, advised the oppressed to be humble and content while awaiting their reward in heaven. The Wobblies, on the other hand, preached a little less hell on earth.

Long-haired preachers come out every night,
Try to tell you what's wrong and what's right;
But when asked how 'bout something to eat
They will answer with voices so sweet:

Chorus:
You will eat, bye and bye,
In that glorious land above the sky;
Work and pray, live on hay,
You'll get pie in the sky when you die.

And the starvation army they play,
And they sing and they clap and they pray.
Till they get all your coin on the drum,
Then they'll tell you when you're on the bum:
Holy Rollers and jumpers come out,
And they holler, they jump and they shout.
"Give your money to Jesus," they say,
"He will cure all diseases today."
If you fight hard for children and wife—
Try to get something good in this life—
You're a sinner and bad man, they tell,
When you die you will sure go to hell.
Workingmen of all countries, unite,
Side by side we for freedom will fight:
When the world and its wealth we have gained
To the grafters we'll sing this refrain:

Last Chorus:
You will eat, bye and bye,
When you've learned how to cook and to fry.
Chop some wood, 'twill do you good,
And you'll eat in the sweet bye and bye.

Although the IWW never attracted more than 5 percent of all trade unionists, and probably never exceeded 150,000 members at the peak of its strength, its impact was enormous. "A movement is judged," said one Wobbly, "not only by what it

Elizabeth Gurley Flynn of the IWW. *(Brown Brothers)*

does itself, but also by what it compels the opposition to do." When the IWW moved east, especially into the textile industry, it won its most notable strike victory at Lawrence, Massachusetts, in 1912. Like so many IWW-led strikes, this one captured the nation's attention with its combination of giant rallies, massive picket lines, flaming oratory, and revolutionary songs. This success marked the peak of IWW influence. In 1913 it participated in the strikes of textile workers in Paterson, New Jersey, and of rubber workers in Akron, Ohio, but both ended in failure.

From the beginning, sectarianism, loose organization, and the withdrawal of key member unions (such as the Western Federation of Miners) weakened the IWW. It failed to consolidate strike victories and to build stable local organizations. Under the growing pressure of patriotism and conformity after the entry of the United States into World War I in 1917, the IWW came under vigilante attack, federal prosecution, and harassment.

The Wobblies had promised to form the new society within the shell of the old. With the conviction of its principal leaders in 1918 for undermining the war effort, however, the IWW, as Dan Wakefield later wrote, had "to form the new society within the jails of the old." What survived were the songs, the legends, and the memory that the IWW had managed to give a new sense of power and dignity to some depressed and alienated workers, if only for a short time.

> *It is we who plowed the prairies; built the cities*
> *   where they trade;*
> *Dug the mines and built the workshops; endless*
> *   miles of railroad laid.*
> *Now we stand outcasts and starving, 'mid the*
> *   wonders we have made;*
> *But the Union makes us strong.*
> *In our hands is placed a power greater than their*
> *   hoarded gold;*
> *Greater than the might of armies, magnified a*
> *   thousand-fold*
> *We can bring to birth the new world from the*
> *   ashes of the old.*
> *For the Union makes us strong.*

For the immediate future, at least, the AFL clearly dominated the portion of labor that was organized. The workers it ignored would have to wait for the emergence of the CIO in the 1930s.

Aspirations and Accommodations

In the decades after the Civil War, American farm boys, taking the new industrial giants such as Rockefeller and Carnegie as their models, swarmed into the cities expecting to work their way to the top. In Europe a similar movement from rural to urban life was under way. Each new influx of immigrants—first the Irish, then the Germans, then the Italians, Poles, Hungarians, and others from central and southeastern Europe—tended to start at the bottom of the economic ladder, only to be pushed upward as less experienced newcomers arrived. Before 1890, for example, most of the miners of Pennsylvania

bituminous coal had been either American-born or English, Scottish, Welsh, Irish, or German immigrants; they would be largely replaced by Slovaks, Magyars, Poles, and Italians. In the garment industries of New York and Chicago, where Germans, Bohemians, and Irish had dominated the work force, Russian Jews and Italians made heavy inroads. And on the Pacific Coast, Chinese contract laborers were employed in railroad construction and in menial jobs deemed undesirable by whites—common labor, laundering, housework, and gardening.

The belief in individual opportunity, shared by both native American workers and newly arrived immigrants, no doubt accounted for much of their indifference to unionization. Organized or not, workers refused to surrender that dream of upward mobility. If they could not accomplish that leap themselves, they would seek it for their children. The trade union journals themselves reprinted selections from popular success novels. Many did manage to move into the middle class (some studies suggest as many as a quarter of the manual workers), but most were not likely to do so.

"They have lost all desire to become bosses now," a machinist said of his fellow workers. "First they earn so small wages; and, next, it takes so much capital to become a boss now that they cannot think of it, because it takes all they can earn to live." As most major industries came to be dominated by a few large companies, the success idea lost some of its credibility. Most workers learned to accommodate themselves to a position of dependency as well as to new uncertainties of livelihood.

WORDS AND NAMES IN AMERICAN HISTORY

Pork is of course meat from a pig, whether it be in the form of ham, bacon, chops, or chitterlings. It was and is a common item in the diet of many Americans. But *pork* is also a kind of legislation passed by the U.S. Congress and all the fifty states of this nation. In the days before electric refrigeration, pork was preserved by smoking or by storage in brine (salt water) in barrels. So sometimes this variety of legislation is called *pork barrel*. The term refers to bills that furnish money for such public projects as bridges, dams, harbor improvements, and military installations, and that are sponsored by a congress-

man or senator who has one eye on benefiting his or her constituents and the other on his or her chances of reelection. In order to get an act passed that will benefit the folks at home, legislators support each other's bills. The general level of governmental expenditure thereby rises on a tide of mutual back scratching in the halls of Congress and other legislative bodies. Scholars are uncertain why this practice came to be called *pork barreling* or why the term seems to have come into common use in the 1880s. The authors of this book would welcome suggestions on this puzzling matter.

SUMMARY

By the turn of the twentieth century, American had undergone a massive economic transformation and become an urban, industrial giant. Settlement of the whole continent had been followed by an industrial boom in the North that turned the United States into a world power. And although economic success had great costs in terms of the dreary, miserable lives of those who labored in the factories, that cost was at first ignored.

What fueled and supported growth was the gospel of success, the idea that anyone could become rich if he or she was willing and able to work hard enough. Darwin's theory of the survival of the fittest was translated into social terms: those who won out over competitors, no matter what methods they used, were fit to survive and therefore deserved rewards. Those who failed did so through their own fault. These ideas justified the careers and the methods of such industrialists as Andrew Carnegie and John D. Rockefeller; they also supported the monopolies and trusts and the strangling of competition.

The first step in this economic revolution was the development of a nationwide mass transportation system—the railroads. Railroads offered a way to move vast quantities of goods easily and quickly to markets. They also offered opportunities for enormous profits, especially where producers of goods had only one line to use. Great fortunes were made—but the cloud of suspicion raised by shady business practices and titanic paper battles among financiers led eventually to calls for reform and for government regulation. But despite the corruption and the "deals," by 1900 the American railroad network of 200,000 miles was the best, the most efficient, and the most efficient system in the world.

The great expansion of northern industry after the Civil War was built on the railroads, which drew European capital to America. This expansion made Americans familiar with money markets and the idea of great corporations. Outstanding examples of the new industrial giants were Carnegie and Rockefeller, whose steel and petroleum empires swallowed competitors like flies and who pioneered new kinds of vertical as well as horizontal expansion. Not only did Carnegie and Rockefeller buy up competitors, but they also bought out processors, distributors, and users of by-products. The Carnegie Corporation and the Standard Oil Company were, in fact, self-sufficient, controlling every aspect of the making, distribution, and sale of their products.

The organizational and managerial problems of these giant new corporations were solved by new technology: the telephone, the telegraph, electric lighting, the typewriter, the adding machine. Public utilities in large cities also profited from economies of scale and became big enterprises. Together with the financiers and the bankers, the heads of these large businesses came to control the American economy. They soon found ways to make even bigger combinations in the form of trusts, pools, and cartels. These monopolies were good for those who controlled them, but not always good for the economy. Americans began to experience the booms and busts of the business cycle, such as the panics of 1873 and 1893.

Workers in particular began to recognize their posi-

TIME LINE

1869	Transcontinental railroad completed Knights of Labor organized
1870	Rockefeller organizes Standard Oil Company
1871	Grand Central Terminal opens in New York City
1872	Carnegie constructs largest steel mill in the world near Pittsburgh
1873–1879	Financial panic and depression
1876	Bell patents the telephone
1877	National railroad workers strike
1879	Edison perfects the incandescent light bulb
1882	Standard Oil trust formed
1886	American Federation of Labor founded Eight-hour Day strikes Haymarket Square bombing and riot
1890	Sherman Anti-Trust Act
1892	Homestead steel workers strike
1893–1897	Financial panic and depression
1894	Pullman railroad workers strike
1901	U.S. Steel Corporation formed
1905	Industrial Workers of the World founded
1912	Lawrence textile strike
1918	IWW leaders convicted and imprisoned

tion in this new economic structure. They could be made to work long hours under unsafe conditions; they could be hired and fired at will; their wages could be lowered when business was bad—and there was nothing they could do about it. Furthermore, they were completely dependent upon their salaries for survival; almost no one in a city owned a house or a piece of land, and there was no such thing as welfare or unemployment insurance.

After 1870, labor conflict in the United States was intense and massive. It led eventually to the formation of trade unions, but at first there seemed little hope of workers ever acquiring any power. The great railroad strike of 1877—a spontaneous, unorganized, and unplanned work stoppage—set the tone for much of the labor strife that followed, such as the Homestead and Pullman strikes and the great Haymarket riot. Workers striking for better conditions or just against a wage cut found themselves at war not only with their employers, but with society as a whole. Governments called out troops to fire upon them, employers hired goon squads to beat them up, and sometimes, after months of struggle, they would have to give in and go back to work under even worse conditions.

Efforts to organize national unions met with mixed success. The National Labor Union, founded in 1866, did not survive the panic of 1873; the Knights of Labor, organized in 1869, was ruined by the Haymarket riot in Chicago in 1886. The only union that grew and survived, the American Federation of Labor under Samuel Gompers, did so in part because it confined itself to economic issues such as hours and wages, and in part because it went along with common practices such as the exclusion of black workers. It avoided the radical social and political activities of such movements as the IWW. But the AFL's survival and growth came at the expense of genuine labor solidarity and the kind of influence that European labor, with its political activism, was to have on major issues confronting industrial society.

Suggested Readings

E. C. Kirkland, *Industry Comes of Age* (1961), is a comprehensive examination of business, labor, and public policy between 1860 and 1897. See also W. E. Brownlee, *Dynamics of Ascent: A History of the American Economy* (rev. ed., 1979). T. C. Cochran and W. Miller, *The Age of Enterprise* (1942), is readable and perceptive. In *Business in American Life* (1972) and *200 Years of American Business* (1977), T. C. Cochran treats business as a social institution and examines how the ideology of business reshaped American life and culture. Matthew Josephson, *The Robber Barons* (1934), is a classic indictment of business ethics. See also W. Miller (ed.), *Men in Business* (1952), and T. C. Cochran, *Railroad Leaders 1845–1890: The Business Mind in Action* (1953). A. D. Chandler, *Visible Hand: The Managerial Revolution in Business* (1977), is a masterful study of the evolution of modern management. D. F. Noble, *America by Design* (1977), examines the impact of science and technology on labor and the rise of corporate capitalism. For this and subsequent chapters, important studies are S. P. Hays, *The Response to Industrialism, 1895–1914* (1957); R. H. Wiebe, *The Search for Order 1877–1920* (1967); and Alan Trachtenberg, *The Incorporation of America: Culture and Society, 1865–1893* (1980).

R. Hofstadter, *Social Darwinism in American Thought* (1955 ed.), is a thoughtful analysis. For the pervasiveness of the success myth, see M. Rischin (ed.), *The American Gospel of Success* (1965); I. G. Wyllie, *The Self-Made Man in America: The Myth of Rags to Riches* (1954); J. G. Cawelti, *Apostles of the Self-Made Man: Changing Concepts of Success in America* (1965); and D. Meyer, *The Positive Thinkers: A Study of the American Quest for Health, Wealth and Power from Mary Baker Eddy to Norman Vincent Peale* (1965).

G. R. Taylor and I. D. Neu, *The American Railroad Network 1861–1890* (1956), is a standard study of railroad development. A. Nevins, *John D. Rockefeller* (2 vols., 1954), is a sympathetic study. M. Klein, *The Life and Times of Jay Gould* (1986), is a reinterpretation of the legendary "robber baron." I. M. Tarbell, *The History of the Standard Oil Company* (1950 ed.), is a classic. J. F. Wall, *Andrew Carnegie* (1970), supersedes earlier biographies. See also Matthew Josephson, *Edison* (1959); R. V. Bruce, *Bell: Alexander Graham Bell and the Conquest of Solitude* (1973); and F. L. Allen, *The Great Pierpont Morgan* (1949). On American technology, see T. P. Hughes, *American Genesis: A Century of Invention and Technological Enthusiasm: 1870–1970* (1989)

The best introductions to the new labor history, which focuses on the social habits, expectations, and adaptations to industrialism of the working class, are H. G. Gutman, *Work, Culture, and Society in Industrializing America* (1976); David Montgomery, *Workers' Control in America: Studies in the History of Work, Technology, and Labor Struggles* (1979) and *The Fall of the House of Labor* (1987) [Note: same author—Montgomery]; J. R. Green, *The World of the Worker* (1980); and P. N. Stearns and D. Walkowitz (eds.), *Workers in the Industrial Revolution* (1974). An excellent brief analysis may be found in M. Dubofsky, *Industrialism and the American Worker 1865–1920* (1975). For critical essays on labor in the twentieth century, see D. Brody, *Workers in Industrial America* (1980). For the reactions of workers to industrialization, see L. F. Litwack (ed.), *The American Labor Movement* (1962), and Rosalyn Baxandall and others (eds.), *America's Working Women: A Documentary History* (1976). On the Knights of Labor, see two autobiographical accounts by T. V. Powderly, *Thirty Years of Labor*

(1889) and *The Path I Trod* (1940). On the AFL, see Samuel Gompers, *Seventy Years of Life and Labor* (2 vols., 1925), and H. C. Livesay, *Samuel Gompers and Organized Labor in America* (1978). On Debs, see N. Salvatore, *Eugene V. Debs: Citizen and Socialist* (1982).

In *The Work Ethic in Industrial America 1850– 1920* (1978), D. T. Rodgers examines the tension between the moral ideal of the work ethic and the reality. That reality is underscored in S. Yellen, *American Labor Struggles* (1936); R. V. Bruce, *1877: Year of Violence* (1959); A. Lindsey, *The Pullman Strike* (1942); M. F. Byington, *Homestead: The Households of a Mill Town* (1910); J. A. Fitch, *The Steel Workers* (1911); and D. Brody, *Steelworkers in America: The Nonunion Era* (1960). On women and work, see A. Kessler-Harris, *Out to Work: A History of Wage-Earning Women in the United States* (1982) and J. Jones, *Labor of Love, Labor of Sorrow: Black Women, Work, and the Family* (1985). On the neglected subject of women and domestic service in industrializing America, see D. M. Katzman, *Seven Days a Week* (1978), and F. E. Dudden, *Serving Women: Household Service in Nineteenth-Century America* (1983). On American anarchism and the Haymarket riot, see P. Avrich, *The Haymarket Tragedy* (1984). The most important works on the IWW are J. L. Kornbluh (ed.), *Rebel Voices: An IWW Anthology* (1964); *The Autobiography of Big Bill Haywood* (1929); and M. Dubofsky, *We Shall Be All: A History of the IWW* (1969). For a more critical assessment of the IWW and American socialism, see A. S. Kraditor, *The Radical Persuasion, 1890–1917* (1981). The best recorded collections of labor songs are *Songs of Joe Hill* (Folkways 2039); *American Industrial Ballads* (Folkways 5251); and *Songs for a Better Tomorrow* (UAW Education Dept., 800 East Jefferson Avenue, Detroit, Michigan 48214). An important oral history is T. K. Hareven and R. Langenbach, *Amoskeag: Life and Work in an American Factory City* (1978).

CHAPTER 21

PARTIES, POLITICS, AND REFORM

When Mark Twain and Charles Dudley Warner coined the expression "the Gilded Age" for their novel of 1873, they wanted to suggest that the corruption of American life had made politics a sordid and shabby affair. Nor were they optimistic about the future. Neither politics nor parties could offer any solution. "The present era of incredible rottenness is not Democratic, it is not Republican, it is national. Politics are not going to cure moral ulcers like these, nor the decaying body they fester upon."

This dismal verdict would be extended by other critics to include the years from 1870 to 1900. The occupants of the White House—Grant to McKinley—were said to have been mediocre and uninspiring, the Senate was a "millionaire's club" dominated by special interests, the House was too chaotic to conduct the nation's business, the political parties differed on no vital issues. Elections offered no real choice, bosses ruled the cities, lobbyists and political machines ruled the legislatures, and the most important decisions affecting the American people were made outside the political arena. Worst of all, the promises of

investigation and reform only deceived the public into thinking abuses would be corrected. "All being corrupt together," E. L. Godkin, editor of the *Nation* wrote in 1873, "what is the use of investigating each other?"

But the politics of the Gilded Age, like that of any period in the nation's history, was many-sided. It was critical and creative as well as callous and corrupt, and the interplay of political, economic, and cultural interests was often complex. If the political candidates were mediocre, the turnout on election day was impressive. If the parties seemed hardly distinguishable on national issues, clear differences emerged on the state and local level and over cultural, religious, and ethnic issues.

If bosses, lobbyists, and the spoils system dominated politics, these abuses also stimulated reform movements. Narrow though these movements were in concept, and limited though they proved to be in action, they still reflected a public willingness to stop corruption. They helped to establish a merit system in the civil service, and public regulation of big business. Finally, the emergence of the Populist movement in the 1890s began a debate about the distribution of power and the role of government that would persist well into the next century.

THE PARTIES

Even today, when public relations specialists and the media are at their command, political parties do not arouse the electorate as the Democrats and Republicans did in the last three decades of the nineteenth century. Speeches, torchlight parades, rallies, and picnics, along with considerable personal abuse, enlivened campaigns and gave the impression of voters making significant choices. Both parties were loose coalitions, alliances of different and often conflicting class, ethnic, and cultural interests. The Republicans were the party of high tariffs and sound money, but they included some who were sympathetic to free trade and monetary reform. The Democrats favored lower tariffs and an expanded currency, but attracted some who favored the protection of domestic industry and sound money.

Each party demonstrated strength among urban and rural, wealthy and poor, working-class and middle-class voters. Both included spokesmen for the dominant economic interests, but they sometimes differed among themselves, depending on the kind of business enterprise they represented. Agricultural regions, for example, had different needs and problems, and politicians who represented these regions might disagree on government policies, depending on whether they spoke for small or large farmers, for a single-crop economy or diversified agriculture, or for primarily agricultural areas versus sections of the country (such as the Ohio Valley) where industry and agriculture were both essential to the local economy.

Industrial enterprises expended substantial amounts of money to bring about beneficial working arrangements in politics. To critics, these arrangements amounted to little more than corruption and bribery in high places. Between 1875 and 1885, the Central Pacific Railroad was said to have budgeted $500,000 annually for bribes. Railroad baron Collis P. Huntington simply explained, "If you have to pay money to have the right thing done, it is only just and fair to do it." But politicians who serviced the needs of business

Joseph Keppler's cartoon "The Bosses of the Senate" (1889). William Allen White, publisher of the Emporia (Kansas) *Gazette,* observed, "A United States senator . . . represented more than a state, more than a region. He represented principalities and powers in business. One senator, for instance, represented the New York Central, still another the insurance interests. . . . Cotton had half a dozen senators. And so it went." *(Library of Congress)*

were not necessarily corrupt or dishonest men. In working for legislation favorable to business, many viewed themselves as working for the national interest and helping to fulfill America's economic destiny. In time, they expected, the benefits would filter down to the great mass of the people. A congressman could argue, for example, that as long as his constituents demanded improved transportation, his friendship toward the major railroads reflected the voters' wishes. Both Democrats and Republicans voiced this kind of thinking, and industrialists often contributed handsomely to both parties. During a federal investigation of the sugar monopoly in the 1890s, a sugar manufacturer was asked about the extraordinary impartiality shown in the contributions he made to the two major parties. He replied, "The American Sugar Refining Company has no politics of any kind . . . only the politics of business."

The "politics of business" commanded the respect of Democrats and Republicans. Both parties affirmed their faith in the essential beneficence of the economic system. Each party contained a reform-minded faction, but the reformers operated within a clear sense of limits. The parties wanted to absorb, deflect, and defuse class issues, not exacerbate them. "Politics," in the estimation of a radical critic, was "the gentle art of getting votes from the poor and campaign funds from the rich by promising to protect each from the other." In the late nineteenth century, it would be left largely to third-party movements to raise issues affecting the day-to-day lives of working Americans and to challenge the prevailing laissez-faire philosophy regarding governmental roles and responsibilities.

Republicans: Stalwarts, Half Breeds, and Mugwumps

For a long time, the Republicans lived off the issues of the past. They waved the "bloody shirt" of the Civil War with success for another quarter of a century. They reinforced party loyalty by attacking the Democrats as "traitors" and by providing liberal pensions for former Union soldiers and their dependents. By identifying Democrats with secession and the Confederate cause, the Republicans were able to avoid the problem of "hard times"—the economic and social issues of industrialization and the growth of the cities.

As the party of high tariffs for industry, liberal aid to railroads, and conservative monetary poli-cies, the Republicans had the support of much of the business community—especially manufacturers, bankers, and the holders of government bonds. There were internal clashes over economic issues, but before the party confronted the voters in national elections, these had usually been resolved.

Factionalism, however, continued to work against party unity throughout this period. The Stalwarts, led by Roscoe Conkling of New York, remained the hard-core machine politicians who put party success and the distribution of offices above any issue or principle. The Half-Breeds, led by James G. Blaine of Maine, gave the appearance of trying to balance party needs against the cries for reform. Essentially, however, the Stalwarts and Half-Breeds differed not over principles and policies, but rather over which group would inherit the spoils. Neither cared to be associated with the Independents (later called Mugwumps), who had deserted the party in 1872 and were prepared to do so again to advance the crusade for good government. On economic questions such as the tariff and sound money, there was little disagreement among the factions. They divided sharply, however, over civil service reform and occasionally over the quality of their party's presidential candidate.

Democrats: Southern Conservatives and City Bosses

The Democrats, despite the treason label, were strong contenders in national elections. After the overthrow of Radical Reconstruction and the defeat of black political aspirations, the South became solidly Democratic. White politicians waved their own kind of bloody shirt, reminding constituents of the "horrors" of "black rule" during Reconstruction and of the need to maintain party unity in the name of white supremacy. In northern industrial cities, where Irish bosses organized the immigrant population, the Democrats developed powerful political machines. They had less support from northern industry than the Republicans, but did have some business backers, mostly northern merchants in the import trade and commercial bankers who had southern business ties.

Conservative southern Democrats sometimes joined with western Republicans to support laws favorable to farm constituents. But they sided with the representatives of eastern commercial and financial interests against the more independent Democrats of the West and against movements espousing economic radicalism. For a share of the spoils, they would also vote in Congress with northern Republicans—a political alliance of convenience and conservatism that lasted well into the twentieth century.

Party Unity

On election day, Democrats came to expect a "solid South." Republicans usually counted on most of New England and the upper Middle West. To obtain votes elsewhere—especially in the key states of New York, New Jersey, Connecticut, Ohio, Indiana, and Illinois—both parties needed to attract as wide a segment of the electorate as possible. That need placed a premium on vagueness. Given a choice between the two parties, voters responded with a certain shrewdness. They refused to trust either one to dominate the federal government for a long period.

The Democrats lost the presidency when Lincoln was elected in 1860 and regained it only temporarily with Cleveland's victories in 1884 and 1892. Yet the two parties showed almost equal postwar strength in numbers. In no election from 1876 to 1896 was the winning side's share of the popular vote greater than 50.8 percent. In two elections, 1876 and 1888, the Republican candidate won with fewer popular votes than his Democratic rival. In the thirteen Congresses elected between 1870 and 1894, the Democrats controlled the House nine times. Such balanced voting made party unity important.

Determined to hold their loose coalitions together, Democrats and Republicans both preferred to sidestep issues that might sharpen intraparty differences. On such questions as the tariff, monetary policy, and regulation of railroads and corporations, both worded their positions so as to attract the widest number of voters. Neither suggested any fundamental dissatisfaction with the pace or cost of industrialization. Nor could they conceive of a need for the federal government to play a major role in the economy. No matter which party won, the industrial sector could feel reasonably secure.

But if business could feel comfortable, the politicians could not: each election rewarded the victors with control of the patronage. With the federal payroll increasing from 53,000 to 166,000 between 1865 and 1891, the number of appointments available made the outcome of an election important. That this often resulted in inefficient

public service was less important than the need to reward the party faithful. The parties depended on the machines to deliver the votes, and the machines depended on the parties to deliver government jobs.

The efforts of the two parties to blur their differences on national economic issues in no way discouraged voter participation. Both Republicans and Democrats looked to their political machines to get out the voters on election day, and their efforts were marked with unusual success. The rate of voter turnout in the Gilded Age exceeded those of most previous elections and the succeeding Progressive Era. Between 1876 and 1896, 78.5 percent of the eligible voters turned out for presidential elections and 62.8 percent for off-year elections, far exceeding turnout in the twentieth century. (In 1980, for example, less than 53 percent of the eligible voters participated in the presidential election, with the result that the winner received the votes of only 27 percent of the eligible voters.)

What voters responded to in the Gilded Age was not necessarily the campaign ballyhoo and political abuse. The closeness of elections encouraged voters to make their votes count and prompted the political machines to mobilize their forces on election day. Voters also responded to issues and tensions important on the state and precinct level that affected them personally. In many sections of the country, ethno-cultural issues cut across class lines, and party identification and voting both reflected and reinforced cultural values and ethnic and religious loyalties. The Democrats drew large numbers of urban Catholics and immigrants. Republicans drew support from native-born, Anglo-Saxon Protestants. The differences and conflicts between these two blocs of voters were often expressed politically and took on added dimensions in a political campaign.

The Democrats, in representing their immigrant constituents, were more likely to oppose prohibition, Sunday closing laws, and any interference with the right of parents to send their children to parochial schools. The Republicans, reflecting the strong evangelical Protestantism that had helped to start the party during the antislavery conflict, were more sympathetic to using government to regulate morals and personal conduct: they favored *blue laws* (statutes regulating work, commerce, amusements, and recreation on Sunday) and restrictions on the sale and consumption of alcoholic beverages, and opposed the use of public funds for parochial schools. At the same time, a revival of nativist agitation in the

1880s and 1890s found a warmer welcome in Republican ranks.

When any of these issues—public schools, prohibition, Sunday-observance laws, or nativism—surfaced at election time, the campaigns on the local and state levels would be bitterly fought. These elections determined not only the fate of the issues themselves, but the outcome of presidential and congressional races. If the voter found it difficult to understand how tariff and currency reform affected his daily life, he could easily see affronts to his cultural values and threats to his personal and religious freedom. And he could be expected to vote accordingly.

The Reformers

Conservatives could more easily dominate parties and politics because their opponents were more divided than they were. Henry George's "single tax" (see Chapter 23), for example, aroused some interest in the cities, but had little political impact. Reformers who wanted inflation to cure rural problems won political followings only in isolated sections of the country. The Patrons of Husbandry (Grangers), who proposed varied solutions to farmers' problems, gained only some short-lived regional political victories in a few midwestern states. Reformers intent on changing the spoils system usually found themselves a minority in their own party. The thrust of these various movements was the need to check abuses of economic and political power. But political and class differences set them apart; the civil service reformers, for one, thought most other reformers were dangerous radicals.

All reformers were confronted by the spectacular development of the nation's resources and the prevailing doctrines of social Darwinism and laissez faire, which supported absolute freedom for economic forces. The rapid pace of social and economic change, and the size of the problems they created, militated against easy solutions. If reformers could agree that unequal distribution of power lay at the root of the trouble, they could not agree on which abuses were the worst and on how to correct them.

Politicians who served the needs of business resented any suggestion that they were abusing

The issue of state aid to private Catholic schools divided the electorate and turned many state and local elections into fierce contests. In this cartoon by Thomas Nast, crocodiles in the regalia of bishops are viewed as menacing the traditional public school system. *(Library of Congress)*

their positions. In helping to fulfill the nation's economic destiny, they viewed themselves as meeting their responsibilities to their constituents. The legislator, however, might need at times to weigh the national interest and that of his own region and political machine. If there was a growing consensus on the need to eliminate tariff abuses, for example, some who wanted reduction were ready to lower tariffs on all goods except those produced in their own district. Candidates elected on a promise to reform the civil service found that once in office they needed to reward those who had helped elect them.

The reform politics of the period was dominated for a time by a group of men variously called Independents, Liberal Republicans, or Mugwumps. To them, the primary source of the nation's moral decline was the corruption of political power and the poor quality of government. The democratic ideals and heritage of the country were threatened because people who had once been given power on the basis of intellect, culture, and experience were no longer in command. The Independents resented the political and economic power of the newly rich industrialists, who flaunted their wealth and influence. They expressed equal resentment for the masses of immigrants in the urban centers, the political bosses who used them, and the patronage system that kept those bosses in power.

Independent spokesmen included Carl Schurz, a German immigrant and former Union officer who had headed the Liberal Republican movement in Missouri in 1872; E. L. Godkin, editor of the *Nation;* George W. Curtis, editor of *Harper's Weekly;* and Charles Francis Adams, Jr., and his younger brother, Henry, descendants of two former presidents. What these liberal reformers worked for was civil service reform and the end of the spoils system. They wanted honest and efficient public service, and that meant a government run by men who were sufficiently disinterested and dedicated to act in the public interest—in other words, men like themselves. "We want government," said Carl Schurz, "which the best people of this country will be proud of."

Elitist, of high social standing, and university-trained, the liberal reformers prided themselves on being "independents" in politics. They were prepared to cross party lines to advance their cause and return government to the hands of the virtuous. But they were committed to orthodox, laissez-faire economics and disliked those who operated outside the mainstream of American politics, particularly socialists and trade unionists.

The railroad strikes of 1877, Godkin thought, must have been conceived "by a tramp by his evening fire, when full of stolen chicken and whiskey."

In the end, disillusion with the results of reform and the refusal of the public to listen to them left reformers such as Godkin bitter and frustrated. "We all expected far too much of the human race," he conceded in 1898. "What stuff we used to talk." Despite the newly established merit system, the quality of those who governed had not improved: the cities remained in the hands of the bosses; immigrants were arriving in even larger numbers; and radical movements continued to threaten the foundations of society.

THE REPUBLICAN YEARS: HARD TIMES AND CIVIL SERVICE REFORM

Despite the lack of results, the cry for reform was never altogether muted. No matter how hard political leaders worked for party unity, the issues simply refused to disappear. In a period of economic fluctuations, rapid industrialization, and growing labor strife, it was difficult to keep issues such as "hard times" and currency inflation out of the political arena. The alliance of business and politicians also kept alive the agitation to eliminate the spoils system. If that movement required a further push, it was soon supplied by a disappointed office seeker when he assassinated a newly elected president.

Hayes and Monetary Policy

When Rutherford B. Hayes won the Republican nomination for president in June 1876, the depression of the seventies was nearing its lowest point. Unrest was widespread. Although the federal government would not assume direct responsibility for individuals, there were traditional political steps to be taken to reverse the downward course of the economy. Most popular with debtors, especially long-term debtors such as western farmers with mortgages, was an inflation of the money supply to cheapen the currency and raise prices. Creditors took the opposite view: they wanted to be paid back in currency at least equal in value in gold to that available at the time the debts were incurred. The changing status of the paper money, or "greenbacks," issued during the Civil War intensified the conflict.

Of the $450 million in greenbacks issued when the government required funds it could not obtain through taxes and borrowing, almost $100 million had been retired by 1868. The rest had risen in value from the wartime low of thirty-eight cents in terms of the gold dollar. That low had resulted from concern over whether the greenbacks would be redeemed in gold or silver. In 1869, in *Hepburn v. Griswold,* the Supreme Court decided that Congress could not simply declare paper money legal tender without gold behind it, as Congress had done in 1862 and 1863 when it created the new currency. This decision sent the value of the greenbacks down. Then, in 1871, the Court reversed itself. In the *Legal Tender* cases, it said Congress could declare paper money legal tender.

With the end of the Civil War, advocates of "hard" or "sound" money wanted the government to withdraw the greenbacks from circulation and return to a standard in which money was redeemable in and backed by gold. But the supporters of "soft" money argued that an expanding economy required an expanding currency; contraction of the currency made no sense to them. And there was a particular urgency about this question. The nation was experiencing deflation, and the prices of agricultural products were declining. Farmers who had gone into debt during the war to increase production found themselves with obligations that had been incurred when prices were high and money was cheap.

Responding to these conflicting needs, Congress in the Resumption Act of 1875 sought a compromise between debtors and creditors. It freed national banks (created under the laws of 1863 and 1864) from limitations on the amounts of bank notes they could issue. It required the Treasury to retire an amount of greenbacks equal in face value to 80 percent of the new bank currency issued to that point, until the amount of greenbacks in circulation was reduced to $300 million. The Resumption Act also postponed until January 1, 1879, the actual resumption of specie payments (payments in gold or silver). But after that date, all government legal-tender notes, such as greenbacks, must be redeemable in gold on demand at banks and at the Treasury.

The question of whether more greenbacks must then be retired or whether the government could keep the remaining $300 million in circulation was left unclear. The distant date for resumption and the question of the greenbacks' future actually forced their value down in 1875 and 1876. Debtors were pleased; creditors were not.

It was just the kind of issue the parties feared the most. The Republican party was known as the party of sound money, but western Republicans openly supported an expanded currency. Democrats were more sympathetic to soft-money policies, but the powerful conservative wing of the party shared with its Republican counterpart an aversion to any policy that undermined public confidence in the economic system.

After Hayes took office in 1877, the issue surfaced. Hayes had backed the Resumption Act of 1875 when he was governor of Ohio. In 1877 his secretary of the Treasury, John Sherman, began to build up government gold reserves for the retirement of greenbacks beginning in 1879, as the act required. Sherman's first step was to sell government bonds for coin. Since the public had little coin, this forced him to negotiate with banking syndicates and money brokers. Despite unfavorable public opinion, Sherman persisted and soon disposed of about $95 million in bonds. The accumulation of additional gold supplies was made easier by a favorable balance of trade when bumper wheat crops were exported to Europe.

As news of Sherman's success spread, greenbacks rose in value until they reached par with gold two weeks before January 1, 1879, the resumption deadline. Knowing there was $200 million in gold in the Treasury, few people bothered to redeem their greenbacks. The greenbacks then remained at par, the creditors' goal. When debtor farmers began to agitate for more greenbacks, their campaign was supported by the newly organized Greenback Labor party, which reached its high point in 1878 by polling over a million votes and electing fourteen congressmen. But with the end of the long depression of the seventies, the drive for currency inflation lessened. Both the Greenback party and greenback agitation declined. The United States returned to the gold standard, and all federal currency issues were redeemable in gold on demand.

But the demand to increase the volume of money in circulation would soon gather new strength and take a different form. The drive for unlimited coinage of silver grew in political importance during the Hayes administration and finally ended in the depression of the nineties and the election of 1896. It had the support of silver mining interests as well as farmers. Its promoters could be found in both political parties, along with its critics.

Some argued that if the government coined large amounts of silver, the economy would be stimulated, interest rates would drop, and the prices farmers received would rise. But to hard-money people, coinage of silver was an invitation to fiscal irresponsibility that would undermine credit and wreck the economic system. The battle lines were drawn early, and each new "crisis" made the conflict worse.

In 1834, Congress had established a ratio of sixteen to one for the silver and gold that backed up the dollar. That is, silver could be legally exchanged for gold at a ratio of sixteen ounces of silver to one of gold. Until 1849, this ratio reflected the market value of the two metals. Then gold came pouring in from the mines of California and other parts of the West, and its value in terms of silver declined. Owners of silver found it more profitable to sell on the open market than to present silver to the mint for coinage. So no one protested when in 1873 Congress adopted a new law ending both the minting of silver dollars and the legal-tender status of the existing supply. In the depression seventies, however, western silver mines began to yield their own enormous wealth. Silver quickly fell in value in terms of gold, and it became worthwhile again to offer it to the mint. With silver overvalued at the ratio of sixteen to one, it was the cheaper metal with which to meet financial obligations. And there was an abundant supply.

On discovering the law against silver coinage, inflationists charged that a sinister group of bankers had engineered the "Crime of '73." They demanded its repeal so that silver could once again be redeemed at the old sixteen-to-one ratio. The first test came in November 1877, when Richard (Silver Dick) Bland of Missouri introduced a bill in the House for the unlimited coinage of silver at sixteen to one. The silver dollar at this time was worth about 89 cents and was falling. Bankers advised Hayes that the passage of the Bland bill would amount to debt repudiation. If silver became legal tender, capitalists would never again buy government bonds for gold; their confidence in the government's credit would be badly shaken. The president believed them, but he knew that Congress would override his veto.

Hayes was rescued when the Bland bill was quietly sabotaged in the Senate by Iowa's smooth-talking William Allison. The amended Bland-Allison bill, a compromise satisfying neither the silver nor the gold factions, substituted limited for unlimited coinage of silver. It required the Treasury to buy not less than $2 million and not more than $4 million of silver every month and coin it into silver dollars at the old ratio of sixteen to one. Until 1890, silver purchases did not drive gold out of circulation or produce the expanded currency that soft-money people wanted. The agitation persisted.

Garfield and Arthur: Civil Service Reform

When Hayes refused to run for a second term, the Stalwarts—with Roscoe Conkling of New York in the lead—turned to Grant. But bad management at the Republican national convention ruined their chances. At the same time, James A. Garfield, a veteran Ohio congressman, brilliantly managed the campaign of another Ohioan, Senator John Sherman. Faced with a deadlock between Sherman and Blaine, the Grant men turned to Garfield as a dark horse. To appease the Stalwarts, the convention backed Conkling's patronage chief in New York, Chester A. Arthur, as Garfield's running mate. The delegates then proceeded to write a platform in favor of veterans' pensions and exclusion of the Chinese, but little else. It expressed pride in the party's accomplishments, and carefully hedged its positions on civil service reform, the protective tariff, and other important issues.

Desperate for a candidate, the Democrats chose Winfield Scott Hancock of Pennsylvania, whose major accomplishment was that he had been a hero of the Battle of Gettysburg. Hancock was described as "a good man weighing 250 pounds"—but he still came close to winning. Garfield squeaked into office with a plurality of 39,000 votes out of more than 9 million cast. His large electoral majority—214 to 155—was the result of narrow victories in two states, Indiana and New York. They had been carried by Republican discipline and plenty of hard cash.

After the election, Garfield rewarded Blaine with the post of secretary of state. Conkling and his Stalwart friends also expected recognition. But the new president, who had reached the top after a brilliant Civil War career and a long apprenticeship in the House, had other ideas. He broke with Conkling right after his inauguration by giving the best patronage post in the United States, Chester Arthur's old job as the collector of the Port of New York, to an anti-Conkling Republican. That infuriated Conkling, and set Republican against Republican in New York.

Before the trouble had subsided, the nation suffered the second assassination of a president in less than twenty years. On July 2, 1881, Garfield entered the Washington railroad depot and was

THE CURSE OF CIVIL SERVICE REFORM

George Washington Plunkitt, a ward boss of the Fifteenth Assembly District in New York City and a powerful figure in the Tammany Hall political machine in the late nineteenth century, prided himself on his "plain talks on very practical politics."

This civil service law is the biggest fraud of the age. It is the curse of the nation. There can't be no real patriotism while it lasts. How are you goin' to interest our young men in their country if you have no offices to give them when they work for their party? Just look at things in this city today. There are ten thousand good offices, but we can't get at more than a few hundred of them. How are we goin' to provide for the thousands of men who worked for the Tammany ticket? It can't be done. These men were full of patriotism a short time ago. They expected to be servin' their city, but when we tell

them that we can't place them, do you think their patriotism is goin' to last? Not much. They say: "What's the use of workin' for your country anyhow? There's nothin' in the game." And what can they do? I don't know, but I'll tell you what I do know. I know more than one young man in past years who worked for the ticket and was just overflowin' with patriotism, but when he was knocked out by the civil service humbug he got to hate his country and became an Anarchist. . . . Isn't it enough to make a man sour on his country when he wants to serve it and won't be allowed unless he answers a lot of fool questions about the number of cubic inches of water in the Atlantic and the quality of sand in the Sahara desert?

Source: William L. Riordon, *Plunkitt of Tammany Hall* (New York: Knopf, 1948), pp. 15–16.

murdered by a deranged job seeker, Charles Guiteau. As Guiteau fired, he exclaimed, "I am a Stalwart and Arthur is President now." Garfield died two months later, and though Arthur filled his cabinet with Stalwarts, his administration saw the beginning of civil service reform.

The assassination dramatized in the minds of many Americans the evils of a patronage and spoils system that had become entrenched in American government and politics. Even veteran machine politicians had grown sick of patronage. Civil service reform, its advocates insisted, was not just one issue among many. The aim, as one reformer expressed it, was to correct the "chief evil" of the day, "the alliance between industrialists and a political class which thinks like industrialists."

The first real step toward the merit system was the Pendleton Act of 1883. This act gave three civil service commissioners, to be named by the president, authority to draw up practical, competitive examinations. The act forbade assessing federal employees for campaign funds or firing them for political reasons. It required that within sixty days Treasury and postal employees be classified in civil service categories, and it permitted the president to extend the coverage to other segments of the federal bureaucracy. During Arthur's administration, about 12 percent of federal employees (compared with 85 percent in the mid-twentieth century) were classified.

The Pendleton Act, by depriving the parties of funds from public employees, forced leaders to turn more and more to big business for campaign

funds. Shrewd party managers such as Matt Quay of Pennsylvania, Tom Platt of New York, and Mark Hanna of Ohio were soon representing big-business clients—and so were the candidates they chose.

THE DEMOCRATIC YEARS: REGULATION AND PROTECTION

Both Democrats and Republicans claimed credit for civil service reform. But more divisive issues now demanded attention. No longer could the federal government afford to ignore corporate abuses, whether these took the form of unreasonably high tariff rates, unfair methods of competition, or industrial combinations that prevented competition. Farmers organized in Granges pushed for laws against railroad malpractices. The great railroad strike of 1877 had dramatized not only the plight of railroad workers, but the degree to which the public shared their grievances against the railroad companies. If nothing else, public concern about the growth and use of corporate power had to be satisfied.

At the same time, the government did not want to tamper with "natural" economic forces by imposing restraints on industrialization. The inhabitants of the White House—Democrat or Republican—believed that the least amount of government was best. And they would cling to that belief even as the nation headed into another depression.

The Campaign of 1884: Cleveland

As president, Chester A. Arthur pleased neither the reformers nor the old guard. The Republican convention in 1884 passed him by in favor of perennial candidate James G. Blaine. Although Blaine had most of the qualities that make a successful presidential candidate, his many years in the House had marked him: he had grown rich without any visible means of outside income and had not allowed anyone to uncover the sources of his wealth. With his nomination, the Independents, or Mugwumps, left the party and supported the Democratic nominee, Grover Cleveland.

Cleveland had attracted notice as a reform mayor of Buffalo and as governor of New York. His defense of sound money and property rights earned him industrial and banking support. Although he was called a reformer, Cleveland carefully pointed out that "a transfer of executive control from one party to another does not mean any serious disturbance of existing conditions."

In the campaign, the parties treated the public to sensational disclosures about the private lives and personal morals of the two candidates. If Blaine's ties to railroad scandals made him unfit to hold public office, the fact that Cleveland, a bachelor, happened to be the father of a seven-year-old child was enough to define him as a moral leper. To the Republican taunt "Ma, ma, where's my pa?" the Democrats replied: "Gone to the White House, ha, ha, ha!" It was that kind of campaign. Neither party claimed to be opposed to tariff revision, as long as it did not endanger any domestic industry. Both parties also agreed

that something had to be done about corporate abuses.

Blaine lost New York by 1149 votes. New York turned out to be decisive in the electoral college, where Cleveland squeaked through, 219 to 182. His popular plurality was only 23,000 out of 10 million votes. But it was enough to bring the Democrats back to the White House after a quarter of a century.

Cleveland's idea of government was almost entirely negative. He especially disliked what he called "paternalism." Early in 1887, in vetoing an act to distribute seeds in drought-stricken Texas counties, he used a phrase that returned to haunt him during the depression of the nineties: "The lesson should be constantly enforced that though the people support the Government, the Government should not support the people." In destroying "paternalism," he foiled pension grabs by veterans and tariff grabs by industry, and even retrieved 81 million acres of the public domain from the railroads. He extended the scope of civil service, but he resisted attempts to regulate business. With public pressure mounting, however, Cleveland could no longer afford to ignore the clamor for reform. By the end of his term, the railroads, tariffs, and big business were heatedly debated subjects of legislation.

Railroad Regulation

After the panics of 1873 and 1884 had forced many speculators to the wall, the movement for railroad regulation and reform increased. Rate and dividend policies came under bitter attack from shippers and investors. When the railroads fought back by spending money to make political friends and hire the best legal talent, they made more enemies. Such open corruption raised protests against the railroads, even by impartial citizens. Reform and regulation eventually won the backing of railroad men who had come to look upon the national government as the only power that could save them from their own competitive and financial practices.

In the late 1870s and throughout the 1880s, *average* railroad freight rates went down steadily because of the competition for traffic. The trouble was that *average* rates included suicidally low ones at junctions where two or more lines crossed, and murderously high ones for shippers at monopoly points. This situation satisfied no one, least of all the railroads, which were under pressure for special consideration from all sides. Shippers at monopoly points along railroads that ended at competitive points were the worst off. They were often required to pay more for short hauls along a small portion of the road than shippers at the

Thomas Nast's cartoon "The Senatorial Roundhouse" in *Harper's Weekly* (1886) illustrated the power of railroad corporations. The bill on which the filibustering senator is stepping would "prevent members of Congress from accepting fees from subsidized railroads." *(Library of Congress)*

terminals paid for long hauls over the road's entire length.

Discriminatory carrying charges were reflected in the decline of land values where shipping costs were highest. In one rich farming area in New York State, served only by the New York Central, the railroad's high short-haul charges contributed to a decline of 20 to 25 percent in land values in 1879 alone. Rebates and other special favors to powerful shippers such as Standard Oil were also a source of anger. The secrecy with which rebating had to be carried on burdened even those who profited from it.

The first regulatory commission was a state effort in Massachusetts in 1869, and it could only investigate railroad abuses and make its findings public. But by 1880, fourteen states had set up railroad commissions, and some had taken more severe measures. Urban manufacturers and distributors and their banker allies sometimes began the fight, but the most persistent organization was the Patrons of Husbandry, which began organizing farmers into local granges in 1867. A year after the panic of 1873, the Grangers had 1.5 million members, mostly in Iowa, Wisconsin, Minnesota, and Illinois. Here they won legislation setting statewide maximum rates for railroad traffic and maximum charges for the use of grain elevators, where farmers had to store their crops while awaiting shipment.

Railroad managers fought Granger legislation in the courts, where they attacked rate fixing by public bodies as nothing less than legalized confiscation. In 1877, in *Munn v. Illinois,* the most important of the Granger cases to reach the Supreme Court, a majority of the justices found against the railroads and grain elevator operators. Owners of property "in which the public has an interest," said the Court, must "submit to be controlled by the public for the common good."

But single states could not regulate corporations chartered by other states and carrying on most of their business across state borders. Pressure for federal regulation mounted in the early 1880s as railroad securities slumped on the stock exchanges. By 1886, nearly 10 percent of the entire railroad system went into receivership.

After the Supreme Court decision in the *Wabash* case (1886), which reflected conservative attitudes, the federal government could postpone action no longer. *Wabash* took much of the strength from *Munn v. Illinois* by forbidding any state to set rates even within its borders on railroad traffic entering from, or bound for, another state. With the states thus removed from the regulatory process, any effective control of the railroads now rested with the federal government.

The Interstate Commerce Act, signed by President Cleveland on February 4, 1887, provided that all charges made by railroads should be "reasonable and just." It forbade higher rates on noncompetitive short hauls than on competitive long ones, and it outlawed rebates to favored shippers. It also prohibited self-regulating practices, such as agreements to pool traffic and maintain high rates. Of particular importance was the establishment of the Interstate Commerce Commission, the first federal regulatory board. But its powers proved inadequate to the tasks it faced: The "cease-and-desist" orders the ICC was empowered to issue could be made to stick only by court action, which the railroads found easy to delay. And in the end the railroads almost always won. In the first ten years of the commission's existence, 90 percent of its orders on rate charges were overruled by the courts. Of the sixteen cases heard by the Supreme Court between 1887 and 1905, the carrier was upheld in fifteen.

When the commission tried more vigorous prosecutions, the railroads responded with an attack on the commission itself. Some people advised them, even as early as 1892, to abandon this approach. In that year, the corporation lawyer Richard S. Olney, soon to become Cleveland's attorney general, wrote to a railroad friend:

My impression would be that, looking at the matter from a railroad point of view exclusively, it would not be a wise thing to undertake to abolish the Commission. . . . The Commission, as its functions have now been limited by the Courts, is, or can be made of great use to the railroads. It satisfies the popular clamor for a government supervision of railroads, at the same time that such supervision is almost entirely nominal. Further, the older such a commission gets to be, the more inclined it will be found to take the business and railroad view of things. It thus becomes a sort of protection against hasty and crude legislation hostile to railroad interests. . . . The part of wisdom is not to destroy the Commission, but to utilize it.

Time proved Olney right. The Interstate Commerce Commission Act did not reduce rates significantly. Nor did it end cutthroat competition. Like many regulatory commissions, the ICC would frequently be staffed by individuals representing the very interests it had been created to control. What mattered was that the public's anxieties about the railroads had been satisfied, at least for a time. Yet the Interstate Commerce Commission Act was not a complete failure. It clearly affirmed the right of the federal government to regulate private interstate business, and it provided the foundation on which a system of effective regulation could be built in the twentieth century.

Protection: The Tariff

Although Democratic politicians advised him to soft-pedal the tariff issue, Cleveland was determined to achieve some reforms in this sensitive area. Beginning with the wartime duties of 1864, protection of domestic industries had increased until it covered at least four thousand items in 1887. Cleveland did not oppose those who sought to nurse "infant industries." But he saw some of the tariff rates as excessive, and he felt that such "unnecessary taxation" only encouraged Congress to spend the annual surplus that accumulated in the Treasury.

Responding to Cleveland's call for tariff reform, the House early in 1888 adopted the Mills bill. It reflected deep study of industry's real needs and recommended the moderate reductions that mild revisionists such as the president wanted. The Senate responded with the "Allison substitute," which called, as usual, for a general rise in the tariff. "We all know," Joseph Wharton, the Pennsylvania iron and steel king, wrote to Senator Allison, "that the legitimate expenses of a general election are heavy, and that failure to provide for them sometimes entails defeat. I am in a position to know that the success of appeals for funds among the steel rail men will be jeopardized if the party they are asked to support proposes a measure that looks to them nearly as fatal as that proposed by the other party." The "Allison substitute" resulted in a congressional deadlock, as intended, and postponed the issue until after the presidential election of 1888.

Republican Interlude

The Democrats renominated Cleveland by acclamation. After Blaine's decision not to run again, the Republicans finally selected Benjamin Harrison, a dreary corporation lawyer from Indiana, and the grandson of President William Henry Harrison. Under the management of national party chairman Matt Quay, the Republicans charged that Cleveland's "free trade" policy (as they insisted on labeling the mild reforms of the Mills bill) would ruin American manufacturing and betray the American worker to the "pauper labor of Europe." Even the Knights of Labor believed this argument and endorsed Harrison.

Although Cleveland's popular vote topped Harrison's by more than 100,000, Harrison won an electoral majority of sixty-five. A switch of only 6500 votes in New York would have given Cleveland that state and the election. Since Cleveland did surprisingly well in protariff regions, the effect of the tariff issue on the election is questionable.

Like so many elections in this period, the national campaign depended largely on the ability of party organizers to mobilize supporters. When Harrison solemnly proclaimed, "Providence has given us the victory," Matt Quay exploded: "Think of the man! He ought to know that Providence hadn't a damn thing to do with it." Quay added that Harrison "would never know how close a number of men were compelled to approach the gates of the penitentiary to make him president."

After the election, Congress took care of the industrial contributors to the campaign with the McKinley tariff (1890), the highest and broadest in the nation's history. By raising already high duties even higher, the new tariff not only protected domestic industries, but made it virtually impossible for foreigners to compete. At the same time, it offered protection to certain industries that had not yet been established, in an apparent effort to encourage their development. Secretary of State Blaine feared that exporting nations hit by the new duties would refuse to buy American farm surpluses. He got Congress to hold a club over resisting nations by inserting a "reciprocity" clause in the new tariff act. The president had the authority to remove remaining items from the free list in retaliation against any discriminatory duties on American produce.

In return for western votes on the McKinley tariff, Congress in 1890 passed the Sherman Silver Purchase Act. This act authorized the Treasury to issue notes that were redeemable in gold as usual but also in greater amounts of silver than had been permitted under the Bland-Allison Act of 1878. Virtually a gift to the silver mining companies, the Silver Purchase Act was defended as an agrarian, cheap-money measure. But the issue was not settled; inflationists wanted unlimited silver coinage.

One more sop offered to the public was the Sherman Anti-Trust Act, which passed Congress in July 1890. Many states had passed antitrust statutes, but these were no more effective against trusts chartered in other states than state regulation of interstate railroads had been. After the Supreme Court's *Wabash* decision of 1886 had undermined stronger state measures against private corporations, the demand for federal trust regulation strengthened.

The Sherman Anti-Trust Act sounded severe. It made combinations in restraint of trade illegal, subjected offenders to heavy fines and jail sentences, and ordered that triple damages be paid to persons who could prove injury by such combinations. Few courts, however, upheld any of the actions brought under the measure. Finley Peter Dunne, the political humorist, said of the act: "What looks like a stone wall to a layman is a triumphal arch to a corporation lawyer."

The Sherman Act did push certain groups of companies to change specific trust arrangements and to merge into huge corporations. Without having to act together, these companies succeeded in dominating industries at least as thoroughly as the trusts had. Other industries employed the *holding company*—an independent corporation that owned enough stock in other companies to control their policies. Dodges such as these neutralized the Sherman Act for a while, but in the twentieth century, political administrations and the courts gradually began to enforce it. Although business consolidation and centralization continued, antitrust legislation did serve as a brake on many combinations considered harmful to the public interest.

WORDS AND NAMES IN AMERICAN HISTORY

The phrase *favorite son* usually refers to politics rather than to families. It is normally used to describe a candidate for the U.S. presidency whose main support comes from his home state and who has little strong support elsewhere. Occasionally, a favorite son has gone on to win the nomination. For example, historians often forget that such a popular president as Andrew Jackson began his political career as a favorite son of the state of Tennessee.

And many historians have failed to note that the Father of His Country was its first favorite son. We have these words from the *New York Daily Gazette* of May 1, 1789: "Yesterday the Great and Illustrious Washington, the favourite son of liberty, and deliverer of his country, entered upon the execution of the office of First Magistrate of the United States of America."

The Election of 1892: Cleveland Again

Running against Cleveland in 1892, Harrison this time got 5,176,000 votes. But Cleveland got 5,556,000. Narrow though this margin was, it was the most decisive victory since 1872. The electoral college count was Cleveland 277, Harrison 145. "I am very sorry for President Harrison," Henry Frick of the Carnegie Steel Company wrote to Carnegie on learning of Cleveland's election, "but I cannot see that our interests are going to be affected one way or another by the change in administration." Carnegie replied: "Cleveland! Landslide! Well we have nothing to fear. . . . People will now think the Protected [Manufacturers] are attended to and quit agitating. . . . Off for Venice tomorrow."

Conservative industrialists may have felt safe, but conservative politicians of both parties had something new to think about: the showing of the People's party, known as the Populists, especially in the new wheat states. Organized in 1890, the party ran General James B. Weaver in 1892 in its first bid for the presidency. The general got over a million votes, more than 8 percent of the total. His party succeeded in capturing four states and brought the silver issue and the needs of the farmers to national attention.

THE POPULISTS AND THE SILVER CRUSADE

The economic crisis of the 1890s and the emergence of a strong third political party made the avoidance of critical economic issues increasingly difficult for the two major parties. Much of the unrest of the decade focused on the farmers, who, like so many industrial workers, sensed that they were no longer in control of their own lives and destiny. Farmers protested declining prices for their products and the growing percentage of their incomes falling into the hands of middlemen—marketing agents, mortgage lenders, grain elevator operators, and railroads. Farmers were joined by other groups experiencing economic hardship and concerned over corporate power and government unresponsiveness. These concerns found expression at all levels of society and soon took on political significance.

For some Americans, the 1890s raised serious questions about the survival of the economic and social order. The depression that followed the panic of 1893 produced tens of thousands of unemployed. Labor strife peaked, with massive showdowns at Carnegie's Homestead steel works in 1892 and in the national railroad strike of 1894. Out of the Midwest emerged an "army" of unemployed who marched on Washington, D.C., to press their case for public relief. The jurist Oliver Wendell Holmes, Jr., identified 1893 as the year when "a vague terror went over the earth and the word socialism began to be heard." In the nation's capital, neither the White House nor Congress seemed responsive to the growing unrest. Against this background, the Populist party made its political appeal. Whatever the ultimate fate of populism as a third party and an economic and cultural movement, it managed to raise critical questions that would outlast both the People's party and the Populist movement.

The Farmers

In 1887 Leonidas L. Polk, a North Carolina editor, expressed the views of farmers in all parts of the country when he wrote:

There is something radically wrong in our Industrial system. There is a screw loose. . . . The railroads have never been so prosperous, and yet agriculture languishes. The banks have never done a better . . . business, and yet agriculture languishes. Manufacturing enterprises never made more money, . . . and yet agriculture languishes. Towns and cities flourish and "boom," . . . and yet agriculture languishes.

What is more, farmers suffered only slightly less in good times than in bad. Broadly speaking, they blamed their plight on the high transportation rates charged by railroads, the high prices charged by producers of farm machinery, the high interest rates charged by mortgage lenders, and the high storage rates charged by monopolistic grain elevator companies. These items consumed a disproportionate share of an income already reduced by falling prices. It was said, for example, that Nebraska annually produced three principal crops: corn, freight rates, and interest, and that the last two were harvested by those who farmed the farmer.

Few enterprises had received more civic support than the railroads of the West. In return, farmers felt that the railroads owed the community moderate rates. But the farther west one moved, the worse conditions grew. In 1887, for instance, the ton-mile charge on the Pennsylvania Railroad east of Chicago was $.95. On the Burlington from Chicago to the Missouri River it was $1.32; on the Burlington west of the Missouri it jumped to $4.80. According to railroad officials, they had to charge high rates in sparsely populated regions. The farmers, dependent on the railroads for getting their crops to market, could hardly agree.

Heavy taxes made the high railroad rates harder to bear. Personal property then consisted chiefly of land and livestock, on which it was relatively simple to assess a personal property tax. Railroads and other corporations created new kinds of personal property—stocks and bonds— that were far easier to conceal. Since the railroads also pushed the politicians for tax exemptions or low rates on their own huge landholdings and other real property, taxes fell more and more heavily on the middle-class farmer. In a free market, he could not pass them along to the consumer, as could many large industrial corporations.

The protective tariff was still another discriminatory tax that angered farmers. In their opinion, it protected the trusts, which had the power to force down the prices for raw materials produced on the farms and to force up the prices of farm machinery and other manufactures.

Falling farm prices, of course, made heavy taxes seem even worse. The price of staples began to fall in the 1880s and hit bottom in the depression years of the nineties. Wheat brought $1.20 a bushel in 1881 and 50 cents in 1895; cotton, 10.5 cents a pound in 1881 and 4.5 cents in 1894. Of course, prices of nonfarm products fell too. But the fall in farm prices hit the growers particularly hard because they were debtors with fixed *money* obligations. Their constant concern with the currency came from their need to keep these obligations stable in terms of the amount of *commodities* needed to pay them. Farmers who

---

THE FARMER IS THE MAN

When farmers gave voice to their grievances, they did so through songs as well as through letters, oratory, and organization. "The Farmer Is the Man" was among the best known of the Populist ballads.

Oh, the farmer comes to town
With his wagon broken down,
But the farmer is the man who feeds them all.
If you'll only look and see,
I think you will agree
That the farmer is the man who feeds them all.

The farmer is the man,
The farmer is the man,
Lives on credit till the fall;
Then they take him by the hand,
And they lead him from the land,
And the merchant is the one who gets it all.

When the banker says he's broke
And the merchant's up in smoke,
They forget that it's the farmer feeds them all.
It would put them to the test
If the farmer took a rest;
Then they'd know that it's the farmer feeds them all.

The farmer is the man,
The farmer is the man,
Lives on credit till the fall;
With the interest rate so high
It's a wonder he don't die,
For the mortgage man's the one who gets it all.

Source: Edith Fowke and Joe Glazer, *Songs of Work and Freedom* (New York: Doubleday, 1960), pp. 96–97. Recorded on *American Industrial Ballads* (Folkways 5251).

had gone into debt in the 1860s to purchase new land and machinery when farm prices were high and money cheap found themselves in the 1880s and 1890s in a period of declining prices and deflation.

Critics told the farmers they received low prices because they produced too much. But the only way the individual farmer could think of to make more money when prices were falling was to raise even larger crops. To the farmers' way of thinking, the price decline reflected a cold-blooded Wall Street conspiracy to squeeze the settlers of the West. The high cost of credit seemed to confirm this view. The credit system helped force the landless southern farmer, and eventually the small southern landholder as well, into the vicious circle of sharecropping and crop lien. Tenancy came later in the West, where land was more easily obtained and more easily mortgaged. But when mortgage money cost 15 percent or more a year, as it did in Kansas and states farther west in the 1880s, the foreclosures began. Farmers faced the prospect of being evicted from the lands on which they lived and worked.

Populist leader Mary E. Lease is said to have advised Kansas farmers to "raise less corn and more hell." *(Library of Congress)*

The Origins of Populism

The roots of the People's party of the 1890s lay in the farmers' alliances and in the idea of cooperatives that would free farmers from private credit merchants and bankers. The alliances had sprung up in the 1880s to replace the Grange. By 1880, many of these had consolidated into two regional groups, the Southern Alliance, which claimed over a million members, and the somewhat smaller National Farmers' Alliance mainly in the Great Plains states. The Colored Farmers' Alliance, begun in 1886 by a white Baptist preacher, reportedly recruited over a million blacks. But it had neither the power nor the influence of the two white organizations.

The Southern and National Farmers' alliances gave a strong stimulus to the social life and the thinking of their members. Like the Granges, they held picnics, conventions, and rallies to help overcome the isolation and bleakness of farm life. They gave out agricultural information and tried to teach their members better business methods. They sponsored economic and political discussions and established circulating libraries, which enabled members to read books of social criticism. At one time perhaps as many as a thousand local newspapers were connected with the movement.

What emerged was both a political and a cultural movement, in which farmers came together to share their experiences and to propose and act upon measures to improve their working lives and free them of the credit system. The talk ranged from the single tax to free silver, from farmers' cooperatives to government ownership of the railroads. "People commenced to think who had never thought before," one alliance sympathizer wrote, "and people talked who had seldom spoken."

In December 1889 all the major farm organizations met in St. Louis at separate sessions. Besides the Northern and Southern alliances, there were the Knights of Labor, the Farmers' Mutual Benefit Association, and the Colored Alliance. But a number of issues kept these groups apart. For one thing, the Southern Alliance regarded secrecy as a distinct advantage because many of its members were tenants, not landowners, and thus more vulnerable. Most northern representatives objected to it. Northern representatives also resented southern insistence that black farmers be excluded, although southern spokesmen were willing to leave to each state organization the right to decide this issue.

Another divisive issue arose over the question of creating a third political party. Certain northerners already were thinking of resorting to this tactic; southerners found it difficult to accept, since they lived in a one-party region. An independent party would have far less of a chance where politics was controlled by a single party than where two major parties were in competition and a third might tip the balance of power. Southern Alliance members also feared that a third party, by dividing voters, would endanger white supremacy.

Although little is known about the Colored Alliance, it did assert its independence of the Southern Alliance on issues such as federal aid to education and enforcement of the Fifteenth Amendment, both of which the blacks supported. More spectacularly, the Colored Alliance called a strike by black cotton pickers that the Southern Alliance (which included employers of cotton pickers) helped to defeat.

Despite organizational differences, the reform programs of the Northern and Southern alliances proved to be very much alike. Northerners gave greater emphasis to the railroad issue, southerners to farm finances and farm credit. The most important proposal for solving the credit problem came from C. W. Macune, organizer of the Texas Alliance. Macune suggested that the federal government set up a subtreasury office and warehouse in every county that would offer for sale more than $500,000 worth of farm products annually. Farmers who placed nonperishable crops in these warehouses would receive as a loan Treasury notes in amounts up to 80 percent of the local market value of their stored crops. This loan was to be repaid when the crop was sold. Macune's plan, later incorporated into the agricultural programs of the 1930s, had the double advantage of allowing the farmer to hold a crop for the best price and of increasing the money supply.

Eastern conservatives laughed off the alliance proposals as "hayseed socialism." But they could not laugh off the political force behind them. Between 1887 and 1890, Southern Alliance men, working at first through the Democratic party, elected three governors and won control of the legislatures of eight states. Northern Alliance candidates, in the major parties or in local third parties in the grain states of the Great Plains states, made impressive gains. It was in Kansas that the third party was first called the People's party. Its members there became known as Populists.

The People's Party

In 1890, radical farmers in the Great Plains states decided to go ahead with a third party. The first step was a convention in Cincinnati in May 1891, which attracted relics of dead organizations such as the Greenback party and visionaries and utopians, as well as Northern Alliance leaders. By 1892 the Southern Alliance, which had initially held back, was ready to break with the Democratic party and cast its lot with the new party. In February 1892 in St. Louis, the national People's party, including the Southern Alliance, was formally organized. The delegates called for a presidential nominating convention to meet in Omaha on July 4—an appropriate date on which to return the country to the creed of its Founding Fathers.

The key to the Populist movement lay in its rhetoric and in its cultural expression. The revivalist zeal that pervaded the Omaha convention very much influenced how the delegates chose to articulate their grievances. In their view, the dominant institutions of society—the presidency, Congress, the legislatures, the courts, and the press—had become so corrupted by industrial interests that they no longer reflected the needs of the great mass of Americans, particularly those who worked with their hands, tilled the soil, and produced the crops. The distribution of power, like the distribution of income, had become so unbalanced that only federal action could correct it. The producing classes were being victimized by mortgage lenders, grain elevator interests, marketing agents, railroads, and the Wall Street bankers who manipulated the currency on behalf of creditors and industrialists. "Wall Street owns the country," Populist leader Mary Ellen Lease told the delegates to the Omaha convention. "It is no longer a government of the people, by the people, and for the people, but a government of Wall Street, by Wall Street, and for Wall Street." The evidence seemed compelling to the delegates: monopolistic enterprises centered in the East conspired to manage on their behalf the economic life of the nation through control of government, the press, and the political parties.

What the Populist platform made clear—and this marked an important break with laissez-faire ideas—was that the federal government would henceforth need to play a far more significant role in the economic life of the nation. To force the railroad, telegraph, and telephone systems to work in the interest of the people, the Populists urged that they be owned and operated by the government. To ease the financial burden on farmers and workers, they demanded a graduated income tax. To increase the money supply and enable farmers to pay their debts more easily, they wanted to replace the rigidly limited money supply created by the gold standard with a flexible currency based on free and unlimited coinage of silver. To facilitate credit, they proposed the subtreasury plan, whereby farmers could borrow government funds at low interest against crops stored in public warehouses. To provide a safe deposit for their earnings, they called for postal savings banks. To return the land to the people, they demanded that all land held by the railroads and other corporations in excess of actual needs be reclaimed by the government and held for settlers only.

To restore government to the people, they advocated the direct election of senators (who were still elected by state legislatures), the secret ballot, and the initiative and referendum. And in the hope of expanding their appeal to urban workers, the Populists promised to support restriction of "undesirable" immigration, the eight-hour day, and abolition of the Pinkerton "standing army of mercenaries." Having adopted a platform, the Omaha convention resounded with the rhetoric of agrarian protest. "The government is the people and we are the people," announced a Populist leader. "Old man Peepul is on top. Aunt Sarah

Jane is on top. We country folk are on top, and everybody is going to be happy."

The party chose James B. Weaver of Iowa as its presidential candidate. The more than one million votes he received (8 percent of the total) had to be a promising political debut. With the exception of the Republicans in 1856, no third party had done nearly as well in its first national effort. After the election, an exultant Weaver confidently predicted the demise of the Republican party. But a sober look at the distribution of the vote might have put a brake on Weaver's optimism. True, he had run well in a few Plains and Mountain states and some southern states. But in such older agricultural states as Iowa, Wisconsin, and Illinois, and in the East, he received less than 5 percent of the vote.

The Populist party hoped to unite various segments of dissent in America, but it proved to be a fragile alliance. The election returns suggested that midwestern and western farmers did not necessarily agree on the causes of their economic plight. Midwestern farmers were noticeably less enthusiastic about currency inflation, and they more readily faced up to the consequences of

The legislative war of 1893. When election results in Kansas were disputed, both Populists and Republicans claimed control of the state legislature. The Republican-dominated Supreme Court decided for the Republicans, and they drove the Populists (pictured) out of the statehouse and assumed control. *(Kansas State Historical Society, Topeka)*

Distribution of the popular
vote for Weaver in 1892

- 48% or over
- 5% to 47%
- Under 5%
- ⊙ Not voting (Territories)

- 🌾 Wheat states
- Cotton states
- Silver states

Populist strength, 1892.

overproduction. In the South it proved difficult to unite farmers with different problems: landowning planters and small farmers, employing farmers and employed farmers, black croppers and tenants. And despite platform pledges to urban workers, Populists failed to understand the new realities of the urban, industrial society they wanted to change.

The Populists had shown enough strength in 1892 to worry the major parties, but no more than that. The next year, one of the worst depressions in American history began. As it spread, it set the stage for another campaign. This time the Populists would alarm conservatives, many of them unable to distinguish among populism, free silver, and socialism.

The Crash of 1893

Many Democrats placed the blame for the panic of 1893 on the Silver Purchase Act, which, they said, destroyed business confidence. Even the withdrawal of foreign capital, they argued, had been prompted by fears that America was going off the gold standard. This move seemed imminent by April 1893, when the Treasury's gold reserve dropped below $100 million.

Cleveland's first thought was to repeal the

Silver Purchase Act, which permitted holders of silver certificates to exchange them for gold. He called a special session of Congress in the summer of 1893, and Gold Democrats and Republicans closed ranks and enacted the repeal in October. By then, however, a run on the Treasury was gaining momentum.

After the failure of other measures to stop it, Cleveland, in February 1895, was forced to borrow $62 million in gold from the Morgan and Belmont banking syndicate on terms decidedly unfavorable to the government. The inflationists denounced the president as a tool of Wall Street. But the bankers, by bringing gold from Europe, succeeded in reversing the drain on the Treasury. With confidence restored, in January 1896 the government floated another loan that ended this crisis.

Cleveland's defense of the gold standard aggravated discontent in the West and South as much as it encouraged eastern financiers. It probably destroyed any hope of getting mass support for the tariff reform he had promised once again. Cleveland regarded the tariff act Congress finally passed in August 1894 (the Wilson-Gorman tariff) as a disgrace to the party, and it became law without his signature. This act did contain one provision that the Populists wanted, a 2 percent tax on incomes over $4000. But in 1895, by a five-to-four decision, the Supreme Court declared the income tax unconstitutional on the ground that "direct taxes" could be apportioned among the states only on the basis of population, not personal wealth. (In 1913, the Sixteenth Amendment made the federal income tax constitutional.)

As the depression deepened, the public mood grew worse. Thousands of unemployed roamed the country, sometimes in large gangs. Since the government offered them nothing, agitators proposed schemes of their own. In 1894, General Jacob S. Coxey of Massillon, Ohio, a rich man himself, convinced frightened propertyholders that a revolution had actually begun. Coxey proposed that Congress authorize a half-billion-dollar public works program. To dramatize his plan, he organized a march on Washington. "We will send a petition to Washington with boots on," he announced.

Soon "armies" all over the country were head-ing for the capital. Not all the marchers made it: Of the thousands who had started out, only Coxey's army of about three hundred men managed to reach Washington. Police speedily dispersed them after arresting Coxey and a few of his aides for illegally carrying banners on the Capitol grounds and for trampling the grass. But Coxey's march helped make an issue of unemployment, an issue the Populists hoped to use in the election of 1896. The silver issue, however, soon became the focus of the campaign and of public attention.

Silver versus Gold

Propaganda produced by western mining interests after the repeal of the Silver Purchase Act in 1893 quickly influenced farmers, who had been demanding inflation for years. They began to see the "conspiracy" against silver as another example

The Coxey army, "a petition with boots," makes its way toward Washington in April 1894 to demand legislation for the unemployed. *(Library of Congress)*

of Wall Street treachery. In 1894 William H. Harvey, author of *Coin's Financial School*, gave the silverites a handbook that reduced the complex subject of money to terms farmers could grasp. By coining silver "you increase the value of all property by adding to the number of money units in the land. You make it possible for the debtor to pay his debts; business to start anew, and revivify all the industries of the country, which must remain paralyzed so long as silver as well as all other property is measured by a gold standard." The book was also a model of Populist rhetoric. Harvey described the country as "distracted" by the hard times, with "the jails, penitentiaries, workhouses, and insane asylums . . . full" and "hungered and half-starved men marching toward Washington."

Well illustrated and distributed in cheap editions, *Coin's Financial School* sold 300,000 copies its first year. No doubt its propaganda hurt the Gold Democrats most and contributed to a 42 percent rise in the Populist vote between the elections of 1892 and 1894. In 1894, when the Republicans won overwhelming control in the House, the Populists elected six senators and seven congressmen. Even more ominous for Democratic prospects, antiadministration rural Democrats in the South, such as "Pitchfork Ben" Tillman of South Carolina, viciously attacked Cleveland. "When Judas betrayed Christ," Tillman charged, "his heart was not blacker than this scoundrel, Cleveland, in deceiving the Democracy." He promised to take his pitchfork to Washington and prod the "old bag of beef in his old fat ribs."

The Election of 1896: The Cross of Gold

Trouble among the Democrats naturally encouraged the Republicans. At their national convention in 1896 they showed solidarity by nominating on the first ballot William McKinley of Ohio, sponsor of the high tariff of 1890. McKinley was handpicked by his fellow Ohioan Mark Hanna, the shipping and traction magnate who was emerging as the Republican national boss.

The platform, however, was a different story. Hanna wanted McKinley to straddle the money issue to keep silverite Republicans from leaving the party. But he yielded to a sound-money plank endorsing the gold standard, in return for eastern financial support in the campaign. Silverite Republicans, led by Senator Henry M. Teller of Colorado, walked out.

The Democratic platform was written largely by Governor John P. Altgeld of Illinois, whose pardon of the Haymarket rioters in 1893 and handling of the Pullman strike the next year had made him hated by conservatives everywhere. The platform repudiated Cleveland's policies and came out flatly for *unlimited* coinage of silver at the ratio of sixteen ounces of silver to one ounce of gold. A sharp debate over the adoption of the silver plank was resolved once a thirty-six-year-old Nebraskan, William Jennings Bryan, had spoken in its favor. The Democratic nomination was also resolved by his speech, for Bryan was voted the candidate on the fifth ballot.

Young as he was, Bryan had already served in Congress from 1890 to 1894 as a member of the growing silver bloc. Defeated for the Senate in 1894, he became editor-in-chief of the influential *Omaha World-Herald*, and soon increased the reputation as a speaker he had made in the House by traveling throughout the country, particularly in the West and South, giving lectures on a variety of subjects. When he made his convention speech, his friends were already working for his nomination.

Bryan's speech was calculated to appeal to the emotions of the delegates: "We are fighting in the defense of our homes, our families, and posterity," he said. He declared firmly that money was by far the most important of the issues. "You come to us and tell us that the great cities are in favor of the gold standard; we reply that the great cities rest upon our broad and fertile prairies. Burn down your cities and leave our farms, and your cities will spring up again as if by magic; but destroy our farms and the grass will grow in the streets of every city in the country." Bryan closed with the striking image by which his speech has ever since been known:

Having behind us the producing masses of this nation and the world, supported by the commercial interests, the laboring interests, and the toilers everywhere, we will answer their demand for a gold standard by saying to them: You shall not press down upon the brow of labor this crown of thorns, you shall not crucify mankind upon a cross of gold.

Despite the fiery images, Bryan's speech was really a plea that farmers too be recognized as businessmen and have equal opportunity to amass property and wealth.

The real tragedy was that the speech doomed the campaign to a debate over the silver issue. If this solution appealed to depressed southern and western farmers, it won little support among labor leaders such as Samuel Gompers, who understood that "the cause of our ills lies far deeper than the question of gold or silver." Nor did this issue generate the necessary enthusiasm among many midwestern farmers, who found more reasons to blame overproduction for agricultural problems.

Even before the election of 1896, many Populists were tired of the emphasis on silver and the neglect of the more radical reforms in the party platform. Thomas E. Watson of Georgia, for example, an early Populist, thought the silver obsession had become "a trap, a pitfall, a snare, a menace, a fraud, a crime against common sense and common honesty."

When the Populists met at their convention they confronted this sad dilemma: to wage a Populist campaign would be to split the silver vote and hand the election to the Republicans; to join the Democrats in support of Bryan would mean the end of their party. Most of the delegates approved of Bryan. But the southern Populists who had joined the third-party crusade now opposed fusion with the Democrats in their section, whom they had been fighting for years. The fusionists pointed out that the Democratic platform, besides demanding the unlimited coinage of silver, did attack Cleveland's deals with the bank-ers, did recommend stricter railroad regulation, and did support a constitutional amendment to make an income tax possible.

The Populists finally nominated Bryan for president, but they could not stand the Democratic vice-presidential candidate, Arthur Sewall, a rich Maine banker. In his place, they nominated Thomas E. Watson, once the staunchest third-party man in the South, who actively sought white and black political unity—but on terms that in no way endangered white supremacy. Theodore Roosevelt, an active McKinley supporter and no friend of the Populists, thought Watson was superior to Bryan: "He represents the real thing while Bryan after all is more or less a sham and a compromise."

The campaign of 1896 was one of the most dramatic in American history. Bryan, handicapped by two running mates who detested and contradicted each other, concentrated on free silver. Hanna, in the meantime, was extracting millions for McKinley from those eager to sink the silver ship. Bryan traveled more than 18,000 miles and delivered over 600 speeches. McKinley stayed on the front porch of his family home in Canton, reading carefully drafted statements to delegations brought there by party leaders:

William Jennings Bryan (left) and William McKinley (right), opponents in the fiercely fought election of 1896. *(Library of Congress)*

This year is going to be a year of patriotism and devotion to country. I am glad to know that people in every part of the country mean to be devoted to one flag, and that the glorious Stars and Stripes; that the people mean to maintain the financial honor of the country as sacredly as they maintain the honor of the flag. What we want, no matter to what political organization we may have belonged in the past, is a return to the good times of years ago. We have good prices and good wages, and when we have them we want them to be paid in good money.

Although Bryan won more popular votes than any previous loser, McKinley's plurality of over 600,000 was the largest of any candidate since Grant defeated Greeley in 1872. McKinley won 271 electoral votes to Bryan's 176. Even such farm strongholds as Iowa, Minnesota, and North Dakota went Republican.

No doubt the flood of propaganda, the pressure employers put on industrial workers, and the identification of Bryanism with anarchy and revolution had something to do with McKinley's success. But there were more obvious causes. The Republican prescription for "hard times" made more sense to the urban and industrial North than Democratic solutions. Republicans argued, with justice, that an inflationary price movement would leave wages far behind and that workers would be the losers. Urban workers failed to provide the mass support Bryan had hoped for. Nor did he do well with the traditional Democratic Catholic vote.

In the midwestern farm states, where the agricultural depression had been less severe than in the prairie states and the South, distrust of free silver and the Democratic analysis of agrarian problems lessened Bryan's appeal. And every middle-class American with savings invested in stocks, bonds, or insurance was, in a small way, a creditor. Recognizing that, Republicans emphasized that inflation would reduce the value of personal holdings. Finally, the Republican party,

learning from past mistakes, succeeded in selling itself to the voters, particularly the growing middle class, as the party of stability, political flexibility, and ethnic and cultural diversity. For a people grown weary of social conflict and alleged conspiracies, that was an attractive appeal.

The election of 1896 did bring about a significant realignment of the party system. Some twenty years of virtual political stalemate gave way to an era of Republican supremacy. The Democrats lost much of their support in the Northeast and the Midwest, maintained Irish Catholic strongholds in the urban North, and commanded some following in the West. But the Republicans made claim to being the national party, the party of Anglo-Saxon Protestant America, the party best attuned to the needs and character of the new society, and (except for Woodrow Wilson's two terms) the majority party until the election of Franklin Delano Roosevelt in 1932.

Republican "Good Times"

"God's in his Heaven, all's right with the world!" Hanna telegraphed McKinley when the returns were in.

McKinley's election in 1896 did not restore prosperity, as the Republicans claimed. But Bryan's defeat did raise the confidence of those who stood to gain most from sound currency and protective tariffs. The Republican administration quickly adopted the Dingley tariff of 1897, which raised schedules even above those of the McKinley tariff of 1890. Three years later, McKinley signed the Currency Act of 1900, which made the gold dollar the single unit of value and required all paper money to be redeemable in gold.

To the losers, the results were disheartening. The silver issue had brought the Democrats their

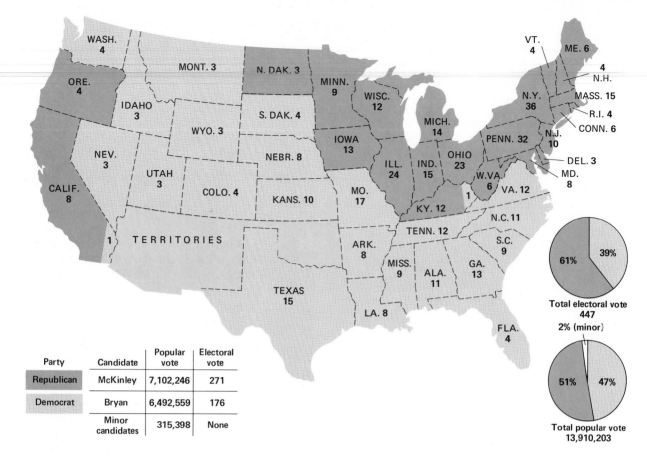

Party	Candidate	Popular vote	Electoral vote
Republican	McKinley	7,102,246	271
Democrat	Bryan	6,492,559	176
	Minor candidates	315,398	None

Total electoral vote 447
2% (minor)

Total popular vote 13,910,203

The election of 1896.

worst defeat in many years, leaving the party more divided than ever. The Populist party was finished. Some Populists joined the Socialist party; in Louisiana, for example, Eugene Debs, the party's perennial candidate, would score heavily in the hill counties where populism had been strong. Some withdrew from politics and voting altogether. Most returned to their old political home—the Democratic party.

History takes strange turns: Not long after the election, the money supply was enlarged by new flows of gold from the Klondike, South Africa, and Australia, and by greater United States production due to a new process for extracting gold from lower-grade ores. Ironically, the inflation the agrarian reformers failed to win through silver came through gold. Good harvests and good prices also brought relief. In the election of 1900, boasting of "Republican prosperity," McKinley again defeated Bryan, this time even more decisively than in 1896. The Republican slogan "The Full Dinner Pail" seemed appropriate for a prosperous country.

The doctrine of populism outlived the party, and McKinley's victory did not stop the forces of protest and reform. Several of the radical planks in the Populist program Bryan and the Democrats had neglected in favor of silver in 1896 soon became law: direct election of senators, the income tax, an improved national currency and credit structure, and postal savings banks. Ultimately, farmers achieved political success by adopting the strategy of Samuel Gompers and concentrating on organizing the most successful farmers in the system. What the farm movement had hoped to accomplish with subtreasuries in the 1890s it did gain in the 1930s with government price supports. But like the AFL, farm organizations in the twentieth century tended to ignore the marginal and dispossessed workers—the tenant farmers, the sharecroppers, the migratory farm workers, the agricultural victims of racism who found themselves trapped in a cycle of indebtedness and dependency that afforded little hope for the future.

The Populists had appealed to the nation's agrarian traditions. But the nation was rapidly becoming more urban. After 1790, the percentage of Americans working in agriculture declined with each census: the figure had dropped to 30 percent by 1910, to 3 percent by 1985. The consequences would be far-reaching, both for the cities and for the new arrivals from the American and European countrysides. In an age of rapid change and industrial power, urban America grew without any real direction or goals—a matter of grave concern to new waves of reformers.

SUMMARY

The Gilded Age in America was a time of corrupt politics, but it was also a time of reform. Some Americans were beginning to realize that government intervention in the economy and in social policy were not necessarily bad. The ideas of the public interest and the public's right to better conditions were gaining strength, though they would not really become effective until the twentieth century.

Despite the corruption and the deals, voters came out in record numbers between 1870 and 1900; campaigns were lively events in which most people were interested. Their interest, however, was generated primarily by local issues. At the national level, both parties used rhetoric and personal attacks to avoid dealing with the hard issues that faced the country. This was the heyday of the machine and the political boss. It was also a time of considerable internal party division. Republicans were split between Stalwarts and Half-Breeds; Democrats, between southern conservatives and city bosses. But all disagreements were papered over for elections. The Democrats had the Solid South, and the Republicans New England and part of the Middle West. The rest of the country was a battleground for votes, and party unity was necessary to win.

Opposed to the parties, which were mostly dominated by conservatives, were the liberal reformers. Their goal was to check abuses of economic and political power. But class and political differences kept them apart. The liberal Republican reformers (the Mugwumps) worked for civil service reform. But they had no patience with economic or social reform and thought labor agitation dangerous to society. So the reformers mostly failed, but the problems they raised did not go away, and the government had taken some steps toward enlarging its role in the economic and social spheres.

During the Republican years from 1876 to 1884, under Presidents Rutherford B. Hayes, James Garfield, and Chester A. Arthur, the issue of monetary policy again became central. The old argument over paper money resurfaced, this time over the "greenbacks" issued during the Civil War to expand the money supply and keep the government going. Afterward, debtors once again wanted cheap money, and creditors did not. The Resumption Act of 1875 had been a compromise that postponed a return to redemption in gold until January 1879. When the government began to prepare for redemption by building up gold supplies in 1877 and 1878, it thereby raised the value of the paper money. It also led to the formation of the Greenback party, which for a time polled a substantial number of votes among farmers.

Although the United States went back to the gold standard in 1879, the issue of expanding the money supply reappeared in the drive for unlimited coinage of silver. This issue finally died in the depression of the 1890s and the campaign of 1896. Until that time, however, it was a focus of nationwide attention.

The election of 1880 brought James Garfield to the presidency, and, after his assassination in 1881, Chester A. Arthur. It also brought the first step in civil service reform and the end of the patronage system—the Pendleton Act of 1883. The Democrats who took power with Grover Cleveland in 1884 faced another explosive issue: corporate abuses, especially by the railroads. Farmers organized into Granges to push for laws against discriminatory practices and high rates. Railroad workers went on strike to protest salary cuts and unsafe working conditions. Despite Cleveland's opposition to federal regulation, by the end of his term the first steps had been taken to regulate railroads. The Interstate Commerce Act of 1887 created not only federal rules, but an Interstate Commerce Commission to oversee them.

Other segments of society were satisfied by the protectionist McKinley tariff of 1890, the highest and broadest in the nation's history to that point. Western silver interests and the farmers were somewhat pacified by the Sherman Silver Purchase Act of the same year. And critics of big business got the Sherman Anti-Trust Act, which passed Congress in July of 1890.

The 1890s brought new agitation over the currency and a new third party, the Populists. Formed by farmers, who were again in trouble because of high transportation costs, heavy taxes, falling prices, and expensive credit, the party was joined by other groups angry about the government's unresponsiveness to their hardships. The panic of 1893 brought depression and widespread unemployment. Workers fought Carnegie Steel at Homestead in 1892, and railroad workers went on another nationwide strike in 1894.

Also in 1894, a march on Washington by an "army" of the unemployed was organized. Only about three hundred ever reached Washington, but the march did make news of unemployment and the Populist cause. The Populists ran their first presidential candidate in 1892. Then came the crash of 1893; the Populists grew strong enough to elect a number of congressmen and senators in the elections of 1894 and to worry conservatives. The tariff of that year, though not a reform, did contain one Populist provision—a 2 percent federal tax on incomes over $4000. But the next year, the Supreme Court declared the tax unconstitutional.

All these forces gathered momentum as the 1896 election approached. But then they were all sidetracked as silver became the focus of the campaign and of public attention. The Republicans, favoring the gold standard, nominated William McKinley of Ohio. The Democrats, taking advantage of the support for silver, chose William Jennings Bryan, whose "cross of gold" speech had swayed the convention. Despite Bryan's skill as a speaker and a campaigner, the Democrats lost. The Populists, who had backed Bryan, lost as well: their party was finished. But some of the Populist program did eventually become law—direct election of senators, the income tax, and a better currency and credit structure.

TIME LINE

1875	Specie Resumption Act
1877	Rutherford B. Hayes becomes president
1878	Greenback-Labor party polls over a million votes and elects 14 Congressmen Bland-Allison Act
1880s	Farm prices fall; emergence of the Southern Alliance, the National Farmers' Alliance, and the Colored Farmers' Alliance
1881	James Garfield assassinated; Chester Arthur becomes president
1883	Pendleton Civil Service Act
1884	Grover Cleveland elected president
1887	Interstate Commerce Act
1888	Benjamin Harrison elected president
1890	Populist (People's) Party organized

	Sherman Antitrust Act Sherman Silver Purchase Act McKinley Tariff
1892	Populist Party convention; adoption of the Omaha Platform Grover Cleveland elected president
1893–1897	Financial panic and depression
1893	Repeal of the Sherman Silver Purchase Act
1894	Coxey's march on Washington, D.C. Wilson-Gorman tariff (including income tax provision)
1895	Supreme Court finds income tax unconstitutional
1896	William McKinley defeats William Jennings Bryan for president
1897	Dingley Tariff
1900	Currency (Gold Standard) Act

Suggested Readings

In addition to the books by Hays and Wiebe cited in Chapter 20, see J. A. Garraty, *The New Commonwealth 1877–1890* (1968). For a conservative interpretation of the American response to industrialism, see Morton Keller, *Affairs of State: Public Life in Late Nineteenth Century America* (1977). E. F. Goldman, *Rendezvous with Destiny* (1952), and Matthew Josephson, *The Politicos* (1938), are lively studies of politics and reform. A revealing personal account is Henry Adams's classic work, *The Education of Henry Adams* (1918).

The best study of liberal reform in the Gilded Age is J. G. Sproat, *The Best Men* (1968). G. T. Blodgett, *The Gentle Reformers: Massachusetts Democrats in the Cleveland Era* (1966), is a solid introduction to the Mugwumps. The new political history, utilizing quantitative techniques and stressing the critical role of cultural and social forces, is best exemplified by P. Kleppner, *The Cross of Culture: A Social Analysis of Midwestern Politics* (1970) and *The Third Electoral System, 1853–1892: Parties, Voters, and Political Cultures* (1979); R. J. Jensen, *The Winning of the Midwest* (1971); S. T. McSeveney, *The Politics of Depression: Political Behavior in the Northeast 1893–1896* (1972); and F. C. Luebke, *Immigrants and Politics: The Germans of Nebraska 1880–1900* (1969). M. Keller, *The Art and Politics of Thomas Nast* (1968), features reproductions of the cartoonist's work.

On the presidents, see H. Barnard, *Rutherford B. Hayes and His America* (1954); A. Nevins, *Grover Cleveland* (1932); and H. W. Morgan, *William McKinley and His America* (1963). On other significant politicians, see C. M. Fuess, *Carl Schurz* (1932); H. Barnard, *Eagle Forgotten: The Life of John Peter Altgeld* (1938); P. W. Glad, *The Trumpet Soundeth: William Jennings Bryan and His Democracy* (1960); and P. E. Coletta, *William Jennings Bryan* (3 vols., 1964–69).

On Populist leaders, see C. V. Woodward, *Tom Watson* (1938), and Martin Ridge, *Ignatius Donnelly* (1962).

I. Unger, *The Greenback Era 1865–1879* (1964), is a solid analysis of the money issue before the rise of populism. On patronage and the civil service reform movement, see A. Hoogenboom, *Outlawing the Spoils* (1968). C. E. Rosenberg, *The Trial of the Assassin Guiteau* (1968), is an imaginative study that goes beyond the patronage issue. D. J. Rothman, *Politics and Power: The United States Senate 1869–1901* (1966), is a sympathetic study. A pressure group that failed is described in D. L. McMurry, *Coxey's Army* (1929). L. Benson, *Merchants, Farmers, and Railroads* (1955), stresses the urban origins of the call for regulation. G. Kolko, *Railroads and Regulation 1887–1916* (1965), emphasizes the frustrations of regulation.

F. A. Shannon, *The Farmer's Last Frontier 1860–1897* (1945), is a good introduction to agricultural problems after the Civil War. S. J. Buck, *The Granger Movement* (1913), and J. D. Hicks, *The Populist Revolt* (1931), are still useful older accounts of farmer unrest and political action. Richard Hofstadter, *The Age of Reform* (1955), remains an important critical assessment of populism and the agrarian mind. L. Goodwyn, *Democratic Promise* (1976), is a sympathetic study that stresses how farmers created a new political consciousness and culture. N. Pollack (ed.), *The Populist Mind* (1967), is a useful documentary collection. For analyses of populism, see also W. T. K. Nugent, *The Tolerant Populists: Kansas Populism and Nativism* (1963); O. G. Clanton, *Kansas Populism* (1969); and R. F. Durden, *The Climax of Populism* (1966). Songs of agrarian protest may be found in P. S. Foner, *American Labor Songs of the Nineteenth Century* (1975). On the aftermath of populism, see J. R. Green, *Grass-Roots Socialism: Radical Movements in the Southwest 1895–1943* (1978).

CHAPTER 22

THE EMERGENCE OF URBAN AMERICA

In moving from the country to the city, Americans in the nineteenth century were sharing in a European movement. The mechanization of agriculture and the competition of new lands in other parts of the world encouraged a continuing exodus to urban centers. But the city in Europe and the city in the United States evoked different images. In Europe the city was always thought of as a center of power and learning, of religion and art. The great city—Athens, Rome, Paris, London, Constantinople, Moscow—traditionally was a place of palaces, emperors, and aristocrats, of universities and cathedrals, of architects, sculptors, painters, poets, philosophers, scholars, doctors. In America, the city was viewed by most with suspicion, and by some as a problem. "When we get piled upon one another in large cities," Thomas Jefferson observed in 1787, "we shall become as corrupt as in Europe, and go to eating one another as they do there."

Despite Jefferson's warning, the cities carved out of the American wilderness were recognized for the role they played in

shaping and reflecting the economic and cultural development of the nation. But Americans never abandoned their mixed feelings toward the city: the more urbanized they became, the more they exaggerated the virtues of their rural origins. It was a rare politician who did not, if he could, boast of his rural past and praise the superior virtues of farm life. Novelists, politicians, pamphleteers, Protestant clerics, and reformers used the same themes in discussing urban life. The city came to symbolize the loss of innocence, the corruption of virtue, and the ultimate triumph of materialism. It was the place that housed the industrialists and bankers, the Catholic church, and the immigrants who refused to conform to American ways.

But love of country life in no way stopped the steady movement toward the city. For every urban worker who chose to migrate to the country and take up farming, twenty farm youths headed for the city; between 1877 and 1910, some small towns lost 90 percent of their high school graduates to the cities. The city may have been the home of corruption, crime, squalor, and stench, but it offered incredible economic opportunities and a sense of freedom.

When thousands of freed slaves moved to towns and cities in the South, they did so, one explained, because freedom in the city was supposed to be "freer." When millions

J. J. Fogerty, *Broadway and Maiden Lane,* 1880. Courtesy of the New York Historical Society, New York City.

of immigrants came to the United States in the late nineteenth century, they settled in the cities because opportunities were said to be better there. And when growing numbers of Americans left the countryside for the city, they did so not only to make their fortunes, but to escape the dreariness, loneliness, and drudgery of farm life. Virtuous living and fresh country air were simply not enough for families confronted with mortgage payments, declining prices, depleted soil, crop failures, and natural disasters.

The number of new city dwellers grew so rapidly that the expansion of the city often was sudden and unplanned. Cities grappled with the problem of supplying water, disposing of sewage, cleaning the streets, and constructing new housing. By the turn of the century, the results were plainly visible: crowded neighborhoods, congested tenements, uncontrolled epidemics, and unworkable governments. The reformers who tried to solve these problems had different degrees of commitment and different political ideas. But their efforts were part of the movement and ideology that came to be called progressivism.

URBAN GROWTH

Although urban growth had proceeded rapidly before the Civil War, in 1840 only one-twelfth of the American people lived in cities of 8000 or more. By 1860 the proportion had grown to one-sixth, and by 1900 to one-third. By 1910, nearly one person in every two lived in the city. The number of cities with more than 100,000 people had increased since 1860 from 9 to 50, and the number of cities holding between 10,000 and 25,000 people had increased from 58 to 369. America was well on its way toward becoming one of the most urbanized nations in the world.

In 1900 more than 25 million Americans were living in cities, most of which had grown in the preceding fifty years. In 1850 New York City and independent Brooklyn together boasted a population of 1.2 million. By 1900 (the five boroughs of present-day New York City had been consolidated in 1898) it was over 3 million; by 1910 it was approaching 5 million. In the same period, again partly by annexation of neighboring communities, Philadelphia grew from 560,000 to over 1.5 million.

No other city quite matched Chicago's rise from a muddy trading post with twelve families in 1831, to 100,000 people in 1860, to nearly 2 million people in the early 1900s, making it the second largest city in the United States. The sudden growth of places that hardly existed in 1860 was equally striking. By the turn of the century, Denver, Minneapolis, Los Angeles, and Birmingham were not towns, they were cities.

Why the Cities Grew

Even before 1860, the steam railroad and the steam engine had begun to transform the urban landscape. The railroad quickly made its presence felt. It took the best sites for rights of way, freight yards, and depots; demolished old landmarks; and established the path and pace of urban expansion. For the local promoters and real estate speculators who had competed to bring the railroad to town, this seemed a small price to pay. The rapid expansion of the railroad network reduced the cost of shipping raw materials and manufactured goods, tapped larger and more distant rural and urban markets, and stimulated large-scale manufacturing. At the same time, the steam railroad and steam power in factories transformed mill towns into soot-laden cities with hundreds of new industries and tens of thousands of new workers.

The rapid growth of American cities after the Civil War was just one sign of the enormous increase in the scale and the pace of American business. The expansion of Pittsburgh and the development of Birmingham were directly related to the modernization and growth of the iron and steel industry. Minneapolis attained city status because of its importance in the grain trade and flour milling. Denver capitalized on the mining boom.

Chicago was first a wheat port, next a railroad hub, then the meat-packing center of the world; its industry and trade boosted business activity so that it became the financial capital of the West as well. Chicago's credit facilities, in turn, attracted a

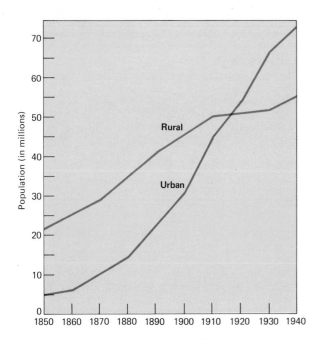

Rural and urban population trends, 1860–1920. *(John A. Garraty,* The American Nation: A History of the United States, *fourth edition, p. 476. Copyright © 1966, 1971, 1975, 1976 by Harper & Row, Publishers, Inc. Reprinted by permission of the publisher.)*

great variety of new industries and business, such as the Marshall Field store and the Sears, Roebuck mail-order house. Philadelphia and New York, still building the commercial life that had been established earlier in their histories, also grew with new industries. One was the manufac-

ture of ready-to-wear clothing, given a great push by the demand for uniforms during the Civil War.

Although tens of thousands of urban residents found employment as industrial workers and laborers, new opportunities were also opening up in white-collar and service occupations. Between 1870 and 1910, the number of wholesalers and retailers tripled. Salespeople and clerks in stores increased elevenfold. Almost equally spectacular was the growth in number of domestics and persons employed in laundries, restaurants, boardinghouses and hotels, barbershops, real estate offices, and banks. In 1910, more than 7 million persons (not all of them white-collar workers) were employed in trade and service occupations, more than four times as many as in 1870. But most newcomers were drawn into the factories and workshops. And many of these were new not only to the city, but to America as well.

The Lure of the City: Immigration

Of the 42 million city residents in 1910, some 11 million had migrated after 1880 from rural homes in the United States. The popular hero of the time was the enterprising youth described in the novels of Horatio Alger, Jr., who typically begins his life in humble circumstances in rural America, seeks fame and fortune in the city, and ultimately realizes the American Dream and becomes a respectable member of the middle class.

Sources of immigrants, 1900–1920.

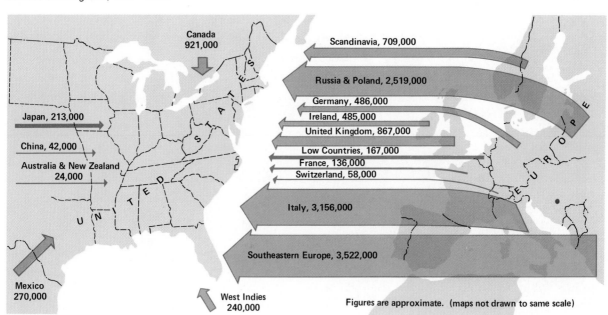

Hold fast, this is most necessary in America. Forget your past, your customs, and your ideals. Select a goal and pursue it with all your might. No matter what happens to you, hold on. You will experience a bad time, but sooner or later you will achieve your goal. If you are neglectful, beware for the wheel of fortune turns quickly. You will lose your grip and be lost. A bit of advice for you: Do not take a moment's rest. Run, do, work and keep your own good in mind. . . . A final virtue is needed in America—called cheek. . . . Do not say, "I cannot; I do not know." *(from a popular immigrant guidebook on how to survive in the United States, 1891)*

Immigrants crossing the Atlantic, December 1906. *(Library of Congress)*

An Italian family on board the Immigration Service boat that carried new arrivals to Ellis Island. Sometimes the number of those waiting to be transferred was so large that they would wait for several days and nights before the little boat could bring them to the island. *(Lewis W. Hine, Library of Congress)*

Newly arrived Russian Jewish immigrants in New York City, 1908.

(Left) An Italian grandmother and (right) a Russian Jewish girl at Ellis Island. *(Lewis W. Hine, Library of Congress)*

(Left) A Finnish stowaway at Ellis Island, 1926, and (right) a Jewish garment worker, New York City, 1920. *(Lewis W. Hine, Library of Congress)*

Mulberry Street, New York City, in the heart of the immigrant area of the Lower East Side, early 1900s. *(Library of Congress)*

DISCOVERING URBAN AMERICA

In 1884, at the age of twenty-four, Hamlin Garland left the midwestern farm on which he had been raised and headed for the city.

With all my pay in my pocket and my trunk checked I took the train for Chicago. I shall never forget the feeling of dismay with which, an hour later, I perceived from the car window a huge smoke cloud which embraced the whole eastern horizon, for this, I was told, was the soaring banner of the great and gloomy inland metropolis, whose dens of vice and houses of greed had been so often reported to me by wandering hired men. It was in truth only a huge flimsy country town in those days, but to me it was august as well as terrible.

Up to this moment Rockford was the largest town I

had ever seen, and the mere thought of a million people stunned my imagination. "How can so many people find a living in one place?" Naturally I believed most of them to be robbers. "If the city is miles across, how am I to get from the railway station to my hotel without being assaulted?" Had it not been for the fear of ridicule, I think I should have turned back at the next stop. The shining lands beyond seemed hardly worth a struggle against the dragon's brood with which the dreadful city was a-swarm. Nevertheless I kept my seat and was carried swiftly on.

Source: Hamlin Garland, *A Son of the Middle Border* (New York: Macmillan Paperbacks edition, 1962) p. 226. © The Macmillan Company, 1962; copyright by Hamlin Garland 1917; copyright renewed 1945 by Mary I. Lord and Constance G. Williams.

Although the Alger heroes were always white, the same dream attracted growing numbers of blacks from the rural South. Of the nearly 5 million black people in the United States in 1870, fewer than 500,000 lived outside the South. By 1890, 12 percent of the black population lived in cities. Like the whites from rural America, black migrants headed first for nearby towns and regional cities, and from there proceeded to the large cities in the North. Some 82,000 blacks migrated from the South between 1870 and 1890; 200,000 left between 1890 and 1910. But the crest of what came to be called the Great Migration would not be reached until World War I (see Chapter 27).

A similar movement from rural to urban life was under way in Europe. Millions would cross the Atlantic in the belief that they could realize a better life for themselves and their children in the cities of the United States. The migration was in such numbers that it overwhelmed the native-born families. By 1900, more than one-third of Chicago's population was foreign-born, and New York City had more foreign-born residents than any city in the world. New York's Italian population in the 1890s equaled that of Naples; its German population, that of Hamburg. Twice as many Irish lived in New York as in Dublin. And yet the real surge of the "new" immigration had hardly begun.

Between 1866 and 1915, some 25 million immigrants came to the United States. "We are the Romans of the modern world," the essayist and poet Oliver Wendell Holmes had said back in

AN IMMIGRANT WRITES HOME

Whatever the optimism with which many immigrants came to the United States, the need to adapt to the realities of day-to-day urban living could produce both cynicism and a reevaluation of expectations, as shown in this letter from Helena Brylska-Dabrowska in the United States to her sister Teofila Wolska in Poland:

January 10 [1909, 1910, or 1911]
Dear Sister: I received the letter with the wafer and I thank you for thinking of me, dear sister. Now, dear sister and brother-in-law, don't be angry if I don't write to you very often, but I don't know how to write myself and before I ask somebody to write time passes away, but I try to answer you sometimes at least. You ask me how much my boys and my man earn. My man works in an iron-foundry, he

earns 9, 10, 12 roubles [dollars] sometimes, and the boys earn 4 or 5 roubles. My dear, in America it is no better than in our country: whoever does well, he does, and whoever does poorly, suffers misery everywhere. I do not suffer misery, thanks to God, but I do not have much pleasure either. Many people in our country think that in America everybody has much pleasure. No, it is just as in our country, and the churches are like ours, and in general everything is alike. I wish to know with which son grandmother is. Write me. And who is farming on that land after Rykaczewski? Perhaps we shall yet meet some day or other, dear sister. . . .

Source: William I. Thomas and Florian Znaniecki, *The Polish Peasant in Europe and America* (Boston: Richard G. Badger, Gorham Press, 1918–20), vol. 2, p. 220.

This view of Dearborn Avenue in Chicago taken in 1910 illustrates the remarkable traffic congestion characteristic of urban America around the turn of the century. *(Chicago Historical Society)*

1858, "the great assimilating people." Toward the end of the century, however, many people no longer shared this faith. Part of the problem was that the new immigrants—Italians, Slavs, Magyars, Croats, Serbs, Slovaks, Greeks, and Jews—came from cultures strikingly different from those of the "natives" who had preceded them.

Of the 15 million newcomers to the United States between 1890 and 1920, 80 percent were from eastern and southern Europe. Between 1900 and 1914, for example, more than 3.1 million Austro-Hungarians entered the United States, more than 3 million Italians, more than 2.5 million from Russia, and nearly 900,000 from the Balkan countries of Europe and the Middle East. At the start of the twentieth century, approximately 9.5 million immigrants engulfed the North Atlantic ports of the United States; four out of five chose to settle in the industrial cities of the Northeast and Midwest, where economic opportunities were the best.

Northern and western Europeans had been the main source of immigration until 1896. Very soon the great numbers of different immigrant groups aroused "native" anxiety about Protestant and Anglo-Saxon supremacy, the survival of republican institutions, and competition over jobs. Actu-

ally, "native American stock," whatever was understood by that phrase, was in no danger of disappearing. Studies of the nation's population in the 1920s revealed that, despite the entry of more than 35 million immigrants since the Revolution (a figure approximately ten times larger than the American population in 1783), 51 percent of the American people were descended from colonial families, and only 49 percent were foreign-born or descended from all the post-Revolutionary newcomers, including those from Great Britain. In 1880, about 12 percent of the American population was foreign-born. Between 1890 and 1910, this figure rose to 15 percent. But by 1930 it was back to 12 percent, and it declined thereafter.

Immigrant life in the cities organized itself largely along lines of nationality. Each immigrant group dominated a particular neighborhood, often replacing another immigrant group. In New York, for example, the Lower East Side experienced periodic changes of population. Once the domain of the Irish and the Germans, the character of the neighborhood underwent profound changes when these groups moved elsewhere in the face of heavy inroads by Russian Jews and Italians in the early twentieth century; the Italians soon assumed control of the old Irish neighborhoods, while the Russian and Polish Jews displaced the Germans. And like those who had preceded them, the new immigrant groups created their own institutions—churches, schools, newspapers, and fraternal and benevolent associations.

The term *melting pot* came into common usage in the early twentieth century as a way of describing the ideal of assimilation that most Americans were said to embrace. But that ideal came into growing question in the face of the accelerated immigration of "new" immigrants from eastern and southern Europe. Among "natives," the spectacle of cities congested with newcomers whose languages, religions, and cultures differed from their own caused considerable debate about unrestricted immigration. In 1885 the Knights of Labor, reflecting concern over job competition, persuaded Congress to forbid the importation of contract laborers (the previous year Hungarians and Italians had been brought in under contract to be used as strikebreakers.) Race prejudice in the West had already resulted in agitation directed at Chinese immigrants, who first came in large numbers in the 1860s to help build the Central Pacific Railroad. The earliest federal law to restrict immigration was passed in May 1882. It forbade Chinese to enter the United States for a decade; in 1902 another act made this exclusion permanent. In 1905 the California legislature urged the exclusion of the Japanese, and extensive negotiations in 1907 and 1908 between the Roosevelt administration and Japan resulted in an agreement (see Chapter 24) sharply restricting Japanese immigration. Not yet satisfied, the California legislature in 1913 enacted an Alien Land Law that barred the Japanese—as aliens ineligible for citizenship—from owning agricultural land in the state.

In the early twentieth century, the advocates of immigration restriction came to focus on the recent immigration from eastern and southern Europe. How to respond to that growing tide remained a source of agitation, heated political controversy, and legislative initiatives until the Immigration Restriction Act of 1921 (see Chapter 27) finally resolved the issue.

CITY LIFE: GROWTH AND DECAY

The full impact of urban growth was not felt in America until early in the twentieth century. Yet even in the nineteenth century, American cities

accumulated ills and evils. Hardships were made worse by ignorance and inexperience. But a major part of the blame goes to the indifference to others that the idea of "success" encouraged.

Most city dwellers took only a halfhearted interest in civic projects that did not immediately affect their own pocketbooks or pleasure. Leaders of older nineteenth-century cities looked with satisfaction on the rising value of the urban land they owned or managed, and left those who were less well off to look after themselves. The industrialists who dominated the newer cities viewed those cities as sites for factories and tenements for the factory workers. Certain areas might be reserved for the industrialists, general managers, superintendents, and other ranking officials. The rest of the populace got miserable housing and almost no public facilities.

To accommodate the surge in population, real estate operators cut up city land into blocks of rectangular lots divided by a grid of roads. The lots themselves were divided simply by lines on a layout. With few restrictions on their operations, builders and landlords made maximum use of the available lots, wiping out all open space. Urban congestion fed upon itself. As sections of a city became thickly populated, more and more transportation was directed there. Water, gas, and electrical utilities might be brought in. Factories, most of them noisy and dirty, then moved in. Eventually, neighboring residential areas were overrun, land values soared, and more and more construction was undertaken to pay for higher taxes.

Under such pressures, private dwellings that had housed single families were remodeled into tenements that housed eight or twelve families or else were torn down to make room for business structures. As living conditions deteriorated, families that could afford to do so moved away. The richer ones went to nearby suburban towns. But as strong as the movement of population to the suburbs was, the flood of newcomers into the cities greatly exceeded it.

Nineteenth-century growth had a decentralizing tendency, but congestion continued to increase. The result was that land values grew every year. Consequently, land utilization became more intensive—indeed, hostile to human life. The cities also had to respond to demands for expanded services: water, gas, sewage disposal, transportation, and electrical power were now the responsibility of municipal departments that had access to large sums of tax money in addition to revenues from bond issues and loans. Municipal debt, in fact, rose from $200 million in 1860 to $1.4 billion in 1902.

The problems created by the fast pace of urban growth were enormous. The existing and often antiquated city governments, some of them still controlled by state legislatures, were simply not equipped to undertake such imposing tasks. Without any developed science of public administration, political machines run by "bosses" accepted the challenge and reaped the financial benefits.

Political Corruption

When a prominent educator called America's cities in 1890 "the worst governed in Christendom—the most expensive, the most inefficient, and the most corrupt," he was underscoring the degree to which the metropolises had fallen under boss or machine rule. Designed to keep themselves and their party in office, the political machine had at its command an impressive army of county, ward, and precinct captains and workers. Few were more impressive in this era than the bosses who headed the machines, men such as William Marcy Tweed and Richard Croker of New York City, "Czar" Martin Lomasney of Boston, "King" James McManes of Philadelphia, Christopher Magee of Pittsburgh, Ed Butler of St. Louis, and "Blind Boss" Buckley of San Francisco. Of course, they charged a price for their presence—and for the essential services they rendered.

Somehow, despite the absence of professional managers, the machines made the cities work—perhaps not efficiently or inexpensively, but with some semblance of order and service. The corruption sometimes became so obvious as to arouse upper- and middle-class residents. But it was the usual indifference of those groups to the needs of city dwellers that had given the bosses their electoral base to begin with.

In most American cities, power resided in the mayor, in the single- or double-chambered city council, and in independent boards. These agencies determined how municipal funds should be raised and spent. They granted the franchises for street railways, awarded contracts for sewers and street paving, constructed public buildings, bought fire-fighting equipment, and contracted for other services and supplies. Since most of these activities were entrusted to committees drawn from elected aldermen or council members

with no training in city management, political bosses found it easy to place their people in positions where they could dip into city treasuries and enter into profitable alliances with local businessmen.

Boss Tweed's career in New York City between 1869 and 1871 became the model for all later political swindlers. As head of Tammany Hall, the New York Democratic machine, Tweed exercised control over patronage. His technique was simple. Everyone who worked for the city was required to pad his bill—at first only by 10 percent, later by 66 percent, and finally by 85 percent. The padding went to Tweed's gang. When Tweed built his famous courthouse, whose final cost ran to many times the original estimate of $3 million, an item charged to the "repair" of fixtures ran over $1,149,000 before the building was even completed. The criticism mounted, particularly in editorials in the *New York Times* and in Thomas Nast's cartoons in that paper and in *Harper's Weekly*. When the corruption and bonded debt reached such proportions that bankers feared the city's credit might be in jeopardy, Tweed was thrown out. Five years later, in 1876, he died in jail.

If older Americans put the blame for corruption on ignorant immigrant hordes, the immigrants themselves were wise enough to back the bosses who helped them survive in harsh new surroundings. While civic reformers talked about honest government, staged periodic "cleanup" crusades, and showed their contempt for the immigrants and lower classes, the boss provided services and earned the loyalty of constituents. His lieutenants welcomed new arrivals at the docks, hastened their naturalization proceedings (to speed them to the polls), gave them gifts at Christmas, found city jobs for them and their sons, encouraged their ethnic customs, and mediated with the police and the courts when immigrants or their children got into trouble. The precinct captain (such as the illustrious George Washington Plunkitt of Tammany Hall) worked a full day and often into the night. Everyone in the neighborhood knew him, and many were indebted to him for some favor. On election day, the voters recalled these services, not the empty promises of do-gooding reformers.

Reform programs to reduce taxes hardly touched the average immigrant's life, for he had no property to tax. Reforms to improve the efficiency of city administration aroused only suspicion, for "efficiency" in government might well mean he and his relatives would be dropped

THE BUSINESS OF URBAN POLITICS

George Washington Plunkitt, a ward boss for Tammany Hall in New York City, discussed the problem of graft in city government in 1905.

Everybody is talkin' these days about Tammany men growin' rich on graft, but nobody thinks of drawin' the distinction between honest graft and dishonest graft. There's all the difference in the world between the two. Yes, many of our men have grown rich in politics. I have myself. I've made a big fortune out of the game, and I'm gettin' richer every day, but I've not gone in for dishonest graft—blackmailin' gamblers, saloon-keepers, disorderly people,—and neither has any of the men who have made big fortunes in politics. There's an honest graft, and I'm an example of how it works. I might sum up the whole thing by sayin': "I seen my opportunities and I took 'em." Just let me explain by examples. My party's in power in the city, and it's goin' to undertake a lot of public improvements. Well, I'm tipped off, say, that they're going to lay out a new park at a certain place. . . . I go to that place and I buy up all the land I can in the neighborhood. Then the board of this or that makes its plan public, and there is a rush to get my land, which nobody cared particular for before. Ain't it perfectly honest to charge a good price and make a profit on my investment and foresight? Of course, it is. Well, that's honest graft.

Source: William L. Riordon, *Plunkitt of Tammany Hall* (New York: Knopf, 1948), pp. 3–4.

While a police reporter, Lincoln Steffens interviewed Richard Croker, who in 1886 became the Tammany Hall boss of New York City—a position he retained for sixteen years.

CROKER: *Now, then, what do you want to ask me?*

STEFFENS: *Well, about this boss-ship. Why must there be a boss, when we've got a mayor and—a council and—*

CROKER: *That's why. It's because there's a mayor and a council and judges and—a hundred other men to deal with. A government is nothing but a business, and you can't do business with a lot of officials, who check and cross one another and who come and go, there this year, out the next. A business man wants to do business with one man, and one who is always there to remember and carry out the—business.*

STEFFENS: *Business? Business? I thought government was all politics.*

CROKER: *Ever heard that business is business? Well, so is politics business, and reporting—journalism, doctoring—all professions, arts, sports—everything is business.*

Source: Adapted from *The Autobiography of Lincoln Steffens* (New York: Harcourt, Brace, 1931), pp. 236–37.

Members of the Tweed ring (Tweed is front left) reply to the question "Who stole the people's money?" by pointing out the next man. This and other Thomas Nast cartoons annoyed Tweed, who once offered Nast $500,000 to stop his attacks. His own followers, Tweed remarked, could not read, but they could "look at the damn pictures!" *(The Granger Collection)*

from the city payroll. Fearful of change, the immigrant disliked the very sound of "reform." And why not, since the typical upper-class reformer seemed to be attacking the very men to whom the immigrant felt most loyal—the bosses who provided the jobs and services. Reformers also had trouble with the well-educated American voter whose party loyalties were exploited by politicians. Many honest people, feeling that local reform movements would only harm their party nationally, tolerated corrupt city and state machines that delivered the vote in national elections. The ties between politics and business strengthened the tolerance of corruption arising from party loyalties. Only when the activities of the political rings became too outrageous did respectable citizens organize for "good government," and then only temporarily.

That the machines survived the challenges and demonstrated considerable staying power is a tribute to the organizational skills they employed and to their relative success in balancing the needs of the city against those of the party. It required a fine sense of priorities to survive. Few expressed it more graphically than the elected official who observed: "There comes a time in politics when a man must rise above principle."

Technical Advances

One great obstacle to good government in the nineteenth century was widespread ignorance of how to make it work. The practice of municipal borrowing, for example, so rewarding to bankers and so much more gentle on taxpayers than paying cash for "improvements," led to huge debts that, even with the best intentions, sucked up great sums for interest and periodic funding. There was no science of sewage disposal, of garbage collection, of budget procedures and effective management.

One of the worst problems was traffic congestion, especially at peak hours when millions of workers had to be carried to and from their jobs. The horsecar, with a maximum speed of six miles an hour, was no longer enough. The steam-driven elevated railroad was tried out in New York City in 1867 and came into everyday use there during the seventies.

Horsecar companies fought the new lines, with the support of citizens who complained of the soot and smoke and hot ashes that dropped on pedestrians' heads. As time passed, elevated steam railroads were abandoned, but not because of discomfort. It simply became too expensive to construct elevated structures strong enough to support heavy locomotives drawing long trains at fast speeds. Some other method had to be found to transport people forced by urban overcrowding to live farther and farther from their work.

The cable car, propelled by a moving underground chain, was used in San Francisco in 1873 and in Chicago ten years later. The most successful innovation, however, was the trolley car, developed by Frank Julian Sprague. Since each of Sprague's trolleys carried its own electric motor and ran on the ground, there was no need for stinking, noisy steam locomotives or the dense network of elevated track that cut off light and air. The operators of the elevated steam railroads fought the trolleys, but soon were forced to electrify their own lines. Electric subways, operating in London since 1886, were introduced in Boston in 1897 and New York City in 1904.

Besides providing energy for urban transportation, electricity helped improve the lighting of city streets and structures. The development of the electric arc lamp for outdoor lighting in 1897 meant the gradual disappearance of flickering gas lamps. Soon after, electric signs on buildings lit up a few streets. Interior lighting by electricity had become commercially feasible in 1879, when Edison perfected the incandescent bulb.

In dealing with such matters as the water supply, waste disposal, and street cleaning, which had been handled relatively well in the past, American cities grew less and less conscientious. By 1870, the disposal of waste had reached a critical stage in the larger cities, where sanitation methods were those used in the villages of a century before. Not one American city filtered its water, even though dumping of sewage and garbage into streams often polluted the supply. The typhoid fever epidemics common in Chicago and Philadelphia in the last decades of the century could be traced to the drinking of contaminated water.

Between 1880 and 1900, cleaner streets, purer water, and more efficient methods of fire fighting made the American metropolis more livable. Yet it retained such ugly and brutal features that Europeans who visited the United States at the end of the century often wondered why people from their country hadn't remained at home. But Europeans who could afford to travel seldom visited Europe's own urban slums, where the most desperate were trying to escape an even grimmer rural poverty.

Housing

Many American cities, especially in New England and along the eastern seaboard, retained something of their small-town character until the Civil War. For many decades, pleasant wooden houses on well-cared-for grounds stood at comfortable distances from elm-lined streets. After 1865, the general appearance of the city changed. New architectural styles came in, and machine-made pressed brick displaced wood as the standard building material.

Not all the houses in the nineties were the architectural absurdities some critics have declared them to be; many streets and districts in the major American cities were attractive and pleasant. Yet the urban landscape, as a whole, became dingier. Even the very rich, with their armies of servants, often lived in mansions near gasworks and slaughterhouses and breathed the same sooty air as the slum dwellers. In middle-class dwellings throughout the country, interiors were dark and crammed with overstuffed furniture peculiarly susceptible to dust.

The bulk and clutter of Victorian living suited a generation that overate, whose women attached bustles to their dresses, and who lived what might be described as upholstered lives. The very poor, constituting half and more of the metropolitan population, and nearly the whole of many factory towns, lived under conditions that were scarcely endurable. The names residents gave to their neighborhoods were appropriate: Hell's Kitchen, Bandit's Roost, Poverty Gap, Kerosene Row, Bone Alley.

Even before 1840 in New York City, rows of abandoned middle-class houses in new industrial districts were being leased for conversion into tenements. After 1865, the practice spread like a disease over metropolitan America. Whole families, sometimes more than one, lived in airless closets, usually without sanitary facilities, lighting, or heat—and were victimized then as now by flourishing populations of rats and other vermin.

The first tenements designed to provide cheap lodging for working-class families were erected in New York in 1850. Driven by rising land costs, their owners built on every available square inch and up to six stories, leaving no space for trees, grass, air, or light. Soon entire districts were occupied by such barracks, into which swarmed the poor, black and white, all paying extortionate rents. Substantial profits, ranging from 15 to 30 percent, were extracted from such buildings and

A one-room tenement apartment in New York. (Jacob A. Riis, the Jacob A. Riis Collection, Museum of the City of New York)

from basements, garrets, outhouses, and stables converted into dwellings. Landlords refused to repair or maintain their property and evicted those who could not or would not pay in advance.

In 1879 the dumbbell tenement, so called because of the shape of its floor plan, was introduced as the model housing unit in New York City. It had fireproof stairways, a toilet at first for every two families, and an outside window for each room, until doubling up cut off this opening. The solid rows of these five- or six-story buildings on twenty-five-by-ninety foot lots discouraged any real tenement reform, and they soon became as overcrowded as the old tenements. By 1894, about 39,000 dumbbell tenement houses had been erected in New York City, and nearly half of the city's population lived in them. Most lacked bathtubs, toilets, running water, and backyards.

Although New York's slums were the worst in the nation, similar conditions prevailed elsewhere. Philadelphia constructed small two-story houses instead of tenements for its working-class population, but overcrowding produced the same hideous results. Other cities used the wooden three-decker apartment building, introduced in Boston during the 1840s. From there it spread west to Chicago, gaining in numbers per acre and numbers per room in the process.

The Black Ghetto

When southern blacks came to the North, they settled largely in the cities. Between 1870 and 1890, the small black population of Chicago more than tripled (from 4000 to nearly 15,000). But that was only a suggestion of what lay ahead. (The 30,000 blacks who lived in Chicago in 1900 made up less than 2 percent of the city's people, compared with nearly 25 percent sixty years later.) The black populations of New York and Philadelphia grew to about 50,000 each in 1900.

But the numbers were larger in Washington, Baltimore, and New Orleans, and the proportion of blacks to whites was far greater in Memphis, Atlanta, Savannah, and Shreveport. Only about 20 percent of whites and blacks in the South were urbanized in 1900, but almost 70 percent of northeastern blacks lived and worked in cities.

In the early postwar decades, the black populations of the older cities of the North, as of the South, often shared neighborhoods with whites. With the spread of racism in the South after 1890, however, the urban black's position declined. Jim Crow laws and attitudes brought segregation in

housing and all other aspects of life. In the North at about the same time, customs and practices subjected blacks to discrimination, police harassment, and a two-faced judicial system.

"To the American white man," a northern black lawyer remarked in 1888, "a 'nigger' is a 'nigger' whether he be a Sixth Avenue dude or a Georgia mule-driver." Although the ghetto—the district marked off for black housing and thus for black life—had not yet taken on the rigidity of later decades, the outlines were already clear in the North.

Tightly knit ethnic neighborhoods were typical of large cities at the turn of the century. But when white immigrants accumulated some money, they could move. That option was closed to blacks; white hostility, often violent, shaped the pattern and quality of black settlement and housing. As the black migration northward gained momentum, the sections of the cities into which blacks could move did not expand. The congestion in the black enclaves increased.

Such housing bred its own misfortunes, which more prosperous white citizens blamed on the blacks themselves. As early as 1885, a black newspaper in New York claimed that house rent consumed at least one-third, and sometimes one-half, the earnings of most black residents, and for dwellings that hardly justified such an expenditure. To meet rent payments, which were higher than for comparable white dwellings, blacks were forced to take in lodgers and convert brownstones into rooming houses.

With the rising tide of foreign immigrants, blacks found that the few jobs to which they could aspire were now threatened. The Irish had already moved them off the docks. Hotels now replaced black employees with immigrants. Even the barbershops, which blacks had once dominated, fell to the Italians in the 1880s and 1890s. Except as members of the "marginal labor reserve," black men—prepared only for menial tasks and kept from apprenticeship training—were bypassed as factory workers.

It was once a mark of standing among the city's rich to have black servants. But as time passed, the glamour of such attendants wore off, and male black employment declined. Black nursemaids, housemaids, and other female domestic workers remained in demand, at least until the new immigrants learned enough English to compete. Many black women became the major, if not the only, breadwinners of their families, which further undermined male morale and multiplied broken homes. Urban conditions ultimately disoriented the black family in ways that even slavery had not succeeded in doing.

Deepening urban segregation did encourage blacks to develop or expand their own social institutions. Black businesses, churches, political clubs, charitable organizations, fraternal and athletic clubs, insurance companies, and similar units grew in number. To serve the expanding ghettos, a black business class emerged, made up largely of self-made men who depended on black patronage and helped to promote community and racial consciousness.

But segregation also heightened the likelihood of racial strife with other segregated groups, especially the white population, which deliberately segregated itself. Race riots in New York in 1900 and in Springfield, Illinois, in 1908 caused much property damage and loss of life. Although the number of victims in no way compared to those killed by lynching in the South, the outbreaks of violence reflected growing urban tensions that would erupt again after World War I.

The Elite

The spread of urban decay depressed many observers, as did sometimes the astonishing growth in numbers and wealth of the urban middle and upper classes. Prosperous merchants and planters of earlier generations had set modest standards of elegance and public virtue on incomes of $10,000 to $20,000 a year. Now industrial magnates and railroad barons boasted incomes in the millions.

So rapid was their rise to power and privilege that few received any training in the social responsibilities of great wealth. Some millionaires, such as Rockefeller and Carnegie, eventually followed the paternalistic pattern by building libraries, universities, and research foundations. But the great majority of the new rich kept their money for business and for personal luxuries.

"Conspicuous consumption" reached absurd heights in the cities during the 1890s, while the business system was sunk in a deep depression. The extravagances of the rich made newspaper copy, as did their debaucheries. At one party the guests, all on horseback, rode their mounts into a luxurious hotel. At another great dinner, cigarettes rolled in hundred-dollar bills were passed out to the guests and smoked after coffee. Harry Lehr staged a dog dinner at which his friends' dogs were invited to sup on rare dainties. Perhaps the most irritating single event was the notorious Bradley Martin ball, given at a cost of $369,000 during the severe depression winter of 1896–1897. The hostess appeared as Mary, Queen of Scots, displaying among her ornaments a massive ruby necklace once worn by Marie Antoinette. One of the guests, August Belmont, wore a $10,000 suit of steel armor inlaid with gold. The reaction to the ball persuaded the Bradley Martins to leave New York and take up permanent residence in England.

Yet the extravagances went on. On upper Fifth Avenue in New York City, the palaces of the rich rivaled those of the titled families of Europe. High-priced architects reproduced ancient forms in limestone and marble, and their clients decorated the interiors with genuine treasures of Europe's artistic past, as well as fraudulent reproductions.

VIEWS OF THE CITY: EDITORS AND ARCHITECTS

When writers, politicians, and clerics focused on the merits of agrarian and urban life, the city almost always suffered by comparison. Its very appearance suggested to many the alienation and depersonalization that typified urban living. In a world dominated by iron, steel, and stone, the people had come to resemble the structures they were erecting. For some, the city newspaper emphasized the differences between the rural and urban ways of life; it fed its readers on murders, scandals, and violence.

There were those who clung to a different vision of the city and what it could become. They talked of altering the physical appearance of the city in order to make it a more decent place to live. That vision was captured in some of the new urban landscapes and architecture and in the Great White City that formed the nucleus of the World's Columbian Exposition in Chicago in 1893. What distinguished that "dream city" from so much of urban America was the fact that it had been planned.

Urban Journalism

The daily press, like the new popular magazines, kept up with the growing complexity of urban life and tried to satisfy the varied tastes of a growing readership. Even before the Civil War, writers and editors had discovered that crusades against corruption or vice paid off in sales. Civic vice gave such a boost to circulation that newspaper editors began to invent causes and to feature crime. Recent arrivals from the farm particularly liked stories that confirmed their ideas of life in the wicked city. Reporters who were able to crash the entertainments of the rich and to describe them from the inside or who could draw a tear by writing authentic reports of the experiences of the poor brought a new individuality and a new glamour to newspaper careers.

The new methods helped to enlarge daily newspaper circulation from 2.8 million in 1870 to 24 million in 1899. Increased revenue from subscriptions and sales, and above all from advertising, helped free editors from political pressure and enabled them to become powerful molders of public opinion.

Joseph Pulitzer, owner of the *St. Louis Post-Dispatch* and later of the *World* in New York, was the model of the new publisher. Combining the crudest sensationalism with effective exposés, the *World* lived up to Pulitzer's promise to publish a "journal that is not only cheap, but bright, not only bright, but large, not only large but truly democratic that will expose all fraud and sham, fight all public evils and abuses."

The *World* exploited all the inventions that were revolutionizing publishing in this period: improved newsprint made from wood pulp, the Linotype machine, typewriters, telephones, and the telegraph. These improvements produced startling rises in circulation—from 20,000 to 40,000 within two months after Pulitzer took over in 1883; to 100,000 by 1884; and to 250,000 by 1886.

Pulitzer's methods were copied by publishers in other large cities and by competitors in New York. William Randolph Hearst, fresh from Harvard and backed by his father's gold-mining millions, managed to outdo Pulitzer in sensationalism in his *New York Journal*. One result of the fierce newspaper rivalry was *yellow journalism*, a name derived from the yellow ink first used by Pulitzer in comics but soon made to stand for the kind of publishing he promoted.

Conservative editors were quick to criticize yellow journalism, but the only effective answer was to produce a good newspaper that sold widely without it. Adolph S. Ochs proved this could be done when he took over the moribund *New York Times* in 1896, cut its price to a penny, and revived its circulation by full and trustworthy coverage of foreign and domestic news.

When Congress in 1879 granted low postal rates to magazines, their circulation grew even more spectacularly than that of newspapers. *McCall's* (1870), *Popular Science* (1872), *Woman's Home Companion* (1873), *Cosmopolitan* (1886), *Collier's* (1888), and *Vogue* (1892) were only a few that benefited from the new postal act. By and large, these publications, as well as established monthlies such as *Harper's*, the *Atlantic*, *Scribner's*, and the *Century*, appealed to the middle-class urban reader.

In the last decade of the nineteenth century, magazines became more sensational in their methods and gave more attention to current issues. New techniques in printing and heavier subsidies from advertisers helped publishers lower magazine prices. By 1900, with the additional benefit of low mailing costs, hundreds of thousands of families could subscribe.

Cyrus H. K. Curtis's *Ladies' Home Journal*, founded in 1883, became the most spectacular magazine success, reaching a million in circulation by 1900. Curtis's brilliant editor, Edward Bok, filled the *Journal* with features for women: advice on how to bring up children, decorate their homes, and preserve their health. Bok bought the fiction of the most popular American and English writers and paid them well. Soon this "monthly Bible of the American home" had become a national force that, among other accomplishments, influenced American domestic architecture and led a campaign to force municipal authorities to clean up their cities.

The New Urban Landscape

To recapture some of the rural virtues lost in an urban environment, a few far-sighted planners tried to bring the country to the city. The vision of a garden city had been caught in 1858 when Calvert Vaux and the landscape architect Frederick Law Olmsted planned Central Park in New York. Not only was the idea of a planned public park itself almost unprecedented, but their ingenious and tasteful efforts to accommodate roads, lawns, and buildings to the topography ushered in a new era in landscape design. At first, many people complained that parks were aristocratic, un-American, and unbusinesslike. But this prejudice soon disappeared, and the resistance of real estate interests was overcome. Between 1872 and 1895, Olmsted and his disciples undertook similar experiments in Boston, Washington, Buffalo, and other cities.

Architects also tried to counteract the ugliness

and imitativeness that characterized so much of urban architecture. It took a different kind of imagination to discover originality and beauty in bridges, railroad stations, grain elevators, viaducts, warehouses, and office buildings. The Brooklyn Bridge, conceived by John Roebling in 1869 and built by his son Washington between 1869 and 1883, performed a practical function. It connected Manhattan Island with Long Island, carried tremendous loads, and eased ferryboat congestion. At the same time, its unadorned steel was breathtakingly beautiful.

Many of the skyscrapers of the period revealed a similar functional beauty, fulfilling what a pioneer Chicago architect called the "ideals of modern business life, simplicity, stability, breadth, dignity." High ground rents made the maximum use of space in business districts necessary, and the vertical, soaring office buildings seemed to escape from the city's limited dimensions. Such buildings were made possible by the electric elevator, perfected in the 1880s, and by cheap steel, which could be constructed as a light, strong cage, instead of bulky masonry walls or stone columns. But city planning or its lack also permitted the skyscraper to turn streets into canyons, to shut out light and air, and to increase congestion.

The 21 million Americans who visited the World's Columbian Exposition in Chicago in 1893 were able to see a "dream city," constructed especially for this occasion, rising miraculously from the shores of Lake Michigan. It had its own transportation facilities, water supply, sewage, and police and fire protection. Frederick Law Olmsted and his assistant, Henry Codman, scored a brilliant success in laying out the grounds. Even their skill, however, could not transform the White City, as it came to be called, into an artistic triumph; only Louis Sullivan's Transportation Building broke with the past. The classic buildings of the Court of Honor produced a dismal succession of pillared banks, town halls, and railroad stations.

But the White City did stimulate experiments in urban planning and beautification. Whatever the artistic merits of the exposition, critics agreed that it was an object lesson in how a well-managed city ought to be administered for the pleasure and convenience of its inhabitants. An electrified railway and electrically powered boats on the lagoons transported hundreds of thousands of visitors. Sanitation squads cleaned up the day's garbage every night. Polite and considerate guards suggested how a model police force should conduct itself. It was a striking contrast to Chicago proper, which was a jungle of disorder.

The exposition began at the outset of a severe depression and ended as the depression deepened. Even before it closed, the temporary buildings had cracked. For some Americans, the exposition was a reflection on the society it had celebrated. But for most it had been an impressive display of American ingenuity. Rather than view the White City as an extravagance in a time of depression, those Americans concerned with the quality of urban life preferred to apply the lessons of planning and efficiency to the social problems that plagued their cities. While landscape architects tried to beautify the city, social reformers tried to help the casualties of city life.

URBAN REFORMERS

Although J. P. Morgan found New York at the turn of the century a "neighborly city," it must have appeared excessively neighborly to the thirty thousand people crowded into a single East Side district of five or six blocks. This area boasted a greater density of population than any similar area anywhere in the world, even in India or China. From his mansion on Millionaires' Row, Morgan could isolate himself from this sore spot. Municipal reformers could confine themselves to developing a science of public administration that would staff city departments with university-trained experts. At the same time, social workers, philanthropists, and clergy began to deal more directly with the social ills of urbanization. Moved by moral considerations and sometimes by fear of revolution, they concerned themselves not so much with altering the structure of city government as with making life more bearable for slum dwellers.

The Humanitarian Response

Traditional explanations of poverty and misfortune had blamed the victims. The virtuous succeeded; the immoral did not. But by the 1870s urban reformers were realizing that the causes of poverty were far more complex. Illness, death of the breadwinner, low wages, and unemployment clearly produced more paupers and criminals than laziness and alcoholism. The advice to be frugal came to be meaningless when unemployment and miserable wages did not permit even the most thrifty families to accumulate any savings. Urban reformers placed more emphasis on the weaknesses of the economy and on the need to do something concrete to assist the victims.

The first step in relief often was simply to keep people alive. During the depression of the 1870s, this problem had grown so vast that private charities could not cope with it. In 1877, Buffalo became the first city to coordinate its relief organizations. A decade later, twenty-five affiliated charities across the country had eliminated much of the inefficiency of earlier social agencies.

By increasing the number of those most susceptible to political agitation and discontent, the slums, many believed, intensified the danger of social upheaval. Hoping to narrow the gulf between the privileged and the underprivileged, middle-class reformers and social workers, most of them women, moved into the immigrant ghettos. They learned through direct experience of the lives of the poor; they opened settlement houses in the poorest neighborhoods to offer guidance, recreation, and companionship.

The idea of the settlement house originated in London in the 1870s, and the opening of Toynbee Hall in the East London slums in 1884 provided a model. Jane Addams became the leader of the settlement house movement in America. In 1889, she and her friend Helen Gates Starr converted the old Hull mansion in Chicago into a settlement house called Hull House. In Boston, Cleveland, Pittsburgh, and elsewhere, college men and women formed clubs for boys and girls, established playgrounds and libraries, conducted classes, transformed settlement houses into a combination nursery, gymnasium, and employment bureau, and campaigned for sanitary regulations, better housing, and penal reform.

The scientific approach to social welfare did not slow down the crusade against alcohol and the saloon. The Prohibition party, which ran its first national ticket in 1872, proved ineffective. But a powerful new organization took shape in 1874—the Women's Christian Temperance Union. Led by Frances E. Willard, a former educator whose creed was "No sectarianism in religion, no sectionalism in politics, no sex in citizenship," the WCTU propagandized against liquor and the people who made and sold it. Its stated policy was "mental suasion for the man who thinks and moral suasion for the man who drinks, but legal suasion for the drunkard-maker." Nothing

seemed to work, however, for by 1898 only five states were legally dry. The women who led the temperance campaign were also at the head of the campaign for women's suffrage (see Chapter 25). But this campaign also had to wait until after World War I.

The Role of the Churches

The response of the churches to slums and poverty was at first slow and indecisive, for few ministers had any knowledge of the lives of working-class families. When demands for shorter hours and for government regulation of working conditions grew loud, one church leader reminded the protesters: "Whatever you suffer here from injustice of others will turn to your account hereafter. Be quiet." But such advice meant nothing in the face of urban and industrial conditions, and during the 1870s the churches began to change their stand.

The social-gospel movement emerged during the last quarter of the nineteenth century. Organized by socially conscious ministers of various Protestant denominations, and concerned over the church's failure to reach large numbers of urban dwellers, the movement attacked the social consequences of urbanization and industrialization. The clergy who made up the movement concluded from examining their own neighborhoods that environmental forces, not immorality, lay at the root of poor living conditions.

Some went no further than to advocate moderate reforms in wages, housing, and working conditions. The more radical insisted that the nation's business system be reformed from the bottom up. Ministers such as Washington Gladden and Walter Rauschenbusch defended labor unions, wrote and preached against laissez faire, and expressed the social-gospel ideal that Christian solutions existed for all social problems. By the 1880s, theological seminaries were offering courses in social Christianity and social ethics.

But despite the need, the social-gospel movement was confined to a minority. Baptist, Methodist, and other churches whose membership consisted largely of artisans, shopkeepers, and farmers preferred to keep the old emphases on individual responsibility for sin and the church's need to deal only with religious salvation. That many of the newly rich were Baptists and Methodists (John D. Rockefeller was a prominent Baptist elder, Daniel Drew a fervent Methodist) may also help to explain why their churches did not quarrel with society as they found it. "People charge Mr. Rockefeller with stealing the money he gave to the church," a Baptist pastor said. "But he has laid it on the altar and thus sanctified it."

Some Protestant ministers, concerned about the "unchurched masses," sought ways to reclaim them. One device was the revival meeting, where evangelists ignored economic and political issues and preached the "old-time" religion. Among the most effective was Dwight L. Moody. In 1870 this former shoe salesman from Boston teamed up with the singer Ira D. Sankey to launch a campaign for saving souls. Moody preached a simple but powerful message: abandon "the cold formalism that has crept into the Church of God" and persevere for Christ.

From Chicago, where Moody had evangelized successfully in Little Hell on the North Side, Moody and Sankey went to England. When they had silenced scoffers there, they returned to take by storm every large city in the United States. The Chicago Bible Institute for Home and Foreign Missions, founded in 1899, was only one of many monuments erected to them.

The evangelist spirit was also expressed in the Young Men's Christian Association, founded as the American offshoot of an English society in 1851, and the Young Women's Christian Association, founded in 1858. Both organizations dedicated themselves to "the physical, mental, social, and spiritual benefit" of men and women everywhere. By 1897, the YMCA had 263,298 members in the United States and the YWCA about 35,000. Another import from England was the Salvation Army, organized by a Wesleyan Methodist, "General" William Booth. This army of Christians helped feed and shelter urban unfortunates. After the first American branch was opened in 1880, the Salvation Army's "slum brigades" marched out into the tenement areas and skid rows and brought comfort and relief to the neglected poor.

Better-off city dwellers sought another sort of spiritual balm, provided by a remarkable woman, Mary Baker Eddy. Her book *Science and Health* (1875) set forth the basic doctrines of the Church of Christ, Scientist, a sect that numbered 35,000 by 1900. Mrs. Eddy taught that "disease is caused by the mind alone" and that "Christian Science," the wisdom of God revealed to humanity by His son Jesus Christ, alone could overcome it. "Mind," she boldly wrote, "constructs the body, and with its own materials instead of matter; hence no broken bones or dislocations can occur." Her message appealed with particular force to Americans for whom science had come to have magical qualities.

The social activities of the dominant Protestant churches hardly touched the millions of Catholics in the United States. Numbering 12 million by 1900, the Catholics were concentrated in the cities and especially among the city poor. Catholic clergymen, unlike their Protestant counterparts, traditionally looked to the needs of the poor. Their organized efforts in America began in 1858 when Isaac T. Hecker, a Catholic convert, organized the Paulist Fathers to serve the New York poor. After the Civil War, the Roman Catholic church enlarged its philanthropic activities and in its schools carried on an effective program of Americanizing Catholic immigrants.

Roman Catholic success with the urban masses led certain Protestant leaders to suspect that the priests were plotting to capture the country. It was not long before anti-Catholic fears surfaced once more. The American Protective Association, a secret society formed in 1887, exploited the bigotry of the rural Middle West against the influence of Roman Catholicism in labor and politics. The irony of APA activities was that they appealed to farmers. The Catholics were in the cities, where the APA leaders had no success.

Many Protestant clerics had to look only to their own congregations to note the disproportionate number of middle- and upper-class members. That perception, along with fears of growing Catholic influence among the urban masses, gradually stirred the Protestant clergy to imitate Catholic methods in the cities. During the post–Civil War decades, nondenominational mission societies were formed. The "institutional church" made its appearance, with clubrooms, reading rooms, gymnasiums, adult education classes, youth organizations, and women's societies. Like the social settlement house, it represented a commitment to urban social reform.

But even as clerics and social workers assisted the victims of urbanization and industrialization, the conditions that bred poverty, unemployment, and urban congestion persisted. There also persisted optimism about improving the quality of urban life—the conviction that the inequalities of society could be corrected by legislation and by arousal of the social conscience of the nation. For those who took up the reform standard in the Progressive Era, urban government and urban living remained formidable challenges.

SUMMARY

After the Civil War, America became an urban nation as well as an industrial one. By 1910, almost one person in two lived in a city. New York had nearly 5 million people, Chicago nearly 2 million. The cities grew because industry and trade grew; there were thousands of new jobs for factory workers and laborers, salespeople, office workers, and clerks. The people who filled these jobs were migrants from rural America seeking success; they were also immigrants from Europe seeking a better life.

Between 1866 and 1915, about 25 million immigrants came to the United States. This great flood led to fear of competition among those already here, and open immigration remained a source of political trouble until the Immigration Restriction Act of 1921.

The exploding nineteenth-century American city had all the problems of rapid, unplanned growth—poor sewage, bad water, inadequate housing, tangled transportation. The difficulties were compounded because no one really knew how to run a large city, and because the prevailing idea about the cause of poverty and misery was that they were the victim's fault. These attitudes led to many opportunities for political corruption, and to the growth of the political machine and the boss.

In return for delivering the votes on election day, political bosses were given control of patronage—city jobs—and power over how tax monies were spent. The boss gave out jobs and favors, and commanded an army of county, ward, and precinct workers. Constituents were taken care of and the city was run in a more or less orderly fashion. In return, bosses such as Tweed of New York pocketed huge amounts of the public's money.

Although the basic problems were not solved, between 1880 and 1900 the American city became a slightly more livable place. Advances in transportation, street cleaning and lighting, and sanitation and water quality helped. So did the activities of editors, architects, and reformers, who planted the idea of a planned city governed in a humane way. Housing, however, remained a mess. The poor were soon crammed into a new kind of building, the dumbbell tenement, introduced in New York in 1879 as model city housing. It and several variants were soon used in cities all over the country.

The black ghetto also began to take shape during this period, as blacks were pushed out of jobs and out of certain areas of the city. Immigrants took over jobs once held by black men, black women became the breadwinners, and the stage was set for the urban black ghetto of the twentieth century.

This was the era of conspicuous consumption by the urban rich. Great mansions were built, and unbelievably extravagant parties were given. The spending continued

TIME LINE

1860	One-sixth of the American people live in cities
1867	Steam-driven elevated railroad tested in New York City
1870	Dwight L. Moody and Ira D. Sankey launch urban revivalist crusade
1871	End of Boss Tweed's rule in New York City
1874	Women's Christian Temperance Union founded
1879	Introduction of "dumbbell tenements" in New York City
1880s–1890s	Social Gospel movement
1882	Chinese Exclusion Act
1883	Joseph Pulitzer buys the *New York World* *Ladies' Home Journal* founded Brooklyn Bridge completed
1887	American Protective Association founded
1889	Hull House (settlement house) opened in Chicago
1890s	Electric trolleys replace horse-driven cars in urban transport
1890–1914	The "new" immigration: 80 percent of the 15 million newcomers are from eastern and southern Europe
1893	World's Columbian Exposition in Chicago
1897	Electric subways introduced in Boston Development of electric arc lamp for outdoor lighting
1900	One-third of the American people live in cities Race riot in New York City
1904	Electric subways introduced in New York City
1908	Race riot in Springfield, Illinois
1920	Majority of the American people live in cities

through the depression of the 1890s, despite public criticism and resentment. The gospel of success said that the rich, after all, were also the righteous and the blessed.

But there were those with a new vision of the city, and those with the attitude that the city was for all people, not just the rich. New York's Central Park became the model for a new idea—the planned public park, maintained by the city for everyone's use. Architects began to design and build public structures that were beautiful as well as functional.

Newspapers and magazines, capitalizing on a growing number of readers and the increase in sales that campaigns against vice and corruption brought, became powerful molders of public opinion. This was the time of yellow journalism, of Pulitzer's *World* and Hearst's *New York Journal.* Special low postal rates helped magazines that appealed to middle-class urban readers. The *Ladies' Home Journal,* founded in 1883, had a circulation of 1 million by 1900.

The problems and evils of city life were also attacked by social reformers, who tried to help those who lived in the slums and worked in the sweatshops. The challenge was great, and they could do little about the underlying conditions that caused poverty and ignorance. But they did begin to change the attitude of blaming the victim, and they involved the churches, especially the Protestant churches, in social work.

A number of the reformers were women. Jane Addams, for example, began the settlement house movement in America. Frances Willard led the crusade against alcohol through the Women's Christian Temperance Union, founded in 1874. The evangelist spirit was expressed in institutions based on English models, such as the YMCA and YWCA and the Salvation Army, all well established in the United States by 1900.

All these organizations and individuals did achieve something to help the poor and to set the climate for change. But nothing substantial would happen until the twentieth century, when government would come to see that social legislation and the solving of urban problems were among its duties.

Suggested Readings

C. N. Glaab and A. T. Brown, *A History of Urban America* (1967), and Z. L. Miller, *The Urbanization of Modern America* (1973), are solid introductions to urbanization. B. McKelvey, *The Urbanization of America 1860–1915* (1963), is a more comprehensive survey. A. M. Schlesinger, *The Rise of the City 1878–1898* (1933), is a pioneering work that touches on many social aspects of city living. Some of the same concerns appear in H. P. Chudacoff, *The Evolution of American Urban Society* (1975), and in Gunther Barth, *City People: The Rise of Modern City Culture in Nineteenth-Century America* (1980). D. Wecter, *The Saga of American Society: A Record of Social Aspiration 1607–1937* (1937), examines the urban life of the elite. Paul Boyer, *Urban Masses and Moral Order in America 1820–1920* (1978), is a study of how the urban middle class sought to combat the social disintegration and moral chaos they saw around them.

Among the important studies of individual cities are C. M. Green, *Holyoke, Massachusetts: A Case History of the Industrial Revolution in America* (1939), and her two volumes on Washington, D.C.: *Village and Capital 1800–1878* (1962) and *Capital City 1879–1950* (1963); B. L. Pierce, *A History of Chicago* (3 vols., 1937–57); S. B. Warner, *The Private City: Philadelphia in Three Periods of its Growth* (1968); and W. D. Miller, *Memphis during the Progressive Era* (1957).

The process of urban growth and expansion is examined in S. B. Warner, *Streetcar Suburbs: The Process of Growth in Boston 1870–1900* (1962). Important examples of the new urban history, using quantitative methods and focusing on social and residential mobility, are S. Thernstrom and R. Sennett (eds.), *Nineteenth-Century Cities: Essays in the New Urban History* (1969); Thernstrom, *Poverty and Progress: Social Mobility in a Nineteenth Century City* (1964) and *The Other Bostonians: Poverty and Progress in the American Metropolis, 1880–1970* (1973); Thomas Kessner, *The Golden Door: Italian and Jewish Immigrant Mobility in New York City 1880–1915* (1977); D. Doyle, *New Men, New Cities, New South: Atlanta, Nashville, Charleston, Mobile, 1860–1910* (1990); and H. P. Chudacoff, *Mobile Americans: Residential and Social Mobility in Omaha 1880–1920* (1972).

M. A. Jones, *American Immigration* (1960), and Philip Taylor, *The Distant Magnet* (1971), provide an introduction to the immigrant. These should be supplemented by the vivid account of the "new" immigrant in Oscar Handlin, *The Uprooted* (1951). On individual immigrant groups, see R. T. Berthoff, *British Immigrants in Industrial America 1790–1950* (1953); C. Erickson, *American Industry and the European Immigrant 1860–1885* (1957); K. A. Miller, *Emigrants and Exiles: Ireland and the Irish Exodus to North America* (1985); W. I. Thomas and F. Znaniecki, *The Polish Peasant in Europe and America* (5 vols., 1918–20); R. Takaki, *Strangers from a Different Shore: A History of Asian Americans* (1989); and M. Rischin, *The Promised City: New York's Jews 1870–1914* (1962). A gripping photographic study is A. Schoener (ed.), *Portal to America: The Lower East Side 1870–1925* (1967), a companion to Irving Howe's sensitive portrayal of East European Jews in New York City, *World of Our Fathers* (1976). The new immigration history has shown how newcomers maintained their cultures and family structure in an alien environment. See, for example, V. Yans-McLaughlin, *Family and Commu-*

nity: Italian Immigrants in Buffalo, 1880–1930 (1977); H. S. Nelli, The Italians in Chicago (1970); and J. Barton, Peasants and Strangers: Italians, Rumanians, and Slovaks in an American City, 1890–1950 (1975). The reactions of native Americans to immigration are examined in J. Higham, Strangers in the Land (1955), and B. M. Solomon, Ancestors and Immigrants (1956).

On blacks in northern cities before the Great Migration, see A. H. Spear, Black Chicago 1890–1920 (1967); G. Osofsky, Harlem: The Making of a Ghetto 1890–1930 (1965); D. M. Katzman, Before the Ghetto; Black Detroit in the Nineteenth Century (1973); K. L. Kusmer, A Ghetto Takes Shape: Black Cleveland, 1870–1930 (1976); and R. Lane, Roots of Violence in Black Philadelphia, 1860–1900 (1986). On black Washington, D.C., see C. M. Green, The Secret City (1967), and J. Borchert, Alley Life in Washington: Family, Community, Religion, and Folklife in the City, 1850–1970 (1980).

L. Steffens, The Shame of the Cities (1904), remains a classic critique of city government. On the urban bosses, see Z. L. Miller, Boss Cox's Cincinnati (1968), and A. B. Callow, The Tweed Ring (1966). L. Hershkowitz, Tweed's New York (1977), is sympathetic to the Tweed machine. A candid and amusing account is W. Riordan, Plunkitt of Tammany Hall (1963 ed.), the personal reflections of a Tammany ward boss. On urban political reform, see B. Brownell and W. Stickle (eds.), Bosses and Reformers: Urban Politics in America 1880–1920 (1973), and B. Stave (ed.), Urban Bosses, Machines, and Progressive Reforms (1972).

R. H. Bremner, From the Depths: The Discovery of Poverty in the United States (1956), is a broad and solid study. J. Riis, How the Other Half Lives (1890), is a classic contemporary account, as is J. Addams, Forty Years at Hull House (1935). A. Mann, Yankee Reformers in the Urban Age: Social Reform in Boston 1880–1900 (1954), and T. L. Philpott, The Slum and the Ghetto: Neighborhood Deterioration and Middle-Class Reform, Chicago 1880–1930 (1978), are important studies of urban social reform. See also the relevant titles among the suggested readings at the end of Chapter 25.

The response of organized religion to industrialism and urban conditions is examined in A. I. Abell, The Urban Impact upon American Protestantism 1865–1900 (1943); R. D. Cross, The Emergence of Liberal Catholicism in America (1958); H. F. May, Protestant Churches and Industrial America (1949); and C. H. Hopkins, The Rise of the Social Gospel in American Protestantism 1865–1915 (1940). For the impact of revivalism, see W. G. McLoughlin, Modern Revivalism: Charles Finney to Billy Graham (1959), and J. F. Findlay, Dwight L. Moody: American Evangelist 1837–1899 (1969).

On urban journalism, see F. L. Mott, A History of American Magazines 1885–1905 (1957). On urban architecture, see L. Mumford, Sticks and Stones (1924) and The Brown Decades (1931); W. Andrews, Architecture, Ambition, and Americans (1955); J. E. Burchard and A. Bush-Brown, The Architecture of America (1961); R. Twombly, Louis Sullivan (1986); and G. Wright, Moralism and the Model Home: Domestic Architecture and Cultural Conflict in Chicago 1873–1913 (1980).

The visions embodied in the international expositions, such as the Chicago world's fair of 1893, are examined in a fascinating account, R. Rydell, All the World's a Fair: Visions of Empire at American International Expositions, 1876–1916 (1984).

CHAPTER 23

CULTURE AND THOUGHT

For all its impressive industrial growth, the United States, in the eyes of some American and foreign critics, remained a cultural dwarf. The Centennial Exposition at Philadelphia in 1876 celebrated the birth of the nation by demonstrating its technological maturity. What Americans came to see were not displays of painting and sculpture, but the new marvels of technology, such as the telephone, the locomotive, and the steam engine.

For the intellectual Henry Adams, however, the World's Columbian Exposition in Chicago in 1893 displayed a world on the brink of disaster:

I apprehend for the next hundred years an ultimate, colossal, cosmic collapse; but not on any of our old lines. My belief is that science is to wreck us, and that we are like monkeys monkeying with a loaded shell; we don't in the least know or care where our practically infinite energies come from or will bring us to.

Even if they had understood him, few Americans in the late nineteenth century would have appreciated Adams. For most of the visitors to the Philadelphia and Chicago expositions, what they had seen confirmed the superiority of their society and the

Joseph Keppler, *Mark Twain Lecturing.* Lithograph from drawing from *Puck,* Vol. XVIII, No. 459, December 23, 1885. New York Public Library.

pioneering tradition that was now conquering new frontiers in technology and science. It mattered to very few that the paintings, murals, and sculptures displayed at the expositions showed hardly a trace of originality or a hint of vitality. If that said something about how Americans chose to measure progress, it was a trait foreign visitors to this country had long recognized.

The same forces so in evidence at the Chicago and Philadelphia expositions exerted a great influence on American attitudes and culture, on educational institutions and churches, on law and philosophy, on the social sciences, and on literature. Educators and editors, economists and sociologists extolled the laws of competition; historians confirmed the superiority of Anglo-Saxon institutions; popular ministers praised money making as the highest form of public service; and writers sentimentalized literature. Defenders of society drew on every kind of belief and knowledge to support their arguments. Some even adapted the new Darwinian ideas to their purposes.

But they did not go unchallenged. Nor did the business ethics, the inequalities, the ostentation, and the vulgarity that were so characteristic of the age. A growing number of respected critics began to question and condemn business values. And in raising critical questions about the changing nature

521

of American civilization, these critics would have a lasting impact on such twentieth-century developments as the Progressive movement and the New Deal.

In literature, too, there was considerable ferment. The McGuffey readers and the Horatio Alger novels may have been widely read, but other books dealt realistically with their society and offered different models of behavior. Mark Twain's Huck Finn, battling the tyranny of the village, would long outlast the boys in the Alger novels, who succeeded only by losing their identity in the urban business world.

SOCIAL DARWINISM

When Charles Darwin published *The Origin of Species* in 1859, the age of the earth, the process of its formation, and the origins of its inhabitants had long been discussed by philosophers, naturalists, and other scientists. But none had reached such firm conclusions from such convincing evidence. Darwin argued that the species of life all around us, far from having been created by separate acts of God in seven days, had gradually evolved over millions of years through the principle of natural selection. According to Darwin, all forms of life were engaged in an unceasing struggle for existence in a constantly changing natural environment. Although some species died, the "fittest" had survived and passed on to their offspring their favorable characteristics. Over long ages, successive adaptations had produced entirely new species, including humans.

Darwin's ideas outraged biblical fundamentalists and offended some leading scientists. More remarkable, however, was the readiness of Americans to embrace the new views, which rapidly gained popularity and acceptance in intellectual circles. Darwin's popularizers in the United States—men such as the Harvard botanist Asa Gray and the historian and lecturer John Fiske—found nothing antireligious in the belief that humans were the product of a long evolutionary process; on the contrary, they viewed that process as nothing less than "God's handiwork." In this way, religion and science could be made perfectly compatible.

Darwin's Popularizers

By combining scientific Darwinism with American optimism, the English philosopher Herbert Spencer achieved an impressive following in the United States. His synthetic philosophy, as he called it, explained the new biology in moral terms easily translated by journalists and other publicists. By ensuring the survival of the fittest, who would in turn pass on their characteristics to their offspring, the evolutionary process promised constant progress. The physical and intellectual power of the fittest would become ever greater. For God, Spencer substituted the Unknowable. This satisfied the many Americans who no longer interpreted the Bible literally, yet clung to a faith in a supernatural agency.

By 1900 about 350,000 copies of Spencer's books had been bought in America—a remarkable sale for sociological and philosophical works. Harvard in 1869 and Yale, Johns Hopkins, and other universities in the 1870s adopted his view in teaching religion as well as the biological and social sciences. William Graham Sumner of Yale, the most independent thinker among American social Darwinists, stressed inevitability more than optimism. "At the banquet of life," wrote Sumner, "there are dinners without appetites at one end of the table and appetites without dinners at the other." Sumner, like Darwin and Spencer, accepted the theory of the English economist T. R. Malthus that population increase outstrips food supply. But he rejected the idea that progress arose out of the resulting struggle for existence.

He saw reformers as meddlers engaged in an absurd attempt to make over the world. Sumner was consistent in his hands-off philosophy: he opposed government handouts in the form of high tariffs to the "fittest" industrialists. Nor had he any sympathy for racists and imperialists who cited Darwin to justify worldwide power.

Critics and Dissenters

To accept Darwin's ideas was not necessarily to accept the social implications stressed by many of his popularizers. Among the most outspoken opponents of Spencer and his American followers was the sociologist Lester Ward. He rejected the theory that "neither physical nor social phenom-

Henry George, social reformer and activist. *(Library of Congress)*

ena are capable of human control" and pointed to the superiority of selectivity over natural breeding in agriculture. Ward believed in social planning and welcomed government intervention in social matters. A democratic government operating in the interests of all, he said, would permit a truer individualism by breaking up monopolies that strangled opportunity.

Ward's first major work, *Dynamic Sociology* (1883), sold only five hundred copies in ten years. Henry George, more of an activist than Ward, reached a far larger audience. He rejected Spencer's talk of the "survival of the fittest." Progress, he said, depended on human association and social equality, which unleashed a person's creative powers. When inequality prevailed, civilization declined. George saw proof of this in California, where he went from his native Philadelphia in 1857. Land speculation was extensive, enormous prices were being paid for agricultural land, and inequalities of wealth had transformed this once simple and egalitarian frontier society. As George wrote, "The tramp comes with the locomotive, and almshouses and prisons are as surely the marks of 'material progress' as are costly dwellings, rich warehouses, and magnificent churches." Sud-

denly George thought he had the answer to the question he had been asking about why advancing wealth entailed advancing poverty. With the growth in population, he observed, "land grows in value, and the men who work it must pay more for the privilege."

George felt that poverty went with progress because of the system of private land ownership. The value of land, he said, was largely a matter of accident. For example, land in metropolitan New York had grown so costly only because "the presence of the whole great population" made it worth millions of dollars an acre. Since land grew in value because of the people who lived on it, George argued, the profit ought to return to the public in the form of a tax on the unearned increase in land values resulting from favorable location, improvements in transportation and production, and community development. He would leave the ownership of land in private hands, but socialize the rent. The single tax on land would make other taxes unnecessary and bring the government funds for many useful social purposes.

George's ideas, set down in *Progress and Poverty* (1879), attracted worldwide attention. He narrowly missed being elected mayor of New York City in 1886. He ran again in 1897, but died five days before election day.

George's contemporary Edward Bellamy also rejected the fatalism of the social Darwinists. But unlike George, he concentrated on the competitive system itself. Bellamy's radicalism had something in common with the utopian experiments of the 1840s and with the social-gospel movement of the 1880s. In *Looking Backward,* a novel published in 1888, Bellamy offered a vision of an ideal society in the year 2000 whose beauty, tranquillity, and efficiency contrasted vividly with the smoky, striving, strike-ridden America of his day. This Golden Age dawned after the nationalizing of the great trusts and the replacement of private with public capitalism.

The millions of Americans who read Bellamy's novel were delighted by the prospect of an immaculate, gadget-filled city of the future in which the people had discarded the profit motive and there were neither rich nor poor. Amazed by the impact of his book, Bellamy concluded that the American people might be ready to put his theories into practice. "Nationalism," as he called his system, was not a class movement. It rested on the idea that all people would join in an effort to build a cooperative society.

To publicize Bellamy's views, "nationalist"

clubs and periodicals advocated public ownership of railroads and utilities, civil service reform, and government aid to education. Before Bellamy's death, "nationalism" had been absorbed by the agrarian reformers. But he had made a large audience familiar with "socialist" ideas.

Academic Rebels

The ideas of George and Bellamy found little support in the universities, where conservatism was firmly fixed. American students learned that inequality in wealth produced the incentives for progress; that labor's wages depended on the number of workers competing for jobs; and that competition was the only way for free individuals to work for "the greatest good of the greatest number." Only in an unregulated society could "natural" economic laws function properly.

These ideas began to be challenged in the mid-1880s by a group of younger scholars, many of them trained in German universities. Richard T. Ely, John R. Commons, Edward Bemis, and other economists grew more and more critical of laissez faire. Under the leadership of Ely, the younger economists and some liberal clergy founded the American Economic Association in 1885. The AEA declared itself in favor of "the positive assistance of the state." While recognizing "the necessity of individual initiative in industrial life," it held that the doctrine of laissez faire was both politically and morally objectionable.

Younger sociologists had also broken out of the Spencerian straitjacket by the 1890s. E. A. Ross argued that individual personality was shaped by *social* institutions that could be controlled. In *Sin and Society* (1907) Ross tried to show that new business conditions demanded a new code of ethics, one that required the corporation to take full responsibility for its acts.

Although the younger social scientists differed in their economic and political programs, by and large they all distrusted a static view of the universe, absolute laws, and fixed conceptions. Society, they felt, was constantly changing and had to be examined in terms of process and growth. They turned to the past in order to understand the present and looked in other disciplines for relevant facts that would help illuminate their own.

Foremost among the academic rebels was the economist Thorstein Veblen. Son of Norwegian immigrants, the Wisconsin-born Veblen had absorbed some frontier populism before he com-

pleted his training at Yale, where he studied under Sumner, and at Johns Hopkins. He emerged as a biting critic of the leisure class, of "the intrusion of business ideals, aims, and methods" into the universities, and of contemporary institutions and values.

According to Veblen, millionaires were not, as Sumner had insisted, products of "natural selection." Nor were they socially useful. Captains of enterprise, he said, actually sabotaged industry through monopolistic practices. Their concern, unlike that of the engineer, was profit, not production. In displaying their wealth so conspicuously, the rich simply wished to show off. In his most widely read book, *The Theory of the Leisure Class* (1899), and in other volumes, Veblen discussed the habits and thoughts of the rich as if they were a primitive tribe.

He introduced ethical, psychological, biological, and anthropological material new to economic studies. He saw an economic community organized under a technical elite whose members would use their mastery of the machine for the good of society. Veblen's ideas seemed odd in the early 1900s, but his influence grew steadily as events made it clear that neither American society nor its economic system was perfect.

NEW IDEAS: PHILOSOPHY, LAW, HISTORY

Although Darwinian ideas won acceptance in academic circles, the ways in which American scholars and intellectuals would choose to apply those ideas differed widely. Rather than use the theory of evolution to defend the economic system and laissez faire, some used it as a basis for questioning everything. Darwinism opened up new areas for exploration and speculation in philosophy, law, history, the social sciences, and education. Traditional findings and interpretations underwent much revision. Most important, the development of pragmatic philosophy, with its emphasis on ideas as tools for solving practical problems, gave social thinkers confidence in their attack on the evils of industrial and urban society.

Philosophy: Pragmatism

Before the Civil War, the standard philosophy taught in the more liberal colleges was Scottish, or "common-sense," realism. It assumed that individuals possessed a natural faculty—common sense—that enabled them to arrive at the truth. In much the same way that Sir Isaac Newton had formulated the natural laws of the universe, it was possible for others to formulate the natural laws of politics, economics, and ethics. In the 1870s and after, German idealism, particularly as developed by Hegel and his followers, made inroads.

Hegel had seen the whole course of history as the working out of divine purpose according to certain general laws of change. But since Hegelians looked upon the present state of affairs as a stage in historical development, Hegelianism served as well as the Scottish philosophy to justify existing conditions. Its uniqueness lay in the fact that it taught reverence for the social order and preached that individuals could be truly free only by subordinating themselves to the advancement of a national government and the institutions of society.

Toward the end of the century, a new school of philosophers appeared: the pragmatists. They rejected the notion of an ideal or eternally fixed system in an evolving society and chose to evaluate ideas and theories in terms of their practical results. William James and John Dewey extended pragmatic thinking into a philosophy of action that would have a profound effect on social and educational reformers.

William James, the brother of the writer Henry James, asserted "the right to believe at our own risk any hypothesis that is live enough to tempt our will." In rejecting absolute truths, James argued for free will and the ability of individuals and societies to arrive at their own truths. The only way to examine those truths was to test them in the real world and see how they worked. Pragmatism, he wrote, prefers to see theories as "instruments" rather than as answers to problems.

As a philosopher and psychologist at Harvard, James developed his case against the "awfully monotonous" Spencerian universe, wrote a brilliant exposition on the active role of the mind that helped to establish psychology as an academic discipline, and preached his views on pragmatism. When James argued that what is true is "whatever proves itself to be good in the way of belief, and good, too, for definite, assignable reasons," he laid himself open to the charge that pragmatism was only a high-sounding name for expediency: Anything is good that works, and the end justifies the means.

The same charge was leveled at John Dewey's instrumentalism, a later version of pragmatism. Dewey was converted to pragmatism in the 1890s

William James, psychologist and philosopher. *(Brown Brothers)*

after reading James, but he had less interest in proving truth than in using it. Like James, he argued the importance of practice rather than theory, and he looked on philosophy as providing an agenda for action. Like Ward, George, and other dissenters, Dewey became an early critic of laissez faire and social Darwinism in politics and business.

He applied his ideas to education, which he felt must be related to the rest of life and made into a tool for social reform. Dewey saw the school as an institution through which the child would be prepared for citizenship in modern society by learning to criticize the customs and beliefs of that society. The child would acquire this knowledge not by absorbing teacher lectures or a specific body of information, but by developing a scientific approach to solving problems. Dewey wanted students to participate directly in the issues or situations that concerned them, to learn by doing. At the same time, he felt strongly that schools should help build children's characters and teach them to be good citizens.

The Law: Holmes and Brandeis

Traditionally, lawyers had acted as though the law was a body of changeless doctrine and as though

John Dewey, philosopher and educator. "Education is growth. Education is not preparation for life; education is life itself." *(Library of Congress)*

judicial decisions followed inevitably from constitutions, statutes, and legal precedents. The man who perhaps did most to shake this conservatism was Oliver Wendell Holmes, Jr., son of the essayist-poet and friend of William James. For twenty years he served on the Massachusetts Supreme Court before being appointed to the United States Supreme Court in 1902. By the time of his retirement in 1932, he had become one of the most celebrated judges in the world.

To Holmes, law, like life, was constantly evolving. In his book *The Common Law* (1881), he demonstrated that even the decisions of judges came as much from human frailty, prejudice, and preconceptions as from logic and authority. He challenged the prevailing faith in decisions based on a mechanical application of precedents and warned that the law must reflect experience. "It is revolting," Holmes said, "to have no better reason for a rule of law than that so it was laid down in the time of Henry IV." Freed of the restraints of precedent and blind tradition, the law could develop and serve society by responding to its needs and reflecting its changes.

Louis D. Brandeis, appointed to the Supreme Court by President Wilson in 1916, agreed with his friend and colleague Holmes that the social beliefs of judges influenced their decisions. But that was all the more reason to consider objective economic and social information in arriving at those decisions. To judge cases fairly, the law's interpreters must understand the revolutionary social and economic changes produced by the industrial transformation. Brandeis's most significant triumph as a lawyer came in the case of *Muller v. Oregon* (1908), in which the Supreme Court, on the basis of Brandeis's overwhelming evidence from physicians, factory inspectors, social workers, and other competent observers, upheld the Oregon ten-hour day for working women.

Even the Constitution became an object of critical study. J. Allen Smith argued in *The Spirit of American Government* (1907) that the framers of the Constitution had intended not to realize democracy, but to check it. In *An Economic Interpretation of the Constitution* (1913), the brilliant Columbia University professor of politics Charles A. Beard showed how the economic holdings and investments of the framers had influenced the decisions they made at the Constitutional Convention. Later historians questioned much of Beard's scholarship as well as his conclusions. Yet few deny the lasting value of his work in depicting the framers as men who shared the prejudices and concerns of their time, and in disclosing how respect for property rights shaped their ideas.

History: Frederick Jackson Turner

The parallel between Darwinian ideas of the evolution of species and the historical evolution of social institutions was too obvious to be missed. By the 1880s some historians were convinced that history could be transformed into as exact a science as biology. Academic historians under the influence of Herbert B. Adams of Johns Hopkins and John W. Burgess of Columbia, proud of their Anglo-Saxon heritage, combined the evolution of species with the evolution of race, and both with the evolution (and improvement) of social institutions. In particular, they saw American democracy as the evolutionary outcome of political practices that began with those of primitive tribes in German forests.

Inspired by popular racist theories and by expansionist sentiment at home, they argued that

Anglo-Saxons had evolved the "fittest" of all political systems. For that reason, they had been entrusted with "the mission of conducting the political civilization of the modern world." At the same time, they gave academic respectability to the suppression of blacks and the exclusion of "inferior" types from American society.

To Frederick Jackson Turner, Wisconsin-born and Johns Hopkins–trained, the conquest of the American frontier was also part of the evolutionary process. It greatly influenced the character and institutions of America, and clearly distinguished the American from the European way of life. Turner argued in his essay "The Significance of the Frontier in American History" (1893) that American democracy began in the American forests and among the European settlers. In the struggle to conquer the New World wilderness, the conquerors were forced to adapt to new conditions or die.

In successive adaptations, as the frontier advanced westward, they removed themselves further from European influences and established institutions and acquired characteristics that were uniquely American. The closing of the frontier in the 1890s, Turner believed, spelled danger for America. From the frontier had sprung the toughness, resourcefulness, individualism, and versatility that made the country great. These qualities were not characteristic of the new industrialized and urbanized America, and he regarded the "new" immigrants pouring into that America as of "doubtful value."

The history taught in the schools reflected the racial, ethnic, and class biases of the historians and the teachers. If the material itself was better than that in the McGuffey readers, the difference lay more in the method of presentation than in the values taught. Controversial subjects were avoided, as were conflicting interpretations of the American past. The student was exposed to a glorification of America in peace and war, to safe models, and to a reverence for the law and private property. History was taught largely as a means of preparation for good citizenship. That, in fact, was the primary mission of American public education.

EDUCATION

Once farm families and the society of small towns had shaped the character of American youth and taught them how to survive. Now this task fell more and more to educators. Public schools, colleges, and universities experienced phenomenal growth in the post–Civil War decades, the result of urbanization and increased support. That the average American received only about five years of schooling at the turn of the century suggests how recent has been the commitment to public education.

Illiteracy declined from 17 percent of the population in 1880 to 7.7 percent in 1910. And the educational system was undergoing significant changes not only in the number of students, but in the curriculum and in methods of instruction. Along with the increase in public libraries and the immense popularity of public lectures, the expanding school system reflected a growing hunger for education.

Public Education

By 1860 about 50 million acres of the public domain had been set aside for the support of public schools and colleges. With the end of the Civil War, the drive for a nationally supported system of public education became stronger. Impressive advances could be seen after 1865 in the lengthening of the school term, the higher dollar expenditure per pupil, the declining illiteracy rate, and the compulsory school attendance laws. The prewar academy that once monopolized American secondary education gave way after 1870 to the public high school. A broadened curriculum included history and literature, as well as vocational and commercial courses designed to prepare students for work.

Between 1870 and 1910, the number of public high schools grew from 500 to more than 10,000, and a high school education began to be the normal expectation of great numbers of young Americans, especially white youths in towns and cities. In this forty-year period, the number of pupils attending public elementary and high schools each year rose from 6,871,000 to 17,813,000. The average number of days in the school year rose from 132 to 157, and the money spent per pupil more than doubled.

But statistics do not tell the full story. With responsibility for schooling still in the hands of local communities, the amount of support varied considerably. In the South, the level of support for black schools was considerably lower than the level for white schools, and the white schools themselves were inadequate.

Contrasting classroom scenes at the turn of the century: (top) immigrant children in the condemned Essex Market School in New York City; (bottom) Milton Academy, a private boys' school in New England. *(Top photograph by Jacob A. Riis, the Jacob A. Riis Collection, Museum of the City of New York; bottom photograph by Charles Currier, Library of Congress)*

Educating Blacks

Before the Civil War, a small minority of blacks (mostly house servants and slaves of urban residents) had learned to read and write. A much larger number had acquired mechanical skills. The vast majority were field hands to whom schooling was unknown. After the Emancipation Proclamation, education acquired almost a religious meaning for the former slave. Not only did northern missionary societies and the Freedmen's Bureau assist blacks in their quest for knowledge, but blacks themselves organized educational associations, built schools, and hired teachers.

White southerners welcomed neither Yankee nor black schoolteachers, and many whites resented paying taxes to support black and white schools. After the overthrow of the Radical governments, white leaders kept the educational provisions in the new state constitutions. But the schools themselves were early casualties of budget-cutting governors and legislators. Statistics of black education in the late nineteenth century confirm W. E. B. Du Bois's charge of "enforced ignorance." By 1910, despite the legal mandate for separate but equal schools, in most of the South twice as much was spent on each white student as on each black student, and the minimum salary for white teachers was nearly twice the maximum salary for black teachers. Poor facilities, a shorter

---

THE EDUCATION OF BLACKS: SEPARATE AND UNEQUAL

When Pauli Murray entered the public schools in Durham, North Carolina, in the 1920s, she inherited nearly half a century of separate and unequal education in the South—what W. E. B. Du Bois called "enforced ignorance."

West End looked more like a warehouse than a school. It was a dilapidated, rickety, two-story wooden building which creaked and swayed in the wind as if it might collapse. Outside it was scarred with peeling paint from many winters of rain and snow. Inside the floors were bare and splintery, the plumbing was leaky, the drinking fountains broken and the toilets in the basement smelly and constantly out of order. . . .

It was never the hardship which hurt so much as the contrast between what we had and what the white children had. We got the greasy, torn, dog-eared books; they got the new ones. They had field day in the city park; we had it on a furrowed stubby hillside. They got wide mention in the newspaper; we got a paragraph at the bottom. The entire city officialdom from the mayor down turned out to review their pageantry; we got a solitary official.

Our seedy run-down school told us that if we had any place at all in the scheme of things it was a separate place, marked off, proscribed and unwanted by the white people. We were bottled up and labeled and set aside—sent to the Jim Crow car, the back of the bus, the side door of the theater, the side window of a restaurant. We came to know that whatever we had was always inferior. We came to understand that no matter how neat and clean, how law abiding, submissive and polite, how studious in school, how churchgoing and moral, how scrupulous in paying our bills and taxes we were, it made no essential difference in our place.

Source: Pauli Murray, *Proud Shoes* (New York: Harper, 1956), pp. 269–70. Photograph courtesy of the Cook Collection, Valentine Museum, Richmond.

school term (often geared to the crops), a higher student–teacher ratio, and a restricted curriculum also set off black schools from white.

Where schools continued to be provided for blacks, vocational training suitable to their low economic position dominated the curriculum. Northern philanthropists, many of whom shared prevailing racist attitudes, funneled their contributions to vocationally oriented black colleges. Among the leaders in the campaign for industrial-vocational education for blacks was Samuel C. Armstrong, founder (1868) and headmaster of the Hampton Normal and Agricultural Institute in Virginia. The son of New England missionaries in Hawaii, Armstrong had come to believe that black people, like other "backward" and "dependent" races, required special training before they could reach the level of white civilization.

If the "Hampton idea" struck Henry M. Turner, a radical black clergyman, as an education in "Negro inferiority," it had no such effect on the young and impressionable Booker T. Washington, who attended the school from 1872 to 1875:

At Hampton, I found the opportunities to learn thrift, economy, and push. I was surrounded by an atmosphere of business, Christian influences, and the spirit of self-help, that seemed to have awakened every faculty in me.

When Washington opened his own normal school in 1881 at Tuskegee, Alabama, with funds supplied by an Alabama banker, he built on Armstrong's theories. Washington could see that for an indeterminate future the southern black majority would be confined to agricultural, domestic, or menial work. The best way to ensure their welfare and the tolerance of the master caste, he reasoned, was to train them in useful pursuits. When Washington made his famous speech at the Atlanta Exposition of 1895—the speech that would bring him national attention—he said little

that he had not already taught at Tuskegee (see Chapter 25).

By 1900 most northern cities, finding a dual educational system too expensive, had abolished segregated schools. But the educational philosophy that had initially supported segregation remained essentially unaltered—the notion that black children had retentive memories and great quickness up to a certain point, beyond which they could not easily advance. Such ideas deflated black aspirations. As a result, few blacks reached high school, and still fewer got to college. (No more than 160 blacks attended white colleges in 1890.)

What black children were taught in the schools, moreover, did little to enhance their self-confidence. "I am ashamed," a twelve-year-old black girl wrote in 1903, "of the names that we are called in the standard history, 'slaves and niggers,' and when we read that part of it the white children look at us real funny." Even such an exceptionally educated black man as W. E. B. Du Bois found his days at Harvard a mixed experience: "I was a crude brown youth, deeply opinionated, painfully aware of my color and race. I not only fiercely held to no desire to cross the color line but rather gloried in my isolation."

Higher Education

Since 1860, American colleges and universities had increased in numbers and enrollments and had grown larger and more bureaucratized in administration. At the same time, they had improved steadily in quality. Public and private donations helped finance the expansion. Within a decade of the Morrill Act of 1862, which had provided for grants of federal land for educational purposes, Wisconsin, Minnesota, California, Texas, Massachusetts, and New York had estab-

---

WORDS AND NAMES IN AMERICAN HISTORY

In educational circles today, the word *deadline* normally refers to the date or even the time of day a student is to hand in an essay, report, or other assignment. The word is also commonly used in business, in government, and even in international relations. The term conveys a certain tension, even though it is quite rare for professors to gun down students who get their papers in late. Originally the word carried much greater tension, but it concerned space rather than time. The term *deadline*, which

came into our language only about a hundred years ago, originally meant something very literal: Cross this line and you're dead. This meaning seems to have come into use in military prisons in the American Civil War. Prison camps were hastily built, often without effective walls. Most had lines surrounding the entire camp that were "drawn" by paint, by a rope, or by shovel, and the guards in the towers had orders to shoot to kill any prisoner who crossed.

530

lished colleges, many of them coeducational. Private money was responsible for other colleges and universities.

Ezra Cornell, who made a fortune from the electric telegraph, founded Cornell, which opened in 1868. Vanderbilt University (1873) and Stanford (1891) were the beneficiaries of two railroad millionaires, and the University of Chicago (1891) received $34 million from the oil magnate John D. Rockefeller. The Johns Hopkins University (1876) bore the name of a wealthy Baltimore banker and railroad executive; Carnegie Institute (1900) in Pittsburgh was named after the multimillionaire steel magnate.

Most of the newly endowed colleges managed to overcome or outlast any interference from their benefactors. But college boards of trustees tended to be dominated by businessmen, some of whom demanded social and economic orthodoxy from faculty members. The same kinds of pressures were often exerted on public universities by legislators and boards of regents. Some faculty members were dismissed for teaching heretical ideas, and others were frightened into silence. Frederick Jackson Turner recalled that the members of the Board of Regents of the University of Wisconsin "used to sit with a red lead pencil in consultation over the lists of books submitted by the professors, and strike out those that failed to please their fancy, with irreverent comments on 'fool professors.'"

Prewar colleges had confined themselves largely to traditional subjects—the classics, mathematics, and theology. The postwar institutions responded to the demand for professional, business, and technical education. The prestige of science had risen so high that such practical additions to the curriculum had to be accepted. By the end of the century, a number of American university scientists had won international reputations, and the number of professional schools in fields such as medicine, law, and business had increased substantially.

Under the direction of Charles W. Eliot, president of Harvard, a new kind of university emerged. Undergraduates elected courses from an expanded curriculum, instead of being limited to required courses. Graduate schools grew, and faculties were assembled. Between 1869 and 1900, Eliot also reformed Harvard's medical and law schools, which then became models for others. Premedical students, who had formerly obtained degrees with a minimum of course and clinical work, were now required to study three full years in medical school, to work in laborato-

ries, and to take examinations. The dean of the Harvard Law School abolished the textbook and introduced a system whereby the law student gained knowledge by examining specific cases.

Not all the changes in university and college life were intellectual or administrative. The introduction of baseball, football, and other organized sports aroused an almost fanatical concern with school rivalries. By the 1890s intercollegiate football had become a mass spectacle attended by crowds of 30,000 or 40,000, and critics were protesting its professional emphasis.

Not all the critics, however, confined themselves to alarm over athletic programs. American universities, said Brooks Adams, graduated narrow, half-educated specialists lacking the breadth of mind needed to administer a complex, centralized economy; Thorstein Veblen, in *The Higher Learning in America* (1918), accused the universities of producing little more than salesmen.

Educating Women

Although much evidence to the contrary existed, many people continued to doubt the intellectual or physical capacity of women to profit from college education. The idea of advanced education for women also had to be reconciled with the prevailing assumption in the nineteenth century that women properly belonged in the home. The experience of higher learning, some feared, would destroy "the loveliness and grace and essential charm of womanhood." The establishment of separate educational institutions for women raised still other concerns, including the danger of unconventional relationships among women and the enhancement of their independence. The idea that women might actually learn, grow, and thrive in the absence of males implied an autonomy and a capacity that the larger society was reluctant to concede. When Smith College opened in 1875, its first president, Clark Seelye, sought to allay such fears and reassure the public: "It is to preserve . . . womanliness that this College has been founded."

Oberlin College in 1837 had been the first American college to admit women, and a number of public and private colleges in the Midwest and West followed its example. But the stubborn refusal of eastern colleges such as Harvard and Yale to admit women led to the establishment of a number of prestigious women's colleges, beginning with Vassar in 1861 at Poughkeepsie, New York. Matthew Vassar, an English-born brewer,

THE EDUCATION OF WOMEN

Two views of the benefits of colleges for women, the first from *Godey's Lady's Book*, a highly popular magazine that celebrated sophistication and refinement in women, and the second from Martha Carey Thomas, a leading educator at the turn of the century and president of Bryn Mawr College:

To that half *education which our countrywomen now receive—the education in science and ornamental arts—add the education in useful arts and domestic knowledge necessary to fit them for the duties of their proper sphere, and they will not merely be, as at present, the "queens of society," but will be far better, the adored rulers of well-ordered and happy households.*

How vast the difference between then [1874] and now [1904] in my feelings, and in the feelings of every woman who has had to do with the education of girls! Then I was terror-struck lest I, and every other woman with me, were doomed to live as

pathological invalids in a universe merciless to woman as a sex. Now we know that it is not we, but the man who believes such things about us, who is himself pathological, blinded by neurotic mists of sex, unable to see that women form one-half of the kindly race of normal, healthy, human creatures in the world; that women, like men, are quickened and inspired by the same great traditions of their race, by the same love of learning, the same love of science, the same love of abstract truth; that women, like men, are immeasurably benefited, physically, mentally, and morally, and are made vastly better mothers, as men are made vastly better fathers, by subordinating the distracting instincts of sex to the simple human fellowship of similar education, and similar intellectual and social ideals.

Sources: *Godey's Lady's Book*, March 1866; Martha Carey Thomas, *Publications of the Association of Collegiate Alumnae* [Bryn Mawr College], 3 (February 1908).

Students at Bacone College in Oklahoma marching from their dormitory. *(Culver Pictures, Inc.)*

believed that women had the same right as men to intellectual development. Completing a course of study as demanding as that of any men's college, Vassar students demonstrated convincingly that women were as intellectually capable as men. Some educators persisted in viewing women's colleges as places to nurture femininity and domesticity, but many of these colleges became instead havens for feminists and independent-minded, career women.

By 1880, most of the important midwestern universities were admitting women. Smith, Bryn Mawr, and Wellesley—founded shortly after Vassar—and other women's colleges offered professional training. The number of women enrolled as undergraduates rose from about 8000 in 1869 to more than 20,000 in 1894, and soared in the twentieth century. But for the graduates of the women's colleges, improvements in educational opportunities were not translated into improvements in economic opportunities. Some women managed to enter status professions, such as medicine and law, from which they had been almost totally barred before the 1860s, but the number of women within these professions remained small. The 21 percent of the nation's women who were at work in 1900 occupied the lowest-paying, least prestigious positions in the work force; college graduates were seldom able to find professional employment outside of elementary-school teaching. Rather than aspire to careers, educated women were still expected to find economic salvation in a well-chosen husband and cultural satisfaction in women's clubs and in the romantic novels that dominated the best-seller lists.

LITERATURE IN THE GILDED AGE

Informed critics after Appomattox often remarked on the poor quality of American literature. Romances, sentimental novels, and tales of success reflected the values, tastes, and stereotypes of middle-class readers. Neither the world depicted in such literature nor the characters themselves suggested that American society was being transformed.

The dividing line of the Civil War was sharpened by the death or withdrawal of the major writers of the past. By 1865 Hawthorne and Thoreau were dead. Emerson retired more and more into himself, while Melville lived virtually forgotten. Emily Dickinson, the one poetic genius of the early postwar years, wrote for herself and a few friends; she was almost unknown to her contemporaries.

If Emerson, Melville, and Dickinson retreated into themselves for private reasons, other postwar writers, reflecting their rural origins and repelled by an industrializing and urbanizing America, retreated to the past. Just when country people were heading for the cities, some writers of the "local color" school, such as Harriet Beecher Stowe and Edward Eggleston, retrieved the scenes and spiritual values of a pastoral America.

Other local colonists, such as Bret Harte, Joel Chandler Harris, Sarah Orne Jewett, and Mary N. Murfree, sought out the "native element" of their distinctive sections—the California mining country, the southern plantation, the New England village, the Kentucky and Tennessee mountains. They did not rule out the city, as George Washington Cable's stories of New Orleans Creoles attested, but in general they stuck to what they considered to be the authentic part of America—the village, the small town, the farm—and lovingly and honestly recorded differences in dialect, manners, and customs.

Already partly visible by the 1870s was a surge of fresh talent, soon to be followed by a new generation. The new writers, many of them influenced by industrialism, Darwinian ideas, and pragmatism, explored subjects largely excluded from "genteel" literature: slums, crime, class conflict, violence, divorce, racism, political corruption, drunkenness, adultery. To be sure, the dominant romantic mood had not disappeared even by the end of the century. But a new realism had given fresh life to literature, making the eventual break with the genteel tradition easier.

Mark Twain

Mark Twain—the pen name of Samuel L. Clemens—belonged by temperament to the local color tradition and was regarded in his own day as a regional author. But he was a writer of far greater dimension than the others. In many respects, Mark Twain was the most revealing figure in postwar American literature, the one who best combined the virtues and defects of the society he analyzed. Born in Hannibal, Missouri, he had been a reporter, river pilot, and popular lecturer before his first literary success with *The Innocents Abroad* (1869), an uproariously funny account of a junket of his countrymen through Europe and the Near East.

Mark Twain. (UPI/Bettman Newsphotos)

Twain wrote about everything from jumping frogs to Andrew Carnegie. But his best works, *The Adventures of Tom Sawyer* (1876), *Life on the Mississippi* (1883), and *The Adventures of Huckleberry Finn* (1884), all derive from his riverboat days. It was his loyalty to the simple America of his boyhood that partly accounts for his rage over the betrayal of democratic ideals in the Gilded Age. "In my youth," wrote Twain, "there was nothing resembling a worship of money or of its possessor, in our region." It took people of the Jay Gould variety, he said, "to make a God of money and the man":

The gospel left behind by Jay Gould is doing giant work in our days. Its message is "Get money. Get it quickly. Get it in abundance. Get it dishonestly, if you can, honestly if you must."

And yet Twain enjoyed "striking it rich" as much as anyone, speculated recklessly, and wrote always with an eye on his large audience. As he put it:

I have never tried in even one single instance to help cultivate the cultivated classes. I was not equipped for it by native gifts or training. And I never had any ambition in that direction, but always hunted for bigger game — the masses.

In his own way, however, Twain was a moralist who looked upon humanity with exasperation because of its cruelty, credulity, and pigheadedness, and with compassion because it was not to blame. *Huckleberry Finn* remains an assault on social hypocrisy, false respectability, and the gospel of success. In renouncing civilization, Huck remains true to his natural goodness, yet without denying human depravity or his kinship with the wicked: "I am the whole human race without a detail lacking . . . .The human race is a race of cowards; and I am not only marching in that procession but carrying a banner."

Realists and Naturalists

William Dean Howells, a friend of Twain, became the leader of the postwar school of realists. Born and reared in Ohio, Howells had come to literature, like many of his contemporaries, through the printer's office and the newspaper. From 1886 to 1891 he wrote his most influential criticism in *Harper's Monthly.* By 1900, many of the younger writers considered him the dean of American letters.

Realism, as Howells used the term, simply meant "the truthful treatment of commonplace material." The romanticism of the popular literature of his day was immoral, in Howells's opinion, because it corrupted American taste and falsified life. He wanted fiction of "fidelity, not merely to the possible, but to the probable and ordinary course of man's experience." Let the novelist, he said through one of his fictional characters, paint "life as it is, and human feelings in their true proportion and relation."

His best-known and probably best-written novels are *The Rise of Silas Lapham* (1885), the story of a self-made businessman, and *A Hazard of New Fortunes* (1890), which reflected his New York experience—the mindless struggle for wealth, the paradox of Fifth Avenue luxury and East Side squalor, the degradation of the republican dream.

Although Howells's friend Henry James could not find enough material for fiction in what he saw as the bleak American scene, he allied himself with the Howells camp. James was born in New York, but he spent a good part of his youth in Europe. After a halfhearted attempt to study law at Harvard, he gave himself entirely to literature, and from 1875 until his death did most of his writing abroad. Because he visited his native land so seldom, and because so many of his novels and short stories have a European setting, many critics put James outside the main current of American literature. Actually, his international plots deal almost exclusively with Americans, and from his vantage point he saw much about the American character that escaped writers who remained too close to home.

Like Hawthorne, by whom he was profoundly

influenced, James liked to place his Americans in what he called "morally interesting situations." He subjected his traveling businessmen (*The American*, 1877), his sensitive and intellectually curious heiresses (*The Portrait of a Lady*, 1881), his artist heroes hungry for culture (*Roderick Hudson*, 1876), to moral tests. Sometimes they passed, sometimes they failed. America remained for him a land of innocence and promise; Europe was beautiful but decadent. A superb technician and psychologist, James was also a social historian who faithfully recorded the moral gaps and strains he detected in upper-class society.

As a result of the realists' efforts, the young writers who came of age in the last two decades of the century could experiment even more boldly with unvarnished truth. Although it no longer took courage to expose a society committed to railroads, stockyards, real estate, and Wall Street, the new literary school went much further than the realists in uncovering the seamy and brutal aspects of American life. Naturalism, as the new movement was called, derived its inspiration from French novelists such as Émile Zola, who believed that literature should be governed by the same scientific laws that guided the physiologist. Human fate was determined by heredity and environment, by inner drives and external circumstances over which people had no control. Theoretically, the naturalist writer put down what he or she saw, no matter how disgusting or shocking it might be.

In America, naturalists such as Stephen Crane and Frank Norris never matched the frankness of the French school. But they dealt with themes from which even Howells flinched. In *Maggie: A Girl of the Streets* (1893), Crane wrote of the seduction and suicide of a New York slum girl; in *The Red Badge of Courage* (1895), he reproduced the animal fear of a young Civil War recruit under fire and his psychological recovery. In all his tales and sketches of derelicts and soldiers, of frightened, abandoned people, Crane suggests that human beings must confront nature without help from the supernatural.

Norris, a less able writer than Crane and more given to melodrama, disliked Howells's realism because it smelled so much of the ordinary, "the tragedy of the broken tea cup." Norris liked huge supermen clashing with titanic natural forces. In *McTeague* (1899), the story of a man's reversion to brutishness, he displayed a power new in American fiction. In his best-known novel, *The Octopus* (1901), Norris depicted an epic struggle between California wheat growers and the railroad. The apparent radicalism of this book was considerably diluted by Norris's message that wheat and the railroad represented natural forces, each governed by the law of supply and demand.

Jack London repeated many of Norris's themes, especially his tendency to exalt the brutal while condemning the brutality of the social order. Born in 1876 and thrown on his own resources at an early age into the waterfront environment of Oakland, California, London became a hobo and a seaman, among other things, before settling down to write. His literary career lasted only eighteen years, but he published over fifty books.

London preached the awful power of the forces of nature as well as the hopeful teachings of socialism. He never reconciled these ideas, but his work expressed one or the other well enough to make him one of the most widely read writers of his time and one of the few American authors to gain recognition in Europe.

London's most interesting books are his autobiographical novel *Martin Eden* (1909) and *The Iron Heel* (1907), concerned with a fight to the death between the exploited classes and an oligarchy. His greatest success was *The Call of the Wild* (1903), a book about the Yukon.

The writings of Theodore Dreiser reflected a naturalism even more uncompromising than that of Crane, Norris, or London. But in Dreiser, the replacement of the good and the bad by the strong and the weak was accompanied by a deeper feeling for character and a profound, almost maternal tenderness. After drifting from job to job, Dreiser spent several years as a newspaper-

Jack London. *(Culver Pictures, Inc.)*

man in Chicago, St. Louis, Cleveland, and Pittsburgh, observing at first hand the hard side of big-city life. His experiences inspired him with the idea of treating a great American city as realistically as Balzac had written of Paris.

Dreiser's first novel and one of his best, *Sister Carrie*, was published in 1900 and then quickly withdrawn after the publisher's wife objected to its "indecency." *Sister Carrie* tells the story of a young girl who comes to Chicago from a small western town and succumbs to a vulgar but generous salesman and then to a restaurant manager. The best chapters of the book trace the gradual downward drift of her second seducer, Hurstwood, who moves toward ruin while Carrie becomes a successful actress.

POPULAR CULTURE

The rapid growth of the cities, an expanding middle class, and changes in patterns of work and leisure produced larger numbers of Americans with the income and the time to seek cultural and recreational diversions. By the late nineteenth century there had emerged a new industry—mass entertainment, ranging from dime novels, pulp fiction, and popular romances to circuses and traveling shows, from vaudeville and opera to baseball, football, and boxing. Although in many ways an urban phenomenon, adding to the allure of the city, the influence of these various forms of leisure extended into rural America.

Like most American industries, popular entertainment underwent consolidation and fell into the hands of a small number of entrepreneurs. By 1900, for example, as vaudeville reached new heights of popularity and respectability, theaters were converted into lavish entertainment palaces, individual theaters gave way to highly organized show-business chains, and the performers themselves came under the control of a few powerful booking agencies. But there was no mistaking the ways in which popular entertainment influenced public attitudes and tastes; many of the performers would reach into the American consciousness in ways that few presidents could match.

Popular Literature: The Romantics

Although realists and naturalists tried to deal honestly with life and gained a following among liberals who wanted to improve conditions, they failed to outsell the sentimental school among the reading public. With love stories, cloak-and-dagger romances, and tales of exotic lands, the sentimentalists helped their middle-class audience, the largest in the world, avoid the raw society around them. A love story, thought the novelist Francis Marion Crawford, should "foster agreeable allusions."

During the last three decades of the nineteenth century, the romanticists and the realists engaged in a kind of journalistic warfare. The realists, said their critics, "taught pessimism in every line of their work. They taught that marriage is a failure, that home is a brothel, that courtship is lewd, that society is an aggregation of animals." The romanticists, replied the realists, supplied flimsy illusions to adults who avoided the issues of the day. In practice, however, both schools made concessions to popular taste and interests.

Since romantic fiction outsold realistic novels four to one, it is hardly surprising that both realists and naturalists injected a little exotic color, mysticism, and pseudoscientific information into their work. They also used flamboyant success stories and sensational romances in which supermen heroes triumphed over the "mongrel" races of the world. "There was a bit of lie in this attitude of mine, a bit of hypocrisy," Jack London confessed of some of his popular works, "but the lie and the hypocrisy were those of a man desiring to live." At the same time, the romantics could not ignore the social turmoil that soon involved so many of their women readers in reform movements. By 1900 the romantic writer and the realist were appearing together in the pages of the *Saturday Evening Post* and the *Ladies' Home Journal*—and it was not always easy to distinguish the one from the other.

Whatever the inroads of the naturalists and realists, the romantics continued to dominate the best-seller lists. Perhaps the major literary craze of the 1890s, however, revolved around the works of an English writer, Rudyard Kipling. Not only were his novels immensely popular, but his poetry was among the most frequently recited by Americans, finding its way even into the halls of Congress.

> *Take up the White Man's burden—*
> *Send forth the best ye breed—*
> *Go, bind your sons to exile*
> *To serve your captives' need;*
>
> *To wait in heavy harness*
> *On fluttered folk and wild—*
> *Your new-caught, sullen peoples,*
> *Half-devil and half-child.*

Published in 1899 in *McClure's Magazine* and reprinted on the front pages of major newspapers, Kipling's "The White Man's Burden" expressed the feelings of a confident and self-satisfied nation in the process of becoming a world power—the America that novelist Herman Melville had once glimpsed with "law on her brow and empire in her eyes."

Popular Literature: The Dime Novels

In a spirit of self-congratulation, Cornelius Vanderbilt once claimed to have read only one book in his life—John Bunyan's *Pilgrim's Progress*, the classic moral allegory published in the seventeenth century but still a best seller in the nineteenth century. He read the book, Vanderbilt added, only after he had turned seventy years of age. Taking the time to acquire a genuine education, he recalled, would have left him precious little time to build his industrial empire. If Vanderbilt was correct, the thousands of workers he commanded were probably better read. The literature they devoured, however, occasioned considerable concern over the decline of both literary and moral standards.

The popularity of the penny newspapers and the cheap editions of pirated English books in the first third of the nineteenth century had already alerted publishers to an expanding American market, especially among leisured middle-class women. After the Civil War, the reading public continued to grow, along with the facilities that enabled more working-class Americans to acquire rudimentary literary skills. The appearance of the public library was in part an effort by reformers to direct this reading public toward books that would be morally uplifting and inspirational. But working-class readers, among others, found themselves drawn instead to books rarely available in the public libraries—the dime novels, the pulp magazines, and romance fiction, usually priced within easy reach of even poorly paid workers.

Denounced by critics as trash, the novels and magazines placed a premium on adventure and romance. For male readers, there were the Beadle dime novels, often set on the frontier, where the heroes displayed remarkable courage and daring. For the women, love stories dominated the literature, providing them entry into worlds scarcely imagined. By the end of the story, more often than not, penniless orphans had become heirs, heroes had triumphed over every adversity, and working-class heroines had found fortune and love simul-

taneously. Few of the novels troubled the reader with the kinds of problems he or she faced on a day-to-day basis. The function they served was largely escapist: they provided working-class readers the rare opportunity to live out their fantasies through the printed page, to glimpse other possibilities in their otherwise tedious working lives. Whether brought surreptitiously into the workplace or read at home or on the long streetcar ride to and from work, the novels helped ordinary working Americans to surmount—if only briefly—the fatigue and discomfort of the real world. The expectations they might raise were no more unrealistic than those purveyed in the inspirational literature on how to achieve success in the new industrial society.

Popular Theater

The theater remained a popular place of entertainment in the nineteenth century, appealing to all classes and literary tastes. Some American playwrights emerged, but the theater still depended heavily on European imports. William Shakespeare's plays were widely performed, and the plots and characters were sufficiently familiar to American audiences to be parodied. The greatest American and British actors performed Shakespeare's plays in elegant eastern theaters and on makeshift stages in the western mining territories; a German traveler in 1882 observed that every log cabin in the Far West contained a bible, and in most of them one could also find a cheap and well-worn edition of Shakespeare's works.

No matter which playwright was being performed, the interplay between spectators and actors made these nineteenth-century performances unique. The audiences intruded on productions in ways that would become unacceptable in the twentieth century: they were often raucous, they interrupted performances, they demanded encores on the spot, and they reviewed the plays with their jeers and cheers rather than await the critic's appraisal.

For much of the nineteenth century, melodrama dominated popular theater. It offered audiences simple moral messages in a language so simple that even the most immature mind could not fail to grasp them. At the same time, the plays gripped the audience emotionally and reflected prevailing American attitudes toward morality, sin, and domestic life. The typical melodrama featured a cast of easily recognizable characters, all of them engaged in some way in the eternal struggle between light and darkness. The vulnerable heroine and the gallant hero pitted their moral strength against the sinister villain. Like the McGuffey readers and the Horatio Alger stories, melodrama taught a simple system of rewards and punishments: good conduct is rewarded, vice and evil are vanquished. The productions offered an abundance of sentimentality, the opportunity to identify vocally with the characters (cheering the heroine and hissing the villain), and staging innovations calculated to dramatize in the most compelling fashion the ultimate triumph of Christian faith, personal integrity, honesty, chastity, and love over sin and evil. The plays also alerted Americans to the family tragedies resulting from the consumption of alcoholic beverages and warned newcomers of the traps and temptations that awaited them in the cities. In this respect, melodrama, in addition to providing diversion, afforded its audiences practical guidance and reinforced moral imperatives.

In the 1870s and 1880s, the minstrel show was still capitalizing on the popularity it had achieved earlier in the century. On the plantations in the antebellum South, slave owners had frequently entertained themselves and their guests by calling out some of their blacks to tell stories and to sing and dance to the accompaniment of the banjo and the bones. Slaves survived by knowing what the master expected of them on occasions such as these, and they performed accordingly, leaving the master and his guests with their racial images confirmed. The origins of minstrelsy may be found in the imitations of these plantation actors and their performances by professional white entertainers who blacked their faces with burnt cork. Many stage careers were based on imitations of the dancing, singing, and humor of black slaves, at least as these were perceived and interpreted by blackface whites. White audiences loved the interpretations and the interpreters, and by the 1870s and 1880s practically every city and town had an amateur minstrel group. If the players had never seen or heard a black, they needed only to purchase any one of the hundreds of low-cost minstrel books containing dialect jokes and songs, hints on makeup and pronunciation, and routines for all occasions and social levels. The total effect of minstrelsy, like so much of popular culture, was to reinforce prevailing caricatures of blacks as simpleminded buffoons, hysterically outlandish in their misuses of white culture, who were addicted to big words they could not pronounce, gaudy apparel, and chicken stealing.

Until the Civil War most of the professional minstrels were white men, like the popular group Christy's Minstrels, for whom Stephen Foster wrote some of his best songs. But in the postwar years, several black minstrel groups toured the country, conforming for the most part to the staging and routines that had been worked out by the white minstrels. The black minstrel, too, blackened his face, thickened his lips, and painted on the grin. These were blacks playing whites playing blacks, and the critics lavished their praise on the performances, one of them observing that "the common every-day Nigger has only to open his mouth to bring laughs."

The use of the term *coon* to describe a black American derived much of its popularity from what came to be called "coon songs." Between 1890 and 1910, as race relations steadily deteriorated, a coon song craze swept the nation. The songs were about and sometimes written by blacks; they were popular in minstrel shows, and in most music halls, vaudeville shows, and sheet music. In their lyrics (and in the visual images that graced the covers of the sheet music), the songs played on those qualities whites associated with black life and character. Over six hundred songs were published during the 1890s, and the more successful songs sold millions of copies. The coon songs, like minstrelsy itself, exerted a profound influence on the black image in the white mind. Long after the songs and the minstrel acts had disappeared from the popular stage, the image persisted.

The minstrel show, while retaining its popularity among amateur groups well into the twentieth century, proved less successful after the Civil War in adapting itself commercially to changing public tastes. By the 1890s, it had been replaced by vaudeville as the most popular form of theatrical entertainment. Vaudeville was essentially a variety show, emphasizing diversity, flexibility, and lavish, carefully crafted productions, always with an eye and an ear to what the public wanted; there was something for everyone. Vaudeville was family entertainment at its best, drawing both material and performers from other highly popular show business forms—minstrelsy, burlesque, the circus, and the musical comedy.

The typical show might have as many as thirty acts—among them songs and dances, dialect and ethnic humor, and dramatic readings—featuring comedians, female impersonators, magicians, jugglers, acrobats, animals, and singers (operatic and comic). By the late nineteenth century, the promoters of vaudeville were merchandizing their shows as respectable, middle-class entertainment suitable for families. Vaudeville produced some of America's most popular entertainers, ranging from magician Harry Houdini and Scotch monologist Harry Lauder to comedians Ed Wynn, Bert Lahr, and Fannie Brice and to legendary women performers such as Eva Tanguay and Lillian Russell. More than minstrelsy and melodrama, vaudeville seemed geared to urban audiences, and many of its stars were themselves city-born, of immigrant origins, and drawn from the working and lower middle classes. Between 1890 and 1920, vaudeville peaked in popularity, but it ultimately declined before the overwhelming competition mounted by the motion picture industry.

Sports

The enthusiasm in the late nineteenth century for competitive athletics and physical culture proved

to be highly contagious. The sports page made its debut in the newspaper, along with the comic page. Once exclusively an amateur undertaking, competitive sports underwent significant changes in an age of rapid urbanization. With an eye on a growing market for their products, entrepreneurs went about the task of professionalizing and commercializing athletics. Before the Civil War, for example, baseball had yielded a number of amateur clubs; the growing popularity of the sport made it an almost obligatory feature at county fairs, and people could see it played on sandlots in small and large cities alike. The National League of Professional Baseball Clubs, formed in 1876, tried to organize a league of rival teams from the large cities. After a period of initial turmoil and controversy over gambling, contracts, and rules, two rival leagues—the American and the National—emerged by 1903, along with a "world series" between the league champions.

Although rivals, both leagues agreed on the rules governing how the game would be played—and on the exclusion of blacks as players. In response, as early as 1887, some seven exclusively black baseball clubs were playing professionally in

A.B. Frost's drawing of the Yale-Princeton football game, November 1879. *(Library of Congress)*

their own league. Occasionally, as in 1907, speculation as to how the black and white teams would fare against each other led the black champions to challenge the champions of the white leagues. But the white leagues declined, fearing the black team might win, alienate white spectators, and thereby undermine popular enthusiasm for the sport.

Prize fighting became so popular that President Theodore Roosevelt, an ardent enthusiast, welcomed matches in the White House. The introduction of the Marquis of Queensberry rules lent the sport greater respectability: five-ounce padded gloves replaced bare knuckles, certain blows were outlawed, a round was limited to three minutes, and a boxer knocked to the canvas who failed to rise by a count of ten lost the match (previously, a knockdown merely ended a round, thereby prolonging the damage). The sport took on growing importance, mostly among men, but in 1908 it faced a crisis of public confidence. Jack Johnson defeated Tommy Burns to become the first black heavyweight boxing champion, and he did so in a fight in which he humiliated his opponent. After he successfully defended his crown against Jim Jeffries, a previously unbeaten champion who had retired, Johnson indisputably was the finest boxer of his generation—and perhaps the greatest heavyweight of all time.

No matter what Jack Johnson did, controversy pursued him. It was not simply his boxing prowess that created all the notoriety, but the way this black champion flouted the prevailing racial code: he lacked humility, he boasted of the ways in which he outboxed his opponents, and he cultivated a lifestyle that shocked whites, dressing ostentatiously and fraternizing with white women, several of whom he eventually married. From 1908 to 1915, he attracted more national attention than any black man of his time, including Booker T. Washington. Many educated, middle-class blacks found him an embarrassment to the race. But for the vast majority of black Americans, he remained a folk hero and legend, celebrated in story and song as a black man who was able not only to outbox and outwit whites but to humiliate them, too. That was a rare triumph in an era of unrelieved racial repression and unchallenged white supremacy.

Football became controversial for a different reason. Introduced into colonial America by English immigrants, football in the nineteenth century became an increasingly aggressive sport, and the number of casualties steadily mounted. President Roosevelt intervened to rescue the sport when it seemed on the verge of being abolished at the major colleges. With the leadership of some brilliant coaches and the introduction of the forward pass, football became both more scientific and more respectable. It was on its way to becoming the outstanding spectator sport in the United States. As early as 1889, the national character of football was underscored by the new custom of selecting an "all-American" team.

On campuses across the country, intercollegiate athletics took on new dimensions, with football exerting a special appeal among the various college sports. Football demanded not only agility, like baseball and basketball (invented in 1891 as an indoor game to keep athletes in good physical condition between the football and baseball seasons), but physical force. Perhaps in saving the sport, Theodore Roosevelt found it particularly conducive in the early twentieth century to his vision of a world of competing nations. Success, Roosevelt once said, came only to players who "hit the line" hard. The same could be said of nations and races, and for Theodore Roosevelt, as for many American presidents in the twentieth century, that was not only an article of faith but the basis for a foreign policy.

SUMMARY

If economic life during the Gilded Age was dominated by laissez faire and the gospel of success, cultural life was dominated by social Darwinism and the gospel of progress.

Darwin's *Origin of Species,* published in 1859, introduced the ideas of evolution and the "survival of the fittest" in biology. These ideas were soon popularized and translated into social terms. The social Darwinism proposed by the English philosopher Herbert Spencer became another support for the gospel of success and brought a new creed—the gospel of progress. All the changes of industrialization and urbanization were not only good, they were all for the better.

Some thinkers—Lester Ward, Henry George, and Edward Bellamy—challenged these ideas and rejected the fatalism of the social Darwinists. In the universities, younger social scientists began to break out of the conservative straitjacket and to question systems such as laissez faire. Among these academic rebels was Thorstein Veblen, whose *Theory of the Leisure Class* (1899) became one of the most influential works of social criticism.

Darwinism also opened up new ways of thinking in philosophy, law, education, and history. Pragmatists aimed to make philosophy useful by looking at ideas as tools for solving practical problems. Pragmatists such as William James and John Dewey had great influence on the new discipline of psychology and the older one of education. The notion that the law too should be responsive to changing needs was practiced by such jurists as Oliver Wendell Holmes, Jr., and Louis D. Brandeis. In the field of history, Frederick Jackson Turner presented new ideas that would influence generations of American historians and students, although they were not generally accepted until the twentieth century.

All these changing ideas found wider and wider audiences as the American people became more educated and more literate. Public schools, colleges, and universities grew rapidly in number and size after the Civil War as government made a genuine commitment to education for all. Public elementary and secondary education, though always remaining under local control, became nationwide, especially in the cities. Compulsory school attendance laws were passed, and illiteracy declined rapidly. A separate system of black education began to develop in the South, but with an emphasis on technical-vocational training. It was set up by blacks themselves and financed largely by northern philanthropists.

Higher education also expanded and changed. Many new colleges were established, and under Charles W. Eliot, Harvard pioneered a new kind of university. Students chose courses from an expanded curriculum, major scholars were recruited for graduate schools, and practical training was required for certification in the professions.

Women also gained access to higher education and to professional training. By 1880, most major midwestern state universities admitted women. Vassar College for women had been founded in 1861; Smith, Bryn Mawr, and Wellesley were established soon afterward. The number of women enrolled as undergraduates rose from 8000 in 1869 to 20,000 by 1894. But education for women still did not mean independence and equal opportunity; it would not be until well into the twentieth century that women would join the labor force on a permanent, though still unequal, basis.

TIME LINE

1869–1870s	Charles Darwin and Herbert Spencer gain acceptance in American intellectual circles and universities
1870–1910	Public high schools grow from 500 to more than 10,000
1876	National League of Professional Baseball Clubs formed Mark Twain, *The Adventures of Tom Sawyer*
1879	Henry George, *Progress and Poverty*
1881	Oliver Wendell Holmes, Jr., *The Common Law* Booker T. Washington opens Tuskegee Institute
1884	Mark Twain, *The Adventures of Huckleberry Finn*
1885	American Economic Association founded William Dean Howells, *The Rise of Silas Lapham*
1888	Edward Bellamy, *Looking Backward*
1889	All-American college football team selected
1890s	Vaudeville becomes the most popular form of theatrical entertainment
1893	Frederick Jackson Turner, "The Significance of the Frontier in American History"
1899	Thorstein Veblen, *The Theory of the Leisure Class*
1900	Theodore Dreiser, *Sister Carrie*
1901	Frank Norris, *The Octopus*
1902	Oliver Wendell Holmes, Jr., appointed to the Supreme Court
1903	First World Series between champions of National and American League
1908	Jack Johnson wins heavyweight boxing championship
1916	Louis D. Brandeis appointed to the Supreme Court

American literature between 1860 and 1900, dominated by romanticism and sentimentality, was designed mainly to be read by middle- and upper-class women who had too much leisure time. But by 1870, a new literature of realism that dealt with the evils and problems of society had begun to emerge. There was also a new generation of American writers who would become prominent not only at home, but throughout the world. Their work would establish American literature as a separate and mature cultural tradition. Among them were Mark Twain, William Dean Howells, Henry James, Stephen Crane, Frank Norris, Jack London, and Theodore Dreiser.

Urbanization, an expanding middle class, and changes in patterns of work and leisure produced larger numbers of people with the income and the time to seek cultural and recreational diversion. By the late nineteenth century, mass entertainment took on an increased importance in the day-to-day lives of Americans. Popular literature attracted a wide readership, offering an assortment of dime novels, pulp fiction, and romances. Circuses and traveling shows brought entertainment to rural America, while the growing urban populations were attracted to the theater, particularly melodrama, opera, minstrelsy, and vaudeville. At the same time, the enthusiasm for competitive athletics helped to transform baseball, football, and boxing into important cultural and commercial enterprises.

Suggested Readings

The best introductions to intellectual life are H. S. Commager, *The American Mind* (1950), and R. Hofstadter, *Anti-Intellectualism in American Life* (1963). More specialized treatments of ideas between 1865 and 1920 include R. Hofstadter, *Social Darwinism in American Thought* (1955); M. G. White, *Social Thought in America* (1949); S. Fine, *Laissez Faire and the General Welfare State* (1957); and P. A. Carter, *The Spiritual Crisis of the Gilded Age* (1971). On sexual attitudes, see R. G. Walters (ed.), *Primers for Prudery: Sexual Advice to Victorian America* (1974); D. U. Pivar, *Purity Crusade: Sexual Morality and Social Control 1868–1900* (1973); and C. Smith-Rosenberg, *Disorderly Conduct: Visions of Gender in Victorian America* (1985).

In a collective biography, *Alternative America: Henry George, Edward Bellamy, Henry Demarest Lloyd and the Adversary Tradition* (1983), J. L. Thomas advances an important reinterpretation of these important thinkers. Individual figures in American thought are examined in C. A. Barker, *Henry George* (1955); A. E. Morgan, *Edward Bellamy* (1944); Joseph Dorfman, *Thorstein Veblen and His America* (1934); R. B. Perry, *The Thought and Character of William James* (2 vols., 1954); G. W. Allen, *William James* (1967); and Ernest Samuels's multivolume biography of Henry Adams: *The Young Henry Adams* (1948), *The Middle Years* (1958), and *The Major Phase* (1964). M. D. Howe's biography of Justice Holmes, *The Shaping Years 1841–1870* (1957) and *The Proving Years 1870–1888* (1963), places the man in his times. See also R. Hofstadter, *The Progressive Historians: Turner, Beard, Parrington* (1968), and B. Kuklick, *The Rise of American Philosophy: Cambridge, Massachusetts, 1860–1930* (1977).

L. A. Cremin, *The Transformation of the School: Progressivism in American Education* (1961), is a solid work, as is M. B. Katz, *Class, Bureaucracy, and Schools* (1975). On higher education, see L. R. Veysey, *The Emergence of the American University* (1965), and B. J. Bledstein, *The Culture of Professionalism: The Middle Class and the Development of Higher Education in America* (1976). For a stimulating critique, see Thorstein Veblen, *The Higher Learning in America* (1918). The expansion of primary and secondary schools is covered in F. Butler and L. A. Cremin, *A History of Education in American Culture* (1953). Other pertinent studies include Merle Curti, *The Social Ideas of American Educators* (1935); R. Hofstadter and W. P. Metzger, *The Development of Academic Freedom in the United States* (1955); and R. Welter, *Popular Education and Democratic Thought in America* (1962). On the education of women, see B. M. Solomon, *In the Company of Educated Women: A History of Women and Higher Education in America* (1985), and the journals and letters of Martha Carey Thomas, president of Bryn Mawr College, in M. H. Dobkin (ed.), *The Making of a Feminist* (1980). For Booker T. Washington's educational views, see his *Up from Slavery* (1901); L. R. Harlan, *Booker T. Washington: The Making of a Black Leader 1856–1901* (1972) and *The Wizard of Tuskegee, 1901–1915* (1983); and A. Meier, *Negro Thought in America 1880–1915* (1963).

A. Kazin, *On Native Grounds* (1942), is a perceptive literary history. See also L. Ziff, *The American 1890s: Life and Times of a Lost Generation* (1966), and the highly readable V. W. Brooks, *New England: Indian Summer* (1940) and *The Confident Years 1885–1915* (1952). On individual literary figures, see D. Wecter, *Sam Clemens of Hannibal* (1952); J. Kaplan, *Mr. Clemens and Mark Twain* (1960); E. H. Cady, *The Road to Realism* (1956) and *The Realist at War* (1958), both on William D. Howells; L. Edel, *Henry James* (5 vols., 1953–69); R. W. Stillman, *Stephen Crane* (1968); P. S. Foner, *Jack London: American Rebel* (1947); and F. O. Matthiessen, *Theodore Dreiser* (1951). Stimulating essays on Norris, Crane, and London appear in M. D. Geismar, *Rebels and Ancestors: The American Novel 1890–1915* (1953).

For an examination of popular culture, see R. B. Nye, *The Unembarrassed Muse: The Popular Arts in America* (1970) and L. W. Levine, *Highbrow/Lowbrow: The Emergence of Cultural Hierarchy in America* (1988). On the theatre, a good place to start is R. C. Toll, *Blacking Up: The Minstrel Show in Nineteenth-Century America* (1974) and *On With the Show* (1976). On sports, see F. R. Dulles, *America Learns to Play* (1940). The role of boxing in American society is examined in J. T. Sammons, *Beyond the Ring* (1988). See also Jack Johnson's autobiography, *Jack Johnson—In the Ring—And Out* (1927).

HARPER'S PICTORIAL HISTORY

OF THE
WAR WITH SPAIN

CHAPTER 24

THE AMERICAN EMPIRE

For more than five hundred years before the age of space, the history of Europeans was the history of expansion overseas. Duty moved them as much as daring, the word of God as much as the spirit of adventure, power as strongly as trade, pride as strongly as profit, the quest for personal independence as strongly as the quest for knowledge. They were impelled to spread "civilization"; they were also impelled to escape from it.

In this long history of expansion, the European discovery of America was a single chapter—the prologue, really—for more than three centuries of rivalry among European nations for dominance in the New World, and in Africa and Asia as well. The wealth and productivity created by the Industrial Revolution stimulated the competition for world markets. France, Belgium, Holland, Russia, and Bismarck's newly unified Germany sought a share of the spoils. They were followed by Italy and a modernizing Japan. What they wanted were the same areas the United States would come to look upon with growing

interest: Latin America, the islands of the Pacific, and China.

The 1890s had been a difficult decade in the United States: economic depression, labor conflict, divisive politics, "new" immigrants, racial violence, corporate abuses. Most Americans, confident of the destiny of their nation, still needed some reassurance, particularly with the closing of the frontier, that the pioneering character, the moral fiber, the power of the society remained intact. To listen to the young New York Republican leader Theodore Roosevelt was to believe that materialism and the pursuit of wealth had made Americans soft. The "great masterful races," he thought, "have been fighting races, and no triumph of peace is quite so great as the supreme triumphs of war." In "strict confidence," he confessed to a close friend in late 1897 that he would welcome "almost any war, for I think this country needs one."

But the new urge to spread American power and influence to other parts of the world was something more than an expression of virility. The rapid transformation of the economy had a great impact on foreign relations. With the United States now producing large quantities of manufactured goods, more than the domestic economy could absorb at profitable prices, the need to find foreign markets became urgent. With American investments abroad soaring between 1900 and 1914—from $455 million to $2.5 billion—there was also the need to protect those investments. With American manufacturers dependent on raw materials from abroad, it became imperative to try to control sources of supplies.

Concern mounted as European competitors, motivated by the same needs, became more and more active overseas. American advocates of the new imperialism sought not so much annexation of other regions as influence. They stressed the need to make arrangements that would secure the national interest and America's position in the world community. If influence could be exerted only through outright possession, however, that would be acceptable.

Whatever the motives or the forms it would take, overseas expansion would be justified in familiar language. Having reached the limits of continental expansion, Americans were "destined" to conquer new frontiers abroad. Confident of the superiority of its institutions and values, the United States by the 1890s was ready to shoulder the "expansionist destiny" of the Anglo-Saxon race, to join "the Christian nations," as an American missionary said, that "are subduing the world, in order to make mankind free."

When applied to the competition among nations, social Darwinism offered a convenient rationale. Progress came to nations that proved themselves superior in the world's ceaseless competition, that cultivated manly, combative instincts. Having proved itself the ablest and strongest in that competition, the Anglo-Saxon race assumed the responsibility to rule the unfit in the interest of all humankind. And why should not the United States, having established the "fittest" of political systems, bestow the blessings of Anglo-Saxon and American civilization on the less fortunate? "In the long run," said Roosevelt, "there can be no justification for one race managing or controlling another unless the management and control are exercised in the interest and for the benefit of that other race."

In the minds of policy makers and the American public, economic and humanitarian considerations reinforced each other. The idea that the United States should plant its institutions and values in the "waste places of the world" while exploiting their economic potential helped to shape American policy in the Caribbean, Mexico, Latin America, and Asia. Perhaps, Senator Albert Beveridge conceded, the "present phase" of American expansion was "personal profit." But he had no doubt about the ultimate objective. "God has marked us as His chosen people, henceforth to lead in the regeneration of the world. American law, American order, American civilization, and the American flag will plant themselves on shores hitherto bloody and benighted, but by those agencies of God henceforth to be made beautiful and bright."

THE NEW EXPANSIONISM

Expansion was hardly a new idea in the United States in the 1890s. Even before the Revolution, American colonists had resisted England's policy of restricting settlement to an area east of the Appalachians. Once independent, the United States rapidly spread westward across the continent. And Mexico to the south and Canada to the north were always part of expansionist plans.

Mexico and Alaska

While the United States was involved in the Civil War, Napoleon III of France attempted to establish a Catholic monarchy in Mexico. Backed by the French military, he installed his puppet, Maximilian of Austria, on a Mexican throne. In 1866, Secretary of State William H. Seward told France that its presence in Mexico was unacceptable, and fifty thousand American troops were sent to the Rio Grande. That was enough, along with new problems in Europe, to persuade France to withdraw. Although Maximilian tried to reign without the French, he was quickly seized, court-martialed, and executed by Mexican nationalists. In his communications with France, Seward never mentioned the Monroe Doctrine. But it had become apparent that the United States now had the strength to enforce its will in the Western Hemisphere.

While avoiding armed conflict with foreign enemies, Andrew Johnson's administration carried out successful negotiations with foreign friends. Among these was Russia, one of the few European states that had not unofficially sided with the Confederates. Russia hoped to build up the United States as a counterweight to Britain, and in March 1867 the Russian minister in Washington offered to unload distant and costly Alaska. Secretary Seward, an expansionist, jumped at the chance and negotiated a purchase treaty. Despite opposition to what the press soon called Seward's Folly, the opportunity to expand America's frontier was enough to win congressional approval. The purchase price was $7.2 million.

Canada

On completing the negotiations with Russia, Seward expressed the hope that Alaska would form the northern arm of a giant pincer movement to bring Canada into the American fold. "I know that Nature," he said, "designs that this whole continent, not merely these thirty-six states, shall be sooner or later, within the magic circle of the American Union."

During the Civil War, Confederate agents and escaping Confederate prisoners of war found sanctuary in Canada, where they could mount attacks on the northern frontier. Soon after the war ended, northerners were again reminded of the potential of British control over Canada. In 1866 the Fenians, an organization of Irish Americans in New York, began a series of assaults on Canada with the bizarre hope of capturing the country and holding it hostage until the British gave Ireland independence. The Irish vote had become an important factor in northern politics, and how to keep it while discouraging adventures of this sort presented a ticklish problem.

Rather than yield to the temptation of supporting or even approving Irish violence, the Johnson administration chose to give Great Britain a lesson in neutral conduct by taking stern measures against anyone who used American bases for foreign intrigues. British leaders chose to ignore the example. They at first refused to receive Seward's claims against Britain for wartime actions by sea raiders such as the *Alabama,* a ship built in England for the Confederacy and used to prey on Union shipping. Resentful Americans began to consider support of the Fenians as a way of forcing Britain to yield. By 1869, however, Europe was in turmoil over Bismarck's expansionist policies on the Continent. Britain, among others, wanted American friendship if these policies led to war. By the Treaty of Washington, ratified in 1871, the two nations agreed to arbitrate their differences. The next year, an arbitration tribunal awarded the United States $15.5 million for its *Alabama* claims.

But the United States continued to cast a hungry eye on Canada. In 1886, Theodore Roosevelt, bursting upon the American political stage, told a Fourth of July audience that he looked forward to the "day when not a foot of American soil will be held by any European power." In 1891, Secretary of State James G. Blaine said he expected that Canada would "ultimately seek . . . admission to the union." Both Roosevelt and Blaine easily qualified as early American *jingoes*—the term applied to those who considered a warlike and expansionist foreign policy to be in the national interest.

THE PACIFIC: TRADE AND EMPIRE

American ambitions did not end with North America or at the water's edge. In the 1850s Commodore Matthew C. Perry thought it "self-evident" that the United States would have to "extend its jurisdiction beyond the limits of the western continent." Cuba had attracted many southern expansionists, and in 1869 President Grant's cronies hungered for the annexation of Santo Domingo (now the Dominican Republic). An island rich in minerals, timber, and fruit, Santo Domingo had won its independence from Spain in 1865. Among those anxious to exploit opportunities there were two Massachusetts promoters who enjoyed influence at the White House through President Grant's secretary, Orville Babcock. While visiting Santo Domingo late in 1869, Babcock was able to negotiate a treaty of annexation. When Attorney General Hoar denounced the treaty as illegal, Grant removed Hoar from office. Charles Sumner, head of the Senate Foreign Relations Committee, then denounced the entire "deal," and in 1870 the Senate defeated Babcock's treaty. But although the United States did not annex Santo Domingo, it would exert a dominant influence in the island.

Large numbers of Americans still believed the nation should concentrate its energies on internal development and avoid foreign entanglements. But internal development would, in fact, make foreign entanglements increasingly desirable, if not absolutely essential. The construction of the transcontinental railroads after the Civil War, along with rapid industrialization, sharpened appetites for Pacific outlets and islands. If the United States was to establish its influence in the Far East and exploit the rich economic possibilities of that region, it would need naval bases and coaling and repair stations for its ships. Both Hawaii and Samoa had already served as stopover stations for American ships in the Pacific trade, and after the Civil War attention focused on them as permanent American outposts. With the prospect of annexation of the Philippines after the Spanish-American War, this matter was quickly resolved.

Samoa

Even before the Civil War, American interest in the Pacific and the Far East had taken on economic and religious significance. Merchants wanted commercial advantages, and missionaries sought converts to Christianity. In the 1840s and 1850s the United States had acquired "most-favored-nation" treaty rights in China, giving American traders terms equal to those of any other country. After Commodore Perry forcibly opened Japan in 1854, Townsend Harris, the first American consul there, negotiated a treaty of friendship by which he became the chief adviser on international relations to the Japanese government. In 1867, the United States Navy took possession of uninhabited Midway Islands in the Pacific. But its inability to dredge the main island's harbor disappointed those who sought to use it as a stopover station for American ships.

After the opening of the first transcontinental railroad in 1869, Americans in the trade between San Francisco and Australia began to think of making Samoa's fine harbor of Pago Pago into a coaling station for steamships. In the mid-1880s, however, Germany, the leading economic power in Samoa, began to enlarge its activities there at the expense of British and American interests. Friction among the three powers persisted until 1899, when Samoa was formally divided between the United States and Germany. Britain received compensation elsewhere in the Pacific. The United States acquired Pago Pago and surrounding territory; Germany got the rest of the land. American Samoa would become a strategic naval station in the twentieth century. The remaining islands, after Germany's defeat in World War I, would be controlled as a League of Nations mandate by New Zealand.

Hawaii

The Hawaiian Islands, closer than Samoa and strategically a natural outpost of the North American continent, had long been known to American traders. New York and New England vessels in the China trade called at the islands in the 1790s, and in the next three decades Hawaiian produce as well as ports played a part in the fur trade. As early as 1820, Yankee missionaries had settled in the islands and transformed Honolulu into a pleasant imitation of a New England town. After 1840 Hawaii became the center of South Pacific whaling. By 1860, many American citizens owned permanent homes there, and a growing local faction was seeking annexation.

After 1850, sugar cane replaced whaling as Hawaii's main industry, and problems of land tenure and labor supply were added to the issues being contested by the government and outside capitalists, and by the outside rivals themselves. Until 1875, American sugar producers in the Louisiana area had succeeded in keeping Hawaiian sugar out of United States ports. That year, however, a reciprocity treaty between the United States and the islands (negotiated under threats by Hawaiian growers to look to Britain for markets and political support) admitted Hawaiian sugar into the United States and American commodities into Hawaii, both duty-free. At the same time, the islands pledged not to give any territory to foreign governments or to extend to them the commercial privileges won by the United States.

Under the treaty, sugar growing boomed, and with it the rest of the business community. Native Hawaiians, however, saw more and more of their land controlled by white planters, and themselves submerged by a flood of Chinese workers.

Negotiations to renew the treaty began in 1884. But the United States Senate would not approve a new agreement until 1887, when, in recognition of the strategic importance of Hawaii, it won an amendment granting the United States exclusive use of Pearl Harbor as a coaling station and repair base for naval vessels. The same year, Hawaiian-born white businessmen, fed up with the corrupt and authoritarian regime of King Kalakaua, brought off a bloodless revolution, forcing him to accept a new government. The Bayonet Constitution, as Hawaiians called it, gave businessmen control of the government and extended the franchise to white foreigners. Property qualifications, in turn, disfranchised most native citizens.

Hawaii became more dependent on the United States. In 1890, sugar for the American mainland made up 99 percent of Hawaiian exports. In that year, Congress admitted other foreign sugars (as well as Hawaii's) duty-free, but gave United States growers a special subsidy to compensate for the drop in sugar prices. Hawaii's economy was badly hurt by these measures. At the same time, Hawaiians grew more and more angry about the new constitution. Discontent spread after 1891, when King Kalakaua died and was succeeded by his sister, Queen Liluokalani, a firm opponent of white rule. By 1893, "Queen Lil's" disregard of constitutional restraints, and her efforts to throw off the constitution altogether, had driven white businessmen into a second rebellion. They had the support of the American minister to Hawaii, John L. Stevens, who helped protect them with American troops landed from a cruiser.

Stevens promptly recognized the provisional government set up by the rebels, who lost no time in sending a five-man commission to Washington to negotiate a treaty of annexation. The retiring President Harrison favored the treaty and sent it to the Senate, where it met Democratic opposition. Suspicious of Stevens's activities in Hawaii, the new president, Grover Cleveland, recalled the treaty and sent a special commissioner to the islands to investigate. His report charged that Stevens, by his abuse of the authority of the United States, had done a great wrong to a "feeble but independent State."

Cleveland tried to restore Queen Lil under a constitutional regime, but the provisional government would not let go. In 1894 it wrote still another constitution, proclaimed the Republic of Hawaii, and confirmed Sanford B. Dole as its first president.

Realizing he would have to use force if he were to unseat the new government, Cleveland recognized it. But he refused its urgent requests for annexation. In 1897, under McKinley, a new annexation treaty was worked out. But the Senate, reflecting popular discontent with imperialist adventures, rejected it. Feelings changed during the Spanish-American War, when Hawaii's strategic value became more evident. In July 1898, by a joint resolution, Congress approved a new treaty making Hawaii "a part of the territory of the United States." In August 1959, about seven months after Alaska became the forty-ninth state, Hawaii became the fiftieth state.

DIPLOMACY AND POWER

After the Civil War, Americans were so intent on developing domestic resources and home markets that the United States merchant marine virtually disappeared. For almost a century, it had been one of the largest in the world. The navy, once as strong as the merchant marine, had shrunk by the 1880s to a small number of wooden sailing ships worse than useless in an age of steel and steam. The United States, especially in competition with a naval power such as Great Britain, hardly appeared to be in a position to establish and maintain its influence anywhere abroad. That weakness became critical as industrialization forced American manufacturers to look elsewhere for markets for surplus goods.

The need for the United States to assert itself more aggressively in its foreign relations won more support in the 1880s and 1890s. A group of spokesmen emerged to provide the necessary direction and momentum. Among these men, two were particularly important: James G. Blaine, secretary of state in 1881 under Garfield and again from 1889 to 1892 under Harrison, and Captain (later Admiral) Alfred T. Mahan, a gifted propagandist who became the model for a later generation of imperialists. Both believed in an aggressive and spirited diplomacy. Blaine focused his energies on Latin America; Mahan concerned himself with making certain the United States had the power to carry out an aggressive diplomacy.

Latin America

Latin America still had strong cultural ties with Spain and Portugal and commercial ties with Britain. In the 1870s Germany began to seek Latin American outlets for its goods and capital. To deflect Latin American trade and development toward the United States, Blaine in 1889 issued invitations to a Pan-American Conference. Delegates from eighteen nations met in Washington and formed the Pan-American Union, but accomplished little else.

Although Latin Americans bought largely from Europeans, they sold mainly to the United States, and mainly items that were duty-free. When the Latin American delegates to the 1889 conference failed to grant tariff concessions to United States exports, Blaine threatened to respond with tariffs on Latin American goods. The so-called reciprocity provision of the McKinley tariff in 1890, which said the United States would respond to favorable treatment, was Blaine's weapon. But his tactics did not work very well. Latin Americans remained hostile and uncooperative.

Sea Power and Trade

As secretary of state, Blaine also pushed for a powerful new American navy. In 1881, Congress set up a Naval Advisory Board to work for larger appropriations. Two years later, Congress appropriated funds for the famous White Squadron—four new steel ships equipped with steam power and a full rigging of white sails. But they were only a token navy, since they had no armor. The establishment of the Naval War College at Newport, Rhode Island, in 1884 gave another push to the idea of a "big navy." At Newport in 1886, just before he was made president of the college, Captain Mahan gave the lectures that eventually became the heart of his famous series of books on sea power in history.

Britain, he said, had grown great on sea power. The United States should profit from Britain's example not simply by rebuilding its merchant marine and its navy, but by adding colonies and naval bases throughout the world. In particular, the United States must have naval bases in the Caribbean to protect a potential canal across the Isthmus of Panama and in the Pacific not only to guard American trade, but also to take part in the coming struggle between Western and Asian civilizations.

Between 1883 and 1890, Congress authorized the building of nine cruisers. Construction began on the first modern American battleship, the *Maine*. After additional pressure from naval expansionists, Congress authorized construction of so many battleships, cruisers, gunboats, and torpedo boats that by 1898 only Britain and France outranked the United States in naval power.

Toward the end of the century, the position of the United States in world trade greatly improved, as Blaine had hoped. American imports, valued at $462 million in 1870, almost doubled in the next thirty years, reaching $850 million in 1900. In the same period, American exports almost tripled, rising from $530 million to approximately $1.4 billion. The panic of 1893, which shrank markets at home, pushed the quest for markets abroad. Senator Albert J. Beveridge, an ardent expansionist, stated the case quite clearly in April 1898: Since American factories and farms were producing more than the American people could use and consume, "the trade of the world must and shall be ours."

Hemispheric Diplomacy

While the United States was using its resources to promote the growth of foreign trade and world power, a series of diplomatic incidents in the Western Hemisphere triggered talk of war and revived the Monroe Doctrine.

One incident arose over the old problem of fishing rights in Canadian waters. Friction over these rights had increased as a result of the other issues in Canadian-American relations during and after the Civil War. The Treaty of Washington of 1871 formally resolved some of these difficulties, but American fishermen continued to be harassed and exploited by local authorities in Canada and Newfoundland. An informal arrangement with Britain, worked out through diplomatic channels by the Cleveland administration, ended the fishing controversy in the Atlantic. But controversy over seal fisheries in the Bering Sea brought trouble once again. In 1890 rumors spread that British warships were policing the region, and some American newspapers suggested firing at British ships in those waters. Cooler heads prevailed, and an arbitration treaty was ratified in February 1892.

A third episode occurred after a revolt in 1891 against the president of Chile, in which the United States had backed the president. When the rebels won, feeling against the United States ran high. In October 1891, the captain of the *U.S.S. Baltimore*, then in Valparaiso, permitted his crew to go ashore unarmed. A riot broke out in which two Americans were killed and others imprisoned. Chilean apologies were slow in coming, and President Harrison hinted that he might invite Congress to declare war. A full apology arrived just in time, and Chile eventually agreed to pay $75,000 to the families of the dead sailors and to those who had been injured.

A more serious affair brought the United States closer to war. It involved disputed territory between British Guiana and neighboring Venezuela, where gold was discovered in the 1880s. When Venezuela broke off diplomatic relations with Britain in 1887, the United States offered to act as mediator. Britain rejected the idea. The last American mediation effort was made in July 1895 by Richard Olney, Cleveland's secretary of state.

In a note to Lord Salisbury, the British foreign minister, Olney charged that Great Britain had violated the Monroe Doctrine by interfering in hemispheric affairs. Olney made it absolutely clear that the doctrine applied to the boundary dispute: "Today, the United States is practically sovereign on this continent, and its fiat is law upon the subjects to which it confines its interposition." Issuing a virtual ultimatum, Olney asked for a quick response to his demand that Britain submit the dispute to "peaceful arbitration." Salisbury took his time in replying. When he did, in November 1895, he refused arbitration and reminded the United States that the Monroe Doctrine was not recognized in international law and therefore did not apply to boundary disputes.

Cleveland made the Olney–Salisbury correspondence public in December, when he himself asked Congress for funds to finance a commission to determine the actual boundary between British Guiana and Venezuela. At the same time, he asserted that "it will . . . be the duty of the United States to resist by every means in its power, as a wilful aggression upon its rights and interests," any efforts by Great Britain to take territory that the United States, after investigation, found to be Venezuela's.

Since the Venezuelan boundary dispute coincided with mounting silverite aspirations for action against England, the alleged center of the "gold power," it was much more serious than any of the earlier episodes. But the peace parties eventually won out both in the United States and in Britain. Cleveland's proposal for a boundary commission gave Americans time to simmer down, since nothing could be done until such a commission reported. Britain, meanwhile, was growing more nervous over its rivalry with Germany, and therefore more interested in American friendship. In February 1897, at America's suggestion, Britain and Venezuela negotiated a treaty turning the boundary dispute over to international arbitration. In 1899 a final settlement was made.

THE SPANISH–AMERICAN WAR

To secure American markets and sources of raw materials, protect the national interest, and increase the influence of the United States in the world community had become principal objectives of American policy makers by the 1890s. Such objectives were also consistent with the American mission of spreading American institutions and habits of mind. The ways in which strong diplomacy, commercial imperialism, and missionary idealism could be combined were best exemplified in the growing American concern over Spanish-held Cuba—a concern that ended in a war and in the debut of the United States as an imperial power.

The Cuban Crisis

When the Cubans rebelled against the Spanish in 1868, Americans had not cared much. The rebellion dragged on for ten years before Spain finally agreed to undertake serious reforms. The Cubans made two major demands: emancipation of the slaves on the island and self-government for the island's inhabitants. Spain took another ten years to free the slaves, and postponed self-government indefinitely. In the meantime, it saddled a ruined Cuban economy with all the costs of the rebellion.

After the emancipation of the slaves, large amounts of European and American capital were invested in Cuba. Modern business practices were introduced, especially in the production of cane sugar. The United States gradually became Cuba's principal market and source of capital. After the removal of the American duty on Cuban sugar in 1884, production of that export reached new highs, and almost all of it went to the United States. Suddenly, events began to work against Cuban prosperity. Europe's production of beet sugar became so great that the world price of sugar fell. The worldwide depression of the 1890s further weakened prices. Finally, the Wilson-Gorman tariff of 1894 restored a 40 percent duty on raw sugar. The acute economic distress that followed, combined with the continuing political trouble, brought another revolt against Spanish rule in 1895. American interests were of course threatened.

Spain sent its best general, Valeriano Weyler (soon to be called Butcher Weyler), and 200,000 men to suppress the uprising. But the Spaniards could not cope with the rebel leaders and their guerrilla followers, who had taken to the hills. The rebels destroyed property in order to exhaust the government and force the withdrawal of the troops. Much American property was also deliberately destroyed in an effort to involve the United States. All this time a *junta*, or council, of Cuban exiles in New York kept pressing for American intervention and Cuban independence. Joseph Pulitzer of the *New York World* and William Randolph Hearst of the *New York Journal* engaged in a circulation battle, each trying to outdo the other in printing sensational accounts of Spanish atrocities. Mahan, Roosevelt, Senator Henry Cabot Lodge, and other expansionists also whipped up the war spirit.

Unlike the American public, however, which focused on the Cuban struggle for liberty, the expansionists sensed higher stakes. The Spanish Philippines were a possible American stronghold in the Far East and a gateway to the potentially lucrative China trade. But President Cleveland refused to be stampeded: He responded to the public frenzy over Spanish atrocities in Cuba by noting that both sides had committed outrages.

Early in 1898, two events combined to make resistance to the jingoes and public pressure difficult. On February 9, a letter stolen from the Havana post office by a rebel sympathizer fell into the hands of Hearst's *New York Journal*. In it, Dupuy de Lome, the Spanish minister to the United States, described President McKinley as "weak and a bidder for the admiration of the crowd, besides being a would-be politician who tries to leave a door open behind himself while keeping on good terms with the jingoes of his party." This was a private letter, but Hearst made it as public as possible. Spain denied any evil intent on the minister's part, and de Lome himself resigned as soon as the letter was published.

The *Maine* tragedy followed in less than a week. The new battleship *Maine* had been sent to Havana in January 1898, after the American consul-general there cabled that American property and lives were in danger. On February 15, the *Maine* apparently hit a mine. Two officers and 258 of the crew were lost. Although an official inquiry left the causes of the explosion uncertain, Assistant Navy Secretary Theodore Roosevelt called it "an act of dirty treachery."

In the absence of his chief, Roosevelt now fired off messages from the Navy Department, among them the famous one to Commodore George Dewey, who was with his Pacific squadron off the China shore. In case of war with Spain, Dewey was to make certain the Spanish squadron did not leave the Asian coast; he was then to undertake "offensive operations" in the Philippine Islands.

With Americans rallying under the slogan "Remember the *Maine!*" Congress unanimously granted the president's request for $50 million for national defense. "There is no stopping place now short of the absolute independence of Cuba," declared the *New York Times*. But many Americans still wanted peace. The business leaders feared that war costs and war taxes would endanger the recent revival from the long depression.

William Randolph Hearst, newspaper publisher: "You furnish the pictures," he instructed his illustrator in Havana, "and I'll furnish the war." The Hearst and Pulitzer newspapers were not alone in whipping up war hysteria over Cuba. The popular magazine *Judge* showed the Spanish as vicious brutes. *(Library of Congress)*

For a time, at least, they thought it possible to protect their investment in Cuban sugar plantations and iron mines without armed intervention. There was considerable doubt, moreover, about the ability of the rebels to set up a stable government if they were to win independence.

"I have been through one war," McKinley told a friend at this time. "I have seen the dead piled up, and I do not want to see another." But the president maintained a public silence, and indecisiveness marked his policies. "I must have money to get ready for war," he told a Republican House leader. "I am doing everything possible to prevent war, but it must come, and we are not prepared for war. Who knows where this war will lead us."

American Intervention

Even a great leader might have found it impossible to reduce the war fever of the American people. For many of them, the struggle of the Cuban people for freedom was like their own struggle in the War of Independence. On March 27, 1898, the president, after consulting his cabinet, made a series of demands on Spain. He called for an armistice on the island, during which the United States would act as mediator between the contestants. But he also made it clear that Cuban independence would be the only satisfactory outcome. Spain was willing to make many concessions, but Premier Sagasta, fearing the end of his government and even the demise of the Spanish monarchy if Cuban independence were granted, refused to accept any armistice that the rebels did not ask for first.

With their hopes for American intervention rising every day, the rebels would make no such request; their demands, in fact, grew harsher. Spain scrambled to find support in Europe, but the German foreign minister, on April 5, expressed the attitude of most other nations when he told the Spanish ambassador: "You are isolated, because everybody wants to be pleasant to the United States, or, at any rate, nobody wants to arouse America's anger; the United States is a rich country, against which you simply cannot

"Dixie" and "The Battle Hymn of the Republic" sounded throughout the halls of Congress after war was declared against Spain, and two Civil War veterans posed in a show of unity. Both North and South favored the war to make Cuba safe for democracy. *(Library of Congress)*

sustain a war." When the pope that same day agreed to suggest an armistice, saving Spain the humiliation of yielding to America, Sagasta gratefully took the offer.

The American minister in Madrid promptly cabled home Spain's consent to an "immediate and unconditonal suspension of hostilities." He added on his own, "I believe that this means peace." But it was too late. The public, the press, the Protestant clergy, and expansionist politicians in both parties had created an atmosphere in which negotiation seemed to mean giving in. On April 11, 1898, President McKinley, "in the name of humanity, in the name of civilization, in behalf of endangered American interests," sent a war message to Congress. He asked for authority to use military and naval force to end the hostilities in Cuba.

On April 20, by a joint resolution, Congress declared Cuba "free and independent," demanded that Spain withdraw from the island, and authorized the president to use military force to assure compliance. Congress added the Teller Amendment, disclaiming any intention to annex Cuba

and promising "to leave the government and control of the Island to its people."

Within a week of the resolution, the United States and Spain formally declared themselves in a state of war. "I think the President could have worked the business out without a war." remarked Wisconsin's conservative Republican senator, "but the current was too strong, the demagogues too numerous, and the fall election too near."

The "Splendid Little War"

The war with Spain was almost too short for those who wanted to display American power, but the results were gratifying. In the Philippines, Commodore Dewey sailed into Manila Bay on April 30. The next day, he blasted the antiquated Spanish fleet sitting there, and by July 25 about 11,000 American troops under General Wesley Merritt had landed. Supported by Filipino insurrectionists under Emilio Aguinaldo, whom Dewey had befriended and helped arm, Merritt took Manila on August 13.

By then, the "splendid little war," as the American ambassador to Britain called it, had already ended in the West Indies. On April 29, a Spanish fleet under Admiral Cervera had sailed west from the Cape Verde Islands. American coastal cities demanded naval protection. A patrol fleet tried to find Cervera before he reached Cuba, where they decided he was headed. They did not locate him, however, until he was safely in Santiago harbor, where American ships bottled him up. A military expedition was now planned to capture Santiago and force Cervera out under the American fleet's waiting guns.

On June 14 a poorly equipped expeditionary force of 17,000 men under General William R. Shafter finally left Tampa, Florida. Typical of this army was the First Volunteer Cavalry Regiment, the Rough Riders, who had few horses. Shafter and his men reached the Cuban coast near Santiago on June 20 and took six days to disembark. After a two-day battle, which saw Roosevelt on July 1 lead the Rough Riders up what "we afterwards christened Kettle Hill" (a flank of San Juan Hill, which became famous for the Rough Riders' charge), the American attack petered out. "We are within measurable distance of a terrible military disaster," Roosevelt wrote Lodge.

Luckily for Shafter, the Spaniards were in even worse shape. On July 3 Cervera decided to escape, but American firepower destroyed his ships. On July 16, General Linares surrendered Santiago to the Americans, and nine days later a second American expeditionary force made a triumphant march through the neighboring Spanish island of Puerto Rico.

The Spanish government had already begun to seek a peace treaty, and on August 12 hostilities were declared over. All told, the United States lost 5462 men in the four-month war, but only 379 in combat. The rest died from disease and other causes. Spain's losses in the fighting were much higher, and in addition it lost the last of a once great New World empire.

The Peace and the Philippines

Few Americans doubted the nobility of their mission in helping an oppressed native people achieve freedom. But there was far less agreement about what the United States should do with some of the spoils of the victory. Did the "liberation" of Cuba require the annexation of the Philippines?

While American negotiators worked on the treaty, hunger for the Philippines kept growing.

The fear that Germany would seize the islands no doubt fed American demands, as did economic, strategic, and racial considerations. The Filipinos were not prepared for self-government, annexationists argued, and the United States had an obligation to give them proper guidance and direction. This was then, as a Presbyterian minister suggested, a special kind of imperialism—"not for domination but for civilization."

The final treaty, insuring the freedom of Cuba and granting the United States the Philippines (for a payment of $20 million), Puerto Rico, and Guam, was signed in Paris on December 10. In the debate on ratification in the Senate, the annexation of the Philippines became the principal issue. To acquire the Philippines and not admit the Filipinos to full citizenship, argued critics, violated a principle in which this nation had long believed—government by consent of the governed. But to admit Filipinos as citizens posed still other dangers. They would be entitled to vote, to send representatives to Congress, and to migrate to the United States, where they would become a source of cheap labor. (That specter helped to link Samuel Gompers of the AFL with

Theodore Roosevelt and his Rough Riders on San Juan Hill in 1898. "Did I tell you," he wrote to his friend Henry Cabot Lodge, "I killed a Spaniard with my own hand, like a jack-rabbit. . . ." *(Library of Congress)*

the anti-imperialists.) Finally, both southern and northern opponents of annexation agreed that annexation would make even worse an already critical race problem. Nothing but trouble might be expected, said the editor of the *Nation,* from "dependencies inhabited by ignorant and inferior races" with whom white Americans had no affinity; indeed, the biracial experiment in the South should be sufficient warning of "the danger and futility of any further attempt in the same direction." The racial argument assumed that Asians, like blacks, could never be assimilated into American life.

The Anti-Imperialist League, organized in November 1898, grew rapidly as the administration's expansionist policies developed. Its supporters included political, business, literary, and intellectual leaders, among them former president Cleveland, William Jennings Bryan, Andrew Carnegie, Samuel Gompers, Mark Twain, William James, and Jane Addams. Some of them were horrified by the behavior of American occupation troops in the Philippines; some were fearful that imperial expansion would involve the United States in an armaments race, foreign alliances, and wars of intervention. A strange coalition of individuals holding conflicting views on domestic political issues, they were drawn together by opposition to colonial expansion.

On February 6, 1899, the Senate ratified the treaty fifty-seven to twenty-seven, only two votes above the required two-thirds majority. The decision might have gone the other way had it not been for the Filipinos themselves. On December 21, 1898, with the debate in the Senate at its peak, McKinley had ordered the War Department to extend the military occupation of Manila to the entire archipelago. This move touched off armed Filipino resistance under Aguinaldo, who headed a group that had suffered imprisonment, exile, and death in its years of struggle for independence from Spain. When the Senate learned that American lives had been lost in the fighting, there were enough votes for the treaty to squeak by.

The commitment to liberate the Cubans now became a war to conquer the Filipinos. "It shows how rapidly we are approaching an imperial form of government," wrote the Massachusetts anti-imperialist Moorfield Storey, "that the President should undertake operations like this without the consent of Congress or without even consulting it." There was nothing "splendid" about this war. The Filipino rebels held off the Americans for three years in a conflict that cost more men and money than the war with Spain itself. Nearly 200,000 American soldiers participated; over 4000 were killed, and 2800 wounded. Some 16,000 Filipinos died in combat. Many more died from diseases that gained an easy foothold in undernourished bodies; the food crops that might have fed them had been destroyed in the fighting. The United States found itself using some of the same brutal methods for which it had condemned the Spanish in Cuba. One American reporter wrote home:

Hundreds of native huts were fired by the Americans to dislodge their occupants. One church, in which Filipinos had fortified themselves, was set on fire by the Americans, and the escaping Filipinos were picked off with rifles as they were smoked out.

As the war deepened, protest at home grew louder. Upon learning that an American general had shot Filipino women and children, Mark Twain bitterly observed that when the general was a youth, his conscience must have "leaked out through one of his pores."

That black American troops were among those helping to suppress the rebellion caused some dissent in the black press. Not a single black soldier, one black newspaper editorialized, should be sent overseas "to kill their own kith and kin for fighting for the cause they believed to be right." Were not black soldiers, another editor asked, "simply fighting to curse the [Philippines] with color-phobia; jimcrow cars, disfranchisement, lynchers, and everything that prejudice can do to blight the manhood of the darker races"? Finally, in assessing the results of American expansionism, a black newspaper observed: "When one of the great Christian countries finds a strip of land it desires to possess, it is quickly seized with a commendable desire to spread the benign influence of civilization over the natives, and what a remarkably small number of natives are left after this process has been completed."

But to Theodore Roosevelt, and to those who shared his obsession about carrying civilization into "the waste places of the earth," the critics were serving only to prolong the war. "We are fighting Filipinos," said Roosevelt, "because they are killing our soldiers. The bullets that slay our men in Luzon are inspired by the denouncers of America here. The Filipino will stop killing our soldiers very soon after he becomes convinced that he will receive no aid in the effort." The certainty of good intentions in the Philippines permitted most Americans to embrace Roosevelt's views. Ultimately, United States military strength prevailed. In Aguinaldo's last wartime proclama-

THE RULES OF CIVILIZED WARFARE

In testimony before a Senate committee in 1902, Brigadier General Robert P. Hughes explained why the troops under his command had destroyed the dwellings of Filipinos suspected of sympathy with the insurgents.

GEN. HUGHES: The destruction was as a punishment. They permitted these people [insurgents] to come in there and conceal themselves and they gave no sign. . . .

SEN. RAWLINS: The punishment in that case would fall, not upon the men, who could go elsewhere, but mainly upon the women and little children.

GEN. HUGHES: The women and children are part of the family, and where you wish to inflict a punishment you can punish the man probably worse in that way than in any other.

SEN. RAWLINS: But is that within the ordinary

rules of civilized warfare? Of course you could exterminate the family, which would be still worse punishment.

GEN. HUGHES: These people are not civilized.

SEN. RAWLINS: But is that within the ordinary rules of civilized warfare?

GEN. HUGHES: No; I think it is not.

SEN. RAWLINS: You think it is not?

SEN. DIETRICH: In order to carry on civilized warfare both sides have to engage in such warfare.

GEN. HUGHES: Yes, sir; certainly. That is the point.

Source: Henry F. Graff (ed.), *American Imperialism and the Philippine Insurrection: Testimony Taken from Hearings on Affairs in the Philippine Islands before the Senate Committee on the Philippines—1902* (Boston: Little, Brown, 1969), pp 64–65. Photograph from the Library of Congress.

tion, he recognized American sovereignty over the Philippines and recommended that the Filipinos make the best of American rule.

In Cuba, meanwhile, General Leonard Wood ruled as military governor until May 20, 1902, when the Cubans were compelled to accept the Platt Amendment. This amendment to an army appropriation bill sharply circumscribed Cuba's

freedom of action. It limited Cuba's treaty-making powers, its right to borrow money, and other rights of sovereignty. Moreover, Cuba could not withhold lands wanted by the United States for coaling or naval stations, or give territory to any other power. Finally, the amendment permitted the United States to intervene in Cuba "for the protection of life, property, and individual liberty."

The United States required that the Platt Amendment be incorporated in any constitution drawn up by Cuba, and also that Cuba make a permanent treaty with the United States using the terms of the amendment. The Platt Amendment remained in force until 1934, when it and related treaties were canceled by agreement. At that time the United States retained Guantanamo Bay and its shore area as a naval base. Until 1959, Cuba remained a safe and tractable neighbor within the American sphere of influence.

The Imperialist Policy

In the middle of public discussion of the new imperialism, the election of 1900 took place. Not a supporter of the peace treaty, William Jennings Bryan, the Democratic candidate, had secured some Democratic votes for it in the Senate. He had done this to guard his party from charges of

wanting the war renewed, and to carry the whole issue of overseas expansion into the campaign. But McKinley's won again, and his victory was interpreted by many as a victory for the new policy. When McKinley was assassinated a few months after his inauguration in 1901 and Theodore Roosevelt became commander in chief, the imperialists expected further expansion.

In May 1901, in the so-called *Insular* cases, the Supreme Court added its approval to that of the president and the people. In these cases the Court held that the Constitution did not follow the flag, that the rights of United States citizens did not automatically belong to the people of the territories. Even though the United States had given Hawaii formal territorial status in 1900, paving the way for statehood, in 1903 the Supreme Court held that these islands had not been "incorporated" into the Union and that the native citizens had not become the equals of citizens of the continental United States.

The United States in the Pacific

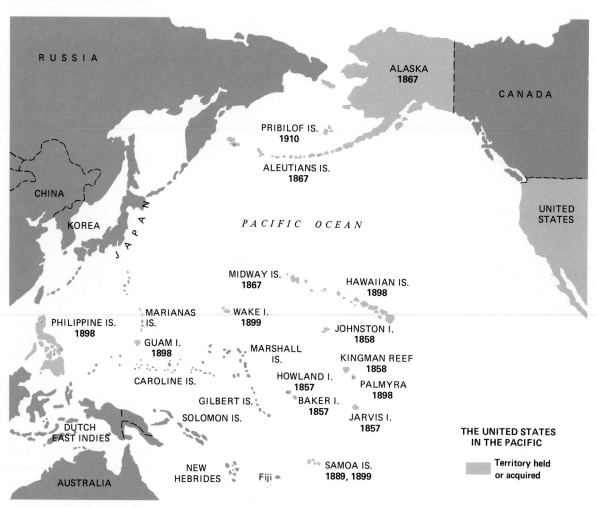

CHAPTER 24 THE AMERICAN EMPIRE

The 1903 decision arose out of the denial of trial by jury to the Hawaiian people. The Court decided it was lawful to follow the existing criminal procedure in the islands instead of using American procedures. In reaching this decision, the Court distinguished between "fundamental rights," which could not be abridged, and "procedural rights," which could be. Trial by jury, the Court held, was a procedural right.

These racist distinctions, however, were soon swept aside, and even the Filipinos were quickly put on the road to self-government. The foundations were laid by the Philippine Commission, appointed in 1900 under William Howard Taft. By 1907 the Filipinos had gained the right to elect the lower house of their legislature, and in 1916 the Jones Act gave them virtual control over their domestic affairs. Some of this ground was lost during the 1920s. But in 1934 the Tydings-McDuffie Act provided for independence after ten years. The Filipinos agreed to the ten-year provision in 1936. After the islands were recovered from Japan during World War II, Filipinos achieved independence, as planned, on July 4, 1946.

POWER POLITICS

With its acquisitions from the Spanish-American War and its industrial supremacy, the United States had become a major world power. It was a position that almost immediately demanded new commitments and entanglements. Other imperial powers were carving out spheres of influence in China. Japan was embarking on an imperial policy very much Western in inspiration. The dominant influence exercised by the United States in Cuba made its presence in the Caribbean and Central America more visible and its meddling more frequent. Expanding American interests in Latin America and the Far East also pointed up the need to construct a canal across Central America to make intercoastal shipping easier and the American navy more maneuverable.

Whether by the Open Door policy in the Far East or by the Monroe Doctrine in the Western Hemisphere, the United States reserved to itself the right to intervene to preserve stability and counteract discrimination by rival powers. These were the principles that would guide twentieth-century foreign relations—principles that bridged the political parties and the occupants of the White House.

China and the Open Door

Along with the American interest in markets, Mahan's ideas about an inevitable struggle for the world between Western and Oriental civilizations had helped push the United States into the Far East. But once there, Americans found the major struggle to be with other Western powers—France, Germany, Britain, and Russia—as well as with Japan. All were staking out spheres of influence in weak and still passive China. Partition of China might well ruin American hopes for further trade with that country. The problem was to find a way to gain and maintain equal trading rights without risking war and without becoming a party to further partition.

In 1898, it appeared that the British were about to use some newly leased territory on the mainland opposite Hong Kong to smuggle imports into China without paying the Chinese tariff. If the other powers followed this example, the Chinese government would soon lose all its tariff revenues. Political as well as commercial chaos would result.

In September 1899, McKinley's new secretary of state, John Hay, sent his famous Open Door notes to Britain, Germany, and Russia—and later to Japan, Italy, and France—inviting them to agree to three points:

1. No nation was to interfere with the trading rights or privileges of other nations within its sphere of influence.
2. Chinese officials were to be permitted to collect duties under existing tariffs, which granted the United States most-favored-nation privileges.
3. No nation was to discriminate against nationals of other countries in levying port duties and railroad rates.

Although none of the powers would make these concessions, Hay refused to accept their vague rejections. He saved himself from disaster by calmly announcing on March 20, 1900, that all had given "final and definitive" consent to his request. Only Japan challenged his bluff.

Hardly were negotiations over the Open Door notes finished when a group of Chinese nationalists rose up against foreigners in their country. The Chinese called themselves the Order of Literary, Patriotic, Harmonious Fists; Westerners called them Boxers. Before they were put down by an international force to which the United States contributed 2500 men, they had killed hundreds of people and destroyed much property. Only swift action by Britain and the United States now prevented the other powers from retaliating by taking more Chinese territory.

Hay advised the imperial rivals that American policy was to "preserve Chinese territorial and administrative entity" and to "safeguard for the world the principle of equal and impartial trade with all parts of the Chinese Empire." This announcement went further than the Open Door notes and had more effect. Eventually, the nations accepted a money indemnity from China rather than new grants of territory. The United States' share of almost $25 million was larger than necessary to meet the losses it suffered. The balance was later returned to China, where it was used to help educate Chinese students in America.

Most important, though, the Open Door policy had laid the basis for greater American influence in the affairs of China and Asia. At the same time, it created an impression of disinterested neutrality. Few explained the American position as clearly as Hay himself. "The ideal policy," he wrote to Henry Adams, "is, as you justly observe, to do nothing, and yet be around when the watermelon is cut. Not that we want any watermelon, but it is always pleasant to be seen in smart colored circles on occasions of festivity."

Japan: The Russo-Japanese War

Theodore Roosevelt's preaching of what he called "the soldierly virtues" frightened many people when he became president at the age of forty-three in September 1901. Four years earlier he had said at the Naval War College: "The men who have dared greatly in war . . . are those who deserve best of their country."

But his first major international venture did not come until his second term, and then he was a peacemaker. Having beaten the Russians in Manchuria in the Russo-Japanese War of 1904–1905, the Japanese in the spring of 1905, temporarily exhausted by their efforts, secretly asked the American president to mediate. Fearful of growing unrest at home, which was to culminate in October in the Revolution of 1905, the Russians were easily persuaded to agree. But Roosevelt would take no steps until Japan consented to respect the principles of the Open Door policy. This Japan did, whereupon the president invited the Japanese and the Russians to meet at Portsmouth, New Hampshire, in August. Here, among

Teddy Roosevelt, policeman of the hemisphere, wields the big stick—an image he cultivated. *(Granger Collection)*

other claims, the Japanese demanded a huge money indemnity to offset their war costs. When the Russians balked, Roosevelt warned the Japanese against pressing their demand. They accepted some small territorial grants instead, along with Russia's promise to vacate Manchuria.

The Japanese people had counted on the Russian indemnity for tax relief and did not quickly forget America's role in depriving them of it. Meanwhile, Japan's emergence as a great power increased anxiety on the West Coast about the "yellow peril." In October 1906 the San Francisco Board of Education ordered that the ninety-three Japanese children in the city be placed in a separate school. Roosevelt's anger over California's action was not lessened by his realization that he had no jurisdiction over California public schools. Only after bringing a great deal of pressure on local authorities did the president succeed in getting the action reversed. At the same time, he promised Californians that Japanese immigration would be curbed. In the Gentlemen's Agreement, a series of notes made up in 1907 and 1908, Japan promised to issue no more passports to workers seeking to emigrate to the United States.

Having pacified the Japanese, Roosevelt was anxious, as he wrote to a friend, "that they should realize that I am not afraid of them." In 1907, as a demonstration of strength, he decided to send the American fleet around the world on a practice cruise. Japan welcomed the visit of the fleet as a friendly gesture, and for a time Japanese-American relations improved. The Root-Takahira Agreement of November 1908 reflected this easing of tensions. An executive agreement, not a treaty, it bound only Roosevelt's administration and its counterpart in Japan. Both powers agreed to maintain the status quo in the Pacific area, to uphold the Open Door in China, and to support that country's "independence and integrity."

Roosevelt's Far Eastern policy was upset by his successor, William Howard Taft, and Taft's secretary of state, the corporation lawyer Philander C. Knox. They favored a policy of promoting American investment and trade abroad, a policy that became known as Dollar Diplomacy. With the full support of the State Department, Taft encouraged investments by American bankers in China and Manchuria. These included financing China's purchase of Manchurian railroads, in which Russia and Japan were interested. His effort only aroused the suspicion of Russia and Japan, driving together the two nations Roosevelt had sought to keep apart.

The Panama Canal

Having become a world power with interests in the Pacific as well as the Caribbean, the United States began to look toward the construction of a canal to link these two great waters. Back in 1850, the United States and Britain had agreed in the Clayton-Bulwer Treaty that they would enjoy equal rights in any canal. Now, the United States pressed Britain to surrender its rights. At last, in 1901, following a new policy of keeping America as a friend, Britain gave in. The Hay-Pauncefote Treaty of that year gave the United States a free hand to build, control, and fortify an Isthmian canal. The United States promised to open the canal without discrimination to the commercial and fighting ships of all nations.

Two routes were possible for this canal—one through Panama in the Republic of Colombia, the other through Nicaragua. Different companies had already been at work across each route for some time. But progress had been slow and costly, and both now wanted to unload their enterprises on the United States. In 1902, after much maneuvering and debate, the United States decided to use the Panama route. This was a triumph for the French New Panama Canal Company, which held the concession from Colombia.

By holding the alternative of a Nicaraguan canal over the heads of Colombia's negotiators, Secretary of State Hay was able to drive a hard bargain in a treaty approved by the United States Senate in March 1903. The treaty stated that $10 million cash and $250,000 annually were to be paid to Colombia for the rights to a canal zone six miles across the Isthmus. The new revolutionary government in Colombia, however, resented some of the terms. Hay responded with such threats that the Colombian Senate, to preserve its own dignity, had to reject the treaty, which it did in August 1903. A furious Roosevelt lost no time in announcing that the "black-mailers of Bogota" must not be allowed "permanently to bar one of the future highways of civilization."

To break this impasse, Roosevelt encouraged Panamanian rebels to declare their independence from Colombia and ordered a warship to the Isthmus to intimidate Colombian forces. With the "revolution" a success, Washington promptly recognized the new Republic of Panama and negotiated a treaty that gave the United States the desired strip of territory for the canal zone for $10 million and $25,000 a year. Roosevelt's behavior created many enemies for the United States throughout Latin America.

Within a decade of the Panamanian revolution, the canal was completed. On August 15, 1914, the first oceangoing steamship passed through it. In the same year, the Wilson administration tried to improve relations through a treaty apologizing for the part played by the United States in the revolution and offering Colombia a $25 million indemnity. Roosevelt's friends in the Senate objected, and the treaty was shelved. In 1921, after Roosevelt's death, the treaty minus the apology at last passed the Senate, and Colombia received its indemnity. If the Senate needed any incentive in this matter, the discovery of oil in Colombia was more than enough.

The Caribbean

The Panama Canal, by giving the United States a great new enterprise to protect, broadened American involvement in the Caribbean. The political and financial instability of the area's smaller

republics was an especially touchy problem. Almost all their public financing had been done in Europe. If any country failed to pay interest due on its bonds, its European creditor, eager for empire, might move in with the idea of staying indefinitely—as France had in Mexico in 1863. To avert this danger, Roosevelt set forth the Roosevelt Corollary to the Monroe Doctrine in a message to Congress on December 6, 1904: In the event of "flagrant cases of . . . wrongdoing or impotence" in Latin America that required outside intervention to set matters right, the United States, "however reluctantly," would undertake the necessary exercise of "international police power."

Between 1900 and 1920, United States Marines and sailors were sent into Central America and the Caribbean at least fifteen times. The first application of the Roosevelt Corollary came in 1905, when the Dominican Republic was unable to pay its debts. After an American show of force, the Dominican government had to invite the

The United States and Latin America

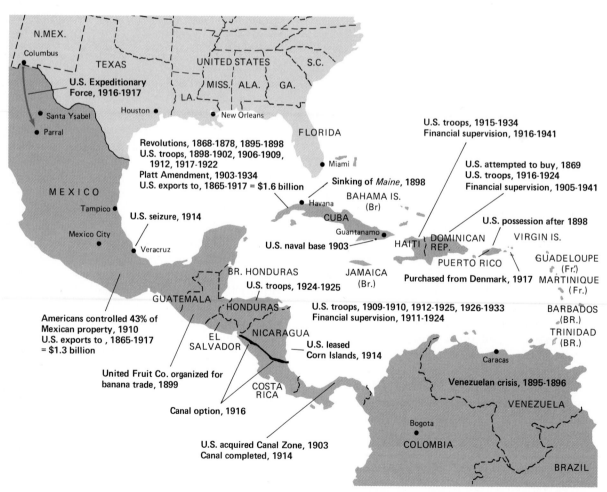

United States to step in. The Dominican foreign debt was then scaled down and transferred from European to American bankers. A percentage of customs collections was allocated to pay future interest and to reduce the principal.

Cuba drew the attention of the Roosevelt administration in 1906, when revolutionary disturbances led the United States to send troops to impose order. They were not withdrawn until 1909. In Taft's administration, Secretary of State Knox persuaded American bankers to increase their interest in the debt of Honduras and to put capital into the National Bank of the Republic of Haiti.

The most provocative case of Dollar Diplomacy took place in Nicaragua, where in 1909 the United States established a sympathetic government, forced it to transfer its public debt from European to American creditors, and persuaded American bankers to take charge of the nation's finances. Three years later, when a nationalist movement threatened to overthrow the American-backed ruler, President Taft rushed in 2700 marines to maintain the "legally constituted good government." Except for a brief withdrawal in 1925, the marines remained there until 1933.

These almost routine displays of force naturally deepened Latin American hostility toward the United States. When Woodrow Wilson succeeded Taft as president in 1913, he promised to correct matters. But Caribbean diplomacy remained essentially the same. The outbreak of the European war in 1914 made the American government even more concerned about maintaining its hemispheric dominance. American Marines entered Haiti in response to revolutionary disturbances in 1915 and stayed there until 1934. American forces also occupied the Dominican Republic again in 1916 and intervened once more in Cuba in 1917. By World War I, the United States had established virtual protectorates over the Dominican Republic, Haiti, Nicaragua, Panama, and Cuba, and President Wilson had become embroiled in a painful adventure in Mexico. In nearly all of these countries, the United States wanted to restore what it considered to be order and stability. And more often than not, United States officials found themselves locked into protecting the new regime they had put in power.

Wilson in Mexico

In May 1911 President Porfirio Díaz, dictator of Mexico since 1877, was overthrown by a revolu-tionary coalition led by the liberal idealist Francisco Madero. Unable to organize a new government rapidly enough, the revolutionaries were themselves suppressed in February 1913 by General Victoriano Huerta, who arranged Madero's assassination. Most European governments recognized the Huerta regime. American businessmen who had made large investments in Mexican industry urged Wilson to do likewise. Wilson refused on the ground that Huerta's was not a free government resting on the consent of the governed. This departure from the American policy of recognizing all governments in power gave the United States the responsibility of deciding which governments were pure and which were not.

Wilson was confident of his judgment. He promised Britain to protect its oil interests in Mexico if it would abandon Huerta, which Britain did. When Huerta's government failed to collapse, as Wilson hoped it would, he offered to help the anti-Huerta Constitutionalist forces under Venustiano Carranza. But Carranza wanted no support from Yankees, and Huerta's regime stood up. Wilson now found himself unable to redeem the pledge he had made to Mexico and to the world that he would guarantee constitutional government in that country.

On April 9, 1914, Wilson was given an excuse for direct intervention. One of Huerta's officers arrested the crew of an American vessel that had landed behind the government's lines at Tampico. Although the Americans were promptly released with expressions of regret, the commander of the American squadron demanded a more formal apology. This Huerta refused to make. Wilson took Huerta's action as an insult to the United States and asked Congress for authority to win an apology by force. Even before Congress could act, Wilson learned of a German steamer about to arrive at Vera Cruz with a load of ammunition for the Huerta government. To stop the delivery of armaments that might be used against American forces, Wilson ordered the navy to occupy the port. This action cost 126 Mexican lives. Even Carranza's Constitutionalists were so angered that they threatened war.

At this crucial point, the ABC powers—Argentina, Brazil, and Chile—offered to mediate. Wilson welcomed the chance to crawl away from his difficulties. Mediation failed, but Huerta's regime collapsed later that year anyway, unable to secure arms from the European nations, who were strengthening their own forces. Carranza took over the presidency, but quickly became embroiled in a civil war with one of his best generals,

Francisco (Pancho) Villa. Disorder spread, and in March 1915 Wilson sent General John J. Pershing across the border on a "punitive expedition" against Villa, who had repeatedly raided American territory and killed American citizens. Carranza replied to this American "invasion" by mobilizing his army. Preoccupied with the war in Europe, Wilson withdrew Pershing's forces. In March 1917, Wilson finally recognized the Carranza regime. Peace was maintained, but only after Wilson had aroused the lasting distrust of a people he meant to help.

The American policy toward Mexico, much like the policy pursued elsewhere in Latin America, suggested a tendency that would persist throughout much of the century. Whether the United States chose to use its growing power for reasons of idealism or out of self-interest, it assumed that its inherent technological and moral superiority obliged it to improve and shape the lives of other peoples. The impact of American policy in the Caribbean and Central America was to fasten upon a number of countries unpopular regimes whose survival rested largely on the military and financial support of the United States. American decision makers often defended this policy on the grounds of military security and the need to serve backward peoples whom they assumed to be incapable of governing themselves. It was the responsibility of the United States, they argued, to teach the peoples of Latin America how to maintain democratic governments and stable institutions.

The same was true of American policy toward Asia. Major General Arthur McArthur's description of his role as military governor of the Philippine Islands in 1900 and 1901 could just as easily have been used by American presidents six decades later:

We are planting in those islands imperishable ideas. We are planting the best traditions, the best characteristics of Americanism in such a way that they never can be removed from that soil. . . . It encouraged me during all my efforts in those islands, even when conditions seemed most disappointing, when the people themselves, not appreciating precisely what the remote consequences of our efforts were going to be, mistrusted us; but that fact was always before me—that going down deep into that fertile soil were the imperishable ideas of Americanism.

If that remained a tenet of American foreign policy for much of the 1900s, it was perfectly consistent with the triumph of progressivism in the first decade of the century. Many of those who became Progressives were expansionists who supported a strong navy and an aggressive foreign policy. To redeem "the waste places of the world" and the slums of American cities were expressions of the same missionary impulse. Both progressivism and imperialism recognized the need to impose order and stability on societies threatened with social upheaval.

SUMMARY

In the 1890s the United States joined the European powers in a new drive for world empire. Americans concentrated on the Caribbean, Central America, South America, the islands of the South Pacific, and the Philippines and China abroad; Canada and Mexico nearer home.

On the continent, American territory was expanded by the purchase of Alaska from Russia in 1867. The idea that Canada would someday be part of the United States persisted, keeping alive the rivalry between the United States and Britain.

In the Pacific, America looked for new markets for manufactured goods, for new sources of raw materials, and for its own system of harbors and coaling stations for its ships. In 1854 Commodore Perry had forcibly opened Japan. In the mid-1880s the United States became involved in a three-way competition for Samoa with Britain and Germany. In 1899 Samoa was finally divided between the United States and Germany. The Hawaiian Islands had been visited by traders in the 1790s and by missionaries as early as 1820, and had a large American colony by 1860. After much political turmoil, the islands were annexed by the United States in 1898.

Part of the push for expansion came from politicians and industrialists eager for world power and wealth. They were supported by the new idea that a nation needed a large and strong military establishment, and particularly a strong navy, to be a world power. But while the United States was using its resources to promote the growth of foreign trade and world power, a series of incidents in the Western Hemisphere brought talk of war and revived the Monroe Doctrine. One was a dispute with Canada over fishing rights, which was resolved by arbitration in February 1892. In 1891 there was an incident in Chile, where the United States had backed the losing side in a civil uprising. A boundary dispute between British Guiana and Venezuela was the most serious; American insistence on arbitrating the dispute brought the United States close to war with Britain.

But the combination of strong diplomacy, commercial imperialism, and missionary idealism was best shown in American actions toward Spanish-held Cuba, which resulted in war with Spain, the independence of Cuba, and the debut of the United States as a world imperial power. War became unavoidable after the sinking of the battleship *Maine* in Havana harbor early in 1898. By the end of April the war was over in the Caribbean but not in the Pacific. There the American fleet under Admiral Dewey sailed into the Philippines, which was still a Spanish possession. Like Cuba, it was in revolt and seeking independence. Hostilities were declared over on August 12. The peace treaty ensured the freedom of Cuba and gave the United States the Philippines (for $20 million), Puerto Rico, and Guam.

Now a world power, the United States naturally became involved in the competition over China, where the European powers and Japan were staking out spheres of influence. To gain entry into what everyone thought would be a rich trade, the United States proposed the Open Door policy, which was in fact a proposal that each nation take its share but not poach on the shares of others. This policy, although it created an impression of disinterested neutrality, laid the foundation for greater American influence in the affairs of China and the rest of Asia.

One of the first exercises of that influence took place after the Russo-Japanese war of 1904–1905. That conflict, which the Japanese had won, was settled by the Treaty of Portsmouth, negotiated in the United States under Theodore Roosevelt, a supporter of American expansion and power. It was during Roosevelt's presidency that the United States began to build the Panama Canal, which was opened to traffic in August 1914. But the president's heavy-handed methods in gaining the consent of the Central American nations and in discour-

---

TIME LINE

1867	United States purchases Alaska from Russia	1898–1902	Philippine insurrection
1870	Senate rejects treaty annexing Santo Domingo	1899	Senate ratifies Treaty of Paris United States and Germany divide Samoa
1871	Treaty of Washington (U.S. and Britain)	1899–1900	Open Door notes
1883–1890s	Naval construction program	1900	Boxer rebellion in China
1884	Establishment of Naval War College; Mahan presides	1901	Supreme Court's Insular cases Hay-Pauncefote Treaty (U.S. and Britain)
1887	United States acquires naval base at Pearl Harbor	1902	Platt Amendment
1889	First Pan-American Conference	1903	Panama "revolution" achieves independence
1893	Hawaiian coup by American businessmen	1904	Roosevelt Corollary
1895	Cuban revolt against Spanish rule intensifies	1904–1905	Russo-Japanese War
1895–1897	Venezuela crisis	1905–1920	United States intervenes in Dominican Republic, Nicaragua, Haiti, and Cuba
1898	Battleship *Maine* sinks in Havana harbor (February) Spanish-American War begins (April) Admiral Dewey captures Manila Bay (May) Annexation of Hawaiian Islands (July) War ends (August) Organization of Anti-Imperialist League (November) Treaty of Paris; annexation of the Philippines (December)	1906	San Francisco Board of Education segregates Asian schoolchildren
		1907	Gentleman's Agreement (U.S. and Japan)
		1908	Root-Takahira Agreement (U.S. and Japan)
		1914	Panama Canal opened
		1915	United States punitive expedition into Mexico

aging British interest in an Isthmian canal earned the United States many enemies in Latin America.

American meddling in the Caribbean after 1900 won no friends either. The Roosevelt Corollary of 1904 to the Monroe Doctrine set up the United States as the police officer for Latin America. In 1905 the United States took over the debt of the Dominican Republic to prevent a European creditor from moving in. Troops were sent to Cuba in 1906 to keep order and protect American investments. American bankers took charge of Nicaragua's finances in 1911, and the following year President Taft dispatched marines to maintain the American-backed government there. Between 1915 and 1917, the United States intervened in Haiti and again in Cuba and the Dominican Republic to maintain its interests.

Although none of this made the United States popular in the Western Hemisphere, perhaps the worst blunder was Wilson's intervention in Mexico in 1914 and 1915. The troops he sent were not withdrawn until 1917, when the United States entered the war in Europe. By that time Wilson, with the best of intentions, had succeeded in arousing the lasting distrust of the Mexicans.

The idea that the United States had a mission to improve and shape the lives of other peoples was to haunt American foreign policy throughout much of the twentieth century. That the result was usually resentment rather than gratitude never seemed to make a dent in the thinking and actions of American presidents and policy makers.

Suggested Readings

Good introductions to the formulation of American foreign policy in this and later periods are G. Kennan, *American Diplomacy 1900–1950* (1950), and R. Osgood, *Ideals and Self-Interest in American Foreign Relations* (1953). Also good are W. A. Williams, *The Tragedy of American Diplomacy* (1972 ed.), and L. C. Gardner, *Imperial America* (1976), who place greater stress on economic influences. E. S. Rosenberg, *Spreading the American Dream* (1982), examines both economic and cultural expansion from 1890 to 1945. W. LaFeber, *The New Empire: An Interpretation of American Expansion 1860–1898* (1963), is indispensable. The new expansionism is also examined in A. K. Weinberg, *Manifest Destiny* (1935); E. R. May, *Imperial Democracy: The Emergence of America as a Great Power* (1961); H. Sprout and M. Sprout, *The Rise of American Naval Power 1776–1918* (1939); and D. Healy, *U.S. Expansionism: The Imperialist Urge in the 1890s* (1970).

On John Hay, see K. J. Clymer, *John Hay: The Gentleman as Diplomat* (1975). A. T. Mahan, *The Influence of Sea Power upon History 1660–1783* (1890), exerted considerable influence on decision makers. Leading expansionists are discussed in H. K. Beale, *Theodore Roosevelt and the Rise of America to World Power* (1956); E. Morris, *The Rise of Theodore Roosevelt* (1979); and J. A. Garraty, *Henry Cabot Lodge* (1953). On Hearst, see W. A. Swanberg, *Citizen Hearst* (1961).

On the Spanish-American War, different perspectives will be found in J. W. Pratt, *Expansionists of 1898* (1936); W. A. Williams, *The Tragedy of American Diplomacy* (1956); W. Millis, *The Martial Spirit* (1931); and R. Hofstadter, "Manifest Destiny and the Philippines," in *The Paranoid Style in American Politics and Other Essays* (1958). H. F. Graff (ed.), *American Imperialism and the Philippine Insurrection* (1969), is a valuable documentary collection. The best study of the Philippine-American war is S. C. Miller,

Benevolent Assimilation: The American Conquest of the Philippines, 1899–1903 (1982). The American occupation of the Philippines is examined in S. Karnow, *In Our Image: America's Empire in the Philippines* (1989).

On the responsibilities of world power, see J. W. Pratt, *America's Colonial Experiment* (1950). The acquisition of Hawaii is examined in S. K. Stevens, *American Expansion in Hawaii 1842–1898* (1945). One approach to American policy in Latin America is to examine case studies. See, for example, D. G. Munro, *Intervention and Dollar Diplomacy in the Caribbean 1900–1921* (1964) and *The United States and the Caribbean 1921–1933* (1975); D. F. Healy, *The United States in Cuba 1898–1902* (1963); A. R. Millett, *The Politics of Intervention: The Military Occupation of Cuba 1906–1909* (1968); H. Thomas, *Cuba* (1971); and H. Schmidt, *The United States Occupation of Haiti, 1915–1934* (1971). More general works focusing on United States policy in the Caribbean and Central America are W. LaFeber, *Inevitable Revolutions* (1983), and L. D. Langley, *The United States and the Caribbean, 1900–1970* (1980) and *The Banana Wars: An Inner History of American Empire, 1900–1934* (1983). On the Panama Canal, see W. LaFeber, *The Panama Canal: The Crisis in Historical Perspective* (1978). On United States policy toward Mexico, consult D. F. Smith, *The United States and Revolutionary Nationalism in Mexico 1916–1932* (1972), and P. E. Haley, *Revolution and Intervention: The Diplomacy of Taft and Wilson in Mexico 1910–1917* (1970). On American policy in the Far East, see A. Iriye, *Across the Pacific: An Inner History of American–East Asian Relations* (1969) and *Pacific Estrangement: Japanese and American Expansion 1897–1911* (1972); M. B. Young, *The Rhetoric of Empire: America's China Policy 1895–1901* (1968); P. A. Varg, *The Making of a Myth: The United States and China 1897–1912* (1968); and J. Israel, *Progressivism and the Open Door: America and China 1905–1921* (1971). On the changing relations with Britain, see B. Perkins, *The Great Rapprochement: England and the United States 1895–1914* (1968).

On the anti-imperialist movement, see E. B. Tompkins, *Anti-Imperialism in the United States: The Great Debate, 1890–1920* (1970), and R. L. Beisner, *Twelve against Empire: The Anti-Imperialists 1898–1900* (1968). For a bitter indictment of American policy overseas, see "To the Person Sitting in Darkness," in Janet Smith (ed.), *Mark Twain on the Damned Human Race* (1962). Of comparable interest is W. B. Gatewood, Jr. (ed.), *"Smoked Yankees" and the Struggle for Empire: Letters from Negro Soldiers 1898–1902* (1971) and *Black Americans and the White Man's Burden, 1898–1903* (1975).

CHAPTER 25

PEOPLE AND POLITICS: THE PROGRESSIVE ERA

The United States entered the twentieth century in a self-congratulatory frame of mind. It had become the world's richest and most productive economic power, its national wealth nearly doubling between 1890 and 1900. It had achieved phenomenal success in the application of modern mass-production methods, and it had no rival as an exporter of foodstuffs and as a producer of coal, iron, and steel. If there were people who doubted the extent of American ingenuity and technological progress, they had only to consider developments such as electric lighting, wireless transmitters, trolleys, phonograph recordings, X rays, and automobiles—new wonders that would profoundly transform American lives in the next several decades. The United States had just emerged from a popular war with Spain, and the American flag had been planted in the Philippines, Hawaii, and Puerto Rico. The prosperity promised by the Republican party was apparently at hand—it was sufficiently impressive, at least, to turn the heads of commercial farmers from notions of free

George Wesley Bellows, *Cliff Dwellers,* 1913. Los Angeles County Museum of Art, Los Angeles County Funds.

silver and third parties to account books, business organization, and pressure politics. The labor wars of Homestead and Pullman were all but forgotten, and the "labor agitator" appeared to be an endangered species. Once a symbol of sectional strife, the black American had become a symbol of national reconciliation on the basis of white supremacy, which was enforced in the South by both legislation and terrorism.

The mood of national unity, optimism, and self-confidence was personified in the president of the United States, William McKinley. His very face and demeanor suggested a confident nation. "I can no longer be called the President of a party," he proclaimed in 1900. "I am now the President of the whole people." Few Americans would have disputed that claim. He was surely the most popular president since Abraham Lincoln. The new vice-president, Theodore Roosevelt, reconciled himself to four years as "a dignified nonentity." But Leon Czolgosz, a self-professed anarchist, decided otherwise. On September 6, 1901, he shot and mortally wounded the president. "It is God's way," McKinley murmured. "His will, not ours, be done." It was an ominous note on which to usher in the new century.

The assassination underscored a contradictory mood in the country. Even as Americans celebrated their triumphs, many were uneasy about the state of the Union. Despite the signs of equanimity and the apparent prosperity, there was, in fact, good reason to be concerned about the health, the moral integrity, and the destiny of the American republic. The danger was sufficiently obvious: a growing fragmentation of American society, made urgent by an accelerated and unregulated industrialization and urbanization. The United States was the world's wealthiest society, but its riches were unevenly distributed, with one percent of the population owning over 40 percent of the gross national wealth. The scale and speed of change had produced problems of unprecedented magnitude: monopolies and corporations had made a mockery of free competition and choked off economic opportunity, the cities were unmanageable and unlivable, public education was producing inferior students. Yet, Americans remained confident that their society was sufficiently durable, flexible, and liberal to handle any social crisis. What emerged in the early years of the twentieth century was a movement of reform designed to impose stability on a society thought to be threatened with fragmentation and social upheaval.

THE PROGRESSIVE SPIRIT

Although the Progressive Era is generally understood to mean the years between 1900 and World War I, progressivism itself was rooted in the concern with government and business abuses that emerged in the post–Civil War decades, and its influence remained apparent as late as the New Deal of the 1930s. But its most intensive period of growth and expression was clearly the first two decades of the twentieth century. It seemed an ideal time for Americans, newly prosperous and buoyantly optimistic about the future, to measure the damage done to their society by the rapid growth of industries and cities. Prosperity had a way of making that damage more obvious by forcing middle-class families to compare their comforts and advantages with those trying to survive below the subsistence level.

Progressive reformers looked for ways to make American society a more decent place in which to live. Within two decades, progressivism had touched nearly every aspect of American life: the structure of city government and the conduct of corporations and trade unions, the education of children and the interpretation of laws, the conservation of natural resources and the socialization of immigrants, the status of women and the labor of children, the quality of food and the content of magazines. Where progressivism did *not* touch peoples' lives was also significant: discrimination against black Americans was relatively unaffected, as were the poverty of tenant farmers and migrant workers and the conditions of labor of most unorganized workers. And Progressive efforts to reform humankind included some odd and contradictory policies: restricting the consumption of alcoholic beverages, limiting the numbers of immigrants, and intervening in the political affairs of peoples in other parts of the world.

Progressives and their concerns varied widely, and so did the innovativeness both of Progressive thinking and of the application of the movement's ideas. But despite their differences, Progressives remained optimistic. National confidence, reinforced by international triumphs and an upswing in the economy, appeared to put nothing beyond the reach of good will. And Progressive reformers expected to tap that good will for the benefit of all classes. The United States, although flawed in places, remained in their estimation a model to inspire the world. To improve the society and its institutions, in fact, was to make them all the more exportable.

The Reform Commitment

The men and women who assumed leadership of the Progressive movement emerged largely from the urban Protestant middle class at a time when the nation more than ever before seemed divided along class lines. The conflict between capital and labor, the changes in the sources of immigration, the squalor of the slums, the corruption of politics, the assassination of three presidents between 1865 and 1901—all had deeply impressed the Progressives in their childhood and adolescent years. Nor had they been blind to the Populist issues of the 1890s or the appeal of socialism in the early twentieth century. The Socialist party reached new sections of the country, and by 1912, 1200 Socialists held public office in 340 cities, including 79 mayors in 24 states, 160 city councilmen, and 145 aldermen. Eugene Debs, the Socialist presidential candidate, increased his vote from 94,000 in 1900 to 900,000 (or 6 percent of the electorate) in 1912. An alarmed Theodore Roosevelt confided to a friend in 1905 "that the growth of the Socialist party in this country [was] far more ominous than any populist or similar movement in the past."

If most Progressives could agree on the need to counter the Socialist challenge by eliminating abuses, they were less agreed on which were the worst abuses and how best to get rid of them. Progressivism was a coalition of many different movements, containing men and women with different degrees of commitment to reform and different priorities. Businessmen might become Progressives to prevent popular displeasure from being channeled in more radical directions. Crusaders for good government thought their cause was critical to progressivism, if only because reform depended on success in making government more responsive and more efficient. Women Progressives seeking to eliminate bias based on sex expanded their struggle to include those who were also oppressed by poverty and the conditions of their employment. They brought to the movement new attitudes toward poverty and a commitment, shown most vividly by the settlement house workers, to reach the people most affected by it. Protestant clerics who joined the movement did so in the spirit of the social gospel, convinced that to save humankind, they must save society first. Many journalists came to progressivism as a result of investigations they had conducted into abuses in almost every phase of American life. Some of the politicians who responded to the exposés with legislation also claimed to be Progressives.

Most Progressives shared a commitment to restore opportunities for the common person, broaden income distribution, rescue the poor, clean up politics, and strengthen the state. Some put strengthening the state first as the best way to deal with the question of social responsibility. The New Nationalism propounded by the Progressive theorist Herbert Croly in his influential book *The Promise of American Life* (1909) set much of the tone of the period. To free Americans from "the energetic and selfish individualism" that had dominated the recent past, Croly argued, the federal government would have to assume major responsibility. What he advocated was a strong, forward-looking state that used professional expertise and social planning.

If progressivism often seemed elitist, it was because it reflected the conviction that the "best men" should govern—those who had the necessary courage and insight to lead the way. Supported by the work of Frederick Winslow Taylor, whose influential *Principles of Scientific Management* appeared in 1911, many Progressives looked to "social engineering" by a trained elite to administer the "means" of government, even if the people determined the "ends."

Taylor had applied his theories only to the factories. Elitist Progressives—the first generation to become aware of the force of technology in amassing power as well as creating wealth—wanted to extend "scientific management" to society as a whole. In this way they hoped to bring both of their primary targets, the economically wasteful wealthy and the politically warped poor, under beneficial control.

Although progressivism was a departure in attitudes and practices, it did not result in any far-reaching redistribution of wealth or power. It aimed largely at corrective legislation and the arousal of the public's conscience, not at the reorganization of society. It sought to reduce conflict and minimize abuses. It showed the ability of American society to absorb economic reforms that in no real way altered the capitalist structure or threatened corporate dominance. That feature in itself made progressivism an attractive movement to some parts of the business community.

Business and Reform

Although most businessmen defended the status quo as actively as they battled the organization of their workers, an impressive number were touched by the Progressive spirit. To some of them, progressivism was a safe and practical way to satisfy the popular demand for reform. Whether motivated by social consciousness or political need, men such as E. A. Filene, the Boston department store merchant, and Joseph Fels, the soap manufacturer, supported reform movements. William Kent, a Chicago real estate operator and cattle-feed producer, became president of the Municipal Voters League and a member of the Illinois Civil Service League. Oil millionaire Samuel M. Jones and streetcar tycoon Tom L. Johnson

Lincoln Steffens (left), muckraking journalist: "If it was privilege that caused what we called evil, it was privilege that had to be dealt with, not men. . . . To shift our votes from one to another of the two political parties, both of which are organized to serve the privileged or the privilege-seekers, was folly." *(Brown Brothers)*   Ida Tarbell (center), whose exposure of the Standard Oil Company earned her the reputation of a muckraker—much to her discomfort: "My conscience began to trouble me. Was it not as much my business as a reporter to present this [favorable] side of the picture as to present the other? . . . The public was coming to believe . . . that the only hope was in destroying the system." *(Library of Congress)*   Upton Sinclair (right), Socialist journalist whose exposure of conditions in the meat-packing plants caused a public uproar and led to demands for reform: "I realized with bitterness that I had been made a celebrity, not because the public cared anything about the workers, but simply because the public did not want to eat tubercular meat." *(Culver Pictures, Inc.)*

emerged as model reform mayors of Toledo and Cleveland, respectively.

Some businessmen supported progressivism because they had something to gain from particular programs. As in the 1880s, many small merchants and shippers, at a disadvantage because railroads favored powerful interests, continued to seek stronger regulation. Some railroad leaders endorsed antirebating and similar federal measures in an effort to keep favor seekers off their backs. Life insurance companies welcomed federal regulation as an alternative to more radical state controls and taxes. Wall Street, small-town, and midwestern bankers could agree that a conservative plan for financial reorganization would be preferable to demands by some Progressives for public control of banking. In the new public utilities that supplied services to the cities, executives sometimes asked for government regulation to avoid municipal ownership.

The effectiveness of business groups in exploiting the reform spirit of the Progressive Era to protect and consolidate their economic gains has been called "the triumph of conservatism." Federal regulation of industry, for example, came partly in response to the demands of businessmen, who not only helped write the legislation but made certain that the regulatory commissions would be staffed with people favorable to their interests. The effect of many of these reforms was to stabilize the industries without making competition any freer, and at the same time to appease the public clamor for reform.

The Muckrakers

To Progressives, disclosure of social and political evils was critical to the success of their efforts. If only the facts were known, the people would demand action. The new muckraking magazines and books supplied the facts in abundance. They exposed malpractices everywhere: in city, state, and national government; corporations; the medical profession; patent medicines; life insurance; the police; the preparation of food products; the banks. It was Theodore Roosevelt who pinned the label *muckrakers* on the young journalists who were exposing the worst aspects of American society. "In Bunyan's *Pilgrim's Progress,*" he said, "you may recall the description of . . . the man who . . . was offered the celestial crown for his muckrake . . . but continued to rake the filth on the floor." Roosevelt agreed that many of the revelations were true, but argued that their effect was simply to make discontent worse. He felt his own Square Deal and other programs could satisfy the clamor for reform. Muckrakers argued that

NATIONAL HOUSECLEANING

The muckraking magazines attracted the attention of Finley Peter Dunne's satirical character Mr. Dooley, the Irish saloonkeeper, and Mr. Hennessy, his steady customer. Despite the uproar created by the muckraking revelations, Mr. Dooley doubted there would be a social upheaval.

"It looks to me," said Mr. Hennessy, "as though this country was goin' to th' divvle."

"Put down that magazine," said Mr. Dooley. "Now d'ye feel betther? I thought so. But I can sympathize with ye. I've been readin' thim mesilf. Time was whin I sildom throubled thim. . . . But now whin I pick me fav'rite magazine off th' flure, what do I find? Ivrything has gone wrong. . . . Graft ivrywhere. 'Graft in th' Insurance Comp'nies,' 'Graft in Congress,' 'Graft in th' Supreem Coort,' 'Graft be an Old Grafter,' 'Graft in Lithrachoor,' be Hinnery James. . . . An' so it goes, Hinnissy, till I'm that blue, discouraged an' broken-hearted I cud go to th'

edge iv th' wurruld an' jump off. It's a wicked, wicked, horrible place, an' this here counthry is about th' toughest spot in it. Is there an honest man among us? If there is throw him out. He's a spy. Is there an institution that isn't corrupt to its very foundations? Don't ye believe it. It on'y looks that way because our graft iditor hasn't got there on his rounds yet. . . ."

"Do I think it's all as bad as that? Well, Hinnissy, . . . I've got to tell ye that this counthry, while wan iv th' worst in th' wurruld, is about as good as th' next if it ain't a shade betther. But we're wan iv th' greatest people in th' wurruld to clean house. . . . An' there ye ar-re Hinnissy. Th' noise ye hear is not th' first gun iv a rivolution. It's on'y th' people iv th' United States batin' a carpet. . . ."

Source: Louis Filler, (ed.), *The World of Mr. Dooley* (New York: Crowell-Collier Press, 1962), p. 148.

the American people would not fight for reform until they had been stirred up.

For many years, reporters had written stories of the kind that made the muckrakers famous. What was new after the turn of the century were the popular magazines, heavily illustrated and selling for as little as ten cents, that provided research funds and nationwide audiences. Even such conservative magazines as the *Ladies' Home Journal* and the *Saturday Evening Post* were forced to publish muckraking articles in order to compete with *McClure's, Cosmopolitan, Everybody's, Arena,* and *Hampton's,* all offering outlets to writers and journalists exposing the shortcomings of American society. Between 1903 and 1906, *McClure's* circulation rose from 370,000 to more than 750,000; *Hampton's,* from 13,000 to 440,000.

Perhaps the muckrakers' most sensational accomplishment was Lincoln Steffens's series on corruption in the cities. Ida Tarbell's almost equally popular exposé of Standard Oil retold the story of the methods by which that huge combine had been built. Charles Edward Russell threw a searching light on the beef trust. Thomas Lawson, a reformed speculator, exposed Amalgamated Copper. Novelist David Graham Phillips wrote for *Cosmopolitan* a lively series of articles called "The Treason of the Senate," exposing that body as a millionaire's club acting for special interests.

Muckrakers offered the public sensational disclosures rather than solutions to the abuses they described. Few had any real quarrel with the basic economic institutions, only with the way some people abused them. "We muckraked," Ray Stannard Baker recalled, "not because we hated our world, but because we loved it. We were not hopeless, we were not cynical, we were not bitter."

Although a Socialist rather than a muckraker, Upton Sinclair wrote the most devastating exposé of the era in his novel *The Jungle* (1906). Having lived among meat-packing workers in Chicago during their 1904 strike, Sinclair described working conditions in the stockyards, corruption in politics and society, and the day-to-day lives of the lower-class victims. But neither his call for Socialist revolution nor his treatment of the working class affected the public nearly as much as the graphic account of how meat was handled and packaged before it reaches the stores:

There would be meat that had tumbled out on the floor, in the dirt and sawdust, where the workers had tramped and spit uncounted billions of consumption germs. There would be meat stored in great piles in rooms; and the water from leaky roofs would drip over it, and thousands of rats would race about on it. It was too dark in these storage places to see well, but a man could run his hand over these piles of meat and sweep off handfuls of the dried dung of rats. These rats were nuisances, and the packers would put poisoned bread out for them, they would die, and then rats, bread, and meat would go into the hoppers together.

The book prompted several investigations of the meat-packing industry (which essentially confirmed Sinclair's findings), and led to the passage of the Meat Inspection Act and the Pure Food and Drug Act. To a bitter Upton Sinclair, who had aimed at the hearts rather than the stomachs of Americans, the people had ignored the real theme and message of his book: "I had not been nearly so interested in the condemned meat as in something else, the inferno of exploitation."

PROGRESSIVISM IN POLITICS

If the revelations of the muckrakers were to be translated into action, Progressive reformers needed to detach government at all levels from the special interests and make it more responsive to the public. Until that had been done, they could not, for example, expect to improve living conditions for slum dwellers, eliminate child labor, regulate the working hours and conditions of women workers, and enforce safety regulations in factories.

The sheer complexity of economic and political life in the early twentieth century often frustrated reform efforts. For example, small businesses had difficulty meeting the new standards established by the Meat Inspection Act and the Pure Food and Drug Act. Control of the industry was thus concentrated in the hands of fewer meat-packers and drug companies. Attempts to eradicate "boss" and machine rule in the cities required Progressives to compromise between greater political participation and efficiency in government. Social reformers could expect resistance in the legislative bodies, which modified their proposals, and in the courts, which often weakened their legislative achievements. But the reformers persisted. If frustrated on a day-to-day basis, they remained confident of ultimate victory. And the new attitudes and policies they introduced eventually worked themselves into the political bloodstream and became permanent features of American government.

City Politics

By the turn of the century, municipal reform efforts had been going on for almost fifty years. The problems of corruption, inefficiency, and special privilege seemed worst on the local level, and so the cities were among the first objects of Progressive attack. The records of mayors such as Samuel M. Jones of Toledo and Tom L. Johnson of Cleveland showed how much could be accom-plished simply by the time-honored practice of throwing the rascals out.

While Johnson was making a fortune in street railways in Indianapolis, Detroit, and Cleveland, he saw the effects of bossism at first hand. Elected mayor of Cleveland in 1901, he won reelection three times and served until 1909. To Johnson, democracy meant public involvement. In order to interest the electorate in its own welfare, he held public meetings in a huge circus tent. And Johnson persuaded good men to work in city government. Lincoln Steffens, the best-informed and severest critic of American city life, called Johnson the "best mayor of the best-governed city in the United States."

In neighboring Toledo, Samuel M. (Golden Rule) Jones ruled from 1899 until his death in 1904. He went beyond reform to the reorganization of society on a "collective" basis, to the establishment of the "Cooperative Commonwealth, the Kingdom of Heaven on Earth." He opened free kindergartens, free playgrounds, and free golf courses, and he organized free concerts. One of his major concerns became police work, so central to the problems of the poor. He substituted light canes for the heavy clubs carried by patrolmen and stopped the system of arrests on suspicion and the jailing of people without charging them. His enemies attacked him for his "laxity" in law enforcement. When they persuaded the state legislature in 1902 to create a police commission appointed by the governor to administer the Toledo police department, Jones fought and won in the Ohio Supreme Court.

Many Progressives were reluctant to depend on the chance availability of good and energetic men such as Johnson and Jones. They wanted institutional safeguards as well. This meant changing the structure of municipal government, removing it from state control through "home-rule" charters, and creating a permanent professional staff to run the city on a nonpartisan basis.

It took a hurricane and tidal wave in Galveston, Texas, in 1900 to point a way. The politicians who made up the Galveston City Council so botched the administration of relief and reconstruction that the state appointed a five-man commission of experts in 1901 to replace them. This commission did so well in rebuilding the city, restoring its credit, and rehabilitating its services that it was kept on to run the city.

Progressives elsewhere soon adopted the Galveston system. By 1914, over four hundred American cities, most of them small or middle-sized, were using the commission form of government. By then, however, the administrative experts had proved themselves less than expert in politics. And the contradiction between the Progressive objectives of greater democracy and citizen participation on the one hand and nonpartisan professional experts on the other could no longer be ignored. By 1914 most city commissioners were required to run for office.

More changes in the direction of greater democracy followed another natural disaster, this one a flood in Dayton, Ohio, in 1913. There, political authority was vested in a small body of elected commissioners who in turn appointed a professionally qualified city manager to run the city departments. By 1923 more than three hundred cities had adopted this system.

Through such reforms, the Progressives claimed to have democratized city government. But the evidence might also suggest the contrary. What they had introduced into municipal government was expert management based in part on corporate models. With decision making centralized in a city manager, commission, or professional staff, city government became more efficient—but not necessarily more responsive. The urban poor, at least, seemed to have enjoyed more influence in city affairs under the "boss" than under the efficiency expert.

The State Governments

No less entrenched than the local bosses were the powerful state machines. Legally, cities are creatures of the states, operating under charters or other limited grants of power from state legislatures. Therefore, to prevent municipal reforms from being undone by the legislative allies of city bosses, urban Progressives extended their attack to the state machines and the business interests they served.

Perhaps the innovation they expected to be most beneficial was the *direct primary*. Reformers hoped that this device, which left the choice of candidates to the people rather than to the party machines, would ensure the selection of abler and more independent officeholders. By 1916 some form of direct primary had been adopted by every state except Rhode Island, Connecticut, and New Mexico. Several states also adopted the *initiative,* a reform that permitted the public to propose legislation, and the *referendum,* which enabled voters to approve or reject measures passed by the legislature.

The *recall* of public officers by popular vote—a means of getting rid of officials before their terms expired—was another reform that received wide support. The thought of exposing the judiciary to the popular will frightened conservatives. But many judges were in low repute for having invalidated social legislation. Seven states, all west of the Mississippi, actually passed laws providing for their recall. Nowhere, however, were these laws used.

The Constitution provided for the election of United States senators by the state legislatures. Since these bodies might be controlled by party machines or by private interests, one of the reforms most in demand by Progressives was direct election of senators by the people. The Seventeenth Amendment, passed by Congress in 1912 and ratified in May 1913, provided for this change.

Although the reformers succeeded in translating many of their political reforms into law, the results often disappointed them. Party bosses quickly found ways to control the primaries. The initiative and referendum often misfired, permitting special interests to saddle the public with their pet projects. Recall was used only rarely.

All too often, outbursts of reform lasted only a short time, rising or falling with the enthusiasm of one outstanding leader. The professional, full-time bosses usually outlasted the amateurs; they became somewhat more careful, perhaps, but they were still powerful. For their part, the reformers held that their occasional victories might at least prevent the machines from doing greater harm.

Progressives attacked not only corrupt state machines but also business interests. Particular targets were the railroads and other public utilities, which relied heavily on government grants of power and political privilege. Wisconsin, where Robert M. La Follette was elected governor in 1900, provided a model for what could be done. La Follette's first step was to replace his party's strong state machine with a Progressive machine of his own. With expert advice from his "brain trust," he proceeded to please his farm constituents by establishing an effective railroad commission. Within a few years, this commission had brought other utilities under its umbrella.

La Follette later agreed that he had not intended to "go after" the corporations. The point of his reforms, he explained, had not been to destroy the corporations, but to curb their political power and to subject them to the same laws that governed other "persons." One of his most useful measures was taxing railroad property like all

A young millworker in Fiskeville, Rhode Island, 1909. Child labor was a target of Progressive reformers. *(Lewis W. Hine, Library of Congress)*

other property. La Follette's career as a reformer in Wisconsin carried him to the United States Senate in 1906 and almost to the Progressive presidential candidacy in 1912.

Social Legislation

Much of the credit for achievements in social legislation belongs to Progressive women. Like Progressive groups in other fields, they based their campaigns on solid study and research, wide publicity, and the use of trained lobbyists in state capitals and Washington. Between 1902 and 1914, under the leadership of the National Child Labor Committee, new child-labor laws or amendments to old ones were adopted in nearly every state. Most of these prohibited the employment of young children (often defined as children under fourteen), at least for factory work. Enforcement was made simpler in many states by laws requiring school attendance until the minimum working age. Other measures prohibited the employment of minors at night and in dangerous occupations.

In 1916 Congress passed the Keating-Owen Act, which prohibited the shipment across state lines of goods made in factories, mines, or quarries that employed children under a specific age. Two years later, in *Hammer v. Dagenhart,* the Supreme Court declared this act unconstitutional on the grounds that it invaded the police powers of the states and attempted to use federal control of interstate commerce to attain noncommercial ends. But the state laws survived.

Until 1908 the courts, while permitting the states to regulate child labor as part of their police power, found that control over the working conditions of women infringed upon their freedom of contract. Then, in 1908, in *Muller v. Oregon,* the United States Supreme Court reversed this position and upheld Oregon's ten-hour law for women. This was another triumph for Progressive research, which was reflected in the 112-page brief submitted by Louis D. Brandeis for the state. Brandeis offered the Court a mere 2 pages of the usual argument buttressed by "authorities." The rest of his brief consisted of historical, sociological, economic, and medical facts providing "some fair ground, reasonable in and of itself," on which the Court might find excessively long hours of work for women injurious enough to "the public health, safety, or welfare" to justify limitations. Brandeis's social "facts" swayed even the most conservative justices. In the decision, which Progressives welcomed, the Court found labor legislation necessary for women because a woman's health "becomes an object of public interest and care in order to preserve the strength and vigor of the race." The effect, however, was less than some Progressives anticipated. Women found themselves excluded from occupations requiring long hours and confined largely to the same menial jobs they had traditionally held.

Insurance covering industrial accidents was another Progressive objective. Under traditional common-law rulings, the burden of all the hazards of industrial labor was on the worker and his or her family. To collect compensation for disabling injuries or death on the job, dependents had to go to court—a long and costly undertaking—and prove that the victim had not willingly assumed the risks of the work, that neither the victim nor any other worker had contributed to negligence that may have caused the accident, and that the employer was solely to blame. Under Progressive pressure, states began to adopt public accident-insurance plans after 1909. By 1920 all but five states had taken such action.

The Progressives also succeeded in establishing a certain amount of public responsibility for the support of children and old people. States had always provided public almshouses, but only occasionally did they offer relief at home. By 1911 state legislatures had begun to accept the idea that it was far better, where possible, to assist dependent children in their own homes than to place them in institutions. By 1913 eight states, and by 1930 all but four, had adopted acts granting financial aid to working mothers. Such acts helped widows with dependent children, as well as families left destitute by divorce, desertion, or incapacity of the breadwinner. In 1914, states began to provide home relief for the aged poor. Urged on by the American Association for Old Age Security, thirteen states passed measures for this purpose during the 1920s. In most cases, persons sixty-five and over became eligible for pensions as high as thirty dollars a month.

Progressive social legislation, especially legislation covering working conditions, was soon challenged, especially by those who would have to foot the bill and who were otherwise affected by bureaucratic interference. After 1900, employer associations, some of them established years earlier to combat unionization, turned their attention to politics. The National Association of Manufacturers, founded in 1895, helped coordinate their activities.

The resistance of business interests to social legislation, and the effectiveness of the propaganda and pressure politics used by those interests, contributed to the decline of progressivism in the states. To satisfy the voters, legislators often found they had no alternative but to enact reform measures. But they did not have to provide funds and machinery for enforcement.

Despite the reforms, the United States continued to lag behind many European countries in providing social benefits for its people. The movement to establish a social security program failed, as did efforts to institute national health care and unemployment compensation. The majority of the poor still had to depend upon the limited funds of private charities and on woefully inadequate poor laws. Finally, the consequences of widespread rural poverty and racism remained relatively unexplored, even by Progressive reformers.

The Progressive faith in legislation was often doomed to bitter disappointment and frustration. Perhaps that explains why Progressives such as Lincoln Steffens eventually turned to socialism. "To shift our votes from one to another of two political parties, both of which are organized to serve the privileged or the privilege-seekers," Steffens concluded, "was folly. To throw out the rascals and put into office honest men without removing that which makes good men do bad things was as irrational as our experience had taught us it was 'unpractical.'" As a muckraker, Steffens had traced evils in government to "the system." The Socialists persuaded him that "the system" embraced the entire society.

Prohibition

The reform impulse scored one of its greatest yet most questionable successes in the Prohibition amendment, the end of more than half a century of agitation to control the production and sale of alcoholic beverages. Much of the strength of the movement to abolish drinking lay in the rural, fundamentalist South and Midwest. It encountered the heaviest resistance among immigrants and Catholics in the urban centers. But it was never entirely a struggle between urban and rural America, nor did it necessarily pit liberals against conservatives. In the Progressive Era it gained urban support, particularly among middle-class women reformers who saw alcohol as a social disease. Its effects on the poor convinced them that it was worth abridging personal freedom in order to improve the quality of human life.

Although women played a leading role in the movement, few of them displayed the aggressiveness that brought such fame to Carry A. Nation of Kansas. Her first husband had died of alcoholism just six months after their marriage in 1867. In 1890 the "wets" of Kansas, encouraged by a favorable Supreme Court decision, opened a strong assault on their state's "dry" laws. Nation organized a branch of the Women's Christian Temperance Union there, but she had as little success with persuasion as the WCTU had elsewhere. So, armed with rocks and brickbats, she embarked on a personal vendetta. Although her crusade was directed against alcohol in general, she singled out the "joints" that dispensed it. Her favorite weapon was her famous hatchet, which she used to smash saloon windows, furniture, fixtures, and supplies in many Kansas towns. "Men!" she would declare to the startled customers. "I have come to save you from a drunkard's grave!" In 1900 she turned to the cities, wielding her weapon to such effect that she was arrested some thirty-nine times, usually for "disturbing the peace."

With the formation of the Anti-Saloon League in 1893, the "drys" at last built up an agency strong enough to combat the saloon and distiller interests and the machine politicians associated with them. The Progressive assault on the machines encouraged the temperance advocates to feel their hour had also come. Anti-Saloon League lobbyists kept the pressure on both major parties, and after 1907 state after state in the West and South fell into the "dry" ranks.

The league's first national success came in March 1913, when Congress passed the Webb-

Kenyon Act over President Taft's veto. This act prohibited the shipment of intoxicating liquors into any state, territory, or district where they were intended to be used in violation of local laws. The "drys" introduced a Prohibition amendment in Congress in December 1913. Four years later, when wartime conditions brought resentment against German brewers and a need for the materials used in distilling, Congress passed the Eighteenth Amendment. It went into effect in January 1920. But to the reformers who had expected so much of this amendment, the results proved to be disappointing (see Chapter 27).

PROGRESSIVISM AND THE PARTIES

To Progressive reformers, who looked more and more to the national government to realize many of their objectives, the president had to be a person who shared their principles. That included a commitment to government as a tool of social and economic change. The first three presidents to serve a full term in the twentieth century—Roosevelt, Taft, and Wilson—all shared that commitment. The differences among them pointed up some of the differences in the movement itself.

The Republicans: Roosevelt

If anyone personified progressivism, it was Theodore Roosevelt. He was a master politician; he knew how to respond to and manipulate public sentiment; and he had a dramatic flair long missing from the presidency. His identification with the outdoors, his relentless pursuit of the "strenuous life," his exploits in the Spanish-American War, and his colorful style excited the public.

To conservatives and liberals alike, Roosevelt was a paradox. Although he came to symbolize Progressive reform, he was often a reluctant reformer. He made no effort to hide his dislike for the men and women who made up the radical and labor movements of his time. But like many Progressives, he saw the need to confront social and industrial abuses and to adopt reforms that would satisfy public fears and demands. As he once told a group of business leaders, he wanted to see "radicalism prosper under conservative leadership" in such a manner "that the progres-

Theodore Roosevelt. *(Brown Brothers)*

sive people will not part company with the bulk of the moderates."

A Republican by family tradition, an aristocrat by temperament, Roosevelt had once flirted with Mugwumpery. His love of power as well as his common touch, however, kept him "regular" enough for McKinley to appoint him assistant secretary of the navy just before the Spanish-American War. His Rough Rider feats added to his popularity, and in the fall of 1898 he was elected governor of New York with full party support.

He soon showed himself so independent of the Republican machine, however, that state party boss Tom Platt determined to bury Roosevelt in the vice-presidency. In the election of 1900. This strategy worked, to the dismay of Mark Hanna. "Don't you realize," he cried, "that there's only one life between this madman and the White House?" In September 1901, when an assassin shot McKinley, that "one life" was removed from Roosevelt's path.

Roosevelt and Big Business

Not since the days of Andrew Jackson had the White House been occupied by a president so devoted to the expansion of the role of chief executive. But where Jackson used his position to strengthen states' rights, Roosevelt used the presidency to build federal power. In confronting private power, however, Roosevelt was always cautious. His attack on the trusts was a case in point. Despite his speeches, Roosevelt aimed not at breaking up the trusts, but at satisfying public concern about corporate power. On March 10, 1902, he ordered Attorney General Philander C. Knox to bring suit under the Sherman Anti-Trust Act to dissolve the Northern Securities Company. This was the company created by the country's greatest bankers to combine the holdings of the country's greatest railroad barons.

So stunning was Roosevelt's attack that J. P. Morgan himself went to Washington to find out what the president had in mind. Two years later, the Supreme Court by a five-to-four vote gave its verdict: the Northern Securities Company must be broken up. The company's directors gained their consolidation goals by other means, but this did not hurt the president's reputation or his self-image. The decision, he said, was "one of the great achievements of my administration. The most powerful men in this country were held to accountability before the law."

The *Northern Securities* verdict was followed in 1905 by *Swift & Company* v. *United States.* In this case the Court broke up the beef trust, reversing its decision of ten years before in *U.S.* v. *E. C. Knight Company,* in which it had disallowed the application of the Sherman Act to manufacturing enterprises. The beef-trust prosecution was one of the earliest results of Roosevelt's success in getting Congress, in 1903, to establish a Bureau of Corporations in the new Department of Commerce and Labor. In keeping with the Progressive belief in publicity as a deterrent to antisocial action, this bureau was authorized to investigate and disclose the affairs of interstate corporations.

The beef-trust suit had been started on the basis of the bureau's information. Its success led to the prosecutions of such "evil" combinations as the oil trust and the tobacco trust. Despite these actions, the wave of consolidations continued, corporate power remained as strong as ever, the same men remained in control, and competition became no freer. The president had simply given notice that *unfair* combinations would be held accountable for their actions. He wanted to make clear to the American public that the government stood ready if necessary to exert its authority over big capital.

Roosevelt also made it clear that big labor was no different from big business. In October 1902, workers in the Pennsylvania anthracite pits had been on strike for months because of conditions in the mines and in the company-owned mining towns. The operators, led by George F. Baer, the Morgan-appointed head of the Reading Railroad, remained unwilling to listen to the complaints. At one stage in the strike, Baer made absolutely clear the divine right of the class he represented: "The rights and interests of the laboring man will be cared for, not by the union agitators, but by the Christian men to whom God in His infinite wisdom has given control of the property interests of the country." With winter coming and coal bins empty, coal riots broke out in northern cities.

When Roosevelt demanded that the strike be arbitrated, the operators refused until the workers went back to the pits. John Mitchell of the United Mine Workers voiced the workers' determination to stay out until their demands were met. Finally, Morgan and Roosevelt were able to agree on an arbitration commission satisfactory also to Mitchell. The resulting settlement awarded the mine workers a nine-hour day and a 10 percent wage increase, which left them only partially satisfied. The union failed to gain recognition as labor's bargaining agent in the coal industry, and the miners were prohibited from striking for another three years.

The public, however, was grateful to the president for the prospect of winter heat, and Roosevelt no doubt felt the coal operators should have been equally grateful. "I was anxious," he recalled, "to save the great coal operators and all of the class of big propertied men, of which they were members, from the dreadful punishment which their folly would have brought on them if I had not acted." After all, as he saw it, he had stood "between them and socialistic action." In reviewing his intervention in the coal strike, Roosevelt felt he had given a "square deal" to all sides. That phrase became a hallmark of his presidency, and it seemed calculated to overwhelm any opposition to him in the election of 1904.

The Square Deal

Not long after he had ordered the prosecution of the *Northern Securities* case, Roosevelt toured the nation and made the Square Deal his principal theme: "We are neither for the rich man nor the poor man as such, but for the upright man, rich or poor." Although such rhetoric was hardly new to politics, Roosevelt's actions in the coal strike and the *Northern Securities* case appeared to lend some substance to these words. By the 1904 presidential campaign, TR was more popular than ever. He won the Republican nomination without opposition.

Judge Alton B. Parker, the Democratic candidate, proved colorless, and Roosevelt's huge majority (7,628,000 popular votes to 5,084,000) took even him by surprise. President at last in his own right, Roosevelt now pursued a broader reform program on the national level. His major achievements were in railroad regulation, protection of consumers, and conservation of natural resources.

By 1904 the Interstate Commerce Act of 1887, designed to regulate the railroads, was practically dead, largely because of the Supreme Court's narrow interpretation of the Interstate Commerce Commission's powers. In 1903, in response to pressure from the railroads themselves, Congress had passed the Elkins Act. This measure made it illegal for railroads to depart from their published freight rates and made shippers as well as railroads liable for punishment for infractions. The act struck at the practice of rebating, which the railroad companies had come to regard as a major nuisance. The Elkins Act, however, failed to give the Interstate Commerce Commission any power to fix rates, which was what farmers and other shippers wanted.

Roosevelt now prodded Congress to strengthen and enlarge the commission's powers. In response, Congress in 1906 passed the Hepburn Act. The commission had been able to order alterations in railroad rates, but the roads did not have to comply until the courts ordered them to do so. Under the Hepburn Act, the commission was authorized to set maximum rates when complaints from shippers were received and to order the roads to comply within thirty days. The roads might still go to court, but in the meantime the new rates were to be in force. Within two years shippers had made more than nine thousand appeals to the commission, and a great many rates were revised downward. With the Hepburn Act, Roosevelt also felt he had helped to blunt the demand for government ownership of the railroads.

In December 1905, in his annual message to Congress, Roosevelt asked for a consumer protection act. His request was made on the basis of investigations by Harvey W. Wiley, a chemist in the Department of Agriculture, and other scientists revealing that adulterants and preservatives were being widely used in canned foods. Naturally, the packing interests fought TR's proposal. But in June 1906, Congress passed the first federal meat-inspection law. The same year, it enacted a Pure Food and Drug Act in response to Samuel Hopkins Adams's exposé of the patent-medicine industry and its misleading advertising.

This law did not ensure full protection for consumers, but it attacked some of the worst abuses and prepared the way for stricter regulation later on.

An amateur naturalist and an outdoorsman with a taste for natural beauty, Roosevelt took an early interest in conservation. Under the Forest Reserve Act, passed in 1891, he set aside almost 150 million acres in Alaska and the Northwest in order to give the United States Geological Survey a chance to study mineral and water resources in those areas. He turned over the supervision of the national forests to the secretary of agriculture, who put a professional conservationist, Gifford Pinchot, in charge.

The "good times" that had helped to sustain the Roosevelt presidency and Progressive reform received a rude jolt in 1907 when a financial panic, brought on by speculation and mismanagement, forced a number of New York banks to the wall. Anxious to avoid a long depression, Roosevelt compromised his earlier position that the federal government could always assert its authority over large corporations. When industrialists and Wall Street representatives advised him that business would recover sooner if he permitted the United States Steel Corporation to acquire control of the Tennessee Iron and Coal Company, a firm whose shaky securities were held by many shaky brokerage houses, Roosevelt nervously approved. Whether his action saved the country from a business collapse remains doubtful.

Although Wall Street and business chose to blame Progressive reforms that were undermining the confidence of financiers, the panic should have pointed up the need for reform of the business and financial community. Roosevelt suggested as much the next year when he called for regulation of the stock market and interstate corporations and for personal income and inheritance taxes.

But Roosevelt would not be in a position to push these ideas from the White House. The day after the election of 1904, he had announced he would not seek a third term. As the 1908 campaign neared, Roosevelt stood well enough with his party to name its next candidate, his friend William Howard Taft of Ohio, the first civil governor of the Philippines and Roosevelt's secretary of war since 1904. The president also stood well enough with the people to put Taft over. The Democrats in 1908 returned to William Jennings Bryan, but Progressive reforms under Roosevelt left Bryan issueless. Taft was swept in by a vote of

7,675,000 to 6,412,000; his margin in the electoral college was 321 to 162.

Taft

Like Roosevelt, Taft recognized the need for social legislation and regulation of the trusts. He supported Roosevelt's Square Deal. He shared Roosevelt's ideas on most questions, and he fully expected to follow Roosevelt's policies. But he was not Roosevelt. He had no charismatic qualities and none of Roosevelt's flair. His administrative skills could not make up for his lack of political skills. And despite his loyalty to the party, Taft himself helped to bring a split in party ranks when he chose to raise an issue Roosevelt had wisely evaded—the protective tariff.

By 1908, call for a reduction of tariff duties were reflecting both urban and rural concern over the steadily rising cost of living. By protecting the trusts from foreign competition, the tariff, critics charged, forced the public to pay higher prices. Responding to pressures within the party, particularly from midwestern Progressives, Taft promised early action. In March 1909, he called Congress into special session to deal with the tariff question. Although Taft may have been genuinely interested in lowering tariff duties, the old guard in the party fought as always. Moderate reductions were adopted in the House. But when Nelson Aldrich and his conservative friends in the Senate finished with the measure, it not only failed to reduce the levies but actually raised them.

Taft had done nothing to stop Aldrich, and this betrayal of a platform pledge so enraged certain western senators that they attacked their own party leaders. They lost the battle, but their revolt shook the old guard to its foundations. When Taft, after signing the Payne-Aldrich Act, declared it the best tariff ever, he shocked the Republican rank and file as well.

With the Republican party increasingly divided between the old guard and Progressives, the battle shifted from the tariff issue to the sweeping powers exercised by House Speaker Joseph G. (Uncle Joe) Cannon, who had repeatedly blocked consideration of reform legislation. Taft backed the old guard; Roosevelt indicated his sympathy for the rebels; and the rebels won when they got enough votes to restrict the Speaker's appointive power.

The Progressives followed up this victory with new railroad legislation that went beyond Taft's wishes. In the Mann-Elkins Act of 1910, Congress empowered the Interstate Commerce Commission to suspend general rate increases (enlarging the power granted by the Hepburn Act to suspend specific increases) and to take the initiative in revising such rates. A Commerce Court was established to speed up the judicial process by hearing appeals directly from the commission. These terms were in line with Taft's desires. But the Progressives also pushed through a provision forbidding railroads from acquiring competing lines, and added another that put telephone, telegraph, cable, and wireless companies under the commission's control.

Any remaining Republican unity was nearly wrecked by the Pinchot-Ballinger affair. The trouble began when the chief forester of the Department of Agriculture, Gifford Pinchot, heard that Secretary of the Interior Richard A. Ballinger had agreed to let private interests take over the reserved coal lands in Alaska. Pinchot attacked Ballinger, but Taft chose to believe his secretary's denials. When Pinchot continued the attack, he was removed. Progressives in Congress now investigated the Interior Department and showed that Ballinger, though not guilty of misconduct, had no sympathy with conservation policies. Somehow Taft gained the same reputation.

Taft did not disappoint the Progressives at every turn. Important measures passed during his tenure included the Sixteenth Amendment, which made the federal income tax constitutional, and the Seventeenth Amendment, providing for the direct election of United States senators, both ratified in 1913. He also initiated about twice as many prosecutions under the Sherman Act in his one administration as Roosevelt had in two.

But Taft's two leading cases, against International Harvester and United States Steel, turned out to be worse than failures. The U.S. Steel prosecution, coming after Roosevelt's virtual guarantee of immunity to the corporation, ended hope for reconciliation between Roosevelt and Taft. The Harvester action alienated the company's promoter and director, the former Morgan partner George W. Perkins, who was to become one of Roosevelt's leading backers in 1912.

The Bull Moose Party

Strife in Republican ranks broke into open warfare over Taft's use of presidential patronage to build up conservative strength for the congressional elections of 1910. At first, Roosevelt made no move that would publicize his difficulties with Taft. But in August he set out through the West for a series of speeches in which he endorsed the concept of the welfare state under the slogan "New Nationalism." Then in 1911, Republican insurgents helped to form the National Progressive Republican League to promote Robert La Follette.

As governor of Wisconsin, La Follette was the most successful Progressive; as United States senator, he was the most militant. Roosevelt, although pressed to head off La Follette as well as Taft, waited almost a year to make up his mind. After La Follette, worn down by campaigning, collapsed during a major speech early in 1912, Roosevelt publicly announced, "My hat is in the ring." A savage fight followed, and by the time of the Republican convention in Chicago in June, Taft's supporters were in control. Roosevelt and nis followers, charging that the president had gained his delegates by fraud, stormed out.

In response to questions about his own physical energy, Roosevelt had said upon arriving in Chicago that he felt "fit as a bull moose." His supporters now hastily organized a Progressive party convention of their own in that city, hoping to send him back to the White House. The delegates adopted a platform calling for the initiative, referendum, and recall, women's suffrage, worker's compensation and social insurance, minimum wages for women, child-labor legislation, and federal trade and tariff commissions to regulate business.

The Democrats: Wilson

Although pleased by the Republican split, the Democrats in 1912 had to mend internal divisions of their own to make the most of their opportunity. Bryan, still a power, helped matters by announcing he would not run again. At the party convention he supported Champ Clark, who had succeeded to the speakership of the House after the 1910 elections. Though strong in the early balloting, Clark failed to get the two-thirds majority needed for the nomination. Finally, on the forty-sixth ballot, the delegates turned to a political newcomer, the Progressive Democratic governor of New Jersey, Woodrow Wilson.

Fifty-five years old at the time of his nomination, Wilson had little political experience. While

Woodrow Wilson. *(Library of Congress)*

president of Princeton University from 1902 to 1910, he had been known as an educational reformer. He proved attractive to the Democratic bosses of New Jersey, who in 1910 were seeking a respectable candidate for governor, preferably one they could control. But when he won the governorship, Wilson broke with the bosses and promoted reforms that earned him Progressive support.

Born in Virginia in an intensely pious community, over which his father presided as Presbyterian minister, he learned his lessons well. The force of moral principle remained very much a part of his character and shaped his view of the world and other people; it was both his strength and his ultimate undoing.

With Roosevelt's third-party candidacy, the stage was now set for a dramatic political showdown within the ranks of progressivism. Taft soon lagged, and the battle narrowed down to Wilson and Roosevelt and the central issue of the trusts. Louis D. Brandeis said that Wilson was for regulated competition, Roosevelt for regulated monopoly. Wilson held that the business combinations were too powerful to be regulated, "that monopoly can be broken up. If I didn't believe it, I would know that all of the roads of free development were shut in this country." A "new freedom" for the individual was more important than a "square deal" from the government.

In the election, the two overwhelmed Taft, who got only 8 electoral votes. Roosevelt won 88, Wilson 435. Eugene V. Debs, running on the Socialist ticket, won no electoral votes, yet his popular vote of over 900,000 was impressive. Although Wilson's popular vote of 6,293,000 was slightly less than 42 percent of the electorate, the Democratic party captured the House and Senate as well as the presidency. Wilson, with the additional support of a bloc of Progressive Republicans, took office with excellent prospects for a Progressive administration.

The New Freedom

Differences on the trust issue may have dominated the election, but other subjects now demanded the president's attention. First on the list was the tariff. In 1913 Wilson called a special session of Congress on this issue. With strong support from Senator La Follette and other Republican Progressives, the Democrats that year passed the Underwood Act, the first satisfactory downward revision since the Civil War. To supply the revenue that would presumably be lost through the tariff reduction, the act also placed a tax of 1 percent on personal incomes of $4000 and graduated surtaxes of from 1 to 6 percent on higher incomes.

Financial reform came next. The panic of 1907 had revealed a poorly functioning financial system and the need for a more flexible currency. Roosevelt's efforts to resolve the crisis had also dramatized the concentration of financial power in the hands of a small group of eastern invest-

The election of 1912.

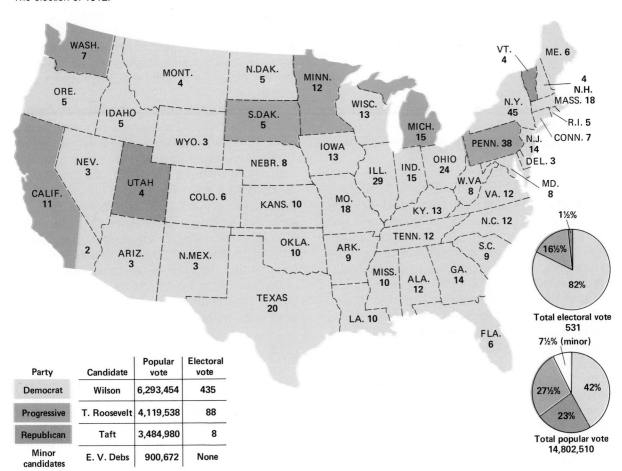

Party	Candidate	Popular vote	Electoral vote
Democrat	Wilson	6,293,454	435
Progressive	T. Roosevelt	4,119,538	88
Republican	Taft	3,484,980	8
Minor candidates	E. V. Debs	900,672	None

Total electoral vote 531

Total popular vote 14,802,510

ment bankers. A commission set up in 1908 under Senator Aldrich had suggested establishing a great central bank with branches dominated by the leading banking interests. Progressives led by La Follette responded with proposals for more public control: remove financial power from the hands of private banking houses and place it in the hands of experts who would be more responsive to the public.

As finally passed on December 23, 1913, the Federal Reserve Act set up twelve regional banking districts, each with a Federal Reserve bank. The Federal Reserve banks were owned by the member banks of the Federal Reserve system. All national banks were required to join; state banks were eligible. Member banks were required to subscribe 6 percent of their capital to the Federal Reserve bank in their region. On the security of this subscription and commercial and agricultural paper, the Federal Reserve banks would create a new currency, Federal Reserve notes, issued by the Reserve banks to member banks and circulated by them to borrowers. The Federal Reserve system was placed under the direction of the Federal Reserve Board, consisting of the secretary of the Treasury and seven other persons appointed by the president.

By 1923, the Federal Reserve system covered 70 percent of the nation's banking. It created a flexible and sound currency and made it available to all sections of the country through the regional Reserve banks. It also left banking a private business under federal supervision and did not really reduce the power of the great New York financial institutions.

To improve the farmer's access to funds, Congress in May 1916 passed the Federal Farm Loan Act, creating a Federal Farm Loan Board of twelve regional Farm Loan banks patterned after the Federal Reserve system. The banks were authorized to lend money to farm Loan cooperative associations on the security of farmlands, buildings, and improvements; up to 70 percent of the value of these assets could be borrowed. Loans were to be long-term, interest was not to be more than 6 percent, and profits were to be distributed to the subscribing Farm Loan associations.

Like his predecessors, Wilson trusted the regulatory agencies to deal with corporate abuses and punish individual wrongdoers. The first Wilsonian antitrust measure, the Federal Trade Commission Act of September 1914, undertook to prevent rather than to punish unfair trade practices. This act created a five-person Federal Trade Commission authorized to investigate alleged vio-

lations of antitrust laws. The commission was empowered to issue "cease-and-desist" orders against corporations found guilty of unfair practices. If this failed, the commission could bring corporations to court.

During Wilson's administration, 379 cease-and-desist orders were issued, and a few dissolutions of trusts were initiated in cooperation with the Department of Justice. Even so, Progressives soon came to feel that the commission was not using its powers vigorously enough. Like the Interstate Commerce Commission earlier, the FTC gradually became a tool of those it was supposed to regulate.

A second antitrust law, the Clayton Act, was passed in October 1914. It prohibited a number of business practices: price discrimination that might lessen or destroy competition; *tying contracts* (contracts that forced purchasers not to buy the products of competitors); the acquisition by corporations of stock in competing firms; and the creation of interlocking directorates in corporations and banks over a specified size as measured by capitalization. Officers of corporations were made personally subject to prosecution if they violated these provisions. Labor unions as such were not to be considered illegal combinations or conspiracies in restraint of trade. Labor injunctions were forbidden except when necessary to prevent "irreparable injury to property, or to a property right."

The domestic record of Wilson's first administration also included legislation controlling child labor (the Keating-Owen Child Labor Act of 1916), improving the condition of merchant seamen (the Seaman's Act of 1915), and establishing an eight-hour day for interstate-railway workers (the Adamson Act of 1916). Like much of the social legislation passed during the Progressive Era, however, many of these measures proved difficult to enforce—because of the way they were written, because of administrative neglect, or because of the hostility of the courts. And two groups in particular continued to struggle on their own: women and blacks.

WOMEN AND PROGRESSIVISM

The women's movement in the United States flourished between 1890 and World War I. With growing numbers of women graduating from college and entering the work force, women not only began to challenge previously male sanctuaries but became more adamant in their refusal to accept second-class citizenship as their legal status and domesticity as their sole vocation. Oliver Wendell Holmes's description of "marriageable girls sittin' like shopkeepers behind their goods" still reflected dominant images of women, but in an era of rapid social and economic change, those images became less credible. The growth of the labor force and the remarkable decrease in the fertility rate of American women (from about 7 births per woman early in the nineteenth century to about 3.5 births at its close), along with a significant increase in the divorce rate and the fact that more women than men were initiating divorce proceedings, suggested a growing independence and assertiveness among women.

By the turn of the century, the General Federation of Women's Clubs, organized in 1889, had grown into a militant organization, especially in the fight for women's suffrage and even on behalf of birth control. The movement of women activists, however, embraced a broad spectrum of voluntary associations, ranging from the General Federation and the suffrage groups to the Woman's Christian Temperance Union. Black women, too, enlisted in campaigns for social improvement, attacking both racial and sex discrimination. The focus of their agitation tended to set them off from the white organizations, whose leaders were sensitive to the need to appease prevailing racial biases. Often excluded from white women's organizations, black women formed their own groups, including the General Federation of Colored Women in 1895.

White, middle-class women played an active role in the Progressive movement. Although the vote remained the first priority, it was viewed not as an end in itself but as a means for attacking a broad range of legal and social problems affecting women's lives. The discovery, for example, that some five million women and nearly one million children under the age of fifteen were now in the labor force (as reported in the census of 1900) prompted women to enter new fields of activity and agitation. Women engaged in campaigns to improve the quality of schools and kindergartens, along with the conditions under which women and children worked. And they confronted a double standard that narrowly defined the rights of women in American society. In most states in 1900 women could neither vote in general elections nor hold public office or sit on juries. In all states discriminatory laws and legal codes restricted the rights of women in property holding, divorces, and contract making.

In seeking to alter such laws and improve their legal status, women challenged the deeply entrenched notion that their proper role in the social order was as wives and mothers. That challenge would in turn raise concern in some quarters about the survival not only of the traditional woman—"the perfect lady"—but of the social order itself. To Mary Heaton Vorse, as to many radical women reformers, the suffrage was, after all, only a way to achieve deeper changes in American society. "I cannot imagine anything that would affect better the moral health of any country," she wrote to a friend, "than something which would blast the greatest number of that indecent, immoral institution—the perfect lady—out of doors and set them smashing and rioting"—much like women in England had done in their campaign for the suffrage.

The Suffrage

Since the 1840s, a small advance guard under the leadership of Susan B. Anthony and Elizabeth Cady Stanton had embraced a broad vision of sexual equality. Rejecting the idea of female inferiority, they advocated full equality with men, including equal access to education, the trades, and the professions. Both Anthony and Stanton devoted their lives to organizing, writing, and lecturing throughout the nation on behalf of women's rights, always aiming broadly at the subordination of women.

After the Civil War, women activists continued to embrace a vision of women liberated not only from political but from economic, social, and marital bondage. But a growing debate persisted over which of these deserved the highest priority and whether it was practical to struggle for the broader vision if it alienated the public from more immediate objectives such as the suffrage.

Angered by their failure to win the vote under the Fourteenth Amendment, suffrage advocates in 1869 formed the American Woman's Suffrage Association. Headed by Lucy Stone and Julia Ward Howe of Boston, the AWSA was concerned almost exclusively with the suffrage. But a more radical contingent, committed to easy divorce laws and more far-reaching institutional changes, soon split off. This group, led by Anthony and Stanton, then organized the National Woman's Suffrage Association. In November 1872 Anthony raised the stakes in the ongoing protest over the exclusion of women from the polls. Asserting her "natural rights" as an American citizen, she tried to vote in Rochester, New York. The men who

A FEMINIST MANIFESTO

Although the social revolution envisaged by feminists failed to materialize in the Progressive Era, the program they set forth anticipated most of the demands that would be made by women's movements in the 1960s and the 1970s. Winnifred Harper Cooley, a writer and journalist whose mother had long been active in the struggle for the suffrage, outlined such a program in 1913.

The abolition of all arbitrary handicaps calculated to prevent woman's economic independence. . . . The woman of the future—married or single—must be absolutely free to earn her livelihood, and must receive equal pay for equal service. The younger feminists consider that the day is rapidly approaching when to be supported by a man in return for sexual privileges, or mere general housekeeping, or to be paid for motherhood, will be morally revolting to every self-respecting wife.

The opportunity for women to serve in all civic capacities—on municipal, educational, institutional and reform boards, on juries, and in every function by which they can be of service to their own sex and to children.

A demand for a single standard of morality. This is not to be interpreted arbitrarily as meaning either a strictly puritanical standard or an objectionably loose standard. It merely means that there should be no unjust and persecuting discrimination against the woman offender, when both man and woman offend.

The abolition of white slavery and prostitution. This is only one form of the age-long insistence of man's ownership of woman. Its manifestations are quite as real in the harem, and in some phases of marriage, as in the poor creature who is sequestered, an absolute prisoner, in "houses" in our cities.

The right to activity of expression and of creating social ideals, quite unhampered by old superstitions. . . . As a matter of fact, public opinion in the future will regard men as quite as essential to the home as are women; and women as quite as essential to the world as are men.

Source: Winnifred H. Cooley, *Harper's Weekly*, 58 (September 1913), 7–8.

Women's suffrage before the Nineteenth Amendment.

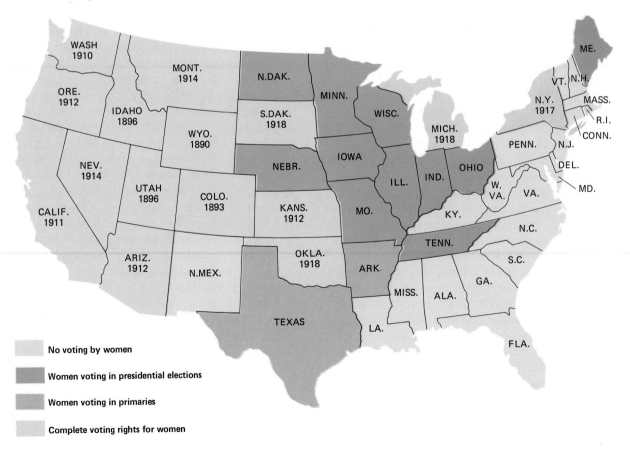

No voting by women

Women voting in presidential elections

Women voting in primaries

Complete voting rights for women

arrested Anthony charged her with "illegal voting."

To maximize support for winning the vote, suffragists in the late nineteenth century sought to avoid potentially divisive issues. Less was heard of the more radical "feminist" demands. Setting aside their differences, the two wings of the movement reunited in 1890 as the National American Woman's Suffrage Association (NAWSA). Focusing on the vote, the movement did little to challenge conventional ideas about woman's place in society. Instead, suffragists chose to emphasize that women were uniquely qualified, based on their experience in the home, to elevate the moral level of government and society.

But the commitment to improve American society led the women's movement in some strange and contradictory directions. Like so many Progressives, women reformers embraced the idea that the "best people" should govern. And like so many Progressives, they were seldom able to overcome their own racial and class biases. To some, in fact, female suffrage promised to counter the growing influence of illiterate European immigrants and to preserve white supremacy in the South. Mobilizing statistics for their cause, suffragists noted the numerical superiority of native-born women to foreign-born men and women combined and the comparable superiority of white women in the South to black men and women combined. In 1893 the NAWSA convention, after noting "there are more white women who can read and write than all negro voters," contended that woman suffrage "would settle the vexed question of rule by illiteracy, whether of home-grown or foreign-born production." Ten years later, a southern white suffragist told the same organization that the vote for women would ensure "immediate and durable white supremacy." Still other suffragists, such as Carrie Chapman Catt, expressed concern over unrestricted immigration. "There is but one way to avert the danger," she declared in 1894. "Cut off the vote of the slums and give it to women." The effect of these positions was to broaden the appeal of the suffragist movement and enhance its respectability. One suffrage banner in 1915 sought to allay any fears that women would exercise the vote irresponsibly: "For the hand that rocks the cradle will never rock the boat." Even so, many women active in the Progressive movement embraced the suffrage as a way to increase and mobilize support for necessary social legislation.

By 1898, Wyoming, Colorado, Utah, and Idaho had given women full voting rights. Other states permitted them to vote for certain offices, such as school board membership. But no federal amendment was passed, despite agitation throughout the nation. Presidents Taft and Wilson preferred to evade the issue, but by the presidential campaign of 1912 women's suffrage was assuming increasing political importance. The election of Wilson, with his conservative southern views on the place of women in society, was a setback. But women went right on agitating, and by 1913 they had won complete voting rights in nine states.

Such limited gains dissatisfied many women, who now decided to concentrate on a federal amendment. They prepared for Congress a petition with 400,000 signatures and opened a lobby in Washington, D.C. Some, such as Carrie Chapman Catt and Anna Howard Shaw, preferred gradual education and propaganda. Others, who followed the lead of Alice Paul, preferred more aggressive tactics. Impatient with the progress of the campaign, they organized the National Woman's Party. Patterning their strategy after that of the English suffragists, they picketed the White House and chained themselves to its fence. Repeatedly arrested and imprisoned, they responded to their harsh confinement by engaging in hunger strikes, requiring that they be force-fed by prison authorities. The protests heightened public awareness, and eventually even President Wilson was persuaded to give the women some encouragement. The active role of women in World War I won the suffragists many new male supporters. When Wilson came before the Senate in the fall of 1918 and urged that body to support women's suffrage, he used an argument similar to that of Abraham Lincoln in his Emancipation Proclamation—he called it "vital to the winning of the war." Ironically, Jeannette Rankin, a Republican from Montana and the first woman elected to Congress, had cast the only vote opposing American entry into the war. She was the only woman to serve in Congress before adoption of the federal suffrage amendment.

In June 1919 Congress passed the Nineteenth Amendment giving women the vote. (The amendment passed the House by a vote of 204 to 90, the Senate by a vote of 56 to 25.) The same year, the League of Women Voters was established to educate women for their new political responsibilities. The amendment was ratified in August 1920; women throughout the country took part in the presidential election that fall. "How much time and patience," reflected Catt, "how much hope, how much despair went into the battle."

Musical comedy star and wife of Florenz Ziegfeld, Anna Held. *(Library of Congress)*

An Italian mother carries home work to be finished by the family. *(Lewis W. Hine, Library of Congress)*

Shirtwaist strikers, New York, 1910. *(Bain Collection, Library of Congress)*

Ladies' luncheon at Delmonico's, 1902. *(Byron Collection, Museum of the City of New York)*

Conforming to the traditional image of American women, the ladies of Black River Falls, Wisconsin, gather in 1905 for one of their regular sessions of tea, talk, and sewing. *(Charles Van Schaick, State Historical Society of Wisconsin)*

Two black women. *(Library of Congress)*

Mother to Son

Well, son I'll tell you:
Life for me ain't been no crystal stair.
It's had tacks in it,
And splinters,
And boards torn up,
And places with no carpet on the floor—
Bare.
But all the time
I'se been a-climbin' on,
And reachin' landin's,
And turnin' corners,
And sometimes goin' in the dark
Where there ain't been no light.
So boy, don't you turn back.
Don't you set down on the steps
'Cause you finds it's kinder hard.
Don't you fall now—
For I'se still goin', honey,
I'se still climbin',
And life for me ain't been no crystal stair.

Reprinted from Selected Poems by Langston Hughes, by permission of Alfred A. Knopf, Inc. Copyright 1926 by Alfred A. Knopf, Inc.; renewed 1954 by Langston Hughes.

May Day parade, 1910. *(Library of Congress)*

A proabortion demonstration. *(UPI/Bettmann Newsphotos)*

Suffragists. *(Bain Collection, Library of Congress)*

Emma Goldman. *(Culver Pictures, Inc.)*

Margaret Sanger. *(UPI)*

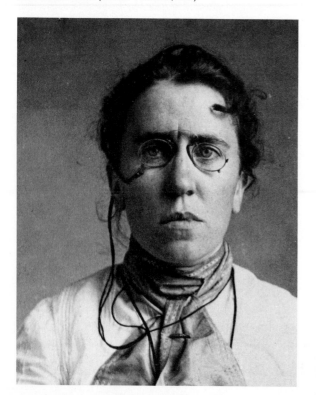

Feminists and Suffragists

The Nineteenth Amendment enabled women to influence the democratic process but it did not usher in the millennium some reformers had anticipated. Nor did the vote necessarily mobilize women to embrace an image of themselves as something more than wives and mothers assigned to a lifetime of domestic drudgery. "All feminists are suffragists, but all suffragists are not feminists," Winnifred Harper Cooley observed in 1913. That is, she explained, the "younger feminists" often digressed from their "elders within the fold," refusing to believe that the ballot alone, like some kind of "magician's wand," would solve the problems confronting women in American society. Many women, she said of the suffragists, claimed the vote as "wives and mothers" and as "homemakers." That posed an obvious problem. "Just why wives should be happier, as *wives*, because they vote, is difficult to see."

Feminism (a term first used in 1910) took on new dimensions in the early twentieth century, as white, middle-class women assumed a variety of public roles. By 1910 nearly 8 million American women were working, many of them in offices and stores as well as in factories. Some had entered law and medicine. Their number in education, even at the college level, had soared. Reflecting the increasing diversity of women's roles, feminism after the Nineteenth Amendment encompassed a variety of issues — the workplace, sexuality, marriage, and the home.

The priorities women assigned to these issues were bound to lead to considerable debate about the proper goals of the movement. The newly organized National Woman's Party proposed in 1923 the first equal rights amendment. For the party leader, Alice Paul, the proposal followed logically upon the adoption of women's suffrage. But advocates of protective labor laws for women thought such an amendment would invalidate hard-won social legislation — laws, for example, limiting working hours for women — that they deemed essential to women's welfare. Supporters of the ERA opposed such laws on the ground that they excluded women from prestigious "male" jobs that required longer hours.

The apparent gains of women in the first three decades of the twentieth century introduced new tensions and anxieties. As the ERA supporters had pointed out, laws limiting the working hours of women barred them from various prestigious occupations. The growing emphasis on female sexuality imposed on women the additional burden of maximizing their attractiveness to men. The prospect of equality in marriage gave women less of an incentive to remain single. With more women embracing the idea of marriage plus career, more women found themselves holding down two jobs — one at the office and one at home. At the same time, studies in child rearing and home economics introduced new anxieties in the home, even as technology and the newly invigorated advertising industry made housewives more aware of what they did not have and exhorted them to be more concerned about the appearance of their person and their home. And finally, the breakthrough by women into the male economic domain came at some cost. For a woman to choose a "man's job" was to risk a loss of respect. The woman, observed anthropologist Margaret Mead some years later, had two choices: she could proclaim herself "a woman and therefore less of an achieving individual, or an achieving individual and therefore less of a woman."

Once the vote had been won, many women returned to the fundamental problems that had plagued feminists throughout much of the nineteenth century — their inferior legal position in American society, their subordinate roles in the social system, and their lack of equal economic and educational opportunities. For working-class women, the abstract recognition of equal rights through the ballot box failed to alter the day-to-day realities they faced in the workplace. Feminism addressed the needs of middle-class women for self-expression and self-fulfillment; working-class women confronted far more urgent needs — safety on the job, food on the table, and a wage that would permit them to enjoy some of the amenities of life.

Some of the middle-class women who dominated the suffrage and feminist movements recognized the importance of addressing the oppression of their working-class "sisters." The campaign for improvement in women's working conditions, whose slogan was "Let Us Be Our Sisters' Keepers," reflected the broadened interests of women's organizations. Although never as large or influential as the General Federation, both the Women's Trade Union League and the National Consumers' League (led by Florence Kelley) publicized the exploitation of working women and won legislation restricting child labor and protecting female workers. Few working-class women belonged to any of the women's organizations, but they did not have to be feminists to recognize that they received less pay for equal work than men and that most of the higher-paying jobs were reserved for men.

Working-class women fought their own significant struggles to improve the conditions of their lives and work. The most dramatic protest was the Uprising of the Twenty Thousand, a general strike by shirtwaist workers in New York City and Philadelphia. The largest strike of women in the nation's history, it involved a rapidly expanding industry in which 80 percent of the workers were female. At the initial mass meeting, Clara Lemlich, still in her teens, proposed turning the walkouts from several shirtwaist factories into a general strike: "I am a working girl, one of those who are on strike against intolerable conditions. I am tired of listening to speakers who talk in general terms."

The young strikers, most of them between sixteen and twenty-five, proved as resourceful as male workers in surviving police harassment, mass arrests, violence, and three hard months on picket lines during the winter of 1909. Although the women failed to win a clear victory, they did lay the groundwork for the successful organizing campaign of the International Ladies' Garment Workers' Union. Two years after the strike, on March 25, 1911, a fire at the Triangle Shirtwaist Company took the lives of 146 women and revealed the grim conditions that still prevailed in the industry: the owners had not installed proper safety equipment and most of the fire escapes had been locked.

The Triangle tragedy made some of the feminists and suffragists realize how little their organizations had addressed the needs of working women. Jessie Ashley, an officer in the National American Woman Suffrage Association, scolded the suffragists for their class biases. Contrasting the "handsome parading ladies" in a recent suffragist parade with the "jammed-in subway girls" on their way home from work, Ashley observed: "Only the women of the working class are really oppressed, but it is not only the working class women to whom injustice is done. Women of the leisure class need freedom too."

Although the women's organizations supported the struggles of working-class women, the question of priorities was never satisfactorily resolved. Some suffragists still insisted that their cause should not be mixed up "with outside interests." Nor did the constructive activities of social workers in the emerging urban ghettos lessen the suspicion with which black women tended to regard the largely white, middle-class women's

movement. Many of the suffragists had themselves emerged from the ranks of the abolitionists. But by the turn of the century, the women's organizations had broadened their appeal and constituency to include thousands of southern white women. To preserve national unity, these organizations were forced to make a series of crippling compromises on the explosive issue of race relations.

After 1920, women would vote in substantial numbers. But men determined their role in society and still demanded conformity to stereotypes. The illusion of independence, based on the vote and the number of women entering the professions, could not obscure for very long the continuing confinement of most working women to low-paid, low-status occupations. Class, race, and ethnic divisions, not sex, largely determined women's voting behavior. And many of those who had made up the suffragist movement were content with their limited gains. It was left to a minority of feminists, such as Crystal Eastman, to argue that the suffrage had only clarified the issues, not finished the debate.

Men are saying perhaps "Thank God, this everlasting women's fight is over!" But women, if I know them, are saying, "Now at last we can begin." . . . Now they can say what they are really after; and what they are after, in common with all the rest of the struggling world, is freedom.

BLACKS AND PROGRESSIVISM

Progressivism coincided with the worst period of race relations in the nation's history. In 1900 some eight million blacks (90 percent of the country's black population) lived and worked in the South. Between 1890 and World War I, the racial creed of the white South manifested itself in the systematic disfranchisement of black men, in rigid patterns of racial segregation, in unprecedented violence, and in the dissemination of dehumanizing racial caricatures. The emergence of a new generation of black southerners who had never known the discipline of slavery only reinforced the determination of whites to maintain racial supremacy.

Early in their lives, then, young blacks would come to appreciate the terrible unfairness of the world they entered—the narrow boundaries, the limited possibilities, the need to curb ambitions, to contain feelings, to weigh carefully every word, gesture, and movement when in the presence of whites. Personal security lay in repressing any impulses toward individuality or assertiveness, in learning how to accommodate to daily indignities. "There is a difference in knowing you are black," remembered a Mississippi woman, "and in understanding what it means to be black in America. Before I was ten I knew what it was to step off the sidewalk to let a white man pass."

Although the Progressive movement also took root in the South, blacks were excluded. More often than not, Progressive and racist leaders were one and the same, the two movements barely distinguishable. With few exceptions, northern Progressives did nothing about the steady deterioration of race relations throughout the country. North and South had come together in the Spanish-American War, and northerners were beginning to face domestic and international racial problems. At home, there were "new" immigrants from eastern and southern Europe. Overseas, "inferior" colored people had to be assimilated into the American empire. When the Supreme Court in 1898 went along with the disfranchisement clause in Mississippi's Constitution, *Nation* magazine thought it "an interesting coincidence that this important decision is rendered at a time when we are considering the idea of taking in a varied assortment of inferior races in different parts of the world—races, which, of course, could not be allowed to vote."

The new academic sciences, such as psychology and sociology, which had become quite fashionable in intellectual and Progressive circles, tended to reinforce racist assumptions. Progressive-minded historians praised the achievements of Anglo-Saxon civilizations and documented the failure of blacks to become intelligent and useful citizens. For those who did not read learned works, there was the first motion picture extravaganza and box-office smash, *The Birth of a Nation,* which premiered in 1915.

The millions of Americans who flocked to this film would find it hard to forget the graphic portrayals of depraved, lustful, dangerous blacks seeking to impose social and political equality on a prostrate South. "It started people to thinking," one reviewer wrote. "The people of Chicago saw more in *The Birth of a Nation* than a tremendous dramatic spectacle. They saw in it the reason the South wants the Negro to 'keep in his place.' They saw in it a new conception of southern problems." President Wilson, who saw the film at a private showing in the White House, thought it "history written in lightning." Thomas Dixon, on whose novel the film was based, assured Wilson that the movie was "transforming the entire population of

the North and West into sympathetic Southern voters."

The motion picture industry simply elaborated upon the stereotypes of black men and women already implanted in the white mind through the minstrel show, vaudeville, popular literature, and merchandised objects that exaggerated and distorted the physical appearance and lives of black people. Popular culture established the image of a race of buffoons, half-wits, and savages—sometimes comic, sometimes bestial, but in either case less than human.

Booker T. Washington: Strategy for Survival

Against this background of white violence, disfranchisement, and segregation, Booker T. Washington followed a pragmatic policy of accommodation: "In all things that are purely social we can be as separate as the fingers, yet one as the hand in all things essential to mutual progress." Rather than agitate, black people should accumulate property: "The trouble with the Negro is that he is all the time trying to get recognition, whereas what he should do is to get something to recognize." Rather than intrude where they were not

Booker T. Washington. *(Brown Brothers)*

wanted, black people should look to their own communities: "Let us, in the future, spend *less* time talking about the part of the city that we cannot live in, and *more* time in making the part of the city that we can live in beautiful and attractive." Once black people had proved themselves, largely by measuring up to white, middle-class standards, their constitutional rights would be recognized. After all, Washington observed, "there is little race prejudice in the American dollar."

Whites—North and South—supported Washington's ideas. The financial support whites funneled through Washington enabled him to monopolize black leadership and virtually control black colleges, churches, and newspapers. The success of this self-made man, who had risen from slavery, also won for him the admiration of many of his own people. "Wherever I found a prosperous Negro enterprise, a thriving business place, a good home," one reporter observed, "there I was sure to find Booker T. Washington's picture over the fireplace or a little framed motto expressing his gospel of work and service." To a small but growing black business class, most of them self-made people with a vested interest in serving a segregated black community, Washington's emphasis on pride and enterprise, rather than political agitation, simply made good sense.

W. E. B. Du Bois: The Talented Tenth

Although Washington remained the dominant personality in black America for nearly two decades, his leadership did not go unchallenged. His principal critics, such as W. E. B. Du Bois, proved to be black intellectuals and professionals, almost all of them northerners who thought Washington had carried accommodation too far and who resented the enormous power "King Booker" wielded in the black community. Unlike Washington, Du Bois had not experienced slavery, poverty, or personal struggle, and he readily acknowledged their diverse social backgrounds:

I was born free. Washington was born a slave. He felt the lash of an overseer across his back. I was born in Massachusetts, he on a slave plantation in the South. My great-grandfather fought with the Colonial Army in New England in the American Revolution. I had a happy childhood and acceptance in the community. Washington's childhood was hard. I had many more advantages: Fisk University, Harvard, graduate years in Europe. Washington had little formal schooling.[*]

*[*]Quoted by permission of the Knaus-Thomson Organization, Ltd.

W. E. B. Du Bois. *(Brown Brothers)*

Highly regarded as an authority on black social and industrial life, largely because of his research at Atlanta University, Du Bois did not openly attack the Washington gospel until 1901, nor did he actively oppose the disfranchisement of the illiterate black farm worker. But he bitterly resented denial of the ballot and other elements of equality to educated blacks, "the talented tenth" destined to lead their people.

Between 1901 and 1903, Du Bois set down his ideas on the dual heritage of black people: Negroes were at once black and American, inheritors of a national culture, yet exhibiting unique gifts. Racial differences were beneficial; racial inequalities were insufferable. The black "would not Africanize America," Du Bois wrote in *The Souls of Black Folk* (1903), "for America has too much to teach the world and Africa. He would not bleach his Negro soul in a flood of white Americanism, for he knows that Negro blood has a message for the world. He simply wishes to make it possible for a man to be both a Negro and an American."[†]

Although Du Bois acknowledged that industrial training was important, he thought blacks should also have the kind of liberating education Washington's philosophy denied them. Black advancement, he felt, depended ultimately on civil equality. Protest was essential if blacks were to maintain self-respect.

The Niagara movement, launched by Du Bois

[†]Fawcett Books Group, Consumer Publishing Division, CBS, Inc.

and his intellectual black friends in 1905, advocated agitation rather than accommodation. But few people, black or white, listened, and the movement had little impact. In 1909, a group of white and black Progressives organized the National Association for the Advancement of Colored People. As editor of its official journal, the *Crisis*, Du Bois became the organization's most militant spokesman. But the NAACP's most practical work from the start was legal action designed to protect civil rights and challenge disfranchisement. Although by 1914 the NAACP boasted six thousand members in fifty branches across the country, the principal officers, except for Du Bois, were white

liberal reformers. The appeal of the organization was largely to college-educated, professional blacks. Its following among the great mass of working-class blacks remained minimal.

Betrayal of Expectations

Despite their differences over strategies, priorities, and the value of agitation, Du Bois and Washington both urged black people to cultivate middle-class virtues: thrift, sobriety, orderliness, cleanliness, and morality. Said Du Bois, "The day the Negro race courts and marries the savings-

Between 1889 and 1941 an estimated 3811 blacks were lynched in this country, frequently with thousands of spectators. *(UPI/Bettmann Newsphotos)*

BLUES FALLING DOWN LIKE HAIL

To listen to Robert Johnson, the country blues singer born in 1911 in the upper Mississippi delta, is to feel some of the tensions that pervaded his youth. In "Cross Road Blues," he finds himself in a predicament every black youth is taught to avoid. He is at a rural crossroads, trying to flag a ride. Night is approaching, he is in a place he should not be, where no one knows him, and where the common expression is: "Nigger, don't let the sun go down on you here." The crossroads are also well known in blues lore as the place where aspiring musicians make their deal with the devil. In "Hell Hound on My Trail," Johnson conveys a similar sense of terror and paranoia, both grounded in the day-to-day experiences of southern blacks in the early twentieth century.

Cross Road Blues
I went to the crossroads, fell down on my knees.
I went to the crossroads, fell down on my knees.
I asked the Lord above, have mercy, save poor Bob
  if you please.
Uumh, standing at the crossroads I tried to flag a
  ride.
Ain't nobody seem to know me, everybody pass me
  by.

And the sun going down, boys, dark gone catch me
  here.
Uumh, oh dark gone catch me here.
I haven't got no loving sweet woman, that love will
  be near.
You can run, you can run, tell my friend, poor
  Willie Brown.
You can run, tell my friend, poor Willie Brown.
Lord, that I'm standing at the crossroads, babe, I
  believe I'm sinking down.

Hell Hound on My Trail
I got to keep moving, I got to keep moving,
  blues falling down like hail,
  blues falling down like hail.
Uumh, blues falling down like hail,
  blues falling down like hail.
And the days keeps on 'minding me,
  there's a hellhound on my trail,
  hellhound on my trail,
  hellhound on my trail.

Source: *Robert Johnson: King of the Delta Blues Singers* (Columbia CL-1654).

---

bank will be the day of its salvation." Washington stated, "It is not within the province of human nature, that the man who is intelligent and virtuous, and owns and cultivates the best farm in his county, shall very long be denied the proper respect and consideration."

But the experience of many black men and women contradicted Washington's optimistic formula for success and recognition. Faithful adherence to the work ethic brought most black southerners nothing. White men and women mobilized their society to maintain the mechanisms of white supremacy, posing formidable obstacles to blacks. Even as Washington preached his self-improvement creed, evidence of blacks making good on that creed was capable of provoking white resentment and violence. When white mobs took to the streets, as in the Atlanta race riot of 1906, much of the violence fell on the respectable, law-abiding, middle-class blacks—the ones whites referred to as the "uppity, aloof, smart-ass niggers."

No wonder many blacks came to believe that education could bring them only frustration and disappointment. They came to believe as well that

WORDS AND NAMES IN AMERICAN HISTORY

The words *lynch, lynching,* and *lynch law* all refer to a mob's seizing a suspected criminal, often from the hands of lawful authorities, sometimes giving him an unauthorized trial, and then executing him, usually by hanging and sometimes after torturing him, in full view of an enthusiastic crowd. Lynching has taken place in the South and on the western frontier. It has been rare in Europe. Lynching reached an epidemic and assumed its most hideous form in the decades after 1889, when mobs of whites seized black men suspected of some outrage (often an attack upon a white woman). Yet the term itself originated during the American Revolution. A Virginia planter and justice of the peace, Charles Lynch, presided over an extralegal court aimed at suppressing Tory activity in his region. At that time, punishment was confined largely to seizure of the offender's property. The modern meaning of the word has been considerably expanded to include mob violence as well as illegality.

it was futile to work hard and obtain wealth and property, because whites would deprive them of their gains, whether by fraud, intimidation, or violence. The historical record provided all too many examples of violence and harassment aimed at blacks determined to improve their condition. To succeed was often to antagonize whites, who deemed such success impossible for an inferior race and who feared and resented any proof to the contrary.

But even as black men and women made their peace with the ruling race, even as they learned to mask their feelings in the presence of whites, many did find ways to carve out a measure of autonomy, to impart meaning and dignity to their lives. If most accommodated, they did so from a sense of limited options, but they did not necessarily submit. There were degrees of accommodation, and the variety of ways, often quite subtle, by which black people sought to influence the terms of their accommodation is very much a part of their history. Excluded from the white world, blacks sought refuge in their own institutions, their own schools, churches, and businesses, their own distinctive forms of expression (the blues—a new musical form—was played in the Mississippi delta as early as the 1890s), in their own increasingly separate world—a nation within a nation.

Frustration confronted Du Bois when he tried to choose among Roosevelt, Taft, and Wilson in the 1912 election. Neither Roosevelt nor Taft had shown any particular regard for the rights of blacks. Both had gone out of their way, in fact, to demonstrate their feeling for the white South.

Although Du Bois preferred Debs, the Socialist candidate, he finally cast his ballot for Wilson:

Wilson is a cultivated scholar and he has brains. We have, therefore, a conviction that Mr. Wilson will treat black men and their interests with foresighted fairness. He will not advance the cause of an oligarchy in the South, he will not seek further means of "jim crow" insult, he will not dismiss black men wholesale from office, and he will remember that the Negro has a right to be heard and considered.

On virtually every point, Du Bois proved to be mistaken. When in 1914 a black delegation registered its outrage over the actions of the new administration, particularly segregation in federal departments, Wilson took offense at their language and all but ordered the black leaders out of his office. Progressivism was apparently for "white folks only."

When President Wilson called upon the American people in 1917 to help make the world "safe for democracy," Francis J. Grimke, a black clergyman, asked: "What kind of a world brotherhood can the United States, with such a man as Wilson at the head of affairs, and the Negro-hating spirit everywhere prevailing in it, represent?"

During World War I, however, some 375,000 blacks were called into military service, and none other than Du Bois urged his people to "close ranks" behind the war effort: "If this is our country, then this is our war." If black people entered the war with any expectations, it was apparently the hope that through their participation both the world and the United States might be made "safe for democracy."

SUMMARY

America early in the twentieth century was the America of the Progressives, as well as the America of big business. The middle-class reformers, mostly urban and Protestant, confronted a broad range of problems: conflict between capital and labor, immigration, the terrible slums, corrupt politics. But although all could agree that there were problems to be solved, they did not agree on which to attack first and how. The movement itself was a coalition of different groups with different aims. No group tried to revolutionize society. The basic idea was to correct the evils of the system, while keeping the system itself intact.

Business groups sometimes supported reform and exploited it to protect and consolidate their economic gains. Regulatory commissions, for example, were often supported by business, which helped to write the

legislation establishing them. But the commissions then became tools of the groups they were intended to control.

Publicity was important for the Progressives, who saw an aroused public as the way to bring pressure for change. All during this period, muckraking—the disclosure of social and political evils in the popular press—was part of the Progressive campaign.

One of the first targets was government at all levels. In the cities, Progressives introduced the commission form of government and the city manager. To protect these reforms, Progressives attacked state machines as well, advocating such innovations as the direct primary, the initiative, the referendum, and the recall. They also pushed to have United States senators elected by the people rather than by the legislatures. (The Seventeenth

Amendment, ratified in 1913, accomplished this.) Business interests, particularly the railroads and the public utilities that depended on government grants and political privilege, were also targets.

In the area of social legislation, Progressives worked for child-labor laws, laws limiting the hours of work, worker compensation, and public responsibility for the support of children and old people.

Another major Progressive campaign aimed at controlling the production and sale of alcoholic beverages and prohibiting drinking altogether. Women played a leading role in this movement. By 1913, its supporters were strong enough to introduce an amendment to the Constitution, which Congress passed and the states ratified. The Eighteenth Amendment went into effect in January 1920 and brought a whole new era: Prohibition, the speakeasy, and large-scale organized crime.

Three presidents during this period shared the Progressive commitment, though in different ways: Theodore Roosevelt, Taft, and Wilson. Roosevelt moved against big business, using the Sherman Anti-Trust Act to bring companies to court and to prosecute the beef trust, the oil trust, and tobacco trust. He considered "big labor" the same as big business, and intervened in the Pennsylvania coal strike of 1902. His theme was the Square Deal—justice for all law-abiding citizens, rich or poor. During his first full term as president, from 1904 to 1908, TR pursued a broad reform program at the

TIME LINE

1889	General Federation of Women's Clubs organized
1890	National American Woman's Suffrage Association formed
1893	Anti-Saloon League founded
1895	General Federation of Colored Women organized
1895	Booker T. Washington advocates a policy of racial accommodation
1901	McKinley assassinated; Theodore Roosevelt becomes president
	Robert M. La Follette elected governor of Wisconsin
	Tom Johnson elected mayor of Cleveland
1902	Anthracite coal miners' strike
1903	W. E. B. Du Bois, *The Souls of Black Folk*
	Elkins Act
1904	Roosevelt elected president
	Northern Securities case
1906	Upton Sinclair, *The Jungle*
	Meat Inspection Act
	Pure Food and Drug Act
	Hepburn Railway Act
	Atlanta Race Riot
1907	Financial panic
1908	*Muller* v. *Oregon*
	William Howard Taft elected president
1909	Women's shirtwaist workers' strike begins

	National Association for the Advancement of Colored People organized
	Herbert Croly, *The Promise of American Life*
	Payne-Aldrich Tariff
1910	Mann-Elkins Act
	Ballinger-Pinchot controversy
1911	Triangle Shirtwaist Company fire
1912	Progressive party founded
	Woodrow Wilson elected president
1913	Underwood Tariff
	Federal Reserve Act
	Sixteenth Amendment (income tax) ratified
	Seventeenth Amendment (direct election of senators) ratified
1914	Federal Trade Commission Act
	Clayton Anti-Trust Act
1915	Seaman's Act
	Premiere of *The Birth of a Nation*
1916	Federal Farm Loan Act
	Keating-Owen Child Labor Act
	Adamson Act
	Wilson re-elected
1918	*Hammer* v. *Dagenhart*
1919	Eighteenth Amendment (prohibition) ratified
1920	Prohibition begins
	Nineteenth Amendment (women's suffrage) ratified

national level. His major achievements were in railroad regulation, protection of consumers, and conservation of natural resources.

Taft, who took office in 1908, attacked the protective tariff, but had a vision of reform different from that of many of the Progressives in his own party. Some reforms were passed during his administration—the Sixteenth Amendment, establishing the federal income tax, and the Seventeenth. But some of his actions led to a split in the Republican party and the rise of a third party for the election of 1912. Taft was the Republican candidate; Wilson ran for the Democrats, and TR was the candidate of the Bull Moose party. Wilson won, and now the country got the Democratic version of progressivism.

Among Wilson's domestic achievements were tariff and financial reform, the latter designed to correct abuses in the financial system that had led to the panic of 1907. The Federal Reserve system, created in 1913, made possible a flexible and sound currency and national supervision of banking, which remained a private business. The Federal Farm Loan Act of 1916 created a financial system for farmers like the Federal Reserve system for banking. Antitrust laws such as the Federal Trade Commission Act of 1914 and the Clayton Act of the same year continued the policy of relying on regulatory commissions to deal with business practices. There was also legislation controlling child labor, improving the condition of merchant seamen, and establishing an eight-hour day for interstate-railway workers.

But like much of the social legislation passed during the Progressive Era, these laws were seldom enforced. The Progressives' major accomplishment seems to have been to satisfy public opinion. Very few structural changes were actually made. And not all segments of society were included: women and blacks continued to struggle on their own. Neither the women's desire for the vote nor black desires for equal opportunity and civil rights received much attention. Both black strategies— Booker T. Washington's "survival" and W. E. B. Du Bois's "talented tenth"—were doomed to betrayal by the continuation of virulent racism and by lack of interest on the part of the nation's leaders.

Suggested Readings

The spirit and thought of the early twentieth century may best be captured by reading the contemporary literature. Of particular value are the autobiographies of Lincoln Steffens, William Allen White, Robert M. La Follette, George Norris, Jane Addams, and Emma Goldman, as well as John Chamberlain, *Farewell to Reform* (1932); Walter Lippmann, *Drift and Mastery* (1914); Herbert Croly, *The Promise of American Life* (1909); Walter Weyl, *The New Democracy* (1912); John Spargo, *The Bitter Cry of the Children* (1906); and Ray Stannard Baker, *Following the Color Line* (1908).

The best introductions to this period are G. W. Mowry, *The Era of Theodore Roosevelt* (1958); A. S. Link, *Woodrow Wilson and the Progressive Era* (1954); O. L. Graham, *The Great Campaigns: Reform and War in America 1900–1928* (1971); J. W. Chambers, *The Tyranny of Change 1900–1917* (1980) and N. I. Painter, *Standing at Armageddon* (1987). In *The Age of Reform* (1955), Richard Hofstadter argued that status anxiety explained the mobilization of the older middle class behind Progressive reform. S. P. Hayes, *The Response to Industrialism* (1957), and R. H. Wiebe, *The Search for Order* (1967), stress that middle-class reformers sought to impose order and efficiency on a society they thought chaotic and fragmented. G. Kolko, *The Triumph of Conservatism* (1963), and J. Weinstein, *The Corporate Ideal in the Liberal State* (1968), emphasize Progressive success in absorbing the reform impulse.

Among the principal studies of Progressive thought are D. W. Noble, *The Paradox of Progressive Thought* (1958), and *The Progressive Mind 1890–1917* (1970); C. Forcey, *The Crossroads of Liberalism* (1961); C. Lasch, *The New Radicalism in America 1889–1963* (1965); S. Haber, *Efficiency and Uplift: Scientific Management in the Progressive Era 1890–1920* (1964); and R. Hofstadter, *The Progressive Historians* (1968).

The revelations of the muckrakers have been anthologized in A. Weinberg and L. Weinberg (eds.), *The Muckrakers* (1961), and H. Swados (ed.), *Years of Conscience* (1962). S. S. McClure, *My Autobiography* (1914); *The Autobiography of Lincoln Steffens* (1931); and I. M. Tarbell, *All in the Day's Work* (1939), tell much about the leading muckraker publisher and his star reporters. See also L. Filler, *Crusaders for American Liberalism* (1950 ed.); D. M. Chalmers, *The Social and Political Ideas of the Muckrakers* (1964); and H. S. Wilson, *McClure's Magazine and the Muckrakers* (1970).

The operations of progressivism on the regional and state level are examined in R. B. Nye, *Midwestern Progressive Politics* (1951); D. P. Thelen, *The New Citizenship: Origins of Progressivism in Wisconsin 1885–1900* (1972); G. E. Mowry, *The California Progressives* (1951); R. M. Abrams, *Conservatism in a Progressive Era: Massachusetts Politics 1900–1912* (1964); S. Hackney, *Populism to Progressivism in*

Alabama (1969); and D. W. Grantham, *Southern Progressivism* (1983). The party politics of progressivism are the subject of L. L. Gould, *Reform and Regulation: American Politics 1900–1916* (1978) and G. E. Mowry, *Theodore Roosevelt and the Progressive Movement* (1947).

The biographical approach to progressivism is also rewarding. The chapters on Roosevelt and Wilson in R. Hofstadter, *The American Political Tradition* (1948), are stimulating and controversial. J. M. Cooper, Jr., in *The Warrior and the Priest: Woodrow Wilson and Theodore Roosevelt* (1983), examines the ideological legacies of the two Progressive reform presidents. On Roosevelt, the best works, each with its own perspective, are H. F. Pringle, *Theodore Roosevelt* (1931); J. M. Blum, *The Republican Roosevelt* (1977 ed.); and W. H. Harbaugh, *Power and Responsibility* (1961). A. S. Link, *Wilson* (5 vols., 1947–65), contrasts in view with J. M. Blum, *Woodrow Wilson and the Politics of Morality* (1956). Principal studies of other political figures include P. E. Coletta, *The Presidency of William Howard Taft* (1973), R. Leopold, *Elihu Root and the Conservative Tradition* (1954); J. Braeman, *Albert J. Beveridge* (1971); J. A. Garraty, *Right-Hand Man: The Life of George W. Perkins* (1960); J. M. Blum, *Joe Tumulty and the Wilson Era* (1951); D. P. Thelen, *Robert M. La Follette and the Insurgent Spirit* (1976); R. M. Lowitt, *George W. Norris* (3 vols., 1963–78); and L. Ashby, *The Spearless Leader: Senator Borah and the Progressive Movement in the 1920s* (1972).

R. M. Crunden, *Ministers of Reform: The Progressives' Achievement in American Civilization* (1982), is a study of the culture, ideology, and politics of Progressive reform. How the Progressives confronted (or failed to confront) social and economic problems is examined in J. D. Buenker, *Urban Liberalism and Progressive Reform* (1973); S. P. Hays, *Conservation and the Gospel of Efficiency* (1959); R. Lubove, *The Progressives and the Slums 1890–1917* (1962); J. H. Timberlake, *Prohibition and the Progressive Movement 1900–1920* (1963); O. E. Anderson, Jr., *The Health of a Nation* (1958); J. R. Barrett, *Work and Community in the Jungle: Chicago's Packinghouse Workers, 1894–1922* (1987); W. Graebner, *Coal-Mining Safety in the Progressive Period: The Political Economy of Reform* (1976); and A. F. Davis, *Spearheads for Reform: The Social Settlements and the Progressive Movement* (1967) and *American Heroine* [Jane Addams] (1973). On changing attitudes and policies toward the criminal, the delinquent, and the mentally ill, see D. J. Rothman, *Conscience and Convenience: The Asylum and its Alternatives in Progressive America* (1980). On judicial reform, see M. I. Urofsky, *A Mind of One Piece: Brandeis and American Reform* (1971), and J. S. Auerbach, *Unequal Justice: Lawyers and Social Change in Modern America* (1976). On radicalism in the Progressive Era, see the assessments of M. Cantor, *The Divided Left: American Radicalism 1900–1975*

(1978), and J. P. Diggins, *The American Left in the Twentieth Century* (1973). Studies of the Socialist party in its heyday include H. H. Quint, *The Forging of American Socialism* (1953); I. Kipnis, *The American Socialist Movement 1897–1912* (1952); D. A. Shannon, *The Socialist Party of America* (1955); N. Salvatore, *Eugene V. Debs* (1982); and J. Weinstein, *The Decline of Socialism in America 1912–1925* (1967).

The social history of women is examined in L. W. Banner, *Women in Modern America* (1974); S. M. Rothman, *Woman's Proper Place: A History of Changing Ideals and Practices, 1870 to the Present* (1978); W. L. O'Neill, *Everyone Was Brave: The Rise and Fall of Feminism in America* (1969); C. N. Degler, *At Odds: Women and the Family in America from the Revolution to the Present* (1980) and S. M. Evans, *Born for Liberty* (1989). N. F. Coit and E. H. Pleck (eds.), *A Heritage of Her Own* (1979), is an important collection of essays, as are Gerda Lerner, *The Majority Finds Its Past: Placing Women in History* (1979), and A. F. Scott, *Making the Invisible Woman Visible* (1984). The history of wage-earning women is examined in A. Kessler-Harris, *Out to Work* (1982). The ideology of women activists is examined in A. S. Kraditor, *The Ideas of the Woman Suffrage Movement 1890–1920* (1965). R. Rosenberg, *Beyond Separate Spheres: Intellectual Roots of Modern Feminism* (1982); and N. F. Cott, *The Grounding of American Feminism* (1987). On feminist-anarchist Emma Goldman, see her autobiography, *Living My Life* (1934), and C. Falk, *Love, Anarchy, and Emma Goldman* (1984). On black activist Ida B. Wells, see A. M. Duster (ed.), *Crusade for Justice: The Autobiography of Ida B. Wells* (1970). Sex and race as issues in American culture are analyzed in W. H. Chafe, *Women and Equality: Changing Patterns in American Culture* (1977). On the changing status of women, as reflected in divorce and birth control, see E. T. May, *Great Expectations: Marriage and Divorce in Post-Victorian America* (1980); W. L. O'Neill, *Divorce in the Progressive Era* (1967); D. M. Kennedy, *Birth Control in America: The Career of Margaret Sanger* (1970); and L. Gordon, *Woman's Body, Woman's Right: A Social History of Birth Control in America* (1976). The Uprising of the Twenty Thousand is described in L. Levine, *The Women's Garment Workers* (1924). R. Rosen and S. Davidson (eds.), *The Maimie Papers* (1977), illuminates the tension between middle-class women reformers and lower-class women immigrants. See also R. Rosen, *The Lost Sisterhood: Prostitution in America, 1900–1918* (1982). On the work and family life of black women, see J. Jones, *Labor of Love, Labor of Sorrow* (1985).

W. E. B. Du Bois, *The Souls of Black Folk* (1903), explores the dilemma of racial identity. On Booker T. Washington, see his autobiography, *Up from Slavery* (1902), and L. R. Harlan, *Booker T. Washington: The Making of a Black Leader 1856–1901* (1972) and *The Wizard of Tuskegee, 1901–1915* (1983). Studies of Du

Bois include E. M. Rudwick, *W. E. B. Du Bois: A Study in Minority Group Leadership* (1960); F. L. Broderick, *W. E. B. Du Bois: Negro Leader in a Time of Crisis* (1959); and A. Rampersad, *The Art and Imagination of W. E. B. Du Bois* (1976). On black ideology in this period, see A. Meier, *Negro Thought in America 1880–1915* (1963). On lynching, see W. White, *Rope and Faggot* (1929), and J. D. Hall, *Revolt against Chivalry* (1979). The best history of the Delta blues is R. Palmer, *Deep Blues* (1981).

AMERICANS ALL!
HONOR ROLL
Du Bois
Smith
O'Brien
Cejka
Haucke
Pappandrikopolous
Andrassi
Villotto
Levy
Turovich
Kowalski
Chriczanevicz
Knutson
Gonzales
Howard Chandler Christy 1919

WORLD WAR AND WORLD REVOLUTION

The incident meant little to most Americans, but it would have great consequences for them and for much of the world. On June 28, 1914, Archduke Franz Ferdinand, heir to the throne of the Austro-Hungarian Empire, was shot and killed by a young Serbian nationalist at Sarajevo in the Austrian province of Bosnia. For more than a generation, the European nations had been living in fear of one another. They had been engaged in an intense competition for world markets and sources of investments and raw materials. As their suspicions and rivalries grew, so did their haste to accumulate arms and allies.

When Ferdinand died, Europe was divided roughly into two camps: the Central Powers (Germany and Austria-Hungary) and the Allied Powers (Great Britain, France, and Russia). Within six weeks, these powerful coalitions were engaged in an armed conflict that would soon engulf the rest of Europe and much of the world—the Great War, or World War I. (Italy remained neutral until May 1915. Then the Allies, in a secret treaty, promised it territory after the war in exchange for intervention on their side.) The Central Powers and the Allies both sought American support and flooded the United States with propaganda.

Concerned with domestic problems, Americans were uncertain of what the European conflict was all about. Few in 1914 could have conceived that national or economic interest might force the country into the war. When Wilson won reelection in 1916, his followers shouting "He kept us out of war!" he could hardly have imagined that in only five months he would go before Congress to ask for a declaration of war. When the United States entered the European conflict, which then became a world war, Wilson explained the American action in the moralistic language Americans had come to expect from him: "This is the People's War, a war for freedom and justice and self-government amongst all the nations of the world, a war to make the world safe for the peoples who live upon it." Whatever doubts Americans had had about the conflict were now resolved; few dared to question the need to work to ensure an American and Allied victory.

When it came to constructing a peace, Wilson was moved by the same moral considerations. What sustained him in his prosecution of the war and in his mission as a peacemaker was the conviction that moral principle would triumph and the world would be made safe for democracy. But the world after the Great War was far different from that of 1914. The Bolshevik Revolution in Russia, social upheavals elsewhere, and colonial and nationalist stirrings complicated and frustrated his peace mission. He would be victimized not only by the legacy of Europe's long history of national jealousies, but by his own self-righteousness and sense of mission. In the end, the Allies denied him the "just" peace he had sought. The Senate denied him the means by which he had hoped to impose a kind of Progressive order on humankind. And the American people seemed to have grown weary of his rhetoric and his crusade.

TOWARD INTERVENTION

The preoccupation of American leaders with world power since the Spanish-American War could not hide the fact that in many ways the United States was a provincial nation in 1914. Most Americans were startled by the outbreak of fighting in Europe. When the president, in the early days of the war, appealed to them to be "impartial in thought as well as in act," they saw no reason why they should be drawn into an overseas war they barely understood.

It was not long, however, before the loyalties of the more than 30 million Americans of European birth or parentage became engaged with one side or the other. Wilson personally shared the sympathy of the majority of Americans with the Allies. Since the turn of the century, England had made an effort to keep American friendship. Language and culture joined the educated classes of both countries; trade and finance, although marked by prewar competition and wartime jealousies, united the British and American business communities. A somewhat vaguer American enthusiasm for France dated back to the days of Lafayette and French help during the War for Independence. Belgium drew sympathy as Germany's first victim—a small, neutral nation overrun by German armies seeking to outflank the French.

In the propaganda battle for the hearts and minds of Americans, the Allies clearly had the advantage. Allied propagandists turned the conflict into a war to preserve the basic values of civilization from the German Hun. The martyrdom of Belgium confirmed in the minds of most Americans the belief that Germany was the wrongdoer. The war at sea also favored Allied public relations. The blockade of central Europe brought hunger and malnutrition to women and children in 1916, but such slow cruelty was hard to dramatize. The German submarine, on the other hand, evoked shocking images of ships lost at sea with no chance of survivors. That warfare took on added significance when it threatened to undermine the American economy.

The Economy and Freedom of the Seas

The disruption of international trade and exchange brought about by the war in Europe threatened the United States with an economic depression. Due to the Allied blockade, American trade with the Central Powers fell in value from almost $170 million in 1914 to virtually nothing in 1916. On the other hand, the Allies looked to the United States for manufactured goods and food, and the British navy controlled the seas. Orders poured into the United States, with the result that American trade with the Allies soared from $825 million in 1914 to about $3.2 billion in 1916. The surge rescued the economy from a recession and started a boom that lasted until 1919.

Even more important was the transformation of the United States from a debtor to a creditor nation. The large amounts of American bond and corporate securities held by British investors were sold to pay for war materials. To finance further buying, on which Allied success in the war depended, the British and their friends had to borrow. The State Department discouraged American bankers from making loans to Allied governments, for fear the American stake in an Allied victory would become so great it would draw the country into war. To grant loans to any of the powers, Secretary of State Bryan informed J. P. Morgan, would be "inconsistent with the true spirit of neutrality." Wilson agreed.

But in June 1915, with Allied gold and dollar resources nearly gone, the administration reversed its position. Secretary of State Lansing, who had replaced Bryan, phrased the problem appropriately: "Can we afford to let a declaration as to our conception of the 'true spirit of neutrality' made in the first days of the war stand in the way of our national interests which seem to be seriously threatened?" To maintain American prosperity, Secretary of the Treasury McAdoo wrote to the president, "we must finance it." By April 1917 loans to Allied governments had exceeded $2 billion.

The United States, then, despite its neutrality, came to have an enormous stake in the Allies' ability to pay for the goods and loans they acquired. The United States had become in effect the principal supplier of the Allied Powers. The assumption of this role was not the work of a small group of American bankers and munitions makers, but reflected the desire of large numbers of American businessmen and farmers to profit from the war needs of the Allies and to make up for the loss of certain peacetime markets. Nor did Americans believe that trade with the Allies compromised their neutrality; on the contrary, they regarded interference with that trade as an unacceptable violation of neutrality.

To Wilson, the rights of neutrals were fully protected under international law, including the right to engage in trade with a belligerent power. He expected the nations involved in the war to respect those rights. To the European powers, engaged in a struggle for survival, modern methods of warfare had made much of international law obsolete. Wilson soon found himself in conflict with both sides over the rights of neutral carriers. One of the earliest disputes with Britain arose over the definition of *contraband*—goods that, according to international law, may not be supplied by a neutral to one belligerent without risk of seizure by another. The British redefined contraband to include *all* articles of importance, including foodstuffs, that might give indirect aid to the enemy.

The liberties the British took with the traditional right of *visit and search* caused additional friction. Under international law, a belligerent vessel had the right to stop and search a neutral merchant ship, sending it to a prize court for legal action if contraband was discovered, releasing it if none was found. The British insisted that the task of searching large, modern vessels had grown too complicated for the usual procedure to be observed any longer. They therefore often took neutral vessels to port for a thorough examination, thereby imposing costly delays on American ships. A third source of trouble was Britain's blockading not only enemy ports, but neutral ports near enough to Germany to serve as entry points to German markets.

In November 1914, the British declared the entire North Sea a military area and mined it so thoroughly that no neutral vessel could cross it safely without first receiving British directions. This again was a radical departure from international practice. To all complaints, Britain replied that it was fighting for its life and would not be bound by laws made under conditions now obsolete. If the United States had chosen to challenge the British action by sending its ships unescorted into the North Sea, no doubt American ships would have been sunk. But the Wilson administration decided instead to protest the British practice through a formal note. In the summer of 1916 the London government drew up a list of eighty-five persons or firms in the United States suspected of giving aid to Germany and forbade British subjects to trade with them. Wilson was outraged.

Yet the United States never really considered going to war against the Allies. "England is fighting our fight," Wilson declared at one point. When members of his cabinet urged him to prohibit exports to Britain in 1915, Wilson replied: "Gentlemen, the Allies are standing with their backs to the wall fighting wild beasts."

But despite his sympathy for the British, Wilson did insist that both sides observe the rights of neutrals. In the first two years of the war, the United States found itself protesting British violations more frequently than German violations. The critical difference between British and German violations, however, was that German violations destroyed American lives and property; British violations did not.

The War at Sea

The more deeply the United States became involved with the Allies, the more likely it was that American ships would be affected by the ongoing submarine warfare. A submarine could easily be sunk once it surfaced, even by the light deck guns of merchant ships. Submarine commanders therefore could not follow the traditional practice of stopping a suspect vessel, discovering its identity, and providing for the safety of passengers and crew before sending it to the bottom. They had to hit and run. British practices on the high seas were less offensive: they involved legal disputes that could be adjusted at the end of the war. On February 4, 1915, the German government announced its intention of establishing a war area around the British Isles in which all enemy ships would be destroyed without warning. It was clear that neutral vessels would not be safe.

The Germans offered to change their tactics if the Allies lifted their food blockade. But there was no hope of altering Allied policy in this respect. By early 1915, as more and more Allied merchant vessels were being sunk, traveling on belligerent ships posed a grave danger. The German government issued warnings about that danger, and Bryan, then secretary of state, urged the president to forbid Americans to take the risk. Wilson refused, insisting that American travelers were simply exercising a traditional right.

On May 7, 1915, a German submarine sank the unarmed British liner *Lusitania;* 1198 passengers were lost, 128 of them Americans. Although the ship was carrying rifle cartridges and other contraband, the toll of lives dramatized the submarine issue. Some Americans demanded an immediate declaration of war. Wilson chose instead to send three strong notes of protest to Germany. One was so close to a threat of war that Bryan resigned rather than sign it and acknowledge a double standard in dealing with British and German violations of neutral rights.

More sinkings occured after the *Lusitania* tragedy, and American protests brought German promises that submarine methods would be modified. But in March 1916 a submarine torpedoed the unarmed French ship *Sussex,* injuring Americans aboard. Wilson warned Germany that if it did not immediately abandon these tactics, "the United States [would] have no choice but to severe diplomatic relations." This threat drew from the Germans the *Sussex* pledge of May 4, 1916, declaring that no more merchant vessels would be sunk without warning, *provided* that the United States held Britain accountable for *its* violations of international law. By ignoring this proviso but accepting the pledge, Wilson succeeded in forcing Germany to place crippling restrictions on its principal maritime weapon.

The Decision to Fight

Wilson became convinced early in the war that the best way to keep the United States at peace was to bring an end to the fighting. In January 1915 and again a year later, he sent his personal adviser, Colonel Edward M. House, on peace missions to Europe. These visits came to nothing. Discouraged, Wilson at last gave in to the agitation for preparedness organized by Roosevelt, Lodge, and others almost from the moment Belgium had been overrun. Late in January 1916 he took off on a nationwide tour to promote the preparedness idea. By June, Congress had adopted his proposals for enlargement of the army, the navy, and the merchant marine, and for the opening of officers' training centers at universities and elsewhere. Plans also were made for industrial mobilization.

In taking these steps, Wilson seized what might have become a useful Republican issue in the 1916 presidential campaign. Although some Progressives felt that much-needed domestic reforms were being sacrificed to military preparedness, they were few in number, even in the Progressive party. Urged to accept the Progressive presidential nomination, Roosevelt asked the party to instead back the Republican nominee, Supreme Court Justice Charles Evans Hughes. Hughes, he said, stood for the "clean-cut, straight-out Americanism" Progressives themselves ad-

---

WORDS AND NAMES IN AMERICAN HISTORY

Nowadays a *running mate* might be someone to jog with. Originally the term was associated with horse racing. But in 1912 Woodrow Wilson, having secured the Democratic presidential nomination, proclaimed about the Democratic candidate for vice-president: "Gov. Marshall bears the highest reputation . . . and I feel honored by having him as running mate." Ever since, the term *running mate* has usually referred to a vice-presidential candidate. "Gov. Marshall" was Thomas Marshall of Indiana, probably the most popular vice-president this nation has ever had. In 1916 he became the first vice-president in a century to succeed himself. He was also a master of one-liners long before that phrase was ever invented. A loyal member of the Democratic party, he announced that "Democrats, like poets, are born not made." Another of his lines, best known to fans of trivia, was "What this country needs is a really good 5 cent cigar." Some seventy years later, the kind of partnership connoted by the term *running mate* proved a bit awkward for Geraldine Ferraro, the country's first woman vice-presidential candidate. During the election of 1984, the advisers of both candidates discussed at length whether they could even put an arm around each other's shoulder in public.

U.S.A.
1917

NORWAY

Oslo •

Stockholm •

SWEDEN

NORTH SEA

FINLAND
Indep. July, 1917

Lake Ladoga

Helsinki •

• Petrograd

Battle of Jutland
May-June, 1916 ✴

DENMARK

BALTIC SEA

ESTONIA
Indep.
Feb. 1918

LATVIA
Indep.
Nov, 1918
Riga offensive
Sept, 1917

Riga

RUSSIA

GREAT
BRITAIN
1914

London •

Copenhagen •

Kiel •

• Hamburg

Memel •

Konigsberg •

Danzig •

Masurian Lakes ✴
Sept, 1914

LITHUANIA
Indep. Feb, 1918

Vilna •

Smolensk •

NETH.

Amsterdam •

Berlin •

Tannenberg ✴
Aug, 1914

Minsk •

Brussels •

BELG.
1914

• Cologne

GERMANY
1914

Leipzig •

POLAND
Indep. Nov, 1918

Pinsk •

GERMAN INVASION
AUG-SEPT, 1914

• Dresden

Warsaw •

Brest-Litovsk •

Paris •

Mainz •

Prague •

• Lublin

Kiev •

LUX.

• Metz

Rhine R.

Strasbourg •

Lemberg •

FRANCE
1914

BAVARIA

Munich •

Danube R.

Vienna •

GALICIA

Cracow •

UKRAINE

Berne • SWITZ.

Pressburg •

Piave June, 1918

• Graz

Odessa •

Milan •

Vittorio-Veneto
Oct-Nov, 1918

Budapest •

AUSTRIA-HUNGARY
1914

Genoa •

Venice •

• Trieste

BLACK SEA

• Marseilles

SPAIN

ITALY
1915

BOSNIA

Belgrade •

RUMANIA
1916

Bucharest •

Danube R.

Withdrew from
Triple Alliance 1914

Sarajevo •

CORSICA

SERBIA
1914

BULGARIA
1915

Rome •

MONTENEGRO
1915

Sofia •

Constantinople •

SARDINIA

Naples •

ALBANIA

OTTOMAN EMPIRE
1914

PORTUGAL
1916

Salonika •

Gallipoli ✴

GREECE
1916

Dardanelles campaign
1915-1916

• Smyrna

SICILY

Athens •

CRETE

1916   Date of entry into the war

━━━━   Maximum advance of the Central Powers

– – –   Maximum Russian advance

•••••••   Line of the Brest-Litovsk Treaty Mar, 1918

━━━━   Armistice lines, eastern front Dec., 1917

0   500

Miles

Central Powers   Allied Powers   Neutral Powers

World War I

mired. This the Progressives agreed to do, although somewere disillusioned enough to vote for Wilson.

The Democrats renominated Wilson on the first ballot. Four years earlier Wilson had been elected only because Republican strength had been split between Roosevelt and Taft. This time, with Roosevelt campaigning for Hughes, it was hard to see how Wilson could win. Hughes, however, straddled the issue of peace and war and failed to excite the voters. Wilson, at the same time, could boast of the *Sussex* pledge, which he had wrung from the Germans while keeping the United States out of war. Wilson's domestic reforms—the child-labor law, the eight-hour day for railroad workers, and low-cost loans for farmers—also helped him. But in the end, the election was close enough to hang for the first time on western ballots. Wilson carried California by a mere 4000 votes, and with it enough states in the electoral college to give him a majority of 277 to 254. In the popular vote, he received 9,127,000, to 8,533,000 for Hughes.

Wilson now renewed his attempts to bring the war to an end through mediation. He sent notes asking all the powers to state acceptable terms of peace. When nothing came of this gesture, Wilson followed with another. In a speech before the Senate on January 22, 1917, he announced to the world his own conception of a just and lasting peace and outlined ideas for a League of Nations to maintain it. "It must be a peace without victory," he said, based on the self-determination of all peoples, freedom of the seas, and disarmament. In making this plea, Wilson claimed to be speaking for "the silent mass of mankind everywhere."

Most Americans greeted this speech with enthusiasm. To the Allies, it seemed to be a withdrawal of the informal sympathy they had come to expect from the United States. Wilson's gestures also came at a time when Germany's military fortunes were high. The bloody stalemate that marked the fighting was wearing down the Allies. Within ten days of Wilson's speech, in fact, the Germans felt confident enough to revoke the *Sussex* pledge and strike for victory. On January 31, 1917, Germany announced that its submarines would again sink all vessels on sight, armed or unarmed, within a specified zone around the British Isles and in the Mediterranean. The Germans realized they now risked almost certain war with the United States, but they hoped to knock Britain out by cutting off its food supply before American forces reached the battlefields. They almost won the gamble.

As Wilson had promised, he now broke off diplomatic relations with Germany. He next called on Congress to authorize the arming of American merchant vessels. When a group of senators blocked this proposal with a filibuster, Wilson called them "a little group of willful men, representing no opinion but their own" and proceeded to carry out his plan by executive order. Wilson thought he still might avoid war, but several factors made this highly unlikely. Suspicion of Germany grew in January 1917, when British naval intelligence intercepted a message in code from German foreign secretary Alfred Zimmerman to the German minister in Mexico, instructing him to propose an alliance with Mexico in case of war with the United States. In return, Germany promised to help Mexico recover "her lost territory in New Mexico, Texas, and Arizona."

Wilson disclosed the message on March 1 to create further support for his armed-ship bill. Two weeks later, the March Revolution in Russia replaced the czarist regime with a provisional representative government, making it easier to describe the war against the Central Powers as a war for democracy and against autocracies. Finally, German submarine warfare in the Atlantic, which resulted in three American ships being torpedoed in March, clarified the issue in the minds of most Americans as a question of defending national honor; neutral rights and international law obviously counted for nothing. Defeat of the Allies, moreover, would endanger both national security and the American economy. Without American troops, as well as a continuing flow of supplies, a German victory seemed certain.

On April 2 Wilson asked Congress for a declaration of war, condemning German submarine warfare as "warfare against mankind." But he placed the conflict on even higher moral grounds. By going to war, the United States intended to fight for the liberation of all peoples, including the German people: "The world must be made safe for democracy." Distinguishing between the "military masters of Germany" and their subjects, Wilson declared that the United States entered the war "not as a partisan" but as everybody's friend; it would defend not only neutrals' rights but the rights of all people. On April 4 the Senate voted for war against Germany, 82 to 6. Two days later the House concurred, 373 to 50. Not until December 7, 1917, was war declared against Austria-Hungary.

THE WAR AT HOME AND OVERSEAS

The decision of the United States to join the fighting against Germany came when the Allies were doing badly almost everywhere. Losses in the Russian armies already exceeded a million men, and the Russian people were prepared to oppose any government that would not call a halt to the slaughter. The Bolshevik Revolution in November 1917 took Russia out of the war altogether, permitting the Germans to move men and supplies from the eastern to the western front. Worst of all, the new German submarine campaign was a great success: 880,000 tons of Allied shipping was sunk in April alone.

The United States entered the war in April 1917. Nineteen months later, with Allied and American troops advancing on all fronts, Germany agreed to an armistice. The role of the United States in achieving this victory was considerable. The American navy almost immediately reduced the amount of tonnage lost to submarines. American ground troops ultimately helped to turn back the German armies. And the continuing flow of American supplies and money sustained the entire war effort.

To make this all possible, the United States needed to mobilize its government, people, economy, and society on a new scale. Americans had to be conditioned to make the necessary sacrifices and commitments. For a nation that had grown accustomed to Progressive ways of thinking, much of this planned effort was only a shift in goals rather than in means.

Mobilization

Even before Congress declared war, thousands of Americans had volunteered to serve with the Allies, and many of them saw the full four years of fighting. When the United States entered the war, the combined strength of the regular army and the National Guard was about 372,000 men, from whom were drawn the officers and noncoms of the new army to be created under the Selective Service Act of May 18, 1917. This act required all men between the ages of twenty-one and thirty (later extended to eighteen and forty-five) to register for military service. Registrants were placed in five classes, headed by able-bodied unmarried men without dependents. From this group alone the nation drew all the 2,810,000 men

actually drafted, although by the end of the war as many as 4,800,000 persons had been enrolled in the army, navy, and Marine Corps.

Some experts recommended that the administration finance the war on a pay-as-you-go basis, by taxing wartime profits and earnings. In fact, about half of the nearly $33 billion spent on the war was raised by taxation. The rest was raised by borrowing, mainly through four Liberty Loan drives in 1917 and 1918. Backed by rallies, parades, and posters, volunteers sold the bonds directly to the public rather than to the banking community. Each issue was oversubscribed.

To mobilize the nation's other resources, Wilson created the Council of National Defense, made up of six cabinet members and an advisory commission of seven additional civilians. Under the council's supervision, huge agencies performed specific wartime tasks. The Emergency Fleet Corporation had been created as early as April 1916 to enlarge the merchant marine. The Food Administration, headed by Herbert Hoover, undertook to supply civilians and combatants. The Fuel Administration doled out coal and oil.

(Library of Congress)

(Library of Congress)

The Railroad Administration consolidated the nation's railroads and, without removing them from private ownership, operated them as a single system.

In March 1918 the Council of National Defense placed the War Industries Board under the direction of Bernard Baruch, a Wall Street broker, and gave him dictatorial powers over American business. Great savings were effected by planning and the standardization of products.

AFL president Samuel Gompers, on becoming one of the civilian advisers of the Council of National Defense, declared that American workers backed the war, but that he hoped the government would prevent exploitation and profiteering at their expense. Early in 1918, in return for its pledge not to strike, organized labor was assured of the right of collective bargaining, maintenance of the eight-hour day where it existed, and other privileges. A National War Labor Board was created to mediate labor disputes, and a War Labor Policies Board to deal with grievances. Between 1915 and 1917, the number of strikes had tripled and the number of strikers had more than doubled. Strikes then fell off. Meanwhile, the AFL pushed its membership from 1,950,000 in 1915 to 2,800,000 in 1918.

The wartime demand for labor pushed wages up as much as 20 percent in purchasing power in key military industries and approximately 4 percent overall. At the same time, salaried employees suffered from wartime inflation, losing as much as one-third of their prewar purchasing power.

Businessmen and farmers fared best of all. Baruch's War Industries Board, unwilling to delay production, gave up the traditional practice of competitive bidding and made war purchases on the basis of *cost-plus contracts*. Such contracts guaranteed sellers profits ranging from 2.5 to 15 percent of production costs. By padding costs, some contractors made enough to increase dividend payments and executive salaries and still pile up profits, despite huge taxes.

Large personal fortunes also grew. In 1914, only 5000 people reported annual incomes in the $50,000-to-$100,000 tax bracket; in 1918, 13,000 did so. Hoover's Food Administration, meanwhile, set such a high government price on wheat and other staples that farmers stretched their resources to acquire more land. Farm operators' real income was 29 percent higher in 1918 than in 1915. Soon after the wartime demand ended, however, the farmers found themselves in deeper financial trouble than ever before (see Chapter 27).

Propaganda and Civil Liberties

Despite the success of the Liberty Loan drives, there was strong feeling against the war. "We are going into war at the command of gold," Senator George W. Norris of Nebraska charged in a popular speech against involvement. At Canton, Ohio, Socialist leader Eugene Debs attacked the war in words that would send him to a federal prison: "The master class has always declared wars; the subject class has always fought the battles. The master class has had all to gain and nothing to lose, while the subject class has had nothing to gain and all to lose—especially their lives." Evidence of antiwar sentiment appeared in the strong showing of the Socialist party in municipal elections in 1917. In some communities, Socialists won as much as 30 or 40 percent of the vote.

To mobilize public thinking, Congress established the Committee on Public Information within two weeks of the declaration of war. Wilson named George Creel, once a prominent muckraker, to head it. Creel enlisted journalists, scholars, and clergy to convince the country that the Germans were depraved. Although the vast majority of German Americans accepted the neces-

WOMEN'S WORK

Although women viewed wartime work as a patriotic duty, not as a way to replace men in industrial jobs, some women managed to keep their positions after the war, deriving considerable satisfaction from the additional income and independence. In their examination of "Middletown" (Muncie, Indiana) in the 1920s, sociologists Robert and Helen Lynd interviewed a forty-two-year-old woman, married to a pipefitter and the mother of two high school boys. She worked six days a week as a cleaning woman in a public building.

I began to work during the war, when every one else did; we had to meet payments on our house and everything else was getting so high. The mister objected at first, but now he don't mind. I'd rather keep on working so my boys can play football and basketball and have spending money their father *can't give them. We've built our own home, a nice brown and white bungalow, by a building and loan like every one else does. We have it almost all paid off and it's worth about $6,000. No, I don't lose out with my neighbors because I work; some of them have jobs and those who don't envy us who do. I have felt better since I worked than ever before in my life. I get up at five-thirty. My husband takes his dinner and the boys buy theirs uptown and I cook supper. We have an electric washing machine, electric iron, and vacuum sweeper. I don't even have to ask my husband any more because I buy these things with my own money. . . .*

Source: Robert S. Lynd and Helen Mercer Lynd, *Middletown* (New York: Harcourt, Brace, 1929), pp. 28–29. Copyright 1929 by HBJ; renewed 1957 by Robert and Helen Lynd. Photograph from the National Archives.

sity of war once the United States joined the Allies, they became the most obvious targets of abuse. Libraries removed German books and sometimes publicly burned them. Schools dropped the German language from the curriculum. A peak in absurdity was reached by restaurants that renamed sauerkraut "liberty cabbage" and kennels that rechristened dachshunds "liberty pups."

But pacifists, Socialists, and left-wing workers suffered the worst repression. Congress made intolerance official by adopting the Espionage Act of June 1917 and the Sedition Act of May 1918. The Espionage Act set a fine of up to $10,000 and a prison term of twenty years for anyone who interfered with the draft or encouraged disloyalty. The Sedition Act set the same penalties for anyone who obstructed the sale of government bonds, discouraged recruiting, or did "willfully utter, print, write, or publish any disloyal, profane, scurrilous, or abusive language" about the American form of government, the Constitution, the flag, or service uniforms, or "advocate any curtailment of production . . . of anything necessary or essential to the prosecution of the war."

Although President Wilson had proclaimed in his war message "the privilege of men everywhere to choose their way of life and of obedience," he maintained a discreet silence on the ensuing widespread violation of civil liberties in the United States. Under the Espionage and Sedition laws, over 1500 persons were imprisoned, including Eugene Debs. Wilson refused to pardon Debs, even after the war had ended. "While the flower of American youth was pouring out its blood to vindicate the cause of civilization," Wilson asserted, "Debs stood behind the lines sniping, attacking, and denouncing them."

But Debs was not the only victim of this curious war for universal liberty and democracy. Several antiwar newspapers lost their mailing privileges, Department of Justice agents conducted illegal raids on antiwar organizations, judges gave harsh sentences to war critics, and patriotic mobs took out their fury in the streets. The House of Representatives voted 309 to 1 not to seat Victor Berger, a Socialist congressman from Wisconsin, because of his antiwar views and consequent indictment under the Espionage Act. "The one and only issue in this case," one congressman made clear, "is that of Americanism."

Only a few Americans protested these abridgments of their fundamental liberties, notably the newly formed Civil Liberties Bureau (the forerunner of the American Civil Liberties Union) under Roger Baldwin. But the bureau found it difficult to publicize its cause or raise funds, and some liberal reformers who were sympathetic decided to keep

World War I: the western front.

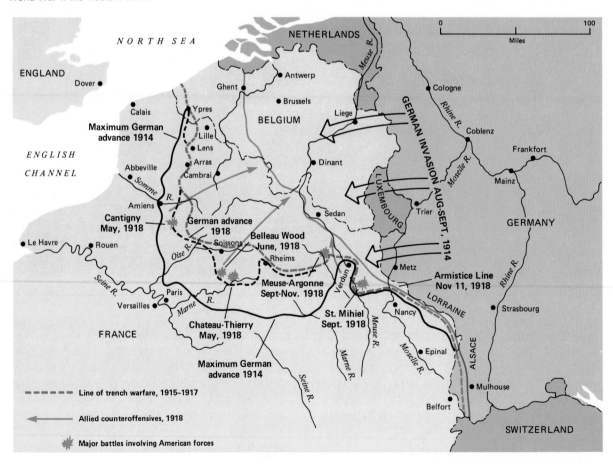

CHAPTER 26 WORLD WAR AND WORLD REVOLUTION

silent. Jane Addams wrote to Baldwin explaining why she could not sign an appeal for funds: "I am obliged to walk very softly in all things suspect."

The Army in Action

The first American troops, under General John J. Pershing, arrived in France in June 1917 and were fed into the sagging Allied lines largely to bolster morale. When the Germans launched a massive offensive in March 1918, hoping to end the war, about 300,000 American soldiers had reached France and more were arriving every day. By war's end, about 1.4 million of the more than 2 million men carried to Europe had become actively engaged, mostly on the western front. In April 1918 the Germans had a numerical superiority of perhaps 320,000 on this front. By November, fresh American troops had given the Allies the advantage by 600,000.

Large numbers of Americans were thrown into battle inadequately trained, but they played a decisive role in the last eight months of the war. The Allies had hoped to continue to use American troops largely as replacements and to integrate them with French or British units. Pershing, however, fought this policy. He felt the Allies had grown too defensive-minded and that the Americans would be more successful conducting independent operations. The greater part of the American army soon took its place in the lines as a separate force under Pershing's command, subject, after April 1918, to the overall command of Marshal Ferdinand Foch of France.

Pershing's men faced their first major test when assigned to help repulse a German thrust toward Paris. By May 30, 1918, the Germans had reached Château-Thierry on the Marne, only fifty miles from the French capital. The Americans drove them back, and from June 6 to June 25 cleared nearby Belleau Wood of enemy forces. In July, when the German General Staff made its last great effort to break through to Paris, between Rheims and Soissons, 85,000 Americans helped check the assault. In its first major offensive assignment, in September 1918, the American army launched an attack on the St. Mihiel salient, a German bulge protruding into the Allied lines across the Meuse River southeast of Verdun. Pershing sent American troops against both flanks of the salient and with some French support reduced it in two days.

The Meuse-Argonne offensive, from late Sep-

Wounded soldier viewing a parade of the 369th Colored Infantry in New York City, 1919. *(UPI/Bettmann Newsphotos)*

tember to early November, became one of the fiercest battles in American military history. Together with the French forces on that front, Americans captured more than 25,000 prisoners and a great deal of equipment, but at a high cost in casualties. This offensive, part of a coordinated drive against the Central Powers all along the western front, helped defeat Germany and its allies. By early November, the German armies were everywhere in retreat, the navy was on the verge of general mutiny, and the civilian population was hungry, exhausted, and dangerously discontented. On November 11, Germany gave up and signed an armistice.

The war was not over, since terms of peace had yet to be worked out. But fighting on the major fronts had ceased at last. American losses— 48,000 killed in battle, 2900 missing in action, 56,000 dead of disease—were light in comparison with the death toll the other nations had suffered since 1914. Before pulling out of the war early in 1918, Russia counted 1,700,000 battle deaths. Germany lost 1,800,000 men, France 1,385,000,

FROM THE FRONT

American Ex. [peditionary] Forces

Dear Wife:

We pulled out about the 19th of Sept, moving towards the Argonne Forest. Finly we came to thair trenches and thair we got lots of prisiners, another fellow and myself got 13 out of one little dugout. We seen a machine gun setting in the mouth of the dugout so we stopped and decided what to do. So I asked him what he wanted to do, go get the machine gun or stay thair and keep his eye on the dugout until I could crawl up and get the gun, so he decided he would let me go.

Thair at that line of trenches one of the boys threw a hand grenade in on a Hun as he started to come out without his hands up and killed him. Well, it was along about eleven o'clock in the day now and as we hadnt had any breakfast we were getting quite tired and hungry.

In a short while we started to advance and by that time Jerry was sending shells over in a jiffy. Right thair was when I saw what war really was. The fellow on my right got hit. It was my luck that I was caught right in an open place so I dropped behind an old stump and thair I had to stay as it looked as if they were going to mow the old stump down. Well, I thought that I was a gone sucker sure. I laid thair until dark looking every minute for Fritzie to sneek up on me but he didn't come. Seven of us was sent back to gather up some ammunition and the Germans saw us and threw the shells into us. Three shells came all at once right on top of us. The man in front of me fell and the one in rear of me. The concussion from the explosion knocked me down and when I went to get up I was bured in dirt and rack and I thought I was killed as they almost knocked me senseless. Will leave out quite a bit that I witnessed now as it is too bad to write. We had 250 men when we started over the top on the 26th of Sept. and when we came out thair want but about 80 of us left. Gee, I did feel lucky, which all of us did that were still alive. Love to you.

Your Husband, Pvt. Jesse M. Maxey

Source: William Matthews and Dixon Wecter, *Our Soldiers Speak: 1885–1919* (Boston: Little, Brown, 1943).

In the thick smoke and fog of the Argonne Forest, Allied and American troops suffered heavy casualties. *(National Archives)*

Britain 947,000, and Austria-Hungary 1,200,000. The war had come close to wiping out an entire generation.

PEACEMAKING AND REVOLUTION

While his administration waged a militant propaganda campaign on the home front, Wilson was seeking to clarify the objectives of the war. When the United States was still neutral, his appeal for "peace without victory" had brought hope to a world already sick of war. After the United States entered the war, he kept asserting that hostilities were directed not against the German people, but against their government. Unaware that the Allies had concluded secret treaties incorporating their own goals, the president held that the real objectives were neither punitive damages nor territorial gains but rather the end of autocratic government and a settlement that would ensure permanent peace.

In the peace treaty he helped to negotiate, as in his proposal for a league of nations, Wilson hoped to translate his idea of the war's objectives into reality. What sustained him in that hope was the conviction that the peoples of the world, if not their governments, shared his views and looked to the United States for leadership and inspiration.

My dream is that as the years go by and the world knows more and more of America it will turn to America for those moral inspirations which lie at the basis of all freedom and that America will come into the full light of day when all shall know that she puts human rights above all other rights, and that her flag is the flag not only of America, but of humanity.

In an age of power politics, nationalist rivalries, and Socialist revolution, such a vision of the world was at best a risk and at worst a reckless denial of reality.

The Fourteen Points

Soon after the United States entered the war, Wilson finally learned that the Allies had secretly agreed to certain territorial readjustments and to the exaction of enormous indemnities from the defeated enemy. To Wilson, such agreements violated his "peace without victory" as well as the principle of self-determination. Diplomatically and militarily, he tried to conduct the American part of the war independently. (The United States, in fact, never became one of the Allied Powers, but only an associated power among them.) The existence of the secret treaties, however, encouraged Wilson to make even clearer the American and the Allied objectives. Events in Russia added to the need for clarification.

After the Bolshevik Revolution of November 1917, the new Russian government invited all the belligerents to end war almost on Wilson's terms—no territory and no indemnities. No response came from the Allies. The Bolsheviks saw their silence as proof of the imperialist nature of the war. Within three weeks, Vladimir Lenin, the Bolshevik leader, began negotiations with the Central Powers to close down the eastern front. This step the Allies viewed as a stab in the back. The Bolsheviks next threatened to publish the secret treaties. (The deposed czar had signed them for Russia.) Wilson, having failed again to win Allied agreement to his peace plan, thought it essential to meet the Bolshevik challenge with a statement of his own. This he did in a message to Congress on January 8, 1918, in which he set forth Fourteen Points summarizing all the ideas he had been proposing during the previous two years.

The first five points were general principles aimed at removing the fundamental causes of conflict. Peace agreements should be arrived at openly, not secretly. Free use of the seas should be guaranteed to all nations, in peace as well as in war. Economic barriers to free trade should be removed, and armaments reduced "to the lowest point consistent with domestic safety." The conflicting claims of the colonial powers should be settled in a way that reflected the interests of the native peoples. The next eight points dealt with territorial readjustments, which should be based, Wilson argued on the principle of self-determination along "historically established lines of nationality." These readjustments would include "autonomous development" for the peoples of Austria-Hungary and the establishment of an independent Poland. The fourteenth point, and the most important in Wilson's eyes, would establish "a general association of nations" designed to guarantee "political independence and territorial integrity to great and small states alike."

To Wilson, the Fourteen Points were "the moral climax of this final war for human liberty." The Allies were less certain. Some of them expressed anger over points that appeared to affect their national honor and imperial ambitions; others found Wilson's proclamation hopelessly naive. "Mr. Wilson bores me with his Fourteen Points," remarked Georges Clemenceau, the French leader. "Why, God Almighty has only ten." Whatever their feelings, however, the Allied leaders saw the propaganda value of Wilson's effort. It was for this reason that they agreed to use the Fourteen Points as at least a basis for the peace negotiations.

Intervention in Russia

When finally forced to sign a separate peace with Germany (the Treaty of Brest-Litovsk) some eight months before the armistice ended the war, the Bolsheviks yielded all of Poland, Lithuania, the Ukraine, the Baltic provinces, Finland, and neighboring territories. All told, they gave up the homeland of 30 percent of the czar's prewar subjects, and the source of 90 percent of Russia's coal and 80 percent of its iron.

By May 1918, the British and French had begun to send troops into Arctic Russia by way of Murmansk on the Barents Sea. Americans soon followed. If they had intended to overthrow the Bolshevik regime—their primary goal, in the opinion of some historians—their more immediate objective was to keep the German military machine busy enough to prevent the transfer of troops to the western front in France. Ideological concerns probably reinforced strategic considerations. If the Bolshevik government collapsed as a result of the intervention, that would have been an added bonus.

The Allied and American presence in Russia encouraged those who opposed the Bolshevik regime. By August 1918, the Westerners had helped set up an anti-Bolshevik puppet government in northern Russia. Anti-Bolshevik groups in Siberia were aided by the arrival there of British, French, American, and Japanese forces. In this way, the Western powers became involved in the "civil war" that raged throughout the Russian Empire until 1920. When the Germans collapsed in the west in November 1918, the Bolsheviks promptly renounced the Treaty of Brest-Litovsk and tried to reclaim the surrendered territories. At the same time, the armistice permitted the Allies and the United States to deal with the upheaval in Russia.

Americans such as Theodore Roosevelt had urged unconditional surrender rather than an armistice. But Secretary of State Lansing recognized the need for a quick end to the war. If

Germany were crushed, he argued, revolution might break out there and spread to other European countries. That bolshevism also threatened to spread was enough reason to end the war immediately and get on with the work of containing the Bolsheviks.

Although the Soviet Union would not be invited to the Paris Peace Conference, the fear of bolshevism played a prominent role in the deliberations. If they disagreed in other matters, the United States and the Allies shared a common alarm over the effect of the Russian Revolution. They continued to support anti-Bolshevik activity within Russia. Allied and American troops remained in northern Russia almost until the end of 1919, and Japanese troops were still in Vladivostok late in 1922. To the charge that this was interference in the internal affairs of Soviet Russia, Clemenceau replied that the only objective was to "help Russia overcome anarchy and restore herself." Wilson wrote to his secretary of state: "If a stable form of government could be established through military intervention in Asiatic Russia, the moral effect upon the balance of Russia would be incalculable."

Years later, Winston Churchill recalled as one of the great mistakes of Allied statesmanship in 1919 "the failure to strangle Bolshevism at its birth and to bring Russia . . . by one means or another into the general democratic system." It remains doubtful, however, that the West could have been persuaded to make the immense effort needed to attain this goal. The White Russians, who offered the only alternative to Bolshevik rule, were in no way committed to a "democratic system." Most important, the Bolshevik regime survived. The Allies' intervention and subsequent policy of economic blockade and nonrecognition won for them the enduring suspicion of the Soviet government and many of the Russian people. As late as the 1930s, Adolf Hitler believed that the Western nations would not intervene if he confined himself to an anti-Soviet crusade.

The Versailles Treaty

Although Wilson's statements on peace were vague enough to be given varying interpretations, he became a hero to people everywhere who were eager for a better world and thought the president could lead them to it. Years later, his portrait could still be found hanging in peasant homes in many parts of Europe. Wilson's welcome in Europe confirmed him in his role as the spokesman for

New independent nations   Plebiscite area

Allied occupation zone

Europe after Versailles.

world humanity. That proved to be a tragic illusion.

Wilson confronted mounting opposition at home. The president knew that his role as peacemaker would be weakened if the American people defeated his party at the polls. And so in October 1918, facing off-year elections, he issued a fatal appeal to voters to express their approval of his leadership by returning a Democratic Congress. His appeal not only failed, it also embittered the Republicans who had supported the war effort. At the polls, the voters elected Republican majorities to both houses of Congress. When Wilson went to Paris in December 1918, he seemed to have been rejected by his own country. By then, he had further angered the opposition by failing to appoint a single Republican leader—or for that matter a single United States senator, even from his own party—to the commission that accompanied him to the peace talks.

The Paris Peace Conference, a meeting of victors to decide the fate of Germany, sat at the Versailles Palace from January to June 1919. Representing Britain was its prime minister, David Lloyd George, who had won a general election the preceding December after calling for the punishment of Germany. Representing France was Premier Georges Clemenceau, a determined promoter of French interests and French security. Vittorio Orlando, the Italian prime minister, was in Paris to see that Allied territorial promises to Italy were kept. When it became clear that they would not be, Orlando went home.

The Big Four became the Big Three—Wilson, Lloyd George, and Clemenceau. Wilson had come to Paris with three cardinal goals: (1) political self-determination for the peoples of Europe and to some extent even the peoples of colonial countries; (2) free trade; and (3) a league of nations. He left Paris with his goals only partially attained. Unfortunately, his concessions were made largely to secure the League of Nations, which the United States Senate was to forbid the United States to join. Wilson did succeed in moderating the Allied demands on Germany. But here too he was far from attaining his goal of "peace without victory." The terms of the final treaty were harsh enough almost to guarantee that the Germans would make every effort to break the agreement when they felt strong enough to do so.

The Treaty of Versailles, signed by the Germans on June 28, 1919, stripped Germany of its colonies in Africa and the Far East, and of Alsace-Lorraine and the Saar Basin north of Lorraine. France won all rights in the coal-rich Saar for fifteen years, after which a plebiscite would decide its future. On the east, German territory was given to Poland, to form the Polish Corridor to the Baltic Sea. This provision split Germany in two and was a bitter pill for Germans. The huge indemnity of $5 billion levied on the Germans and the provision for additional "reparations" later on made them look upon the Allies as vultures.

Perhaps most distressing was the "war guilt" article, which attempted to justify the indemnity and reparations by forcing Germany to acknowledge responsibility for starting the war. In an effort to prevent future aggression, the treaty deprived Germany of a navy and merchant marine and limited its army to 100,000 men. Other treaties in conjunction with the Versaillies treaty established such new states as Czechoslovakia and Yugoslavia by dismembering the Austro-Hungarian Empire.

For all its harshness, the Versailles treaty was no worse than the terms Germany would have imposed on the Allies had it won. (The Treaty of

Brest-Litovsk had made that clear.) The treaty, however, failed to satisfy Clemenceau. He refused to sign until Britain and the United States in a separate agreement promised to come to the aid of France in the event of a future attack on that country. Wilson probably suspected the Senate would reject such an "entangling alliance," which it did. His own expectation was that the League of Nations would play the role of this alliance, and he worked successfully to get the Allies to include the league's convenant in the treaty.

Under the covenant, responsibility for maintaining peace rested with an assembly (in which every member nation would be represented), a council (consisting of the United States, Britain, France, Italy, and Japan, and four others chosen by the assembly), and a Permanent Court of International Justice. Each member nation pledged itself to respect the "territorial integrity" and "political independence" of other members; to recognize the right of any nation to bring any threat to peace to the league's attention and to submit dangerous disputes to arbitration; and as a last resort to use military and economic sanctions against aggressor nations.

Like the Versailles treaty, however, the League of Nations Covenant failed to confront the fundamental causes of conflict—the industrial, commercial, and imperial rivalries. To some critics, in fact, it looked much more like a device to maintain the past rather than the peace.

PEACE AT HOME: WILSON, THE LEAGUE, AND THE SENATE

When Wilson returned to the United States, he faced a difficult battle. He needed to persuade a divided Senate to ratify the Versailles treaty, and he needed to keep the support of the American people, who were now concerned with unemployment and inflation. The president was confident. He had fought for the people of Europe over the heads of their rulers; he would now wage a similar struggle for the minds of Americans.

The Senate Debate

On July 10, 1919, two days after Wilson's return from Paris, he formally presented the Versailles treaty, including the League of Nations Covenant, to the Senate. He was confronted by the Republican majority elected in 1918 and especially by

his enemy, Henry Cabot Lodge, now chair of the Foreign Relations Committee. In addition, a strong group of "irreconcilables," including such western Progressives as William E. Borah, Hiram Johnson, and Robert La Follette, were determined to resist the treaty and the league. "We may become one of the four dictators of the world," Borah warned, "but we shall no longer be master of our own spirit." Nevertheless, more than the needed two-thirds of the Senate seemed ready to vote for the Versailles treaty, with some form of league membership. There is every evidence that the majority of the people would have backed them, despite the opposition of German Americans because of the harshness of the treaty, of Italian Americans because of the frustration of their homeland's demands, of Irish Americans bitter over the failure of the treaty to secure Irish independence, and of the American Left, which regarded the treaty and the league as nothing more than props for a decaying economic and social order.

As the Senate and the people debated the league through the summer of 1919, however, Wilson grew more and more stubborn about even minor changes in the covenant and more tactless about his all-or-nothing stand. When the irreconcilables opened a tremendous propaganda barrage, the president, though exhausted by work and illness, decided to take his own case to the country. In more than forty speeches delivered in some twenty-two days, he pressed home his point. For what had American youths died? he asked. "For the redemption of America? America was not directly attacked. For the salvation of America? America was not immediately in danger. No; for the salvation of mankind. It is the noblest errand that troops ever went on." If the United States rejected the treaty and league membership, it turned its back on those troops.

While the president was gone, Lodge proposed a series of reservations to the covenant, which he knew Wilson would reject and over which the Senate might talk the whole treaty to death. Lodge's strategy worked. By the time his reservations were introduced in the Senate, Wilson had had a physical breakdown, forcing him to cancel the rest of his trip. Early in October he suffered a stroke that left him half-paralyzed. His sickbed appeal to "all true friends of the treaty" to reject the Lodge reservations helped defeat them in the Senate in November. But a resolution to ratify the treaty and the league without reservations also failed, by thirty-eight to fifty-five, with every Republican but one voting against it.

Enough support for the league remained even in the Senate for the treaty to be brought up again in March 1920. Although a majority (forty-nine to thirty-five) voted for the treaty with the modified Lodge reservations, that was seven short of the necessary two-thirds. Wilson supporters remained opposed to compromise. Both the treaty and league membership were dead.

The Election of 1920

Even so, Wilson did not give up hope. The election of 1920, he announced, must be "a great and solemn referendum." The people would now vote directly on the issue. But it has rarely been possible in peacetime to make an American presidential election a clear referendum on foreign policy, and 1920 was no exception.

Deprived of their most popular leader by Roosevelt's death early in 1919, the Republicans at their national convention split so badly over the candidacy of Roosevelt's friends General Leonard Wood and Governor Frank O. Lowden of Illinois that they gave in at last to the backers of Warren G. Harding of Ohio. This small-town newspaperman, owner and editor of the *Marion Daily Star,* had been elected United States senator in 1914. When reminded that Harding remained unknown outside Ohio, Senator Frank Brandegee of Connecticut shouted: "There ain't any first-raters this year. Harding is the best of the second-raters." Perhaps second best was the equally surprising nominee for vice-president. Calvin Coolidge, even more obscure than Harding, was governor of Massachusetts when he suddenly came to national fame by breaking the Boston police strike of September 1919.

To run against Harding, the Democrats named another Ohioan, Governor James M. Cox, who had not been closely identified with Wilson's policies. As his running mate they chose Franklin Delano Roosevelt, Wilson's assistant secretary of the navy. Meanwhile, the Socialists decided to offer an alternative by again nominating Eugene Debs. Since the president refused to pardon him, Debs would have to conduct his campaign from behind prison walls.

Although Cox strongly favored the league, he wavered on what amendments he might be willing to accept. The Republicans caught the mood of the public by evading this and all other issues. "Keep Warren at home," advised Boies Penrose, the political boss of Pennsylvania. "Don't let him make any speeches. If he goes out on a tour somebody's sure to ask him questions, and Warren's just the sort of damned fool that will try to answer them." The Republican platform condemned the League of Nations Covenant but Harding, who had voted against the league in the Senate, promised to work for "an association of nations."

Tired of the whole debate, the American people reacted not so much to the league as to the rising cost of living, the number of people out of work, high taxes, and labor violence. Cox was crushed at the polls, 16 million to 9 million, receiving only 34 percent of the popular vote. No major-party candidate had ever been defeated so badly.

In commenting on the election, the *New York World* wrote: "The American people wanted a change, and they have voted for a change. They did not know what kind of a change they wanted, and they do not know what kind of a change they have voted for." But the American electorate may have been sharper than some observers thought possible. Although Harding said little, what he did say may have been the key to his overwhelming success at the polls. He promised the American people no new crusades, no calls for self-sacrifice to save humanity, but simply a return to stability and to minding America's own business—a return to "normalcy." After eight years of Wilson's drives, that in itself was a welcome change.

SUMMARY

World War I officially brought the United States into European power politics. At the same time, the entry of the United States made the European war into a world war. At first, Americans did not understand why they should be involved, and the loyalties of Americans of European background were divided. But the Allies (Britain and France) soon won the public relations campaign. In addition, the Allies' wartime demand for goods rescued the American economy and started a boom that lasted until 1919. Even more important, the United States was transformed from a debtor to a creditor nation. And since the debtors were the Allied countries, America now had a huge economic stake in the outcome of the conflict.

Problems involving freedom of shipping brought the United States into conflict with both Britain and Germany, since both were battling for control of the seas and their sources of supplies. Wilson's policy at the beginning was to try to bring the war quickly to an end. He was eventually forced to give in to the idea of preparing for war. The climax came in January 1917, when Germany broke its pledge on submarine warfare in a gamble to win the war before America could come to the Allies' rescue. The Allies were in deep trouble, and their defeat would have meant an economic disaster for the United States. In April 1917 the United States declared war on Germany. Nineteen months later, the Germans were forced to agree to an armistice.

The American navy reduced the amount of tonnage lost to submarines. American ground troops helped to turn back the German armies, and the flow of American supplies and money sustained the entire war effort. These achievements required the United States to mobilize its resources on an unprecedented scale. A new army was created by the Selective Service Act of May 1917. A Council of National Defense supervised huge federal agencies that managed the merchant marine, food and fuel supplies, transportation, and industry. The war also brought official intolerance and a loss of civil liberties in the form of the Espionage Act of June 1917 and the Sedition Act of May 1918.

When it was over, Wilson hoped to realize in the peace treaty his dream of "making the world safe for democracy." But in an age of power politics, national rivalries, and Socialist revolution, such ideas were hopelessly and dangerously naive. His Fourteen Points were an effective propaganda device, but the Allies, bound by secret agreements, had no intention of negotiating anything but a punitive peace. This they did in the Treaty of Versailles, drawn up at the Paris Peace Conference from January to June 1919. The treaty stripped Germany of its colonies abroad and some of its territory in Europe, saddled it with a $5 billion indemnity, deprived it of military forces, and declared it responsible for the war.

Wilson did get his League of Nations, for which he sacrificed all his other objectives. But then the United States Senate, in a bitter campaign, refused to ratify the treaty and allow the United States to become a member of the league. Wilson, exhausted and ill, suffered a stroke that left him paralyzed and removed him from politics. In the election of 1920, Republican Warren Harding of Ohio became the new president. His slogan was a return to "normalcy."

TIME LINE

1914	Archduke Ferdinand assassinated; World War I begins		(May) Selective Service Act
	United States declares neutrality		(June) Espionage Act
	Britain declares North Sea a war zone		(November) Bolshevik Revolution in Russia
1915	United States extends loans to Allied governments	1918	Wilson announces Fourteen Points
	Germany announces submarine blockade of Britain		Sedition Act
			Allied and U.S. troops intervene in Russia
	Lusitania sunk		Eugene Debs imprisoned
1916	*Sussex* pledge		American Civil Liberties Bureau founded
	Wilson re-elected president		Armistice ends World War I
1917	(January) Germany resumes unrestricted submarine warfare		Republicans win congressional elections
	(January, disclosed in March) Zimmerman telegram	1919	Paris Peace Conference; Treaty of Versailles
	(March) German submarines sink three American ships	1919	Senate rejects Treaty of Versailles
	(April) U.S. declares war on Germany	1920	Warren G. Harding elected president

Suggested Readings

Barbara Tuchman, *The Proud Tower* (1965), is an extremely readable chronicle of Europe on the verge of war. For the diplomatic background, see A. J. P. Taylor, *The Struggle for Mastery in Europe 1848–1918* (1954), and Fritz Fischer, *Germany's Aims in the First World War* (1967).

CHAPTER 26 WORLD WAR AND WORLD REVOLUTION

The most comprehensive account of Wilson and World War I is the multivolume biography by A. S. Link (5 vols., 1947–65). For a briefer presentation, see his *Wilson the Diplomatist* (1957) and *Woodrow Wilson and the Progressive Era* (1954). Among the numerous works examining American intervention in the war are E. R. May, *The World and American Isolation 1914–1917* (1959); R. Gregory, *The Origins of American Intervention in the First World War* (1971); P. Devlin, *Too Proud to Fight: Woodrow Wilson's Neutrality* (1975); C. P. Parrini, *Heir to Empire: United States Economic Diplomacy 1916–1923* (1969); and J. Cooper, Jr., *The Vanity of Power: American Isolationism and the First World War 1914–1917* (1969). N. G. Levin, *Woodrow Wilson and World Politics: America's Response to War and Revolution* (1969), stresses Wilson's commitment to a liberal, democratic, capitalist world order.

Walter Millis, *Road to War: America 1914–1917* (1935), and C. C. Tansill, *America Goes to War* (1938), are critiques of intervention from the isolationist view of the thirties. R. E. Osgood, *Ideals and Self-Interest in America's Foreign Relations* (1953), is a perceptive examination of the nation's motivations.

The impact of the war on American society is examined in D. M. Kennedy, *Over Here: The First World War and American Society* (1980). The mobilization of the American mind is described in G. Creel, *How We Advertised America* (1920), and S. L. Vaughn, *Holding Fast the Inner Lines: Democracy, Nationalism, and the Committee on Public Information* (1980). For wartime restraints on opinion, see D. Johnson, *Challenge to American Freedoms: World War I and the Rise of the American Civil Liberties Union* (1963); H. N. Scheiber, *The Wilson Administration and Civil Liberties 1917–1921* (1961); H. C. Peterson and G. C. Fite, *Opponents of War 1917–1918* (1957); and W. Preston, Jr., *Aliens and Dissenters: Federal Suppression of Radicals 1903–1933* (1963). The mobilization of the universities for the war effort is described in C. S. Gruber, *Mars and Minerva: World War I and the Uses of the Higher Learning in America* (1975).

The economic conversion to war is the subject of R.

D. Cuff, *The War Industries Board: Business-Government Relations during World War I* (1973). The position of the military in American life is examined in R. D. Challener, *Admirals, Generals, and American Foreign Policy 1898–1914* (1973), and J. G. Clifford, *The Citizen Soldiers: The Plattsburg Training Camp Movement 1913–1920* (1972). J. W. Chambers II, *To Raise an Army* (1987), examines how the United States raised its armies, focusing on the adoption, operation, and legacy of the modern national draft. On the military experience, see E. M. Coffman, *The War to End All Wars* (1968); J. J. Pershing, *My Experiences in the World War* (2 vols., 1931); and F. E. Vandiver, *Black Jack: The Life and Times of John J. Pershing* (1977).

The reaction of the United States to the Russian Revolution is examined in G. F. Kennan, *Russia Leaves the War* (1956) and *The Decision to Intervene* (1958); C. Lasch, *The American Liberals and the Russian Revolution* (1962); P. G. Filene, *Americans and the Soviet Experiment 1917–1933* (1967); and L. C. Gardner, *Safe for Democracy: The Anglo-American Response to Revolution, 1913–1923* (1984). For the impact of the Russian Revolution on the peace, see W. A. Williams, *American-Russian Relations 1781–1947* (1952); J. M. Thompson, *Russia, Bolshevism, and the Versailles Peace* (1966); and A. J. Mayer, *Political Origins of the New Diplomacy 1917–1918* (1959) and *Politics and Diplomacy of Peacemaking: Containment and Counterrevolution at Versailles 1918–1919* (1967).

T. A. Bailey, *Woodrow Wilson and the Lost Peace* (1944) and *Woodrow Wilson and the Great Betrayal* (1945), analyze Wilson's performance at Versailles and American opposition to the league. See also J. A. Garraty, *Henry Cabot Lodge* (1953). J. M. Keynes, *The Economic Consequences of the Peace* (1919), is a critical assessment of the Big Four, including Wilson. See also R. Lansing, *The Peace Negotiations: A Personal Narrative* (1921), and Harold Nicolson, *Peacemaking 1919* (1939). On the meaning of the war for those who lived through it, see the deeply moving account by P. Fussell, *The Great War and Modern Memory* (1975).

CHAPTER 27

THE TWENTIES: BUSINESS AND CULTURE

Few decades evoke as many different and conflicting images as the twenties, and few have been subjected to more distortion and exaggeration. High-spirited college students and "flappers," emboldened by bootleg gin, danced the Charleston and the Black Bottom and went to "petting" parties. Marathon dancers competed with flagpole sitters for public attention, and both were outranked by Babe Ruth, Clara Bow, Henry Ford, and Al Capone. Sophisticated urbanites violated Prohibition in speakeasies; young and old alike satisfied their fantasies in the movie houses; the small-town elites found their outlets in Rotary, Kiwanis, or Lions clubs. Advertising became a major industry in its own right, rewarding its armies of salespeople better than most of the businesses whose products it tried to sell. The automobile became a necessity, along with the radio, the washing machine, and the refrigerator. Easy credit made these and countless other commodities available to millions of Americans.

The cultural tastes of the decade were as varied as the newly available consumer goods, and both came to be increasingly standardized. Edgar Guest, whose work appeared daily in the press, was a more widely read poet than either T. S. Eliot or Ezra Pound. Bruce Barton, the ad man who peddled an updated version of Jesus Christ, outsold Ernest Hemingway, who spent much of the decade out of the country. The *Saturday Evening Post,* whose covers and contents mirrored the middle-class vision of themselves and America, was far more popular than Henry L. Mencken's irreverent *American Mercury.* Highbrows and lowbrows alike were thrilled by young Charles Lindbergh's dramatic solo flight from New York to Paris—the story of the decade. Lindbergh seemed to personify the individualistic and pioneering spirit Americans still revered and the new technology they were embracing so feverishly.

But there is another side to the twenties that tends to get lost in the nostalgia Americans still feel for the Jazz Age. If the decade was a carefree fling for some, many sections of the population experienced little of the fun and none of the "good times." While ad men made a virtue out of conspicuous consumption, a lopsided distribution of income made reduced consumption necessary for millions of Americans. Although the twenties tolerated bobbed hair, short skirts, cosmetics, and a

John Sloan, *The Lafayette,* 1928 (detail). Oil on canvas, 30½ × 36⅛". The Metropolitan Museum of Art. Gift of Friends of John Sloan, 1928.

relaxation of sexual rules—the trademarks of a new subculture based on age—that same decade was intolerant of radicals, union organizers, immigrants, and blacks. Even the "flaming youth" more often than not reflected and reinforced the dominant business culture. The same decade in which some Americans flaunted their liberation also witnessed a revival of the Ku Klux Klan, the Red Scare, racial violence, a court test of the right to teach evolution in the public schools, and the first restriction on the number of immigrants admitted to the United States.

The family underwent much change, as did the role of women in the household. The size of urban middle-class families continued to decline, and in the 1920s the impact of this change became more obvious. The smaller family and labor-saving devices enabled mothers to spend more time on the personality and education of their children. Knowledge of birth control, advances in the technology of contraception, and more open discussion of sex not only resulted in earlier marriages, but influenced the dominant middle-class sexual ethic. Women were encouraged to be more sexually responsive and to expect sexual gratification in marriage. This improved the quality of sexual relationships, but it may also have contributed to the rapid increase in the divorce rate. In 1890, 6 out of every 100 marriages ended in divorce; in 1930, it was 18 out of every 100 marriages.

The number of working women increased, as did the number of women attending college. On the other hand, the percentage of women in the work force and in professional employment declined. For middle-class women, college and career were still an interval between adolescence and marriage. The ideal woman of the 1920s was encouraged to be more feminine in order to further her husband's career, not her own. Dorothy Dix, in her widely syndicated column, advised that "a man's wife is the show window where he exhibits the measure of his achievement. . . . The woman who cultivates a circle of worth-while people, who belongs to clubs, who makes herself interesting and agreeable . . . is a help to her husband."

Women's suffrage in no way changed the quality of men elected to public office. The White House in this decade was occupied by Harding, Coolidge, and Hoover. They differed widely in talent, but were united in the conviction that "the chief business of the American people is business."

Scandals marked the Harding administration and complacency the Coolidge years, but the highest expectations greeted the Hoover presidency. "Big business in America," said a much impressed Lincoln Steffens, "is producing what the socialists held up as their goal: food, shelter, and clothing for all. You will see it during the Hoover administration." Within a year of Hoover's inaguration, these expectations had been dashed. The decade closed with a mood of panic and desperation. The unemployed and the depressed of the twenties suddenly found themselves with plenty of company.

AFTER THE WAR: REPRESSION AND INTOLERANCE

The kind of planning that had enabled the United States to go to war was not used for demobilization afterward. With controls on the economy suddenly lifted and several million soldiers returning to civilian life, the nation found itself in a brief recession. Inflation and unemployment took their toll. Lingering wartime emotions and tensions found new outlets in hysteria over radicalism, in immigration restriction, and in racial violence. At the same time, the rapid pace of urbanization (the 1920 census revealed that for the first time most Americans lived in urban areas) fed traditional rural–urban antagonisms. And many of the 19 million Americans who moved from the farms to the cities in the twenties brought rural ways of thinking with them.

While President Harding talked of returning the nation to "normalcy," the head of the newly revived Ku Klux Klan talked of returning power to the people—"the everyday, not highly cultured, not overly intellectualized, but entirely unspoiled and not de-Americanized, average citizen of the old stock." Most Americans did not need the Klan to remind them of what they could see all too well for themselves: that traditional ways, morals, and beliefs were changing, along with the old ethnic makeup of the nation. Dangers from within had replaced the enemy abroad.

The Red Scare

During the war, Americans had grown used to the suppression of dissent. With the war's end, the intolerance that had been directed mainly against those suspected of sympathizing with Germany came to cover a wider range of people—foreigners in general, Catholics, Jews, blacks, radicals, strikers. The new wave of fear found a scapegoat in the Bolshevik Revolution in Russia and the threat of worldwide revolution against capitalism. Actually, Socialists were split over the virtues of the new Soviet government. The Russian Revolution had fragmented rather than united an already demoralized American radicalism. The number of Communists in the United States did not exceed half of 1 percent of the population—and most were intellectuals, not workers. But violence in labor relations right after the war deepened concern about the safety of the social order, and bomb scares turned that concern into panic.

No longer bound by wartime no-strike pledges, trade unions made new wage demands after the armistice, using their traditional weapon. They were seeking not only to maintain previous gains, but to keep up with the soaring cost of living. In 1919 alone there were 3630 strikes involving about 4 million workers. Whatever the few gains workers were able to make, industrialists quickly blamed them for the rise in prices. In February 1919 Seattle found itself paralyzed by a general strike called by the Central Labor Council in support of shipyard workers seeking higher pay and shorter hours.

The tactic of a general strike revived fears of the IWW, which had been active in the Northwest, and the mayor exploited those fears in calling out troops to crush the strike. Even more spectacular was a strike in September 1919 by the Boston police after the city's police commissioners refused to recognize a union organized to raise low wages. Governor Calvin Coolidge, who had done nothing to encourage a settlement, called

out the state guard to maintain order in the state capital. When AFL president Samuel Gompers protested the firing of several leaders of the policemen's union for their organizing activities, Coolidge replied: "There is no right to strike against the public safety by anybody, anywhere, anytime." Despite his timid role in the entire affair, this statement established Coolidge as a national hero and led to his nomination for the vice-presidency in 1920.

The attempts to link strikes with radicalism came to a head in September 1919, when AFL unions struck the United States Steel Corporation plants in Pittsburgh, in Gary, Indiana, and elsewhere. Since the last major steel strike, at Homestead in 1892, conditions in the steel mills had only grown worse. Hours, shop conditions, and union recognition, as well as wages, were at issue. But the corporation blamed the strike on some of its Communist organizers. Using its own "security" forces along with state militia and federal troops, it broke the strike in January 1920, after eighteen workers had been killed and hundreds beaten.

The strike was thoroughly investigated by a commission of inquiry of the Interchurch World Movement under Bishop Francis J. McConnell of the Methodist Episcopal church. Among the leading causes of the strike's defeat, said the commission, was U.S. Steel's "effective mobilization of public opinion against the strikers through charges of radicalism, bolshevism, and the closed shop, none of which is justified by the facts." The working conditions that had brought on the strike, it concluded, "continue to exist."

Some union demands supported charges of radicalism. In an unsuccessful strike, the United Mine Workers had demanded nationalization of the coal pits. Railroad unions endorsed the widely discussed Plumb Plan, which called for the continuation of government operation of the railroads. The agitation sped passage of the Esch-Cummins Act of 1920, which provided for the return of the railroads to private control and also, for the first time, authorized the roads to plan combinations that would make rail service more efficient.

Using as their excuse the influence of "foreign ideologies" in the labor movement, employer associations spent large sums of money promoting the American Plan—a set of attitudes, the most important of which was that collective bargaining and the closed or union shop were "un-American." Eventually, American Plan associations were organized in every state and nearly every industrial city in the country. Chambers of commerce, local

Seeking union recognition and an end to the twelve-hour working day, steelworkers went on strike in 1919, but without success. The bosses and the newspapers claimed the strikers were led by Communist agitators. *(UPI/Bettmann Newsphotos)*

boards of trade, "constitutional associations," and other groups all helped. The National Grange mobilized farm support.

In 1919 and 1920 a series of bomb scares intensified the Red Scare. A time bomb was discovered in a parcel addressed to the mayor of Seattle. Another bomb blew off the hands of a Georgia senator's house servant. No less than thirty-six bombs addressed to such prominent people as J. P. Morgan, John D. Rockefeller, and Justice Holmes of the Supreme Court were discovered in various post offices. A bomb exploded in front of the Washington home of the attorney general, and in September 1920 a bomb exploded in Wall Street, killing thirty-eight and injuring hundreds. Although the work of only a few anarchists, the bombs lent support to fears of a massive conspiracy to overthrow the government.

Wilson's attorney general, A. Mitchell Palmer,

who had presidential ambitions of his own, did nothing to discourage fears of revolution. He claimed to see Reds almost everywhere he looked, and the end of the war provided him with the opportunity to hunt them down. "Like a prairie fire," he explained, "the blaze of revolution was sweeping over every American institution." On New Year's Day 1920, Palmer ordered simultaneous raids on every suspected Bolshevik cell in the country. In about a week, more than 4000 persons were arrested and their property confiscated. Friends who visited them were jailed on grounds of "solicitude for revolutionaries." Though supposedly armed to the teeth, the captives yielded the imposing total of three pistols and no explosives.

The Palmer raids were followed by the eventual deportation of 556 aliens convicted of no crime. Vigilantism spread across the nation. Students, professors, editors, writers, actors, and others suspected of harboring subversive ideas or engaging in un-American activities were the victims. In January 1920, five Socialist members of the New York State Assembly were expelled simply because of their party affiliation.

A few months after the Palmer raids, two Italian anarchists, Nicola Sacco and Bartolomeo Vanzetti, were arrested for a murder committed in connection with a payroll robbery in South Braintree, Massachusetts. Upon the jury's finding them guilty, Judge Webster Thayer sentenced the two defendants to death. The actual evidence against them was not conclusive, and the suspicion grew that they had been convicted not because they had committed the crime, but because of their political beliefs. Judge Thayer's conduct of the trial, in which he made little secret of his feelings about anarchists, only deepened

suspicion of the verdict. Responding to protest in this country and abroad, Governor Alvan T. Fuller of Massachusetts appointed an advisory commission that included the president of Harvard and instructed it to review the evidence. The commission concluded that the trial judge had been guilty of a "grave breach of official decorum," but that justice had been done.

Appeal motions delayed the execution of the two men for years. Vanzetti's dignity and both men's quiet persistence in their anarchist beliefs while their lives hung in the balance won them additional sympathy. When they were electrocuted in 1927, in the middle of a new wave of worldwide protest, millions were convinced they were innocent. Millions more were convinced that, guilty or innocent, they had not been given a fair trial. "What more can the immigrants from Italy expect?" asked columnist Heywood Broun.

Nicola Sacco and Bartolomeo Vanzetti, convicted anarchists who were electrocuted on August 23, 1927. "Never in our full life could we hope to do such work for tolerance, for justice, for man's understanding of man, as now we do by accident. . . . That last moment belongs to us—that agony is our triumph." *(UPI/Bettmann Newsphotos)*

"It is not every prisoner who has a president of Harvard throw on the switch for him."

Although the Red Scare quieted down after the Palmer raids, the atmosphere was hardly promising for radical activity and expression in the twenties. And the linking of radicals and immigrants added to the growing pressure for restrictions on their admission to the United States.

The "Race Suicide" Alarm: Immigration

The conception of the United States as a melting pot was as old as the Republic itself. When in the early twentieth century President Theodore Roosevelt exulted, "We Americans are the children of the crucible," most Americans took pride in having achieved a blending of various nationalities and cultures. Not only did Americans appear to embrace the goal of assimilation but they supported institutional mechanisms designed to accelerate the Americanization of new arrivals. Perhaps the most extraordinary of such mechanisms was the Ford English School, attached to Henry Ford's automobile factory in Highland Park, Michigan, where thousands of Ford employees in the 1920s would learn English and American citizenship. Employees who successfully completed the course earned the right to participate in a unique graduation ceremony held in the largest hall in the city.

On the stage was represented an immigrant ship. In front of it was a huge melting pot. Down the gang plank came the members of the class dressed in their national garbs and carrying luggage such as they carried when they landed in this country. Down they poured into the Ford melting pot and disappeared. Then the teachers began to stir the contents of the pot with long ladles. Presently the pot began to boil over and out came the men dressed in their best American clothes and waving American flags.

Whatever assurances this ceremony afforded Henry Ford and the audience, it failed to dispel growing concern over the ability of American society to assimilate immigrants from eastern and southern Europe. With their rapid increase before World War I and the prospect of renewed immigration from those regions after the war, the debate turned from assimilation and Americanization to restriction.

Xenophobia (antiforeign feeling) after the war brought to a head the anti-immigration sentiment that had been growing in the United States since the 1880s. The Immigration Restriction League, organized by a group of New England intellectu-als in 1894, reflected fears that the "new" immigrants from southern and eastern Europe would destroy the "American character." This group had pushed for a literacy test for immigrants. During the Progressive Era, xenophobes and labor and business leaders who shared hostility to newcomers were joined by liberals who feared that immigration was threatening the American way of life. The flood of "new" immigrants in the fifteen years before World War I brought some Americans to the verge of panic over "race suicide."

In the pages of the widely read *Saturday Evening Post,* Kenneth Roberts cautioned against the admission of so many Polish Jews, who were "human parasites." He argued that the mixture of Nordic with Alpine, Mediterranean, and Semitic stocks would result in "a hybrid race of people as worthless and futile as the good-for-nothing mongrels of Central America and Southeastern Europe." Such arguments were given wide national exposure and helped to pave the way for a complete reversal of the old, easygoing terms of admission to the United States.

The Immigration Restriction Act of 1921 established a quota system based on national origin. Each European nation was assigned an annual quota equal to 3 percent of the number of its nationals residing in the United States in 1910. Most Asians were already barred. This law was expected to limit immigration to about 350,000 persons a year, largely from the United Kingdom and northwestern Europe.

The National Origins Act of 1924 cut quotas to 2 percent and made the base year 1890, when the proportion of "Nordics" in the American population had been much higher than in 1910. The National Origins Act also shut the door on Japanese immigrants—a national humiliation for Japan, which warned that the measure would have "grave consequences." This act was to last only until 1927. Afterward, no more than 150,000 immigrants were to be admitted annually, according to quotas based on the ratio of each country's nationals to the whole American population in 1920.

In fact, the desire to restore the "Nordic" proportion of the American population was frustrated because these laws did not apply to immigrants from Western Hemisphere countries. During the 1920s, almost a million Canadians, many of them French-speaking Catholics, and at least half a million Mexicans crossed their respective borders to work in the factories of New England and the fields of the South, the Southwest, and the West.

President Warren G. Harding (left) and Vice-President Calvin Coolidge (right). Their traditional Americanism and optimistic faith in business set the political tone of the decade. *(Culver Pictures, Inc.)*

But nothing would ever again approach the earlier waves of European immigrants. With the restrictive legislation enacted in the 1920s, the idea of America as the promised land for the "huddled masses yearning to breathe free" came to an abrupt end. Only in the 1960s and 1970s — when the doors were opened to thousands of political refugees from Southeast Asia, Cuba, and Haiti — would that idea be momentarily revived.

The Great Black Migration

Although restrictions on immigrants affected the ethnic makeup of the nation, the movement of southern blacks to northern cities during and after World War I altered the racial map of the United States and introduced new tensions. Between 1910 and 1940, more than 1,750,000 black people left the South, nearly 500,000 during the war and another 800,000 in the twenties. By 1940, the black population outside the South had more than doubled. In cities such as New York, Chi-cago, Detroit, Cleveland, and Buffalo, the percentage of blacks in the population grew by 100 to 250 percent. Within only a few decades, a largely rural black population had become more urban than the white population. The Jim Crow restrictions, the alarming rate of lynchings and beatings, the absence of adequate educational facilities, and the impossible tenantry and credit systems led large numbers of southern blacks to look for a better life elsewhere.

Until 1915, the North had offered the southern black migrant very little. But the labor demands created by World War I and the decline in European immigration changed that situation, opening up opportunities in northern industry at wages unknown in the South. In 1914 Henry Ford promised to pay his workers no less than $5 a day — a sensational announcement in itself — and agreed at the same time to hire black workers for his assembly line. Before, blacks had been barred from industrial work; now, self-interest won out over racial considerations. "These same factories, mills, and workshops that have been closed to us," said the Chicago *Defender,* "through necessity are being opened to us. We are being given a chance, not through choice but because it is expedient. Prejudice vanishes when the almighty dollar is on the wrong side of the balance sheet."

Stimulated at first by labor agents, black newspapers, and the letters of friends, the Great Migration soon had a momentum all its own. It was not uncommon for entire communities to transplant themselves. Although all classes of blacks made up the movement, many in the early waves were young, unskilled, and unmarried, the sons and daughters of sharecroppers and tenants. The chances for a rewarding life in the South had seemed increasingly dismal to these migrants, and they hoped for something beyond what their parents and grandparents had been forced to accept.

If their expectations were often disappointed, the hope persisted that somehow they could improve the quality of their daily life. After nineteen years in Mississippi, Arkansas, and Tennessee, young Richard Wright headed for Chicago in 1927, having concluded that life in a "hostile and forbidding" South made it impossible to maintain self-respect.

I had been what my surroundings had demanded, what my family—conforming to the dictates of the whites above them—had exacted of me, and what the whites had said that I must be. . . . I headed North, full of a hazy notion that life could be lived with dignity, that the personalities of others should not be violated, that men should be able to confront other men without fear or shame.[*]

<hr>

[*]From Richard Wright, *Black Boy.* Copyright 1945 by Harper & Brothers.

A black family from the South arrives in Chicago in 1910. *(Historical Pictures Service, Chicago)*

THE PROMISED LAND

I'm tired of this Jim Crow, gonna leave this Jim
  Crow town.
Doggone my black soul, I'm sweet Chicago bound,
  Yes, I'm leavin' here, from this ole Jim Crow
  town.
I'm goin' up North where they say, money grows
  on trees.
I don't give a doggone, if ma black soul leaves,
I'm goin' where I don't need no B.V.D.s.
Lord well, if I get up here—where they don't
  suit—
I don't start no cryin'; go tell that ole ma'am of
  mine,
Lord I'm ready to come back to my Jim Crow
  town.

Source: Paul Oliver, *The Story of the Blues* (Chilton Book Co.,
1969), p. 75.

Philadelphia, Pa., Oct. 7, 1917

Dear Sir: . . . With the aid of God I am making very
good I make $75 per month. I am carrying enough

insurance to pay me $20 per week if I am not able to
be on duty. I don't have to work hard. dont have to
mister every little white boy comes along I havent
heard a white man call a colored a nigger you no
now—since I been in the state of Pa. I can ride in
the electric street and steam cars any where I get a
seat. I dont care to mix with white what I mean I am
not crazy about being with white folks, but if I have
to pay the same fare I have learn to want the same
acomidation. and if you are first in a place here
shoping you dont have to wait until the white folks
get thro tradeing yet amid all this I shall ever love
the good old South and I am praying that God may
give every well wisher a chance to be a man
regardless of his color. . . . when you find time I
would be delighted to have a word from the good old
home state. Wife join me in sending love you and
yours.

Source: Emmett J. Scott (ed.), "Letters of Negro Migrants of
1916–1918." *Journal of Negro History*, 4 (Oct 1919), 290–340.

The Great Migration took place in an atmosphere of growing racial intolerance. Despite the optimism with which many blacks had participated in World War I, in the first year of the armistice 70 blacks were lynched, 10 of them soldiers still wearing their uniforms. Between 1918 and 1927, more than 416 blacks were lynched; 42 of them were burned alive. Nor was this brutality confined to the old Confederacy. On July 2, 1917, East St. Louis, Illinois, was the scene of a savage attack on the black community; 39 blacks and 9 whites died. Fear of black competition for white jobs and the use of black strikebreakers triggered the riot, but ignorance and

Two years later, on July 27, 1919, the worst race riot in the nation's history erupted in Chicago; it lasted six days and nights. By the time the state militia restored some order, 38 persons (15 whites and 23 blacks) had died, 537 had been hurt, and more than a thousand were homeless. The riot started after a seventeen-year-old black youth, swimming off a Chicago beach, accidentally crossed the unmarked line dividing the water into sectors for blacks and whites. He was stoned by white bathers until he drowned. Enraged by police indifference, black bathers attacked the whites. The bloodshed then spread to the city streets. Quick to respond, Attorney General A. Mitchell Palmer blamed outside agitators, particularly Bolshevik sympathizers seeking black support for an insurrection. "If to fight for one's rights is to be Bolshevists," a black newspaper replied,

"then we are Bolshevists and let them make the most of it."

As the black migration grew, so did white fears, resistance, and discrimination. During the Red Summer of 1919, as it came to be called, there were more than twenty-five riots in various parts of the country. Several outbreaks were provoked by incidents involving urban police, bringing the charge that law-enforcement officers practiced a double standard when dealing with black communities. In the black urban enclaves known as *ghettos*, the residents also faced high rents for substandard housing, high prices, poor municipal services, and white economic control. "Our money is being used by the white man," one black resident charged, "to pay us for being his cook, his valet, and his washerwoman."

Despite the expectations with which Richard Wright arrived in Chicago, he soon came to realize, as did many southern migrants, that racial oppression did not always show itself in lynchings, Jim Crow laws, or disfranchisement:

Slowly I began to forge in the depths of my mind a mechanism that repressed all the dreams and desires that the Chicago streets, the newspapers, the movies were evoking in me. I was going through a second childhood; a new sense of the limit of the possible was being born in me. What could I dream of that had the barest possibility of coming true? I could think of nothing. And slowly, it was upon exactly that nothingness that my mind began to dwell, that constant sense of wanting without having, of being hated without

The Ku Klux Klan marching in full regalia past the White House in 1925. Hiram Wesley Evans, Imperial Wizard and Emperor of the Ku Klux Klan: "The outstanding proof of both our influence and our service . . . has been in creating, outside our ranks as well as in them, . . . a growing sentiment against radicalism, cosmopolitanism, and alienism of all kinds." *(Library of Congress)*

reason. A dim notion of what life meant to a Negro in America was coming to consciousness in me, not in terms of external events, lynchings, Jim Crowism, and the endless brutalities, but in terms of crossed up feeling, of emotional tension. I sensed that Negro life was a sprawling land of unconscious suffering, and there were but few Negroes who knew the meaning of their lives, who could tell their story.*

The Ku Klux Klan

The revival of the Ku Klux Klan in the 1920s reflected a concern not about blacks alone, but about the general erosion of the nation's moral fiber. The Klan of Reconstruction days had almost

---

*Paul R. Reynolds, Inc., for Richard Wright, "The Man Who Went to Chicago," from *Eight Men*. Copyright 1960 by World Publishing Co. Reprinted by permission.

died out in the 1870s. The new Klan, founded in Georgia in 1915, grew rapidly after 1920. At its peak in 1924, no fewer than 4.5 million "white male persons, native-born Gentile citizens," as they said, had joined the hooded group. On its night rides, the Klan burned fiery crosses to advertise its presence. It flogged or kidnapped blacks and whites, acted as a moral censor—and especially as the enforcement arm for Prohibition—made and unmade local politicians, and frightened union organizers.

This time around, the Klan had a much wider appeal, both geographically and ideologically. "We are a movement of plain people," explained Hiram Evans, the grand wizard of the Klan, "very weak in the matter of culture, intellectual support, and trained leadership. . . . It lays us open to the charge of being 'hicks' and 'rubes' and 'drivers of second hand Fords.' We admit it."

The Klan did well in portions of the Midwest and Far West, broadening its targets to include Jews and Catholics as well as blacks. It found support among the people who felt most threatened and frustrated by the changes in American society. "One by one all our traditional moral standards went by the boards," Evans declared, "or were so disregarded that they ceased to be binding. The sacredness of our Sabbath, of our homes, of chastity, and finally even of our right to teach our own children in our own schools fundamental facts and truths was torn away from us."

By 1924 the Klan's political influence had become so great that the Democratic national convention, after days of debate, could not adopt a resolution condemning the group by name. Nor did the Democrats have a monopoly on the Klan problem. In Indiana, the group's leader, D. C. Stephenson, had built up an organization powerful enough to dominate the Republican party. But in 1925 Stephenson was convicted of second-degree murder of a young woman who took poison after he had abducted and assaulted her. He insisted he had been framed and took his revenge by giving newspapers details about state officials associated with him. Other exposés disclosed the depths of Klan corruption and soon drove people away. The Klan revival was short-lived, though it would reappear in the 1960s as one of several organizations seeking to preserve white supremacy in the South.

The Dry Decade

Although never exclusively a rural movement, Prohibition enjoyed its greatest support in the countryside and among the fundamentalist denominations. After decades of agitation, the goal would finally be realized in the twenties. In anticipation of the Prohibition Amendment's becoming law in 1920, Congress in October 1919, over President Wilson's veto, passed the Volstead Act to implement it. This act defined intoxicating liquor as any beverage containing more than one-half of 1 percent of alcohol. It forbade any person, except for religious or medical purposes, to "manufacturer, sell, barter, transport, import, export, deliver, furnish, or possess" such beverages without a license. The commissioner of internal revenue was to enforce the act.

Making liquor illegal nationwide had two immediate results. The old saloon was replaced by the speakeasy, where drinking soon took on a new glamour. At the same time, by putting outside the law a personal habit millions of Americans would not give up, Prohibition opened up a new field for city gangs. National Prohibition made liquor a major source of gang income, raised that income to phenomenal levels, and strengthened gang domination of local police and local politics. Congress never voted enough money for more than token enforcement of the Volstead Act. The commissioner of internal revenue rarely had as many as two thousand agents to police the entire country; the Capone gang alone had a private army in Chicago of at least a thousand. They and hundreds of other gangs gained control of the undercover liquor business—bootlegging, smuggling, and speakeasies. At its peak, the Capone gang took in $60 million a year, with gambling and liquor the principal sources of income.

Criticism of the noble experiment, as Prohibition was called, gradually mounted. The Democratic party, although deeply divided over the issue, had to think of its urban constituents, for whom drinking in public was a social custom. It became an issue in the campaign of 1928, when Alfred E. (Al) Smith, the Democratic candidate, proposed to do away with the federal law and return the problem to the states. Herbert Hoover, his Republican opponent, did not take a stand. After his election, Hoover named a commission headed by the distinguished lawyer George W. Wickersham to study enforcement problems. Its report, published in January 1931, reviewed in frank detail all the evils of the "experiment." Yet a majority of the commission urged that it be continued.

After the Democratic landslide in the election of 1932, Congress adopted the Twenty-first Amendment, repealing the Eighteenth, in February 1933. By the end of the year it had been ratified. With control of liquor returned to the states, only seven chose to continue Prohibition. Mississippi, in 1966, became the last of the seven to go "wet."

Fundamentalism and Civil Liberties

The repression of foreigners and foreign ideologies and habits soon carried over to the repression of thought and speech. Here, as among the Klansmen and the "drys," Protestant fundamentalists, demanding an absolutely literal reading of the Bible and resisting all modifications of theology in the light of modern science and biblical criticism, led the assault. The object of their attack became the public schools, where, they insisted, Darwin's theory of evolution should not be taught.

In Tennessee in 1925, the fundamentalists won passage of a state law forbidding the teaching of evolution in the state's schools and colleges. The American Civil Liberties Union was eager to test the law, and the same year, John T. Scopes, a young high school teacher in the country town of Dayton, Tennessee, violated it and was arrested. Reporters from all over the country swarmed into Dayton (population 1700) to cover the court proceedings.

To defend the Bible, William Jennings Bryan, bald and aging, joined the prosecution. Clarence Darrow, perhaps the most brilliant trial lawyer in the country, headed the defense. Bryan began by attacking the city slickers, come all the way from the Gomorrah of New York to expose the true believers. The climax came when Darrow subjected Bryan to questioning that exposed his ignorance and inconsistencies. Bryan then allowed himself to be lured into a concession that made his followers gasp. "Do you think the earth was made in six days?" asked Darrow. "Not six

days of twenty-four hours," answered Bryan. In the end he conceded that the Creation might have lasted for "millions of years." The presiding judge mercifully cut the questioning short. Scopes, found guilty, was fined only $100. The national ridicule sustained by the fundamentalists took much of the strength from their efforts to retain a system of values by legal compulsion.

Those who cared deeply about American traditions of freedom of expression and personal liberty were most discouraged by the right-wing hysteria, ethnic intolerance, and anti-intellectualism of "normalcy." Nor could they look with much confidence to the Supreme Court, although Justice Oliver Wendell Holmes, Jr., did use several cases to caution against *indiscriminate* attempts to suppress unpopular ideas. In *Schenck v. United States* (1919), Holmes upheld the conviction of Schenck, a Socialist, for conspiracy in distributing a circular urging draftees to refuse to report for induction into the army. In doing so, he tried to draw the line between those forms of speech that must be protected and those that were dangerous to the state. "The character of every act depends upon the circumstances in which it is done," he

Clarence Darrow and William Jennings Bryan at Dayton, Tennessee. *(Brown Brothers)*

declared. The right of free speech would not, for example, permit anyone to shout "Fire!" in a theater and cause a panic.

The determining question, then, is whether the words are used in such a way as to create "a clear and present danger" to the national interest. Schenck, in the opinion of the Court, had clearly interfered in wartime with the power of Congress to raise armies. (In 1951 the Court would cite the *Schenck* decision in upholding the conviction of Communist party leaders for conspiring to teach the violent overthrow of the American government.)

Holmes applied his principle in a dissenting opinion in a case superficially similar to Schenck's, *Abrams v. United States* (1919). Here a majority of the Court upheld the conviction of a group of Russian immigrants for distributing leaflets opposing American intervention in Russia in 1918. Holmes, with Justice Brandeis concurring, held that the specific statements made by the defendants did not constitute a threat to the government or to the conduct of its war against Germany. The Court had departed, he insisted, from the reasonable line it had drawn in the *Schenck* case: "Congress certainly cannot forbid all effort to change the mind of the country." Holmes closed his dissent with an appeal for "free trade in ideas."

The twenties proved less than hospitable to "free trade in ideas." Even so, there were fervent practitioners of that trade. Most of them could be found in literary and artistic movements, which were experimenting with new ideas, undermining established beliefs, exposing absurdities in society, and promoting nonconformity.

THE CULTURE OF DISSENT

With a number of other protesters, novelist John Dos Passos stood outside the walls of Charlestown Prison on August 23, 1927, when the switch was thrown that sent Nicola Sacco and Bartolomeo Vanzetti to their deaths in the electric chair. Several years later, in his novel *The Big Money* (which completed the trilogy *U.S.A.*), Dos Passos declared that with that execution America had become two nations:

they have clubbed us off the streets they are stronger they are rich they hire and fire the politicians the newspapereditors the old judges the small men with reputations the collegepresidents the wardheelers (listen businessmen collegepresidents judges America will

not forget her betrayers) they hire the men with guns the uniforms the policecars the patrolwagons
all right you have won you will kill the brave men our friends tonight . . .
America our nation has been beaten by strangers who have turned our language inside out who have taken the clean words our fathers spoke and made them slimy and foul . . .
all right we are two nations*

For a number of American intellectuals, writers, and artists, America had become two nations much earlier. The invasions of civil liberties, Prohibition, fundamentalism, Klansmen, Rotarians, the triumph of business values, the small-town, service-club mentality of the White House—all had confirmed their belief that materialism, intolerance, and hypocrisy were making a shambles of American civilization. But unlike some of the prewar rebels, they did not look for a political solution. The problem with America was simply too deep to be resolved by legislation. Although the nation could boast of mass consumption on an unparalleled scale, the American people, in their view, were suffering from emotional and aesthetic poverty.

Whether in novels, poetry, paintings, or plays, the quality of their work would vary considerably. There emerged no single writer of greater stature than Melville, Emerson, Hawthorne, Whitman, Mark Twain, or Henry James. But in their willingness to question the sanity of their society and in their experiments with new ideas and forms, this generation of writers stood out from all others. Probably more good writing and more important books were produced in these years than in any period in the nation's history.

Prelude to Rebellion: The Optimistic Years

The spirit of freedom and experimentation so eagerly taken up by writers and artists in the 1920s had found outlets for expression in the prewar years. Across the country, in large cities and in small towns, "intellectually liberated" Americans, as they liked to think of themselves, began to meet and exchange ideas. They included political radicals as well as revolutionary poets and painters. Some of them formed groups with artistic, cultural, or political programs; others preferred to work alone. Although small artist communities formed in places such as Chicago,

---

*Copyright by Elizabeth H. Dos Passos.

St. Louis, and even Davenport, Iowa, the mecca by 1914 had become a few blocks of downtown New York known as Greenwich Village.

The wildest young rebels from all over America came to the Village to experience "freedom," to flout convention, and to debate all the "new" ideas, from penology and poetry to birth control and sexual repression. Although the influence of Sigmund Freud, the Austrian founder of psychoanalysis, was not fully felt until the twenties, his visit to the United States in 1909 and the translation by 1925 of some of his early works had brought him to the attention of Village intellectuals. In the teens and the twenties, the popularized and distorted version of Freudian thought ignored his more complex explanations of the role of unconscious motivation in determining behavior and focused instead on the theories that seemed to advocate sexual freedom. Even to talk of Freud's ideas (few actually read his works) was to feel liberated.

The cultural interlude that ushered in Wilson's presidency in 1912 has been called "the innocent rebellion." It continued the artistic war begun by writers such as Mark Twain, Frank Norris, Stephen Crane, Jack London, and Theodore Dreiser (Chapter 23). The writers who came of age around 1912, like their predecessors, attacked the "genteel tradition" for its deliberate avoidance of reality, its polite evasions. More freely experimental, this group promised, as one of its manifestoes said, to be "skeptical of inherited values" and "ready to examine old dogmas." In the many "little magazines" that suddenly appeared, they published their works and criticisms. In art galleries and shows, they saw the latest experimental painting from abroad—postimpressionists such as Matisse, Braque, and Picasso. In contrast, the Ashcan school of American painters chose to represent life around them as it really looked.

Experimental theater flourished, as did the new poetry. Both broke sharply with traditional forms and expression. In *Bound East for Cardiff*, a one-act play produced in 1916, Eugene O'Neill (1888–1953) recalled the world of tramp steamers, waterfront dives, and seamen's talk he had known. The poet Carl Sandburg (1878–1967) crowded into his verse the midwestern life he had observed in the prairie towns of Illinois and in the raw metropolis of Chicago. Robert Frost (1874–1963) evoked the black beauty of the New Hampshire hills and celebrated the taciturn and self-contained Yankees who seemed to blend into the New England landscape.

Both as a critic and as a poet, Ezra Pound (1885–1972) had considerable influence: he promoted and associated himself with the imagists, who departed from conventional poetry by using common speech and new rhythms to evoke images of everyday life. Pound had been confident of an intellectual awakening in America, but in 1909, seemingly in despair, he chose to live as an expatriate. Others would soon join him abroad, convinced that individual artistic fulfillment could never be realized in the machine culture of America.

The prewar writers and artists had had a certain confidence about themselves and their ability to change society. Although some were committed to socialism, the prevailing spirit was more often anarchistic or free-thinking. It was a rejection of all rigid ideologies. But even before America entered the war, much of the optimism had vanished. And what remained failed to survive the war and the postwar repression.

Disillusion and Disenchantment

The *lost generation* was the term Gertrude Stein used to describe the postwar writers and artists, because in their youth the war had broken the continuity of their lives. But Malcolm Cowley (1898–1989) said of himself and his literary and artistic contemporaries that they had actually lost their innocence before the war. To come of age in the America of the Progressive Era was to suffer from "a sense of oppression." He and his friends could feel little passion or optimism. Progressive reform threatened to create only "an intolerable utopia of dull citizens"; morality was "a lie told to our bodies"; what they learned in school was "useless or misdirected"; and "society in general was terribly secure, unexciting, middle-class, a vast reflection of the families from which we came."

But World War I, in which many of the young writers and artists participated, had a deep effect on their lives. It left them bitter, resentful, and thoroughly disillusioned. Ernest Hemingway (1899–1961) had only recently graduated from high school when he enlisted in a volunteer ambulance unit in France. What he experienced of the war convinced him of its senseless brutality, stupidity, and insensitivity. "I was embarrassed," says Lieutenant Henry in Hemingway's *A Farewell to Arms* (1929), "by the words *sacred, glorious,* and *sacrifice.* . . . We had . . . read them, on proclamations, now for a long time, and I had seen nothing sacred, and the things that were glorious had no glory and the sacrifices were like the stockyards in Chicago, if nothing was done with the meat except to bury it. . . . Abstract words such as *glory, honor, courage* were obscene."*

Like Cowley and Hemingway, many of those who fought found it difficult to return to an America that had, in their eyes, betrayed and deceived them. The soldiers, Ezra Pound wrote,

> *walked eye-deep in hell*
> *believing in old men's lies,*
> *then unbelieving*
> *came home, home to a lie,*
> *home to deceits,*
> *home to old lies and new infamy;*
> *usury age-old and age-thick*
> *and liars in public places.†*

To the question of what men had died for in the war, Pound delivered the classic response of the "rebel" generation:

> *For an old bitch gone in the teeth,*
> *For a botched civilization.†*

Hemingway, like Pound, settled in Paris after the war. The American writers and artists who went abroad before the war had gone mostly to look, to compare, to criticize, to learn. America remained their homeland, and they believed it would yet produce a vital culture. The expatriates of the 1920s felt differently. To be sure, they considered themselves cultural representatives of their land. But few wished ever again to endure its narrow-mindedness, provincialism, and stifling conformity. In a place such as Paris, artists would be free to express themselves in any way they chose. What attracted so many to France, explained e. e. cummings, the unconventional poet and writer who had also served with an American ambulance corps in the war, was that "France has happened more than she is happening, whereas America is happening more than she has happened."

Although Paris remained an intellectual and artistic center throughout the twenties, many of the expatriates eventually returned to their Native America, some of them having found that even Europe afforded no lasting excape. After Hemingway returned to New York, he wrote *The Sun Also Rises* (1926), which told of expatriates, broken by the war, amusing themselves in a postwar wasteland—drinking, boxing, watching bullfights, making love, all to no purpose.

What made postwar America such a stifling place for the rebel writers and artists who made up the lost generation was its business mentality, its machine standardization, and its spiritual sterility. To these critics, the businessman was the symbol of bourgeois culture. They mocked and condemned him not as an exploiter of labor or a corrupter of politics but for his blind conformity and emotional emptiness. His motto was "Gotta hustle"; he spoke in clichés, worried about trivia, and practiced bigotry and moral censorship.

George Follansbee Babbitt, the main character in Sinclair Lewis's (1885–1951) novel *Babbitt*, entered the American vocabulary as a way of defining business or professional men who conform unthinkingly to middle-class standards. Babbitt was the product of standardization and mass marketing; his very character was shaped by the goods he consumed and the material objects he worshiped:

> *Just as he was an Elk, a Booster, and a member of the Chamber of Commerce, just as the priests of the Presbyterian Church determined his every religious belief and the senators who controlled the Republican Party decided in little smoky rooms in Washington what he should think about disarmament, tariff, and Germany, so did the large national advertisers fix the surface of his life, fix what he believed to be his individuality. These standard advertised wares—toothpastes, socks, tires, cameras, instantaneous hot-water-heaters—were his symbols and proofs of excellence; at first the signs, then the substitutes, for joy and passion and wisdom.*

The need to probe the sources of America's troubles required many of the writers of the twenties to analyze the very places in which they had been born and nurtured—the small towns of Middle America and the Bible Belt, where "dullness is made God." Hemingway, for example, grew up in Oak Park, Illinois. "What did he fear?" he asks of one of his characters. "It was not fear or dread. It was a nothing that he knew too well."

In *Main Street*, Sinclair Lewis, whose birthplace was Sauk Center, Minnesota, drew caricatures of small-town types obsessed with material success and standardized in their thoughts and emotions. With more compassion, Sherwood Anderson (1876–1941), born in Ohio, tried to convey how the industrial machine had destroyed the community and poetry of the village and

---

*Copyright 1929 by Charles Scribner's Sons; copyright renewed. Reprinted with permission from Charles Scribner's Sons.

†Ezra Pound, *Personae*. Copyright 1926 by Ezra Pound. Reprinted by permission of New Directions Publishing Corporation.

*From *Babbitt* by Sinclair Lewis. Reprinted by persmission of Harcourt Brace Jovanovich, Inc.

MAIN STREET, USA

In the novel *Main Street* (1920), Sinclair Lewis probed his own midwestern origins. Through the character of Carol Kennicott, a recent college graduate who has married a physician of Gopher Prairie, Minnesota, Lewis sought to expose "the unsparing unapologetic ugliness" of small-town America. At a party welcoming her to the town, Carol tries to divert the conversation from small talk to more serious topics.

"There hasn't been much labor trouble around here, has there, Mr. Stowbody [president of the Ionic Bank]?" she asked innocently.

"No, ma'am, thank God, we've been free from that, except maybe with hired girls and farmhands. Trouble enough with these foreign farmers; if you don't watch these Swedes they turn socialist or populist or some fool thing on you in a minute. Of course, if they have loans you can make 'em listen to reason. I just have 'em come into the bank for a talk, and tell 'em a few things. I don't mind their being democrats, so much, but I won't stand having socialists around. . . ."

"Do you approve of union labor?" Carol inquired of Mr. Elder.

"Me? I should say not! It's like this: I don't mind dealing with my men if they think they've got any grievances—though Lord knows what's come over workmen, nowadays—don't appreciate a good job. But still, if they come to me honestly, as man to man, I'll talk things over with them. But I'm not going to

have any outsider . . . butting in and telling me how to run my business!"

Mr. Elder was growing more excited, more belligerent and patriotic. "I stand for freedom and constitutional rights. If any man don't like my shop, he can get up and git. Same way, if I don't like him, he gits. And that's all there is to it. . . . The half-baked thinker that isn't dry behind the ears yet, and these suffragettes and God knows what all buttinskis there are that are trying to tell a business man how to run his business, and some of these college professors are just about as bad, the whole kit and bilin' of 'em are nothing in God's world but socialism in disguise! And it's my bounden duty as a producer to resist every attack on the integrity of American industry to the last ditch. Yes—SIR!"

Mr. Elder wiped his brow.

Dave Dyer added, "Sure! You bet! What they ought to do is simply to hang every one of these agitators, and that would settle the whole thing right off. Don't you think so, doc?"

"You bet," agreed Kennicott. . . .

The talk went on. It did go on! Their voices were monotonous, thick, emphatic. They were harshly pompous, like men in the smoking-compartments of Pullman cars. They did not bore Carol. They frightened her. . . .

Source: Sinclair Lewis, *Main Street* (New York: Harcourt, Brace, 1920), pp. 49–52.

---

alienated its inhabitants from each other. The loneliness of Americans—the reaching out for human contact and finding none—produced the behavior and outlook he described in *Winesburg, Ohio* (1919). The procession of grotesque characters that moved through his tales—the drunkards, keyhole peepers, bedroom murderers—had become twisted and deformed because their emotions found no outlet. As Anderson wrote of one of his characters: "The living force within could not find expression."

More concerned with a region than the small town, William Faulkner (1897–1962), a native of Mississippi, broke with conventional literary forms in novels such as *The Sound and the Fury* (1929), *Light in August* (1932), and *Absalom, Absalom!* (1936). No writer, no chronicler probed more deeply into the interior life of the South, into the recesses of the white southern mind. Nor did any novelist write as compellingly about the South's tragic past—the terrible burden of the Civil War and the decadence, violence, and terror that marked the transition from the old values and

civilization to the New South. Human relationships fascinated Faulkner, and few American writers conveyed as many terrible truths about those relationships. "I listen to the voices," he remarked, "and when I put down what the voices say, it's right. Sometimes I don't like what they say, but I don't change it."

With little compassion of any kind, Henry L. Mencken (1880–1956), a critic and essayist, took on Babbitts as well as social idealists in the *American Mercury*, which he helped found in 1924. In America, he insisted, the conventional middle classes, the pillars of society, even more than the masses, were boobs, yokels, or peasants. The United States was their paradise, and Harding, "the Marion stone-head," was their president. The intellectual Woodrow Wilson, on the other hand, was that "self-bamboozled Presbyterian, the right thinker, the great moral statesman, the perfect model of the Christian cad." Mencken expressed distaste for the political reformers of his time—"the army of uplifters and world-savers," the "jitney Messiahs," and "saccharine liberals."

Democracy itself was a failure, though it provided "the only really amusing form of government ever endured by mankind." Monogamy was against nature; romantic love, a lie based on "the delusion that one woman differs from another."

In one of his annual volumes of *Prejudices*, which he began publishing in 1919, he asked of himself: "If you find so much that is unworthy of reverence in the United States, then why do you live here?" He replied with another question: "Why do men go to zoos?" Mencken's ferocious assault on every sacred conviction of "the booboisie" made the *American Mercury* an overnight sensation, delighting even those he parodied. That in itself should have forced him to consider the shallowness and sophomoric quality of many of his barbs.

Few writers came closer to symbolizing the lost generation than F. Scott Fitzgerald (1896–1940). He emerged as the principal spokesman for a generation "grown up to find all Gods dead, all wars fought, all faiths in man shaken." Fitzgerald, along with his wife Zelda, followed a lifestyle of reckless and decadent abandon. *This Side of Paradise*, published in 1920 when Fitzgerald was twenty-four, made him a celebrity overnight with its vivid and daring depiction of "flaming youth."

But in his best novel, *The Great Gatsby* (1925), Fitzgerald managed to suggest both the glitter of American prosperity and the treacherous foundations on which it rested. With particular skill, he exposed the success ethic for the ways in which it consumed and destroyed individuals. Jay Gatsby, the romantic bootlegger who believes every dream can come true simply by wishing for it hard enough, is betrayed by his gangster friends and by the privileged rich, who "smashed up things and then retreated back into their money and their vast carelessness."

That "vast carelessness" helped to bring "the greatest, gaudiest spree in history," as Fitzgerald once called it, to a sobering end. In 1931, against the background of economic distress and widespread unemployment, Fitzgerald wrote an obituary for the decade.

Now once more the belt is tight and we summon the proper expression of horror as we look back at our wasted youth. Sometimes, though, there is a ghostly rumble among the drums, an asthmatic whisper in the trombones that swings me back into the early twenties when we drank wood alcohol and every day in every way grew better and better, and there was a first abortive shortening of the skirts, and girls all looked alike in sweater dresses, and people you didn't want to know said, "Yes, we have no bananas," and it seemed

Claude McKay. *(Brown Brothers)*

Langston Hughes. *(New York Public Library)*

*only a question of a few years before the older people would step aside and let the world be run by those who saw things as they were—and it all seems rosy and romantic to us who were young then, because we will never feel quite so intensely about our surroundings any more.**

Some years later, a friend visited Fitzgerald and found him reading Karl Marx. It was an odd scene—at least the visitor thought so—but Fitzgerald, like many of the other literary and artistic rebels of the twenties, was heeding the call to social responsibility. As Fitzgerald explained to his friend, "I've got to examine all my characters in the light of their class relationships."

The Harlem Renaissance

While seeking equality in white America, W. E. B. Du Bois had advised his people in *The Souls of Black Folk* (1903) not to sacrifice their racial heritage or their individuality. For too long, he felt, blacks had been forced to look at themselves through white eyes, calculating every move and word in terms of white expectations. In the 1920s, the rapid urbanization of blacks in the North, along with the postwar racial violence and the new cultural influences, helped to promote a movement among black writers and artists to express the "true self-consciousness" Du Bois had urged.

As Greenwich Village lured white artists, so Harlem—that part of northern Manhattan formerly occupied by the Dutch, the Irish, and the Jews—became the center of black America, and an exotic attraction for the white pleasure seeker. Black people flocked to Harlem because that was the only place to be. To young, aspiring black writers and artists, many of whom came there in the twenties, Harlem was a remarkable place that deserved to be celebrated and loved for what it was. "Where else could I have all this life but Harlem?" asks the principal character in Claude McKay's *Home to Harlem* (1928):

Good old Harlem! Chocolate Harlem! Sweet Harlem!. . . . The deep-dyed color, the thickness, the closeness of it. The noises of Harlem. The sugared laughter. The honey-talk on its streets. And all night long, ragtime and "blues" playing somewhere, . . . singing somewhere, dancing somewhere Oh, the conta-

*gious fever of Harlem. Burning everywhere in dark-eyed Harlem.**

Like the young white rebels, Harlem intellectuals and artists, in large part the children of middle-class parents, rejected many of the values and standards of their seniors. What had stood in the way of "true Negro art in America," Langston Hughes (1902–1967) insisted, was that unfortunate "urge within the race toward whiteness, the desire to pour racial individuality into the mold of American standardization, and to be as little Negro and as much American as possible." Hughes rejected such assimilationist notions:

We younger Negro artists who create now intend to express our individual dark-skinned selves without fear or shame. If white people are pleased we are glad. If they are not, it doesn't matter. We know we are beautiful. And ugly too. The tom-tom cries and the tom-tom laughs. If colored people are pleased we are glad. If they are not, their displeasure doesn't matter either. We build our temples for tomorrow, strong as we know how, and we stand on the top of the mountain, free within ourselves.†

The older generation of cultural leaders, Du Bois's "talented tenth," had been so fearful of reinforcing white stereotypes about blacks that they ignored or obscured the artistic resources of black folk forms. The more conservative among them frowned on the poets, novelists, musicians, and entertainers who celebrated black vitality and substituted anger and irony for the old strategy of humiliation or imitation. But that did not stop a new generation of black activists from preferring the black vernacular, the mournful blues of Bessie Smith, the "hot jazz" of Duke Ellington and Louis Armstrong, the soft-shoe shuffling of Bojangles Bill Robinson, the singing sermons of evangelist Elder Lightfoot Solomon Michaux.

By whatever means, the Harlem artists were intent on revealing the freshness and variety of black culture. They found inspiration and spiritual identity in their African origins. They rediscovered the spirituals, the work songs, the sermons, and the rich plantation folklore. They sought to describe, honestly and realistically, the lives and troubles of their people, both in the slave past and in the urban present. Having arrived in Harlem in 1921, Langston Hughes would spend the remainder of his life there celebrating in his poetry, novels, and humor the beauty, spontaneity, and genuine folk wisdom he found.

> Folks, I'm telling you
> birthing is hard
> and dying is mean—
> so get yourself
> a little loving
> in between.*

Of the scores of talented men and women who gave Harlem its unusual distinction in the twenties, certain names stand out. One was the Jamaican Claude McKay (1890–1948), a gifted poet and prose writer and an early leader in the Harlem movement. McKay dramatized in his life and work the new Negro's rebellion against bourgeois inhibitions. Cosmopolitan, Marxist, idealist, and realist, his serious treatment of primitivism and his militant protest against capitalism and racial bigotry linked him with both the white literary experimentalists and the radical publicists of the postwar decade.

Like McKay and Hughes, Zora Neale Hurston (1901–1960) wanted to celebrate the common folk. She felt "on fire" about her people, appreciating their complexity, beauty, and agony. Several of her stories and novels focused on the oppression and daily drudgery of black women and the struggles they waged to overcome their predicaments. Endeavoring to be loyal to the rhythms, nuances, and poetic imagery of rural black speech, Hurston had her characters express their feelings in a simple eloquence. For example, a former slave imparts to her granddaughter a harsh version of reality, hoping she might be able to avoid the same fate.

> Honey, de white man is de ruler of everything as fur as Ah been able tuh find out. Maybe it's some place way off in de ocean where de black man is in power, but we don't know nothin' but what we see. So de white man throw down de load & tell de nigger man tuh pick it up. He pick it up because he have to, but he don't tote it. He hand it to his womenfolks. De nigger woman is de mule uh de world as fur as Ah can see. Ah been prayin' fuh it tuh be different wid you. Lawd, Lawd, Lawd!†

Perhaps the most brilliant single achievement of the renaissance was Jean Toomer's (1894–1967) novel *Cane* (1923), a series of portraits that ranged over unexplored parts of black life in the South. But *Cane* sold less than five hundred copies the year it was published, emphasizing the problem black artists faced not only in reaching their own people, but in having to cater to white expectations. If McKay's *Home to Harlem* made the best-seller charts, that was because his portrayal of Harlem life confirmed what so many whites were discovering for themselves.

The twenties, Langston Hughes recalled, was a period "when the Negro was in vogue." That is, downtown whites and tourists went to Harlem to see the action, to listen to the music, to drop their inhibitions and find emotional release. Harlem soon had a reputation among whites that few Harlemites might have recognized. Some years later, Hughes would bitterly recall the white man's addiction:

> A party of whites from Fifth Avenue
> Came tippin into Dixie's to get a view,
> Came tippin into Dixie's with smiles on their
>   faces,
> Knowin they can buy a dozen colored places.
> Dixie grinned. Dixie bowed.
> Dixie rubbed his hands and laughed out loud—
> While a tall white woman
> In an ermine cape
> Looked at the blacks and
> Thought of rape,
> Looked at the blacks and
> Thought of a rope,
> Looked at the blacks and
> Thought of flame,
> And thought of something
> Without a name.*

When Carl Van Vechten wrote *Nigger Heaven* (1926), a best-selling novel, he caught the essence of the Harlem appeal: "Jungle land. Hottentots and Bantus swaying under the amber moon. Love, sex, passion, hate." Although Van Vechten was white, he promoted black artists and helped find patrons and publishers for them. Their recognition, however, proved to be double-edged, and such relationships were bound to fail. "She wanted me to be primitive and know and feel the intuitions of the primitive," Hughes recalled of his white patron. "But, unfortunately, I did not feel the rhythms of the primitive surging through me, and so I could not live and write as though I did. I was only an American Negro—who had loved the surface of Africa and the rhythms of Africa—

---

*Reprinted by permission of Harold Ober Associates Incorporated. Copyright 1951 by Langston Hughes. Copyright renewed 1979 by George Houston Bass.

†From Zora Neale Hurston, *Their Eyes Were Watching God.* Fawcett World Library, 1969, p. 16. Originally published by Lippincott, 1937. Copyright renewed 1965 by John C. and Joel Hurston.

---

*From *Death in Harlem.* Reprinted by permission of Harold Ober Associates Incorporated. Copyright © 1942 by Langston Hughes; copyright renewed.

but I was not African. I was Chicago and Kansas City and Broadway and Harlem."

Once the Great Depression struck, the patrons departed, as did the publishers. In Harlem, the exclusive clubs that had catered to white customers closed their doors. "We were no longer in vogue," Hughes recalled. Besides, he noted, the Harlem artists who thought the renaissance would bring acceptance and success had only deceived themselves. "For how could a large and enthusiastic number of people be crazy about Negroes forever? . . . The ordinary Negroes hadn't heard of the Negro Renaissance. And if they had, it hadn't raised their wages any."

In 1932, Hughes and twenty-one other Harlem writers visited the Soviet Union. Claude McKay became briefly interested in the Communist experiment, but came away disillusioned and entered the Catholic church. The light-complexioned Jean Toomer found an outlet in mysticism and crossed the color line altogether. The task of expressing "our individual dark-skinned selves without fear or shame" would be largely taken on in the thirties by Hughes, Du Bois, and a newcomer, Richard Wright.

THE POPULAR ARTS

Applied to the popular or "lively" arts, technology had an enormous impact on the twenties. It shaped American attitudes and tastes in ways that few if any books could. Radio reached into the homes of millions, and similar numbers flocked to the movie houses and listened to phonograph records. The effects were both liberating and conditioning. Rural isolation broke down. Americans everywhere were introduced to make-believe worlds, new styles of music, new levels of sophistication, different lifestyles, and new models to imitate. Movies and radio programs nationalized popular culture, revolutionized people's expectations, and standardized society even more. With their vast potential for molding the habits and tastes of Americans, the popular arts by the end of the decade had become big businesses in their own right.

The Movies

The liveliest of the lively arts of the twenties, the movies, was also the most highly mechanized, the most highly capitalized, the one closest to big business in production and distribution methods. The movie began as a peep show in a penny arcade. The viewer put a nickel in a device called a kinetoscope (invented by Thomas A. Edison about 1889) and saw tiny figures moving against blurred backgrounds. Edison thought little of his invention, but others took it up and soon succeeded in projecting images on a screen for large audiences. By 1905, more than five thousand

A chorus line of women who satisfied the exacting demands of theatrical producer Florenz Ziegfeld. *(Culver Pictures, Inc.)*

This is the great picture upon which the famous comedian has worked a whole year.

6 reels of Joy.

Charles Chaplin IN "THE KID"

Written and directed by Charles Chaplin

A First National Attraction

(Granger Collection)

John W. Considine, Jr. presents.

RUDOLPH VALENTINO IN 'The Son of the Sheik'

a Sequel to The Sheik

with VILMA BANKY

from the novel by E. M. HULL Adapted to the Screen by FRANCES MARION

A GEORGE FITZMAURICE PRODUCTION

(Granger Collection)

WINGS

With CLARA BOW

CHARLES (Buddy) ROGERS, RICHARD ARLEN and GARY COOPER

(Granger Collection)

"nickelodeons," housed in converted stores and warehouses, were showing films for five cents' admission.

Peep shows had prospered by showing short, comic action. The new films introduced endless variations on the chase: cowboys after rustlers; sheriffs after badmen; city cops after bank robbers. Comedians threw pies at one another, slipped on banana peels, fell into manholes. The first movie with a recognizable plot was *The Great Train Robbery* (1903), and its instant success set every producer to turning out thrillers. But there were still no stars, no sex, no culture. David W. Griffith liberated the movie camera from nickelodeon themes and the limitations of the stage set. In *The Birth of a Nation* (1914), a partisan and intolerant film about the Civil War and Reconstruction, Griffith showed sweeping panoramas of massed armies, fade-outs, close-ups, and other kinds of shots revealing the scope and flexibility of camera and screen. Budgeted at an unheard-of $100,000 and directed with imagination, *The Birth of a Nation* was a financial and artistic model.

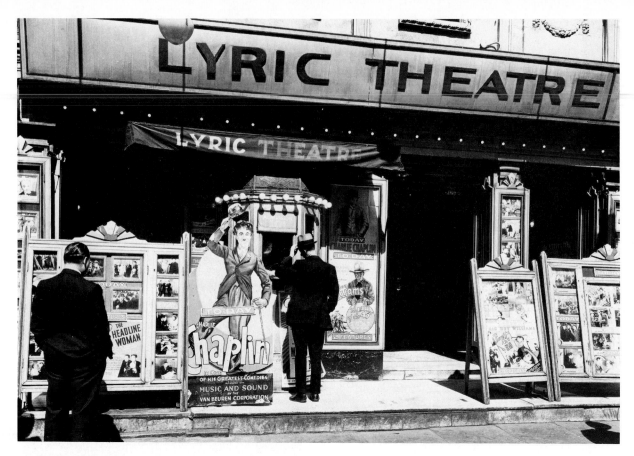

The Lyric Theatre, New York. *(Berenice Abbott, for the federal art project "Changing New York," courtesy Museum of the City of New York)*

The Rex Theatre, Lelaud, Mississippi. *(Dorothea Lange, Library of Congress)*

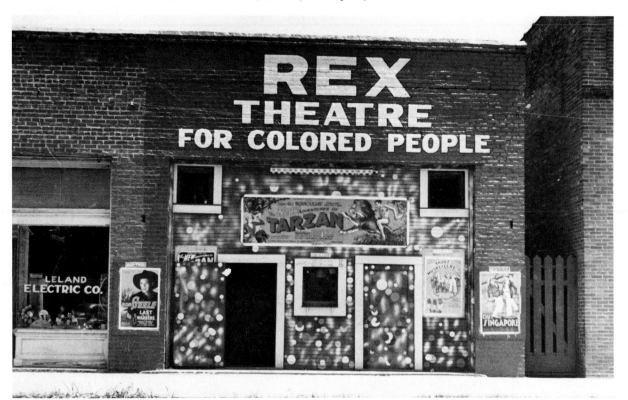

The most successful of Griffith's imitators in the twenties was Cecil B. De Mille, whose religious spectacles—*The Ten Commandments* (1923) and *The King of Kings* (1927), for example—exploited the mechanical possibilities of the camera and proved that sex could be worked into almost any subject. By 1917 the movies had become a multimillion-dollar industry, and Hollywood, California, the film capital. Luxurious movie theaters were rapidly replacing the nickelodeons, and Americans were spending $175 million a year on admissions.

The first stars—Mary Pickford, Roscoe (Fatty) Arbuckle, Douglas Fairbanks, Marie Dressler—earned fabulous salaries, lived glamorous lives, and attracted incredible newspaper and magazine attention. Much of it was promoted by movie press agents to keep the stars in the public eye. The stars themselves cooperated so well, on and off stage, that Hollywood soon achieved a reputation as the Sodom of America. As if to confirm that view, films such as *Sinners in Silk, Ladies of Pleasure, The Joy Girl,* and *Women Who Give* exposed audiences, in the words of one press agent, to "brilliant men, beautiful jazz babies, champagne baths, midnight revels, petting parties in the purple dawn, all ending in a terrific smashing climax that makes you gasp!"

These films promised considerably more than they gave, but moralists worried about their effect on youth and agitated for official censorship. To forestall their critics, film producers in 1922 hired Will H. Hays, former chairman of the Republican National Committee and Harding's postmaster general, to act as their conscience. Hays devised a production code setting limits on lovemaking, décolletage, crime, and profanity.

Besides sex and spectacles, slapstick comedy featuring such stars as Arbuckle, Harold Lloyd, and Buster Keaton quickly became a movie staple. The greatest comic of all, Charlie Chaplin, achieved an international reputation as the wistful little tramp with the battered derby hat, cane, and funny walk. In *Modern Times*, in which he had to escape from the clutches of enormous machines, Chaplin captured the tyranny of the assembly line.

With the opening of Al Jolson's *The Jazz Singer* in 1927, the era of sound films began. Within two years, "talkies" had replaced silents, and Hollywood, with what John Dos Passos called "its great bargain sale of five and ten cent lusts and dreams," was reaching even larger audiences.

The Phonograph: Ragtime and Jazz

What the film projector did for motion, the phonograph, another Edison invention, did for sound. By 1905 the phonograph had become a successful commercial device. Comedians, actors, singers, and musicians could be heard in the home or in places of public entertainment. In 1914 more than half a million phonographs were manufactured, and soon it was nearly a million.

Before the radio, the phonograph gave the greatest impetus to the spread of popular music, much of it ragtime and jazz. Ragtime had emerged in the 1890s, with Scott Joplin its best-known composer. It borrowed heavily from black work songs and both black and white minstrel songs—"a music," writes LeRoi Jones, that "the Negro came to in imitating white imitations of Negro music."* Stressing rhythm rather than melody, the instrument rather than the voice, ragtime would have a significant influence on jazz.

With the wartime and postwar migration of blacks, jazz and blues spread northward, especially to Chicago's South Side and New York's Harlem. Dixieland bands first played in these cities around 1915, the year W. C. Handy wrote his "St. Louis Blues."

In 1920, the Okeh Record Company made the dramatic decision to permit a black singer to make a commercial recording. With Mamie Smith's rendition of "Crazy Blues," race records, as they were called, made a successful debut. The first jazz records were made in 1917 by a white group. Within the next several years, Paul Whiteman became known as the King of Jazz. Blues and jazz recordings multiplied, and attending jazz concerts became fashionable. But as LeRoi Jones would later observe in *Blues People:* "With such displays as Whiteman's Aeolian Hall concert, complete with 'European Style' orchestra and Heifetz and Rachmaninoff in the audience, jazz had rushed into the mainstream without so much as one black face." But, he added, Americans had come to realize that there existed an American music "as traditionally wild, disenchanted, and unfettered as it had become fashionable for them to think they themselves had become."†

---

*From *Blues People* (1963) by Imamu Amiri Baraka (LeRoi Jones) by permission of William Morrow & Company.
†From *Blues People* (1963) by Imamu Amiri Baraka (LeRoi Jones) by permission of William Morrow & Company.

Bessie Smith, Empress of the Blues. *(Culver Pictures, Inc.)*

Preach them blues.
Sing them blues . . .
Moan them blues.
Let me convert your soul.

Radio

Unlike the movies, whose commercial possibilities were obvious from the first, the early development of radio was haphazard and accidental. In 1920, perhaps twenty thousand amateurs listened on homemade sets to wireless messages sent mainly from ships at sea. That year, as an experiment, the Westinghouse Electric and Manufacturing Company in Pittsburgh began to broadcast musical programs. Amateurs in the area responded enthusiastically, and soon popular demand induced Westinghouse to air the programs on a regular basis and to introduce reports of baseball scores. In 1920 the first commercial broadcasting station, KDKA, was set up in Pittsburgh in time to broadcast the results of the Harding–Cox election.

Overnight, radio became big business. Within four years, 562 stations were sending out music, stock-market and news reports, bedtime stories, and church services. The ringside account of the Dempsey–Carpentier fight in 1921 first realized radio's potential to tap the rage for mass spectator sports. By the end of the decade, broadcasts of prizefights, as well as the World Series and the Rose Bowl, had ensured large audiences. The sales of radio sets boomed. Radio stations covered the country, approximately a fourth of them controlled by newspapers or newspaper chains bent on dominating news outlets. Stations were combined into networks so that programs could reach mass audiences simultaneously. In 1926, the Radio Corporation of America (RCA) established the National Broadcasting Company with nineteen stations.

Once established as a national habit, radio listening became the object of intensive study by advertisers, who paid for most of the entertainment. As a selling medium, it seemed unsurpassed. The advertiser could reach into the homes of millions and repeat a message hour after hour. Most people seemed to have accepted "commercials" as the price of free radio entertainment. But to Lee De Forest, whose technical breakthrough had made national radio possible, the price was too high. "What have you done with my child?" he asked. "You have sent him out on the street in rags of ragtime to collect money from all and sundry. You have made of him a laughingstock of intelligence, surely a stench in the nostrils of the gods of the ionosphere."

Now that Americans could listen to nominating conventions and campaign speeches in their homes, interest in politics increased. But that did not appear to affect the quality of politics in the twenties. Radio did enable millions to follow the Smith–Hoover campaign of 1928. Millions more would hear Franklin Delano Roosevelt seek to calm fears over the collapse of the economic order.

THE POLITICS OF COMPLACENCY

To sell their candidate in the 1920 presidential election, the Republicans chose Albert Lasker of the Lord and Thomas agency, a creative genius in the newly glamorous advertising business. The selection was entirely appropriate. Having already made household words of Pepsodent and Puffed Wheat, Lasker undertook to "humanize Harding." He implanted the image of "an old-fashioned, safe, honest-to-the-core Middle Westerner who could be trusted never to rock the boat." To make that case required no distortion of Harding's character or political record.

Even without Lasker's salesmanship, the American people were bound to respond favorably to Harding. He was an easy man to like, a public favorite as long as he held office. He embodied the nation's small-town virtues. He belonged to the right clubs; he was a self-made man; he "looked like a president ought to look"; and he had a warm personality.

Unlike Wilson, Harding had no difficulty pardoning Eugene Debs for his wartime statements: "I could pick you out a half dozen members of the House and Senate," Harding explained, "who deserved quite as much to be in the penitentiary as did Debs." But he could not understand why radicals and some trade unionists persisted in their agitation rather than place their faith, as he had, in the American Dream. He had made it, and he assumed any American who had the right kind of hustle and determination would also succeed.

When Harding died, in August 1923, Coolidge's oath of office as president was administered to him by his father in their Vermont farmhouse, by the light of an old-fashioned kerosene lamp. This ceremony successfully projected a taciturn Yankee rustic in the Lasker image of his unfortunate predecessor. If Harding made a virtue of humility, Coolidge made one of inactivity and dedication to the principle that "civilization and profits go hand in hand." Both men reflected the dominant business culture of the decade. And in their policies both of them helped promote the maldistribution of wealth and the speculation that were speeding the nation toward economic disaster.

The Tragedy of Harding

When Harding said, "We must strive for normalcy to reach stability," he had in mind his campaign promise to encourage less government in business and more business in government. To help him in that task, he said, he would bring the "best minds" to Washington. He kept this promise in part by appointing to his cabinet such able men as Charles Evans Hughes (secretary of state), Herbert Hoover (secretary of commerce), Henry C. Wallace (secretary of agriculture), and Andrew W. Mellon (secretary of the Treasury). But he also brought with him some lesser minds, his small-town "Ohio gang." They proceeded to make a shambles of the Harding administration.

At the head of the Ohio gang was Harry M. Daugherty, a small-time lobbyist for tobacco, meat, and utility interests; it was he who launched the Harding presidential boom. Rewarded with the attorney generalship, he held that position until dismissed by President Coolidge in 1924, when his malfeasance was revealed. While in office Daugherty had made a business of selling liquor permits, pardons, and paroles to criminals at fancy prices. (Two divided juries in 1926 enabled him to escape prison.) Jesse Smith, who conducted a clearinghouse for the Ohio gang's graft, committed suicide, and the gang's worst secrets died with him. Even so, a number of administration insiders were soon sent to jail.

Charles R. Forbes, whom Harding had met on a vacation trip, so charmed the president that he was made director of the Veterans' Bureau. In that position he swindled the country of no less than $250 million by demanding kickbacks from contractors and suppliers and by condemning sup-

WORDS AND NAMES IN AMERICAN HISTORY

The development of a national economy in the United States eventually brought with it *brand names* and *brand-name products*—products manufacturers hoped would be recognized by and appeal to an unprecedented number of people spread out over an enormous area. Of course, the mass media would eventually help to place these names in the living rooms of millions of Americans. But it wasn't until late in the nineteenth century—about fifty years after newspapers became daily, cheap, and widely available—that patent medicines became the first widely known brand-name products. Lydia Pinkham's syrup (which actually contained alcohol) was downed in great quantities by teetotaling folks as a cure for almost any ailment. By the 1920s, some new products were beginning to be known by their brand names: record players were Victrolas, and paper handkerchiefs Kleenexes.

plies meant for veterans and selling them at reduced prices in return for rebates for himself. In 1925 he was sent to Leavenworth Prison. Thomas W. Miller, the alien-property custodian, was convicted of conspiracy to defraud the government. In return for lavish gifts, Miller distributed to American firms the valuable German chemical patents confiscated during the war; the firms paid far less than the patents were worth.

Most notorious was the Teapot Dome scandal. Since 1909, when the conservation movement was in full swing, three tracts of oil-rich public land had been set aside under the jurisdiction of the secretary of the navy for naval needs. In 1921, with navy secretary Edwin Denby's consent, these lands were transferred to the custody of Secretary of the Interior Albert B. Fall. A friend of private oil men, Fall secretly leased the Teapot Dome Reservation in Wyoming to Harry F. Sinclair's Mammoth Oil Company. Soon after, he leased a second reserve, at Elks Hill, California, to a company headed by Edward F. Doheny. Fall received about $300,000 in cash and negotiable securities and a herd of cattle from Sinclair, and a "loan" of $100,000 from Doheny. The wealth soon attracted the interest of watchful senators.

A committee headed by Senator Thomas J. Walsh of Montana gradually untangled the story. The Supreme Court voided the leases, and Fall, convicted of accepting a bribe, was fined $100,000 and sentenced to a year in prison. Although Doheny and Sinclair, oddly enough, were acquitted of having bribed Fall, Sinclair went to jail for contempt of the Senate and for contempt of court. He had refused to answer questions, and had hired detectives to shadow the jury at his trial.

From the start, Harding was overwhelmed by the presidency. Every decision cost him endless torment. He expected his friends to operate as a "team" now that they were in the "big league." He found it difficult to deal with their betrayal of him. "My God, this is a hell of a job," he told a journalist. "I have no trouble with my enemies. . . . But my damned friends, my Goddamned friends, . . . they're the ones that keep me walking the floor nights!" While on a speaking tour in the West, Harding became ill; he died on August 2, 1923, in San Francisco.

Still ignorant of the worst of this administration (as the president himself had been to the end), the public went into a period of mourning as deep as that for any leader since Lincoln. It was as though they had lost a personal friend. Disclosures of corruption after his death only slowly eroded his popularity.

"Normalcy" in Government: Economic Policies

The transition from Harding to Coolidge was bound to be smooth. To Coolidge, as to the man he replaced, business values were sacred. "The man who builds a factory builds a temple," Coolidge observed. "The man who works there worships there." The government justified itself by its success in encouraging the business community. Beyond that objective, it needed only to cut expenses and reduce taxes.

The beginning of a business revival for which the Republicans took full credit permitted them to confront the electorate in 1924 with the slogan "Keep Cool with Coolidge." The Democrats were

WORDS AND NAMES IN AMERICAN HISTORY

Today the word *lobby* often suggests political activity, but it retains its ancient meaning of an entrance room or hallway. Modern hotels still have lobbies. But so do state and national legislatures—just outside the chambers where legislative business is carried on by elected members only. A *lobby* is a usually well financed group of people formed with the intent of influencing legislation. Various interest groups hire *lobbyists* to *lobby* for or against certain legislation that might affect the welfare of the group; often a great deal of money is at stake. In its political sense the term originated in the Jacksonian era, when American political practices changed so dras-

tically. In 1841 an English visitor to this country described what he saw with accuracy but obvious aristocratic distaste: "A practice exists in the State capitals, called *lobbying*. . . . A certain number of agents, selected for their skill and experience in the arts of deluding, persuading, and bribing members, are employed by public companies and private individuals, who have bills before the legislature which they are anxious to get passed. These persons attend the lobby of the House daily, talk with the members, . . . invite them to dinners and suppers, etc."

badly divided. William G. McAdoo, Wilson's son-in-law and former secretary of the Treasury, had the support of the rural Protestant segment of the party. Alfred E. Smith, New York's Catholic governor, drew support from the city machines and the "wets." There was a deadlock until the two factions finally settled on John W. Davis, a conservative New York corporation lawyer.

Convinced that the American people needed a choice in the election, Robert M. La Follette ran as a third-party candidate on a revived Progressive ticket. The platform called for nationalization of railroads, recognition of labor's right to bargain collectively, and a popular referendum for any declaration of war in cases other than invasion of the United States. Although attacked by both major-party candidates as a dangerous radical, La Follette managed to poll nearly 5 million votes. Davis received over 8 million, and Coolidge well over 15 million. The vote ensured the Republican party virtually a free hand during Coolidge's administration.

"No one can contemplate current conditions," said Coolidge in his inaugural address of March 1925, "without finding much that is satisfying and still more that is encouraging." The good times seemed to have justified the economic measures taken during Harding's term. Many of those measures were inspired by Andrew W. Mellon, the immensely wealthy head of the aluminum trust, owner of oil companies, steel mills, utilities, and banks, and a lavish contributor to the party, who became secretary of the Treasury in 1921. Believing that government should promote private enterprise, he sought to reduce the national debt by reducing government expenses and by insisting that the Allies repay the United States in full. At the same time, he wanted lower taxes for the upper-income groups to provide an incentive for the wealthy to become even wealthier.

Despite the $24 billion national debt, Congress adopted the Revenue Act of 1921, which repealed the wartime excess-profits tax and reduced the maximum personal income tax from 73 to 50 percent. After Coolidge's reelection, Congress went even further in reducing the maximum income tax. During the debate on the 1925 tax cut (many more were to come during the next four years), a Nebraska Progressive observed that "Mr. Mellon himself gets a larger personal reduction than the aggregate of practically all the taxpayers in the state of Nebraska."

As taxes went down, tariffs went up. As early as 1916, Americans feared a postwar domestic market flooded by European manufactures. Primed by this threat, Congress raised duties to high levels in the Fordney-McCumber Act (1922). This prevented the Allies from reducing their war debts by exporting goods to the United States; it also caused many nations to adopt tariffs against American imports. Nevertheless, protectionism remained an essential part of Republican economic policy in the twenties. During the Hoover administration duties would be raised even higher, in the Hawley-Smoot tariff (1930).

Under Harding and Coolidge, the principal regulatory agencies—the Interstate Commerce Commission, the Federal Trade Commission, and the Federal Reserve Board—were staffed by men who shared the belief that government serves the people best by serving the needs of business. The FTC, for example, encouraged business conferences in which industrywide agreements for corporate benefit were negotiated. Hoover continued this policy as secretary of commerce. Through trade associations in which companies shared product and market information, Hoover hoped to achieve his goal of industrial cooperation and standardization. In addition, the Commerce Department helped businesses find overseas markets for materials and investments.

The Supreme Court cleared the way for cooperation and combination. By introducing the "rule of reason" into its decision dissolving the Standard Oil Company in 1911, the Court implied that its antimonopoly rulings would thenceforth be even less severe. This promise was tested in the antitrust suit involving the United States Steel Corporation. In 1920, the Court ruled that although the billion-dollar enterprise controlled about 40 percent of the steel industry, this did not make it powerful enough to act in "unreasonable" restraint of trade. Encouraged by the favorable judicial atmosphere, as well as by federal agencies and cabinet-level departments, business in the 1920s went on a new merger spree. In the field of public utilities, 3744 firms were swallowed up. Comparable consolidations occurred in manufacturing, banking, transportation, and wholesale and retail trade.

Organized labor, by contrast, lost ground. Between 1919 and 1922, strikes failed against the great steel, coal, and railroad industries. Employers pushed workers into subservient company unions, whose members numbered more than 1.5 million by 1929. AFL membership, at a peak of over 4 million in 1920, had fallen below 3 million by 1923 and continued to fall thereafter. Most workers, particularly in the new mass-production industries, remained unorganized. Employers

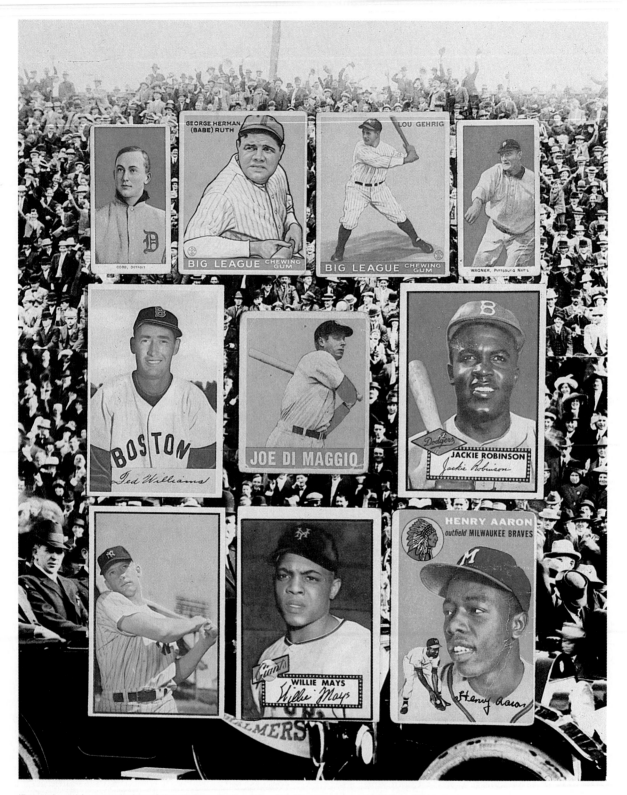

(Reproduced by permission of the players, Topps Chewing Gum Inc., and Leaf Brands, Inc.)

Babe Ruth. *(Culver Pictures, Inc.)*

Joe DiMaggio. *(UPI/Bettmann Archive)*

George Bellows's painting of Argentina's Luis Firpo, "the Wild Bull of the Pampas," knocking Jack Dempsey out of the ring in 1923. Dempsey came back to win. *Dempsey and Firpo*. (1924) Oil. 52 x 63¼ inches. (Collection of Whitney Museum of American Art. Acq. #31.95)

Red Grange. *(Culver Pictures, Inc.)*

Mud-spattered football players in a game between the Cleveland Browns and the Green Bay Packers, 1966. *(Arthur Rickerby/Life Magazine, Time, Inc.)*

used various methods, including paid informers and blacklists, to keep them that way. Although workers gained modest annual improvements in real wages during the decade, the average annual income for many of them fell below the $1800 thought necessary to maintain a minimum decent standard of living.

Social legislation designed to help workers fared badly in the courts. Two Supreme Court decisions in 1921 exposed strikers to injunctions thought to be illegal under the Clayton Act of 1914. In 1922, the Court held that child labor could not constitutionally be regulated by a discriminatory tax levied on products manufactured by children. The next year, the Court struck down an act of Congress establishing minimum wages for women and children in the District of Columbia. Only in 1932, after the Depression had created a new political mood, did organized labor succeed in pushing through Congress the Norris–La Guardia Act against labor injunctions.

The economic problem most troublesome to the Republicans was the distress of farmers deeply in debt from wartime overexpansion. Dairy, vegetable, and fruit farmers prospered from nearby city markets. Staple farmers had to sell in world markets, where increased competition after the war worsened the problem of overproduction. When women turned from cotton to rayon fabrics and families changed their diets to include more fruits and vegetables at the expense of pork, beef, and flour, the pinch on staple farmers tightened. Republican leaders again urged higher tariffs as the solution. But tariffs harmed exporters by forcing up the prices of farm families' purchases and by bringing foreign tariff regulation on American agricultural exports.

Net farm income, including that of prosperous dairy and truck farmers, fell by nearly 50 percent in the 1920s—from $9.5 billion in 1919 to $5.3 billion in 1928. A strong farm bloc in Congress responded with the McNary-Haugen bill for federal support of staple prices. It passed in 1927 and again in 1928, but the president vetoed it both times. "Farmers have never made money," Coolidge said. "I don't believe we can do much about it."

"COOLIDGE PROSPERITY"

New production techniques and new consumer industries gave a golden glow to "Coolidge prosperity." Electricity was applied to machines, and the "scientific management" theories of Frederick Winslow Taylor and his followers were applied to the people who made machines produce. The result was a substantial increase in industrial efficiency and production.

Between 1921 and 1929, industrial output almost doubled, even though the size of the labor force remained stable. At the same time, population and economic growth, as well as the wartime construction lag, pushed the demand for housing to record levels. This stimulated the private construction industry, which traditionally used more capital and labor than any other.

But "Coolidge prosperity" rested on a slippery footing. The profits of increased production were not shared adequately with workers, resulting in an unequal distribution of purchasing power. Technological unemployment increased. Farmers failed to recover from the postwar recession. The construction and auto booms, along with speculation in real estate and securities, sustained the "good times," but only for a while.

New Industries

World War I itself contributed much to the prosperous side of the 1920s. The Liberty Loan drives accustomed millions to investing in securities. After the war, stock or bond issues made it easier for corporations to finance new or expanded ventures. Many corporations made so much money during the war that they could pay for expanded or improved facilities without going to the money market at all. The excess-profits tax of the war years had prompted corporations to plow back earnings into modernized plant and equipment. This paid off in productivity and profits when the war was over.

Many industries that came of age in the twenties had been created by the war or streamlined by its demands. In 1903 at Kitty Hawk, North Carolina, Wilbur and Orville Wright made the first successful flight in a motor-driven heavier-than-air contraption. But there was little interest in airplanes until they were needed in the war for scouting and combat. Transcontinental airmail service began in 1920; in 1923 came the first regularly scheduled flights, between Chicago and Cheyenne, Wyoming. The Air Commerce Act of 1926 gave substantial mail subsidies to private airlines and helped make commercial flying a big business. In May 1927, Charles A. Lindbergh, Jr., made his solo flight from New York to Paris, and flying became more popular than ever. Three years later, 122 American airlines were carrying almost half a million passengers over 50,000 miles of air routes.

The war gave the American chemical industry an even greater boost. Before 1914, American chemical companies had produced little but the simple heavy acids and alkalis used in basic industrial processes. During the war, explosives became the principal product of the industry, and many new chemical plants were built to supply Allied needs. Once the war was over, two government actions fostered the growth of a huge chemical industry. The first was the confiscation of German coal-tar patents and their assignment to American chemical corporations. The second, motivated by popular demand for chemical self-sufficiency in the event of another war, was high duties on chemical imports. By 1929, the corporate beneficiaries of these measures, such as Allied Chemical, Union Carbide, and the old DuPont company, were outproducing by far all foreign chemical firms or cartels.

An Electrochemical Revolution

During the twenties, the efficiency of the power industry improved significantly. By the end of the decade, 70 percent of American factory machinery was operated by electricity, compared with 30 percent fifteen years before. The most striking gains from the combination of electricity and chemical processes were made in the petroleum industry. Between 1913 and 1928, electrochemical processes tripled the quantity of gasoline that could be refined from a gallon of crude oil. Electrochemical processes in the steel industry led to higher-quality parts for internal-combustion engines, which as a result made more efficient use of gasoline. The combination of electricity and chemistry in metallurgy also brought gains in the manufacture of phonographs, refrigerators, radios, washing machines, vacuum cleaners, and other adjuncts of the good life.

Electricity revolutionized not only industrial technology but also factory organization and procedures. By permitting the transmission of power over tremendous distances, it freed the factory from the river valley and the coal field; management could now give much greater weight to markets and other "location" factors in deciding on factory sites. By permitting the even flow of power throughout huge plants, electricity added immensely to the flexibility of organization within the factory. It established the economies of the production line and put a premium on standardization of jobs and materials. *Rationalization* became the catchword of industrial planners, much as *systems* would forty years later.

The Automobile Age

No industry was more firmly rooted in the technological and managerial changes of the postwar years than automobiles. For the rubber, glass, and alloys of which body and engine parts were made, automobile manufacturers depended on the new chemical and electrical knowledge and the new electrochemical processes. Automobile manufacturers became the greatest users of each of the commodities that went into their product, and work on auto assembly lines became highly mechanized and repetitive.

American technological experience led to the growth of automobile production. From the nation's earliest days, carriage manufacturers had made bodies, springs, and wheels. Since the 1850s, the building of farm machinery had developed familiarity with small engines. In the last decades of the nineteenth century, bicycle manufacturers pushed the development of pneumatic tires. The American environment, in turn, reinforced the impact of American technological experience. The United States was a country of majestic distances and of a growing middle class prosperous enough to purchase thousand-dollar commodities that could cross the wide-open spaces with satisfying speed. Railroads had helped concentrate population in metropolises; the automobile tended to disperse it, speeding the decline of cities.

Many attempts had been made to build a "horseless carriage" run by steam, electricity, alcohol, or some other fuel. After a series of experiments with a gasoline engine, in the United States and abroad, the automobile became commercially feasible about 1903. In seven years, some sixty American companies were producing cars. William C. Durant formed General Motors to control the competition, but failed to get Henry Ford to join him. Ford was already a prominent automobile manufacturer in 1908. The next year he introduced the Model T, at a list price of $950, in "any color you choose so long as it's black." By 1913, Model Ts were down to $550. Ford sold 168,000 cars, representing about a third of the nation's entire automobile business that year.

In 1914 Ford opened his revolutionary plant at Highland Park, Michigan. It was equipped with the first electric conveyor belt, which carried the gradually assembled car at a uniform—and rapid—speed past stationary workers. Each worker used certain materials and tools to perform one simple mechanical task. In 1913 it had taken fourteen hours, on the average, to assemble a Model T. In the new plant it took ninety-three minutes. In 1914, Ford built 248,000 cars—45 percent of the total automobile output—at a base price of $490. His profit that year exceeded $30 million. By 1925 Ford was turning out a complete car every ten seconds. People, however, were beginning to tire of the Model T and drift toward distinctive models with more comfortable appointments.

In 1920 about 9 million automobiles were registered in the United States. In ten years it was nearly 30 million. Millions of Americans came to see the automobile as part of the minimum standard of living. It broke down distances and encouraged a movement into the suburbs, created a new kind of tourist industry, and stimulated government expenditures for street and highway construction. For some, the automobile became a status symbol. In Sinclair Lewis's *Main Street,* the hero confesses four loves: his wife, his medical practice, hunting, and his automobile. He found it impossible to rate them in order of preference.

The Election of 1928

When Coolidge let slip the announcement that he did not choose to run in 1928, Republican leaders turned to his secretary of commerce. Born in modest circumstances on an Iowa farm, Herbert Hoover had had a rewarding career as an engineer and promoter. He won acclaim for his relief work in Europe during the war. After the war, he was credited with having used American wealth to stop the advance of communism. These activities gave him a reputation for practicality and humanitarianism. His attacks on the many unwise aspects of peacemaking also gave him standing as a statesman.

To oppose Hoover, the Democrats united behind Al Smith. As governor of New York, Smith had built an outstanding record of backing liberal legislation and ideas. But that record meant nothing to the nation at large. An Irishman, a Catholic, a New Yorker, and a "wet," Smith was the incarnation of everything that aroused rural and small-town suspicions.

With Hoover's initial advantages, it seems unlikely that any Democrat could have beaten him. His popular *majority* exceeded 6 million votes, and he carried all but eight states, including, for the first time since Reconstruction, five in the Solid South. Many Catholics blamed bigotry for Smith's defeat. But "Coolidge prosperity" and Hoover's promise of continued economic health were more likely the decisive factors.

Despite Smith's defeat, the Democrats found some satisfaction in his showing. His vote doubled that of Davis in 1924. In the country's twelve largest cities, strongly Republican in the two preceding elections, his total exceeded Hoover's. And the future lay with the urban voter.

Calvin Coolidge left the White House confident that his administration had achieved its objective. The business community, with the active support of the government, was working economic wonders. The pockets of unemployment, the imbalance between farm and business income, the difference between wages and increases in productivity, the speculation in bonds and securities did not seem to concern him. "The country," he told Congress in 1928, "can regard the present with satisfaction, and anticipate the future with optimism."

Most Americans shared that optimism, and in 1928 they had voted accordingly. But even as the new president took the oath of office, the shaky foundations on which "Coolidge prosperity" had rested were cracking. When the collapse came, there was little left but the dreary statistics of depression.

SUMMARY

The twenties were an extraordinary decade in America—a time when life and culture changed rapidly, when the "good times" and the prosperity of some contrasted sharply with the struggles and poverty of others.

The decade began with postwar depression and repression. Wartime tensions carried over into hysteria

over radicalism, restriction of immigration, and racial violence. The Ku Klux Klan was revived, and the Red Scare engulfed and defeated a labor movement once again pushing for better wages and working conditions. The murder trial of two Italian anarchists and their execution brought worldwide protest from millions convinced of their innocence. The "race suicide" alarm resulted in the Immigration Restriction Act of 1921 and the National Origins Act of 1924.

In the South, Jim Crow laws, lynchings and beatings, lack of educational facilities, and the misery of the sharecropper's life brought tens of thousands of blacks to northern cities. Between 1910 and 1940, more than 1.7 million blacks left the South, and the black population outside the South more than doubled. But the Great Migration took place in an atmosphere of growing racial intolerance in the North as well as in the South. The worst race riot in the nation's history took place in Chicago in July 1919.

Prohibition was another feature of the twenties. Making liquor illegal nationwide had two immediate results: drinking moved from the old saloon to the speakeasy, where it took on a new glamour, and a new field was made available for organized crime. Not until 1933 did Congress, with a new Democratic majority, passed the Twenty-first Amendment to repeal the Eighteenth.

The war between fundamentalism and "foreign" ideologies led in 1925 to the trial of a schoolteacher in Tennessee for teaching the theory of evolution. The contest set two great figures, William Jennings Bryan and Clarence Darrow, against each other as opposing legal counsel. It ended by destroying Bryan's reputation and subjecting the fundamentalists to national ridicule.

For American intellectuals, writers, and artists, the twenties were enormously productive. In their willingness to question the sanity of their society and to experiment with new ideas and forms, the members of this generation stood out; more good writing and more important books were produced in those years than in any similar period in the nation's history. Paris and New York's Greenwich Village became centers of a new American culture, of new writing, new theater, new poetry, new art. Ernest Hemingway, Ezra Pound, Malcolm Cowley, e.e. cummings, Sinclair Lewis, Sherwood Anderson, William Faulkner, Henry L. Mencken, and F. Scott Fitzgerald—these and others were the writers and artists of the lost generation. Some became expatriates for a while because they felt they could not work at home.

This was also the time of the Harlem Renaissance, a flowering of black culture that was to spread to the white

TIME LINE

1914	Henry Ford opens modernized automobile plant in Michigan		Teapot Dome scandal Jean Toomer, *Cane*
1915–1920s	Great Migration (black southerners to the North)	1924	National Origins Act *American Mercury* magazine founded Coolidge re-elected
1917	Race Riot in East St. Louis, Illinois	1925	Scopes trial F. Scott Fitzgerald, *The Great Gatsby*
1919	Seattle general strike Race riot in Chicago Boston police strike Strike of U.S. Steel workers *Schenck v. United States; Abrams v. United States*	1926	RCA establishes the National Broadcasting Company Ernest Hemingway, *The Sun Also Rises*
1920s	Harlem Renaissance Revival of the Ku Klux Klan	1927	Sacco and Vanzetti executed Lindbergh's transatlantic flight *The Jazz Singer,* first movie with sound
1920	Prohibition begins First commercial radio broadcast Transcontinental airmail service begins Red Scare, Palmer raids, and deportations Sinclair Lewis, *Main Street*	1928	Herbert Hoover elected president Claude McKay, *Home to Harlem*
		1929	William Faulkner, *The Sound and the Fury* Ernest Hemingway, *A Farewell to Arms*
1921	Immigration Restriction Act		
1922	Sinclair Lewis, *Babbitt* Fordney-McCumber Tariff	1930	Hawley-Smoot Tariff
1923	Harding dies; Calvin Coolidge becomes president	1933	Twenty-first Amendment repeals Eighteenth; Prohibition ends

world as well. New York's Harlem became the center of culture for blacks, the "place to be." Black music—jazz and blues—became known worldwide. Among the black writers and intellectuals of this period were Langston Hughes, Claude McKay, Zora Neale Hurston, and Jean Toomer.

The new popular arts—movies, radio, records—were all the result of technology. They shaped American attitudes and tastes in new ways. They reached mass audiences, nationalized popular culture, and speeded up the standardization of society.

Politics during the twenties was marked by a return to the American Dream—the notion that anyone who had the right kind of ambition and determination could succeed. It was a politics of complacency, shaken but not shattered by the scandals of the Harding administration. To Harding, as to Coolidge, who succeeded him, business values were sacred. Taxes were lowered; tariffs were raised. The regulatory agencies and the Supreme Court cooperated to make life easier for business. But organized labor lost ground, social legislation had a hard time in the courts, and staple farmers were in deep trouble.

"Coolidge prosperity" was marked by new production techniques and new consumer industries. The airplane became a commercial business. Electrochemical technology made possible a revolution in the petroleum industry and the mass production of consumer goods such as phonographs, refrigerators, radios, washing machines, and vacuum cleaners. Factory organization and operation changed because of the availability of electric power. And the automobile became part of every American's life. In 1920, about 9 million automobiles were registered in the United States; ten years later, it was nearly 30 million.

This prosperity rested on a shaky foundation. Workers did not receive a large enough share in the profits of increased production to raise their purchasing power; technological unemployment grew; the farmers did not recover; and wild speculation on the stock market inflated the economy to the bursting point. The election of 1928 brought Herbert Hoover to the presidency with promises of continued Republican prosperity. But the good times were not to last much beyond his inauguration in March of 1929.

Suggested Readings

The stereotypical twenties are vividly chronicled in F. L. Allen, *Only Yesterday* (1931). W. E. Leuchtenburg, *The Perils of Prosperity, 1914–1932* (1958), A. M. Schlesinger, Jr., *The Crisis of the Old Order 1919–1933* (1957), and E. W. Hawley, *The Great War and the Search for a Modern Order* (1979), are more substantial introductions to this period. The many-sided character of the twenties is underscored in two anthologies—Isabel Leighton (ed.), *The Aspirin Age* (1949), and Loren Baritz (ed.), *The Culture of the Twenties* (1969). R. S. Lynd and H. M. Lynd, *Middletown* (1929), is a revealing analysis of ordinary American life in Muncie, Indiana. P. S. Fass, *The Damned and the Beautiful: American Youth in the 1920s* (1977), examines the culture of youth, focusing on the values, manners, and activities of native-born, white, middle-class college students. The changing social, economic, and political role of women is examined in W. H. Chafe, *The American Woman 1920–1970* (1972).

On Harding, see S. H. Adams, *Incredible Era* (1939), and Andrew Sinclair, *The Available Man* (1965). R. K. Murray, *The Harding Era* (1969) and *The Politics of Normalcy* (1973), are positive assessments. D. R. McCoy, *Calvin Coolidge: The Quiet President* (1967), is a revisionist biography, but W. A. White, *A Puritan in Babylon* (1938), remains rewarding reading.

The postwar repression is described in R. K. Murray, *Red Scare* (1955); W. Preston, Jr., *Aliens and Dissenters: Federal Suppression of Radicals 1903–1933* (1963); S. Coben, *A. Mitchell Palmer: Politician* (1963); and G. L. Joughin and E. M. Morgan, *The Legacy of Sacco and Vanzetti* (1948) and R. Polenberg, *Fighting Faiths: The Abrams Case, the Supreme Court,* *and Free Speech* (1987). On anti-immigrant feeling and legislation, see J. Higham, *Strangers in the Land: Patterns of American Nativism 1860–1925* (1955), and R. A. Divine, *American Immigration Policy 1924–1952* (1957).

D. Brody, *Steelworkers in America: The Non-Union Era* (1960), provides background for the steel strike of 1919, described in Brody's *Labor in Crisis* (1965). On the struggles of workers and farmers and their failure to share in the prosperity of the decade, see I. Bernstein, *The Lean Years: A History of the American Worker 1920–1933* (1960), and T. Saloutos and J. D. Hicks, *Twentieth Century Populism: Agricultural Discontent in the Middle West 1900–1939* (1951). Based in part on oral testimony, the lives of cotton mill workers are graphically portrayed in J. D. Hall et al, *Like a Family: The Making of a Southern Cotton Mill World* (1987).

The authoritative study of the South in the twentieth century is G. B. Tindall, *The Emergence of the New South 1913–1945* (1967). On the Great Migration, the best study is J. R. Grossman, *Land of Hope: Chicago, Black Southerners, and the Great Migration* (1989). Black life in the urban North is examined in G. Osofsky, *Harlem: The Making of a Ghetto 1890–1930* (1966); A. H. Spear, *Black Chicago: The Making of a Negro Ghetto 1890–1920* (1967); S. C. Drake and H. R. Cayton, *Black Metropolis* (1945); K. L. Kusmer, *A Ghetto Takes Shape: Black Cleveland 1870–1930* (1976); and J. Borchert, *Alley Life in Washington, D.C.: Family, Community, Religion, Folklife in the City, 1850–1970* (1980). The personal accounts of James Weldon Johnson, *Along This Way* (1933), A. Clayton Powell, *Against the Tide* (1938), and Richard Wright, *Black*

CHAPTER 27 THE TWENTIES: BUSINESS AND CULTURE

Boy (1945), illuminate the Afro-American experience, as does L. W. Levine, *Black Culture and Black Consciousness* (1977). On racial violence, see the Chicago Commission on Race Relations, *The Negro in Chicago: A Study of Race Relations and a Race Riot* (1922); W. M. Tuttle, Jr., *Race Riot: Chicago in the Red Summer of 1919* (1970); and E. M. Rudwick, *Race Riot at East St. Louis, July 2, 1917* (1964). The views of the most popular black leader of this period will be found in A. Jacques-Garvey (ed.), *Philosophy and Opinions of Marcus Garvey* (1969 reprint ed.), and J. Stein, *The World of Marcus Garvey* (1986). The best collection of black urban folklore is R. D. Abrahams, *Deep Down in the Jungle: Negro Narrative Folklore from the Streets of Philadelphia* (1964). On urban blues, see C. Keil, *Urban Blues* (1966) and R. Palmer, *Deep Blues* (1981).

D. M. Chalmers, *Hooded Americanism* (1965), K. T. Jackson, *The Ku Klux Klan in the City* (1967), and C. Alexander, *The Ku Klux Klan in the Southwest* (1965) examine the impact of the KKK in the twentieth century. On Prohibition, see A. Sinclair, *Era of Excess: A Social History of the Prohibition Movement* (1962), and N. H. Clark, *Deliver Us from Evil* (1976). The battle over evolution theory is examined in N. F. Furniss, *The Fundamentalist Controversy 1918–1931* (1954), and the Scopes trial is vividly related in R. Ginger, *Six Days or Forever?* (1958). L. W. Levine, *Defender of the Faith: William Jennings Bryan; The Last Decade, 1915–1925* (1965), is a study of Bryan and the period.

George Soule, *Prosperity Decade: From War to Depression 1917–1929* (1947), is a good introduction to the economy. See also J. W. Prothro, *The Dollar Decade: Business Ideas in the 1920s* (1954). On the advertising industry, the most important works are O. Pease, *The Responsibilities of American Advertising* (1958) and R. Marchand, *Advertising the American Dream: Making Way for Modernity, 1920–1940* (1985). On the auto industry, see A. P. Sloan, Jr., *My Years with General Motors* (1964); C. E. Sorensen, *My Forty Years with Ford* (1956); A. Nevins and F. E. Hill, *Ford* (3 vols., 1954–62); and the more critical K. Sward, *The Legend of Henry Ford* (1948). On the impact of the automobile, see J. B. Rae, *The Road and the Car in American Life* (1971), and J. Fink, *The Car Culture* (1975).

H. May, *The End of American Innocence* (1959), is a solid analysis of American culture between 1912 and 1917. The impact of radical ideas is assessed in D. Aaron, *Writers on the Left* (1961). The avant-garde periodicals are analyzed in F. J. Hoffman and others, *The Little Magazine* (1946). Malcolm Cowley, *Exile's Return* (1951), is an indispensable personal account; see also the memoirs of Floyd Dell, Max Eastman, Mabel Dodge Luhan, Van Wyck Brooks, and Randolph Bourne.

G. Seldes, *The Seven Lively Arts* (1957 ed.), is a classic account of popular culture. The impact of the motion picture is examined in L. Jacobs, *The Rise of the American Film* (1939); E. Rosow, *Born to Lose: The Gangster Film in America* (1978); R. Sklar, *Movie-Made America: A Social History of American Movies* (1975); R. Schickel, *The Disney Version* (1968); and L. May, *Screening Out the Past: The Birth of Mass Culture and the Motion Picture Industry* (1980). J. E. O'Connor and M. A. Jackson (eds.), *American History/American Film: Interpreting the Hollywood Image* (1979), examines film as historical evidence. On radio and American life, see J. F. MacDonald, *Don't Touch That Dial! Radio Programming in American Life from 1920 to 1960* (1979), and A. F. Wertheim, *Radio Comedy* (1979).

A. Locke (ed.), *The New Negro* (1925), is indispensable as an introduction to the Harlem Renaissance. N. I. Huggins, *Harlem Renaissance* (1971), is a modern assessment. See also Huggins (ed.), *Voices from the Harlem Renaissance* (1976). The personal accounts of Langston Hughes, *The Big Sea* (1940), Zora Neale Hurston, *Dust Tracks on a Road* (1942), and Claude McKay, *A Long Way From Home* (1937), are important, as are their literary works. Among the best biographical studies are A. Rampersad, *The Life of Langston Hughes* (2 vols., 1986, 1988); W. F. Cooper, *Claude McKay: Rebel Sojourner in the Harlem Renaissance* (1987); R. Hemenway, *Zora Neale Hurston* (1977); and C. E. Kerman and R. Eldridge, *The Lives of Jean Toomer* (1987).

F. J. Hoffman, *The Twenties* (1955), is a thorough literary history. See also M. Geismar, *The Last of the Provincials* (1949) and *Writers in Crisis* (1947). Edmund Wilson is a perceptive social commentator in *The Shores of Light* (1952) and *The American Earthquake* (1958). On some of the principal critics and writers, see C. Bode, *Henry L. Mencken* (1969); I. Howe, *Sherwood Anderson* (1951); M. Schorer, *Sinclair Lewis* (1961); A. Mizener, *The Far Side of Paradise* (1951); A. Turnbull, *Scott Fitzgerald* (1962); C. Baker, *Ernest Hemingway: A Life Story* (1969), and F. R. Karl, *William Faulkner* (1989). F. Scott Fitzgerald, *The Crack-Up* (1945), is an impressionistic account based on his letters and notes.

CHAPTER 28

THE GREAT DEPRESSION AND THE NEW DEAL

The presidential inaugurations of 1929 and 1933 provided a striking contrast in personalities, issues, and the state of the Union. In his somewhat muffled, droning voice, Herbert Hoover spoke of the "many satisfactions" he derived from surveying "the situation of our Nation at home and abroad":

Ours is a land rich in resources; stimulating in its glorious beauty; filled with millions of happy homes; blessed with comfort and opportunity. In no nation are the institutions of progress more advanced. In no nation are the fruits of accomplishment more secure.

Less than eight months later, on Black Tuesday, October 29, 1929, stock prices at the New York Stock Exchange fell in the most disastrous trading day in the history of the market. Within a few hours, more than $10 billion of America's "fruits of accomplishment" were gone. In the next three years, consumer purchasing declined and manufacturers closed plants or reduced the work force. Some 100,000 workers, on the average, were fired each week. The number of unemployed stood at 2 million in 1929, 4 million in 1930, 8 million in 1931,

William Gropper, *Construction of a Dam* (detail). Oil on canvas, 68 × 221 cm. National Museum of American Art, Smithsonian Institution.

12 million in 1932. National income was cut more than half. Over 5000 banks and 9 million savings accounts were wiped out; tens of thousands of mortgages were foreclosed.

Families found themselves evicted from their homes and barely able to survive. More than a million homeless people took to the road or settled in "Hoovervilles," shantytowns made out of old packing cartons and car bodies. They came to symbolize not only the depths of the Depression, but the president's inability to do anything about it.

By March 4, 1933, when Franklin D. Roosevelt took the oath of office as president of the United States, three and a half years had passed since the stock-market crash, the number of unemployed had reached 13 million, and the nation was experiencing failure on a scale unprecedented in its history. But the new president, even as he described "the dark realities of the moment," conveyed a sense of confidence and determination in his voice and manner that comforted his audience:

This nation asks for action and action now. Our greatest primary task is to put people to work. . . . It can be accomplished in part by direct recruiting by the Government itself, treating the task as we would treat the emergency of a war.

The American people would respond to FDR's appeal for confidence—"the only thing we have to fear is fear itself"—with an enthusiasm matched only by the contempt they had shown for Hoover's plea for confidence—"all the evidences indicate that the worst effects of the crash. . . will have been passed during the next 60 days." But the Great Depression, as both Hoover and Roosevelt would learn, could not be solved with psychology. Confidence was not enough. Confidence alone could not feed hungry people or create jobs for the unemployed, and there was much more to fear than fear itself. Americans were thrilled by FDR's pledge to treat the economic crisis as he would treat a war. Few had any reason to suspect that only a war would ultimately bring them out of the crisis.

THE CRASH

The crash centered in the New York Stock Exchange on Wall Street, the scene in 1929 of an enormous amount of activity in stock securities. The talk was of good times and striking it rich. Overnight success stories, the assurances of business and political leaders, and easy credit terms fed the fever. Thousands of small investors, along with the wealthy, poured their savings into common stocks. The warning signs went unheeded: cutbacks in private construction, large business inventories, the decline in consumer purchasing. Industry was not making enough profit to justify the soaring stock prices. The market wavered, and on October 29, 1929, it came crashing down.

President Hoover had tried to assure the public that there was no reason to panic: "The fundamental business of this country, that is, production and distribution of commodities, is on a sound and prosperous basis." But he was wrong. And with every new assurance that the worst had passed, the depression deepened. The president would act in more decisive ways to restore confidence in the economy. But there were limits beyond which he refused to go.

A Flawed Economy

The stock-market crash dramatized fundamental weaknesses in the economy. It revealed more "pockets" of economic hardship than had been acknowledged, larger ones than had been supposed, and their tendency to grow. Farm receipts had already bottomed out, and farmers throughout the twenties had to deal with large surpluses, declining prices, and higher expenses. For many years chronic unemployment had characterized certain industries, in particular textiles and coal mining. In the twenties, the uneven distribution of income should have suggested that the nation was risking economic disaster. The slowly rising real wages of industrial workers were outdistanced by the salaries, savings, and profits of those higher on the economic ladder. In 1929, the 24,000 richest families had an aggregate income more than three times as large as that of the nearly 6 million poorest families. Forty percent of all families had incomes under $1500.

No wonder the purchasing power of Americans did not keep up with the production potential of the industrial plant and the promotional techniques of advertising. Those who were getting

WORDS AND NAMES IN AMERICAN HISTORY

One of the most famous streets in the world is a rather short one in New York City. The name *Wall Street* has come to suggest the world of U.S. banking and trading in stocks and bonds. One of the country's foremost financial newspapers is called, simply, the *Wall Street Journal*. The New York Stock Exchange, the nation's most important center for trading in stocks and bonds, has a Wall Street address. In Communist countries, *Wall Street* is often a shorthand way of referring to the "evils" of capitalism. The street got its name innocently enough: it runs along the site of what was once a wall that stood at the northern edge of the little town of New Amsterdam some three hundred years ago. The original Dutch settlement occupied only a tiny part of the downriver end of Manhattan, and the street is located near the southern tip of that island.

rich, meanwhile, found their savings piled up out of all proportion to need. Looking for opportunities for sound investment, they turned to speculation in real estate and securities, both blown up into a bubble sure to burst.

The federal government had failed to deal with these matters. Tax policies favored the rich, making even more unequal the distribution of income. Labor policies were antiunion. The economic situation abroad only aggravated the domestic crisis. European nations needed goods and credit from America to restore their economies and stabilize their currencies. But American tariffs, such as the Hawley-Smoot tariff passed during the Hoover administration, presented obstacles to exports and limited Europe's buying power. American manufacturers found it ever more difficult to sell abroad. And the American and European economies were so closely linked that the Depression soon became worldwide.

Hoover himself scorned the fear of others. "Prosperity is just around the corner," he kept saying. To demonstrate his own confidence, the president made a point of attending the World Series in 1931. At the same time, he urged the American people not to give in to despair. "What the country needs," he told a newspaperman, "is a good big laugh. There seems to be a condition of hysteria. If someone could get off a good joke every ten days, I think our troubles would be over." Hoover supplied his own brand of humor with this observation: "Many persons have left their jobs for the more profitable one of selling apples." Meanwhile, Hoover's Democratic rivals made the most of the crisis. Since the Republicans had taken full credit for "Coolidge prosperity," the Democrats promptly called the new era the "Hoover depression."

Hoover and the Depression

For all his stress on confidence, Hoover acknowledged the need for direct federal intervention. That decision in itself marked a significant break with the past. In 1930, when the slide of wheat and cotton prices became catastrophic, Hoover tried to reverse the price trend by extending agricultural credit and using the new Federal Farm Board to make open-market purchases. It was not long, however, before government warehouses bulged with surpluses. Private dealers, fearful of this glut being unloaded on the market, sold their own holdings for instant cash. By 1932,

cotton was six cents a pound, down from sixteen cents in 1929; wheat, thirty-eight cents a bushel, down from a dollar.

To help labor and industry, Congress granted the president $700 million early in 1930 for public works. This was the start of a new program that saw Hoover spend almost $3 billion on public construction. The president also tried to get companies to delay firing workers and cutting wages. But even the best-willed industrialists could not keep people at work at a living wage when there were no markets for products. By 1932, wages had plummeted and 12 million were unemployed. Great companies faced bankruptcy.

In an effort to save insurance companies and philanthropic organizations that had invested in their securities, Congress created the Reconstruction Finance Corporation. By the end of 1932, the RFC had loaned $1.5 billion to about 5000 shaky firms. But this shot in the arm did little to help the economy.

No previous administration had ever taken such extensive measures to revive the private economy or help the victims of an economic collapse. Yet they proved wholly inadequate. The crisis became even more acute when local and private welfare agencies also crashed. But Hoover's principles—his belief in market forces, voluntarism, and self-help—did not permit him to undertake the massive federal intervention the crisis demanded. Direct federal aid, he feared, would make the unemployed the wards of the state and endanger the ethic of individualism. "You cannot extend the mastery of the government over the daily working life of a people without at the same time making it the master of the people's souls and thoughts." Even as the Depression deepened, Hoover clung to the belief that the principal function of government was "to bring about a condition of affairs favorable to the beneficial development of private enterprise."

Hoover, the "great humanitarian" of the war years, soon was portrayed as the heartless villain of the Depression. Nor did the president's attempts to minimize the extent of the human crisis enhance his image. "Nobody is actually starving," Hoover told a group of reporters. "The hoboes, for example, are better fed than they have ever been. One hobo in New York got ten meals in one day." In the summer of 1932, Hoover's image suffered another blow over the way he responded to the Bonus Army, some 12,000 jobless veterans who had marched to Washington in hopes of persuading Congress to appropriate a bonus for veterans.

On Hoover's orders and under the personal direction of Chief of Staff Douglas MacArthur, the marchers were driven from the city with tear gas and bayonets.

The Election of 1932

With unemployment increasing and local and state welfare funds nearly exhausted, Hoover faced a grim electorate in 1932 and a formidable Democratic opponent. Aware that they had to renominate Hoover to deflect the charge of a Hoover depression, the Republicans did so on the first ballot. The Democrats named Franklin D. Roosevelt, governor of New York. Roosevelt's victory in that state in 1928 stood out boldly against the Republicans' overwhelming national success that year. In 1930, FDR was reelected governor almost by acclamation. On receiving the presidential nomination, Roosevelt flew to Chicago to accept the honor in person, something no candidate had done before. "I pledge you, I pledge myself," he told the delegates, "to a new deal for the American people."

Despite the urgency of the Depression, neither the platforms of the two major political parties nor the candidates themselves suggested that the federal government might need to play a central role in the industrial society. Hoover stressed international economic difficulties as the main causes of the crash. Roosevelt did not deny the Depression's international character, but he zeroed in on the flaws it revealed in the American economy. Hoover warned that too much government intervention would destroy individual liberty. Roosevelt called for novel methods to meet novel conditions—"bold and persistent experimentation." But his few specific commitments were conventional, and his pledge to assist the victims of the Depression while reducing government expenditures and balancing the budget must have baffled economic analysts.

Yet more voters were heartened by his promises, however vague, than were impressed by Hoover's warnings. Roosevelt received 22,809,638 votes; Hoover 15,758,901. The victor's electoral-college margin, 472 to 59, reflected his success in carrying all but six northeastern states—Maine, New Hampshire, Vermont, Connecticut, Pennsylvania, and Delaware. The Democratic party, moreover, won overwhelming majorities in both houses of Congress.

Since the campaign had turned largely on a clash of personalities rather than ideologies, few knew how to judge the new president. The people looked to Roosevelt to exert vigorous leadership, but they had only a vague notion of the direction in which he intended to lead them. The president-elect was also uncertain. He knew, however, what was expected of him. "I have looked into the faces of thousands of Americans," he told a friend during the campaign. "They have the frightened look of lost children. . . . They are saying: 'We're caught in something we don't understand; perhaps this fellow can help us out.'" That typified the kind of sensitivity FDR brought with him into the White House, and it was good enough to keep him there for twelve years.

FDR'S NEW DEAL

Charming, self-assured, energetic, and fearless, FDR was the New Deal's greatest asset. Whatever was hidden behind the famous Roosevelt smile, it was an extraordinarily effective tool in private and public relations. Unlike Hoover, the new president seemed to have both compassion and confidence, and the people responded. However erratic his actions, and despite the uncertainty with which he sometimes moved, Roosevelt knew how to communicate.

In his radio "fireside chats," he made the people feel he was discussing important national questions with them directly, that he understood their problems and frustrations. Few expressed that

Franklin D. Roosevelt. *(AP/World Wide Photos)*

reaction more clearly than the North Carolina millworker who explained to an anti–New Deal journalist why he stood by the president: "Mr. Roosevelt is the only man we ever had in the White House who would understand that my boss is a sonofabitch."

Roosevelt was deeply moved by the plight of the poor. Unlike Cleveland and Hoover, he believed the underprivileged had a legitimate claim on the federal government. During the early years of the New Deal, many people spoke of it as an attempt at economic planning. Economic experimentation would be a more accurate description. No one knew of a single solution, and Roosevelt's policies proved as varied as the men around him. Those men included veteran politicians.

Postmaster General James A. Farley of New York had a card-index mind in which deserving and undeserving Democrats alike were sorted out. Secretary of State Cordell Hull, a national legislator with many years of service, reflected his Tennessee background in his support of the traditional southern quest for lower tariffs and freer world trade. William H. Woodin, a conservative industrialist who enjoyed the confidence of business, became secretary of the Treasury. When Woodin resigned after the bank crisis of 1933, he was succeeded by Henry Morgenthau, Jr., an old friend of the president.

The reform element was represented in the cabinet by a veteran Progressive, Harold L. Ickes of Illinois, who became secretary of the interior. Henry A. Wallace, the son of Harding's and Coolidge's secretary of agriculture, now filled this post himself. Frances Perkins had worked with Roosevelt in Albany, and, as secretary of labor, became the first woman cabinet member. Harry Hopkins also had strong reform leanings. Hopkins became perhaps the most influential of all Roosevelt's advisers, though he wasn't appointed to the cabinet until 1939.

Even less formally related to the administration than Hopkins were the members of the "brain trust," especially three Columbia University professors who had advised Roosevelt during the campaign: Raymond Moley, A. A. Berle, Jr., and Rexford Tugwell. Tugwell, an economist, voiced the sentiments of the social planners, who looked for more government control over the nation's economic life, including control of prices and profit margins.

Hoover's approach to the problem of recovery had been largely the traditional one of allowing the deflation to run its course. The New Dealers experimented with currency inflation and with heavy government spending to prime the pump of business. Some of them, such as Tugwell, hoped also to make the crisis an occasion for reforms that would reach far beyond those of the Progressive movement. They began tentatively. But as the Depression grew worse, public pressure for change grew stronger. Led by the president, they moved to rescue the banks, stabilize business and agriculture, reduce unemployment, and provide assistance for the victims of the Depression.

The Bank Crisis

One of the most dangerous developments of the Depression—the plunge of the banks toward bankruptcy—was the first to be attacked. The first steps were taken within a day or two of Roosevelt's inauguration and gave the public a welcome taste of energetic new leadership.

So many banks had failed that even solvent institutions were menaced by frightened depositors rushing to withdraw their money. To stop the panic, the governors of almost half the states had declared "bank holidays," and most of the banks were closed when Roosevelt took office. By proclamation on March 6, Roosevelt suspended all banking operations and gold transactions. Three days later Congress, called into special session, passed the Emergency Banking Act. This measure ratified the president's actions and established procedures for getting sound banks back in business.

Roosevelt then went on the air with his first fireside chat, a brilliant effort to reassure people that a sound banking system was about to emerge from the reorganization. Before the end of March, most of the sound banks had reopened and the unsound ones were on the way to being permanently closed. Within another month, more than twelve thousand banks, with 90 percent of the country's deposits, were functioning normally.

"In one week," wrote columnist Walter Lippmann of the bank crisis, "the nation, which had lost confidence in everything and everybody, has regained confidence in the government and in itself." Roosevelt's avoidance of the more radical solution of nationalizing the banks quieted conservative suspicions. His actions also made it clear that the New Deal was designed to patch up the old order rather than replace it. As adviser Raymond Moley recalled, Roosevelt intended to preserve and revive, not destroy, the free enterprise system: "If ever there was a moment when things hung in the balance, it was on March 5, 1933—

when unorthodoxy would have drained the last remaining strength of the capitalistic system." But to keep intact the basic structure of American capitalism, he would have the federal government play an unprecedented role.

Bank reform soon followed. One of the best reform measures was the Glass-Steagall Act of June 1933, which created the Federal Deposit Insurance Corporation (FDIC) and authorized it to guarantee bank deposits up to $5000 per depositor. Many banks had got into trouble using depositors' money to speculate in the stock market, investing through their affiliates in the securities business. The Glass-Steagall Act forbade national banks to maintain such affiliates, and it contained other reforms aimed at divorcing commercial from investment banking. The simple sanity of this law did not prevent the American Bankers Association from fighting it "to the last ditch," as its president had vowed to do. Finally, the Banking Act of 1935 greatly increased federal authority over the banking system by empowering the Federal Reserve Board to regulate interest rates.

The administration also pressed for closer supervision of the stock market. The Securities Act of 1933 required greater publicity for the details of stock promotion and closed the mails to sellers failing to provide it. This measure was followed by the Securities Exchange Act of June 1934, which created the Securities and Exchange Commission. The SEC was authorized to require registration of all securities traded on the stock exchanges and to cooperate with the Federal Reserve Board in regulating the purchase of securities.

Playing with Money

Business recovery proved more difficult than banking reform. The New Deal experimented with various plans aimed at stimulating industrial activity, mostly with no success. One of the earliest ideas was to cheapen the dollar. That would reduce the burden of fixed debts, which had become a drag on expansion. At the same time, it would raise domestic prices, and encourage output. Cheapening the dollar was also expected to stimulate exports, because foreign currency would buy more goods. In May 1933, Congress authorized the president to issue greenbacks, reduce the gold content of the dollar, and provide for unlimited coinage of both gold and silver at a ratio that he could set.

The president used his new authority with great caution. To retain his flexibility with the dollar, and insisting that the United States be free to pursue its own course, Roosevelt refused in mid-1933 to join the London Economic Conference in its efforts to stabilize world currencies. In a new effort to increase the money supply and boost commodity prices by currency manipulation, Roosevelt ordered the purchase of gold on the open market. This action, he hoped, would raise the price of gold, which in turn would help to raise the general price level. But at the end of January 1934 even this was given up, and the president chose to fix the price of gold at $35 an ounce—about 40 percent higher than its pre-1933 level. Despite these experiments, the price level did not rise.

Business: The NRA

The idea behind currency experiments was that under favorable monetary conditions, ordinary market mechanisms might push prices up. But the New Dealers were not alone in realizing that the market mechanisms themselves needed artificial respiration and probably a permanent iron lung. To help the economy breathe once more, Congress passed the National Industrial Recovery Act (NIRA) in June 1933. The president hailed it as "the most important and far-reaching legislation ever enacted by the American Congress."

The point of the NIRA was not so much to expand the economy as to ration the nation's business among the surviving corporations. It had the support, and in some cases the sponsorship, of businessmen and leaders of the United States Chamber of Commerce. Under its provisions, the antitrust laws were, in effect, suspended. Trade associations and other business groups were permitted to draw up "codes of fair competition," which would include comprehensive price agreements, firm production quotas, and wage scales high enough to improve the condition of the lowest-paid workers.

Each type of business was empowered to draw up its own code. The government reserved the right to accept or reject the codes, to set up its own when companies in any industry failed to agree, and to enforce them. Section 7(a) of the NIRA guaranteed labor the right of collective bargaining. A National Recovery Administration (NRA) was formed to administer the codes. It was chaired by General Hugh Johnson, who had worked on the War Industries Board during World War I.

To put the NRA on something like a war footing, administrators organized parades and mass meetings. They adopted as a symbol a placard with a blue eagle, and awarded it for display to businessmen and even to consumers who cooperated. One of their hoped-for effects was to stir up boycotts of uncooperative firms, substituting public pressure for legal enforcement. General Johnson blared forth in his characteristically grandiloquent way: "When every American housewife understands that the Blue Eagle on everything she permits to come into her home is a symbol of its restoration to security, may God have mercy on the man or group of men who attempt to trifle with this bird." Violators of the codes or objectors such as Henry Ford, who met code requirements but refused to subscribe to their industry code in writing, were seldom prosecuted. NRA administrators may have thought that the entire scheme would collapse if put to the judicial test.

No less than 746 NRA codes were adopted by businessmen eager to get started again. But there were problems. The paperwork required to supply needed information to the government quickly reached fantastic proportions and was resented. Big corporations resisted all further signs of bureaucratic interference. Small firms complained that the codes, drawn up by the larger firms in each industry, discriminated against small business. Workers, who at first supported the NRA, soon nicknamed it the National Run Around. Code administrators, they said, sided with antiunion employers in labor disputes. Employers detested the very existence of Section 7(a) and the expansion of organized labor it would allow. Moreover, when the codes succeeded in reviving production by raising prices, they aroused consumer discontent.

The NRA had reached a low point in popularity when the Supreme Court killed it in May 1935. In *Schecter Poultry Corporation v. United States*, the Court unanimously found that the National Industrial Recovery Act was unconstitutional on two counts. First, it improperly delegated legislative powers to the executive. Second, the provisions of the poultry code constituted a regulation of intrastate, not interstate, commerce.

The NRA had not been entirely worthless. For example, when the codes were adopted, some of the most exploited workers in the textile industry had been paid as little as five dollars a week. To such workers the cotton textile code, which set minimum wages of twelve to thirteen dollars a week, was heaven-sent. The NRA also established the principle of maximum hours and minimum wages on a national basis. It reduced child labor. It made collective bargaining a national policy. In many instances cancellation of the codes brought a return to poor working conditions, to which the labor movement soon turned its attention.

Agriculture: The AAA

Two months before Roosevelt's inauguration, the normally conservative head of the Farm Bureau Federation, Edward A. O'Neal, warned a Senate committee: "Unless something is done for the American farmer we will have revolution in the countryside within less than 12 months." Even as he spoke, farmers were beginning to take matters into their own hands. They brought eviction sales and mortgage foreclosures to a stop. They intimidated and assaulted public officials and agents of banks and insurance companies. Violence had become so widespread in Iowa by April 1933 that the governor put several counties under martial law and called out the National Guard. "Americans are slow to understand," commented the *New York World-Telegram*, "that actual revolution already exists in the farm belt. . . . When the local revolt springs from old native stock, conservatives fighting for the right to hold their homesteads, there is the warning of a larger explosion."

The New Dealers were well aware of the need for quick action to raise the prices of agricultural products to a level that would increase farmers' purchasing power. They therefore approached the farm problem in the same mood with which they approached the problems of industry. The farm plan was incorporated in the Agricultural Adjustment Act of May 1933, which established the Agricultural Adjustment Administration (AAA).

Abandoning all hope of regaining lost foreign markets for staples, the AAA envisioned cutting back farm production to the level of domestic needs and rationing the domestic market among producers. In this way it planned to bring farm prices up to parity with those of the prosperous years of 1909 to 1914. To compensate farmers for cooperating with the government plan, the AAA would pay various subsidies for acreage withdrawn from production and for certain marketing practices. The program would be financed by taxes on the processors of farm products, such as millers, cotton ginners, and meat-packers. At first, the act provided for reductions only in cotton, wheat, corn, hogs, rice, tobacco, and milk. Later, other products were included.

THE FARMERS BECAME DESPERATE

Oscar Heline, an Iowa farmer, recalled the impact of the Great Depression:

The struggles people had to go through are almost unbelievable. A man lived all his life on a given farm, it was taken away from him. One after the other. . . . Not only did he lose the farm, but it was impossible for him to get out of debt. . . . First, they'd take your farm, then they took your livestock, then your farm machinery. Even your household goods. And they'd move you off. . . .

Grain was being burned. It was cheaper than coal. Corn was being burned. . . . You couldn't hardly buy groceries for corn. . . . People were determined

to withhold produce from the market—livestock, cream, butter, eggs, what not. If they would dump the produce, they would force the market to a higher level. The farmers would man the highways, and cream cans were emptied in ditches and eggs dumped out. They burned the trestle bridge, so the trains wouldn't be able to haul grain. Conservatives don't like this kind of rebel attitude and aren't very sympathetic. But something had to be done.

Source: Studs Terkel, *Hard Times* (New York: Pantheon, 1970), pp. 252–53. Photograph by Dorothea Lange, Library of Congress.

To cut production when people were hungry was bound to bring criticism. But farm spokesmen insisted that if the profit system meant anything, then the farmers had the same right as businessmen to do this. The contradiction between a program of planned scarcity and the food and clothing shortage suffered by millions of Americans was never really resolved. The United States, Secretary of Agriculture Wallace conceded, had "the largest wheat surplus and the longest breadlines in its history." But he saw no way out: "We must play with the cards that are dealt. Agriculture cannot survive in a capitalist society as a philanthropic enterprise."

To make matters worse, the AAA did not begin to work until after the spring planting of 1933. Farmers who had not sufficiently reduced their acreage were ordered to plow under a large part of their crops. With people reportedly starving in the cities, the AAA's action seemed heartless. It also fell short of its goal. Many farmers accepted government checks for reducing acreage and then calmly cultivated their remaining acres more intensively. In 1934 Congress added production quotas to acreage restriction and imposed taxes on violators. The new and old laws helped double and triple farm-staple prices. Total net income of farm operators rose dramatically, from $1.8 billion in 1932 to $5 billion in 1936.

The Supreme Court ruled in January 1936 that it was unconstitutional for Congress to impose a tax on processors for the purpose of regulating farm production. Congress responded with the Soil Conservation and Domestic Allotment Act, which put crop restriction on a sounder constitutional basis. The object now was to increase soil fertilization and conserve resources. The AAA was authorized to pay farmers for using soil-conservation measures and for reducing acreage used for soil-depleting crops. Congressional appropriations were to finance the new program.

When prices tumbled again in 1937, Congress passed a second Agricultural Adjustment Act, intending to put into action Secretary Wallace's idea of the ever-normal granary. The price fall in 1937 had come from bumper crops produced in 1936. The new act aimed to keep such bumper crops off the market—in effect, to keep the supply of staples "ever normal"—by compensating farmers for storing them. Large amounts were paid to farmers, but staple growers did not really do well until wartime demand in the 1940s pushed prices up.

Millions of farm families gained nothing from such legislation, which was designed to help commercial, landowning farmers. By 1935, an estimated 46 percent of all white farmers in the country were tenants, as were some 77 percent of black farmers. The problem of tenancy was worst in the South. If tenant farmers or sharecroppers owed money to the landlord or to the storekeeper—and most did—they were required by state law to work the land until the debts had been paid. They lived in crudely built shacks, suffered from malnutrition, and looked forward to little except a lifetime of drudgery and debt. Few observers described this life more vividly than James Agee in *Let Us Now Praise Famous Men* (1941).

Rarely did the benefits of the AAA seep down to the tenants and sharecroppers; 90 percent of the government payments went to the planters and landlords, and these same people usually controlled the local and county committees to which the tenants would have to appeal their cases. Landlords who removed acreage from cultivation to qualify for AAA payments evicted many tenants rather than split the payments with them, thereby stimulating a movement of these tenants to the cities, where they could join the army of the unemployed.

As the Depression wore on, concern for sharecroppers, farm tenants, and hired farm laborers grew. The New Deal's response was the Resettlement Administration, created in 1935. The RA withdrew 9 million acres of wasteland from cultivation and moved the families on them to resettlement areas. It extended loans to farmers who could not obtain credit elsewhere, and it encouraged cooperation among those farmers who had always insisted on going it alone.

In response to the report of a presidential committee on rural poverty, Congress passed the Farm Tenancy Act in 1937. This measure provided loans to sharecroppers, tenant farmers, and farm laborers for the purchase of land, livestock, supplies, and equipment. By June 1944, 870,000 rural families had been helped. And it was the Farm Security Administration, set up under this act, that sent out photographers such as Walker Evans, Dorothea Lange, Russell Lee, and Arthur Rothstein to portray these people in all their simple dignity.

Although they recognized the problem of rural poverty, the New Dealers had still done very little about it. When sharecroppers and farm laborers—white and black—began to attack their troubles through the newly formed Southern Tenant Farmers' Union, they found violent resistance from the farming interests that had benefited

most from New Deal legislation. The union's newspaper finally concluded that under President Roosevelt, "too often the progressive word has been the clothing for a conservative act. Too often he has talked like a cropper and acted like a planter."

The kind of social planning necessary to deal with rural poverty and tenantry never received adequate thought or money. Instead, those who strongly supported such planning found themselves out of the Department of Agriculture. "Of course," Secretary Wallace wrote, "the liberals presented a strong case for the tenants, but the reforms they wanted would have blown the department out of the water at that time."

Rural Redevelopment: The TVA

One of the poorest of all American farm areas was the Tennessee Valley, which was immensely rich in natural resources. Government projects to harness the mighty Tennessee River were begun at Muscle Shoals during World War I. Senator George W. Norris of Nebraska tried to continue them under government management. But the private power companies opposed all efforts to keep Muscle Shoals a public project, and Coolidge and Hoover vetoed the necessary legislation.

After his election, Roosevelt visited Muscle Shoals and soon had a grand plan for the whole valley. On May 18, 1933, Congress created the Tennessee Valley Authority and empowered it to buy, build, and operate dams in the valley. The TVA would generate and sell electric power, and plan reforestation and flood control. It could withdraw marginal lands from cultivation and undertake regional planning to improve the standard of living of the people who lived in the valley.

Of all the New Deal experiments in government, the TVA was probably the boldest and most original. It was an independent public corporation, and its area of responsibility embraced 40,000 square miles in seven states. The TVA built sixteen dams and took over five others. By 1940, four of the dams were generating electric power in the TVA region. Over 40,000 users, many of them farmers with no previous access to electricity, were directly or indirectly served. TVA rates were kept low, and served as a yardstick by which to measure private rates. The result was to force private companies in the area to keep rates down. Land redeemed by the TVA from flooding was made productive for the first time.

Like earlier valley plans, the TVA was fought by the power companies. They gained the support of disinterested conservatives who saw in the experiment a threat to the private enterprise system. Like other New Deal measures, the TVA was soon taken to court. But unlike some other measures, it survived.

Unemployment: The CCC, PWA, and WPA

When Roosevelt took office, at least 13 million workers were unemployed. They and their fami-

BROTHER, CAN YOU SPARE A DIME?

They used to tell me I was building a dream,
And so I followed the mob;
When there was earth to plow or guns to bear
I was always there, right there on the job.

They used to tell me I was building a dream
With peace and glory ahead;
Why should I be standing in line
—just waiting for bread?

CHORUS: Once I built a railroad, made it run,
Made it race against time.
Once I built a railroad, now it's done—
Brother, can you spare a dime?

Once I built a tower, to the sun,
Brick and rivet and lime;

Once I built a tower, now it's done—
Brother, can you spare a dime?

Once in khaki suits—gee, we looked swell,
Full of that Yankee Doodle-de-dum.
Half a million boots went sloggin' thru Hell,
I was the kid with the drum.

Say, don't you remember, they called me Al,
It was Al all the time;
Say, don't you remember, I'm your pal!
Buddy, can you spare a dime?

Source: Words by E. Y. Harburg, music by Jay Gorney. Copyright 1932 by Harms, Inc. Copyright renewed. All rights reserved. Used by permission of Warner Bros. Music. Photograph by Dorothea Lange, Library of Congress.

lies added up to about 50 million people, many of them on the verge of starvation. The writer Martha Gellhorn, touring the country in 1933, reported to Harry Hopkins on the unemployed: "I find them all in the same shape—fear, fear driving them into a state of semicollapse; cracking nerves; and an overpowering terror of the future . . . each family in its own miserable home going to pieces."* The issue was no longer whether the federal government should act, but how. Should it give handouts to the poverty-stricken, which was the cheapest plan, or should it provide work, which seemed less wasteful and more humane?

The first New Deal assistance to the unemployed was the Civilian Conservation Corps, aimed at the youth of the country. At one point the CCC had on its rolls 500,000 young men, eighteen to twenty-five. Recruited from cities to live in camps built by the War Department, they worked on reforestation, road and dam construction, control of mosquitoes and other pests, and similar tasks. Of the thirty dollars a month they received in wages, twenty-two dollars was sent to their families. By the end of 1941, some 2,750,000 youths had spent part of their lives in CCC camps.

The first comprehensive New Deal relief measure was the act of May 1933 creating the Federal Emergency Relief Administration (FERA). Under Harry Hopkins, the FERA had half a billion dollars to be used for direct emergency relief. Although the federal government provided the money, the relief itself was to be administered by the states. Cash payments were distributed at first, but Hopkins thought work relief was psychologically and economically superior. He also was concerned with quick results. Whenever someone approached him with a project that would "work out in the long run," Hopkins snapped, "People don't eat in the long run—they eat every day."

In time, almost half of those receiving relief were put to work on jobs that presumably did not compete with private business. Pay began at thirty cents an hour. In all, FERA spent about $4 billion before it was succeeded in December 1935 by the Works Progress Administration.

The Civil Works Administration, set up in November 1933, was run entirely from Washington and devoted wholly to work relief. Widely criticized by opponents of the New Deal on the ground that it "made work," the CWA in fact performed many useful services, such as repairing roads and improving schools and parks. The Public Works Administration (PWA), under Secretary of the Interior Harold Ickes, was more a pump-priming than a relief agency. Its duties included planning bridges, dams, hospitals, and other public projects and contracting for their construction by private companies.

Many people complained that New Deal relief agencies, besides duplicating tasks, made no effort to distinguish between employable persons who needed relief and "unemployables"—those who could not have found work even in good times. Early in 1935 Roosevelt proposed a reorganization of the entire relief program. The federal government would aid employables only. The care of others would be left to the states and municipalities. The Emergency Relief Act of 1935 put these proposals into effect. The CCC and the PWA were continued. All other federal relief was brought under the new Works Progress Administration (WPA), directed by Harry Hopkins. When its operations ended in July 1941, the WPA had spent $11.3 billion. At its peak, in November 1938, nearly 3.3 million persons were on its payroll, and all told it provided work for 8 million people. Among its more than 250,000 projects were hospitals, bridges, municipal power plants, post offices, school buildings, slum clearance, and the rehabilitation of army posts and naval stations.

The WPA also took into account the plight of the humanities and the arts, whose practitioners, like other workers, were left stranded by the Depression. Its projects in the fine arts, music, and the theater gave employment to painters, writers, actors, singers, and musicians, stimulating what *Fortune* magazine called "a kind of cultural revolution in America." Authors of WPA guides conducted research in local history to write the first composite survey of the American states. Other projects resulted in the recovery of American folklore, interviews with more than two thousand former slaves, and the recording of white and black spirituals, Indian songs, and folk tunes. On post office walls all over the country WPA artists painted regional scenes and memorable local episodes. Americans who had never gone to a theater or concert flocked to Federal Theatre Project performances, which charged no admission from those unable to pay.

The cultural work of the WPA was supplemented by the National Youth Administration, which helped meet the needs of young persons with intellectual interests. Through the NYA young people aged sixteen to twenty-five found part-time employment in high schools, colleges, and universities.

---

*Hopkins Papers, quoted in Arthur Schlesinger, Jr., *The Coming of the New Deal*, p. 272. Houghton-Mifflin, 1959.

In 1930, when the number of unemployed went over 4 million, unemployment lines such as this one were a common sight. One worker described his experience in Studs Terkel's book *Hard Times:* "I'd get up five in the morning and head for the waterfront. . . . Outside the gates there would be a thousand men. You knew dang well there's only three or four jobs. The guy would come out with two little Pinkerton cops. 'I need two guys for the bull gang. Two guys to go into the hold.' A thousand men would fight like a pack of Alaskan dogs to get through there." *(Library of Congress)*

Isaac Soyer's painting *Employment Agency* (1937). Oil 34¼ x 45 inches. *(Collection of the Whitney Museum of American Art. Juliana Force Purchase acq.#50.23)*

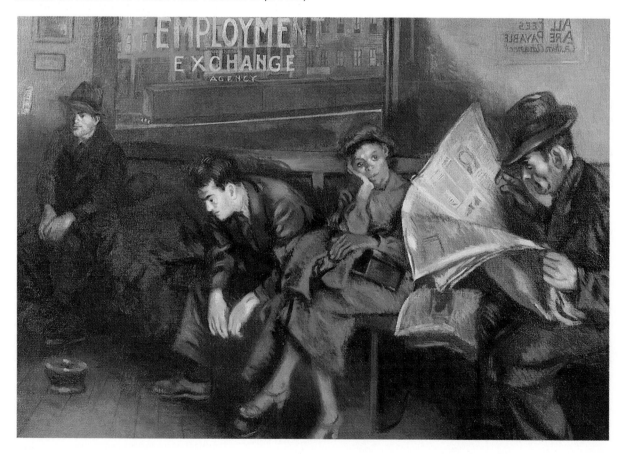

No part of the New Deal drew more criticism than its relief program. The cost was truly enormous for the times, and the tax burden had to be shouldered by the depressed private sector of the economy. Many critics charged, usually inaccurately, that relief was inefficiently handled. Others, often justly, accused the administration of using relief for political purposes. No part of the relief program drew more criticism than its support of cultural activities. Many Americans had no sympathy with the idea that musicians, writers, and artists had as much claim on the community as workers in other fields.

Even at its peak, however, the WPA reached fewer than half of the unemployed. Despite the New Deal experiments in economic legislation, only once, in 1937, did the number of unemployed fall below 8 million. In 1940 it was back above that figure, at a level five times that of 1929. This failure, some critics suggested, revealed a flaw in the New Dealers ideas about the essential soundness of the economic system they were trying to revive.

CHALLENGE AND RESPONSE

Most of the New Deal's famous "alphabet agencies"—the NRA, TVA, AAA, SEC, CCC, and PWA—came into being in the first hundred days of the Roosevelt administration. The opposition was for the moment shamed, shocked, or stunned into silence. Supported by the president's optimism, relief and reform measures were adopted almost unanimously. That same enthusiasm carried over to the polls. In the congressional elections of 1934, the Democrats scored overwhelming victories, swelling their majorities in the House and Senate.

But if the election of 1934 buried the conservative critics who thought Roosevelt was going too far too fast, it might have reminded him, if he needed reminding, of several things: The spirit of protest was still rising; recovery had not yet been achieved; and those who believed the New Deal moved too little and too slowly would be heard from. The most troublesome critics in the next several years would be those who took advantage of the growing despair of the lower middle class, many of whom had been badly shaken by the collapse of a system they had never thought to question. The despair was widespread enough to move the New Deal into some new areas.

Critics and Crusaders

Most formidable among the new breed of critics was Senator Huey Long, the Kingfish of Louisiana. A skilled politician and a champion of poor whites, he had engineered some needed reforms in his state while governor, though not without corruption and invasions of constitutional liberties. He built up a national following, especially in the Mississippi Valley and on the Pacific Coast, on the strength of his Share Our Wealth plan. This called for confiscatory taxes on the wealthy, which would provide every family with an income of $2500, a homestead, and an automobile. In 1935 a Democratic National Committee survey disclosed that Long might win from 3 to 4 million votes on a third-party presidential ticket, thereby gaining the balance of power in American politics. This potentially disastrous threat to Roosevelt's chances in the 1936 campaign disappeared with Long's assassination in September 1935.

A second popular challenge was mounted in California by Francis E. Townsend, an elderly physician. In January 1935 he announced a plan by which the government would give $200 a month to every citizen over the age of sixty. The cost would be paid by a sales tax. Each pensioner would be required to spend his or her allowance within the month. This would start such a wave of consumer buying that business would boom and make it easy for the rest of the country to bear the cost. Responsible economists dismissed the plan as a crackpot scheme; one of them estimated it would require half the national income to be turned over to 8 percent of the population.

But Townsend Clubs, organized throughout the country, attracted desperate older men and women. Their combined membership was said to be about 3 million in 1935, and there were perhaps as many as 7 million additional supporters. When frightened politicians began to endorse Townsend's scheme, Roosevelt had to face the possibility that a large proportion of the voters over sixty would be forged into a bloc.

More forceful and yet more vague than Dr. Townsend was the "radio priest," Charles E. Coughlin, who broadcast weekly from Royal Oak, Michigan. Coughlin won an enormous audience with assaults on Wall Street and the international bankers, phrased in such a way that no one could doubt the role of these groups in the Depression. His harangues seemed more satisfying to his followers than his more rational demands for a "living wage" and nationalization of banks, utili-

THE GREAT DEPRESSION

Missouri migrant farm laborer in California, 1936: "What bothers us travellin' people most is we cain't get no place to stay still." *(Dorothea Lange, Library of Congress)*

Cotton farmer on inherited but mortgaged farm, Green County, Georgia, 1937. *(Dorothea Lange, Library of Congress)*

Migrant workers' camp near Prague, Oklahoma, 1939. *(Russell Lee, Library of Congress)*

Hard Times Blues

Well, I went down home 'bout a year ago,
Things so bad, Lord, my heart was sore.
Folks had nothin', it was a sin and a shame,
Ev'rybody said hard times was to blame.

    (CHORUS) Great God a-mighty, folks feelin' bad
             Lost ev'rything they ever had.
             Great God a-mighty, folks feelin' bad
             Lost ev'rything they ever had.

Now the sun was a-shinin' fourteen days and no
   rain,
Hoein' and plantin' was all in vain,
They had hard, hard times, Lord, all around,
Meal barrels empty, crops burnt to the ground.

They had skinny lookin' children, bellies pokin' out,
That old pellagra without a doubt.
Old folks hangin' round the cabin door
Ain't seen times so hard before.

Well, I went to the boss at the commissary store,
Folks all starvin', please don't close your door.
We want more food and a little more time to pay.
Boss man laughed and walked away.

Now your landlord comes around when your rent is
  due.
And if you ain't got his money, he'll take your home
  from you.
He'll take your mules and horse, even take your cow,
Says, "Get off my land, you're no-good, no-how!"

Source: This Land Is Your Land: Songs of Social Justice. Music by Josh White; lyrics by William Waring Cuney. Copyright 1957 Charles Street Publishing Company.

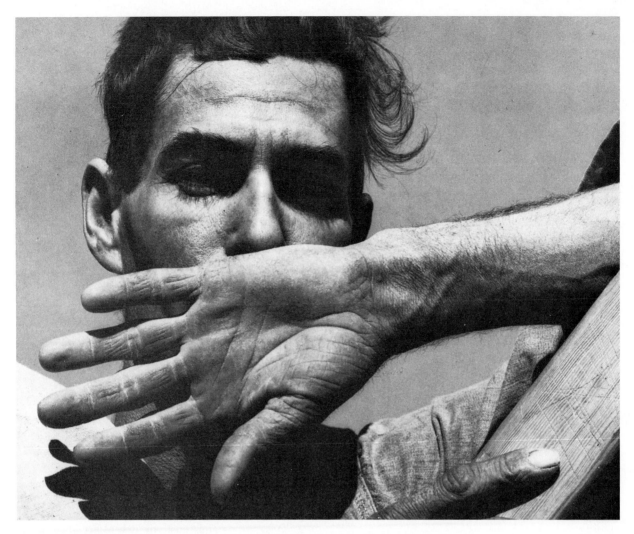

Migratory worker, 1940: "When they need us they call us migrants. When we've picked their crops we're bums and we've got to get out." *(Dorothea Lange, Library of Congress)*

"I can count twenty-three farmers in the west half of this county that have had to leave the farms to give three men more land. Was waiting to see what would be the outcome of my hunt for a place, and the outlook right now is that I will move to town and sell my teams, tools, and cows. I have hunted from Childress, Texas, to Haskell, Texas, a distance of 200 miles, and the answer is the same. I can stay off the relief until the first of the year. After that I don't know. I've got to make a move, but I don't know where to go."

Texas Plains
June 20, 1938.

Migratory worker's wife: "If you die, you're dead—that's all." *(Dorothea Lange, Library of Congress)*

Evicted sharecropper, 1939: "Tractors are against the black man. Every time you kill a mule you kill a black man. You've heard about the machine picker? That's against the black man, too." *(Arthur Rothstein, Library of Congress)*

Victim of the drought, 1937: "I want to go back to where we can live happy, live decent, and grow what we eat." *(Dorothea Lange, Library of Congress)*

Seven Cent Cotton and Forty Cent Meat

Seven cent cotton and forty cent meat,
How in the world can a poor man eat?
Flour up high and cotton down low,
How in the world can we raise the dough?
Clothes worn out, shoes run down,
Old slouch hat with a hole in the crown.
Back nearly broken and fingers all sore,
Cotton gone down to rise no more.

Seven cent cotton and eight dollar pants,
Who in the world has got a chance?
We can't buy clothes, we can't buy meat,
Too much cotton, and not enough to eat.
Can't help each other, what'll we do?
I can't explain it, so it's up to you.
Seven cent cotton and two dollar hose,
Guess we'll have to do without any clothes.

Seven cent cotton and forty cent meat,
How in the world can a poor man eat?
Mules in the barn, no crop laid by,
Corn crib empty and the cow's gone dry;
Well water low, nearly out of sight,
Can't take a bath on a Saturday night.
No use talking, any man is beat,

With seven cent cotton and forty cent meat.
Seven cent cotton and forty cent meat,
How in the world can a poor man eat?
Poor getting poorer all around here,
Kids coming regular every year.

Fatten our hogs, take them to town,
All we get is six cents a pound.
Very next day we have to buy it back,
Forty cents a pound in a paper sack.

Source: Pete Seeger (ed.), *American Industrial Ballads.* Words and music by Bob Miller and Emma Dermer (Folkways 1929).

Cotton chopper, White Plains, Georgia, 1941. *(J. Delano, Library of Congress)*

Migrants moving on, 1936: "Damned if we'll work for what they pay folks hereabouts." *(Dorothea Lange, Library of Congress)*

Harvest hand in Ohio, 1938: "We must make enough for beans, and when we have to buy gas it comes out of the beans." *(Ben Shahn, Library of Congress)*

Goin' Down the Road

I'm goin' down the road feelin' bad,
I'm goin' down the road feelin' bad,
I'm goin' down the road feelin' bad, Lord
And I ain't gonna be treated this-a-way.

Lord I can't live on cornbread and beans, . . .
Lord I'm goin' where the water tastes like wine, . . .
Lord I'm goin' where the climate fits my clothes, . . .
Lord where I go nobody knows, . . .
I'm not goin' to be treated this-a-way.

(an old Oklahoma folk song)

Sources: Dorothea Lange and Paul S. Taylor, *An American Exodus* (NY: Retnal & Hitchcock, 1939), p. 68; John Greenway, *American Folksongs of Protest* (Philadelphia: University of Pennsylvania Press, 1953), pp. 206–7.

Source: Dorothea Lange and Paul S. Taylor *An American Exodus* NY: Retnal & Hitchcock, 1939), p. 82.

New York City bootblack, 1937. *(Arthur Rothstein, Library of Congress)*

ties, and natural resources. Originally one of Roosevelt's supporters, Coughlin broke with the New Deal in 1935, drifted toward fascism and anti-Semitism, and lost most of his popular appeal.

The popularity of Long, Townsend, and Coughlin, coming as it did with organized labor's growing discontent, suggested in the spring of 1935 that Roosevelt's mass appeal, so strong in the early months of the New Deal, might soon dissolve. The president well understood the genuine grievances underlying the broad appeal of these critics, and privately he even spoke of doing something "to steal Long's thunder." The Revenue Tax Act, the Social Security Act, the National Labor Relations Act, and other actions were all responses to this pressure. "I am fighting Communism, Huey Longism, Coughlinism, Townsendism," Roosevelt told one of his critics. "I want to save our system, the capitalistic system; to save it is to give some heed to world thought of today. I want to equalize the distribution of wealth." The result was more reform.

New Directions: The 1935 Reforms

Three reform measures were enacted in one month, August 1935. One was inspired by the administration's desire to stop the growth of gigantic personal fortunes. This was the Revenue Tax Act, sometimes called the "wealth tax" or the "soak the rich" law. Some also suspected it was Roosevelt's way of responding to Long's Share Our Wealth scheme. Tax rates, which had already been raised by earlier New Deal measures, were now pushed much higher, reaching 75 percent on individual incomes over $5 million. Holding companies used for the management of private fortunes were also heavily taxed, and corporation taxes were raised.

Roy W. Howard, the publisher of a chain of newspapers until then sympathetic toward Roosevelt, now wrote the president in an open letter that businessmen believed the wealth tax to be a punishment. Roosevelt replied that the act was intended to "create a broader range of opportunity" and to impose taxes according to ability to pay. He did promise, however, that business would now have a "breathing spell."

The second August law was the Public Utility Holding Company Act. Holding companies were corporations permitted to hold the securities of other corporations. By holding only a tiny fraction of a great corporation's securities, but a fraction large enough to mean strong influence if the other holdings were scattered, the holding company could dominate policies to its own advantage. Consumers as well as investors had suffered from public utility holding companies. In 1932, thirteen such companies controlled no less than 75 percent of the electric-power market.

The new act required the dissolution of those holding companies that could not demonstrate within five years that they had made economies in management. This "death sentence" clause started a bitter struggle in Congress, and holding companies spent large sums trying to defeat it. After some compromises, the clause remained in the law and the Supreme Court eventually upheld it. Every effort to impose the "death sentence," however, was stubbornly resisted, at immense legal costs. The law became a windfall for lawyers.

The third measure was the Social Security Act, designed to secure "the men, women and children of the nation against certain hazards and vicissitudes of life." For the first time, the federal government would make payments, directly or through the states, for pensions to the aged and the infirm, for unemployment insurance, and for benefits to dependent mothers and children. Federal pensions of up to fifteen dollars a month to the poor over sixty-five years of age were expected to be matched by the states. Federal retirement funds, ranging from ten to eighty five dollars a month, were to be paid to workers who retired at sixty-five and who had participated in the plan before their retirement. Agricultural workers, household servants, government employees, and those working for nonprofit religious or charitable organizations were among those excluded.

The money for those included was to be raised by a payroll tax on employers and employees. Most states promptly set up old-age pension and unemployment-insurance systems conforming to the provisions of the act. A worker who lost his or her job could collect from five to fifteen dollars a week for about fifteen weeks while looking for new work.

By 1940, about 50 million workers were protected by social security. From time to time since then, new classes of workers have been covered, money payments increased, and the period for receiving unemployment insurance extended. A nonpartisan Social Security Board administers the program. The Social Security Act passed the House and Senate with far larger majorities than the other measures. Its opponents, however, made up in loudness what they lacked in numbers. Several of them asserted that the measure would mean the end of free government, and one critic thought social security would "take all the romance out of life."

Labor

In May 1935 the Supreme Court had found the National Industrial Recovery Act unconstitutional, and had thereby invalidated its labor guarantees. Congress responded in July of that year with the National Labor Relations Act—often called the Wagner Act, after the New York senator who championed it. The act guaranteed collective bargaining and prohibited employer interference with organizing activities. It provided that the representative of the majority of the employees in any plant be the *exclusive* bargaining representative of *all* the employees. It empowered the newly established National Labor Relations Board (NLRB) to investigate and certify the proper representatives and to hold supervised elections when there was a dispute over which union should represent employees.

The long-run effects of this measure for the political future of the New Deal, for the Democratic party, and for the country were as profound as its economic consequences. Under the new act, no less than 340 company unions were broken up. Membership in trade unions continued to grow, particularly in the unorganized mass-production industries, until in 1941 it had reached 10.5 million. By then, the NLRB had handled 33,000 cases affecting more than 7 million workers.

The rise of organized labor was accompanied by conflict not only between workers and employers, but also within labor. The AFL was badly split. The leaders of the old craft unions that had first come together in the federation sought to retain their power and standing as the "aristocracy of labor." Not wanting to bring in the unskilled and semiskilled workers in the mass-production industries, they also refused to permit other leaders to organize such workers in new unions. The issue came to a head at the national AFL convention in October 1935, when a majority of the delegates stood fast for craft unionism.

Police attack strikers at the Republic Steel plant near Chicago on May 30, 1937. Republic Steel president Tom M. Girdler was quoted as saying, "I won't have a contract, verbal or written, with an irresponsible, racketeering, violent, communistic body like the C.I.O., and until they pass a law making me do it, I am not going to do it." *(AP/Wide World Photos)*

A month later, John L. Lewis of the United Mine Workers and seven other AFL leaders organized the Committee for Industrial Organization (CIO), intending to advise the AFL on how to organize the mass-production industries. Lewis became chairman of the committee. In January 1936 the AFL executive council ordered the CIO to disband. The leaders refused, and in August they were suspended. Expelled in March 1937, they took with them unions representing 1.8 million workers. A massive organizing campaign followed, contributing to a record 4740 strikes that year. Early in 1938, when the CIO had nearly 4 million members, the leaders formed a new organization with the same initials, the Congress of Industrial Organizations.

One of the CIO's new weapons, outlawed by the Supreme Court in 1939, was the sit-down strike. Instead of walking off the job and picketing, workers went to their posts in the plants and stayed there, making it difficult for others to replace them. Sit-down strikes against two giant automobile companies, General Motors in January 1937 and Chrysler in April, won the CIO recognition as the bargaining agent for their workers. In March 1937 the United States Steel Corporation, once the terror of organized labor, also gave in.

"Little Steel" proved harder to crack. On Memorial Day 1937, Chicago police killed ten pickets during a strike against the Republic Company, Little Steel's leader. Other strikes brought violence in Youngstown, Massillon, and Cleveland, Ohio. The Little Steel companies did not fall until 1941, when they signed contracts conforming to an NLRB order to reinstate workers fired during the 1937 struggle.

As labor grew more aggressive and important in politics as well as business, the split in its ranks caused many difficulties. A peace movement finally brought about a merger of the AFL and the CIO in 1955. By then, the complacency and conservatism of the AFL appeared to be characteristic of much of organized labor. The energy and spirit that had marked the organizing drives of the thirties were only distant memories.

The Roosevelt Coalition: White and Black

Although serious economic problems persisted, the New Deal did give the American people a sense of direction and hope. Through his personal leadership and the legislation he had helped to bring about, Roosevelt had managed to build an extraordinary political coalition by the end of 1935. Its elements were partly old and partly new: (1) the solidly Democratic South (commercial farmers in cotton and tobacco had benefited from the agricultural program); (2) Democratic machines in northern cities (FDR preferred to use, not destroy them); (3) new immigrant groups and blacks (who were hit especially hard by the Depression); and (4) organized labor, intellectuals, and many normally Republican farmers and businessmen.

Among the ethnic elements, blacks had good reason not to support the administration. Almost all the NRA codes, for example, discriminated against black workers in the areas of employment, wages, and job-improvement opportunities. AAA crop-control payments went mostly to farmers with large acreage, which left black sharecroppers in a precarious economic position and forcing many of them off the land altogether. The CCC began as a lily-white agency: fewer than 3 percent of the first quarter-million enrolled were blacks. Even when black participation grew, segregation remained the rule. This was also true in the model towns established by the TVA. And the New Deal housing program encouraged the development of racially segregated neighborhoods.

Most important, the New Deal did not make a significant dent in black unemployment, and blacks were not sharing in relief. When black grievances in Harlem finally exploded into a riot in 1935, the white press blamed Communist agitation. The field secretary of the Harlem YMCA saw it differently:

It is true there were Communists in the picture. But what gave them their opportunity? The fact that there were and still are thousands of Negroes standing in enforced idleness on the street corners of Harlem with no prospect of employment while their more favored Negro neighbors are compelled to spend their money with business houses directed by white absentee owners who employ white workers imported from every part of New York City.

The New Deal approached relief, reform, and recovery on a national and a general basis. Many of its leaders did not want established social patterns attacked. Party solidarity also made Democratic leaders cautious on race. They did little or nothing, for example, to fight the poll tax, which disqualified most blacks of voting age in the South, or to stop lynching. Between 1930 and 1934, more than sixty blacks were hanged, shot, or burned by vigilante mobs.

Black leaders, as they had in the 1920s, pressed for federal legislation against lynching. Once again, however, southern filibusters in the Senate defeated every antilynching bill. The practical-minded Roosevelt had to explain to Walter White, an NAACP official: "If I come out for the antilynching bill now, they will block every bill I ask Congress to pass to keep America from collapsing. I just can't take that risk." The best that could be said of the president on this issue, Du Bois remarked, was that he had called lynching "collective murder," and that at least offered black people some hope.

And yet the president managed to convince American blacks that he cared about them. Black voters responded to the New Deal with enthusiasm and formed a strong part of the Roosevelt coalition. However little their share, they, like others, did get relief under the New Deal; under Hoover there had been little or none. Despite almost universal second-class treatment, blacks, like others, did benefit from New Deal reforms. And they, like others, did share in economic recovery, perhaps most through the new labor movement the New Deal fostered. Roosevelt and many of his aides showed the same warmth to black leaders as they did to others, and the New Deal hired many black administrators. Finally, Eleanor Roosevelt's liberality of spirit and constant support of minorities helped to move urban black voters to the FDR bandwagon.

The success of the New Deal's agricultural program also brought many normally Republican westerners into the Democratic ranks. Iowa, for example, had gone Republican in every election from 1916 to 1928, often overwhelmingly so. In 1932 it swung to Roosevelt, and in 1936 it remained solidly behind him. Labor's newly organized millions also swung heavily into the Roosevelt camp in 1935 and 1936. John L. Lewis and other CIO leaders organized Labor's Non-Partisan League to mobilize the labor vote in industrial centers. The CIO gave half a million dollars to the 1936 Democratic campaign. Roosevelt was not hurt by the split in labor's ranks. AFL president William Green, after visiting FDR, announced that 90 percent of labor's vote would be his.

Labor's lead was followed by many intellectuals throughout the country. Suspicious at first of some of the features of the NRA and the AAA, and troubled by the inadequacy and inconsistency of many New Deal measures, teachers, writers, clergy, artists, and journalists rallied behind the New Deal after the 1935 reforms. Intellectuals were encouraged by the administration's receptivity to ideas and experts and by its readiness to help unemployed artists, scholars, and writers.

Nor was business altogether absent from the coalition. Roosevelt counted many loyal personal friends among businessmen. Other business people, especially antitariff merchants and bankers, were traditionally Democrats. Still others represented the socially concerned rich. A large number came from sectors of the economy that benefited directly from the gains in mass purchasing power brought by New Deal reform and relief legislation. From them—consumer-goods manufacturers, for example, and chain- and department-store owners and other retailers—Roosevelt won a gratifying response when the chips were down. Their contributions were feeble compared with what the Republicans got from corporate and personal holders of "the big money." But Roosevelt needed much less money than his opponents to win votes.

The Election of 1936

By the time of the 1936 elections, the New Deal had made most of the progress it was going to make. It had fostered business recovery and furthered labor organization. It had relieved distress on the farms and helped the unemployed. Economic statistics suggested that a good deal of recovery had been achieved in certain sectors of the economy. Farm income had gone up dramatically. Average weekly earnings of workers in manufacturing had risen since 1932 from $17 to almost $22. Although some 7 million remained unemployed, this figure had dropped by 4 or 5 million since Roosevelt took office, and the unemployed were receiving enough to live. The rise in national income from $40.2 billion in 1933 to $64.7 billion in 1936 reflected the general advance.

The Republicans attacked every aspect of the New Deal. "America is in peril," their 1936 platform began. "We invite all Americans, irrespective of party, to join us in defense of American institutions." For president, the Republican convention nominated Governor Alfred M. Landon of Kansas; for vice-president, Frank Knox, a Chicago publisher. The Democrats renominated Roosevelt by acclamation. "These economic royalists," Roosevelt told the convention, "complain that we seek to overthrow the institutions of America. What they really complain of is that we seek to overthrow their power."

The critics came together in Cleveland to form a third party, the Union party. They nominated William Lemke, a Republican congressman from North Dakota. But the critics were far fewer now. The Social Security Act of 1935 had stolen much of Dr. Townsend's thunder, and Huey Long had been assassinated. Coughlin had received unmistakable evidence that the Roman Catholic church hierarchy found his political behavior embarrassing. Lemke polled fewer than a million votes and did not carry a single state.

Some Democrats, including Al Smith, went over to Landon during the campaign. But the Republican candidate's main support came from the Liberty League, financed by conservative millionaires. Near the end of the campaign, before a wildly enthusiastic crowd in New York's Madison Square Garden, Roosevelt declared that the New Deal had been struggling with "business and financial monopoly, speculation, reckless banking, class antagonism, sectionalism, war profiteering." He went on: "Never before in all our history have those forces been so united against one candidate as they stand today. They are unanimous in their *hate* for *me*—*and I welcome their hatred.*"

In the balloting, Roosevelt carried all but two states, Maine and Vermont. His 27.75 million popular votes represented more than sixty percent of the total cast. In the cities, his margins reached record levels. By winning even more overwhelmingly than in 1932, he made the Democratic party the accepted majority party of the country.

The fate of the minor parties testified to the strength of the Roosevelt coalition. Lemke's showing disappointed the Republicans as well as his followers. Republicans had hoped he would deprive Roosevelt of enough conservative farm votes to swing some states to Landon. The record of the Socialist and Communist candidates showed that the New Deal had completely broken independent political radicalism. Four years earlier, Norman Thomas, the Socialist party nominee, had won 881,000 votes; in 1936, he won only 187,000. William Z. Foster, the Communist candidate in 1932, had won 102,000 votes; Earl Browder, his successor in 1936, got only 80,000.

THE CLIMAX OF THE NEW DEAL

In his second inaugural address, FDR expressed no complacency over his victory or his achievement. The problems of depression and deprivation, as he frankly confessed, persisted: "I see one-third of a nation ill-housed, ill-clad, ill-nourished." Before attacking these problems, however, Roosevelt set out to neutralize a major obstacle to the realization of his reform vision—the Supreme Court.

The Court Fight

The president's attack on the Supreme Court came as a surprise. On February 5, 1937, apparently having consulted no one but his attorney general, Roosevelt proposed to Congress what was then called his "court-packing bill": whenever a federal judge failed to retire within six months after reaching the age of seventy, an additional federal judge should be appointed. Although the proposal applied to the entire federal judiciary, it was obviously aimed at the Supreme Court, where six of the judges were already over seventy. Thus, as many as six judges could be added, bringing the full Court to fifteen.

Although the announcement came as a shock, the need for the bill seemed clear enough. The people had approved of the New Deal, but the Supreme Court had opposed its early legislation. In 1935 and 1936, the Court had struck down the NRA and the AAA. It had rejected a railroad retirement plan and the Bituminous Coat Act, which was intended to reorganize a sick industry. It had invalidated congressional legislation designed to protect those with farm mortgages, and it had thrown out a municipal-bankruptcy act. To those who sympathized with the New Deal social program, the Court seemed to be creating an area where neither state nor federal power could be used to solve critical problems.

The number of Supreme Court justices had, in fact, been changed several times in the past, but the present total of nine had become fixed for so long it almost had the sanction of constitutional authority. To attempt to reduce the Court's power by a constitutional amendment would take years, if ever. Roosevelt's plan was a shortcut. But his assertion that it was intended simply to help federal courts catch up with their business seemed not altogether true. Even for a large number of New Dealers, it gave weight to the charge that he was indeed seeking the dictatorial powers his opponents had said all along he wanted.

During debate on the bill, several events weakened its chances. Most important, within a few weeks of Roosevelt's bombshell, Justice Owen J. Roberts began to vote on the liberal side in some cases. On March 29, 1937, the Supreme Court sustained a state minimum-wage law five to four, overruling a recent decision by the same majority. Even more important for the New Deal, on April 12 the Court upheld the National Labor Relations Act. Six weeks later, in two five-to-four rulings, the Court sustained the social security legislation.

In May, Justice Van Devanter, one of the most conservative justices on the bench, struck another blow at the court-reform bill when he announced his intention to retire. Roosevelt would have at least one appointment of his own. On July 22, the Senate voted overwhelmingly, seventy to twenty, to recommit the bill to the Judiciary Committee, where it died. And yet Roosevelt had a sort of triumph after all. In August 1937 he appointed the liberal Hugo L. Black of Alabama to Van Devanter's place.

In the next few years, six other aging justices took the cue and announced their intention to retire. To five of the vacancies thus created, Roosevelt appointed liberals and New Dealers; to the sixth, the southern Democrat James F. Byrnes. To the chief justice–ship vacated by Hughes, Roosevelt shifted the learned, liberal Harlan Fiske Stone, a firm supporter of federal power. New Dealers had lost the battle but won the war, even though the whole procedure opened a lasting rift in the party and cost voter support.

Housing and Labor Standards

Many reforms were gained or extended during FDR's second term. As in the Court fight, however, the political costs were high. The reform potential of the Democratic coalition was becoming exhausted.

New reforms attempted to strike harder at poor housing and low wages. As early as 1933, the administration had created the Home Owners Loan Corporation and given it huge resources to protect householders from losing their property through mortgage foreclosure. In June 1934 it had set up the Federal Housing Administration as a source of loans mainly to middle-income families for the purpose of repairing old homes or building new ones. But positive action on low-income housing came only with the Wagner-Steagall Housing Act of September 1937.

It created the United States Housing Authority and authorized it to make long-term, low-interest loans to state or city public housing agencies that would clear slums and build new houses to federal standards. Occupancy of these homes was to be limited to those who could not pay rents high enough to induce private builders to construct dwellings for them. By 1941 the USHA had torn down more than 78,000 substandard buildings and built new homes for 200,000 families. This accomplishment met only a tiny portion of the need, but private building interests succeeded in stopping the program at this point.

The last major New Deal reform measure was the Fair Labor Standards Act of June 1938. The outcome of liberal agitation, this measure had failed to pass Congress on its first try. Finally, after Roosevelt gave it his open endorsement, it became law over the opposition of southern Democrats. The law included most industrial workers but, at the insistence of rural congressmen, omitted farm labor. It aimed to secure a minimum wage of forty cents an hour and a maximum work week of forty hours for those covered. Even these modest goals were to be reached gradually: Beginning at forty-four hours, the work week was to be lowered to forty hours in three years. Beginning at twenty-five cents an hour, the minimum wage was to be raised to forty cents after eight years. The law called for time-and-a-half pay for overtime. Many Americans were shocked to discover that over 750,000 workers were so poorly paid that they received immediate wage increases when the law went into effect in August 1938. At the same time, the hours of 1.5 million workers were shortened.

Farewell to Reform

Even before Congress unwillingly passed the Fair Labor Standards Act, a Democratic member had begged the White House not to send any more controversial legislation. Much of FDR's political difficulty came from the so-called Roosevelt recession of 1937, when no less than 4 million workers returned to the rolls of the unemployed.

The reversal appears to have happened partly because the administration, encouraged by the business advance, had called for reduced spending by the WPA and other New Deal agencies. The high taxes enacted in 1935 and 1936 seem to have cut private investment, and the accumulation of funds in the Treasury under the social security laws cut purchasing power.

The speed with which decreased government expenditures started the downward trend sug-

LEGACY OF THE DEPRESSION

For those who lived during the Great Depression, the memories of that event remained vivid. In Studs Terkel's *Hard Times,* Virginia Durr and Tom Sutton offered their assessments.

Virginia Durr

Oh, no, the Depression was not a romantic time. It was a time of terrible suffering. The contradictions were so obvious that it didn't take a very bright person to realize something was terribly wrong.

Have you ever seen a child with rickets? Shaking as with palsy. No proteins, no milk. And the companies pouring milk into gutters. People with nothing to wear, and they were plowing up cotton. People with nothing to eat, and they killed the pigs. If that wasn't the craziest system in the world, could you imagine anything more idiotic? This was just insane.

And people blamed themselves, not the system. They felt they had been at fault. . . . People who were independent, who thought they were masters and mistresses of their lives, were all of a sudden dependent on others. Relatives or relief. People of pride went into shock and sanitoriums. My mother was one.

Tom Sutton

Those who went through the Depression have a little more pride in their possessions, have a little more pride in the amount *of possessions they have. They know that it was a fortunate person in the Thirties who had as much as they have today. . . .*

I don't think we're basically a revolutionary country. We have too large a middle class. The middle class tends to be apathetic. An apathetic middle class gives stability to a system. They never get carried away strongly, one way or the other. Maybe we'll have riots, maybe we'll have shootings. Maybe we'll have uprisings as the farmers did in Iowa. But you won't have revolution.

Source: Studs Terkel, *Hard Times* (New York: Pantheon, 1970), pp. 531, 511–12.

---

gested that neither the administration nor private industry could maintain economic growth without large-scale public spending. Early in 1938, the president and Congress put the spending program back into high gear. The business revival was resumed, but at a slower pace. In the meantime, FDR attacked the "economic royalists," who, he said, were choking American opportunity. "Big Business collectivism in industry," he told Congress, "compels ultimate collectivism in government." He now launched the broadest trust-busting campaign since Taft. At his urging, Congress created the Temporary National Economic Committee and charged it with restudying the whole structure of American private enterprise.

These drastic steps seemed only to strengthen the growing dissatisfaction with the New Deal. Just before the congressional elections of 1938, Roosevelt took actions similar to his efforts to pack the Supreme Court. He attempted to purge the Democratic party of conservative southerners and others who were alienated by the growing prestige of labor in the New Deal. Again, he succeeded only in adding numbers to the discontented while purging almost no one. In the elections, the Democrats—northern and southern—kept their majority in both houses. But Republicans made large gains, raising their number in the House from 89 to 164 and in the Senate from 16 to 23.

The president acknowledged that the reform urge in the New Deal had lessened considerably. In his annual message to Congress in January 1939, he talked about the need "to invigorate the processes of recovery in order to *preserve* our reforms." Two years earlier, Harry Hopkins had concluded that America was "bored with the poor, the unemployed and the insecure." Recovery had not been achieved. It was not as though the "ill-housed," "ill-clad," and "ill-nourished" were any less visible. But the need to do something about them seemed less urgent, and the chances of getting more reform legislation were much poorer. By 1939, moreover, the crisis in Europe and Asia was occupying the president's time and energy and tended to overshadow domestic problems.

The New Deal: An Assessment

Although the New Deal commanded the loyalty of the great majority of Americans, as shown by election results, it was fought at every turn. Conservative critics pointed out invasions of individual liberty, the failure to balance the budget, the enormous increase in the national debt (from $22.5 billion in 1933 to almost $43 billion in 1940), and the growing federal bureaucracy (from 600,000 civilian employees in 1932 to more than a million in 1940).

At the same time, critics noted that the New Deal had failed to restore the confidence of the business community, which held the real key to recovery. Critics on the Left raised questions about the soundness of the economic system that was being restored and the refusal of the New Deal to undertake the massive national and social planning that would really redistribute income. In 1939, when all the experiments were over, more than 8.7 million workers remained unemployed, and millions more were poor.

New Dealers preferred to emphasize the rise in national income from $40.2 billion in 1933 to $72.8 billion in 1939. Furthermore, if unemployment were measured in terms of real human suffering and social waste, then it appeared to be less burdensome than a few years earlier. Whatever the methods by which reforms were achieved, farm prices did rise, enabling farmers to recover some lost purchasing power. Workers did gain from wage and hours legislation, and even more from protection of unionization and collective bargaining. The benefits of the New Deal may have gone mostly to the middle class, which had been given the means to preserve their savings and their homes.

The New Deal placed on the statute books a number of measures intended to make life more comfortable and secure, measures that would benefit millions yet to be born. To achieve such results, the federal government assumed a greater role in the lives of Americans—social security, minimum wages and hours, collective bargaining, improved housing for low-income families, and the insuring of bank deposits. By the end of the New Deal, only a few, even among Republicans, quarreled with this role.

When Roosevelt came into office in 1933, many Americans were flirting with thoughts of violence and doubts of democracy—political solutions of the extreme Right and the extreme Left. The New Deal restored their confidence in the ability of government to assume responsibility and to act. What the New Deal failed to restore was prosperity. Only with rearmament and World War II did the American people finally achieve economic recovery; the question of whether the New Deal alone could have solved the economic crisis was left unanswered. To win the war, the government embarked on ambitious spending programs and national mobilization, including a commitment to full employment. The eagerness with which all Americans accepted national planning for the purpose of waging war raised some troublesome questions that would persist long after the war had ended.

SUMMARY

The Great Depression, which began with the stock-market crash of Black Tuesday, October 29, 1929, had a lasting effect not only on the United States, but on the entire world. Americans were devastated. There were bread lines, people were homeless and starving, and there seemed to be no hope for the future. Franklin Delano Roosevelt's election and the Democratic landslide in 1932 brought the first attempt at a turnaround, but even the New Deal did not solve the problem.

The stock-market crash pointed up the flaws in the economy. The Hoover administration did not see these flaws until much too late, and used only inadequate measures to try to fix them. The Republicans still believed that federal intervention in the economy was to be avoided. FDR and his New Dealers thought the opposite: only massive federal programs, they held, could solve some of the most urgent problems.

Almost from the day of his inauguration in March 1933, FDR moved to rescue the banks, stabilize business and agriculture, reduce unemployment, and assist the victims of the crash. Most banks were closed when Roosevelt took office. Using the Emergency Banking Act, passed by a special session of Congress, the government got the sound banks back in business and the bad ones closed permanently within a month. More bank reform followed, along with laws providing for closer supervision of the stock market. The president was given authority to devalue the dollar.

Business recovery was attacked through the National Industrial Recovery Act, which set up the NRA, the first of the "alphabet" agencies of the New Deal. Agriculture was put under the AAA, the Agricultural Adjustment Administration. Laborers, sharecroppers, and farm tenants were helped by the RA, the Resettlement Administration. The federal government's first large-scale attempt at rural redevelopment was the TVA, the Tennessee Valley Authority. Unemployment was addressed by several agencies: the CCC (Civilian Conservation Corps), the PWA (Public Works Administration), and the WPA (Works Progress Administration). Thousands of roads, hospitals, bridges, schools, post offices, and other public facilities were built under their direction.

But all these efforts still did not break the back of the Depression. A new burst of reform was attempted in 1935, after the congressional elections of 1934. By this time, the administration had to contend with a variety of dissent movements, including those inspired by Huey Long in Louisiana, Dr. Townsend in California, and the "radio priest," Father Coughlin, in Detroit. Three reform laws were passed in August 1935: the Revenue Tax Act, designed to stop the growth of great personal fortunes; the Public Utility Holding Company Act, intended to stop manipulation and control of companies through the holding company device; and the Social Security Act, which for the first time set up the federal government as guarantor for Americans in economic trouble.

The National Labor Relations Act addressed the problems of the labor movement. It guaranteed collective bargaining and prohibited employer interference with organizing activities. It also set up the National Labor Relations Board, authorizing it to investigate and certify the proper bargaining representatives and to hold supervised elections if several unions wanted to organize a company. The effects were deep and lasting. Company unions were broken up, and nationwide membership in trade unions grew to 10.5 million by 1941. Also during this decade, organized labor split into two large organizations, the AFL and the CIO. The two remained separate until 1955, when they merged in the AFL–CIO.

The New Deal gave Americans a sense of direction and hope. Under FDR's leadership, the Democrats built a huge coalition that joined Americans of all classes and colors: the solidly Democratic South, the Democratic machines in northern cities, the new immigrant groups and blacks; organized labor; intellectuals; and many farmers and businessmen. Although the New Deal did nothing about the discriminatory poll tax or the lynching of blacks in the South, FDR convinced American blacks that he cared about them, and they responded.

In the election of 1936, despite fierce criticism and even the defection of Al Smith to the Republicans, FDR carried every state except two. This landslide made the Democrats the majority party of the country. But the problems remained. This time Roosevelt set out to pack the Supreme Court with his own people to make it more cooperative. The attempt failed, and cost FDR political support.

Yet the coalition held, and in Roosevelt's second term many new reforms were gained and old ones extended, particularly housing for the poor and a minimum wage. But the reform drive was slowing, and by 1939, with millions still unemployed, it was dead. By that time too, the crisis in Europe and Asia overshadowed all else.

TIME LINE

1929	Stock market crashes (October 29); Great Depression begins
1930	4 million unemployed
1931	8 million unemployed
1932	12 million unemployed Bonus March on Washington, D.C. Reconstruction Finance Corporation established Franklin Delano Roosevelt elected president
1933	13 million unemployed Federal Emergency Relief Administration (FERA) Bank crisis Glass-Steagall Act, creating Federal Deposit Insurance Corporation National Industrial Recovery Act (NIRA) Agricultural Adjustment Act (AAA) Tennessee Valley Authority (TVA) Civilian Conservation Corps (CCC) Civil Works Administration (CWA) Public Works Administration (PWA) Home Owners Loan Corporation (HOLC)
1934	Securities Exchange Act, creating Securities and Exchange Commission

	Federal Housing Administration (FHA)
1935	Works Progress Administration (WPA) Supreme Court finds NIRA unconstitutional Resettlement Administration Revenue Tax Act Public Utility Holding Act Social Security Act National Labor Relations (Wagner) Act Committee for Industrial Organization (CIO) formed Huey Long assassinated Harlem riot
1936	Supreme Court finds AAA unconstitutional Roosevelt re-elected
1937	Organizing strikes in auto and steel Farm Security Administration Roosevelt proposes "court-packing" plan, rejected Supreme Court upholds state minimum wage and NLRA Wagner-Steagall Housing Act
1938	Fair Labor Standards Act
1939	8.7 million unemployed

Suggested Readings

On the causes of the Great Depression, J. K. Galbraith, *The Great Crash* (1955), is brief and clear. The best biography of Hoover is D. Burner, *Herbert Hoover: A Public Life* (1978). A. U. Romasco, *The Poverty of Abundance* (1965), examines Hoover's policies and the Depression. On the Bonus Army, see R. Daniels, *The Bonus March* (1971).

The impact of the Depression is clearly conveyed in the interviews collected by S. Terkel for *Hard Times* (1970), several of which have been recorded in a two-record album, *Hard Times* (Caedmon TC2048). Equally compelling are the letters collected in R. S. McElvaine, *Down and Out in the Great Depression* (1983). In addition, anyone seeking to understand how people lived during the Depression should look at its rich photographic images, which may be found in H. O'Neal (ed.), *A Vision Shared: A Classic Portrait of America and Its People 1935–1943* (1976); R. E. Stryker and N. Wood, *In This Proud Land: America 1935–1943 as Seen in the FSA Photographs* (1973); F. J. Hurley, *Portrait of a Decade: Roy Stryker and the Development of Documentary Photography in the Thirties* (1972); D. Lange and P. S. Taylor, *An American Exodus* (1939); and W. Evans, *American Photographs* (1938) and *First and Last* (1978). Critical discussions of the photography may be found in W. Stott, *Documentary Expression and Thirties America* (1973) and C. Fleischauer and B. W. Brannan, *Documenting America, 1935–1943* (1989). Two of the finest social commentaries in American literature deal with the thirties: J. Agee and W. Evans, *Let Us Now Praise Famous Men* (1941, 1960), focusing on three tenant families, and T. Rosengarten, *All God's Dangers: The Life of Nate Shaw* (1974), the personal account of a black cotton farmer in Alabama. On the legacy of the people depicted in *Let Us Now Praise Famous Men,* see D. Maharidge and M. Williamson, *And Their Children After Them* (1989). The quality of life in the thirties is also illuminated in the Federal Writers' Project, *These Are Our Lives* (1939); T. E. Terrill and J. Hirsch, *Such as Us: Southern Voices of the Thirties* (1978); R. S. Lynd and H. M. Lynd, *Middletown in Transition* (1937); B. Sternsher (ed.), *Hitting Home: The Great Depression in Town and Country* (1970); and W. Guthrie, *Bound for Glory* (1943). The songs of the Depression may be heard in the New Lost City Ramblers, *Songs from the Depression* (Folkways 5264); Woody Guthrie, *Talking Dust Bowl* (Folkways 2011); and two sets of Library of Congress recordings, *Woody Guthrie* (Elektra 271/272) and *Leadbelly* (Elektra 301/302).

Two popular works that assess the impact of the Depression are C. Bird, *The Invisible Scar* (1966), and E. R. Ellis, *A Nation in Torment* (1970). The best introduction to the New Deal is W. E. Leuchtenburg, *Franklin D. Roosevelt and the New Deal* (1963). See also P. Conkin, *The New Deal* (1967); A. M. Schlesinger, Jr., *The Coming of the New Deal* (1959) and *The Politics of Upheaval* (1960); R. H. Pells, *Radical Visions and American Dreams* (1973); R. S. McElvaine, *The Great Depression* (1984); S. Fraser and G. Gerstle (eds.), *The Rise and Fall of the New Deal Order, 1930–1980* (1989); and two anthologies, H. Zinn (ed.), *New Deal Thought* (1966), and H. Swados (ed.), *The American Writer and the Great Depression* (1966). On FDR, see F. Freidel, *Franklin Delano Roosevelt* (4 vols., 1952–76); J. M. Burns, *Roosevelt: The Lion and the Fox* (1956); and R. Hofstadter, "Franklin D. Roosevelt: The Patrician as Opportunist," in *The American Political Tradition* (1948).

The best "inside" narratives include R. G. Tugwell, *The Democratic Roosevelt* (1957), *The Brain Trust* (1968), and *In Search of Roosevelt* (1972); F. Perkins, *The Roosevelt I Knew* (1946); R. Moley, *After Seven Years* (1939); R. E. Sherwood, *Roosevelt and Hopkins* (1948); D. E. Lilienthal, *Journals: The TVA Years 1939–1945* (1964); J. M. Blum, *From the Morgenthau Diaries: Years of Crisis 1928–1938* (1959) and *Years of Urgency 1938–1941* (1964); and H. L. Ickes, *The Secret Diary of Harold Ickes* (3 vols., 1953–54). Eleanor Roosevelt, *This I Remember* (1949), is a valuable personal account.

Two important New Dealers are examined in G. McJimsey, *Harry Hopkins: Ally of the Poor and Defender of Democracy* (1989), and J. A. Schwarz, *Liberal: Adolf A. Berle and the Vision of an American Era* (1989). On FDR and the business community, see A. U. Romasco, *The Politics of Recovery* (1983). On the AAA and farm policy, see V. L. Perkins, *Crisis in Agriculture* (1969) and R. S. Kirkendall, *Social Scientists and Farm Politics in the Age of Roosevelt* (1966). J. L. Shover, *Cornbelt Rebellion: The Farmers' Holiday Association* (1965), and D. E. Conrad, *The Forgotten Farmers: The Story of Sharecroppers in the New Deal* (1965), are both valuable accounts, as is S. Baldwin, *Poverty and Politics: The Rise and Decline of the Farm Security Administration* (1968). C. McWilliams has written the classic account of migratory farm labor: *Factories in the Field* (1939). J. N. Gregory, *American Exodus: The Dust Bowl Migration and Okie Culture in California* (1989) is a vivid and authoritative exploration of the Oklahomans, Arkansans, Texans, and Missourians who sought out the reputed land of opportunity. On the changing rural South and its people, see P. Daniel, *Breaking the Land* (1985); J. T. Kirby, *Rural Worlds Lost: The American South 1920–1960* (1987); and W. Flynt, *Poor But Proud: Alabama's Poor Whites* (1989).

On the WPA and the arts, see W. T. MacDonald, *Federal Relief Administration and the Arts* (1969); F. V. O'Connor, *Art for the Millions* (1973); and R. D. McKinzie, *The New Deal for Artists* (1973). On the Federal Theatre Project, H. Flannagan, *Arena* (1949), a memoir, may be supplemented by J. D. Matthews, *The Federal Theatre 1935–1939* (1967), a scholarly account. On the Federal Writers' Project, see J. Mangione, *The Dream and the Deal* (1972).

Labor under the New Deal is examined in I. Bernstein, *Turbulent Years* (1970); S. Fine, *Sitdown: The General Motors Strike of 1936–1937* (1969) and B. Nelson, *Workers on the Waterfront: Seamen, Longshoremen, and Unionism in the 1930s* (1989). See also E. Levinson's vividly told *Labor on the March* (1938). On the CIO, see M. Dubofsky and W. Van Tine, *John L. Lewis* (1977). On black workers, see H. R. Cayton and G. S. Mitchell, *Black Workers and the New Unions* (1939), and W. H. Harris, *Keeping the Faith: A. Philip Randolph, Milton P. Webster, and the Brotherhood of Sleeping Car Porters 1925–1937* (1977).

B. Mitchell, *Depression Decade* (1947), is a solid economic history. On economic planning, social programs, and the New Deal, see R. Lubove, *The Struggle for Social Security* (1968); P. Conkin, *Tomorrow a New World* (1959); E. W. Hawley, *The New Deal and the Problem of Monopoly* (1966); and O. L. Graham, Jr., *Toward a Planned Society: From Roosevelt to Nixon* (1976).

N. J. Weiss, *Farewell to the Party of Lincoln* (1983), examines black politics during the 1930s. On blacks in the New Deal, consult H. Sitkoff, *A New Deal for Blacks* (1981). See also R. Bunche, *The Political Status of the Negro in the Age of FDR* (1973); R. Wolters, *Negroes and the Great Depression* (1970); and H. Cruse, *The Crisis of the Negro Intellectual* (1967). On urban whites in the Roosevelt coalition, see J. J. Huthmacher, *Senator Robert Wagner and the Rise of Urban Liberalism* (1968), and an engrossing study of the mayor of New York, T. Kessner, *Fiorello H. La Guardia and the Making of Modern New York* (1989). On the old Progressives and the New Deal, see O. L. Graham, Jr., *An Encore for Reform* (1967).

The challenge to the New Deal is best examined in A. Brinkley, *Voices of Protest: Huey Long, Father Coughlin, and the Great Depression* (1982). See also T. H. Williams, *Huey Long* (1969). I. Howe and L. Coser, *The American Communist Party* (1957), and L. De Caux, *Labor Radical* (1970), discuss the radical Left. For the memoir of a black radical, see N. I. Painter, *The Narrative of Hosea Hudson: His Life as a Negro Communist in the South* (1979). For a study of race relations and the Left, see D. T. Carter, *Scottsboro: A Tragedy of the American South* (1969) and M. Naison, *Communists in Harlem During the Depression* (1983). On student activism, see J. Wechsler, *Revolt on the Campus* (1935). On the challenge from the Right, see J. T. Patterson, *Congressional Conservatism and the New Deal 1933–1939* (1967), and G. Wolfskill, *The Revolt of the Conservatives: A History of the American Liberty League 1934–1940* (1962).

CHAPTER 29

THE AGE OF VIOLENCE: WORLD WAR II

Already shaken by the experience of the Great Depression, most Americans in the 1930s refused to believe that the United States might become involved in another world war. But the news from abroad was ominous. The English writer W. H. Auden called this decade the age of anxiety. The enthusiasm with which the embittered and depressed German people rallied around Adolf Hitler's pledge to redeem their pride, race, and economy was but one example. So was Mussolini's war on the Ethiopians, Stalin's purges of Communist officials, Japan's aggression in Manchuria and China, and the civil war in Spain. All these events fed and reinforced the insecurity the deepening worldwide depression had helped set in motion.

When Americans began to understand the events unfolding in Europe and Asia, they felt almost unanimous that the United States should avoid any involvement in another war. The poor reputation of American business leaders during the Depression fed the belief that international bankers and munitions makers had conspired to draw the United States into World War I. Public opinion polls in 1937 showed that 70 percent of the American people thought it had been a mistake for

the United States to enter World War I; 95 percent thought the United States should stay out if another war developed in Europe.

But the desire to avoid involvement was not the same thing as indifference. Nazi Germany's aggressiveness and inhumanity troubled Americans. Although as late as 1939 popular polls showed 90 percent of Americans still opposed to involvement in the European war, 80 percent expressed sympathy for the Allies—Great Britain and France. Sensing this divided mood, FDR tried to balance the nation's desire to stay out of the war against the growing fear of Nazi Germany and the wish to help the Allies defeat Germany.

Hitler's invasion of Poland in September 1939 set off a new general war. The distress of America's old allies, as well as the continuing struggle for supremacy in the Pacific, encouraged Japan to strike at the United States. What confronted Americans after the attack on Pearl Harbor, December 7, 1941, was quite simply the preservation of a way of life. In a series of articles on "What I Am Fighting For," which appeared in the popular *Saturday Evening Post,* the theme was clear enough: "I am fighting for that big house with the bright green roof and the big front lawn." The United States fought because it had been attacked, not to make the world safe for democracy. Recognizing such feelings, Roosevelt called World War II the War for Survival and indulged in far less speculation about the postwar world than had Wilson.

In that war some 45 million people did not survive at all: among them were 20 million Russians, 6 million Jews, 4.2 million Germans, 2.2 million Chinese, 1.4 million Japanese, and 405,000 Americans. Methods of mass annihilation were brought to new levels of scientific efficiency. Of the 344,000 people who lived in Hiroshima, Japan, nearly 100,000 died as a result of the atomic bomb. On the night of February 13, 1945, and into the next day, at least 135,000 died in Dresden, Germany, after an Allied saturation bombing.

What happened in the Nazi extermination camps, where 6 million Jews died, had even more fearful implications. Drawing on its much-revered traditions in science, medicine, and engineering, Germany demonstrated to humankind unprecedented techniques of extermination as well as bestial cruelty based on race and nationality. The Germans employed assembly-line efficiency in carrying out the executions, and the men and women—the technicians, engineers, and physicians— who acted as executioners and engaged in grisly experiments with human life looked upon themselves as perfectly normal human beings. Of all the literature that came out of World War II, few documents could approach the poignancy of a letter written by a child in a Nazi death camp in Poland. It said all that needed to be said about this costliest war in history: "Now I must say goodbye. Tomorrow mother goes into the gas chamber, and I will be thrown into the well."

It was a time of extraordinary violence and brutality. While the casualties soared, the technology of extermination became even more sophisticated. With the dropping of the atomic bombs on Hiroshima and Nagasaki, World War II came to a close and the Atomic Age dawned. A world in upheaval found itself gripped by new tensions and anxieties.

BETWEEN THE WARS: 1920–1937

Having rejected membership in the League of Nations, the United States went its own way in international affairs. For Americans, the wisdom of this course was reinforced by the failure of the Allies to make good on their enormous war debts to the United States, and the uneasy peace in Europe. The United States made a few gestures toward international cooperation, such as joining the other world powers in naval disarmament and in vague agreements to renounce war and respect national interests. At the same time, it actively pursued its economic goals abroad, especially in Latin America and Asia, and contributed to the tariff war. And it remained alert to any international developments that posed a threat to national and economic security.

The sources of international conflict after World War I increased as the worldwide depression deepened. The economic crisis became so severe that many peoples supported totalitarian movements that promised a solution to their insecurities. Benito Mussolini in Italy and Adolf Hitler in Germany came to power at the head of two such movements; they replaced democratic forms with police states and adopted militant and expansionist foreign policies. In Asia, Japan emerged as the dominant power after World War I. The Japanese took formerly German islands in the Pacific, kept troops in Siberia, cast an eye on the raw materials of Southeast Asia, and tried to shut the Open Door in China.

In the thirties, the United States often tried to interest European nations in collective action that would restrain Japan's ambitions. At the same time, the United States remained outside Europe's system of collective security. Both policies failed. Weakened by American isolation, European collective security collapsed in the face of Nazi aggression. With the Europeans in trouble at home, American efforts to involve them in the Far East were doomed.

Disarmament and Stability: The Washington Conference, 1921–1922

To show that it had not abandoned its role as a great power, the United States took the lead after

World War I to stop the naval race and to impose some kind of stability on the Far East. President Harding invited Britain, Japan, France, Italy, and China to meet with the United States in Washington beginning on Armistice Day, November 11, 1921.

Secretary of State Charles Evans Hughes presided over the conference. He electrified the delegates with a proposal for a ten-year suspension of construction of capital ships—battleships and cruisers. He also proposed that the capital-ship tonnage of the United States and Britain be limited to 500,000 and that of Japan to 300,000. This was in keeping with the existing power ratio of 5:5:3 among the three countries. But it also meant that Britain and Japan would have to get rid of no less than sixty-six ships, and the United States thirty ships. The conference ended in February 1922 with a five-power naval treaty that endorsed the 5-5-3 ratio almost at Hughes's tonnage figures. France and Italy were permitted capital-ship tonnage of 175,000. Although smaller ships were not covered by the agreement, the naval race was at least partially stopped.

Two other important agreements made at the Washington meeting were the so-called Four-Power Pact and the Nine-Power Pact. The first replaced an Anglo-Japanese alliance with a new agreement including the United States and France as well as England and Japan. Those four powers pledged to keep the peace in the Pacific. In the second agreement, China, Italy, Belgium, the Netherlands, and Portugal joined the other four. They reaffirmed the Open Door in China and guaranteed that nation's sovereignty, independence, and territorial integrity. But these treaties contained no real enforcement mechanism and said nothing about land and air forces or economic barriers to trade.

The Washington Conference was welcomed in most of the world as a triumph of diplomacy. When it was followed in 1928 by the Kellogg-Briand Pact, which renounced war as an instrument of national policy (sixty-two nations signed), a fragile international world seemed safer. Japan, however, was simply marking time.

Japan in China

Having shattered the myth of the invincibility of the white man by its triumph over Russia in 1904–1905, Japan came out of World War I with renewed strength, determined to compete with the Western powers for economic advantages in Asia. If Japan came to believe that its destiny was a unified Asia under Japanese control, it was only asserting imperial ambitions that Great Britain, France, Germany, and the United States, among others, had asserted more than once in Africa, Asia, and Latin America. Japan's ambitions reflected its need for sources of raw materials to sustain its rapid industrialization and modernization. The Great Depression would make quite clear its economic vulnerability.

Since 1905, Japan had enjoyed special privileges in southern Manchuria, in the northeastern part of China. In the 1920s, Chinese Nationalists under Chiang Kai-shek, intent on uniting the country and ridding it of foreign powers, threatened the Japanese in Manchuria; Japan chose to strike back. In September 1931, using as an excuse an incident on the Japanese-controlled Manchurian Railway, Japanese forces moved into Manchuria. The United States and the League of Nations promptly reminded Japan of its treaty responsibilities. But by January 1932 the Japanese army had crushed all resistance in Manchuria and turned it into a puppet state.

When it became clear that reminders would have no effect, Western diplomats raised the possibility of economic sanctions. Secretary of State Henry L. Stimson suggested this option to President Hoover. But feeling that sanctions might lead the United States into war, the president opposed them. His decision, and the reluctance of the league powers to go beyond it, limited Western action to moral pressure. This Japan felt free to ignore. On January 7, 1932, Secretary Stimson stated in a note to Japan and China that the United States could not recognize any treaty or agreement in Asia that infringed on China's rights or violated its territorial integrity. This policy of refusing to recognize territorial changes achieved by force of arms became known as the Stimson Doctrine.

The situation deteriorated after January 28, 1932, when Japan invaded Shanghai, wiped out the Chinese force there, and killed civilians. For the first time, militant sentiment against Japan appeared in the United States, but President Hoover continued to oppose even economic pressure. Secretary Stimson decided to issue a message to the world through a letter to the chairman of the Senate Committee on Foreign Relations. In it, Stimson asserted that the United States would stand on its treaty rights in the Far East, especially those recognized in the Nine-Power Pact, and invited other nations to do the same. He warned that violation of one of the Washington treaties released the parties from the other treaties. The move was greeted with strong approval in the American press, but it had little effect on Japan.

The League of Nations condemned the Japanese aggression and refused to recognize the puppet regime in Manchuria. In March 1933, Japan responded by withdrawing from the league. Less than two years later, it renounced the Washington Conference naval agreement. In 1936 the United States and Britain refused to grant Japan naval equality with themselves, prompting it to begin an expansion program they felt they had to match. The more Japan viewed its interests as endangered by the refusal of the United States to recognize its conquests and ambitions, the closer it came to taking the chance of war.

The Soviet Union

Fear of Japan on the Asian mainland and of Hitler in Germany made the Soviet Union anxious to establish relations with the United States. All other major powers, including Japan, had long since recognized the Soviet government. The United States had equally strong reasons to extend recognition. Mutual concern over Japanese intentions in Asia might have been sufficient justification. With the Great Depression, the pressure mounted. The prospect of trade with the Soviet Union attracted American businessmen, especially those in the machine-tool and agricultural-implement industries. At the same time, there was growing interest among American intellectuals and writers in the Communist experiment.

Formal relations between the United States and the Soviet Union were set up by an exchange of notes in Washington on November 16, 1933. Maxim Litvinov, Stalin's emissary, gave up Soviet damage claims against the United States for its actions during the 1918–1919 intervention (see Chapter 26). Litvinov in turn agreed to negotiate the claims of American and European creditors for the debts of czarist Russia. He also agreed to stop Soviet propaganda in the United States and to remove Soviet government influence from any organizations in the United States heretofore "under its direct or indirect control."

Trade relations did not really grow, but recognition gave the United States an official observation post in Moscow. Mutual suspicion persisted. It was aggravated in the Soviet Union by memories of the postwar intervention and in the United States by negotiations over debts and continued Communist activity in the Western Hemisphere.

Latin America

Despite the pretense of isolationism in American foreign affairs after World War I, the United States pursued an active policy in Latin America. Strategic, diplomatic, and economic considerations led the United States to interfere in the governments of no less than ten countries. If any justification was necessary, the Roosevelt Corollary to the Monroe Doctrine (see Chapter 24) was enough.

Often American armed forces became involved—in Panama in 1921, in the Dominican Republic from 1921 to 1924, and in Honduras in 1923. United States Marines had been in Nicaragua since 1912. When they were withdrawn in 1925, Nicaragua again became so unstable that Coolidge almost immediately sent them back. This time they encountered a guerrilla force raised by Augusto Cesar Sandino, a Nicaraguan nationalist. His success in eluding the marines frustrated both the occupation forces and the United States government. "Until now," a State Department official wrote in 1927, "Central America has always understood the governments which we recognize stay in power, while those which we do not recognize and support fall. Nicaragua has become a test case. It is difficult to see how we can afford to be defeated." But Sandino persisted until mounting marine casualties and the cost of maintaining the intervention exceeded the willingness of Congress to support the undeclared war. Congress cut off appropriations for further troop deployment to Nicaragua, and in 1933 United States troops were withdrawn. But they left behind the Nicaraguan National Guard, organized, trained, and armed by the United States. In 1934, after emerging from the hills to back the new civilian government, Sandino was ambushed and killed. The head of the National Guard, Anastasio Somoza, soon assumed dictatorial rule and remained in power for the next forty-five years, using the guard as his army. (It was Somoza of whom President Franklin Delano Roosevelt said, "He may be a son of a bitch, but he's our son of a bitch.")

Protection of private economic interests influenced United States policy in Mexico. The Mexican Constitution of 1917 had reaffirmed the old Mexican principle, violated during the long Diaz regime (1877–1911), that the government retained ownership of all Mexican mineral and oil resources. American businessmen, encouraged by Diaz, had invested heavily in Mexican development. Now they feared confiscation of their properties. When President Plutarco Calles took office in 1924, he announced his desire to make just such a change. The Mexican Congress then provided that petroleum rights acquired in 1917 would be limited to fifty years.

The pressure of American oil interests and the influence of American Catholics, who resented Calles's anticlerical policy, together with the policy of intervention in Latin America, soon brought talk of a new war with Mexico. But in 1927 President Coolidge sent Dwight L. Morrow to Mexico with this instruction: "Keep us out of war." Morrow worked out a compromise by which American investors could retain permanently the oil properties they had held before the Constitution of 1917. Confiscation under the Cárdenas regime in 1938 infuriated American oil companies, brought charges of Communist influence, and revived talk of intervention. The matter was negotiated, but not until one Mexican newspaper had said: "Poor Mexico. So far from God, and so close to the United States." Under the settlement reached in 1941, the Mexican government bought out American oil properties and other claims.

In March 1933, in his first inaugural address, Franklin Delano Roosevelt said he hoped "to dedicate this nation to the policy of the good neighbor." His intentions were soon tested in Cuba, where in August 1933 the regime of Gerardo Machado was overthrown, perhaps with a push from Roosevelt's ambassador, Sumner Welles. The new government of Ramón Grau San Martín, however, was far too reformist to please Cuban business interests, including the substantial American business community. On the advice of Ambassador Welles, the president withheld recognition. With the encouragement of the United States, Martín's military backers, led by Sergeant Fulgencio Batista, conducted an election in January 1934. It brought the United States–backed candidate, the first in a string of Batista puppets, to the presidency. Roosevelt quickly recognized the new government.

As a gesture of good will, the United States negotiated a treaty with Cuba in May 1934 in which it gave up its right of intervention under the Platt Amendment. But it seemed clear that the United States reserved the right to impose order on the island if American economic interests or citizens were in any danger. And in keeping the naval base at Guantánamo, the United States, as the New York Times noted, gave "a clear indication that Cuba is embraced within the plans of the United States for national defense."

To improve the image of the United States in Latin America, Secretary of State Cordell Hull attended the Montevideo Conference of American States in 1933 and agreed to a proposal that "no state has the right to intervene in the internal or external affairs of another." Hull also announced a new plan to reduce tariffs through reciprocal trade agreements, further pleasing the delegates. In the spirit of the Montevideo agreement, United States representatives signed a treaty with Panama in March 1936 surrendering American rights to interfere in that nation's affairs and raising the annual payments for the canal. Not until 1939, however, when Panama agreed to permit the United States to defend the canal in emergencies, did the Senate approve the treaty.

Despite the deep resentment of Latin Americans toward Yankee imperialism, relations were sufficiently improved by the time of the attack on Pearl Harbor for the United States to be assured of cooperation in the hemisphere. But American economic domination persisted, setting the stage for more conflict after World War II.

Neutrality and Aggression

The need to do something in Latin America was made more urgent by the rapid decline in sympathy and understanding between America and Europe. American immigration and protectionist policies in the twenties shut out European peoples and European goods. The arguments over Allied war debts, which the United States refused to cancel and European nations neglected to pay, reflected the breakdown in mutual respect. Nor had the United States relaxed its opposition to membership in the League of Nations. Before his nomination for the presidency, even FDR allowed himself to be pressured into attacking the league.

The desire to keep out of alliances and military confrontations became stronger in the mid-thirties. The sensational "merchants of death" investigation of 1934 conducted by a Senate committee gave weight to the view that wars were fought for the benefit of international bankers and munitions makers. The best way to stay out of war was to make it unprofitable under the law for citizens to trade with belligerents.

The first test of this policy came in mid-1935 when the fascist dictator Benito Mussolini made it clear that Italy intended to annex Ethiopia. By the time the Italians had launched a full-scale attack in October 1935, Congress had passed the first of a series of Neutrality Acts authorizing the president, after proclaiming that a state of war existed between foreign nations, to forbid Americans to sell or ship munitions to them. Basic war materials such as oil, steel, and copper were not included in the ban. Under administration pressure, Congress put a six-month limit on this embargo, which Roosevelt then reluctantly signed. The arms embargo, he said later, by penalizing unprepared victims while leaving untouched those who had built up massive military machines, "played right into the hands of the aggressor nations," which "were actually encouraged by our laws to make war upon their neighbors." (In February 1936, Congress extended the Neutrality Act to May 1, 1937, and added to the ban loans and credits to belligerents.

After his triumph in Ethiopia, Mussolini embarked on other adventures. In July 1936, when Spanish fascists under General Francisco Franco rebelled against their country's republican gov-

ernment, Mussolini promptly sent 50,000 to 75,000 "volunteers," along with planes and supplies. Not to be outdone, Hitler also sent help.

Opinion in the United States was deeply divided over the Spanish war. Many Americans sided with the government, which the United States had long recognized. Some even went to Spain to fight for it. Soviet support of the government, however, lent weight to the fascist charge that it was Communists they were opposing. It also made it easier for American fascist sympathizers and Catholic supporters of Franco's uprising to get a joint resolution from Congress forbidding the export of munitions to either side (January 6, 1937). Naturally this action hurt the government more than the fascists, who were receiving much foreign assistance.

In May Congress adopted a new measure authorizing the president to decide not only when wars between nations existed, but also when civil wars such as that in Spain endangered world peace. In such situations, an embargo was to begin at once on the export of munitions and on credits for them. A cash-and-carry plan, limited to

Adolf Hitler: "Today there must remain no vestige of doubt—it is not a Führer or a man who speaks, but the whole German people!" *(Brown Brothers)*

CHAPTER 29 THE AGE OF VIOLENCE: WORLD WAR II

two years, empowered the president to require belligerents buying *nonmilitary* goods in this country to take them away in their own ships. The act also made it unlawful for Americans to travel on vessels of belligerents.

In March 1939, after an exhausting war, Franco's forces won. General Franco was under heavy obligation to Mussolini and Hitler. He managed to outlive both of them, and his anticommunism would win him new friends in the post–World War II era.

THE ROAD TO WAR

After Japanese and Chinese forces clashed near Peking in July 1937, the Japanese overran North China. Roosevelt attacked this aggression in his famous quarantine speech of October 5, 1937.

Ninety percent of the people of the world wanted peace, he said, but their security was threatened by the other 10 percent. Peace-loving nations must act together to quarantine aggressors; otherwise the disease would spread uncontrolled:

There is a solidarity, an interdependence about the modern world, both technically and morally, which makes it impossible for any nation completely to isolate itself from economic and political upheavals in the rest of the world, especially when such upheavals appear to be spreading and not declining. . . . We are determined to keep clear of war. . . . We are adopting such measures as will minimize our risk of involvement, but we cannot have complete protection in a world of disorder in which confidence and security have broken down.

The president gave no indication of what kind of collective action he had in mind. The response to the speech was so mixed in the United States that Roosevelt remarked to one of his close

The European theater, 1939–1942.

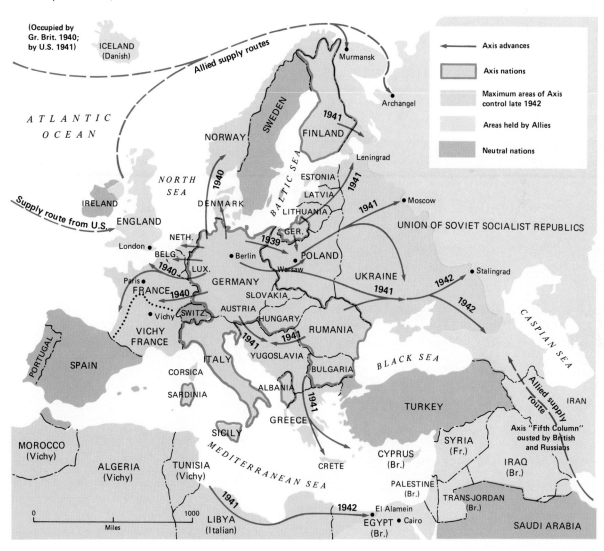

advisers, "It's a terrible thing to look over your shoulder when you are trying to lead—and to find no one there."

The Crisis in Europe

Although he took no action against Japan, Roosevelt got a billion dollars from Congress in May 1938 to enlarge the navy. Within the year, aggression in Europe brought on a crisis there. Hitler had come to power in Germany in January 1933. Fifteen months later he renounced the Versailles Treaty's terms on German disarmament. In March 1936, while Mussolini's invasion of Ethiopia held the attention of western Europe, German forces occupied the Rhineland. Hitler had long been campaigning for the return of German territory lost in World War I. Now, in September 1938, he was poised to grab the Sudetenland of Czechoslovakia.

France, along with Great Britain, remained unprepared to confront a rearmed Germany. At a disastrous meeting in Munich on September 29,

1938, they let Hitler have what he wanted. The world had gained "peace with honor . . . peace in our time," British prime minister Neville Chamberlain subsequently told his people. But his words carried little conviction.

Having gained the Sudetenland, Hitler promised to leave the rest of Czechoslovakia alone. But in March 1939 he swallowed up the remainder of the small republic. Not to be outdone, Mussolini took Albania three weeks later. Hitler's word obviously was worthless. Yet the world applauded FDR when he wrote to Hitler and Mussolini in April 1939 asking them to pledge not to attack any one of a list of thirty-one nations for a period of ten years.

Hitler replied for both by suggesting that the danger existed only in Roosevelt's mind. The reality was brought closer in May 1939, when a stubborn group of Senate isolationists blocked an administration request for revisions of the neutrality laws that would permit economic aid to Britain and France in case of war.

Apparently safe on his western front, Hitler shocked the world by making a nonaggression

In August 1940 Congress enacted the first peacetime conscription in American history, and on October 29 the first draft numbers were drawn. Within two weeks, these draftees (on their way to Fort Dix, New Jersey) and others were drilling in camps all over the country. *(UPI/Bettmann Newsphotos)*

pact in August with the Soviet Union on his eastern front. For their part, the Soviets could now strengthen their western frontier. Meanwhile, Hitler was free to attack Poland. He had demanded that Poland return territory lost by Germany at Versailles, but Poland resisted, encouraged by France and Britain. On September 1, 1939, Hitler's troops invaded Poland while his air force bombed Polish cities.

Two days later, Britain and France honored their commitments to Poland by declaring war on Germany. As the law still required, Roosevelt invoked the Neutrality Act. But he did not repeat Woodrow Wilson's appeal for neutrality in thought as well as in deed. "Even a neutral," said Roosevelt, "cannot be asked to close his mind or his conscience."

Before Munich, public opinion polls showed only a third of the American people in favor of selling arms to Britain and France in case of war. By mid-September 1939, when Roosevelt called a special session of Congress to revise the neutrality laws, and specifically to repeal the arms embargo so that munitions could be sold to the old Allies, he appeared to have the support of at least two-thirds of the people. In his message to Congress, Roosevelt also asked for authority to prevent American ships from sailing into danger zones. Belligerents would have to carry their own cargoes. All these requests were voted by Congress on November 3, 1939. Lifting the arms embargo pleased the interventionists; restoration of cash-and-carry pleased the isolationists.

In September 1940, with the support of big-business opponents of the New Deal, the America First Committee was formed. Robert E. Wood, board chairman of Sears, Roebuck, was national chairman. The committee drew many well-known people before being dissolved when Pearl Harbor was attacked. Charles A. Lindbergh, Jr., who had thrilled Americans in 1927 with his solo flight from New York to Paris, expressed the sentiments of the committee when he declared: "In the future we may have to deal with a Europe dominated by Germany. . . . An agreement between us could maintain peace and civilization throughout the world as far into the future as we can see."

Interventionists found their voice in the Committee to Defend America by Aiding the Allies. The chairman was William Allen White, a Kansas editor and Republican. White replied to Lindbergh that many countries, trying to be neutral, had been destroyed: "Hitler's whole philosophy, his idea of government, his economic setup, his insatiable ambitions, all make it impossible for a free country and a free people to live beside Hitler's world enslaved."

The mood in America remained sharply divided. One month after the Nazi invasion of Poland, polls revealed that 62 percent of the American people favored aiding the Allies short of war. Less than 30 percent wanted the United States to enter the war if it seemed the Allies would be defeated. On college campuses, students demonstrated on Armistice Day 1939 to express their desire for peace and disarmament. And the president himself insisted, "I hope the United States will keep out. . . . Every effort of your government will be directed toward that end."

Aid Short of War

When Hitler delayed moving on the Western Front, many even in Europe were lulled by the "phony war." But when Hitler did move in April 1940, he did so with terrifying speed and force. Neutral Denmark, Norway, and the Low Countries—Belgium, Holland, and Luxembourg—and France itself were all defeated in seven weeks. When Belgium fell, Britain had to use every resource to rescue its own army from the Continent. Between May 28 and June 4 every available boat, including small pleasure craft piloted by their owners, evacuated the last of more than 335,000 men from Dunkirk, France, under the pounding of German planes and guns. On June 10, Mussolini attacked France from the south. On June 22, a crushed France signed an armistice.

The British now stood alone against the Berlin-Rome Axis. During the summer and fall of 1940, in a tremendous effort to bring Britain to its knees, Hitler sent clouds of planes to bomb English cities. Tens of thousands of civilians were killed and wounded. But the Royal Air Force fought back with extraordinary courage, and by autumn it was clear that Hitler's attempt would fail. If Britain was to be conquered, it must be by invasion. Winston Churchill, at the time of Dunkirk, had promised to resist "whatever the cost may be . . . until, in God's good time, the New World, with all its power and might, steps forth to the rescue and liberation of the Old."

Two months after the fall of France, Roosevelt talked with a close adviser on the situation in which he found himself. "Bill," FDR remarked, "if my neighbor's house catches fire and I know that fire will spread to my house unless it is put out, and I am watering the grass in my back yard, and

I don't pass my garden hose over the fence to my neighbor, I am a fool. How do you think the country and the Congress would react if I should put aid to the British in the form of lending them my garden hose?"

Even as Roosevelt pledged to keep the nation out of war, he strengthened American defenses and took steps to assist Britain. Throughout the summer of 1940, aid was being rushed overseas. Military equipment that could not be legally transferred directly from government to government was sold to private firms, which resold it to Britain.

On September 3, Roosevelt took his most daring step. By executive agreement, he made the famous deal transferring fifty old but still useful destroyers that Britain needed to keep off German submarines. In exchange, Britain gave the United States sites for naval bases in Newfoundland and Bermuda and rent-free leases on other sites in the Caribbean and South Atlantic. Although outraged by this trade, Hitler did nothing to push the United States to join the Allies. Even so, Congress passed the first peacetime draft in American history and appropriated about $16 billion for airplanes, warships, and other defense needs.

The climax of the debate came at about the same time as the presidential election of 1940. The Democrats broke the two-term tradition and renominated FDR, naming Secretary of Agriculture Wallace as his running mate. Republicans leaned toward Senator Robert A. Taft of Ohio and the young district attorney of New York, Thomas E. Dewey. But the bright young men in the party rallied behind a newcomer to politics, Wendell L. Willkie of Indiana, and put him across on the sixth ballot.

A public-utilities executive, Willkie had been a leader of the private power interests that fought the TVA. His charm grew with his liberalism. By 1940 his stand on the war in Europe was close to Roosevelt's. This left him with a popular position, but without an issue on which to set himself off from his opponent. Willkie lost by a popular vote of 22,321,018 to 27,307,819 and an electoral vote of 82 to 449. But he restored the Republican party to a strong position without accepting the views of its isolationist wing—an outstanding personal success.

Roosevelt renewed the debate over foreign policy in a fireside chat to the people on December 29, 1940: "There will be no 'bottlenecks' in our determination to aid Great Britain," he said; "all our present efforts are not enough. . . . We must be the great arsenal of democracy." One week later, the president took steps to fulfill that role.

The cash-and-carry system worked only as long as the British had the cash, and Churchill had warned Roosevelt that Britain's financial resources were nearly exhausted. On January 6, 1941, in his annual message to Congress, Roosevelt came up with a clever solution. He proposed *lend-lease* as the most practical means by which the United States, remaining at peace itself, could help arm Britain and its allies. The lend-lease bill, which would supply Britain and its allies with arms, to be carried in their own ships and returned or replaced when the war ended, was fiercely opposed in Congress. Senator Burton K. Wheeler of Montana called it the "New Deal's 'triple A' foreign policy—to plow under every fourth American boy." But public opinion favored lend-lease, and Congress approved it.

Lend-lease had an effect on British finances and morale even before the flow of material began. It also made American intervention seem definite. Admiral Harold R. Stark, United States chief of naval operations, promptly wrote his fleet commanders: "The question as to our entry into the war now seems to be *when*, and not *whether*."

To ensure that lend-lease ended up at its destination and not at the bottom of the sea, Roosevelt took steps to help Britain fight the packs of German submarines in the Atlantic. He soon extended American "defense" lines all the way to Greenland and Iceland. On March 31, 1941, he made a more aggressive move, ordering the Coast Guard to seize German or German-controlled ships in American ports. On May 15, a German torpedo sank the American merchant ship *Robin Moor* in the South Atlantic. Roosevelt responded by proclaiming an unlimited national emergency. On June 16, he requested Germany and Italy to close their consulates in the United States.

Thereafter the United States moved steadily closer to war in the Atlantic. In July the president announced that the United States, by agreement with the Icelandic government, was taking over the defense of Iceland for the duration of the war, and that the navy would keep convoy lines open as far as that island.

In August he met with Churchill on a British battleship at sea. The two leaders drew up the eight-point Atlantic Charter, in which they proclaimed "certain common principles" that would ensure "a better future for the world": (1) no territorial aggrandizement; (2) self-government for all peoples; (3) free access to trade and raw materials; and (4) the abandonment of war as an instrument in international relations.

The Atlantic Charter goals were very much like Wilson's Fourteen Points. Churchill accepted the "self-government" principle only with strong reservations. "We mean to hold our own," he said a year later. "I have not become the King's First Minister in order to preside over the liquidation of the British Empire."

Meanwhile, the war at sea continued. When a German submarine fired on the American destroyer *Greer* in September 1941, Roosevelt ordered the navy to "shoot on sight" any Axis raiders they encountered, although the *Greer* had provoked the attack. In October, the American destroyer *Kearney* was damaged near Iceland in a battle with German submarines. Roosevelt said: "America has been attacked. . . . The shooting has started." At the end of October the destroyer *Reuben James* was sunk off Iceland while engaged in convoy duty. Congress responded in November by authorizing American merchant ships to sail well armed and to carry lend-lease supplies directly to Britain.

Thus, by the fall of 1941 the United States had become an open ally of Britain without formally having declared war. By then Hitler had begun his invasion of the Soviet Union, so recently his partner in the nonaggression pact. What led Hitler to take this step remains uncertain. Most likely he hoped to capture the wheat of the Ukraine, the oil of the Caucasus, and the greater part of the Soviet Union's industrial resources. Such conquests might make Britain and its friends across the sea more likely to negotiate rather than fight. Success might also inspire Germans with new hope of total victory.

Whatever his calculations, Hitler had obviously underestimated the Soviet potential for resistance. Others did the same. In June 1941, for example, immediately after the Nazi attack, Henry L. Stimson, now Roosevelt's secretary of war, estimated it would take Hitler from one to three months to conquer the Soviet Union. Secretary of the Navy Knox thought it would take "anywhere from six weeks to two months." Yet when winter came, the Nazi armies still were outside Moscow and Leningrad, and the Soviet Union was still mustering its strength.

Churchill welcomed the Russians as comrades in arms, just as he had welcomed the American "arsenal." "I have only one purpose, the destruction of Hitler," he told his secretary. "If Hitler invaded Hell I would make at least a favorable reference to the Devil in the House of Commons." Predictably, the notion of reversing a generation of hostility and aiding the Soviet Union created a controversy within the United States. Public opinion polls revealed that most Americans wanted the Soviet Union to defeat Germany. There was less enthusiasm about outright American aid. Charles Lindbergh reacted with anger to such a proposal. He preferred an alliance with Nazi Germany than with the "godlessness and barbarism that exist in the Soviet Union." The persistence of anti-Soviet feeling was perhaps best summed up by Harry S. Truman, then a senator from Missouri: "If we see that Germany is winning we ought to help Russia and if Russia is winning we ought to help Germany and that way let them kill as many as possible, although I don't want to see Hitler victorious under any circumstances. . . ."

Fortunately, Roosevelt listened to no arguments about who should win. In November 1941, the United States extended lend-lease to the Soviet Union. "Give us anti-aircraft guns and the aluminum and we can fight for three or four years," Stalin told Harry Hopkins, Roosevelt's emissary. Despite predictions in the United States of a quick German victory, the Red Army proved Stalin correct.

Toward Pearl Harbor

Since his quarantine speech, Roosevelt had been cautious in dealing with the Japanese. As early as December 1937, when Japanese planes sank the American gunboat *Panay* in the Yangtze River in China, war had seemed possible. But Japan quickly apologized and paid reparations for the lives lost. From then on, the United States followed an unclear line. Roosevelt refused to invoke the Neutrality Act, because to do so might have stopped the movement of supplies over the Burma Road to Chinese forces opposing Japan. Yet Americans continued to sell large quantities of scrap metal, steel, copper, oil, lead, and machinery to the Japanese.

It would have been possible after January 1940 to end this traffic by embargo. But the president hesitated to take this step, thinking it would only spur Japan to further conquests in Asia in search of these commodities. In May 1940, as a deterrent to Japan, Roosevelt ordered the transfer of the United States Pacific Fleet's base from San Diego, California, to Pearl Harbor in Hawaii.

As a further deterrent, after the fall of France in

June 1940, Congress passed a law requiring Americans to obtain federal licenses for the export of oil and scrap metal. Under this law, Roosevelt, on July 26, ordered aviation gasoline withheld from Japan, a step that drew a strong Japanese protest. The next month, Japan forced the helpless Vichy government in France to surrender bases in northern Indochina. This move prompted Roosevelt, on September 25, to extend the embargo to iron and steel scrap and to grant a large new loan to Chiang Kai-shek. Two days later, Japan joined the German-Italian coalition.

The formation of the Berlin-Rome-Tokyo Axis to promote Hitler's "New Order" in Europe and the prosperity of "Greater East Asia" under Japan was intended to warn the United States to keep hands off both. The three partners agreed that if America attacked any of them, the other two would come to the aid of the victim. The first

major change in the Pacific followed the Nazi invasion of the USSR in June 1941, which removed the last possibility that Soviet forces could be used against Japan.

That July, Tokyo compelled the Vichy government to yield bases in southern Indochina. Roosevelt responded by freezing all Japanese assets in the United States. Japan reciprocated, thereby paralyzing trade between the two countries. On August 17, 1941, Roosevelt warned the Japanese that if they made any further moves to impose military domination on neighboring countries, the United States would take "all steps which it may deem necessary toward safeguarding [its] legitimate right and interest."

The previous December, United States Naval Intelligence cryptographers had broken Japan's secret diplomatic code, and Washington could listen in on messages from Tokyo to its envoys in

The Japanese assault on Pearl Harbor. Millions of Americans first learned of the surprise attack when they turned on their radios to hear their favorite Sunday programs. *(National Air and Space Museum, Smithsonian Institution)*

CHAPTER 29 THE AGE OF VIOLENCE: WORLD WAR II

the American capital. One thing seemed certain from these messages: Japan intended to conquer China. At the same time, the United States had no intention of sacrificing Chiang Kai-shek to Japan's ambition. Negotiations between the two countries came to a halt principally on this issue.

In Japan the government of Prime Minister Fumimaro Konoye was forced to resign in favor of General Hideki Tojo in mid-October 1941. Tojo feared that the army's morale would suffer if after years of sacrifice it had to yield China under American pressure. "If a hundred million people merge into one iron solidarity to go forward," Tojo declared, "nothing can stop us." He would have been glad to have China without war with the United States.

On October 23 his cabinet agreed to speed up military preparations. By November 3 his government had decided to attack Pearl Harbor if negotiations did not permit Japan to have its way. At the same time, talks in Washington were to continue. After November 17 they were under the direction of Saburo Kurusu, a special envoy.

From the secret code, Washington knew that if a satisfactory agreement were not completed by November 29, "things are automatically going to happen." On November 20 Kurusu and the Japanese ambassador presented Secretary of State Hull with proposals that seemed to be a demand that the United States approve and aid Japan's conquest in Asia. Six days later, the State Department presented counterproposals. Favorable trade relations were offered in exchange for Japan's withdrawal of forces from China and Indochina and its signature to a nonaggression pact with other nations that had interests in the Far East. Japan obviously would not accept such terms. "I have washed my hands of it," said Hull to Secretary of War Stimson that day, "and it is now in the hands of you and Knox, the Army and Navy."

Hull did not realize how right he was. Unknown to the American negotiators, a Japanese carrier force had just set out. On December 1, dismissing the American demands as "fantastic," Kurusu nevertheless asked that discussions continue. Washington already knew of Japanese troop movements, which Roosevelt thought meant only an attack in the Southwest Pacific on Thailand, Malaya, and the Dutch East Indies—which were, in fact, the main Japanese objectives. On December 6 he sent the Japanese emperor a hasty peace appeal. The next day Japan made its move.

Early in the morning of Sunday, December 7, 1941, a strong carrier-borne force of Japanese planes swooped down on the American naval base at Pearl Harbor. Most of the American aircraft were destroyed on the ground, and the unprotected naval vessels suffered terrible damage. In this one assault, 2355 American servicemen and 68 civilians died; 1178 were wounded. The next day a shocked Congress voted to declare war on Japan.

Roosevelt's critics later accused him of having provoked Japan to attack in order to bring the United States into the war in Europe, and of having deliberately exposed the navy at Pearl Harbor in order to create a situation that would unite Americans behind his war. That Roosevelt wanted to enter the war by November and that he knew a firm stand against Japan might bring drastic action seem beyond doubt. However, had the United States stood quietly by while Japan built an immensely rich empire in China and Asia, Roosevelt would have been criticized for inaction.

The notion that Roosevelt conspired to destroy a substantial part of the navy he had served and built up and that his administration and high military authorities were involved in the plot is most unlikely. No doubt there was fault both in Washington and in Pearl Harbor. But to the very end it was thought the Japanese would strike elsewhere.

On December 11, four days after Pearl Harbor, Japan's Axis partners, Germany and Italy, declared war on the United States. Congress responded immediately with declarations of war against them. The United States was now engaged in global warfare.

THE HOME FRONT

Two weeks after the attack on Pearl Harbor, Jonathan Daniels, a newspaper editor who would soon become Roosevelt's administrative assistant, wrote that the war had brought a new era in American history: "The twenties are gone with self-indulgence. The thirties have disappeared with self-pity. The forties are here in which Americans stand on a continent as men—men again fighting in the crudest man terms." Unlike World War I, there was little discussion about the need to fight. The American people—men and women—were asked to mobilize their human and physical resources for total war. It was the men who would ultimately take the war into the enemy's terrain; it was the women who built most of the bombers and fighters that pounded the enemy's cities.

To mobilize a people for war, to generate the kind of enthusiasm that will lead them to make sacrifices, it is almost always necessary to portray the enemy as an inhuman force. World War II was no exception. The Germans were the very incarnation of evil, prepared to invade the homes of American families. The Japanese were subhuman and treacherous. *Time,* the popular newsmagazine, caught the proper tone when it entitled the article on the Battle of Iwo Jima "Rodent Exterminators." "The ordinary unreasoning Jap is ignorant," *Time* observed. "Perhaps he is human. Nothing . . . indicates it." Near the close of the war, when *Time* featured on its cover Admiral William F. (Bull) Halsey, it also used his motto: "Kill Japs, kill Japs, and then kill more Japs."

Japanese Americans

To unleash such hatred against a foreign enemy could be expected of any nation engaged in war. Less understandable was the decision in early 1942 to single out 110,000 Japanese Americans— two-thirds of them citizens of the United States— remove them from their homes on the West Coast, and confine them in inland relocation centers. Except for President Jackson's removal of the Indians from Georgia, the action was without precedent in the nation's history.

What caused the decision was race prejudice rather than military security. It was the result of more than forty years of anti-Japanese sentiment and racial tension on the West Coast. No removal was ordered in Hawaii, where 32 percent of the population was of Japanese descent. Nor did anyone ever seriously consider doing the same to German Americans or Italian Americans. Earl Warren, then the California attorney general, tried to explain:

We believe that when we are dealing with the Caucasian race we have methods that will test the loyalty of them, and we believe that we can, in dealing with the Germans and the Italians, arrive at some fairly sound conclusions because of our knowledge of the way they live in the community and have lived for many years. But when we deal with the Japanese we are in an entirely different field and we cannot form any opinion that we believe to be sound.

The lack of evidence of Japanese sabotage on the West Coast after Pearl Harbor only confirmed the suspicions of those who advocated removal.

Lieutenant General J. L. DeWitt, head of the Western Defense Command, in recommending removal to the secretary of war, concluded: "The very fact that no sabotage has taken place to date is a disturbing and confirming indication that such action will be taken."

Despite such hysterical racial repression, many units of Nisei (persons born in the United States of parents who emigrated from Japan) performed heroically in the United States armed forces. Their work, along with the realization of how unfairly Japanese American families had been treated, finally induced the federal government to pay more than $35 million to the evacuees for property losses. But this was very little compensation for the immense damage that had been done.

Near the end of the war, the Supreme Court, in a series of decisions, upheld the essential features of the removal program. If Justice Frank Murphy found in that program "a melancholy resemblance" to the Nazi treatment of the Jews, Justice Hugo Black expressed the more popular opinion: "Hardships are a part of war, and war is an aggregation of hardships."

Nearly half a century later, on August 10, 1988, President Ronald Reagan signed legislation containing an apology for the forced relocation of Japanese Americans during World War II and establishing a $1.25 billion trust fund for reparations to those who were placed in camps and to their families.

Black Americans

Black America had responded with some uncertainty to the outbreak of war in Europe. "Our war," said one black newspaper, "is not against Hitler in Europe but against the Hitlers in America." After the attack on Pearl Harbor, a black sharecropper reportedly told his landlord, "By the way, Captain, I hear the Japs done declared war on you white folks." What these reactions reflected was not only skepticism about a "white man's war," but the contrast between wartime democratic slogans and the realities of black–white relations.

The vast majority of blacks no doubt reached the same conclusion that one of their contemporary heroes, heavyweight champion Joe Louis, did: "America's got lots of problems, but Hitler won't fix them." During World War I, W. E. B. Du Bois and other black leaders had urged their people to set aside their grievances and rally to the war effort. But now the black press and leadership vowed that World War II would be fought on two

"A JAP'S A JAP"

As head of the Western Defense Command, General John L. DeWitt defended the removal of Japanese Americans: "A Jap's a Jap. . . . It makes no difference whether he is an American citizen or not. . . . There is no way to determine their loyalty." In subsequent testimony before a congressional committee, he advised against returning the Japanese to the West Coast.

GENERAL DEWITT: . . . I don't want any of them here. They are a dangerous element. There is no way to determine their loyalty. . . . There is a feeling developing, I think, in certain sections of the country that the Japanese should be allowed to return. I am opposing it with every proper means at my disposal.

MR. BATES: . . . would you base your determined stand on experience as a result of sabotage or racial history or what . . . ?

GENERAL DEWITT: I first of all base it on my responsibility. I have the mission of defending this coast and securing vital installations. The danger of

the Japanese was, and is now—if they are permitted to come back—espionage and sabotage. It makes no difference whether he is an American citizen, he is still a Japanese. American citizenship does not necessarily determine loyalty.

MR. BATES: You draw a distinction then between Japanese and Italians and Germans? We have a great number of Italians and Germans and we think they are fine citizens. There may be exceptions.

GENERAL DEWITT: You needn't worry about the Italians at all except in certain cases. Also, the same for the Germans except in individual cases. But we must worry about the Japanese all the time until he is wiped off the map. Sabotage and espionage will make problems as long as he is allowed in this area—problems which I don't want to have to worry about.

Source: Hearings before Subcommittee of House Committee on Naval Affairs on H.R. 30, 78th Cong., 1st sess., 1943, pp. 739–40. Photograph by the War Relocation Authority, National Archives.

fronts—"victory over our enemies at home and victory over our enemies on the battlefields abroad."

The outlook for winning the war at home was often very bleak. While more than one million blacks were entering the armed forces, over half of them to serve overseas, discrimination and segregation continued in the army, navy, and marines, in USO and other service clubs, even in Red Cross blood banks and entertainment centers. Nor did the war change traditional restrictions and practices. Under a "V for Victory" sign, for example, bus riders in Charleston, South Carolina, were advised, "Victory demands your cooperation. . . . Avoid friction. Be patriotic. White passengers will be seated from front to rear; colored passengers from rear to front." Between 1940 and 1943 seventeen blacks were lynched. In 1943 race riots broke out in Los Angeles, Beaumont, Mobile, New York, and, worst of all, Detroit, where twenty-five blacks and nine whites died. "There ain't no North any more," a Detroit black woman observed. "Everything now is South."

Still, World War II marked a significant turning point in race relations. Even before Pearl Harbor, in early 1941, a threatened march of 100,000 blacks on Washington, D.C., forced Roosevelt to prohibit racial discrimination in defense industries and to establish a Fair Employment Practices Commission to protect minorities from job discrimination. During the war, blacks shared in employment opportunities. Migration of southern blacks to northern and western cities continued to change the nation's racial map. Overseas experience made black servicemen less willing to accept racial restrictions at home.

Nor was the lesson of what had happened to 6 million Jews in Europe lost on black Americans. World War II also generated revolutionary ferment in Africa and Asia that would eventually force the United States to reassess its own racial policies. "The thesis of white supremacy," a State Department official remarked in 1944, "could only exist so long as the white race actually proved to be supreme."

Mobilization and Politics

At the time of Pearl Harbor, an American army of 1.6 million men already existed, most of them recruited through the first peacetime draft. Eventually, all men between eighteen and forty-five were subject to military service, and for the first time women were permitted to volunteer for the armed forces. By the war's end, 15 million men and more than 200,000 women had served in the army, navy, marines, and Coast Guard.

Behind these men and women stood American industry, agriculture, labor, and science. Critics of the president had dismissed as wishful thinking his call in 1940 for 50,000 planes a year. In 1942, over 47,000 aircraft were built. For 1944, the figure rose above 96,000. By 1945 no less than 55 million tons of merchant shipping and 71,000 naval vessels had been launched by American yards. Because supplies of Malaysian and East Indian raw rubber had been cut off early in the war, a synthetic-rubber industry had been established. In other American industries, first lend-lease and then American war production ended the Depression.

The "hate Roosevelt" attitude of big business did not die with mobilization. Until Pearl Harbor, the steel industry, for example, was slow in responding to appeals to expand. The automobile industry's business-as-usual policy reflected its reluctance to convert to armaments just when the boom was reviving the market for cars. Almost complete conversion was achieved, but private industry's fear of excess plant capacity forced the government, through the Defense Plant Corporation, to build about 85 percent of the new facilities needed for war production. Most of the government-built plants were run during the war by private corporations under liberal contracts with the armed services, and were purchased afterward on generous terms.

Depression unemployment also ended. Millions of women joined or replaced men on the assembly lines and kept war plants going day and night. A War Manpower Commission shifted workers into areas where they were most needed and made arrangements for efficient use of the labor force. The incentive to work in war plants grew as average weekly earnings rose from $23.86 in 1939 to $46.08 in 1944. After Pearl Harbor, the AFL and CIO made no-strike pledges. Later, as prices rose and as the worst period of the war passed, strikes became frequent. Workers were widely criticized for strikes. The slogan "There are no strikes in foxholes" was easily met, however, with the reply "There are no profits either." Corporate profits after taxes rose from $5 billion in 1939 to almost $10 billion in 1944, and many new fortunes were made.

With the drafting of men into the armed forces, large numbers of women found wartime employment, particularly in the defense industries. By the fall of 1943, with war production reaching peak levels, an estimated 17 million women made up a third of the total work force. Of these, some 5 million worked in war factories. Posters of Rosie the Riveter, along with popular songs, persuaded women to leave the home for war work as a patriotic duty and reassured them they could do factory work as easily as household work: "If you've sewed on buttons, or made buttonholes, on a machine, you can learn to do spot welding on airplane parts," one billboard proclaimed. "If you've used an electric mixer in your kitchen, you can learn to run a drill press. If you've followed recipes exactly in making cakes, you can learn to load shell."

Rosie the Riveter was conventionally depicted as a temporary worker, usually a middle-class housewife who left her comfortable home to serve her country and was anxious to return to her domestic duties after the war. But some 78 percent of the women who held wartime industrial jobs had already been working; many eagerly left lower-paying positions (usually menial and service employment) for the more attractive and remunerative jobs in the war industries. Although women war workers welcomed their increased income, independence, and self-esteem, men continued to dominate the supervisory positions. And the wage scales, despite government promises to the contrary, discriminated against women. After the war, women were expected to give up their jobs to returning veterans and to resume domesticity and war-deferred motherhood. Many women who remained in the labor force, however, faced a painful return to lower-paying and less fulfilling work.

Although the farm population fell during the war (despite draft exemptions for many agricultural workers), farm production soared in response to favorable weather and scientific aids. Output per farm worker in 1945 was almost double that from 1910 to 1914, agriculture's golden years. Farm income also doubled. The war showed that a small farm labor force using improved agricultural techniques could meet the normal needs of the domestic market. This realization soon influenced farm and financial policies.

The Office of Price Administration under Leon Henderson made a major effort to control inflation during the war. It set price ceilings on a wide variety of consumer goods. A few products, such as sugar, coffee, meat, and butter, were rationed. Prices had already risen about 25 percent when controls were first authorized in January 1942, and they continued to rise slightly. But serious inflation was avoided.

Wartime science in the United States came under the direction of the Office of Scientific Research and Development, headed by Vannevar Bush, president of the Carnegie Institution of Washington and former vice-president of the Massachusetts Institute of Technology, and James Conant, since 1933 president of Harvard. Their work profited greatly from the contributions of refugee scientists from Axis countries and the cooperation of British scientists. Among the major developments were those in radar, a British invention. The most lethal development was the atomic bomb.

Even before Munich, German scientists had

(Library of Congress)

(Gordon Parks)

THE ROSIES

We were happy to be doing it. We felt terrific. Lunch hour would find us spread out on the sidewalk. Women welders with our outfits on, and usually a quart of milk in one hand and a salami sandwich in another. It was an experience that none of us had ever had before. Workers from other ships would look at us and see that we were welders and it was a terrifically wonderful thing. We had a happy attitude toward our work that they [the men] of course did not have because they were in the middle and the end of their stories and we felt we were at the beginning. (Lola Weixel, in the documentary film *The Life and Times of Rosie the Riveter*)

Women are working only to win the war and will return willingly to their home duties after the war is won. They will look on this period as an interlude, just as their men who have been called to service will consider military duties as an interlude. The women are like Cincinnatus, who left his plow to save Rome and then returned to his plow. Women will always be women. (Betty Allie, state worker compensation official, in the *Detroit News*, November 26, 1943)

Well, the war ended. The black man went first, and I went second, and everybody else remained. We were laid off within a day of each other. In a way, I felt then that it was right. We had in us a philosophy that man is the breadwinner, and that if there's a choice between himself and you, he's entitled to more than you. . . . I finally ended up going to an office. I readjusted, but I never really liked it. (Celia Yanish)

After the war it was completely different. I went around and applied to different factories, but there were no jobs for me. So I had to fall back on the only other work I knew, and that was doing domestic work. And it was a very defeating feeling, very. (Margaret Ridell)

Source: Interviews conducted by Connie Field, director, *Rosie The Riveter Film Project* (Clarity Educational Productions, Inc., Emeryville, CA.

Rosie the Riveter

While other girls attend their fav'rite cocktail bar—
Sipping dry Martinis, munching caviar—
There's a girl who's really putting them to shame
Rosie is her name.

All the day long whether rain or shine—
She's a part of the assembly line—
She's making history working for victory,
Rosie the Riveter.

Keeps a sharp lookout for sabotage—
Sitting up there on the fuselage—
That little frail can do more than a male can do,
Rosie the Riveter.

Rosie's got a boy friend Charlie,
Charlie, he's a marine—
Rosie is protecting Charlie
Working overtime on the riveting machine.

When they gave her a production "E"
She was as proud as a girl could be.
There's something new about red, white and blue about
Rosie the Riveter.

Ev'ry one stops to admire the scene—
Rosie at work on the B-Nineteen—
She's never twittery nervous or jittery,
Rosie the Riveter.

What if she's smeared full of oil and grease
Doing her bit for the old Lend lease
She keeps the gang around
They love to hang around,
Rosie the Riveter.

Rosie buys a lot of war bonds
That girl really has sense
Wishes she could purchase more bonds
Putting all her cash into national defense.

Source: Red Evans and John Jacob Loeb. Copyright renewed 1969 Ahlert-Burke Corp. & John J. Loeb Co.

---

become the first in the world to release energy by splitting the uranium atom. They worked feverishly to find a way to use this incredible energy in a deliverable weapon. Late in 1939 Albert Einstein, who had fled Germany when Hitler took power, and two other refugee scientists had managed to make FDR understand what atomic science could do. Roosevelt promptly established an advisory committee on uranium. But the crash program to produce an atomic bomb was not decided upon until the spring of 1941.

At that point the British, whose atomic research was considerably ahead of that in the United States, agreed to share their knowledge. From the very first, the scientists knew they could keep

their findings from political leaders who would want to use atomic energy in warfare. Almost to a man, however, they had suffered under Axis regimes. Their hatred and fear of the Nazis had grown as strong as the new physical force itself. Either way, civilization seemed doomed. Perhaps Hitler's defeat might offer the better chance. In any case, it was they who pressed the bomb on governments, and not the other way around.

The most fruitful work on the atom was done at the University of California at Berkeley, the University of Chicago, and Columbia University in New York City. This work showed that a practical bomb could be made by using plutonium—a new element produced by splitting the uranium atom in a cyclotron, or atom smasher. On May 1, 1943, the job of producing plutonium in large quantities was given to the secret Manhattan District Project established at Oak Ridge, Tennessee, where the immense hydroelectric resources of the TVA were available.

At about the same time, the responsibility for building a practical bomb was given to Robert J. Oppenheimer and the brilliant team of British, American, and European scientists he gathered at Los Alamos, New Mexico. On July 12, 1945, final assembly of the first atomic bomb began. Four days later, at the Alamogordo air base in New Mexico, the weapon was detonated.

By mid-1943 American war costs, including those for atom-bomb development, were running at $8 billion a month—as high as the *yearly* budgets of the peacetime New Deal. In 1945, for the first time in history, the federal government spent over $100 billion. The total cost of the war to the United States was about $350 billion—ten times the cost of World War I.

After July 1, 1943, employers began to collect income taxes for the government by withholding them from employee payrolls. This innovation continued to be used after the war. It assured the government of its revenues and kept workers up to date with taxes. Income and other taxes paid for two-fifths of the war's huge cost. Yet between 1941 and 1945, the national debt rose from about $48 billion to $247 billion.

Politics was not suspended in the war years. In the congressional elections of 1942, Republicans gained by capitalizing on public discontent with military defeats. But by 1944 the military situation had changed, and the Republicans had to contend once again with Roosevelt's popularity. Thomas E. Dewey, now governor of New York, became their candidate. The Democrats, having already shattered the third-term tradition, renominated Roosevelt.

Since FDR's health and age were matters of concern, the convention spotlight focused on the choice for vice-president. After a stormy session, Henry Wallace, unpopular with city bosses and southern conservatives, was dropped in favor of Senator Harry S. Truman of Missouri. Truman had gained attention as chairman of a Senate committee investigating malpractices in the fulfillment of wartime production contracts.

Dewey had no real issue on which to campaign, since he and his party had accepted most of the administration's program, including the president's commitment to a new international organization. The Republicans focused on Roosevelt's

health, but this tactic boomeranged. Dewey's freshness appeared to reflect his limited participation in war work, at which the president exhausted himself to save the country.

Roosevelt won by a popular vote of 25,606,585 to 22,014,745 and by 432 to 99 in the electoral college. The Democrats' choice of vice-president proved fateful indeed, for Roosevelt was to serve less than four months of his fourth term.

THE WAR FRONTS

In the spring of 1942, the United States and the Allied powers did not expect to win the war quickly, if they could win at all. They outnumbered the Axis powers, but the Axis had enormous labor resources in central Europe, the occupied part of the Soviet Union, and the Southwest Pacific. Occupied France and friendly Spain could contribute by helping to make the Atlantic and the western Mediterranean dangerous for Allied shipping. Axis forces occupied North Africa from Tunis to the Egyptian border, and Germany's formidable Afrika Korps, under Field Marshal Rommel, seemed about to smash eastward to Alexandria, closing the Suez Canal and forcing Turkey to join the Axis.

When the eastern Mediterranean became impassable, Allied ships had to take the long route around the Cape of Good Hope to supply British forces in the Middle East. In southern Russia, the Germans were hammering at the Caucasus, threatening to drive through to Iraq and Iran and complete the conquest of the routes to the East. Britain would then have been cut off entirely from its empire.

The situation was no better in the Pacific. Japan followed up Pearl Harbor with successful attacks on the Philippines, Wake Island, Guam, Hong Kong, British Malaya, and Thailand. American troops in the Philippines under General Douglas MacArthur made brave stands on the Bataan Peninsula and on the fortress island of Corregidor. But after MacArthur managed to escape to Australia, Bataan surrendered in April 1942 and Corregidor in May. In the Southwest Pacific, the Japanese paralyzed the British navy and then captured Singapore and crushed resistance in the Netherlands East Indies. By March 1942, they had conquered Burma and closed the Burma Road, the supply route to China.

At best, a war lasting seven to fifteen years seemed the future for the Allies. But this forecast neglected some Allied assets, notably American resources and American industrial capacity. Allied planning and administration proved vastly superior, both in individual countries and in joint efforts. The United States and Britain in particular, through their combined chiefs of staff and the collaboration of Roosevelt and Churchill, worked together with remarkable harmony during most of the war. At an early point in their joint effort, their military planners made an important overall decision. They would conduct a holding operation in the Pacific until the United States could mobilize enough aid for Britain and Russia to take the offensive in Europe. After the Axis had been defeated in Europe, Japan's turn would come.

To win the war in Europe, the Western powers had to gain control of the sea and the air. For months after the United States entered the war, German submarines roamed the Caribbean and the waters off the Atlantic and Gulf coasts. Ship sinkings were extremely high. Few submarines were sunk, however, until a new system of convoys was worked out and coastal waters were patrolled. Still, the cost in tonnage and lives continued, and it was only the tremendous rate of American merchant-ship production that allowed the United States to absorb the submarine damage.

In the air, supremacy had passed to Britain's Royal Air Force during the clashes over England in 1940. In 1941, when British aircraft production surpassed Germany's, the RAF went on the offensive. It returned the terrible attacks Germany had inflicted on British cities. Sustained RAF bombing reached a peak during July 1943, when night raids over Hamburg destroyed more than a third of that port and killed over sixty thousand

The European theater, 1942–1945.

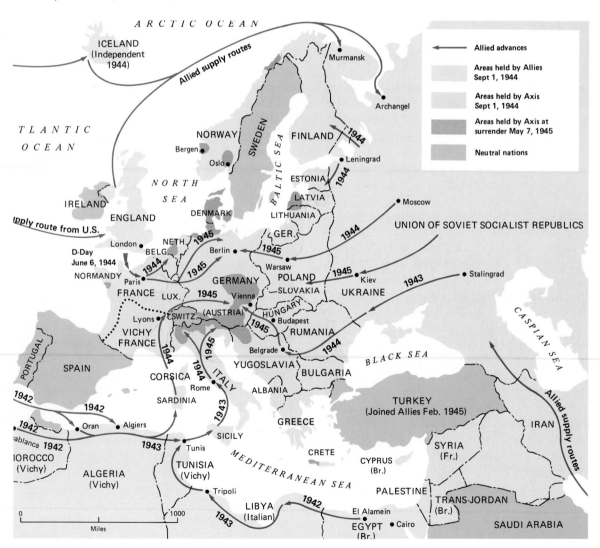

CHAPTER 29 THE AGE OF VIOLENCE: WORLD WAR II

people. In August 1942 American airmen joined the British in raids over the Continent, supplementing RAF nighttime saturation bombings with precision daylight bombing. Between them, the two air forces dropped more than 2.6 million bombs.

At one point, there was talk among the Allies of trying to bring Germany down by air attack alone. This would avoid the casualties a land invasion would almost surely mean. But the idea had to be abandoned. Air attacks never succeeded in stopping Axis production of planes, submarines, or synthetic rubber, although in the long run they crippled transportation and refineries. When the time came for the Allies to invade the Continent, Germany found its defenses gravely weakened by the damage inflicted on railways, roads, and bridges at home and in France, and by shortages of fuel for planes, tanks, and other vehicles.

North Africa and the Casablanca Conference

With an all-out assault on France still too risky, Churchill and Roosevelt decided to attack in Egypt, where Rommel's Afrika Korps was pressing toward the Suez Canal. On October 23, 1942, the first great Allied land offensive of the war confronted Rommel at El Alamein, on the Mediterranean, and sent his forces streaming back toward Libya. Broadening the assault, three Allied armies under General Dwight D. Eisenhower (who had been named supreme Allied commander in the Mediterranean theater) began landing at Algiers, Oran, and Casablanca in French North Africa on November 8, 1942.

These landings had both military and political results. They affected two sets of touchy relations involving the Allies. One was with the Vichy government, which controlled unoccupied southern France and French North Africa. The other was with General Charles de Gaulle, exiled leader of the Free French and an enemy of Vichy. Most of the French administrators and the French navy in North Africa had remained loyal to Vichy, so the Allied invaders were not necessarily greeted as liberators.

The landings at Algiers met little resistance. Those at Casablanca and Oran encountered heavy fire from the French fleet, parts of which were sunk. To make matters even more difficult, French land forces would have nothing to do with General Henri Giraud, a hero of the fall of France who had escaped from prison in Germany and had been brought to North Africa by Eisenhower. The troops proved more responsive to Admiral Jean Darlan, chief of all Vichy forces, who happened to be in Algiers. Impressed with Allied strength, he agreed to an armistice.

Conveniently for the Allies, Darlan was assassinated, and Giraud succeeded him as head of the French government in North Africa. De Gaulle became chief of the Committee of National Liberation, which the United States recognized in July 1943 as the de-facto government of all liberated parts of France. Although he became a thorn to Churchill and Roosevelt, de Gaulle and his Free French forces contributed to victory and to the French revival after the war.

The momentum of El Alamein, strengthened by the Soviet stand at Stalingrad in late 1942, gave hope to the Allies. When Churchill and Roosevelt met at Casablanca in January 1943, they made plans for victory on all fronts. The Allied leaders decided to invade Sicily and Italy after securing North Africa. They agreed to send enough forces to the Pacific to take the offensive there, and promised to ease the pressure on the Russians by setting up another front in Europe.

They also announced that they would accept only the "unconditional surrender" of the Axis.

WORDS AND NAMES IN AMERICAN HISTORY

Unconditional surrender is a phrase first associated with Ulysses S. Grant. During his siege of Confederate-held Fort Donelson in Tennessee in 1862 his opponents suggested a stop to the fighting; Grant replied, "No terms except an unconditional and immediate surrender." That he was able to enforce this demand made him a hero in the North. The same words were used during World War II, when the Allies agreed not to negotiate a peace, or separate peaces, with Nazi Germany or with Japan. During that war, "Unconditional surrender!" became a rallying cry even among civilians in the United States. These facts are well known. What is not widely recognized is that surrendering an army (let alone an entire nation) without agreed upon protections for the losers was a new phenomenon in Western warfare. Some historians argue strongly that Grant's demand marked the beginning of the modern age of war.

"[We] mean that [the] will power to resist . . . of the Nazi, Fascist, and Japanese tyrannies . . . must be completely broken," Churchill explained, "and that they must yield themselves absolutely to our justice and mercy."

After the war, when searching for strong allies with whom to rebuild the balance of power on the Continent, Churchill reopened the controversy over unconditional surrender by asserting that it had made enemy resistance desperate and prolonged the slaughter. But that is not what he thought at Casablanca, where he took credit for the idea. But he and the others who thought the ultimatum might shorten the war by leading the enemy to sue for an early peace were soon proved wrong, at least where the Germans and the Japanese were concerned.

Following the Casablanca Conference, the Allies took full possession of North Africa. General Von Arnim surrendered Rommel's army of 350,000 men in Tunisia (the Desert Fox himself evaded capture). Destruction of Nazi North African submarine and air bases followed. The southern Mediterranean again became available to the Allies at normal wartime risk, and pressure on the Middle East was eased.

The Italian Campaign

The attack on Italy began on July 10, 1943—the earliest that enough landing craft could be assembled. By August 17, when Sicily was cleared, 100,000 German prisoners had been taken. Meanwhile, King Victor Emmanuel and members of the Fascist Grand Council had deposed Mussolini and set up a new government under Marshal Pietro Badoglio, who immediately sued for peace. On September 8, 1943, the Italian government signed an unconditional surrender.

But Italy itself was still occupied by strong German forces, which Hitler reinforced. The Allied objective was to wipe out these forces, or at least to occupy them so they could not be used against the Russians. At the same time, the Western powers had another objective. Control of Italy would permit them to move east into the Balkans and stop the Soviets from overrunning southern Europe when the final push against Hitler came.

The Italian campaign turned into an agonizingly slow and costly war. The Allies captured Naples on September 28, 1943. Rome, only one hundred miles north, did not fall until June 4, 1944—only two days before the cross-channel

invasion of France was to begin. On April 28, 1945, Italian partisans captured Mussolini, murdered him, and mutilated his body. But the Nazis in Italy fought on until May 2, five days before the Reich itself collapsed.

Conference Diplomacy: Cairo and Teheran

Although Roosevelt and Churchill met several times after the Casablanca Conference, the need to include Stalin in these meetings became more and more important. In October 1943, the foreign ministers of the Big Three—Hull for the United States, Eden for Britain, and Molotov for the USSR—met in Moscow and drew up a general understanding. The Western spokesmen promised the Russians to open the invasion of France in 1944. All three declared their intention to establish a general international organization "for the maintenance of international peace and security." They also proposed a democratic future for Italy. Poland, where Russia's dominance was unnegotiable, proved troublesome, but Roosevelt remained satisfied with the progress made.

And he was determined to meet with Stalin personally. This occasion, with Churchill joining the other two, was set for Teheran, the capital of Iran, late in November 1943. On the way to Teheran, FDR met with Chiang Kai-shek and Churchill at Cairo. To keep Chiang willing to fight to the finish, the three leaders promised to continue the struggle until Japan surrendered unconditionally. Occupied territories, including Manchuria and Formosa, would then be returned to China. They also foresaw a "free and independent Korea."

All of this was in the Cairo Declaration, announced December 1, after the Russians had endorsed it at Teheran. At Cairo, Roosevelt and Churchill also agreed that Eisenhower would become the supreme commander of the forces that would invade Europe.

The Big Three conference at Teheran set the Normandy invasion, under the code name Overlord, for May or June 1944. It was to be linked with a Russian offensive against Hitler from the east. Stalin also confirmed a promise made at the Moscow Conference to enter the war against Japan after Germany was defeated.

The Grand Alliance agreed to aid Marshal Tito and the Yugoslav partisans in ridding their country of German forces. Poland would again be sliced, the USSR taking some of its eastern land.

On June 6, 1944 (D-Day), Allied forces established a beachhead on the Normandy coast in the largest amphibious operation in history. "I took a walk along the historic coast of Normandy in the country of France. . . . Men were sleeping on the sand, some of them sleeping forever. Men were floating in the water, but they didn't know they were in the water, for they were dead," wrote Ernie Pyle, noted war correspondent. *(Bettmann Archive)*

But the Poles would be compensated on the west at Germany's expense. Germany was to be destroyed as a military power.

At the close of the meeting the Big Three announced: "We came here, friends in fact, in spirit, and in purpose." Roosevelt's optimism was apparent when he told Congress on his return that he "got along fine with Stalin," and predicted: "We are going to get along with him and the Russian people—very well indeed."

D-Day and the German Defeat

Victory in the Battle of Britain gave the Allies command in the air. Victory in the Battle of the Atlantic and in North Africa had given them command of the seas. The amphibious landings and the establishment of beachheads at Casablanca, Oran, Sicily, and Salerno had gained them good experience. Even the stalemate in Italy, which tied down needed Allied forces, also tied down troops and equipment Hitler needed desperately in France.

For four years Hitler had concentrated on making northern France the strongest wall of his fortress. For six weeks Allied air attacks pulverized this wall and the communication lines leading to it. By June 1944, a force of nearly 2.9 million men, supported by 2.5 million tons of supplies, 11,000 airplanes, and a vast armada of ships, had been assembled in England for the invasion. On D-day, June 6, the first assault troops established beachheads along the coast of Normandy.

Although caught by surprise because they had expected the attack elsewhere, the Nazis were able to mobilize quickly. But by July 24, more than a million Allied troops had taken 1500 square miles of Normandy and Brittany. The next day, General George S. Patton, Jr.'s, Third Army swept after the Germans and turned their retreat into a rout. On August 25, assisted by a Free French division, Patton liberated Paris. Two days later, de Gaulle installed himself as president of a provisional government. Patton kept going, with Omar Bradley's First Army moving more slowly on his left. Farther north, British field marshal Bernard

The Big Three—Churchill, Roosevelt, and Stalin—at Yalta, February 1945. *(Franklin D. Roosevelt Library)*

Montgomery was hurtling through Belgium with Canadian and British forces.

Having lost half a million men and virtually all of France, the Germans decided to take refuge behind their long-neglected west wall in the homeland across the Rhine. Patton was ready to burst after them. Montgomery wanted permission to make "one powerful and full-bodied thrust toward Berlin." But the Allied offensives had stretched supplies of trucks, tires, and fuel. Rather than let either Patton or Montgomery go, Eisenhower decided to regroup for a final general advance into the German interior. The Germans used the time to rally their forces. On December 16, 1944, they startled the Allies with a strong counterattack in the thinly defended Ardennes forest in southern Belgium. In ten days the German armies advanced fifty miles. Finally they were stopped by the Americans at the crossroads town of Bastogne. By mid-January 1945, in the costly Battle of the Bulge (77,000 American casualties), the Germans had been pushed back to

their old lines. Eisenhower now had to delay his final assault another month.

If Hitler had any thoughts about reinforcing his troops in the west, the Red Army made that impossible. After devastating the Crimea, the Nazis had reached the height of their invasion of the USSR in the summer of 1942 at the approaches to the industrial city of Stalingrad on the Volga River. The battle for Stalingrad, which had few natural defenses and could be saved only by massed manpower, opened in July. Five months later, Marshal Zhukov ordered a sweeping counterattack that encircled the German forces. On January 31, 1943, after one of the "dourest, bloodiest, and most prolonged" battles of the war, the trapped German armies surrendered.

By D-Day in Normandy, the Red Army had recaptured the Crimea and was advancing along the entire eastern front. Elimination of Nazi forces in the Balkans started in the summer of 1944. In Greece, Churchill sent troops to turn the civil war there to the conservative side. Elsewhere in the Balkans, the Soviets were able to establish Communist regimes. By February 1945, Finland was in Soviet hands and Poland had been organized as a Communist state. Hungary had fallen, Czechoslovakia had been penetrated. Vienna was about to collapse.

At the time of the Yalta Conference (February 4 to 11, 1945) Soviet armies were only fifty miles from Berlin. No people besides the Jews had suffered more from Nazi atrocities than the Russians. None of the Western Allies had sacrificed as much in the fighting itself. Understandably, the Soviet Union was concerned about its future security. Stalin now pressed that concern in all discussions over how the postwar world would be reorganized.

Although Stalin agreed at Yalta to hold "free and unfettered elections as soon as possible" in Poland, he was determined to have no unfriendly governments on his borders. To negotiate Soviet dominance in eastern Europe now was like asking the United States to negotiate the Monroe Doctrine. Critics would charge that Roosevelt had given up too much at Yalta. But the fact remains that in the final phase of the war, the Red Army had overrun eastern Europe. Stalin gave no indication of withdrawing his troops, and the United States was not about to drive them out. Neither Roosevelt nor Churchill gave Stalin anything that was in his possession.

Anxious to get Soviet participation in the Asian war, Roosevelt made some territorial concessions to Stalin at the expense of Japan. Stalin, in turn, promised to join the war "two or three months"

When Allied and Soviet troops finally broke through into Germany, they found the victims of the Nazi concentration camps—both the dead and the walking ghosts. One camp commander testified at Nuremberg to the cold efficiency of the Nazi plan: ". . . when I set up the extermination building at Auschwitz, I used Zyklon B, which was a crystallized prussic acid which we dropped into the death chamber from a small opening. It took from three to fifteen minutes to kill the people in the death chamber, depending on climatic conditions. Another improvement we made over Treblinka was that we built our gas chambers to accommodate 2,000 people at one time, whereas at Treblinka their ten gas chambers only accommodated 200 people each." *(AP/Wide World Photos)*

after the surrender of Germany. Tentative decisions at Yalta provided for the multiple administration of Berlin, the partitioning of Germany, and trials of "war criminals." (These decisions would be confirmed at the Potsdam Conference in July and August 1945.)

Finally, Stalin agreed to a United Nations Conference to be held in San Francisco in April 1945, at which a permanent international organization would be established. In Roosevelt's eyes, Stalin's agreement to participate in a United Nations was an important achievement. And with the atomic bomb still untested, American leaders welcomed Soviet action in Manchuria to help bring about the surrender of Japan.

The European war ended after tough and costly fighting. On March 7, 1945, the Allies at last crossed the Rhine, using the railroad bridge at Remagen, the only bridge still standing. On April 25, American and Soviet troops made contact at the Elbe River. On or about May 1, Hitler committed suicide in Berlin, and the next day the capital surrendered. On May 7, General Jodl, chief of staff of the German army, signed an unconditional surrender at Eisenhower's headquarters. Within a week, half the American air force in

The war in the Pacific.

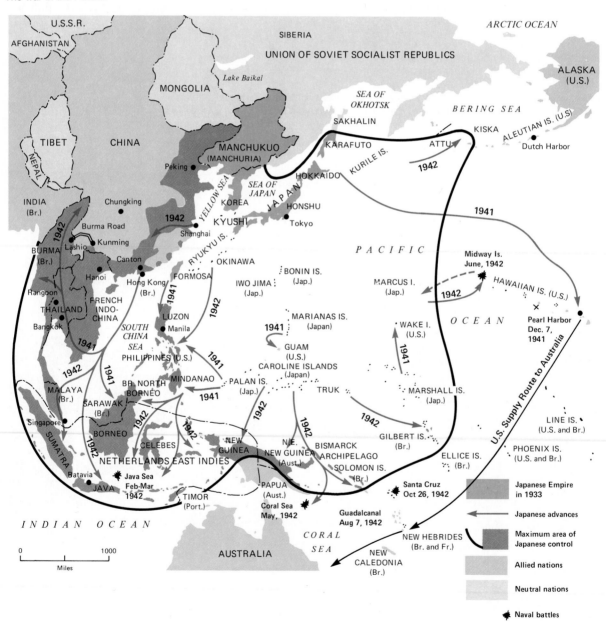

GIs invade Makin Island. "Always the rain and the mud, torrid heat and teeming insect life, the stink of rotten jungle and rotting dead, malaria burning the body and fungus infection eating away the feet, and no hot chow for weeks. And fury by day and terror by night and utter weariness all the time. And death." Major Frank O. Hough, U.S. Marine Corps, quoted in *The Island War*. (UPI/Bettmann Archive)

Europe was bound for the Pacific and the demobilization of the massive American army had begun.

On April 12, 1945, in Warm Springs, Georgia, Roosevelt died suddenly of a cerebral hemorrhage. Not since the assassination of Lincoln had the death of a president so moved the American people. Many could not even recall living under any other president. Asked if she had heard the radio bulletin, a Bronx housewife replied in tears, "For what do I need a radio? It's on everybody's face." Most appalled of all, perhaps, was FDR's successor, Harry Truman, who even as vice-president had not known the war's best-kept secret, the atomic bomb.

The War in the Pacific

In April 1942, Japan had a taste of the future. Sixteen American B-25s led by Colonel James H. Doolittle dropped a load of bombs on Tokyo. These planes had come from the aircraft carrier *Hornet*. *Hornet's* own planes had too little range to reach Tokyo, and her deck was too short to receive Doolittle's raiders on return. All the bombers were lost in China, where their crews had to bail out. Although the raid did little damage to the target, it had great consequences and boosted American morale.

The Japanese had mounted a new offensive even before they had had time to absorb the great area conquered in their initial thrusts after Pearl Harbor. This offensive was aimed at nailing down a naval and air line of defense from Attu, the westernmost of the Aleutians, to Port Moresby, the best harbor in New Guinea. Anchor points were to be at Japanese-held Wake and American-held Midway. Inside this line Japan expected to chew up China and perhaps India.

But these plans were changed in the spring of 1942 in two important naval engagements. One was the Battle of the Coral Sea, in which a Japanese assault on Port Moresby was turned back. Coral Sea, said Admiral Ernest J. King, was "the first naval engagement in . . . history in which surface ships did not exchange a single shot." In fact, they never saw one another. The entire battle, which set a pattern for the Pacific engagements, was fought by carrier-based planes.

The second Allied victory came in the Battle of Midway Island, June 3 to 6. Japanese capture of Midway would have made Pearl Harbor unusable. To save the island, Admiral Chester Nimitz mobilized what was left of the American fleet in Pearl Harbor and sent it out to meet the much larger Japanese force. Despite heavy losses, the Americans gave the enemy its first major naval defeat.

After their failure at Midway, the Japanese took Attu and Kiska in the Aleutians. Alaska seemed on the verge of occupation, and Seattle was threatened. Men and materials needed elsewhere were rushed to Alaska. The Alcan Highway through Canada was begun, and plans were made for operations that would regain Attu in May and Kiska in August 1943.

The Japanese were even less successful in a second attack on Port Moresby, this one begun over land in July 1942. To protect this attack, they had begun to clear an airstrip on Guadalcanal, one of the nearby (as South Pacific distances go) Solomon Islands. At the same time, the United States was looking at Guadalcanal as the starting point of its own offensive on Japan's more exposed positions.

On August 7, 1942, the first combined American and Australian landings on Guadalcanal were begun against sharp resistance. Two days later, a Japanese cruiser force swooped down on half-unloaded Allied transports in the Solomon's Savo Sea. In "the worst defeat ever suffered by the United States Navy," the cruisers sank virtually all the protective fighting ships. The transports ran, and the Japanese, mission accomplished, moved off. For six months, ill-equipped, half-starved Marines clung to Guadalcanal's airstrip while huge naval actions surrounding reinforcement attempts by both sides raged in the surrounding waters. Finally, on February 9, 1943, the Japanese evacuated the island.

After Guadalcanal, the Japanese became occupied with defending the Pacific and mainland positions they still held as a screen for the home islands. The defense was fierce, often fanatical. The military chiefs of staff in Washington became so impressed with the Japanese that even at the time of the Yalta Conference, when the brilliance of Allied strategy had been well demonstrated, they advised Roosevelt that the Pacific war had at least two years to run with full Soviet assistance, and much longer without it.

Allied success in the South Pacific encouraged General Douglas MacArthur, chief of Southwest Pacific operations, in his determination to make a return to the Philippines his last step before taking Tokyo. But the Gilbert Islands, the Marshalls, and, farther north still, Wake Island stood in the way. Even barren atolls had been armed with an airstrip, artillery, and men. To the west of this arc lay the Carolines, Guam, and the Marianas. They were closer to Japan, and even more heavily armed. Farther north and west lay Iwo Jima and, in the shadow of Japan itself, Okinawa. This defense in depth, extending more than three thousand miles, shielded Tokyo. Any invasion from the Philippines would meet murderous flanking fire.

To roll back this defense, island by island, atoll by atoll, man by man, would occupy a generation and still not guarantee success. MacArthur's command devised the bold alternative of island hopping, a strategy designed to open a path to the heart of Japan. Air power would neutralize the uncleared rear. Even so, armies as large as those that once conquered nations fought hundreds of battles on tiny, unknown atolls.

The burden of this offensive was on Admiral Chester W. Nimitz and his Central Pacific Fleet. But every assault involved coordination of sea, land, and air forces. None was easy. Tarawa established the Allied hold on the Gilberts in November 1943; Kwajalein, control of the Marshalls in February 1944. In May, Wake was taken. In the immense Battle of the Philippine Sea (June 19 and 20), Admiral Raymond Spruance stopped a Japanese effort to reinforce the Marianas. By August 1, Saipan and Tinian, as well as Guam, had succumbed.

Tokyo was now within range of land-based bombers. The capital and other home-island cities were systematically assaulted with fire bombs that consumed their wooden buildings and devastated the civilian population.

The island-hopping strategy had opened a path from New Guinea to the Philippines. On October 9, 1944, a grand armada carrying MacArthur and 250,000 men set out for the Philippine island of Leyte. Four days later, virtually the entire Japanese navy converged on Allied transports in Leyte Gulf, and from October 23 to 25 the greatest sea battle in history was fought. At its end the United States emerged in complete command of the Pacific. Manila fell to MacArthur's forces on February 23, 1945. But not until July 5 were the last of the Japanese rooted out. By then, Iwo Jima and Okinawa had been taken at a cost of 70,000 men.

Kamikaze attacks by Japanese suicide fliers who plunged their bomb-laden planes into American ships accounted for many of the American casualties at Okinawa. Both campaigns—Iwo had been gained by March 16, 1945, and Okinawa by June 21—wiped out any lingering doubt that the Japanese would resist to the last knife or bullet or breath.

The island-hopping campaigns had finished all but the remnants of the Japanese navy and air force. American submarines had sunk more than half of the Japanese merchant marine, which had kept Japan supplied with the oil, rubber, tin, and grain of its mainland conquests. These conquests had been under strong attack by British and American forces since the winter of 1943.

The Allies struggled to get Chiang Kai-shek to fight harder in China. But Chiang was preparing for a showdown with the Communists, who were gathering forces in the Chinese north. The most progress against the Japanese was made in Burma, where Rangoon, the principal port, was retaken in May 1945. But Japan did not give up the other mainland territories until its collapse at home.

The Atomic Victory

On July 16, 1945, at precisely 5:30 a.m., an atomic bomb was successfully detonated in the New Mexican desert. For those who witnessed the explosion, it was a terrifying sight. "It was as though the earth had opened and the skies had split," one journalist wrote. "One felt as though one were present at the moment of creation when God said: 'Let there be light.' "

Ten days later, Allied leaders assembled at Potsdam sent an ultimatum to the enemy: "The alternative to surrender is prompt and utter destruction." No surrender came, because Japanese military leaders overruled the government. On August 6 the first atomic bomb to be used in warfare was dropped on Hiroshima, killing instantly nearly 75,000 people and injuring 100,000 more in a city of 344,000; many more would die from the effects of radiation. Still no word from the government. Two days later, as it had promised in Yalta, the Soviet Union entered the war and overran Japanese forces in Manchuria.

On August 9, a second bomb was dropped, this time on Nagasaki. At last, on August 10, Tokyo sued for peace, but on one condition: that Emperor Hirohito be permitted to retain his throne. This condition was accepted by the Allies. On September 2, 1945, formal surrender ceremonies were conducted in Tokyo Bay on the battleship *Missouri*, with General MacArthur accepting for the victors.

The most terrible war in history had ended in the most terrible display of force. The decision to use the bomb on a country already on the brink of collapse aroused much controversy in the world community. Those who defended the decision argued that it actually saved the lives of hundreds of thousands of Americans and Japanese by bringing the war to a quick end and making unnecessary an invasion of the Japanese mainland. If the United States had confined itself to "conventional" fire bombing of Japanese cities, the cost in human lives would presumably have been much greater than the cost of the Hiroshima and Nagasaki bombs. But critics contended that Japan would have surrendered soon even if there had been no atomic bomb, invasion, or Soviet entry into the war.

Still another factor was suggested by Secretary of State James F. Byrnes: the new weapon would "put us in a position to dictate our own terms at the end of the war" and "make Russia more manageable in Europe." To American soldiers in

The mushroom cloud rises over Nagasaki, August 9, 1945. *(Official U.S. Air Force Photo)*

the battle areas, of course, as to their families at home, anything that contributed to a quick end to the war outweighed all other considerations.

President Truman had no misgivings about his decision. "I regarded the bomb as a military weapon and never had any doubt that it should be used. The atomic bomb was no great decision, not any decision you had to worry about." No policy maker, in fact, seriously questioned the assumption that the atomic bomb would be used against Germany or Japan once it was ready. Most likely, then, the bomb was dropped to force Japanese leaders to agree to a quick surrender. That its use would also dramatize to the Soviet Union the supremacy of the United States reinforced more immediate military objectives. In any event, the United States, by becoming the only nation to have used the bomb, assumed an awesome image in the world. The atom bomb, said Truman, had become "merely another powerful weapon in the arsenal of righteousness."

The massive national mobilization of the war had significantly enlarged the role of the military in the economy, in education, and in other areas of American life. The unleashing of atomic energy at the moment of final victory, and then the international rivalry for atomic power, gave militarism new life. It also invited new worldwide responsibilities and irresponsibility—and speeded up change at home.

The war brought the end of empire: colonial domains established by Europe in Asia and Africa over some three centuries—sources of immense labor power and natural wealth—were almost entirely dissolved in the fifteen years that followed the war. Contending for the loyalty and resources of the new nations would be the two superpowers—the United States and the Soviet Union. Both were intent on remaking the postwar world in their own image.

SUMMARY

From 1920 to about 1937, the United States went its own way in world affairs. The Washington Conference, an effort to stop the naval arms race after World War I, began late in 1921. It ended in early 1922 with a five-power naval treaty, a four-power pact, and a nine-power pact. But none of these agreements had an enforcement mechanism, and they were no more effective than the Kellogg-Briand Pact of 1928, which renounced war as an instrument of national policy and was signed by sixty-two nations.

The first signs that all these international agreements and the League of Nations were worth nothing came with Japanese expansionism. In the face of Japanese moves into Manchuria in 1931, the United States offered only the Stimson Doctrine, a policy of refusing to recognize territorial changes achieved by force of arms. Japan continued its war in China, resigned from the league in 1933, and renounced the naval agreements of 1922.

Fear of Japan and of Hitler's Germany finally led the United States to recognize the Soviet Union in November 1933. But mutual suspicion between the two continued. In Latin America, an active, interventionist policy had made the United States no friends. Roosevelt's Good Neighbor policy brought only slow improvement.

The need to do something about Latin America and the Soviets was made urgent by the deterioration of relations between America and Europe. Fascist governments had come to power in Italy and Germany. In 1936 Spanish Fascists under Franco began a civil war that

lasted until 1939. With the help of Germany and Italy, Franco won.

All these governments favored aggressive, expansionist foreign policies centered in military conquest. Mussolini took Ethiopia in 1935; German forces occupied the Rhineland in 1936; in September 1938, Hitler took the Sudetenland. At the Munich Conference, Britain and France, unprepared, let him get away with it. In March 1939, Hitler took the rest of Czechoslovakia; three weeks later, Mussolini took Albania. In August, Hitler made a nonaggression pact with the Soviet Union to protect his eastern flank. Then, on September 1, Nazi troops and planes invaded Poland. Two days later, Britain and France, honoring their Polish commitments, declared war on Germany.

The United States was officially neutral, and public opinion was sharply divided. But then in April 1940, Hitler unleashed a *blitzkrieg* ("lightning war"), rolling over Denmark, Norway, Belgium, Holland, Luxembourg, and even France in seven weeks. The British were left to stand alone. During the summer and fall of 1940, Hitler made a tremendous effort to bomb them into surrender. He did not succeed, and at the end the British had regained control of the air.

American policy was to strengthen its own defenses while aiding Britain to keep it from collapsing. Roosevelt, reelected in 1940 for a third term, began pressing the foreign-policy debate in public. The lend-lease program was passed by Congress in early 1941, and the United States moved steadily closer to war in the Atlantic. At an

August meeting, Churchill and Roosevelt drew up the Atlantic Charter, which set forth their goals for the postwar world. By the fall of 1941 the United States had become an open ally of Britain without having formally declared war. In November, lend-lease was extended to the Soviet Union, now under attack as Hitler opened his eastern front.

In the Pacific, the American response to Japanese pressure had been first to embargo aviation gasoline and then iron and steel-scrap shipments to Japan. Two days after the extension of the embargo in September, Japan joined the German-Italian coalition. Although negotiations with Japan continued in Washington through the autumn, the Japanese made plans to attack if the outcome was not satisfactory. These plans were carried out on Sunday, December 7, 1941, when a carrier-borne force of Japanese planes destroyed the Pacific Fleet at Pearl Harbor in Hawaii. The next day Congress declared war on Japan, and four days later Germany and Italy declared war on the United States. America was again engaged in global war.

The home front was mobilized for war; it was also mobilized in a propaganda campaign of hatred for the enemy. One result was the internment of Japanese Americans in camps far from their West Coast homes. At the time of Pearl Harbor, an American army of 1.6 million

TIME LINE

1921–1933	United States intervenes in Panama, Dominican Republic, Honduras, and Nicaragua
1921	Washington Disarmament Conference
1928	Kellogg-Briand Pact
1931	Japan invades Manchuria
1932	Stimson Doctrine
1933	Hitler comes to power in Germany
	United States recognizes the Soviet Union
	Good Neighbor policy announced
	Germany begins rearmament
1935	Italy invades Ethiopia
	First Neutrality Act
1936	Spanish Civil War begins
	Second Neutrality Act
1937	Japan overruns North China
	Third Neutrality Act
	Roosevelt's Quarantine Speech
1938	Munich Conference (France, Britain, Germany)
1939	Nazi-Soviet Pact
	Germany invades Poland; World War II begins
	Congress repeals arms embargo
1940	Germany overruns Western Europe
	Air battle over Britain
	Japan joins German-Italian coalition (Axis)
	Congress passes first peacetime draft
	Destroyer-bases deal (U.S. and Britain)
	Roosevelt re-elected
1941	Lend-lease Act

German submarines attack American merchant ships
Germany attacks the Soviet Union
March on Washington; Roosevelt prohibits racial discrimination in defense industries
Atlantic Charter
Japan attacks Pearl Harbor; U.S. enters World War II

1942	Internment of Japanese-Americans
	Allies invade North Africa
	Battles of Coral Sea and Midway
	Soviet victory at Stalingrad
1943	Casablanca Conference (Roosevelt and Churchill)
	Allies invade Sicily and Italy
	Teheran Conference (Roosevelt, Churchill, Stalin)
	Race riots in Los Angeles, Beaumont, Mobile, New York, and Detroit
1944	Allied forces land in France (D-Day)
	Battles of Philippine Sea and Leyte Gulf
	Roosevelt re-elected
1945	Battles of Iwo Jima and Okinawa
	Yalta Conference (Roosevelt, Churchill, Stalin)
	Roosevelt dies; Harry Truman becomes president
	Soviet-Allied offensive defeats Germany
	Potsdam Conference (Truman, Churchill/Atlee, Stalin)
	Atomic bombs dropped on Hiroshima and Nagasaki; Japan surrenders

men had been recruited in the first peacetime draft. The draft was extended to all men between certain ages, and women were allowed to volunteer.

Behind the 15 million men and more than 200,000 women in active service were American industry, agriculture, labor, and science. Depression unemployment ended. Many women went to work, especially in the defense industries. Men continued to dominate in supervisory positions, and wage scales discriminated against women. Blacks continued to be segregated, even in the armed forces.

The Allied powers did not expect to win quickly. Germany had conquered most of Europe, and Japan had taken a good bit of the Pacific islands and Southeast Asia. The Allied decision was to concentrate on Europe first. The next decision was that the Allies would have to gain control of the sea and air before land invasions could begin.

The first land operation was conducted in North Africa, where the Germans were moving toward the Suez Canal. It was followed by the invasion of Italy in July 1943, and then by the invasion of Normandy by a huge force on D-Day, June 6, 1944. Throughout the war, Allied leaders met constantly to plan strategy and conduct diplomacy. Conferences were held in 1943 at Casablanca (January), Moscow (October), and Cairo and Teheran (November). By the time of the Yalta Conference in February 1945, Soviet armies were only fifty miles from Berlin. The European war ended on May 7, 1945, with the unconditional surrender of Germany.

President Roosevelt died on April 12, and Harry Truman became president. By this time the campaign in the Pacific, based on an island-hopping strategy, was close to Japan itself. It was Truman's decision to use the atomic bomb for the first time ever in war, to bring the conflict to a quick end and avoid a long and costly land campaign. The most terrible war in history thus ended in the most terrible display of force. And at the end there were two superpowers, the United States and the Soviet Union, both out to reshape the postwar world according to radically different ideologies.

Suggested Readings

G. Wright, *The Ordeal of Total War 1939–1945* (1968), is a solid overview of the European and world situation. G. F. Kennan, *American Diplomacy 1900–1950* (1951) and *Memoirs 1925–1950* (1967), provide valuable commentary and analysis. On prewar American attitudes, see S. Adler, *The Isolationist Impulse* (1957) and *The Uncertain Giant* (1965).

R. H. Ferrell, *American Diplomacy in the Great Depression* (1957), and J. E. Wiltz, *From Isolation to War 1931–1941* (1968), provide background. But see also W. A. Williams, *The Tragedy of American Diplomacy* (1972) ed. On the development of a Far Eastern policy, see D. Borg, *The United States and the Far Eastern Crisis 1933–1938* (1964), and A. Iriye, *After Imperialism: The Search for a New Order in the Far East 1921–1931* (1965) and *Across the Pacific: An Inner History of American–East Asian Relations* (1967). On Latin American relations, see B. Wood, *The Making of the Good Neighbor Policy* (1961) and *The United States and Latin American Wars 1932–1942* (1966), and D. Green, *The Containment of Latin America* (1971). On Soviet-American relations, see W. A. Williams, *American-Russian Relations 1781–1947* (1952), and R. P. Browder, *The Origins of Soviet-American Diplomacy* (1953).

On Hitler's rise and the response, see A. Bullock, *Hitler: A Study in Tyranny* (1952); A. A. Offner, *American Appeasement: United States Foreign Policy and Germany 1933–1938* (1969); and S. Friedlander, *Prelude to Downfall: Hitler and the United States 1939–1941* (1967). See also W. S. Cole, *Senator Gerald P. Nye and American Foreign Relations* (1962) and *America First: The Battle against Intervention 1940–1941* (1953). On the Spanish civil war, see G. Jackson, *The Spanish Republic and the Civil War 1931–1939* (1965), and A. Guttman, *The Wound in the Heart: America and the Spanish Civil War* (1962).

On FDR and the war, the definitive studies are R. Dallek, *Franklin D. Roosevelt and American Foreign Policy 1932–1945* (1979), and J. M. Burns, *Roosevelt: The Soldier of Freedom 1940–1945* (1970). For the policy makers around FDR, see E. E. Morrison, *Turmoil and Tradition: A Study of the Life and Times of Henry L. Stimson* (1960); H. L. Stimson and M. Bundy, *On Active Service in Peace and War* (1948); R. N. Current, *Secretary Stimson* (1954); Cordell Hull, *Memoirs* (2 vols., 1948); J. W. Pratt, *Cordell Hull* (1964); R. E. Sherwood, *Roosevelt and Hopkins* (1948); and J. M. Blum, *From the Morgenthau Diaries: Years of Urgency* (1965).

On the road to war, W. L. Langer and S. E. Gleason, *The Challenge to Isolation 1937–1940* (1952) and *Undeclared War 1940–1941* (1953), provide a detailed treatment. See as well R. A. Divine, *The Illusion of Neutrality* (1962) and *The Reluctant Belligerent* (1965). On the mounting crisis in the Far East, see J. C. Grew, *Turbulent Era: A Diplomatic Record of Forty Years* (1952), and H. Feis, *The Road to Pearl Harbor* (1962). Critical of American policy are C. A. Beard, *American Foreign Policy in the Making 1932–1940* (1946) and *President Roosevelt and the Coming of the War* (1948), and C. C. Tansill, *Backdoor to War* (1952). More recent revisionist studies include L. C. Gardner, *Economic Aspects of New Deal Diplomacy* (1971) and *Architects of Illusion* (1970).

S. Terkel, *The Good War* (1984) is a compelling oral history. J. M. Blum, *V Was for Victory* (1976), is a solid study of American politics and culture during the war.

The home front is also examined in G. Perrett, *Days of Sadness, Years of Triumph* (1973); R. Polenberg, *War and Society* (1972); and B. Catton, *War Lords of Washington* (1948). Wartime mobilization is examined in E. Janeway, *The Struggle for Survival* (1951), and D. M. Nelson, *Arsenal for Democracy* (1944), provides an "inside" account. On the military and the economy, see R. M. Leighton and R. W. Coakley, *Global Logistics and Strategy 1940–1945* (2 vols., 1955, 1968); on labor, J. Seidman, *American Labor from Defense to Reconversion* (1953) and N. Lichtenstein, *Labor's War at Home: The CIO in World War II* (1983); on farmers, W. W. Wilcox, *The Farmer in the Second World War* (1947). On women in the war effort, see K. T. Anderson, *Wartime Women: Sex Roles, Family Relations, and the Status of Women During World War II* (1981); D. A. Campbell, *Women at War with America* (1984); S. M. Hartmann, *The Home Front and Beyond* (1982); and L. J. Rupp, *Mobilizing Women for War: German and American Propaganda, 1939–1945* (1978), and the engrossing documentary film *The Life and Times of Rosie the Riveter* (Clarity Educational Productions, P.O. Box 315, Franklin Lakes, NJ 07417).

Wartime dissent is examined in L. S. Wittner, *Rebels against War: The American Peace Movement 1941–1960* (1969). See also P. E. Jacob and M. Q. Sibley, *Conscription of Conscience* (1952), and the personal account of FDR's attorney general, Francis Biddle, *In Brief Authority* (1962). The role of the Communist party is examined in M. Isserman, *Which Side Were You On?* (1982). On black life and attitudes, see R. M. Dalfiume, *Desegregation of the U.S. Armed Forces 1939–1953* (1969); G. Myrdal, *An American Dilemma* (1944); H. Garfinkel, *When Negroes March* (1959); R. W. Logan (ed.), *What the Negro Wants* (1944); W. White, *A Rising Wind* (1945); P. McGuire (ed.), *Taps for a Jim Crow Army: Letters from Black Soldiers in World War II* (1982); P. S. Washburn, *A Question of Sedition: The Federal Government's Investigation of the Black Press During World War II* (1986); and N. A. Wynn, *The Afro-American and the Second World War* (1976). On the internment of the Japanese, see R. Daniels, *The Politics of Prejudice* (1962) and *Concentration Camps USA* (1971), P. Irons, *Justice at War: The Story of the Japanese American Internment Cases* (1983) and J. Tateishi (ed.), *And Justice for All: An Oral History of the Japanese-American Detention Camps* (1984). On the United States and the German death camps, see D. S. Wyman, *The Abandonment of the Jews: America and the Holocaust, 1941 and 1945* (1984) and R. Abzug, *Inside the Vicious Heart* (1985).

On the scientific community and the development and use of the atomic bomb, see A. K. Smith, *A Peril and a Hope: The Scientists' Movement in America 1945–1947* (1965); R. G. Hewlett and O. E. Anderson, Jr., *The New World* (1962); N. P. Davis, *Lawrence and Oppenheimer* (1968); M. J. Sherwin, *A World Destroyed: The Atomic Bomb and the Grand Alliance* (1975); D. J. Kevles, *The Physicists* (1977) and R. Rhodes, *The Making of the Atomic Bomb* (1987). The cultural fallout of the atomic bomb in the United States is imaginatively explored in P. Boyer, *By the Bomb's Early Light: American Thought and Culture at the Dawn of the Atomic Age* (1985).

A. R. Buchanan, *The United States and World War II* (2 vols., 1964), surveys all phases of American military involvement. See also D. D. Eisenhower, *Crusade in Europe* (1948), D. MacArthur, *Reminiscences* (1964), S. A. Ambrose, *Eisenhower: Soldier, General of the Army, President-Elect, 1890–1952* (1983); D. C. James, *The Years of MacArthur, 1941–1945* (1975); and F. C. Pogue, *George C. Marshall* (4 vols., 1963–1987). The most comprehensive account of Japan's path to war and of the fighting and its aftermath is J. Toland, *The Rising Sun: The Decline and Fall of the Japanese Empire 1936–1945* (1970). See also R. H. Spector, *Eagle against the Sun: The American War with Japan* (1985); H. Feis, *Japan Subdued: The Atomic Bomb and the End of the War in the Pacific* (1945); and J. Hersey's unforgettable *Hiroshima* (1946).

J. W. Dower, *War Without Mercy: Race and Power in the Pacific War* (1986) is a brilliant and indispensable inquiry into the racial ideas that underlay the war against Japan. Based on first-hand accounts, both literary and autobiographical, P. Fussell, *Wartime: Understanding and Behavior in the Second World War* (1989) contrasts actual combat and wartime rhetoric. The ordinary soldier is best described in E. Pyle, *The Story of G.I. Joe* (1945); B. Mauldin, *Up Front* (1945); and three novels: J. H. Burns, *The Gallery* (1947); N. Mailer, *The Naked and the Dead* (1948); and J. Heller, *Catch-22* (1961). See also the illuminating sociological study by S. A. Stouffer and others, *The American Soldier* (2 vols., 1949).

H. Feis, *Churchill, Roosevelt, Stalin* (1957), is a study of conference diplomacy. See also J. L. Snell, *Illusion and Necessity: The Diplomacy of the Global War* (1963); G. Smith, *American Diplomacy during the Second World War* (1965); R. B. Levering, *American Opinion and the Russian Alliance 1939–1945* (1976); and the Cold War studies cited at the end of Chapter 30.

CHAPTER 30

THE SEARCH FOR SECURITY

The United States emerged from World War II as the most successful and dominant nation in the world, possessing, as its president said, "the greatest strength and the greatest power which man has ever reached." If greatness was measured by national income, industrial productivity, a trained work force, natural resources, scientific expertise, or the average daily caloric intake of the population, the United States had no equal.

By contrast, the Soviet Union had seen its industrial capacity reduced by more than 40 percent. Great Britain and France faced desperate problems of economic recovery; nationalist movements in Africa, Asia, and the Middle East threatened to topple their colonial empires. Germany and Japan were shattered and conquered territories. China was about to be engulfed by civil war. As if to underscore the position of the United States in the world community, it was also the only nation that had the atomic bomb.

But within two years after V–J Day, Americans discovered that despite all the power they commanded, their position in

the world was by no means secure. Not only were nationalist movements shaking colonial empires and threatening to upset the political balance of power, but the Soviet Union refused to bend to the wishes of policy makers in Washington, D.C., or of the peoples who lived on their eastern borders.

The United States and the Soviet Union were engaged in a Cold War, a new experience for Americans. It was a war of rhetoric, the subversion and countersubversion of other governments, direct intervention in the affairs of other nations, and an armaments race with no limits. Over the next two decades, this unresolved conflict would use up a large portion of the national wealth for the perfection and accumulation of weapons designed to defend the country from nuclear destruction. It would demand from the American people the kind of loyalty usually reserved for a hot war.

The search for security was unlike anything in the American past. A nation that had always avoided "entangling alliances," the United States now entered into mutual defense pacts with forty countries. For a nation that had confined its intervention to the Caribbean and Central America, the United States found reasons to intervene, covertly or openly, in the Middle

East (Iran and Lebanon) and in Asia (Korea, Vietnam, Cambodia, and Laos), as well as in its own "sphere of influence" (Cuba, the Dominican Republic, and Chile).

But even with this commitment, and with American forces occupying bases in some thirty countries, the security Americans sought still eluded them.

THE NEW INTERNATIONAL ORDER

Once Japan had surrendered and the secret provisions at Yalta were revealed, Roosevelt's territorial concessions to the Soviet Union—in Eastern Europe and the northernmost islands of Japan—caused an outburst of criticism. Some of the outcry was politically inspired; there were those who wished to pin the label of appeasement on the Democrats. The critics conveniently ignored the military situation at the time of Yalta, the urgent need for Soviet entry into the Asian war, and Stalin's determination to establish a defense perimeter in Eastern Europe to secure the USSR from future attack. None of the "concessions" included territory actually controlled by the United States or its Western allies at the end of the war.

FDR apparently thought them necessary to reassure the Soviet Union about its security and to win Stalin's participation in the United Nations once the fighting was over. On returning from Yalta in March 1945, Roosevelt declared that the agreement there "spells the end of the system of unilateral action and exclusive alliances and balances of power" in favor of "a universal organization in which all peace-loving nations will finally have a chance to join."

The old League of Nations had failed at least as badly as traditional balance-of-power arrangements in keeping world peace. Whatever stability the new United Nations would be able to impose on the world rested largely on cooperation between the two dominant powers, the United States and the Soviet Union. But mutual suspicions had been aroused before the UN even had a chance to take shape. Only eleven days before his death, Roosevelt sent Stalin a sharp message about "the lack of progress" in implementing the political decisions reached at Yalta, particularly those regarding free elections in Poland.

Likewise, Stalin had grown skeptical of Western actions and intentions. No less disturbing to him was the Western challenge to Soviet domination of Eastern Europe after the war. Stalin held off until the last moment before sending a delegation to San Francisco, where work on the United Nations charter began April 25, 1945. His delay only deepened Western suspicion.

The United Nations

Even before the United Nations Charter was written, certain international structures had been created to handle wartime relief and postwar reconstruction. As early as November 1943, forty-four nations had set up the United Nations Relief and Rehabilitation Administration to assist areas liberated from Germany, Italy, and Japan. The first of two conferences in 1944 to plan the postwar world was held at Bretton Woods, New Hampshire. This conference created an International Monetary Fund to stabilize national currencies and an International Bank for Reconstruction and Development, called the World Bank, to extend rehabilitation loans. The second conference, at Dumbarton Oaks in Washington, D.C., drafted plans for the United Nations Charter.

The charter of the United Nations Organization provided for two major agencies, the General Assembly and the Security Council. Each member nation had a seat in the General Assembly, which was primarily an arena for discussion and debate of international questions falling within the scope of the charter. But it could recommend action to the Security Council, and if the council failed to act, the assembly, as of 1950, could recommend action to member nations.

The Security Council, which was to remain in continuous session in order to settle international disputes as they arose, consisted of five permanent members—the United States, the Soviet Union, Great Britain, France, and China—and six others elected for two-year terms. The council had the power to apply diplomatic, economic, or military sanctions against any nation threatening the peace. Any of the permanent members, however, could block action by a veto. This decision virtually ensured that the council would be unable to oppose aggression by the major powers. But it may have helped save the world from a collision of such powers by allowing them to check the use of force by the UN itself.

The United States Senate had debated the Covenant of the League of Nations for eight months before rejecting it. It debated UN membership for six days, and approved it by a vote of eighty-nine to two. After the charter had been signed at San Francisco, the UN held its first meetings in London in 1946 and then moved to New York City, its permanent home. Founded with 51 charter nations, the UN had by the 1980s tripled in membership to 159 nations, more than two-thirds of them in the Third World.

In the early years, the United States exercised considerable influence over the organization. In 1950, it obtained General Assembly sanction for military intervention in Korea. And until 1961 it saw to it that the question of seating the People's Republic of China was not placed on the agenda. By the early 1970s, however, that dominance had clearly passed. China had been seated, and the United States ambassador to the UN was openly expressing his concern over a new "tyranny of the majority."

If only as a discussion body, the United Nations ensured that some questions affecting world peace would be debated with words rather than with weapons. Some of its subsidiary units, such as the World Health Organization (WHO) and the United Nations Educational, Scientific, and Cultural Organization (UNESCO), made important strides toward international cooperation in vital areas. But the UN failed to control the postwar armaments race, deal with the dissolution of the overseas empires of Western powers, or resolve the question of what to do with the conquered Axis powers. As the Cold War developed, those issues became more and more important.

Atomic Energy

The UN was forced to confront atomic warfare and a potential atomic-arms race as its first major problem. Scientists in all industrial countries knew of the research on the atom that had been conducted since the 1930s, although only those in the United States could mobilize the funds, labor, and technical equipment required for A-bomb development and manufacture during the war. Once the bomb was dropped, many of the scientists involved wanted to harness the monster they had created. At the same time, the evidence of its power spurred others to develop the bomb in self-defense.

In 1946, Bernard M. Baruch, the American delegate to the recently created UN Atomic Energy Commission, submitted a plan for control of atomic weapons. It called for the creation of an international agency to which the United States would turn over its atomic secrets. The agency would be able to inspect atomic installations in any country and see that weapons were not being manufactured. It could punish violators and its decisions would not be subject to veto. As soon as the inspection system was working, the United States would destroy its stock of weapons and manufacture no more.

But the USSR was suspicious of any international agency likely to be dominated by the United States, and was unwilling to tolerate inspection. It proposed instead an international agreement to abandon atomic warfare and prohibit the making of weapons. The Soviet plan had no provision for inspection. This was unacceptable to the United States. Once the USSR detonated its own first atomic bomb in September 1949, security by balance of terror became part of the new world order. That balance may have done more to avert atomic warfare than the long and fruitless pursuit of control and disarmament.

While progress toward regulation dragged, the United States proceeded with the development of atomic energy. In August 1946, Congress created the Atomic Energy Commission. It was placed under civilian control, and a proposal to give the armed-service chiefs a veto on its actions was defeated. The commission was to promote private and government research into the peaceful as well as military uses of atomic energy and to develop facilities for its production.

Cost and technical problems delayed peaceful applications for almost two decades. In the mid-sixties, nuclear generating plants began to be built by utility companies. But the danger of radioactive emissions was a source of considerable alarm. The disastrous potential of the accidents at the Three Mile Island nuclear plant near Harrisburg, Pennsylvania, in April 1979 and at the Chernobyl nuclear plant near Kiev in the Soviet Union in April 1986 threw the entire future of the nuclear industry into question.

The Conquered Nations

The problem of settling the fate of the conquered nations also revealed the tension between the Soviet Union and the West. On July 17, 1945, Truman, Churchill, and Stalin met at Potsdam, Germany, to deal with the future of the old Axis members. (Following the startling defeat of his party in the British elections on July 26, Churchill gave way to the new prime minister, Labour party leader Clement Attlee). At Potsdam the new Big Three reaffirmed the four-power occupation of Germany, worked out details of German reparations payments, and tentatively settled the Polish-German frontier.

During 1945 and 1946, the leading Nazis were tried at Nuremberg before an international military court on charges of having started the war and conducting it in ways that violated fundamental human decency. The trial revealed the full story of Nazi barbarity: the systematic torture and murder of millions of Jews and Slavs, along with other defenseless civilians. Never before had such brutality been so fully documented. Ten leading war criminals were executed. In all, over 500,000 Nazis were found guilty in the American zone and received sentences of varying severity.

Similar trials in Japan led to the execution of former premier Tojo and six other war leaders. Lighter sentences were passed on about four thousand other war criminals. A generation later, these trials were to be recalled to the discomfort of some of the accusers, including the United States. For in the fighting against formerly colonial peoples, Europeans and Americans themselves broke many of the rules of war.

In 1948 the Soviets, irked by the friction arising from the administration of Germany, ordered a blockade of Berlin. That city, though situated deep in their zone, was jointly administered by the USSR and the Western powers. By threatening the Germans in the Western zone of Berlin with starvation, the Soviets hoped to force the Allies to leave Berlin. The challenge was met with an airlift. Food and supplies were delivered to the city by continuously shuttling cargo planes. In the end, it was the USSR that gave in and lifted the blockade, in May 1949.

Frustrated by the failure to reach agreement on Germany, the Western powers met in June 1948 and consented to the creation of an unarmed German Federal Republic, embracing the three Western zones. The new state was launched in September 1949. One month later, the Soviets established the German Democratic Republic in the east.

No such divisions occurred in conquered Japan, where the United States assumed full command under General Douglas MacArthur. A new constitution went into effect in May 1947, turning the fundamental powers of government over to representatives elected by the people. The emperor renounced his claim to divinity, and the constitution renounced war as a right of the nation. Social reforms were carried out, including the dissolution of the great industrial and commercial monopolies and the restoration of large tracts of land to the poor in rural areas.

In September 1951, following the Communist triumph in China (1949) and the outbreak of the Korean conflict (1950), forty-nine nations signed a general peace treaty with Japan restoring its "full sovereignty," including the right to redevelop an armaments industry and armed services. (The USSR did not sign.) The treaty was negotiated at the urging of the United States, which wished to rebuild Japan in order to offset communism in Asia—as Germany was soon to be strengthened so that it could offset communism in Europe. At this time, mutual-security agreements were also made with the Philippines, Australia, and New Zealand.

A sailor and a nurse celebrate the end of World War II on V–J Day, August 14, 1945, in New York's Times Square. (As recently as 1980, various individuals have claimed to be the man or the woman in this classic photograph by Alfred Eisenstaedt.) *(Life Magazine © 1945, Time, Inc.)*

THE TRUMAN ADMINISTRATION AT HOME

The death of Roosevelt in April 1945 had brought to the presidency Harry Truman, a relatively obscure New Deal Democrat whose bland folksiness contrasted sharply with FDR's urbanity. During World War I, Truman, a farm boy from Independence, Missouri, became an artillery captain. Soon after demobilization in 1919, he opened a men's clothing store in Kansas City. When this business died in the postwar depression, the Pendergast political machine, which controlled Kansas City politics, invited Truman to run for county judge.

When the same machine needed a "clean" candidate for the United States Senate in 1934, it chose Truman. He won easily. After his reelection in 1940, he became chairman of a Senate committee that investigated defense contracts. His zeal in working over wartime big business brought him notice and won him the Democratic vice-presidential nomination four years later.

Upon becoming president, he said: "I felt like

United States population, 1950–1960.

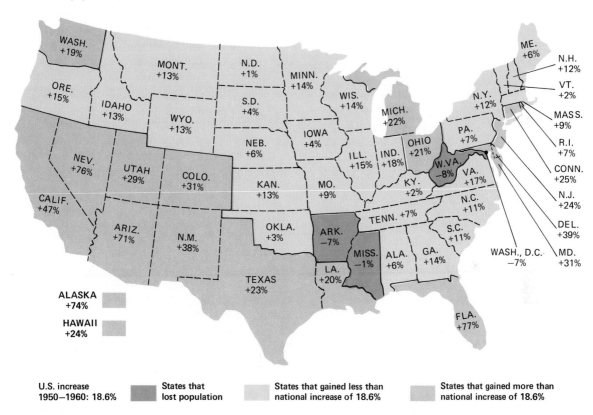

| U.S. increase 1950–1960: 18.6% | States that lost population | States that gained less than national increase of 18.6% | States that gained more than national increase of 18.6% |

Total Population (in millions)

150.7 1950
179.5 1960

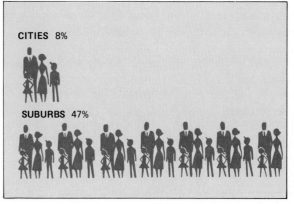

Suburban Growth, 1950–1960

CITIES 8%

SUBURBS 47%

the moon, the stars, and all the planets had fallen on me. I've got the most terribly responsible job a man ever had." Neither in political wisdom nor in the ability to command confidence was he a match for FDR. But it was left to Truman to lead the nation out of one war while alerting it to the threat of still another. The problems he faced at home were enough to worry the most experienced of statesmen: a people eager to return to a peacetime footing but wanting to give up none of the economic benefits the war had brought them. The memories of the Great Depression were still much too vivid.

Demobilization

Once the war ended, in August 1945, Americans' profound war weariness manifested itself in troop demonstrations and riots from Manila to Frankfurt, all of them protesting delays in getting home. The failure of military authorities to agree upon the postwar strength of the rival services explained the delays, but only added to the frustration of soldiers eager to return to civilian life.

Congress and the president bent under all this pressure. By midsummer 1946, army and air force personnel had been cut from over 8 million to under 2 million; navy personnel, from nearly 4 million to 980,000. "I termed this," Truman wrote in his *Memoirs,* "the most remarkable demobilization in the history of the world, or 'disintegration,' if you want to call it that."

Although Truman had suggested the need for universal military training. Congress hesitated until June 1948, when the growing friction with the Soviet Union led it to reenact selective service. In the meantime, the army and navy had begun offering assistance to college men who enrolled in Reserve Officer Training Corps (ROTC) units on their campuses. The expansion and extension of various veterans' benefits placed a college education within reach of a far greater proportion of high school graduates. Under the Servicemen's Readjustment Act of June 1944, commonly known as the GI Bill of Rights, and later measures, $13.5 billion in federal funds was spent between 1945 and 1955 for veterans' education in colleges and vocational schools. Veterans of Korea were included.

This act also entitled discharged servicemen and women to medical treatment at veterans' hospitals, vocational rehabilitation for the crippled, one year's unemployment insurance, and government loans for building homes and establishing businesses.

Not long after the demobilization of military personnel, the Truman administration moved to reorganize the military establishment. The National Security Act of 1947 unified the administration of the armed services and enlarged their duties. A National Military Establishment, soon to be renamed the Department of Defense, was created under a cabinet-level secretary of defense, to "be appointed from civilian life." (Navy Secretary James V. Forrestal became the first secretary of defense). Each service—army, navy, air force—was to be headed by a secretary below the cabinet level, and a uniformed chief of staff or chief of operations. The uniformed chiefs of the three services, along with the president's chief of staff, were to make up the Joint Chiefs of Staff and be the principal military advisers to the president.

The act also created a National Security Council, to be presided over by the commander in chief, and placed under it a Central Intelligence Agency, which would coordinate all government intelligence activities. Though forbidden by its charter to do so, the CIA would also play a role in domestic surveillance of politically suspect activity.

The Economy

With the end of the war, Americans longed for the material comforts that had been denied them when industry converted to wartime production. Backing up this longing was the massive $140 billion in savings accounts and government war bonds that Americans had come out of the war anxious to spend. "The American people," Fred M. Vinson, director of war mobilization and reconversion, declared late in 1945, "are in the pleasant predicament of having to learn to live 50 percent better than they have ever lived before."

The many new luxuries available to consumers, such as television sets, freezers, and automatic dishwashers, clothes dryers, and garbage disposals, were quickly made into necessities by a revitalized advertising industry. At the same time, Americans were able to make certain decisions the war had postponed, such as marrying and having children. The average age of marriage declined, and birthrates increased rapidly, producing a remarkable baby boom. In 1950, 3.5 million babies were born, compared with 2.5 million in 1940; between 1950 and 1980, the American population increased by 50 percent. To

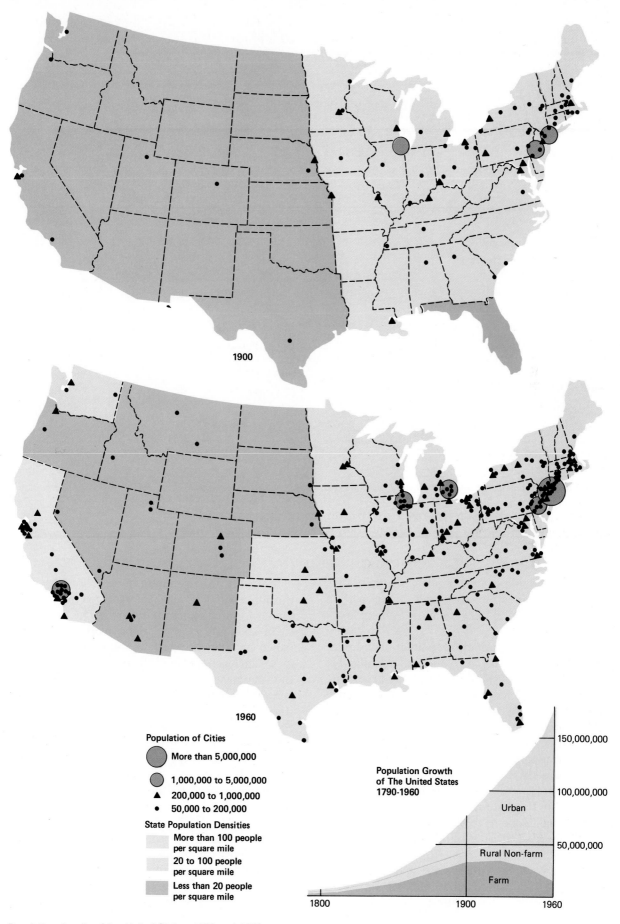

1900

1960

Population of Cities

⬤ More than 5,000,000

⬤ 1,000,000 to 5,000,000

▲ 200,000 to 1,000,000

• 50,000 to 200,000

State Population Densities

More than 100 people
per square mile

20 to 100 people
per square mile

Less than 20 people
per square mile

**Population Growth
of The United States
1790-1960**

150,000,000

100,000,000

Urban

50,000,000

Rural Non-farm

Farm

1800   1900   1960

Population density of the United States, 1900 and 1960.

Fun seekers crowd Jones Beach, New York. In the 1950s the population increased sharply as women of childbearing age averaged 3.35 children; by the late 1960s, the average had fallen to 2.45. *(UPI/Bettman Newsphotos)*

accommodate more and larger families, a new American frontier also emerged, along with a society and culture new to most Americans—suburbia.

The improved economic condition of the middle class, the availability and affordability of automobiles and gasoline, and easy credit and the readiness of the federal government to subsidize interest rates for mortgages—most notably for single-family houses—provided additional incentives for many Americans to reconsider their living arrangements. Of the 13 million homes built between 1948 and 1958, 11 million of them—or 85 percent—were built in the suburbs. By 1960, for the first time, more Americans owned homes than rented them, and by 1970 more Americans lived in the suburbs than in the central cities.

Not only did the American people experience significant population movements, separated mostly by race and class, into and out of the inner cities (as the urban centers came to be called), but the suburban way of life transformed the environment in some extraordinary ways. The first major retail shopping center in the world was established in Raleigh, North Carolina, in 1949. The idea soon swept through the country, and by 1984 the nation's twenty thousand large shopping centers accounted for about two-thirds of all retail trade. The major retail stores either abandoned the central business districts or established branches in the suburbs.

The liberal heritage of the New Deal survived the war, but the sense of urgency about social and economic reform was no longer present and the mood of the country was more conservative. President Truman tried to interest Congress in a liberal legislative program that included broader social-security coverage, public housing, medical insurance, a higher minimum wage (from forty to sixty-five cents), a permanent Fair Employment Practices Commission, and a full-employment bill. In February 1946, after a long debate on the relative roles of business and government, Congress passed the Maximum Employment Act.

This act committed the federal government for the first time to utilizing the nation's economic resources to ensure "maximum employment, production, and purchasing power." It created a Council of Economic Advisers and authorized it to keep the president informed on economic trends and on the proper public measures for softening business downswings and sustaining prosperity. Although the country did not return to prewar levels of unemployment, it did permit an unemployment rate unacceptable to many industrialized democracies. Even in a time of relative prosperity, as in the early 1960s, more than 5 percent of the work force remained unemployed, and a much higher rate prevailed for blacks.

The reconversion of industry to peacetime production and the elimination of wartime controls preoccupied government and business leaders. Once the war ended, private companies that had operated Defense Plant Corporation facilities took advantage of their liberal purchase options to buy them up. The business community also went

on a spree of new plant construction. To stimulate postwar business, Congress cut taxes an estimated $6 billion in November 1945. In November 1946, Congress swept away all wartime price controls except those on rents, sugar, and rice. (Truman had vetoed a similar measure, calling it "a sure formula for inflation.") With these incentives, industrial production soared, as did the inflationary spiral. Between 1945 and 1947, food prices increased more than 25 percent.

So strong was the pent-up demand for consumer goods that shortages soon intensified the already sharp inflation caused by everyone's catching up at once. Inflation in turn broadened the wave of strikes that swept the country after the removal of wartime restraints. Labor found that wages were simply not keeping pace with the cost of living. One of the most far-reaching strikes was that of the United Mine Workers in April 1946. Although Truman ordered government seizure of the coal pits, the mine workers eventually made important wage gains.

A nationwide railroad strike, followed by fruitless labor–management negotiations, prompted Truman to seize the railroads in May 1946. Only a

After winning the election in a great upset, Harry Truman waved a copy of the staunchly Republican *Chicago Daily Tribune,* which had gone to press confident of a Dewey landslide. *(UPI/Bettmann Archive)*

last-minute settlement halted the passage of stern anti-union legislation. The president's actions no doubt reflected the lingering spirit of wartime discipline. Yet the atmosphere had changed: militant unionism received no encouragement in the postwar decades. That was in step with the prevailing conservative mood, which suddenly brought life and hope back to the Republican party.

The Eightieth Congress

Even as Truman grew more confident in the White House, the postwar inflation and labor conflicts hurt the Democratic party, especially in the cities. Despite Truman's tough anti-Soviet stand in foreign relations, the Republicans harped on the New Deal's "softness" on communism and the possibility that highly placed Americans had participated in spy rings. Using these issues, the Republicans won majorities in both houses of the Eightieth Congress in the elections of 1946. In March 1947 Congress passed the Twenty-second Amendment to the Constitution, limiting the president to two terms, a backhanded slap at FDR. This amendment was ratified in 1951. As the incumbent, Truman was exempted from its provisions.

With his eye on the 1948 presidential campaign, Truman pressed on the Republican-dominated Congress the liberal measures with which he hoped to rebuild Democratic urban strength. Among his proposals were comprehensive medicare and civil rights bills. As anticipated, this program died in Congress, the victim of a Republican–southern Democrat coalition. Seeking to save something of the civil rights program, and perhaps to maximize the effectiveness of the armed forces, Truman used his authority as commander in chief to issue an executive order in July 1948 for racial equality (desegregation) in the armed services.

The Eightieth Congress's most controversial domestic measure, adopted over Truman's veto in June 1947, was the Taft-Hartley Act. This measure, first, outlawed the closed shop (unions could not compel employers to hire only union members) but allowed the union shop (unions could negotiate contracts with employers by which newly hired workers would have to join the union). Second, it legalized "right-to-work" laws, by which states could prohibit the requirement of union membership as a condition of employment. Third, it permitted the government to impose on

unions a sixty-day "cooling-off period," before the end of which they could not strike. Last, it required union leaders to file affidavits that they were not Communists. If they did not do so, their unions could not be certified as bargaining agents under the National Labor Relations Act.

Labor leaders denounced Taft-Hartley, but the act did not prevent them from making substantial gains. From 1945 to 1952, union membership rose from 14.6 to 17 million. Although the act made it more difficult to organize new kinds of workers, it did weld unions together and speed the move toward unification of the AFL and the CIO. It also assured Truman of solid union support in the 1948 election.

The Election of 1948 and the Fair Deal

As the presidential election neared, Truman's prospects appeared poor. The Eightieth Congress had blocked most of his social legislation. Southern Democrats were angry over the growing concern of party liberals with civil rights. As early as 1946, moreover, Henry A. Wallace, Truman's secretary of commerce, had broken with the president over his Cold War policies and been dropped from the cabinet. In December 1947, Wallace announced he would run for president on a third-party ticket. Some analysts believed he might win 5 to 8 million votes, enough to sink any Democratic candidate. The Republicans renominated Governor Thomas E. Dewey of New York for president and Governor Earl Warren of California for vice-president. Their platform was internationalist on foreign policy and moderate on domestic issues.

For months before the Democrats convened, feverish efforts were made to hold the party together. Liberals led by Mayor Hubert H. Humphrey of Minneapolis formed Americans for Democratic Action (ADA) to help stop the Wallace challenge. When a broad-based movement to draft the immensely popular General Eisenhower failed, the Truman regulars closed ranks and put the president over.

The ADA group, meanwhile, had carried a liberal platform defending the FDR–Truman tradition, denouncing Taft-Hartley, and promising antilynching and anti–poll tax laws. As a sop to southerners, the convention named acting president of the Senate Alben W. Barkley of Kentucky for vice-president.

The ADA's tactics and Barkley's nomination both fell short of their goals. The so-called Dixiecrats, meeting in Birmingham, Alabama, formed the States' Rights Democratic party and nominated Governor J. Strom Thurmond of South Carolina for president. Five days later, the Wallace liberals formed the Progressive party and named their favorite as standard-bearer. Wallace had hoped to offer an alternative to Truman's bipartisan Cold War foreign policy and the growing repression of civil liberties in the name of that policy. On still another emerging issue—civil rights—the Wallace movement broke with both major political parties in challenging the entire apparatus of racial repression in the South, from disfranchisement to segregation.

But the Wallace movement was unable to overcome either its identification with individuals and ideas deemed subversive in the atmosphere of the Cold War, or the growing obsession with loyalty. The Communist party's endorsement of Wallace and its active role in his campaign, along with the failure of the Progressive party to condemn Soviet imperialism, served to alienate prospective supporters and tarnish the Wallace candidacy. Although Wallace's views on the Cold War and civil rights deserved a wider hearing, he found himself harassed during the campaign and driven out of public life.

The failure of the efforts at unity made Truman's cause seem hopeless. But the Dixiecrat defection enhanced his appeal to the strategically important black voters of the North, and Wallace's campaign clearly illustrated that Truman was no friend of the radical Left. Dewey, on the other hand, never caught the imagination of the voters. Truman, aware of the fight he had to make, stormed up and down the country denouncing "the do-nothing, good-for-nothing Eightieth Congress."

When the ballots were counted, Truman had pulled off the greatest upset in American political history, winning 24,105,812 popular and 303 electoral votes to Dewey's 21,970,065 and 189. Thurmond carried only four Deep South states, Wallace no state at all. For the Eighty-first Congress, moreover, the Democrats gained a Senate majority of twelve and a House majority of ninety-three.

Convinced that he had received a popular mandate to carry on what he now called the Fair Deal, Truman drew up a program designed to go

The election of 1948.

Truman

Democratic gains from election of 1944

Dewey

Republican gains from election of 1944

Thurmond

the New Deal one better. At vital points the newly influential coalition of conservative Democrats and Republicans blocked him, but he made headway. In 1949 he secured an amendment to the New Deal's Fair Labor Standards Act raising the minimum wage from forty to seventy-five cents an hour. A new Social Security Act, passed in August 1950, added almost 10 million people to those eligible for benefits. A National Housing Act, passed in July 1949, provided large sums to cities for aid in slum clearance and the construction of over 800,000 units for low-income families.

Congress, however, defeated the Brannan Plan (an ambitious program for stabilizing farm income), turned down a strong civil rights program for blacks, and refused to repeal or significantly amend the Taft-Hartley Act.

THE TRUMAN ADMINISTRATION AND THE COLD WAR

While Americans attempted to resume politics as usual at home, the United States and the Soviet Union clashed over the reorganization of the postwar world. Even before Winston Churchill's famous pronouncement at Fulton, Missouri, that "an iron curtain has descended across the Continent," Truman's new secretary of state, James F. Byrnes, caught the mood of American decision makers: "In many countries throughout the world our political and economic creed is in conflict with ideologies which reject both of these principles." No doubt Stalin saw things much the same way.

These conflicting ideas affected how the United States and the Soviet Union perceived each other and how they defined threats to their national security. To the United States, the USSR was a revolutionary monolith dedicated to the triumph of world communism, whether by subversion or by force of arms. The foreign policy of the United States was based on the inevitable danger of Soviet military aggression and the need to contain it.

With equal conviction, the USSR perceived the United States as a power anxious to preserve and extend American institutions and capitalism, whether by atomic diplomacy, subversion, or force. The foreign policy of the Soviet Union rested in part on the conviction that its security demanded a weak Germany and friendly governments on its borders—the kind of security the United States enjoyed in the Western Hemisphere. With the horrors of World War II and Nazi

occupation still paramount in the minds of his people, Stalin felt the need to prepare for anything.

The United States and the Soviet Union viewed each other's moves in the world arena as a confirmation of these perceptions and fears. And decision makers in each nation capitalized on those perceptions and fears to justify greater expenditures for arms and military alliances with friendly nations. It was imperative as well for each nation to keep intact its own sphere of influence (Eastern Europe and Latin America) and to win friends among the noncommitted nations of the world. New nations only recently emerged from colonial domination became targets of competition.

Containment through Foreign Aid

With the Communists in firm control of Eastern Europe, the first skirmishes of the Cold War were fought in the Middle East, Turkey, and Greece. Seeking to establish Soviet influence in oil-rich Iran, Stalin backed a Communist movement in Azerbaijan, Iran's northernmost province on the Soviet border, and tried to secure oil concessions similar to those enjoyed by Anglo-American companies. To maintain the pressure, he chose to ignore the Big Three agreement at Teheran in 1943, which had called for the removal of all Allied troops from Iran by March 2, 1946.

On March 5, after Iran had complained to the UN of Soviet interference, Truman sent Stalin a stiff note. By May 1946 the Soviet troops had been withdrawn, but only after the USSR had obtained an agreement for participation in Iranian oil production. With American aid, Iran regained control over Azerbaijan, and in early 1947 the Iranian government rejected the proposed Iranian-Soviet oil company.

For centuries Russia had sought access to the Mediterranean by way of the Turkish straits leading out from the Black Sea. In 1945 the Soviet Union renewed its demands for joint control of the straits. The United States responded by sending a naval task force. This action, in addition to stern American and British notes, deterred the Russians but also led them to shift the pressure westward onto Greece.

Until February 1947, British forces had assisted the Greek government against Communist guerrillas who sought the overthrow of the right-wing monarchist regime. But the British were in financial trouble. On February 24, they notified the United States that they could no longer afford the burden of resisting communism in the Mediterranean. They planned to withdraw troops from Greece and to terminate aid to Turkey.

This step was an acknowledgment of the end of British supremacy in the Mediterranean. In March 1946 Britain had acknowledged the independence of Trans-Jordan (renamed Jordan in 1949). In April 1947, it turned over the future of Palestine to the UN. This led to the creation, with mixed United States reactions, of the independent state of Israel in May 1948. France, meanwhile, had completed its promised withdrawal from Syria and Lebanon by August 1946. If only by default, leadership of the non-Communist world, with all the obligations it entailed, fell to the United States.

Determined to bolster the pro-Western governments in Greece and Turkey, Truman went before Congress on March 12, 1947, to enunciate what has been known since as the Truman Doctrine. He asked Congress for $400 million to assist Greece and Turkey. In addition, he wanted authority to send American civilian and military advisers to those countries, at their request, to oversee the use of American grants and to train Greek and Turkish soldiers.

To sell this program to the American people and a budget-minded Congress, Truman set down the classic justification for Cold War policies. The images and language he used would be repeated by every succeeding president from Dwight D. Eisenhower to Ronald Reagan. The issues, as Truman portrayed them, were clear:

At the present moment in world history nearly every nation must choose between alternative ways of life. The choice is too often not a free one.

One way of life is based upon the will of the majority, and is distinguished by free institutions, representative government, free elections, guarantees of individual liberty, freedom of speech and religion, and freedom from political oppression.

The second way of life is based upon the will of a minority forcibly imposed upon the majority. It relies upon terror and oppression, a controlled press and radio, fixed elections, and the suppression of personal freedom.

I believe that it must be the policy of the United States to support free peoples who are resisting attempted subjugation by armed minorities or by outside pressures. . . . If we falter in our leadership, we may endanger the peace of the world—and we shall surely endanger the welfare of our own Nation.

If some American critics felt Truman had oversold the Communist menace, others questioned aid to regimes whose only virtue was their opposition to communism. But Congress responded favorably. Between 1947 and 1950, the United States spent about $660 million in aid to Greece and Turkey, and the political stability of those nations was preserved. Even before success had been assured, however, Secretary of the Navy James V. Forrestal was urging Truman to wage an economic offensive to stabilize the Western world before the "Russian poison" overwhelmed Europe, South America, "and ourselves."

Through the development of the Marshall Plan in 1947, the United States again took the initiative in the Cold War. Britain's retreat from its Mediterranean lifeline brought home to the United States the economic predicament of Western Europe and underscored this region's political vulnerability as well. Britain, almost entirely dependent upon outside food supplies and on world trade to pay for them, was by far the worst off economically. The situation in France, however, appeared more ominous because a large Communist party was able to capitalize on a century of deprivation among the working classes.

Deprivation had an even longer history in Italy than in France, and communism an even stronger hold. In defeated Germany, hunger was common and chaos ruled. To restore "the confidence of the European people in the economic future of their own countries," the United States proposed to help reconstruct the entire European economy. General George C. Marshall, the first military man to become secretary of state, announced the new program in his commencement address at Harvard on June 5:

Our policy is directed not against any country or doctrine, but against hunger, poverty, desperation, and chaos. Its purpose should be the revival of a working economy in the world so as to permit the emergence of political and social conditions in which free institutions can exist.

The Soviet Union, though invited to participate in the Marshall Plan, saw it as a project to revive and preserve Western capitalism. Most likely the United States neither expected nor wanted Soviet participation, particularly with a Republican Congress controlling appropriations. Western European leaders welcomed the program and immediately drew up plans for using it. They were probably moved as well by the Communist coup in Czechoslovakia in February 1948. After considerable debate, Congress provided $5.3 billion in April 1948 for the first twelve months of Marshall Plan aid. Between 1948 and 1952, about $12 billion was distributed, more than half of it going to Britain, France, and West Germany. By 1952, economic recovery in these countries had been completed. Western Europe began a long business boom, and the advance of communism within the West was checked.

To solidify American influence elsewhere in the world, Truman proposed the Point Four program in 1949 "for the improvement and growth of undeveloped areas," so that resistance to communism could be strengthened. Between 1951 and 1954, Congress appropriated nearly $400 million for technical assistance to such regions. Such aid was both a response and a stimulus to the growing "revolution of rising expectations" in Asia, Africa, and Latin America.

Containment through Military Alliances: NATO

The idea behind the Truman Doctrine, the Marshall Plan, and Point Four was *containment,*

which after 1947 became the cornerstone of American foreign policy. The concept was set forth by George F. Kennan, a senior foreign-service officer and Soviet expert who had spent five years in the USSR. He warned that the Soviet Union was committed to an "aggressive intransigence with respect to the outside world." But it should not be assumed that the Russians would commit themselves to some "do-or-die program" to overthrow Western society. Their own belief in the inevitable fall of capitalism had convinced them that time was on their side.

The history of Russia and the teachings of Lenin suggested to Kennan that the Soviets would move with caution, retreating when necessary "in the face of superior force." Under such circumstances, American policy must be one of "long-term, patient but firm and vigilant containment of Russian expansive tendencies" based on the "application of counter-force."

The containment policy gave little hope for an

NATO and Eastern Europe.

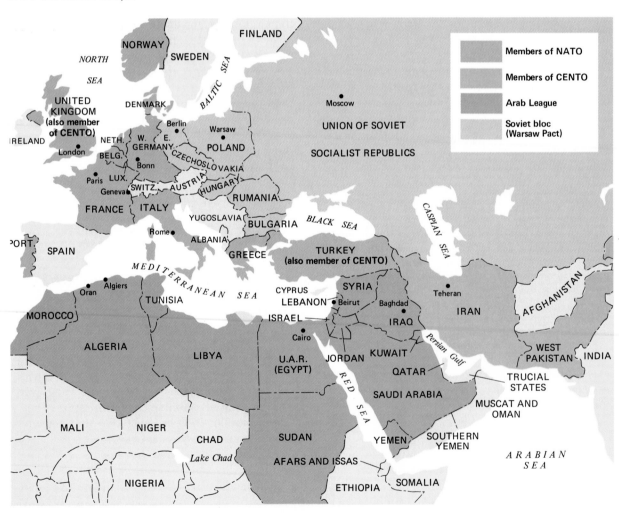

early end to the Cold War. With every new diplomatic move, the United States and the Soviet Union made assumptions about the other's motives that resulted in even more rigid policies. As an alternative to containment, the right wing of the Republican party became infatuated with the idea of "liberation"—that is, direct action to free captive peoples behind the Iron Curtain. With far greater realism, Truman moved to consolidate recent gains. What had begun as economic and military aid to nations threatened by communism evolved into a policy of military alliances.

The UN Charter permitted "collective self-defense" arrangements until the Security Council could act "to maintain peace and security." In March 1948, under the sanction of this article and of the Marshall Plan, Britain, France, the Netherlands, Belgium, and Luxembourg signed a treaty of economic cooperation and military alliance. This step prompted the United States Senate in June 1948 to adopt the Vandenberg Resolution, by which the United States promised "to exercise the right of individual or collective self-defense" in the event of an armed attack "affecting its national security."

The ground was thereby laid for the North Atlantic Treaty, signed April 4, 1949, by twelve Western nations and ratified overwhelmingly (eighty-two to thirteen) by the United States Senate. An armed attack upon any member would be considered an attack upon all; each member promised to assist the one attacked by whatever action was thought necessary, "including the use of armed force." When asked if the signatories to the treaty contemplated a rearmed Germany, Secretary of State Dean Acheson replied: "We are very clear that the disarmament and demilitarization of Germany must be complete and absolute." (In 1954 West Germany was granted full sovereignty, admitted to NATO with full equality, and permitted to raise an army of twelve divisions to become part of the NATO force.)

On September 22, 1949, President Truman made the momentous announcement that the Soviet Union had successfully exploded an atomic bomb. "This is now a different world," Senator Arthur Vandenberg remarked. That same month, Congress passed the Mutual Defense Assistance Act, aimed at building up the military strength of the members of the North Atlantic Treaty Organization (NATO). During the next four years, the United States would supply almost $6 billion worth of arms and other material to European allies and another $1.7 billion to other countries.

Although the European allies strained to make their own contributions to NATO, they failed by and large to do so. NATO therefore soon came to depend on air power as the principal deterrent to the Soviet Union. It relied particularly on the American Strategic Air Command, organized in 1951. SAC, in turn, imposed on the United States the need for air bases in many parts of the world. And this need sometimes awkwardly but decisively influenced diplomatic decisions.

Latin America

During World War II, all Latin American countries except Argentina and Chile had cooperated with the Allies to the extent of supplying strategic materials and making bases available. Brazil and Mexico also sent troops overseas against the Axis. Argentina, aspiring to leadership in competition with both Brazil and the United States, grew especially envious of Brazil because of the United States' lend-lease aid Brazil received.

After the strongly pro-Axis Colonel Juan D. Perón became virtual dictator of Argentina in 1944, relations between his country and the United States deteriorated. Latin American nations began to fear that the war with the Axis would be extended to their hemisphere. To act upon this threat, they met at the Castle of Chapultepec in Mexico City in 1945; Argentina was excluded and the United States represented. On March 6 the conference adopted the Act of Chapultepec, an informal agreement declaring that an attack by any state against the territory, sovereignty, or political independence of an American state would be considered an act of aggression against the signers.

Argentina, aware of its growing isolation, declared war on the Axis on March 27, 1945, and a few days later accepted the Chapultepec agreement. In return the United States, over Soviet opposition, helped Argentina win a seat at the San Francisco Conference in April. It and all the Latin American countries became charter members of the UN.

The end of the war meant the end of the profitable markets for strategic raw materials that Latin American countries had enjoyed during the conflict. It also saw the frustration of their hopes for industrialization, on which they had counted as a springboard for economic growth. When neglect by the United States followed the restoration of peace, suspicion grew that the Good Neighbor policy declared by FDR had been merely a screen for wartime exploitation. A crushing blow came in June 1947 when Latin America found itself excluded from the Marshall Plan.

The urgency of the Cold War stirred the Truman administration to solidify hemispheric defenses. At the Inter-American Conference near Rio de Janeiro in August and September 1947, the United States helped draw up a hemispheric mutual-defense pact. A second step was the creation at Bogotá, Colombia, in March 1948 of the Organization of American States, which would oversee the Rio Pact and other inter-American contacts. Through the OAS, new requests were made—for aid like that offered under the Marshall Plan. When the United States rejected them, whatever small gains had been made were undone.

The Rio Pact and the OAS underscored the United States' concern for political stability. But the depth of poverty in Latin America, combined with a growing revolutionary ferment, made the status of some United States–backed regimes increasingly uncertain.

The People's Republic of China

Containment worked well enough in Europe, but in the Far East an entirely different situation developed with the triumph of the Communist forces in China in October 1949. These forces, under Mao Tse-tung, had come into existence long before World War II. Throughout the war the United States and Britain, each for its own purposes, had tried to get Mao and the Nationalists under Chiang Kai-shek to work together to defeat Japan. The policy failed dismally. General Joseph W. Stilwell, who was in charge of coordinating Chinese wartime efforts against Japan, concluded that Chiang's government "is a structure based on fear and favor, in the hands of an ignorant, arbitrary, stubborn man."

At the war's end, nevertheless, the United States did what it could to expedite the dominance of Chiang and the Nationalists, preferring them to the Communist challengers, who were deemed to be subservient to the Soviet Union. The United States turned over key positions in China to the Nationalists, carried Chiang's troops to areas that had been controlled by the Japanese, tried to arrange for the surrender of Japanese units to the Nationalists, and finally helped to transport nine Nationalist armies into North China to confront Mao's troops. At the same time, the Chinese Communists, encouraged by the Soviet Union, received the surrender of Japanese armies inde-pendently, amassed their own arms, and engaged in skirmishes with the Nationalists. By late 1945, they controlled 225,000 square miles and more than 105 million Chinese.

In an attempt to stave off further civil war in China and the extension of Communist rule there, United States ambassador Patrick J. Hurley arranged a meeting in Chungking, the Nationalist capital, between Chiang and Mao Tse-tung in September 1945. After a full six weeks of talks, no agreement was reached. Embittered by his failure, Hurley resigned, blaming career officers in the United States Foreign Service for undermining his efforts to "prevent the collapse of the Nationalist government."

As Chiang's regime continued to falter, Truman sent General Marshall to the divided country. But he could do nothing. At one point Marshall warned Chiang that the Communist forces were too strong for him to defeat militarily, and urged negotiations. On his return to Washington in January 1947 to become secretary of state, Marshall was most discouraged. Sincere efforts to reach a settlement, he said, had been frustrated not merely by the Communists, but also "by irreconcilable groups within the Kuomintang [Nationalist] party interested in the preservation of their own feudal control of China."

In July 1947, Truman made still another effort to avert disaster. This time he sent General Albert C. Wedemeyer, who had served as Chiang's chief of staff from late 1945 until the middle of 1946, to appraise the entire situation. Wedemeyer's report of September 19, 1947, though recommending aid to the Nationalists, reflected so harshly on Chiang's ability to control his own territory that Truman and Marshall kept the report from the public until the summer of 1949. Wrote Wedemeyer:

Today China is being invaded by an idea instead of strong military forces from the outside. . . . The Central Government cannot defeat the Chinese Communists by the employment of force, but can only win the loyal, enthusiastic and realistic support of the masses of the people by improving the political and economic situation immediately.

From the end of the war to August 1949, the United States spent $2 billion in a futile attempt to prop up Chiang. But his government was far too corrupt, undemocratic, and inept to make the changes essential to winning popular support. The Truman administration, conceding it had "bet on a bad horse," reluctantly decided that

Chiang's prospects did not merit further assistance. In the great civil war that developed, the Communists swept all the way to Shanghai by May 1949.

Having rested his power on military strength, continued American assistance, and an oppressive landlord class, Chiang was unable to withstand the well-disciplined Communist forces, who had the support of millions of poverty-stricken peasants. Large numbers of Nationalist troops defected, and nearly 80 percent of the American supplies sent to Chiang fell into Communist hands. By December 1949, Chiang had fled to the island of Formosa (now Taiwan), bringing with him 300,000 troops and an impressive gold supply.

In the meantime, on October 1, scarcely a week after the Soviet Union had exploded its first atomic bomb, the People's Republic of China was proclaimed. In February 1950, the PRC concluded a treaty of alliance and mutual assistance with the USSR.

With the collapse of Chiang, the State Department in August 1949 issued a lengthy white paper on the Chinese question. In his introduction Secretary of State Acheson claimed that "the ominous result" of the civil war in China had been beyond the control of the United States. Nevertheless, Acheson still anticipated a time when the Chinese people would overthrow the "foreign yoke" of communism.

Perhaps to speed that day, the United States, unlike Britain and other major nations, continued to view Chiang's government in Taiwan as the legitimate government of China and refused to recognize the People's Republic of China or consent to its admission to the UN. In October 1971, the United Nations admitted the People's Republic and expelled Nationalist China. President Nixon's trip to China in February 1972 finally opened the way for United States recognition of the People's Republic (see Chapter 33).

The white paper failed to silence the small but vocal China bloc in the United States, which urged continued military aid to Chiang. Former ambassador Hurley denounced the white paper as a "smooth alibi for the pro-Communists in the State Department who had engineered the overthrow of our ally." A number of congressmen joined Hurley, and bitterness rose to the point where Marshall and his advisers were charged with the deliberate betrayal of American interests. The criticism capped more than a year of controversy over how far the United States should have committed itself in defending Chiang.

The Republicans used the issue to brand the opposition as "the party of treason." Democrats too had been critical of the administration: On February 21, 1948, for example, a young congressman from Massachusetts, John F. Kennedy, charged that the State Department had betrayed China by attempting to force Chiang into a coalition with Mao and by listening to the wrong advisers. "This is the tragic story of China, whose freedom we once fought to preserve," Kennedy concluded. "What our young men saved, our diplomats and our President have frittered away."

Although China had been "lost," the United States was determined to maintain its position in the Far East. On January 12, 1950, Secretary of State Acheson announced that the "defense perimeter" of the United States ran from the Aleutians to Japan, the Ryukyus, and the Philippines. Significantly, he did not include South Korea. In case of attack west of the defense perimeter, he added, "the initial reliance . . . must be on the people attacked to resist it," and then on "the entire civilized world under the Charter of the United Nations." The day after Acheson's declaration, the UN Security Council refused to seat the People's Republic of China. The Soviet delegate promptly walked out, not to return until August 1 — more than a month after the Security Council voted to support United States efforts to sustain South Korea.

The Korean Conflict

The hot war between Chiang and the Communists in China had an almost instant sequel in nearby Korea. During World War II, the Allied powers had agreed that Korea, occupied by Japan, should be made independent. In August 1945, the Soviet Union agreed to accept the surrender of the Japanese in Korea north of the thirty-eighth parallel. The United States, on the arrival of its forces in September, was to accept the surrender below that line.

Although both the United States and the Soviet Union favored a united Korea, mutual suspicion and the unwillingness to accept unification under Communist or anti-Communist control led to the establishment of separate regimes. The United States referred the question of Korean unity to the UN in September 1947. Although opposed by the USSR, the General Assembly voted to set up a temporary commission to supervise an all-Korean election.

Elections were held in May 1948 for a national

MY GENERATION

Let me try to define my generation . . . as those of us who approached our majority during World War II, and whose attitudes were shaped by the spirit of that time and by our common initiation into the world by that momentous event. . . . By contrast [with World War I] our war, despite a nervous overlay of the usual frivolity (do you recall Rosie the Riveter and Slap the Jap or aching erotic schmaltz that suffused those "Back Home for Keeps" ads?), was brutally businesslike and anti-romantic, a hard-boiled matter of stamping out a lot of very real and nasty totalitarianism in order to get along with the business of the American Way of Life, whatever that is. Our generation was not only not intact, it had been in many places cut to pieces. The class just ahead of me in college was virtually wiped out. Beautiful fellows who had won basketball championships and Phi Beta Kappa keys died like ants in the Normandy invasion. Others only slightly older than I—like myself young Marine Corps platoon leaders, primest cannon fodder of the Pacific war—stormed ashore at Tarawa and Iwo Jima and met ugly and horrible deaths on the hot coral and sands. . . .

We were traumatized not only by what we had been through, but by the realization that the entire mess was not finished after all: there was now the Cold War to face, and its clammy presence oozed into our nights and days. When at last the Korean War arrived, some short five years later (it was this writer's duty to serve his country in the Marines in that mean conflict, too), the cosmos seemed so unhinged as to be nearly insupportable. Surely by that time . . . we were the most mistrustful of power and the least nationalistic of any generation that America has produced.

William Styron, American novelist

Source: Reprinted by permission of Don Congdon Associates, Inc. Copyright © 1968 by William Styron.

---

assembly in the United States zone. The new assembly then adopted a constitution, elected Syngman Rhee (a devout anti-Communist who had spent many years in the United States) as the first president, and on August 15 proclaimed the Republic of Korea. The United States and thirty other nations promptly recognized the new nation. That very day, elections above the thirty-eighth parallel led to formation of the rival Democratic People's Republic of Korea, which the Soviet Union and its allies promptly recognized.

By December the USSR had recalled its troops, but it left the North Koreans heavily armed. At the General Assembly's suggestion, the United States recalled its troops from South Korea in June 1949, leaving behind much material and about five hundred "advisers."

North and South Korea thus faced each other across an artificial border, each backed by a rival great power and committed to unification on its own terms. Border skirmishes soon threatened to broaden into civil war. To bolster South Korea, Truman approved an act in February 1950 providing it with $110 million in economic aid. Military aid was also enlarged. On June 25, 1950, North Korea sent its forces across the thirty-eighth parallel in reprisal for border raids. The UN commission called it a "well-planned, concerted, and full-scale invasion."

Truman, concluding that the attack endangered American interests, both in Asia and Europe, responded decisively. At his urgent request,

the UN Security Council met on the afternoon of the invasion and by a vote of nine to zero held North Korea accountable for a "breach of the peace." (Yugoslavia abstained; the Soviet Union was still boycotting the council over the China issue.) Within forty-eight hours, and without consulting Congress, Truman ordered American naval and air units to help push the North Koreans back over the thirty-eighth parallel. Not wishing to draw China into the war, he also ordered the fleet to keep Chiang Kai-shek from attempting to invade from Formosa.

After the Security Council had urged positive action to assist South Korea, Truman broadened his earlier military instructions and with other nations sent ground troops. Although the operation was ostensibly under UN auspices, American troops made up about four-fifths of the UN forces in Korea, and General Douglas MacArthur was in firm command. "The entire control of my command and everything I did came from our Chiefs of Staff," MacArthur later recalled. "I had no direct connection with the United Nations whatsoever." To avoid asking Congress for a declaration of war, Truman chose to describe American military engagement in Korea as a "police action."

The Korean fighting was as savage as many World War II campaigns, and losses ran high. By the end of August 1950, the outnumbered UN forces had been pushed almost into the sea in the area around the port of Pusan. After being heavily reinforced, however, MacArthur opened a coun-

U.S. soldiers move slowly down a muddy road on the central Korean battle front. "It looks like World War III is near," President Truman wrote in his private notebook. *(Feldman, official U.S. Army photo)*

terattack with an amphibious landing at the port of Inchon behind the North Korean line. A full-scale offensive in November drove the North Koreans back toward the thirty-eighth parallel and destroyed a considerable part of their army. Although Truman had declared in late June that the United States aimed only to reestablish peace in Korea and "restore the border," he told the American people several months later that the Koreans "have a right to be free, independent, and united." By late September, he had accepted the recommendation of his National Security Council that MacArthur be permitted to move into North Korea.

Taking advantage of their momentary military superiority, UN forces pushed across the thirty-eighth parallel on October 9, 1950, and pressed on toward the Yalu River—the boundary between North Korea and China. Through diplomatic channels, China had already warned the Western world that it would not "sit back with folded hands and let the Americans come to the border." The United States, however, thought such interven-

tion unlikely. MacArthur called for the surrender of North Korea, American troops advanced northward, and Chinese forces began to mass across the Yalu.

Truman, Acheson, and MacArthur all doubted that China would intervene in the war. At a conference on Wake Island in mid-October 1950, MacArthur assured Truman: "We are no longer fearful of Chinese intervention. We no longer stand hat in hand." With the United States Air Force controlling the skies, "there would be the greatest slaughter" if the Chinese should move across the border. The slaughter came, but the principal victims were American and South Korean troops. Few had anticipated either an attack or a well-disciplined and aggressive Chinese army. On November 26, Chinese forces moved into Korea, trapped and inflicted heavy casualties on American and Korean troops at Chosin Reservoir, and pursued the fleeing armies below the thirty-eighth parallel. The United States had made a gross miscalculation. Although American troops finally regrouped and counterattacked, the

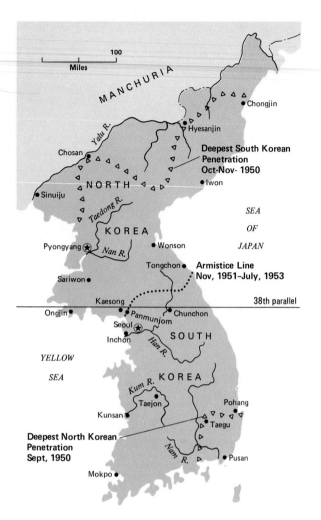

The Korean War.

war was now an increasingly brutal military stalemate.

Restive over the restraints imposed on him by the strategy of conducting a limited war for the limited objective of restoring South Korea's frontier, General MacArthur publicly expressed his dissatisfaction with the UN and President Truman. Even at the risk of becoming involved in an open war with China—a development many observers believed might lead to war with the Soviet Union—MacArthur urged an all-out effort that included the bombing of Chinese troops and supplies in Manchuria, a naval blockade of mainland China, and the use of Nationalist Chinese troops.

General Omar N. Bradley, chairman of the Joint Chiefs of Staff, warned that a major war against China would be "the wrong war at the wrong place, in the wrong time and with the wrong enemy." MacArthur rejected this decision. Condemning him for recklessness, Truman fired him on April 11, 1951, for insubordination, reliev-

ing him both of his Korean command and of his control of the occupation forces in Japan. MacArthur returned to the United States, where he received a hero's welcome from the public.

On June 23, 1951, the head of the Soviet delegation to the UN suggested that the Korean conflict might be settled if both parties were willing. This announcement led to armistice negotiations, which began on July 10, 1951, and proceeded for two entire years, during which fighting often broke out. During the 1952 presidential campaign, General Eisenhower, the Republican candidate, dramatically announced that if elected he would fly to Korea to bring about a cease-fire. In December, a month after his victory at the polls, Eisenhower made the trip. But the cease-fire was delayed another seven months. It would have been delayed even longer, in his opinion, had he not threatened once more to extend the war beyond the Korean peninsula, unleash Chiang Kai-shek, and—despite the deep misgivings of the British and other Europeans—to employ "tactical" atomic weapons.

The touchy armistice, resolved on July 27, 1953, restored the prewar division at the thirty-eighth parallel. By then, some 1.3 million Americans had served in Korea. The war cost the United States over $15 billion and more than 140,000 casualties, including 33,629 dead. (After the armistice, 3597 returned from Communist prisoner-of-war camps.) The outcome was a military and political draw, with Korea still divided but now war-ravaged as well. Although they remained separate nations, North and South Korea both seemed determined to suppress political opposition at home and rigidly control the lives and liberties of their people.

MCCARTHYISM: REPRESSION AT HOME

Within the United States, the strains of the Cold War manifested themselves in a desperate search for internal security. Nothing in their historical experience had equipped the American people to deal with a cold war. The same level of unity and bipartisanship asked of a people at war was now demanded in different circumstances. Never before had an individual's loyalty to country seemed more important. How to measure that loyalty was sufficiently clear—the intensity and consistency of a person's anticommunism. "I think that Owen Lattimore is not a Communist," someone observed of that well-known China specialist, "but the policies he has advocated certainly cannot be described as anti-Communist." That was the essence of the new loyalty.

In conducting foreign policy, Truman reinforced traditional American fears of the Soviet Union and of communism itself. At times, the threat seemed real enough. The spectacular revelations of spy rings, such as that uncovered in Canada in 1946, fed the growing suspicion that certain highly placed people were conspiring to overthrow or subvert American institutions.

For confirmation, they had only to listen to Truman's own attorney general, J. Howard McGrath: "There are today many Communists in America," he warned an audience in May 1950. "They are everywhere—in factories, offices, butcher shops, on street corners, in private business—and each carries with him the germs of death for society." At this very moment, he cautioned, they are "busy at work—undermining your government, plotting to destroy the liberties of every citizen, and feverishly trying, in whatever way they can, to aid the Soviet Union." Sounding an almost identical warning, *Life* magazine observed as early as July 1945: "The 'fellow traveler' is everywhere, in Hollywood, on college faculties, in government bureaus, in publishing companies, in radio offices, even on the editorial staffs of eminently capitalistic journals."

Actually, the U.S. Communist party exerted little influence in the postwar period, even on the American Left. What had robbed it of power was not so much anti-Communist vigilance as previous disillusion with the Stalin purges, the Hitler-Stalin pact, and the repressive character of Soviet communism. That helps to explain why the sensational exposures of the late forties and the fifties were so often exposures of past political sins, committed largely during the Great Depression, when the party was respectable in intellectual circles. But if the postwar Communist hunt did little for internal security, it did serve up numerous scapegoats. By 1950, substantial numbers of Americans were ready to believe Senator Joseph R. McCarthy of Wisconsin when he branded "the whole group of twisted-thinking New Dealers" as Communists who had "led America near to ruin at home and abroad."

Loyalty Tests

Before Senator McCarthy embarked on his crusade, the groundwork for what came to be called *McCarthyism* had been laid by Republicans and Democrats, by both the Truman administration and the Republican-controlled Eightieth Congress. Responding to fears of internal subversion, President Truman in March 1947 ordered a full-scale "loyalty investigation" of all present and prospective federal employees. No source of information, however questionable, was to be ignored. Along with all "loyalty" data worked up by government bureaus since 1939, the new dossiers were to become part of a "central master index." Among the "standards for refusal of employment or removal from employment" was "sympathetic association" with any foreign or domestic organization designated by the attorney general as "subversive." A Loyalty Review Board was empowered to oversee this extensive security program.

In compliance with the president's order, Attorney General Tom C. Clark, in December 1947, issued a list of ninety organizations considered disloyal to the United States. None of these organizations had the right to defend itself. Since the list had been prepared by the federal government, with the assistance of the FBI under J. Edgar Hoover, it quickly became the principal reference for the detection of disloyalty. Not only federal agencies but private organizations, businesses, trade unions, newspapers, entertainment agencies, and schools consulted it to discover "subversives."

During the 1948 presidential campaign, even Americans for Democratic Action published in major newspapers the names of leading Progressive party supporters along with their alleged Communist affiliations, based on the attorney general's list. Only in retrospect, in a speech nearly fifteen years later at Columbia University Law School, did former attorney general Clark confess to the arbitrary nature of the list he had compiled: "Perhaps we should, as I look at it now, have given the parties an opportunity to be heard before we issued it."

When the federal investigation of loyalty was completed in April 1951, the records of no less than 3,225,000 civil servants had been examined. Under the pressure of the inquiry, 2900 had resigned, and only 300 had been dismissed. Because of the broad criteria for what constituted subversion, it is possible that none of these individuals was a Communist, although some might have been at one time. Little that Joseph McCarthy ever managed to do in the United States Senate could compare with the steady, although less spectacular, subversion of constitutional liberties under Truman's loyalty program.

In the name of internal security, Americans had been encouraged to spy on each other. Almost any "derogatory information" uncovered could deprive a person of job and livelihood. Rather than soften any abuses of the system, the Loyalty Review Board conducted proceedings that denied the accused the right to confront the witnesses against them.

HUAC

Even as President Truman established his own anti-Communist credentials, Republicans in the Eightieth Congress revived the House Un-American Activities Committee. The HUAC was formed in 1938 as a temporary investigation unit, largely to advance the personal political fortunes of its chairman, Democrat Martin Dies of Texas. With a strong push from the freshman California congressman Richard M. Nixon, victorious after a calculated Red-baiting campaign, the committee proceeded to hunt Communists and alleged Communists. In doing so, it advanced individual political careers and the fortunes of the Republican party generally.

Before long, the HUAC's chief investigator reported: "We were to expand to many rooms, to agencies in leading cities, a staff of 75, and 600 filing cases containing more than one million names, records, dossiers, and data pertaining to subversion. About 20,000 accredited agents of the FBI, Treasury, Army, Navy, Civil Service, Atomic Energy Commission, and other Federal officers have used our growing files."

What the HUAC did was to manipulate various channels of publicity to reveal the political associations of individuals who had unorthodox ideas. By holding over each witness a threat to his or her career, the committee exerted tremendous power. Refusal to answer the committee's questions or cooperate with its investigation was like an admission of guilt.

The committee's most audacious adventure was a two-week foray into Hollywood in October 1947 "to expose those elements that are insidiously trying to . . . poison the minds of your children, distort the history of our country, and discredit Christianity." The attempt to prove extensive Communist influence in the film industry was a dismal failure. Even a leading Republican newspaper, the *New York Herald-Tribune,* conceded that the Hollywood investigation had "dissolved into the ludicrous." Nevertheless, it did frighten movie executives into an indiscriminate housecleaning, which soon spread to radio and television. Actors, writers, directors, and others were blacklisted; some could not get work twenty years later.

The Hollywood probe had been preceded by the HUAC's attempt to question Communist party officials, starting in February 1947. Many of them preferred citations for contempt to answering the summons. Eugene Dennis, general secretary of the Communist party in the United States, was among those who defied the summons. At Congressman Nixon's suggestion, the HUAC agreed to ask the House to bring contempt charges against Dennis and also to ask the Justice Department to investigate the Communist "conspiracy" to violate the Smith Act of 1940. This act made it illegal for a person to advocate "overthrowing . . . any government in the United States by force," or to "affiliate" with groups teaching this doctrine.

In July 1948, the Justice Department got the indictment of Dennis and ten other high-ranking Communist leaders under this act. Their conviction by the federal district court in New York in October 1949 and their heavy fines and prison terms were upheld by the Supreme Court, six to two, in June 1951.

In upholding the conviction, the Supreme Court lent its weight to the frantic search for internal security. "Certain kinds of speech are so undesirable," Chief Justice Fred M. Vinson said for the Court in the *Dennis* case, "as to warrant criminal prosecution." This view diminished the value Justice Holmes in 1919 had put on "the free trade in ideas" under the guarantees of the First Amendment. The *Dennis* ruling also encouraged states and municipalities, under local acts and ordinances similar to the Smith Act, to pursue thousands of alleged subversives, sometimes on the basis of hearsay or even lies.

The Hiss case, the HUAC's most far-reaching triumph, began on August 3, right after the Dennis indictment in July. On that day, Whittaker Chambers, an admitted former Communist who said he had quit the party in 1937, was brought before the committee to support earlier testimony about the Communist "apparatus" in Washington. Chambers, an editor of *Time* magazine, told a sensational story. He named members of the Washington Communist apparatus of the 1930s, including Alger Hiss, a former State Department official and since 1947 president of the Carnegie Endowment for International Peace. On learning of Chambers's accusation, Hiss telegraphed a full denial to the committee and asked for a hearing, which was granted on August 5.

"ARE YOU NOW OR HAVE YOU EVER BEEN?"

Typical of the quality of the investigation of the Hollywood film industry by the House Un-American Activities Committee was the testimony of actor Adolphe Menjou on October 21, 1947. Robert E. Stripling acted as the committee's secretary, and Congressman Richard M. Nixon was a member (and would continue to be until 1950).

MR. STRIPLING: *Do you have your very definite suspicions about some members of the Screen Actors Guild?*

MR. MENJOU: *I know a great many people who act an awful lot like Communists.*

MR. STRIPLING: *As an actor, Mr. Menjou, could you tell the Committee whether or not an actor in a picture could portray a scene which would in effect serve as propaganda for Communism or any other un-American purpose?*

MR. MENJOU: *Oh, yes. I believe that under certain circumstances a Communistic director, a Communistic writer, or a Communistic actor, even if he were under orders from the head of the studio not to inject Communism or un-Americanism or subversion into pictures, could easily subvert that order, under the proper circumstances, by a look, by an inflection, by a change in the voice. I have never seen it done, but I think it could be done. . . .*

MR. NIXON: *In answer to a question by Mr. Stripling, you indicated that, although you might* not know whether a certain person was a Communist, I think you said he certainly acted like a Communist.

MR. MENJOU: *If you belong to a Communist-front organization and you take no action against the Communists, if you do not resign from the organization when you know the organization is dominated by Communists, I consider that a very, very dangerous thing.*

MR. NIXON: *Have you any other tests which you would apply which would indicate to you that people acted like Communists?*

MR. MENJOU: *Well, I think attending any meeting at which Mr. Paul Robeson appeared, and applauding or listening to his Communist songs in America. I would be ashamed to be seen in an audience doing a thing of that kind.*

MR. NIXON: *You indicated you thought a person acted like a Communist when he stated, as one person did to you, that capitalism was through.*

MR. MENJOU: *That is not Communistic per se, but it is [a] very dangerous leaning, it is very close. I see nothing wrong with the capitalistic system, the new dynamic capitalism in America today. . . .*

Source: *Communist Infiltration of Hollywood Motion-Picture Industry: Hearings before the Committee on Un-American Activities.* 80th Cong., October 21, 1947, Photograph from UPI/Bettmann Newsphotos.

Alger Hiss. *(AP/Wide World Photos)*

Richard Nixon. *(UPI/Bettmann Newsphotos)*

This and subsequent hearings, interspersed with reexaminations of Chambers, brought additional details of Hiss's activities in the thirties, including membership (with Chambers) in a Soviet spy ring in Washington and the passing of classified government documents to the Russians. Hiss persisted in his denials. Neither could be prosecuted for espionage, since the acts had taken place more than seven years before and thus, under the statue of limitations, were beyond legal reach. But Hiss was indicted for perjury. After two trials, the first one ending in a hung jury, Hiss was found guilty and sentenced to five years in prison and fined $10,000. Appeals to higher courts upheld the verdict, and Hiss went to prison in March 1951.

A Harvard Law School graduate and secretary to Justice Holmes, Hiss had served as one of the early New Dealers in the AAA before joining the State Department. He helped to plan the United Nations Organization and was a member of Roosevelt's Yalta delegation. Before leaving the government in 1946, he served as director of the State Department's Office of Special Political Affairs. All in all, he lent some substance to the charge that privileged individuals in high places had helped to betray the country. The controversy about Hiss's guilt or innocence continued for several decades and remains unresolved.

Despite the Hiss coup, the HUAC failed to turn up any significant number of "subversives" in

government, at least none that could safely be brought to trial. Meanwhile, J. Parnell Thomas, chairman of the HUAC during the Eightieth Congress, was convicted of fraud on December 3, 1949, and sent to prison.

While the Hiss case was in progress, the HUAC made other accusations, and the FBI bestirred itself to uncover Soviet agents. The news of the first Soviet atomic bomb explosion late in September 1949, followed in October by the Communist triumph in China and in February 1950 by the mutual-security pact between the People's Republic and the USSR, all deepened the shock of Communist gains and provoked charges that the State Department itself was filled with Communists. Senator McCarthy, having learned his lessons well from Democrats and Republicans who had successfully used the Communist issue, now pounced on this theme.

McCarthy and McCarthyism

In a speech in Wheeling, West Virginia, on February 9, 1950, Senator McCarthy declared that the United States, the strongest nation on earth on V–J Day, had been shorn of its strength "because of the traitorous actions of those who have been treated so well by this nation." None were worse than "the bright young men" in the State Department "born with silver spoons in their

Senator Joseph R. McCarthy: "We've been losing to international Communism at the rate of 100 million people a year. Perhaps we should examine the background of the men who have done the planning, and let the American people decide whether . . . we've lost because of stumbling, fumbling idiocy, or because they planned it that way." *(UPI/Bettman Newsphotos)*

mouths." To add substance to his charges, McCarthy added: "I have here in my hand" the names of "two hundred and five men that were known to the Secretary of State as being members of the Communist party and who nevertheless are still working and shaping the policy of the State Department."

McCarthy could never make good on his startling revelation. He gradually backed away from the figure of 205, keeping in the limelight with new numbers, but in the end he was unable to substantiate a single name. Nothing, however, was done to restrain the accuser. On the contrary, the respected conservative Republican leader Senator Robert A. Taft of Ohio gave the full benefit of his own prestige: "McCarthy should keep talking, and if one case doesn't work he should proceed with another."

Events soon played into McCarthy's hands. While he was playing "the numbers game" with Communists in the State Department, British authorities arrested for atomic espionage Klaus Fuchs, a German-born nuclear physicist and naturalized British subject who had worked on the American bomb at Los Alamos in 1944. Fuchs admitted the charges and was sentenced to fourteen years in prison. He also implicated certain American Communists in his activities.

Acting on Fuchs's information, the FBI arrested Ethel and Julius Rosenberg and their friend Morton Sobell in the summer of 1950. They were charged with passing atomic secrets to the Soviets and speeding up Russian success with the bomb. For a crime "worse than murder," in the words of the trial judge, the Rosenbergs were sentenced to death in March 1951. Sobell was sentenced to thirty years. After many appeals failed, the Rosenbergs were executed on July 19, 1953. The punishment in this case suggested the kind of fear and hysteria that had overtaken the American people and the judiciary.

Meanwhile McCarthy's charges grew in reach and recklessness as the "limited" Korean conflict eroded American morale. A low point was touched on June 14, 1951, after General MacArthur's recall. McCarthy made a bid to retrieve the headlines with a sixty-thousand-word attack in the Senate on MacArthur's rivals, General Marshall and General Eisenhower. Marshall, perhaps the most respected military figure in the country, was accused of "serving the world policy of the Kremlin." Deeply involved with him, "in a conspiracy so immense and an infamy so black as to dwarf any previous such venture in the history of man," was Marshall's "firm supporter" and "fast-rising protege, 'Ike' Eisenhower."

McCarthyism had by then passed into the language as an expression for wild and unfounded charges of disloyalty. But many Americans came to believe, as the senator himself told his home following in Wisconsin, that "McCarthyism is Americanism with its sleeves rolled." Money began to pour in on McCarthy, and superpatriot societies took up the cause. His most spectacular feats still lay ahead of him. So did his downfall.

The McCarran Acts

Congress also responded to the national obsession with anticommunism. On September 23, 1950, over Truman's veto, it passed the McCarran Internal Security Act, making it unlawful to conspire "to perform any act which would substantially contribute to the establishment within the United States of a totalitarian dictatorship." All "communist-action" and "communist front" organizations were assumed to be such conspiracies and were required to register with the attorney general. The act authorized the president, in the case of an "internal security emergency," to arrest and detain any individuals for whom there was "reasonable ground" to suspect that they would "probably" engage in acts of espionage or sabotage. Any alien, moreover, with the slightest "subversive" taint was to be excluded from admission to the United States.

Even Senator McCarran denounced the Internal Security Emergency amendment to his bill as "a concentration-camp measure pure and simple." In his veto message, Truman characterized parts of the Internal Security Act as "the greatest danger to freedom of speech, press, and assembly since the alien and sedition laws of 1798." Far from protecting the nation from dictatorship, he added, the McCarran Act took the United States "a long step toward totalitarianism."

On June 30, 1952, Congress supplemented the Internal Security Act with the McCarran-Walter Immigration Act, passed again over Truman's veto. This act updated but hardly liberalized the widely attacked quota system, which imposed exceptional hardship on displaced persons and refugees from Communist countries. More to the point, it required the attorney general to screen out "subversives" within the permitted quotas and empowered him to deport such persons even after they had become naturalized American citizens.

"Seldom," said Truman, "has a bill exhibited the distrust evidenced here for citizens and aliens alike—at a time when we need unity at home and the confidence of our friends abroad." Despite Truman's vetoes, the McCarran acts might be viewed as the logical result of earlier attacks on individual liberties, beginning with the president's federal-loyalty directive. What he had already done, Truman insisted, was enough to deal with the problem.

The McCarran acts, like Truman's loyalty program and the actions of the FBI, intensified the preoccupation with internal security. McCarthy had effectively used the issue in the congressional elections of 1950 to defeat a Maryland senator, Millard F. Tydings, who had been bold enough to oppose his reckless charges. With equal effectiveness, McCarthy capitalized on fears of communism to win reelection in 1952, and the Republican party employed such fears that same year to return to the White House.

The Election of 1952: Eisenhower

Once recovered from the shock of losing the 1948 election, Republican leaders who had opposed the nomination of Thomas E. Dewey and had favored Taft blamed the defeat on bipartisanship in foreign policy, which they proceeded to attack. The decision in 1951 to constrain MacArthur and "contain" the Korean conflict gave weight to their charge of betrayal. At the same time, they made a calculated attempt to win the votes of millions of "ethnics"—those who had roots in countries behind the Iron Curtain—by endorsing a policy of "liberation." In their 1952 platform the Republicans thus promised to repudiate any commitment such as Yalta, that aided "Communist enslavement," and attacked the containment policy that had "abandoned" so many millions to that fate.

Yet many Republicans remained committed to bipartisanship in principle and to the Truman version of it in practice. Many of them also loathed McCarthy as deeply as most Democrats, a feeling they found it easy to transfer to his misguided friend Taft. Their own choice for the nomination was the immensely popular wartime hero Dwight David Eisenhower, who had turned down the Democrats four years earlier. After unseating southern delegates for Taft, the Eisenhower convention team put Ike across on the first ballot. The Taft people took what solace they could from the nomination for vice-president of Richard Nixon, the former HUAC luminary who had won a seat in the United States Senate after still another demonstration of Red-baiting politics.

The Republicans' snaring of Eisenhower only deepened the pessimism with which the Democrats approached their national convention two weeks later. Many voters believed the McCarthyite charge that their reign had been "twenty years of treason." On the home front, the inflation brought by the Korean conflict also worked against the Democrats. The inflation was dramatized by the steel strike in 1952, which Truman failed to arbitrate and which resulted in higher

WORDS AND NAMES IN AMERICAN HISTORY

A great many American students have suffered through the lines of a school *cafeteria* and scarcely need to have the word defined for them. Yet the word has a somewhat curious history. It comes from the Spanish *cafetera*, which means a coffeepot, not a place where coffee is served. The word seems to have come into American usage not directly from

Spain but from Mexico, since it was first used in its modern sense in the Mississippi Valley rather than along the Atlantic seaboard. Some scholars trace its earliest use to the late nineteenth century. Visitors to this country are sometimes confused to learn that a *café* and a *cafeteria* are both eating and drinking establishments, but not necessarily the same kind.

AMERICAN SOCIETY IN THE TWENTIETH CENTURY: LEISURE

(Bruce Davidson/Magnum Photos)

Marilyn Monroe, by Andy Warhol. *(Leo Castelli Gallery, New York)*

An outdoor movie in South Dakota. *(J. R. Eyerman/Life Magazine,* © *1958, Time, Inc.)*

Audience at a 3–D movie. *(J. R. Eyerman/Life Magazine,* © *1952, 1980, Time, Inc.)*

steel prices. Moreover, beginning in 1951, certain petty scandals came to light involving the use of influence by persons close to Truman.

After Truman announced in March 1952 that he would not be a candidate, the leading Democratic aspirant became Senator Estes Kefauver of Tennessee. Kefauver had gained a national reputation as head of the special Senate Committee that had uncovered so much Democratic graft. When Kefauver failed to win on the first two ballots at the Chicago convention, the delegates drafted Truman's choice, Adlai E. Stevenson, governor of Illinois. Senator John J. Sparkman of Alabama became his running mate.

Stevenson conducted a vigorous and unusually eloquent campaign that won him many supporters among intellectuals. He particularly attacked the Republicans' "liberation" promises as "cynical" attempts "to play upon the anxieties of foreign nationality groups in this country."

During the campaign, Nixon's successful use of innuendo to smear opponents came back to haunt him. Even as he charged that a Stevenson triumph would ensure "more Alger Hisses, more atomic spies, more crises," newspapers revealed the existence of a "secret" contingency fund that had been raised by friends to keep Nixon in "financial comfort." With Eisenhower now on the verge of dropping him from the ticket unless he placed "all the facts before the people, fairly and squarely," Nixon took to nationwide television to explain that the fund had been used for campaign expenses, not for himself or his family. The public responded favorably to what came to be known as the Checkers speech (referring to the family dog Nixon refused to give up), and Eisenhower reaffirmed his confidence in Nixon's integrity. But relations between the two men would be strained for some time.

To no one's surprise, Eisenhower's vast appeal, enhanced by his campaign pledge to fly to Korea and end the stalemate there, carried him to a striking triumph. He received 33,936,234 popular votes to Stevenson's 27,314,992. In the electoral college, his margin was 442 to 89, with the Solid South contributing to the Republican total for the first time since 1928. Yet the Republicans had grounds for worry. Even Eisenhower's great popularity brought the party a mere majority of eight in the House and a standoff in the Senate. With a Republican–southern Democratic coalition able to control Congress, however, the conservative mood still prevailed.

The election of Eisenhower ended twenty years of Democratic rule in the White House. But few Americans anticipated any startling changes. By this time, much of the New Deal social legislation, such as social security, had become so much a part of American life that no Republican leader thought of tampering with it. The foreign policy of the United States, despite Republican charges, was still bipartisan. Democrats and Republicans alike operated from the premise that the Soviet Union represented a constant and inevitable threat to the "free world" and needed to be contained. Even the search for internal security had been largely a bipartisan effort. Finally, no political figure so exemplified the spirit of bipartisanship to the American people as did Eisenhower, a candidate both parties had eagerly sought.

SUMMARY

The United States after World War II was a superpower engaged in a rivalry with the other superpower, the Soviet Union, for world domination. Wartime cooperation soon returned to mutual suspicion and distrust.

The United Nation, created as the war ended in an attempt to set up an international organization that would be more effective than the old League of Nations, began with fifty-one members. Its charter set up two major agencies, the General Assembly, to which all members belonged, and the Security Council, made up of the great powers as permanent members plus a few rotating members. The council was given authority to apply sanctions to maintain peace, but each of the permanent members could block action with a veto.

By the 1980s the UN had 157 members. Over the years, it influenced some world issues. But the arms race, the dissolution of overseas empires, and the Cold War were beyond its power to solve. So was the development of more and more sophisticated nuclear weapons. For once the Soviet Union had detonated its own atomic bomb in September 1949, security by balance of terror became part of the new world order.

In Europe, the map was far different from what it had been before the war. Germany had been divided into two states, and the leading Nazis had been tried for war crimes by an international tribunal. In Asia, Japan was occupied by the United States until 1950, when a general peace treaty was signed. At home Truman, taking office after Roosevelt's death, had to face the problems of demobilization, reconversion of the economy to a peacetime footing, reorganization of the military establishment, and satisfaction of the pent-up demand for consumer goods.

The year 1948 is remembered for the greatest national-election upset in American history, when Truman won the presidency in his own right against Thomas E. Dewey, whom everyone had expected to win. Truman's domestic program was called the Fair Deal, and it was designed to expand the New Deal's social programs.

In foreign affairs, Truman had to deal with the Cold War and the new postwar world. The Soviets had moved to secure their borders in Europe by creating a sphere of influence in Eastern Europe like American control in the Western Hemisphere. The rest of the world became a battleground for an ideological war between the United States and the Soviets. And the American policy set during this period—containment of Russia and the spread of communism through foreign aid and military alliances—was to last unchanged for more than a generation.

The Truman Doctrine provided aid that bolstered proWestern governments in Greece and Turkey. The Marshall Plan, developed in 1947, helped restore the shattered European economy and stop the advance of communism in Western Europe. In 1949 Truman pro-

TIME LINE

1945–1946 Nuremberg war crimes trials	NATO established
1945 United Nations founded	Soviet Union explodes an atomic bomb
Act of Chapultepec	U.S. Communist party leaders convicted under Smith Act
1946 Atomic Energy Commission created	Truman launches Fair Deal
Baruch plan	First major retail shopping center opens
Iran crisis	
Union strike wave, including miners and railroad workers	1950 Treaty of alliance between Soviet Union and China
Maximum Employment Act	Hiss convicted of perjury
Republicans win control of Congress	Senator McCarthy's Wheeling, West Virginia speech
1947 National Security Act	Korean War begins
Federal Employee Loyalty Program	U.S. troops enter North Korea
Truman Doctrine	China enters Korean War
Marshall Plan announced	McCarran Internal Security Act
Taft-Hartley Act	1951 Truman dismisses MacArthur
HUAC investigation of "subversion" in Hollywood	Strategic Air Command (SAC) organized
Attorney-General's list of subversive organizations issued	1952 McCarran-Walter Immigration Act
1948 Berlin blockade and airlift	Dwight D. Eisenhower elected president
East and West German governments organized	U.S. explodes a hydrogen bomb
Communist coup in Czechoslovakia	1953 Korean War ends
Organization of American States (OAS) formed	Julius and Ethel Rosenberg executed
Executive order desegregates the armed forces	1955 Soviet Union explodes a hydrogen bomb
Hiss-Chambers case	1970 More Americans live in the suburbs than in the central cities
Israel created	
Truman elected president	
1949 Communists come to power in China	

posed Point Four, a program of aid to Asia, Africa, and Latin America designed to strengthen resistance to communism on those continents.

Collective defense in Europe was set up through NATO, the North Atlantic Treaty Organization. Its counterpart in Latin America was the Rio Pact of 1947 and the Organization of American States (OAS), set up in 1948. In the Far East, the victory of the Communists in China in 1949, despite all the aid America had given Chiang Kai-shek and the Nationalists, led the United States to extend its defense perimeter to include Japan, the Ryukyu Islands, and the Philippines.

The first open conflict came in Korea, which had been divided in two after the war. When North Korea, backed by the Soviet Union, invaded the South on June 25, 1950, Truman went to the UN and then ordered American forces into the conflict. The fighting went on for three years, and at the end no one had won; Korea remained divided, and the armistice of July 1953 was a return to the prewar boundary of the thirty-eighth parallel. The futile conflict had cost the United States more than 140,000 casualities and more than $15 billion.

At home, Cold War tensions erupted in an obsessive concern with internal security and widespread fears of subversion. The House Un-American Activities Committee looked for Communists everywhere, even in Hollywood. The Hiss case was its only "triumph." But the shadow the HUAC spread ruined careers and poisoned lives. Senator Joseph McCarthy, who came to symbolize the mania for loyalty, took as his special target the State Department. *McCarthyism* became a new word in the American vocabulary, and it came to mean wild and unfounded charges of disloyalty. McCarthy never managed to prove one of the many accusations he hurled in public. The McCarran Acts of 1950 and 1952 were the congressional response to the national obsession with communism at home.

All these tensions and fears, plus the popularity of General Dwight D. Eisenhower, brought a Republican president in 1952 after twenty years of Democrats in the White House. But there were to be no startling changes; the New Deal was not dismantled, and bipartisanship and the Cold War continued.

Suggested Readings

E. F. Goldman, *The Crucial Decade—and After: America 1945–1960* (1960), H. Zinn, *Postwar America 1945–1971* (1973), G. Hodgson, *America in Our Time* (1976), and W. E. Leuchtenburg, *In the Shadow of FDR: From Harry Truman to Ronald Reagan* (rev. ed., 1985), are stimulating and often contrasting interpretations. The suburbanization of the United States is described in K. T. Jackson, *Crabgrass Frontier* (1985). On Truman, see M. Miller, *Plain Speaking* (1973), and R. Donovan, *Conflict and Crisis* (1977) and *Tumultuous Years* (1982). B. J. Bernstein, *Politics and Policies of the Truman Administration* (1970), is a critical assessment. A. L. Hamby, *Beyond the New Deal* (1973), is a sympathetic treatment of Truman and liberal reform. For commentary by a probing contemporary critic, see I. F. Stone, *The Truman Era* (1953).

The Yalta Conference and its aftermath are examined in H. Feis, *Churchill, Roosevelt, Stalin* (1957); W. L. Neumann, *After Victory: Churchill, Roosevelt, Stalin and the Making of the Peace* (1967); and D. S. Clemens, *Yalta* (1970). On the Potsdam Conference, see C. L. Mee, *Meeting at Potsdam* (1975), and H. Feis, *Between War and Peace: The Potsdam Conference* (1960). The conflict over control of atomic weapons is examined in R. G. Hewlett and F. Duncan, *Atomic Shield 1947–1952* (1970); M. J. Sherwin, *A World Destroyed* (1975); and two personal accounts—B. M. Baruch, *Baruch: The Public Years* (1960), and D. E. Lilienthal, *Journals* (2 vols., 1964). Telford Taylor, *Nuremberg and Vietnam: An American Tragedy* (1970), is a thoughtful review of the implications of war-crime trials by one of the American prosecutors at Nuremberg.

The best introductions to the United States and the Cold War are W. LaFeber, *America, Russia, and the Cold War* (rev. ed., 1976), and S. E. Ambrose, *Rise to Globalism: American Foreign Policy 1938–1980* (rev. ed., 1988). On the origins and development of the Cold War, see L. C. Gardner, A. Schlesinger, Jr., and H. Morgenthau, *The Origins of the Cold War* (1970); J. L. Gaddis, *The United States and the Origins of the Cold War* (1972); D. Yergin, *Shattered Peace: The Origins of the Cold War and the National Security State* (1977); and T. G. Paterson, *Meeting the Communist Threat: Truman to Reagan* (1988). The changes in George Kennan's views are revealed in his *American Diplomacy 1900–1950* (1951); *Realities of American Foreign Policy* (1954); *Russia and the West under Lenin and Stalin* (1961); *On Dealing with the Communist World* (1964); and *Memoirs 1925–1963* (2 vols., 1967, 1972). The critical "revisionist" view is presented in T. G. Paterson (ed.), *Cold War Critics* (1971); W. A. Williams, *The Tragedy of American Diplomacy* (1962); G. Kolko, *The Politics of War* (1968) and *The Limits of Power* (1972); G. Alperovitz, *Atomic Diplomacy* (rev. ed., 1985); R. G. Barnet, *Intervention and Revolution: The United States in the Third World* (1968); L. C. Gardner, *Architects of Illusion* (1970); and T. J. Paterson, *Soviet-American Confrontation: Postwar Reconstruction and the Origins of the Cold War* (1973). For an additional assessment, see R. E. Osgood and others, *America and the World: From the Truman*

Doctrine to Vietnam (1969). J. L. Gaddis, *Strategies of Containment* (1982), is a critical appraisal of postwar American national-security policy. The military influence on decision making is analyzed in R. K. Betts, *Soldiers, Statesmen, and Cold War Crises* (1977).

The personal accounts of decision makers are useful and revealing. Among the most important are H. S. Truman, *Memoirs* (2 vols., 1955, 1956); D. Acheson, *Present at the Creation* (1969); J. Byrnes, *Speaking Frankly* (1947); W. Millis (ed.), *The Forrestal Diaries* (1951); Kennan's memoirs, previously mentioned; and Arthur Vandenberg, *Private Papers* (1952). See also R. H. Ferrell, *George C. Marshall* (1966), and G. Smith, *Dean Acheson* (1972).

Henry Wallace's break with Truman is examined in N. D. Markowitz, *The Rise and Fall of the People's Century* (1973); A. Yarnell, *Democrats and Progressives* (1973); and J. S. Walker, *Henry A. Wallace and American Foreign Policy* (1976).

On the Truman Doctrine, J. M. Jones, *The Fifteen Weeks* (1955), conveys the crisis atmosphere in which it was formulated. The implications are discussed in R. M. Freeland, *The Truman Doctrine and the Origins of McCarthyism: Foreign Policy, Domestic Politics and Internal Security 1946–1948* (1972). On the Marshall Plan, see J. Gimbel, *The Origins of the Marshall Plan* (1976). On NATO, see R. E. Osgood, *NATO: Entangling Alliance* (1962).

The Far East and the Cold War are examined in A. Iriye, *The Cold War in Asia* (1974), and Y. Nagai and A. Iriye (eds.), *The Origins of the Cold War in Asia* (1977). The United States and China may be profitably examined in the State Department's *China White Paper, August 1949* (2 vols., 1967). See also H. Feis, *The China Tangle* (1953); T. Tsou, *America's Failure in China* (1963); and M. Schaller, *The United States Crusade in China 1938–1945* (1979).

On the Korean War, the important works are D. Rees, *Korea: The Limited War* (1964); M. Hastings, *The Korean War* (1987); B. Cumings, *The Origin of the Korean War* (1981), and B. Cumings and J. Halliday, *Korea: The Unknown War* (1988). For a vigorous contemporary dissent, see I. F. Stone, *The Hidden History of the Korean War* (1952). On Truman and MacArthur, see J. W. Spanier, *The Truman-MacArthur Controversy and the Korean War* (1959); Douglas MacArthur, *Reminiscences* (1964); and D. C. James, *The Years of MacArthur: Triumph and Disaster 1945–1964* (1985).

The Fair Deal is examined in the general works cited in the first paragraph. See also S. M. Hartmann, *Truman and the 80th Congress* (1971). On labor, see A. F. McClure, *The Truman Administration and the Problems of Postwar Labor 1945–1948* (1969). On agriculture, see A. J. Matusow, *Farm Policies and Politics in the Truman Years* (1967), and John Shover's broader analysis of the transformation of rural life in America in *First Majority—Last Minority* (1976).

Preelection voter polling became a powerful political device after World War II. For its use in political analysis, see S. Lubell, *The Future of American Politics* (1952) and *Revolt of the Moderates* (1956). The nature of political power is examined in R. E. Neustadt's influential *Presidential Power* (1960). On the far Right in American politics, see R. Hofstadter, *The Paranoid Style in American Politics and Other Essays* (1965). On the radical Left, see D. A. Shannon, *The Decline of American Communism: A History of the Communist Party of the United States since 1945* (1959); J. R. Starobin, *American Communism in Crisis 1943–1957* (1972); A. Richmond, *A Long View from the Left: Memoirs of an American Revolutionary* (1972); and M. B. Duberman's exhaustive and evocative biographical study, *Paul Robeson* (1988). On liberalism, see Reinhold Neibuhr's influential works, such as *The Irony of American History* (1952) and *The World Crisis and American Responsibility* (1958); A. M. Schlesinger, Jr., *The Vital Center* (1949); Christopher Lasch's critical assessment in *The New Radicalism in America 1889–1963* (1965); and R. H. Pells, *The Liberal Mind in a Conservative Age: American Intellectuals in the 1940s and 1950s* (1985). On the Democratic party, see H. S. Parmet, *The Democrats: The Years after FDR* (1976).

David Caute, *The Great Fear: The Anti-Communist Purge under Truman and Eisenhower* (1978), surveys the deterioration of civil liberties. For the particulars, see E. Bentley (ed.), *Thirty Years of Treason: Excerpts from Hearings before the House Committee on Un-American Activities 1938–1968* (1971); W. Goodman, *The Committee* (1968); M. Lowenthal, *The Federal Bureau of Investigation* (1950); E. Bontecou, *The Federal Loyalty-Security Program* (1953); W. Gellhorn (ed.), *The States and Subversion* (1952); L. Ceplair and S. Englund, *The Inquisition in Hollywood: Politics in the Film Community 1930–1960* (1980); and V. Navasky, *Naming Names* (1980) and E. W. Schrecker, *No Ivory Tower: McCarthyism and the Universities* (1986). On J. Edgar Hoover and the FBI, see M. Lowenthal, *The Federal Bureau of Investigation* (1950); R. G. Powers, *Secrecy and Power: The Life of J. Edgar Hoover* (1987); and A. G. Theoharis and J. S. Cox, *The Boss: J. Edgar Hoover and the Great American Inquisition* (1988). R. Rovere, *Senator Joe McCarthy* (1959), is a critical assessment but ignores the context in which the senator launched his crusade. That context is provided in R. Griffith and A. Theoharis (eds.), *The Specter: Original Essays on the Cold War and the Origins of McCarthyism* (1974); A. D. Harper, *The Politics of Loyalty: The White House and the Communist Issue 1946–1952* (1970); R. M. Freeland, *The Truman Doctrine and the Origins of McCarthyism* (1972); R. Griffith, *The Politics of Fear* (1970); A. Theoharis, *Seeds of Repression: Harry S. Truman and the Origins of McCarthyism* (1971); and R. M. Fried, *Men against McCarthy* (1976). On the nature of McCarthy's appeal, M. P. Rogin, *The Intellectuals and McCarthy* (1967), is an important study. See also T. C. Reeves, *The Life and Times of Joe McCarthy* (1982), and D. M. Oshinsky, *A Conspiracy So Immense: The World of Joe McCarthy* (1983). The Hiss and Rosenberg cases remain controversial and unresolved. The Hiss case is examined in A. Cooke, *A Generation on Trial* (1950), but no verdict is rendered. J. C. Smith, *Alger Hiss* (1976), is a strong defense; A. Weinstein finds him guilty in *Perjury* (1978). W. Schneier and M. Schneier, *Invitation to an Inquest* (1965), raises questions about the guilt of the Rosenbergs; R. Radosh and J. Milton, *The Rosenberg File* (1984), finds them guilty.

CHAPTER 31

SUPERPOWERS IN THE MISSILE AGE

With the presidency of Dwight D. Eisenhower, the United States embarked on a unique period of peace and relative good times. Since the end of World War II, the American people had been involved in economic reconversion, an obsessive concern with internal security, and a cold war that defied resolution. And there was no assurance that the Eisenhower presidency would bring relief. His victory came at a moment in the Cold War when the American way of life seemed threatened by events around the world and at home.

The nuclear arms race had assumed terrifying proportions. The Soviet Union had exploded its first atomic weapon in 1949. The United States produced the even more destructive hydrogen bomb three years later and tested it on November 1, 1952, on the Pacific island of Elugelab. The island, one mile in diameter, disappeared. The bomb's power was about seven hundred times greater than the atomic bomb dropped on Hiroshima. The Soviet Union in turn developed its hydrogen bomb in 1955; two years later it reported the first successful tests of an intercontinental ballistic missile (ICBM). Although much would be made of

how the Soviets had used spies to secure information about the hydrogen bomb, nuclear experts concluded some years later that the Soviet Union may have deduced the necessary information by analyzing radioactive fallout from American nuclear blasts.

Confronted with this balance of terror and with international developments they could neither control nor at times understand, the American people found in President Eisenhower the security and self-assurance they so badly needed. Although his "dynamic conservatism" envisioned a less interventionist role for the federal government, he did little to undo the Fair Deal or the New Deal. Although his foreign policy took on a "new look" and used the language of "massive retaliation" and "brinksmanship," the substance and goals remained the same: containment by alliance and superior military power.

His conservative approach satisfied most Americans, as did his refusal to commit American youth to combat situations. Through two terms, he remained for most Americans the symbol of order, stability, and military might in the White House—precisely what the times seemed to demand.

With its avoidance of controversy, belief in organization, and celebration of "togetherness," the fifties would be called the Plastic Decade. The creative energies of the American people appeared to be absorbed in the task of combating an alien

Los Alamos National Laboratory.

ideology. Dissent was not fashionable. What remained of the American Left had been demoralized and splintered; liberals were preoccupied with demonstrating their own anticommunism. The storm of protest that would be unleashed in the sixties was barely visible on the college campuses.

Those who made up the silent generation, as the college students of the fifties came to be called, embraced the prevailing values of the adult society. They aspired to affluence, dressed modestly, avoided controversy. They listened to Perry Como, Frank Sinatra, and the Crewcuts—music that could easily be reconciled with the middle-class homes and suburban enclaves from which most of them came. The distinguishing characteristic of the class of 1949, *Fortune* magazine observed, was its aversion to risk and passion for security: "These men don't question the system. Their aim is to make it work better—to get in there and lubricate the machinery. They're not rebels; they'll be social technicians for a better society."*

Whatever dissent managed to surface in the fifties often took unlikely forms. Among the critics, and perhaps the most deeply probing, was a stand-up nightclub comic, Lenny Bruce. "People should be taught what is, not what should be," he told his audiences. "All my humor is based on destruction and despair. If the whole world were tranquil, without disease and violence, I'd be standing in the breadline—right in back of J. Edgar Hoover."

Equally alienated but more popular in intellectual circles was a small group of young Bohemian writers and artists who frequented the coffeehouses of San Francisco and came to be known as *beatniks*, or *beats*. Like Lenny Bruce, they scorned all ideologies, parodied the most cherished American myths and beliefs, celebrated absurdity, and frankly questioned the nation's sanity.

But if Bruce and the beats anticipated the rebellion of the sixties, most Americans in

the fifties found them incomprehensible and in poor taste. The literary, stage, and film success of the period was Herman Wouk's *The Caine Mutiny,* which celebrated the virtues of conformity and authority. "The idea is," one of the novel's characters declares, "once you get an incompetent ass as a skipper there's nothing to do but serve him as though he were the wisest and the best, cover up his mistakes, keep the ship going, and bear up."*

The same decade that would see rebellion on the campuses and a counterculture based on youth began with the election to the presidency of John F. Kennedy, the youngest person elected to that office and the first president born in the twentieth century. Perhaps it was his youth that underscored the difference between Kennedy and his predecessor in the White House, that seemed to inspire hope in the youthful population of the entire world. He conveyed the impression of new and imaginative approaches to old problems, even if his actual policies were not so different.

Two events of 1960, seemingly unrelated, heralded the decade of turbulence that lay ahead. On February 1, four black students in Greensboro, North Carolina, violated segregation laws and customs by taking seats at the lunch counter of the local F. W. Woolworth store. On May 13, the House Un-American Activities Committee tried to hold hearings in San Francisco and ran into a massive demonstration, made up in part of students from the nearby Berkeley campus of the University of California.

These rumblings were barely understood in 1960—but comprehension came soon enough. The optimism with which the sixties began and with which many young Americans responded to Kennedy's vision of a New Frontier would be shattered by assassination, racial strife, and a deepening involvement in a small Asian country previously unknown to most Americans—Vietnam.

CONSERVATIVES IN POWER

In campaigning for the presidency, Eisenhower had promised to clean up the "mess in Washington," purge the disloyal, spend less money, and stem the tide of "creeping socialism." The America he venerated was exemplified by his own boyhood home of Abilene, Kansas, which lay almost at the exact geographic center of the United States. No one stressed more than the president his dedication to the "middle way." But Eisenhower discovered, like any new president, that it was not so easy to put campaign rhetoric into action.

He pledged to bring into government "men and women to whom low public morals are unthinkable," only to find his own administration afflicted with scandals by 1958. The president's loyalty program, an elaboration of Truman's, purged some dissenters, but few who were disloyal. His dislike for centralized government failed to uproot "creeping socialism." The traditional virtue of individualism was celebrated by Eisenhower, even as most Americans were embracing "togetherness" and submerging their individuality in the organizations that employed them. He also spoke frequently of "preserving" each person's "equality before the law," as though each person enjoyed this fundamental right. But even while Eisenhower was taking, as he believed, "that straight road down the middle," events were polarizing the nation and the world in profound and disconcerting ways.

The Businessman's Government

To rise in the chain of command, Eisenhower wrote in *Crusade in Europe,* the individual needed personal characteristics of a special sort: "The teams and staffs through which the modern commander absorbs information and exercises his authority must be a beautiful, interlocked, smooth-working mechanism. Ideally, the whole should be practically a single mind; consequently misfits defeat the purpose of the command organization."*

Misfits were few and short-lived on the Eisenhower team. Successful businessmen and corporation lawyers dominated the cabinet. The most controversial appointment was that of Charles E.

*Reprinted by permission of Doubleday & Co., Inc.

Wilson, president of General Motors, as secretary of defense. Since GM was a major supplier of defense material, the appointment raised a possible conflict of interest between the public good and company profits. Wilson tried to defuse the issue with his much-quoted assertion: "I thought what was good for the country was good for General Motors, and vice versa." Eisenhower thought the conflict-of-interest law had been carried beyond reason. The time may come, he warned, when presidents would "be unable to get anybody to take jobs in Washington except business failures, political hacks, and New Deal lawyers."

Best known for his diplomatic experience, John Foster Dulles became secretary of state. At certain crises in foreign relations, the president overruled Dulles. Yet in this field even more than in others, his normal policy was to leave decisions to his top administrator. Operating almost independently of the State Department, Dulles established a close working relationship with the new president. His long experience in foreign affairs, dating back to a diplomatic mission under President Wilson, was enough to silence any potential critics within the administration. "After all," Eisenhower's assistant said of Dulles, "how are you going to argue with a

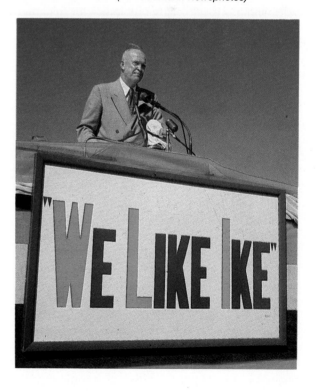

Eisenhower prepares to make his acceptance speech at the Republican National Convention in 1952, which nominated him on the first ballot. *(UPI/Bettmann Newsphotos)*

The search for national security was a bipartisan effort involving senators of such diverse politics as (left to right) Sam Ervin, Jr., Henry Jackson, John McClellan, and Joseph McCarthy. Standing behind them is Chief Counsel Robert Kennedy. *(UPI/Bettmann Newsphotos)*

man who has lived with a problem—for instance in respect to Iran—for longer than most of us knew there was such a country?"

Upon becoming president, Eisenhower had promised his business friends a more favorable political climate. His cabinet selections went far to fulfill that pledge. But the president was less successful in his efforts to cut government expenses and stabilize the agricultural sector. Although few New Deal and Fair Deal programs were enlarged, few were canceled. In September 1954, on the eve of the congressional elections, Eisenhower signed an act adding more than 7 million people to those eligible for social security benefits. The Republicans were less generous about extending the public housing program, and their attitude toward public power development clearly favored private enterprise.

Declining farm prices proved to be the most serious domestic challenge. Faced with higher distribution costs, farmers found themselves getting less for their products but paying more for what they purchased. Under the price-support policy, farm surpluses were accumulating in

government warehouses. (The public was not willing to buy farm products at the prices being supported by the government.) To reduce the surpluses, the secretary of agriculture decreased the government's support and secured congressional authorization for a flexible system. The result of this program was to aggravate the plight of small farmers. So many stayed poor that *Time* magazine called the new program "the $5 billion farm scandal."

Significant gaps in economic performance appeared during the first Eisenhower administration. But the business boom, with a strong boost from government spending and government guarantees of home mortgages and other private credit, was sufficiently genuine for the Republicans to campaign in 1956 with the slogan "Peace, Progress, and Prosperity."

The Decline of McCarthy

No sooner had Eisenhower come to power than Senator McCarthy used his chairmanship of the

Government Operations Committee to renew his assault on his favorite target, the State Department. In February 1953, Eisenhower nominated Charles E. Bohlen as ambassador to the Soviet Union. A veteran foreign service officer, Bohlen had served as Roosevelt's interpreter at Yalta. After vicious condemnations of the nominee, McCarthy and his friends permitted the Senate to approve him. But their reward was the appointment of their own man as the State Department's new "security officer." Henceforth few worked there without McCarthy's consent.

Having cleansed the stables at home, as he thought, McCarthy turned to operations abroad. His first target was the Voice of America, the overseas broadcasting unit of the United States Information Agency. After the most demoralizing search, he failed to uncover a single Communist there. The next victim was the State Department's International Information Administration, which disseminated printed materials through libraries in many parts of the world. Many books by eminent American writers, one of them Secretary Dulles's cousin, were ordered withdrawn. To the shock of the world, some were publicly burned.

Determined to expand the dragnet for Communists, the president issued his own "loyalty order" on April 27, 1953. The categories for "security risks" in government employment were made broader and vaguer. If charges were brought against a federal employee, he or she could now be suspended. Although the administration boasted it had fired 1456 federal employees under this program, not one Communist could be found. Truman's program had yielded even more "risks." The result of the Democratic-Republican loyalty purges was the demoralization of federal employees and the elimination of a generation of dissenters from public service.

The search for internal security knew few limits. In December 1953, Eisenhower dismayed the scientific community by ordering a "blank wall" to be placed between J. Robert Oppenheimer, the distinguished nuclear physicist who had directed the making of the first atomic bomb, and all secret atomic data. Oppenheimer, at this time head of the Institute for Advanced Study at Princeton, also served as chairman of the general advisory committee of the Atomic Energy Commission. The administration learned that McCarthy was on Oppenheimer's trail, and it wanted to get him first. After a humiliating hearing, a special review board cleared Oppenheimer of disloyalty. But in the eyes of the AEC he remained a "misfit,"

unemployable because of "fundamental defects in his character."

Although Congress and the presidency had often knuckled under to McCarthy, the senator's star began to wane in the summer of 1954. His reckless attack on the "coddling" of Communists in the United States Army led to the spectacular Army–McCarthy hearings. Before a nationwide television audience, McCarthy failed to sustain his charges. He conducted himself in a manner that embarrassed many of his associates. In December 1954, the Senate censured him by a vote of sixty-seven to twenty-two for "conduct unbecoming a member." Less than three years later, he died virtually unsung.

Although *McCarthyism* entered the American vocabulary as a word for indiscriminate allegations and unsubstantiated charges, such fame actually distorted the senator's importance. He had exploited the art, yet the origins lay in the Cold War itself. The earliest practitioners had been Democrats and Republicans, conservatives and liberals, including many who thought McCarthy had simply carried the tactic too far. Columnist Murray Kempton perhaps best summed up the legacy of the Wisconsin senator: "The enormities of the musician who abuses the piano have a way of obscuring the disharmonies of the score which was appointed as entirely appropriate for him to play. Overattendance upon the excessive can distract us from noticing how bad the normal is."

Despite vigilance, extensive loyalty programs, the continued operations of the HUAC, and loyalty oaths in businesses, public schools, and universities, the internal security of the nation seemed as much in danger as ever. Two years after Kennedy assumed office, J. Edgar Hoover explained to a House subcommittee why his FBI needed additional appropriations to combat Communist influence: "They have infiltrated every conceivable sphere of activity: youth groups; radio; television; and motion picture industries; nationality minority groups and civil and political units." And Kennedy's promptness in reappointing Hoover suggested the power and influence the FBI director still commanded.

Black Rights and White Laws

Even as the United States posed abroad as a defender of oppressed peoples, it found its credentials seriously undermined and challenged at home by its own black citizens. The revolution of rising expectations in the newly liberated colonial empires in Africa and Asia also stirred the black community in the United States. Despite the persistence of traditional racial practices, a new mood emerged in black America. "We're going to take over the world," jazz artist Dizzy Gillespie told a white audience, "so you'd better get used to it. You people had better just lie down and die. You've lost Asia and Africa, and now we're cutting out from white power everywhere. You'd better give up or begin to learn how it feels being a minority."

The presidency could no longer feel immune to the international implications of racism in the United States. During the Truman administration, a Committee on Civil Rights, composed of leaders of both races, made clear the extent to which the American image abroad and the Cold War demanded a new and more realistic view of race relations:

Our position in the post-war world is so vital to the future that our smallest actions have far-reaching effects. We cannot escape the fact that our civil rights record has been an issue in world politics. The world's press and radio are full of it. Those with competing philosophies have stressed—and are shamelessly distorting—our shortcomings. They have tried to prove our democracy an empty fraud, and our nation a consistent oppressor of underprivileged people. This may seem ludicrous to Americans, but it is sufficiently important to worry our friends. The United States is not so strong, the final triumph of the democratic ideal is not so inevitable that we can ignore what the world thinks of us or our record.

In May 1954, the Supreme Court's momentous decision in *Oliver Brown et al. v. Board of Education of Topeka, Kansas*, ordered the end of public-school segregation. Even earlier, the Court had begun to erode the "separate but equal" principle established by the *Plessy v. Ferguson* decision (1896).

In the 1930s the National Association for the Advancement of Colored People (NAACP) attacked the inequality of black educational facilities and especially of black teachers' salaries in the courts. A turning point came in the Supreme Court decision in 1938 in *Missouri ex rel. Gaines v. Canada*, one of a series of cases in higher education through which the idea of the inherent inequality of separate facilities was developed. The University of Missouri Law School, in the absence of a law school for blacks in that state, attempted to meet the "equal" requirement by offering to pay the tuition of Lloyd Gaines, a black, for an out-of-state school. The Court held, seven to two, that he must be trained in Missouri, in whose courts he would practice. In the absence of a law school for blacks there, he must be admitted to the one at the University of Missouri.

Similar decisions covering medical as well as law schools led the NAACP to challenge not only the inequality of facilities, but segregation itself. At the time of the *Brown* ruling, cases were pending from South Carolina, Virginia, Delaware, and the District of Columbia, as well as from Kansas. All were covered by *Brown*. The Department of Justice, in submitting the segregation cases to the Supreme Court, also revealed a deep concern over their implications in the Cold War struggle, claiming that racial discrimination must be viewed in the context of a world struggle between competing ideologies. "Racial discrimination furnishes grist for the Communist propaganda mills, and it raises doubt even among friendly nations as to the intensity of our devotion to the democratic faith."

In September 1953, Chief Justice Fred M. Vinson died. In his place Eisenhower named Governor Earl Warren of California. Privately, the president was to call that appointment "the biggest damn fool mistake I ever made." By that time, however, Warren had directed the Court toward a far greater protection of the civil rights of racial and political minorities. Speaking for a unanimous Court in May 1954, including three southern justices, Warren reversed the *Plessy* decision:

To separate [black children] from others of similar age and qualifications solely because of their race generates a feeling of inferiority as to their status in the community that may affect their hearts and minds in a way never to be undone. . . . We conclude that in the field of public education the doctrine of "separate but equal" has no place. Separate educational facilities are inherently unequal.

Although welcoming the decision, E. Franklin Frazier, a prominent black sociologist, recognized the mixed motives that had made it possible: "The white man is scared down to his bowels, so it's be-kind-to-Negroes-decade at last."

Much has been made of the sudden and shocking character of the Warren Court's ruling. No doubt it shocked millions who had never given a thought to the issue. It probably stunned the president. Yet the particular cases had been before the courts for years. And great care was taken in the ruling's implementation, which was placed in the hands of local courts. They were permitted to use guidelines reflecting local situations.

In the border states, considerable progress was made toward compliance within two years. In the

LITTLE ROCK

For a moment all I could hear was the shuffling of their feet. Then someone shouted, "Here she comes, get ready!" . . . The crowd moved in closer and then began to follow me, calling me names. I still wasn't afraid. Just a little bit nervous. Then my knees started to shake all of a sudden and I wondered whether I could make it to the center entrance a block away. It was the longest block I ever walked in my whole life. . . .

I stood looking at the school—it looked so big! Just then the guards let some white students go through. The crowd was quiet. I guess they were waiting to see what was going to happen. When I was able to steady my knees, I walked up to the guard who had let the white students in. He didn't move. When

I tried to squeeze past him, he raised his bayonet and then the other guards closed in and they raised their bayonets.

They glared at me with a mean look and I was very frightened and didn't know what to do. I turned around and the crowd came toward me. They moved closer and closer. Somebody started yelling, "Lynch her! Lynch her!" I tried to see a friendly face somewhere in the mob—someone who maybe would help. I looked into the face of an old woman and it seemed a kind face, but when I looked at her again, she spat on me.

(Elizabeth Eckford)

Source: Daisy Bates, *The Long Shadow of Little Rock* (New York: David McKay, 1962), Photograph by Wide World Photos.

Deep South it became clear that compliance would take time and might involve violence. In September 1957 Little Rock, Arkansas, became the focal point of southern resistance. Governor Orval E. Faubus used the National Guard to prevent nine black children from entering that city's Central High School.

President Eisenhower countered by providing the children with federal military protection, and

they were subsequently enrolled. Explaining his decision to send troops to Little Rock, Eisenhower revealed on nationwide television his own awareness of Cold War pressures. After speaking of "the harm that is being done to the prestige and influence and indeed to the safety of our nation and the world," he concluded: "Our enemies are gloating over this incident and using it everywhere to misrepresent our whole nation."

Faubus's overwhelming election to a third term as governor in August 1958 was an endorsement of his segregation stand and a signal to the rest of the South. When the election returns were in, Harry Ashmore, liberal editor of the *Little Rock Gazette,* asserted that the moderate position was now "clearly untenable for any man in public life anywhere in the region. A period of struggle and turmoil lies ahead." The handful of black students in Little Rock were subjected to such harassment that the local school board soon asked for a suspension of the integration program. Attorneys for the school board argued that it could not at present put integration into effect because of "the total opposition of the people and of the State Governor of Arkansas." Over a reasonable length of time, perhaps, the situation would change.

Attorneys for the NAACP, led by their chief counsel, Thurgood Marshall, replied: "There can be no equality of justice for our people if the law steps aside, even for a moment, at the command of force and violence." The Supreme Court agreed and on September 12, 1958, unanimously denied the request. Seventeen days later it delivered an unprecedented written opinion on the case in which, to underscore their unanimity, all nine justices listed themselves as coauthors. This opinion declared that

the constitutional rights of respondents [Negro children] are not to be sacrified or yielded to . . . violence and disorder. . . . The constitutional rights of children not to be discriminated against in school admissions on grounds of race or color declared by this court can neither be nullified openly and directly by state legislators or state executives or judicial officers, nor nullified by them through any evasive scheme for segregation.

The outlook, however, remained bleak. By 1959, of the 2985 biracial southern school districts, only 792 had been integrated. None were in the Deep South or Virginia. Those states had taken the lead in adopting an official policy of "massive resistance," whereby the governor could close any school ordered integrated by the courts.

Concentrating first on the school issue, blacks soon broadened their campaign to every phase of life. What was at issue was not only school integration, but the entire range of southern laws and customs that confined black people to separate and almost always inferior facilities. On December 1, 1955, Rosa Parks, a middle-aged black woman, refused to give up her seat to a white on a bus in Montgomery, Alabama. After her arrest, local blacks under the leadership of a young Baptist clergyman, Martin Luther King, Jr., organized a boycott of the city buses.

The boycott lasted for an entire year, until the Supreme Court ruled in favor of the blacks and forced the city to desegregate its public transportation system. That proved to be only the beginning of a massive nonviolent campaign to disrupt and undermine the racial caste system in the South.

Responding to the rising militancy, Congress passed the first federal civil rights acts in almost a century in 1957 and in 1960. Broad at the outset, these acts, as adopted, were confined largely to the right to vote, and they made the procedure for federal intervention in this critical field so difficult that any gains were nullified. Nevertheless, the two measures revived dormant federal commitments. "I don't believe you can change the hearts of men with laws or decisions," Eisenhower had said, urging caution in implementing the *Brown* ruling. A few years later, Martin Luther King, Jr., observed: "The law may not change the heart— but it can restrain the heartless." That much and more, sometimes with far-reaching consequences, the law and continued black agitation were to undertake.

THE NEW LOOK IN FOREIGN POLICY

The Republicans took office promising a "new look" in foreign policy. Rather than pursue the negative Democratic policy of containment, they proposed to "liberate" the nations in communism's grip, "roll back" Soviet power in Eastern Europe, and "unleash" Chiang Kai-shek in Asia. The architect of this ambitious program, John Foster Dulles, was an intractable and evangelical anti-Communist. But despite the considerable influence Dulles exerted on foreign policy, the Eisenhower years showed no significant break with the containment policies of the previous administration.

Eisenhower moved more cautiously than Dulles's rhetoric dictated. His military experience had taught him to hate war, and his search for "conciliation and compromise" appeared to be genuine. Dulles actively pursued a diplomacy of rhetoric and alliance. He sought to bolster anti-Communist regimes and to undermine Communist ones. But even if Eisenhower placed few restraints on this policy, he kept American troops out of combat.

Diplomacy by Rhetoric

Having ended the war in Korea with the armistice of July 27, 1953, the Eisenhower administration tested its "new look" in Europe. The death of Stalin in 1953 had resulted in a shared leadership in the Soviet Union, with Georgi Malenkov emerging as the new premier. He suggested "peaceful coexistence" with capitalist countries. He also relaxed controls over the peoples of Eastern Europe. That step led to an uprising in East Berlin in June 1953 that quickly spread across East Germany. This revolt, a forerunner of others in 1956, had to be suppressed by Soviet tanks and troops. "You can count on us," Dulles had told the peoples of Eastern Europe in January 1953. But in this instance, as in the others, he did nothing to implement his pledge.

The president had promised "fiscal morality," by which he meant balancing the budget—a goal attainable only by reductions in military spending. Conforming to the president's guidelines, the National Security Council announced a new military strategy as early as October 1953. Dulles soon called it "massive retaliation." Others justified it by another phrase, "more bang for the buck." Under this new policy, dependence on the army's costly ground forces would be reduced or eliminated. As a bonus, the United States would no longer be lured into "police actions" such as that in Korea.

Security would be attained by emphasis on air power, in which the United States still led the world. The administration would simply let the Communists in Moscow and Peking know that any new menace to American security would be met by nuclear and thermonuclear assaults on their cities and civilians. Since the United States had already used two nuclear bombs and had threatened to employ nuclear weapons in Korea, its NATO allies shuddered at this threat, for any military showdown with the Soviet Union could easily obliterate all of Europe.

Despite the president's great prestige, the new policy also caused trouble in the armed services. Within the Department of Defense, it fanned dangerously tense interservice rivalry with its massive favoritism toward air power. The reasoning behind it was soon proved wrong by the steeply rising prices of modern air equipment and installations.

By the end of 1954, "massive retaliation" had become synonymous with massive annihilation. The USSR had detonated its own thermonuclear bombs and had developed delivery systems like SAC's. America was confronted with a "balance of terror." Dulles responded with still another empty verbal triumph: brinksmanship, the art of going "to the brink of war without being scared." But when it came to new nationalist movements that threatened American interests, the United States would not rely on rhetoric alone.

The New Nationalism: Iran, Guatemala, and Vietnam

With the collapse of colonial rule in Asia, Africa, and the Middle East, the United States faced the task of converting nationalist movements into anti-Communist allies. There were times when it could realize that objective only by helping to destroy or immobilize the movements themselves.

In Iran, Mohammed Mossadegh headed a movement that seized power in 1951 and proceeded to nationalize the Anglo-Iranian Oil Company—a combine that exploited Iran's oil reserves largely for the profit of non-Iranians. Iran was not only an oil-rich nation, but one that bordered the Soviet Union. When American officials concluded that the new government was coming under Communist influence, the United States stopped aid to Iran. It sent CIA agents to help subvert the Mossadegh regime, and provided the military equipment that enabled the Shah of Iran to regain control in August 1953.

The payoff came in the form of a pro-Western ally, a much larger percentage of Iranian oil production, and a legacy of American intervention in the internal affairs of Iran that came back to haunt the United States twenty-six years later when the Shah's repressive regime was overthrown and replaced by an equally repressive but staunchly anti-American government.

Encouraged by its success in Iran, the United States prepared to deal with a challenge in its own hemisphere. In Guatemala, a Communist-backed reformist, Colonel Jacobo Arbenz Guzmán, headed a new government and confiscated lands belonging to the monopolistic United Fruit Company. In March 1954 Dulles pushed through a resolution at the Tenth Inter-American Conference declaring "international communism . . . incompatible with the concept of American freedom." Meanwhile, the CIA engineered a coup that toppled the constitutional Arbenz regime.

The deposed president appealed to the UN, but in vain. This was an internal matter, Dulles argued; it concerned only the OAS. When the USSR presented a similar argument to justify intervention in Czechoslovakia and Hungary, the United States reacted with outrage.

With considerably less success, the United States sought to bolster its defenses in Asia, where a nationalist movement was threatening to undermine one of the last bastions of colonialism: Indochina, a mid-nineteenth-century creation consisting of three ancient kingdoms of Laos, Cambodia, and Vietnam. With Britain and Holland on their way out as Asian powers, the United States wished to help the French retain these valuable possessions, especially after the Chinese intervention in Korea.

The situation in Indochina differed in one major way from that in other European colonies overrun by Japan. Elsewhere, the Japanese had found it advantageous to use Western-educated native leaders as occupation administrators. In Indochina, the Japanese had less need of native leaders because of the pro-Vichy French there. The nationalist Indochinese, more profoundly hostile to imperialism than most people under British rule, were driven underground. Like the partisans in the Nazi-occupied countries of Europe during the war, they soon fell under the domination of highly skilled Communists, led in this case by the Russian-trained Ho Chi Minh, who had begun to work against French rule long before World War II.

The principal nationalist group in Indochina was the Vietminh, whose standing by the end of World War II was enhanced by its success in liberating portions of the north from the Japanese. In September 1945, its leaders had proclaimed the Democratic Republic of Vietnam, with Hanoi its capital and Ho Chi Minh its president. While colonialism crumbled elsewhere, the French sought to maintain full control over Indochina.

In September 1946, Ho Chi Minh returned from consultations in Paris disenchanted with the French attitude toward independence. By December, clashes in the north had grown into a general war. The rivalry grew more intense after June 1949. The French, having set up former native rulers as puppets in Cambodia and Laos, now tried the same tactic in Vietnam. Their puppet here was Bao Dai, from an old ruling family, who had no popular following and preferred life in Paris or the French Riviera to Saigon.

This challenge led the Vietminh to intensify and extend its military activity. The emergence of the People's Republic of China in October 1949 gave a tremendous boost to Vietminh morale and soon to Vietminh strength. Early in 1950 China formally recognized the Hanoi regime. The United States and Britain, concerned at this time about French support for NATO in Europe, responded by recognizing the Saigon regime of Bao Dai. More than that, the Truman administration began to offset Chinese aid to Ho with American aid to Bao.

When the Korean conflict ended, the United States greatly enlarged its assistance to the French. By the end of 1953, American taxpayers were paying two-thirds of the cost of the French military effort, or about $1 billion per year. But it could not save the French after their main army allowed itself to be trapped at Dienbienphu early in 1954.

The siege of Dienbienphu intensified the debate in Washington. Eisenhower had already stated that Southeast Asia was of "transcendent importance" to American security: "You have a row of dominoes set up, and you knock over the first one, and what will happen to the last one is the certainty that it will go over very quickly."

But while taking this stance, Eisenhower resisted advice from close associates to commit American troops. As he told a press conference on February 10, 1954: "I say that I cannot conceive of a greater tragedy for America than to get heavily involved now in an all-out war in any of those regions, particularly with large units."

Within the next several months, Eisenhower made good his promise to avoid American involvement. The French, their forces near exhaustion in Dienbienphu, urgently requested United States intervention. On April 3, 1954, Dulles, with Admiral Arthur W. Radford, chairman of the Joint Chiefs of Staff, met in private with congressional leaders to request authorization for an American air strike on Dienbienphu from navy carriers. The congressmen said no. Eisenhower refused to sanction unilateral American military action. On April 10, Dulles flew to London to seek British support, but did not get it.

On April 16, in a speech before the American Society of Newspaper Editors (intended apparently as an administration trial balloon), Vice-President Nixon declared that "if to avoid further Communist expansion in Asia and Indochina we must take the risk now of putting our boys in, I think the Executive has to take the politically unpopular decision and do it." The reaction was clearly negative. The House at this time had under consideration a rider to an appropriations bill seeking to limit the president's authority to send troops anywhere in the world without congressional consent. Eisenhower's threat to veto the bill helped kill the rider.

By the time Dienbienphu surrendered to Ho Chi Minh on May 7, 1954, the representatives of nine powers—France, the People's Republic of China, the USSR, Britain, the United States, the two Vietnams, Cambodia, and Laos—had already convened at Geneva to work out some arrangements in the light of the inevitable collapse. Dulles did not attend these discussions, which were certain to end with something less than complete victory over the Communists. The

Postwar alliances.

Members of SEATO

Nations having bilateral treaties with the U.S.

Communist bloc

Geneva settlement, complicated and ambiguous, was meant to be temporary.

Its armistice agreement, secured on July 20, provided for a military truce between the Vietminh and the French military command, the latter openly acting for its Saigon puppet regime. The truce divided Vietnam along the seventeenth parallel. North of the line, Vietminh armies were to "regroup"; south of it, the armies of the French. Although Ho Chi Minh controlled two-thirds of the country, he withdrew his forces to the north, convinced that he would easily win the country-wide elections in July 1956.

Not until January 1955 did the French turn back the Saigon regime to Bao Dai and his strong man, Prime Minister Ngo Dinh Diem. Fearful of a Communist victory, Diem found reasons for putting off the elections. Meanwhile, the United States gradually replaced the French in South Vietnam and increased its aid to Diem's regime, despite a campaign of suppression and political and religious murders that offended even his American friends. Although American aid was based upon the willingness of South Vietnam to undertake "needed reforms," Diem's government proved slow in doing anything. But the United States was reluctant to cast him adrift.

Within South Vietnam, the pro-Communist guerrillas stepped up their attacks on the regime. By 1959 the North was openly aiding these attacks, and in September 1960 Ho formally recognized the Vietcong as the National Front for the Liberation of South Vietnam. Within the first year of the Kennedy administration, the Vietcong had grown to nearly 10,000. The South Vietnamese army was unable to restrain them, and the new president felt it necessary to send his vice-president, Lyndon B. Johnson, on a fact-finding mission. Obviously, the debate over the United States role in Vietnam had by no means been settled.

Diplomacy by Alliance

Frustrated in his efforts to "liberate" Eastern Europe, Dulles envisioned encircling the Communist world with a series of military alliances in which the United States promised to defend member nations against aggression. Diplomacy by alliance would become, in fact, a hallmark of the Dulles approach to foreign affairs. The policy met with varied success. In Asia, repeated failures to check communism led Dulles to seek a counterpart to NATO in Europe. But he was turned down by significant new countries such as India, Burma, Indonesia, and Ceylon. They resented American intrusion and feared that efforts to isolate China might just provoke that country.

Two mainland countries, Pakistan and Thailand, along with the Philippines, Australia, and New Zealand, proved more responsive. In September 1954 they met with the United States, Britain, and France at Manila and created the Southeast Asia Treaty Organization (SEATO). The signers agreed to meet any "common danger" from "Communist aggression" in accordance with their own "constitutional processes." In case of Communist threats short of armed attack, they would simply "consult" on what should be done. In the meantime, by a provision often overlooked, and perhaps meant to be, they were obliged "to strengthen their free institutions" in order to prevent Communist provocation. No SEATO armed force similar to NATO's was contemplated or created; thermonuclear weapons were to provide security.

Between the SEATO countries in the Far East and the NATO countries in the West lay the oil-rich Middle East. Arab nationalism, already inflamed by the creation of Israel in 1948, was reinforced after 1952 by the overthrow of King Farouk in Egypt. A new Egyptian republic emerged, with Colonel Gamal Abdel Nasser as its strong man. He had ambitions to unite the neighboring Arab lands under Egyptian leadership. An obvious first step was eliminating the remains of colonialism, most evident in Britain's control of a powerful military base at the Suez Canal. Dulles hoped to draw Nasser toward the West by pressing the British to yield the base. Reluctantly, they did.

To close the gap between SEATO and NATO, and thereby "create a solid band of resistance against the Soviet Union," Dulles had been promising a Middle East defense organization. In February 1955, Turkey and its neighbor Iraq, meeting at Baghdad, signed a mutual-defense treaty. Britain, Pakistan, and Iran also subscribed. These arrangements became known as the Baghdad Pact, under which the Middle East Treaty Organization (METO) was formed. The United States agreed to "cooperate with" but not join the organization. Widespread sympathy for Israel, especially among American Jews, who contributed heavily to the urban vote, made the administration reluctant to appear too close to the Arab powers, who had sworn to destroy the Jewish state. Dulles also feared that open American participation in METO, which ran across the

USSR's southern frontier, might provoke the Soviets.

To Dulles's great discomfort, Egypt also stayed out. Nasser wished freedom of action in playing off the USSR and the West against each other. His policy paid dividends in September 1955, when Egypt and the Soviet Union made an arms deal. Dulles, along with Britain and the World Bank, soon offered to help Egypt build the Aswan Dam, which would make much more of the Nile's water available for irrigation. Nasser accepted the American offer in July 1956. But within a week, certain anti-Western gestures prompted Dulles to withdraw it. On July 26, Egypt responded by announcing the nationalization of the Suez Canal. Egypt would use the canal tolls to construct the dam itself.

Rising tensions led Israel to launch an invasion of Egypt in October 1956, with the declared objective of destroying the bases from which raids had been made on its territory. Israel's action was followed by the remarkable Anglo-French invasion of the Suez region. Even more remarkable was the collaboration of the United States and the Soviet Union in the United Nations General Assembly, where they jointly condemned this resort to arms by NATO nations. The General Assembly then voted to organize a force to supervise a cease-fire.

But the UN call for peace went unheeded until the USSR threatened to intervene unilaterally with "volunteers." American threats combined with those of the USSR brought the Israeli invasion to a stop a week later. The first detachments of the United Nations peacekeeping force arrived on November 15. But this was only a stopgap measure that solved nothing in the Middle East. And the NATO alliance was slow to recover.

When the Soviets continued to arm Arab nations, METO members called on the United States to join the Baghdad Pact. This the administration refused to do. Instead, in a message to Congress in January 1957, the president asked for endorsement of the Eisenhower Doctrine, a unilateral warning to the USSR that the United States would defend the entire Middle East against Soviet attack.

Congress foresaw no direct Soviet attack, only increased Soviet subversion. It withheld approval until March of that year. Then, by a joint resolution, it gave the president discretional power to use American forces to help any Middle East nation, at its request, to resist "armed attack from any country controlled by international commu-

nism." In July 1958, following an anti-Western revolution in Iraq that led eventually to that country's withdrawal from the Baghdad Pact, the United States and Britain sent troops to Lebanon and Jordan to prevent similar uprisings in those countries.

CONCILIATION AND CONFRONTATION

Soviet-American cooperation in the UN on the issue of Egypt and Israel early in November 1956 was the last glimmer of a momentary thaw in Cold War tensions. After Stalin's death in 1953, the Soviet Union had made a series of conciliatory moves. It recognized the Federal Republic of West Germany, signed a peace treaty with Japan, and ended the four-power occupation of Austria and recognized its independence. In June 1955, Premier Nikolai Bulganin, who had succeeded Malenkov, and Nikita Khrushchev, the Communist party head, paid a visit to Marshal Tito's Yugoslavia.

In defiance of Stalin in 1948, Tito had set up his own version of a Communist state. Now, Tito, Bulganin, and Khrushchev declared openly that "differences in the concrete forms of socialist development are exclusively the concern of the peoples of the respective countries." This acknowledgment of the first break in the Soviet structure was to have far-reaching consequences in Europe and Asia.

The high point of peaceful coexistence came in July 1955, when the Big Four—the United States, the USSR, Britain, and France—met in Geneva for the first summit conference since World War II. On the agenda were such troublesome old subjects as the unification of Germany, European security, and disarmament. But since they were abrasive issues, they were not pressed. The best that could be said of the conference was the "spirit of Geneva" that it fostered.

Eisenhower took a conciliatory stance: "There are no natural differences between our peoples or our nations. There are no territorial or commercial rivalries. Historically, our two countries have always been at peace." But upon returning from Geneva, Eisenhower sounded a note of warning: "We must never be deluded into believing that one week of friendly, even fruitful negotiations can wholly eliminate a problem arising out of the wide gulf that separates East and West."

Although the United States and the USSR remained militarily the world's superpowers, each capable of annihilating the other, both were to find themselves increasingly frustrated in their attempts to control other nations. Preoccupied with each other, the two superpowers seemed unable or unwilling to grasp the implications of the revolutions that were transforming large segments of the world. All too often, they failed to understand the need of colonial and oppressed peoples to determine their own destinies. That failure would have profound consequences for the future of peaceful coexistence in a rapidly changing world.

The Second Eisenhower Administration

As the election of 1956 approached, the Republicans had every right to feel confident. "By virtually every economic measure," wrote *Time*, "1956 was the greatest year in history." Setbacks in foreign affairs had not dimmed Ike's popularity, and his heart attack in 1955 and serious surgery in 1956 brought him closer still to the people. Dependent on the general's personal appeal, Republican leaders urged him to run again, despite his health. He was renominated by acclamation, along with Vice-President Nixon.

Eisenhower's illnesses and Nixon's controversial reputation made many Democrats feel they had a chance at the White House. Despite Truman's opposition, Adlai E. Stevenson easily won renomination, with Senator Kefauver as his running mate. The Democrats made what they could of the threat of a Nixon succession, of economic discontent in the farm belt, and of the failure of the "new look" in foreign affairs. But Eisenhower's personal appeal carried him to victory even more decisively than in 1952.

With 35,590,472 votes to Stevenson's 26,022,752, he won 58 percent of the ballots. In the electoral college his margin was 457 to 73. At the same time, the Democrats maintained their margin of forty-nine to forty-seven in the Senate, and enlarged by two seats their comfortable majority in the House. Not since the time of Zachary Taylor had a president been elected without carrying at least one house of Congress for his party.

In his second inaugural address, January 21, 1957, Eisenhower expressed his continuing hopes for coexistence when he said: "We honor, no less in this divided world than in a less tormented time, the people of Russia. We do not dread, rather do we welcome, their progress in education and industry." A few months later the president and the American people suffered a shock that suggested they would not, after all, welcome Soviet progress quite so heartily.

On October 4, 1957, within six weeks of reporting the first successful tests of an intercontinental ballistic missile, the Soviet Union electrified the world by using the missile's rocket engine to launch the first unmanned space satellite, Sputnik I. The launching of four American satellites the following year brought some comfort. But this was dissipated by the Soviet success on January 2, 1959, with Lunik I, the first space vehicle to traverse the full distance of about 250,000 miles to the moon. Lunik did not hit the moon, but soared into space to become the first artificial planet in orbit around the sun. Two months later, on March 10, the United States put a planet of its own in orbit. The next stage in space exploration involved putting a human in orbit around the earth. This feat, and more spectacular ones, were accomplished in the sixties.

During Eisenhower's second administration, the United States suddenly found itself with a slowdown in business expansion, a disturbingly high level of unemployment, inflation, and serious racial strife. In distressed areas such as the coal regions of Pennsylvania, West Virginia, Kentucky, and the old industrial regions of New England, structural unemployment had become part of the way of life. In other sections of the country, unemployment among blacks grew especially acute. Besides encountering almost universal discrimination in the job market, blacks were prevented by lack of educational opportunities from seeking white-collar work.

The continued rapid mechanization of agriculture, meanwhile, and the price-support program for staples both so favored large farm corporations that the income of farming families fell off. Those who fled the land for the towns swelled the ranks of the unemployed.

The Eisenhower administration had come into office after crusading against Democratic corruption. In mid-1958, however, the administration was hit by revelations of scandals so far-reaching that Sherman Adams, the confidential assistant to the president, was forced to resign. The depth of the party's trouble on all fronts was disclosed in the 1958 congressional elections, when it suffered a defeat like those of the early New Deal years. The shadow cast by these elections was deepened during the administration's last two years when Dulles's death in May 1959 left the president largely on his own to face new crises in foreign affairs.

Coexistence and New Tensions

At the Twentieth Party Congress in February 1956, Nikita Khrushchev startled the world by revealing the crimes of Stalin, supporting the idea of "different paths to socialism," and suggesting the need for less rigid restrictions than those sanctioned by Stalin. This bold move, along with Khrushchev's endorsement of peaceful coexistence, his trip to the United States, and his refusal to support Mao Tse-tung's call for wars of national liberation, would soon drive a wedge between the USSR and China.

The Soviet Union found itself charged with appeasement of capitalism and betrayal of Marxist-Leninist principles. When de-Stalinization led Poland and Hungary to seek those "different paths to socialism," the Chinese used the occasion to exploit the weaknesses in Soviet leadership and to assert their own leadership in the Communist world.

Both the Polish and Hungarian "counterrevolutions" had reached their turning points in October 1956, when the world and the UN were absorbed in the Mideast crisis. Convinced that the uprisings had been "provoked by enemy agents" rather than Stalinist oppression, Khrushchev sent troops to crush the Hungarian revolt and tightened controls elsewhere. At the same time, he secured his position at home. In March 1958 he became premier as well as party chief.

Bolstered by space triumphs and missile gains, Khrushchev took some steps to ease the Cold War tensions. During Vice-President Nixon's visit to Moscow in July 1959, Khrushchev engaged in such a high-spirited TV debate with the vice-president that Nixon decided the premier should get to know more about the United States at first hand. This led to a prompt invitation from the president, and on September 14, Khrushchev arrived. After a peaceable address at the UN and a lively cross-country speaking tour, he met with Eisenhower with such success that a summit conference was informally agreed upon to continue "the spirit of Camp David," the site of their talks.

But the thaw proved to be short-lived. On May 5, 1960, less than two weeks before the scheduled summit conference in Paris, an American U-2 reconnaissance plane was shot down over Soviet territory. Before acknowledging the truth of Soviet protests that the plane was on a regular spying mission, the administration trapped itself in a web of denials and half-truths. "Up until now," the *Wall Street Journal* observed, "it has been possible to say to the world that what came out of the Kremlin was deceitful and untrustworthy but that people could depend on what they were told by the Government of the United States. Now the world may not be so sure that this country is any different from any other."

Although Eisenhower announced that surveillance flights over the Soviet Union would not be resumed, the damage had been done. The spirit of Camp David instantly dissolved in Paris, with Khrushchev demanding American apologies for "aggression" and punishment of those responsible. The conference ended within three hours.

While East–West relations deteriorated, relations among the anti-Communist powers also worsened. Relations with Charles de Gaulle, who had become premier of France in June 1958, became so bad that he refused to allow the United States to build NATO missile bases in France or to store nuclear weapons there. The violence that broke out in the Congo when Belgium reluctantly agreed to the formation of the Republic of the Congo in June 1960 further weakened Western unity and raised the curtain on a new stage of East–West conflict. Many Japanese resented the continuing United States occupation of Okinawa and the militarization of their homeland. When Eisenhower visited the Far East in June 1960, anti-American demonstrations in Tokyo became so militant that he was officially advised to omit Japan from his itinerary because his personal security could not be assured. Meanwhile, much closer to home, Latin America had begun to erupt.

Cuba and Castro

The deterioration of the American position in Latin America had become dramatically evident in April and May 1958, when Vice-President Nixon visited a number of countries in an effort to revive friendliness toward the United States. He was hostilely received, and in Venezuela mobs stoned and spat upon him. When Eisenhower responded by sending warships and alerting marines at nearby Caribbean bases, he succeeded only in reviving the image of Yankee imperialism. The most important challenge to United States dominance, however, came in Cuba. On January 1, 1959, Fidel Castro successfully completed a five-year struggle to overthrow the Batista regime.

Determined to make a radical social revolution, Castro moved to end the colonial relationship that had bound the Cuban government and economy to the United States. The massive confiscation of foreign holdings he ordered simply reflected the extent of outside control. More than 40 percent of sugar production, for example, and 90 percent of the cattle ranches and mineral resources belonged to American interests.

Of course, Castro's economic program and repression of civil liberties angered the United States. It led many middle-class Cubans to flee to the United States. The rapid shift of Castro to the radical Left and the Soviet trade bloc came as no surprise to the last American ambassador to Cuba: "It was not Castro's predilection for Communism," he explained, "but his pathological hatred of the American power structure as he believed it to be operative in Cuba together with his discovery of the impotence of Cuba's supposedly influential classes, that led him eventually into the Communist camp. Only from that base, he thought, could he achieve his goal of eliminating American influence."

With the threatened spread of *Fidelismo* elsewhere, the United States chose to rely on the traditional ways of dealing with hemispheric trouble. Before Eisenhower left office, he agreed to a CIA plan by which an anti-Castro army of Cubans would be trained in the United States and then landed in Cuba in early 1961. Meanwhile, the Cuban issue played a curious role in the 1960 presidential election. Kennedy talked vaguely of intervention and support of "non-Batista democratic anti-Castro forces." Nixon tried to cover his awareness of the preparations already under way to overthrow the Castro regime.

Eisenhower's Farewell

Eight years in office proved a great strain on the Republican party, especially since it had failed to balance the budget, reduce the national debt, end the upward wage–price spiral, restore farm income, or significantly cut taxes. It had also failed to roll back the Communists and restore the good old days of continental security. When Republican delegates convened in the summer of 1960 to choose a candidate, the conservatives were in command of the party machinery. On the first ballot the convention named Richard M. Nixon for president. As a sop to the party liberals, it chose Henry Cabot Lodge, United States delegate to the UN, as his running mate.

After his extraordinary performance in a series of primaries, Senator John F. Kennedy of Massachusetts clearly overshadowed the other presidential aspirants at the Democratic convention in Los Angeles. He won on the first ballot. Fearful of the effects of their strong civil rights plank and of Kennedy's Catholicism, the Democrats nominated Senator Lyndon B. Johnson of Texas for vice-president in an attempt to hold the South. In Kennedy's acceptance speech, he talked about "a New Frontier—the frontier of the 1960s—a frontier of unfulfilled hopes and threats."

The campaign was highlighted by the first television debates between presidential candidates, from which Kennedy seemed to have gained more than his opponent. Nixon, moreover, had aroused considerable controversy in his political past, much of it revolving around the tactics he had used to advance his career. Nor did Eisenhower's lukewarm support help. (When asked at a press conference to name the major decisions in which his vice-president had participated, Eisenhower replied, "If you give me a week, I might think of one.")

When the results were in, Kennedy had become the first Catholic president and, at forty-three, the youngest ever to be elected. But his winning margin was a mere 118,550 out of a record 68.8 million votes cast. He won by less than

WORDS AND NAMES IN AMERICAN HISTORY

There could scarcely be a more American word than *Yankee,* but few people seem to agree about its original meaning or even about how the word came into being. It is clear, though, that the word was known—though not commonly used—before the American Revolution. The meaning of the term depends entirely on the context in which it is used. For foreigners outside the United States, *Yankee* applies to all Americans. To American southerners, it means anyone from the North (which in this context includes folks from California). In the northern states, it denotes people from New England. In that northeastern corner of the country it is often used to distinguish people of old English descent from newer immigrants from Ireland, Italy, Canada, and so on. Most of these later immigrants were members of the Roman Catholic church, so the term *Yankee* has overtones of even Protestantism and Puritanism. Finally, we should bear in mind that "the Yankees" are for millions of Americans first and foremost a baseball team.

two-thirds of 1 percent of the popular vote, and there were reports of election irregularities in Illinois and Texas, which Kennedy narrowly carried. What probably saved him from defeat was the solid support he received from Catholics and blacks. At least 70 percent of these voters, according to reliable estimates, endorsed him. No doubt his personal intervention on behalf of Martin Luther King, Jr., who had been jailed in October for violating a Georgia Jim Crow law, helped to bring out the black vote.

Before leaving the White House, the still popular Ike wanted to give the American people the "most challenging message" possible, and he did so admirably in his famous farewell speech of January 17, 1961:

This conjunction of an immense military establishment and a . . . permanent armaments industry of vast proportions . . . is new in the American experience. The total influence—economic, political, even spiritual—is felt in every city, every state house, every

office of the federal government. We recognize the imperative need for this development. Yet we must not fail to comprehend its grave implications. . . .

In the councils of government we must guard against the acquisition of unwarranted influence, whether sought or unsought, by the military-industrial complex. The potential for the disastrous rise of misplaced power exists and will persist. We must never let the weight of this combination endanger our liberties or democratic processes.

The warning came too late. By 1961, the "military-industrial complex" had virtually overrun the traditional instruments of American government. With confrontation in Asia and the Caribbean, the military ascendancy, like the Cold War itself, seemed destined to remain a part of the American way of life. The newly elected president must have sensed that, and he paid little heed to Eisenhower's warning. During the first year of the Kennedy administration, the military budget increased 15 percent.

The election of 1960.

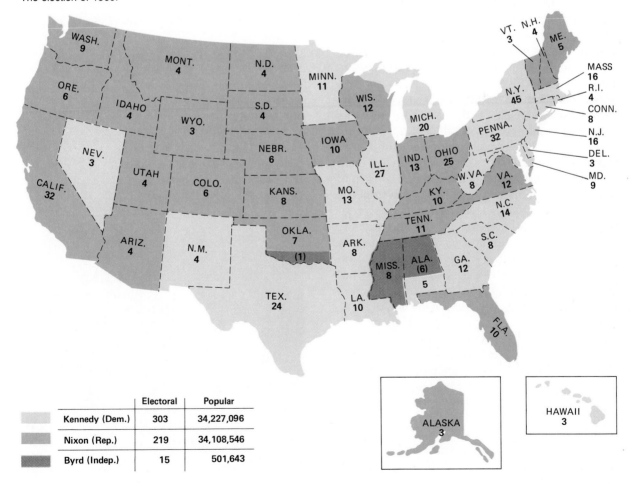

	Electoral	Popular
Kennedy (Dem.)	303	34,227,096
Nixon (Rep.)	219	34,108,546
Byrd (Indep.)	15	501,643

JFK AND THE NEW FRONTIER

Young as he was when he delivered his first State of the Union message in January 1961, John F. Kennedy had already served fourteen years in Congress, the last eight in the Senate. He had been exposed to politics even earlier, in the home of his father, millionaire Joseph P. Kennedy, ambassador to Britain under FDR. It took time for the politically conservative environment to wear off. In Congress, he had associated with the severest critics of his party's China policy, helped carry the McCarran Internal Security Act over Truman's veto, and refrained from criticizing McCarthy. Elected to the Senate in 1952, Kennedy made an unsuccessful bid four years later for the Democratic vice-presidential nomination.

Despite his congressional experience, the young senator still lacked a national reputation. Moreover, he had to overcome a political tradition in which no Catholic had ever been elected to the presidency. But he did have some important assets. His long contact with politics had not affected him personally: his candor was credible, his humor fresh, his modesty unfeigned. And he possessed, besides, an excellent war record and an efficient campaign organization. These assets proved to be more than enough to win the Democratic nomination, but only barely so to defeat Nixon in the election.

No sooner had Kennedy taken office than he surrounded himself with youthful advisers pledged, like himself, to get the country moving again. The members of the Kennedy team, David Halberstam would later write, "carried with them an exciting sense of American elitism, a sense that the best men had been summoned forth from the country." The dynastic heir apparent, the president's younger brother Robert, became attorney general with perhaps broader powers than any previous holder of that office. Robert S. McNamara, one of the statistical geniuses of the Ford Motor Company, was named secretary of defense. His assignment was, with the aid of computers, to bring Pentagon feuding under civilian control. McGeorge Bundy, a Harvard intellectual, became Kennedy's special assistant for national security affairs. In that position he may have exerted more influence than the secretary of state, Dean Rusk. Walter C. Heller, chairman of the Council of Economic Advisers, offset the traditional attitudes of the secretary of the Treasury, the banker C. Douglas Dillon. During the campaign, Kennedy had compared himself with his also youthful rival.

Nixon, said Kennedy, "has the courage of our old convictions." But "the New Frontier is here, whether we seek it or not." The New Frontier promised to pioneer new approaches to old problems and to get the country moving again. The direction in which the country moved—toward confrontation at home and abroad—suggested how dependent Kennedy's approaches remained on the policies of his predecessors.

Civil Rights and Civil Conflict

In his first State of the Union message, Kennedy enumerated the "unfinished and neglected tasks" that faced his administration. Because of financial need, "one-third of our most promising high school graduates" prematurely ended their education. Persistent recession resulted in the "highest peak in our history" of "insured unemployment." Long-term "distressed areas" continued to decay. The drain of American gold abroad, largely for military assistance, menaced the stability of the dollar. Growing numbers of poor old people, the ill, and others in need were neglected. Natural resources as basic as the water supply were being wasted.

President John F. Kennedy. *(John F. Kennedy Library)*

Segregated drinking fountains symbolized the separate worlds of the South until the 1960s. *(Elliott Erwitt, Magnum Photos)*

But all these issues paled before that of racial equality, which Kennedy failed to mention in 1961. By the summer of 1963, the hundredth anniversary of the Emancipation Proclamation, it dominated the headlines. It had been nearly a decade since the Supreme Court had ruled school segregation illegal, yet the pace of integration had made a mockery of the court-ordered "all deliberate speed." When blacks sought admission to state universities, moreover, the resulting showdowns required the application of federal force. At the University of Mississippi, Governor Ross Barnett tried to block the admission of James Meredith. At the University of Alabama, Governor George Wallace stood in the doorway, as he had promised, to stop two black students from entering.

Meanwhile, the attack on segregation had broadened. The sit-in at the Woolworth lunch counter in Greensboro, North Carolina, on February 1, 1960, mushroomed into hundreds of similar demonstrations, all designed to desegregate public facilities and transportation. By deliberately violating Jim Crow laws, black youths defied traditions and customs that had maintained generations of white supremacy in the South. By 1963, an estimated 70,000 blacks and white sympathizers had participated in these demonstrations, and more were to come.

To the embarrassment of American foreign policy, the headlines of 1963 made known around the world the brutality with which civil rights demonstrations were suppressed. Several weeks after Kennedy proposed his first civil rights legislation to Congress, mass demonstrations began in Birmingham, Alabama. Before the summer was over, more than eight hundred cities and towns had held peaceful protests, often in the face of dogs and fire hoses employed by the police.

Leadership in the black nonviolent movement rested with Martin Luther King, Jr., a young minister from Atlanta barely in his thirties. If black people directed their appeal to the Christian conscience of white America, King argued, the walls of segregation and race hatred would inevitably crumble. What he asked of his followers was nonviolence, Christian love, and a belief in the essential decency of people. It would not be easy.

The climax of the nonviolent campaign came on August 3, 1963, when over 200,000 blacks and sympathetic whites marched on Washington, D.C., demanding "freedom now." Although an impressive demonstration, it was not the massive show of nonviolent civil disobedience that had been planned. Less radical organizations and leaders prevailed, and President Kennedy invited them to the White House. The March on Washington is best remembered for Martin Luther King's eloquent speech ("I have a dream. . . .") and the assembled multitude singing the anthem of the civil rights movement, "We Shall Overcome."

At the same time, however, the Washington rally revealed growing restlessness and divisiveness within the ranks of black leadership. These trends were most evident in the rapid emergence of Malcolm X, a brilliant Black Muslim leader and separatist. "They took it over," he said bitterly of the March on Washington.

It's just like when you get some coffee that's too black, which means it's too strong. What do you do? You

Martin Luther King: "We will match your capacity to inflict suffering with our capacity to endure suffering. We will meet your physical force with our soul force. We will not hate you, but we cannot obey your unjust laws. Do to us what you will and we will still love you. Bomb our homes and threaten our children; send your hooded perpetrators of violence into our communities and drag us out on some wayside road, beating us and leaving us half dead, and we will still love you. But we will soon wear you down by our capacity to suffer. And in winning our freedom, we will so appeal to your heart and conscience that we will win you in the process." *(Declan Haun/Black Star)*

integrate it with cream, you make it weak. But if you pour too much cream in it, you won't even know you ever had coffee. It used to be hot, it becomes cool. It used to be strong, it becomes weak. It used to wake you up, now it puts you to sleep. This is what they did with the march on Washington. Why, it even ceased to be a march. It became a picnic, a circus.

Several months before the March on Washington, on June 10, Medgar Evers, field secretary of the Mississippi NAACP, was murdered by a sniper. Less than a month after the March, a bomb exploded in the Sixteenth Street Baptist Church in Birmingham, killing four black children. Perhaps, some argued, Martin Luther King had demanded too much of his people. His movement had yielded some positive results, but at a cost in human lives and frustration that many blacks found difficult to bear. "It's simply not possible," said Malcolm X, "to love a man whose chief purpose in life is to humiliate you, and still be what is considered a normal human being." The black movements, increasingly independent of white liberal sympathizers, began to take on different dimensions.

Although much of the activity was confined to the South, there were no grounds for optimism or smugness in the North. If anything, the frustration and betrayal of expectations were even deeper and potentially more explosive. Even as northern whites reacted with anger to the televised brutalities inflicted on southern blacks, they paid little attention to the discrimination in housing, employment, and education in their own region. Black sharecroppers and farm laborers were flowing to northern cities in record numbers in the 1950s and 1960s. Many whites fled to safer urban areas and to the suburbs, leaving the urban areas more and more isolated and explosive. Between 1950 and 1960, for example, the twelve largest cities lost more than 2 million white residents and gained over 2 million blacks. These cities rapidly succumbed to the poverty and frustration of their new residents.

Although northern blacks had the vote and civil rights, these were not of much value to someone facing unemployment and hunger. That was the message Malcolm X was hammering home, and he found an audience. "Well, I am one who doesn't believe in deluding myself," he said of white America. "I'm not going to sit at your table and watch you eat, with nothing on my plate, and call myself a diner. Sitting at the table doesn't make you a diner, unless you eat some of what's on that plate."

In Birmingham, Alabama, fire hoses and police dogs were used to disperse civil rights demonstrators. *(AP/Wide World Photos)*

Space, Militarism, and Prosperity

"To get the country moving again" in the economic sphere, the new economists of the Kennedy administration explored every avenue for using the energies of the entire population. Early in 1962, the president proposed a broad tax cut for consumers as one way to stimulate demand for goods. But this measure, like so many of his proposals, made little headway in Congress.

The president enjoyed far more success when he asked for appropriations for defense and space. "Anybody who would spend $40 billion in a race to the moon for national prestige is nuts," Eisenhower said after he had retired from the presidency. Kennedy, although at first as doubtful as his conservative predecessor, soon held other ideas. In May 1961, under the heading "Urgent

National Needs," he told Congress: "No single space project in this period will be more impressive to mankind" than that of "landing a man on the moon and returning him safely to earth."

During Kennedy's administration, annual space appropriations soared to over $5 billion. To those who questioned such an expenditure, he responded in kind at Rice University: "But why, some say, the moon? . . . And they may well ask, why climb the highest mountain? Why, thirty-five years ago, fly the Atlantic? Why does Rice play Texas?"

The business upswing in 1962 and 1963 followed new expenditures and appropriations not only for the space program, but for the related missile program and other "national security" items. While the strength of the country in foreign affairs depended on the strength of the domestic economy, it seemed that the strength of the domestic economy depended on the volume of military spending. Kennedy, as a senator, had become by 1959 one of the most active opponents of the growing militarization of the foreign-aid program. As president, his efforts to reverse this trend were strengthened by his opposition to the military straitjacket of "massive retaliation" that so confined the Eisenhower-Dulles policy of deterrence. "We intend," he declared in July 1961, "to have a wider choice than humiliation or all-out nuclear action."

THE DIPLOMACY OF FLEXIBLE RESPONSE

Although Kennedy hoped to identify the country's power with its political ideals, its strength with its social values, he warned that "we must never be lulled into believing that either [the Soviet Union or China] has yielded its ambitions for world domination." Kennedy's acceptance of this basic premise of the Cold War points up a tragic irony in his attempts to find new approaches to foreign policy and to use the advantages of cooperating with different cultures and governments.

While he tried to apply political solutions to "limited" international incidents, he felt obliged to build up the armed services. The "big stick" could still reduce the likelihood of extreme provocation. Admitting that, he could not stop the rapid development of the instruments of "massive retaliation." In 1962, military expenditures went over the $50 billion mark for the first time since the Korean conflict.

By then, Kennedy had taken certain steps in pursuit of a more "flexible response" in foreign policy. The Peace Corps, in which young men and women would volunteer their technical skills to help underdeveloped nations, was a different and more creative approach to diplomacy. Far less imaginative was the president's response to continuing trouble in Latin America. Determined to try to stop the spread of *Fidelismo,* Kennedy in March 1961 outlined a plan, modeled on the Marshall Plan, for an Alliance for Progress with Latin American nations. With United States assistance, these nations were expected to put into practice much-needed land reforms and accelerate economic development.

But even while proposing such a program, the Kennedy administration, like its predecessors and successors, bolstered repressive regimes whose primary virtue was their opposition to communism. If that suggested inconsistency or even political bankruptcy, the response of the United States to the revolutionary upheavals in Cuba and Southeast Asia provided tragic confirmation.

Cuba: The Bay of Pigs and the Missile Crisis

In one of his last acts as president, Eisenhower had broken off diplomatic relations with Cuba in protest against "a long series of harassments, baseless accusations, and vilifications." At least one of those accusations, however, was soon proved far from baseless. For nine months, as Castro had charged, about 1500 anti-Castro Cuban exiles had been secretly training in Guatemala under United States CIA men for an invasion of their island. Mass internal uprisings were certain to follow their arrival, the exile leaders promised, and the Castro regime would be overthrown.

After repeated assurances by a unanimous Joint Chiefs of Staff, some of his own "new frontiersmen," and an enthusiastic Allen Dulles (who reminded Kennedy of how his CIA had overthrown Guatemala's Marxist government), the new president permitted the invasion to start. He assured the press that "there will not be, under any conditions, any intervention in Cuba by United States forces." Five days later, on April 17, 1961, the exile forces attempted to land at the Bay of Pigs, ninety miles from Havana. At the same time, a CIA-hired firm on Madison Avenue was issuing press releases in the name of the "Cuban Revolutionary Council," which called for a "coordinated wave of sabotage and rebellion."

The anticipated popular uprising never materialized. United States air support was inadequate; the few B-26s furnished the exiles were no match for Castro's air force, and the assault instantly collapsed. Over 1200 of the invaders were taken prisoner and held for almost two years.

The day after the abortive invasion, the president cautioned Castro that "our restraint is not inexhaustible" and that the United States would act "alone, if necessary" to protect its security. Using an odd analogy, he also warned the Soviet Union that "we do not intend to be lectured on intervention by those whose character was stamped for all time on the bloody streets of Budapest."

Castro tried to strengthen his defenses against any further United States aggression. But the

Soviet Union's seizure of this opportunity to install missile sites in Cuba, manned by Soviet technicians and capable of obliterating targets within a range of two thousand miles, was more than the United States was willing to tolerate. On October 22, 1962, on nationwide television, Kennedy took a calculated risk that brought the world to the brink of nuclear war. He ordered Khrushchev to remove the missiles and instructed the navy to intercept and turn back Soviet ships headed for Cuba. (The Joint Chiefs of Staff and former Secretary of State Acheson had argued instead for a direct air strike on the missile sites.)

Recognizing the gravity of Kennedy's stand, the Soviet Union agreed to recall the ships and to remove the missile bases. Kennedy, on his part, assured the Soviet leader—but only in the form of a tacit understanding—that the United States would refrain from offensive action to overthrow the Castro regime. Both leaders had made their point. Kennedy emerged with enhanced prestige. The Soviet Union came out of the crisis determined never again to be placed in a position of military disadvantage.

What small chance for success the Alliance for Progress may have had was gone in the face of Castro's performance. By 1963 it had become evident that countries below the border would find it impossible to carry out the reforms that would allow the development of broad-based capitalist economies. Nor would the United States tolerate "anti-imperialists" with a popular following who might undertake even more fundamental social changes. This was made clear in Guatemala before the elections scheduled there in November 1963.

Juan José Arévalo, a former president with a Marxist following and a strong record in agricultural reforms, was the leading candidate. As one high-level Kennedy official said of Arévalo early that year: "I don't give a damn whether he is or is not a communist. He talks like a communist, he acts like a communist, and if he's elected he'll be soft on communists." In March 1963, while CIA men at least turned the other way (some suppose they helped engineer the shift), President Miguel Ydígoras Fuentes was deposed by a military faction that installed the minister of defense as president, and the November elections were not held.

Despite the Cuban confrontation and the ongoing Berlin crisis, new hopes for a détente between the Soviets and the West came out of the deepening split between the USSR and China. These hopes were strengthened in July 1963 when the three nuclear powers (the United States, Britain, and the USSR) signed a treaty pledging themselves to end nuclear testing that "causes radioactive debris" outside their own borders. This was only a first step toward "the speediest possible achievement of an agreement on general and complete disarmament."

The three powers invited others to sign the treaty. In the West, Germany had misgivings. France, eager for nuclear arms of its own, was openly hostile. In the East, China denounced the Soviets and the Western powers. In the United States, and no doubt in the USSR, armament had gained the irreversible momentum of which Eisenhower had spoken in his farewell.

Kennedy and Southeast Asia

During the early months of his administration, Kennedy found himself spending a great amount of time on the struggle to control Laos. By May 1962 the Pathet Lao, a Communist guerrilla movement, controlled almost two-thirds of the small country, apparently with little popular opposition. The conservative, pro-Western regime, which the Eisenhower administration had supported, was finally forced to flee.

While Kennedy hurriedly sent protective naval and military contingents to neighboring Thailand, the United States and the Soviet Union used diplomatic channels to pave the way for a coalition government in Laos under Souvanna Phouma, an avowed neutralist. The Pathet Lao maintained its pressure. More important, it kept open the path of North Vietnamese aid to the Vietcong in South Vietnam over the Ho Chi Minh Trail through southeastern Laos. Meanwhile, the CIA began to supply anti-Communist guerrillas operating behind the Pathet Lao lines, and the United States soon undermined the coalition government. With the Pathet Lao now on the offensive and the United States retaliating with secret bombing raids, the situation in Laos deteriorated.

Despite Kennedy's emphasis on developing political options, the most obvious product of "flexible response" became the elaboration and application of the concept of limited war. The fatal test of this policy came in Vietnam. Although Diem had refused to hold all-Vietnam elections in 1956 (correctly fearing he would lose), and had violated his pledge to Eisenhower to make needed reforms, the United States remained committed to his regime. In October 1961, General Maxwell D. Taylor went to South Vietnam as Kennedy's

The map legend reads:

O 200
Miles

CHINA

Deinbienphu
Hanoi
Haiphong

NORTH

Red R.

Luang Prabang

Gulf of Tonkin

HAINAN

VIETNAM

17th parallel—the
temporary division between
North and South Vietnam
established by the Geneva
Conference in 1954

Vientiane   LAOS

Mekong R.

Hue
Danang

SOUTH
CHINA
SEA

THAILAND

Bangkok

CAMBODIA

SOUTH
VIETNAM

Gulf of Thailand

Phnom Penh

Saigon

Mekong
Delta

Communist countries

Allied with U.S.

Neutral countries

The two Vietnams.

special representative to appraise the situation. The result of that mission was a speedup in the flow of American instructors, pilots, and other military personnel to that country.

By the end of 1962, after Taylor had become chairman of the Joint Chiefs, the number of Americans in South Vietnam had reached 10,000. Within five years, Under Secretary of State George Ball warned the president, the United States might have as many as 300,000 troops in Vietnam. Kennedy refused to believe it. "George," he replied, "you're crazier than hell."

Although Kennedy at first resisted both the "overmilitarization" and "over-Americanization" of the war in Vietnam, he soon found himself approving the growing military intervention. Embracing Eisenhower's domino theory, he declared in July 1963 that a United States withdrawal would "mean a collapse not only of South Vietnam

but Southeast Asia. So we are going to stay there." American military assistance to the Diem regime soared, and the number of American military personnel edged toward 17,000.

Earlier, the Joint Chiefs had assured the president that 40,000 troops would "clean up the Vietcong threat." McNamara had concluded: "Every quantitative measurement we have shows we're winning this war." In the meantime Diem stepped up his attacks not on the Vietcong but on the Buddhists, who made up most of the opposition to the French-oriented Catholic ruling class.

As early as 1954, military experts had continued right up to the fall of Dienbienphu to forecast that "the French are going to win." (A decade later, they shamelessly forecast the always imminent but yet somehow elusive American triumph.) But Kennedy had said, "I am frankly of the belief that no amount of American military assistance in Indochina can conquer . . . 'an enemy of the people' which has the sympathy and covert support of the people." The emergence of the Vietcong some years later apparently did not alter his conviction that "counterinsurgency" must fail "if its political objectives do not coincide with the aspirations of the people, and their sympathy, cooperation and assistance cannot be gained."

In keeping with these deeper feelings, Kennedy, in September 1963, declared of the South Vietnamese: "In the final analysis, it's their war. They're the ones who have to win it or lose it. We can help them as advisers but they have to win it." To improve the prospects of winning, South Vietnamese General Duong Van Minh, with American encouragement, overthrew the Diem regime on November 1, 1963, and shortly thereafter executed Diem and his brother. The new government (the first of nine in the next five years) was given prompt American recognition. By the time of Kennedy's assassination on November 22, however, it had won few military laurels.

On October 2, 1963, Kennedy had McNamara and Taylor announce from the White House the administration's intention of withdrawing most United States forces from South Vietnam by the end of 1965. Whether Kennedy could have done this will never be known. Within three weeks of Kennedy's assassination, McNamara and CIA chief John A. McCone visited Saigon. On their return, on New Year's Day 1964, they announced they had "told the junta leaders that the United States was prepared to help . . . as long as aid was needed." This only seconded President Johnson's

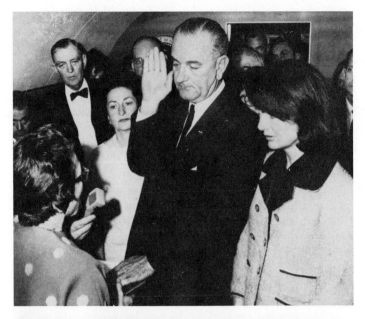

(top) Hours after the assassination of John Kennedy, Lyndon Johnson was sworn in as president, as Jacqueline Kennedy and Lady Bird Johnson looked on. *(AP/Wide World Photos)* (bottom) Two days later, Lee Harvey Oswald, the suspected assassin, was shot to death in the Dallas city jail. *(Copyright 1963 by the Dallas Times Herald and photographer Bob Jackson)*

New Year's Eve promise to them of "the fullest measure of support . . . in achieving victory."

While these commitments were being made, the American people and Congress were not informed of the full implications of United States involvement. That "credibility gap," as historian Walter La Feber would argue, "did not begin with Lyndon Johnson's presidency. In 1963 the gap measured the growing abyss between the actual situation in Vietnam and the self-assurance of the Kennedy Administration that it could manipulate military power to control nationalist revolutions."

Death of the President

On reviewing his first two years in office, Kennedy acknowledged a large degree of frustration. "The responsibilities placed on the United States are greater than I imagined them to be and there are greater limitations upon our ability to bring about a favorable result than I had imagined them to be. . . . It is much easier to make speeches than it is finally to make the judgments."

The German problem remained unsolved. The Communists made it even more vivid by building a wall, early in August 1961, separating East from West Berlin. Periodic crises raised the threat of armed confrontation. In Africa, emerging nations were throwing off the last vestiges of colonialism and moving toward a neutral position in the East–West conflict. In Asia, the United States deepened its involvement in Vietnam.

In space, Soviet scientists continued to set the pace. The big breakthrough came on April 12, 1961, when Major Yuri Gagarin successfully orbited the earth in a Soviet space capsule. On February 20, 1962, after preliminary flights in space by Commander Alan B. Shepard, Jr., (May 5, 1961) and Captain Virgil I. Grissom (July 21, 1961), Colonel John H. Glenn, Jr., became the first American to orbit the earth.

Congress generously appropriated funds for defense and space, but proved more reluctant when it came to social legislation and the protection of civil rights. As the black movement spread, white resistance hardened. Black frustrations made Martin Luther King's hold on black leadership more precarious, and the prospect of violent confrontation grew. Meanwhile, Kennedy's civil rights program went nowhere in Congress, along with his proposals to enlarge federal aid to education and extend medicare to the aged.

This was the state of the world and the nation in the summer of 1963. The previous November, 51 million Americans, the largest ever in a nonpresidential year, went to the polls and broke tradition by fully supporting the administration in power. The Republicans were surprised as well by Richard Nixon's defeat in the California race for governor. The leading candidate for the Republican nomination in 1964 appeared to be Senator Barry Goldwater of Arizona, a staunch conservative who told an audience in November 1963 that

the New Frontier had produced "1,026 days of wasted spending, wishful thinking, unwarranted intervention, wistful theories, and waning confidence." When asked to respond to such charges, Kennedy smiled and replied, "Not yet, not yet."

On November 22, 1963, Kennedy was in Dallas, Texas, to bolster his political position in that state. While riding in an open car, to the cheers of crowds lining the streets, the president was shot in the neck and head by an assassin. He died almost instantly. The tragic death of the young president threw the nation and the world into shock, mourning, and disbelief. The disbelief was compounded by the bizarre series of events that followed.

While a nationwide television audience looked on, Lee Harvey Oswald, the suspected assassin, was shot to death two days later by Jack Ruby, the proprietor of a small Dallas nightclub, who confronted Oswald as he was being escorted to the county jail. Although a special committee headed by Chief Justice Earl Warren could find no conspiracy in Kennedy's assassination, doubts and rumors persisted. In 1979, a congressional inquiry raised serious questions about whether Oswald had acted alone. Given all the bizarre events of the decade, the American people were prepared to believe almost anything.

SUMMARY

The eight years of the Eisenhower presidency were a time of relative peace and prosperity, although both domestic and international pressures were building beneath the surface.

The Eisenhower administration, dedicated to the "middle way," was led by businessmen and lawyers. But even they were unable to cut government spending or stabilize agriculture. And the search for internal security continued, although Senator McCarthy's star began to wane in 1954, when he was censured by the Senate.

The most important domestic event of Eisenhower's first term was the Brown v. Board of Education decision by the Supreme Court, which ordered the desegregation of the public schools. Under Chief Justice Earl Warren, the Court began actively to protect the civil rights of racial and political minorities. The mood of black America now was far different; there was a new militancy and a new determination. The events at Little Rock, Arkansas, in 1957, when the president sent federal troops to enforce the desegregation of a high school, symbolized both the depth of the resistance and the national commitment to change. The bus boycott in Montgomery,

Alabama, in 1955–1956 marked the beginning of a massive nonviolent campaign to end the racial caste system in the South.

The "new look" in foreign policy, carried out by Secretary of State John Foster Dulles, was based on the idea of rolling back communism all over the world. It was a diplomacy of rhetoric, threat, and alliance in which the United States sought to bolster anti-Communist regimes and undermine Communist regimes. It relied on massive retaliation and brinksmanship to meet threats to world peace.

As a result of this policy, the United States intervened actively in Iran, Guatemala, and Vietnam to convert nationalist movements into anti-Communist allies. In Vietnam, the French were losing the war against the Vietminh, the Communist regime based in the North. Eisenhower had resisted the pressure to commit American troops, although the United States did extend aid to the French and did join in the truce negotiations at Geneva after the disaster of Dienbienphu in May 1954.

Gradually, the United States replaced the French in South Vietnam in support of a repressive anti-Communist regime. Pro-Communist guerrillas, supported by the North Vietnamese, continued the war—but now against the South Vietnamese army instead of the French. These events and others in Southeast Asia led Dulles in 1954 to set up a new collective security alliance, SEATO, the counterpart of NATO in Europe. But no military force was created; thermonuclear weapons were to provide security.

In the Middle East, conflict between the oil-rich Arabs and the new state of Israel was a source of constant tension. In 1955 Dulles engineered the Baghdad Pact, under which METO, another collective-security alliance, was formed. But the United States, because of Israel, did not openly join. Nor did Egypt, now under the leadership of Nasser and a new government. In July 1956, Egypt responded to American machinations in the Middle East by nationalizing the Suez Canal. In October, Israel invaded Egypt; this act was followed by an Anglo-French invasion of the Suez.

It took American-Soviet cooperation through the United Nations to force a cease-fire and avoid a new world war. But the peace was shaky, and the Middle East continued to be a powder keg. Soviet-American hostility and tension soon returned to pre-Suez levels. The Geneva summit of 1955 had been the high point of "peaceful coexistence," and it had dealt with none of the real issues that divided the superpowers. The arms race and the rivalry continued.

TIME LINE

1952	Nasser comes to power in Egypt
1953	Eisenhower expands loyalty program
	Oppenheimer loses security clearance
	Earl Warren appointed Chief Justice
	Stalin dies
	Shah of Iran returns to power with U.S. support
1954	Supreme Court orders end to racial segregation in the schools
	Army-McCarthy hearings
	Senate censures McCarthy
	CIA coup topples Guatemalan government
	Vietnamese defeat French at Dienbienphu
	Geneva Conference on Vietnam
	SEATO created
1955	Rosa Parks arrested, Montgomery bus boycott begins
	Baghdad Pact
1956	Suez crisis
	Khruhschev reveals Stalin's crimes
	Soviet-Chinese relations deteriorate
	Soviets crush Hungarian revolt
	Eisenhower re-elected
1957	Little Rock school integration crisis
	Soviet Union launches Sputnik satellite
	Eisenhower Doctrine
1958	U.S. intervenes in Lebanon
1959	Khruhschev visits United States
	Castro comes to power in Cuba
1960	U-2 spy incident; Paris conference dissolves
	Civil rights sit-in in Greensboro, North Carolina
	Anti-HUAC demonstration, San Francisco
	Martin Luther King, Jr. arrested and jailed
	John F. Kennedy elected president
1961	Eisenhower's farewell address
	Peace Corps founded
	Bay of Pigs invasion
	Berlin wall constructed
	Khrushchev and Kennedy meet in Vienna
	Yuri Gagarin orbits earth in space capsule
1962	Cuban missile crisis
	University of Mississippi crisis over admission of black student
	Number of Americans in South Vietnam reaches 10,000
	John Glenn orbits earth in space capsule
1963	Civil rights demonstrations in Birmingham
	Crisis at University of Alabama over admission of black student
	Assassination of Medgar Evers
	Limited ban on nuclear testing
	March on Washington
	Church bombing in Birmingham
	Kennedy assassinated; Lyndon Johnson becomes president

Eisenhower's second administration was marked by spectacular Soviet advances in rocketry, a business slowdown, inflation, and racial strife. It was also marked by dissent within the Communist camp between China and Russia, by harshly suppressed uprisings in Poland and Hungary in 1956, and by the U-2 crisis in 1960, when an American reconnaissance plane was shot down over Soviet territory.

In addition, relations among the anti-Communist powers also worsened. Eisenhower had to omit Japan from his itinerary for a Far East tour in 1960 because of anti-American feeling there, and Vice-President Nixon was stoned on a visit to Venezuela. Nearer home, on January 1, 1959, Fidel Castro successfully completed a five-year struggle to overthrow the American-supported Batista regime. His hatred of the United States, fueled by American business's exploitation of Cuba, changed the whole situation in the Caribbean.

The election of 1960 brought to the White House John F. Kennedy—a Democrat, a Catholic, and the youngest president in American history. The Kennedy administration was staffed by youthful advisers and pledged to get the country moving again, to the New Frontier. But many of its approaches to foreign and domestic problems were no different from those of preceding administrations.

Conflict over civil rights escalated, and the attack on segregation broadened. Before the summer of 1963 was over, peaceful protests had occurred in more than 800 towns and cities, and 200,000 blacks and whites had marched on Washington. But by this time there was division within the black leadership between the more moderate Martin Luther King, Jr., and separatist militants such as Malcolm X.

On the domestic front, the administration had far more success with defense and space programs than with measures to aid the economy. In foreign affairs, Kennedy attempted to reverse the trend toward the militarization of the foreign aid program by a diplomacy of "flexible response." It included such new ventures as the Peace Corps and the Alliance for Progress in Latin America. It also included the continuation of Cold War policies and the rapid development of new weapons.

Cuba continued to be a problem. Its leader had turned not only to the Soviet Union, but to the task of spreading *Fidelismo* throughout Latin America. American responses were conventional: an American-supported invasion, the Bay of Pigs, which ended in a fiasco in April 1961, and the threat of nuclear war in October 1962 over Soviet missile bases installed on the island, which was only ninety miles from the United States.

In Southeast Asia, Laos and Vietnam continued to be plagued by guerrilla wars, and the United States continued to be involved. The policy of flexible response became focused on the concept of "limited war," put into practice in Vietnam. By the end of 1962, there were 10,000 Americans in South Vietnam. By late 1963, the number was 17,000 and the predictions were still for an early and easy victory.

What would have happened can only remain conjecture, because on November 22, 1963, John F. Kennedy was assassinated in Dallas while riding through the city in an open car. The New Frontier was over.

Suggested Readings

Many works cited for Chapter 30 are valuable for this chapter as well. The best introduction to cultural developments in the 1950s is D. Miller and M. Nowak, *The Fifties: The Way We Really Were* (1977). Among the principal commentaries on society and culture in the fifties are D. Riesman, *The Lonely Crowd* (1950) and *Individualism Reconsidered* (1954); W. H. Whyte, Jr., *The Organization Man* (1956); C. W. Mills, *White Collar* (1951) and *The Power Elite* (1956); P. Goodman, *Growing Up Absurd* (1960); M. Mead, *And Keep Your Powder Dry* (1965); D. Bell, *The End of Ideology* (1959); D. M. Potter, *People of Plenty* (1954); M. Kempton, *America Comes of Middle Age* (1963); J. Gilbert, *A Cycle of Outrage: America's Reaction to the Juvenile Delinquent in the 1950s* (1986); L. May (ed.), *Recasting America; Culture and Politics in the Age of the Cold War* (1989); and E. T. May, *Homeward Bound: American Families in the Cold War Era* (1988). A different kind of commentator, but often compelling in his ability to probe society, was Lenny Bruce, whose reflections are available in J. Cohen (ed.), *The Essential Lenny Bruce* (1967), and on several records. On the beat generation, see *Evergreen Review* (vol. 1, no. 2), devoted entirely to the "San Francisco Scene"; L. Lipton, *The Holy Barbarians* (1959); B. Cook, *The Beat Generation* (1971); A. Charters, *Kerouac* (1973); and D. McNally, *Jack Kerouac, the Beat Generation, and America* (1979). To understand the 1950s is also to visualize the decade, as in the photographs of Robert Frank in *The Americans* (reprint ed. 1969).

Insight into Eisenhower will be gained from his two volumes on the White House years, *Mandate for Change* (1963) and *Waging Peace* (1965). The best biographical study is S. Ambrose, *Eisenhower: Soldier, General of the Army, President-Elect, 1890–1952* (1983) and *Eisenhower: The President* (1984). See also H. S. Parmet, *Eisenhower and the American Crusades* (1972), and C. S. Alexander, *Holding the Line: The Eisenhower Era, 1952–61* (1975). The most perceptive memoir is E. J. Hughes, *The Ordeal of Power* (1963). Accounts by insiders also include A. Larson, *Eisenhower: The President Nobody Knew* (1968); C. Bohlen, *Witness to History, 1929–1969* (1973); and R. M. Nixon, *Six Crises* (1962). For more critical views, see R. H. Rovere, *Affairs of State: The Eisenhower Years* (1956); I. F. Stone, *The Haunted Fifties* (1964); E. J. Dale, Jr., *Conservatives in Power: A Study in Frustration* (1960); and Herblock's contemporary cartoons and comments in *Here and Now* (1955) and *Special for Today* (1958). On farm policy, see L. Soth, *Farm*

Trouble in an Age of Plenty (1957). On Robert A. Taft, see J. T. Patterson, *Mr. Republican* (1972); on Adlai E. Stevenson, see J. B. Martin, *Adlai Stevenson and the World* (1977).

P. L. Murphy, *The Constitution in Crisis Times 1918–1969* (1972), is the best introduction to the Supreme Court. See also A. M. Bickel, *Politics and the Warren Court* (1965); P. B. Kurland, *Politics, the Constitution and the Warren Court* (1970); R. H. Saylor and others (eds.), *The Warren Court: A Critical Analysis* (1969); and E. Warren, *Memoirs* (1977). The desegregation decision is examined in R. Kluger, *Simple Justice: The History of Brown v. Board of Education and Black America's Struggle for Equality* (1976). On the southern response, see A. Lewis, *Portrait of a Decade* (1964); N. V. Bartley, *The Rise of Massive Resistance* (1969); R. Coles, *Children of Crisis* (1967); and a personal memoir, E. Huckaby, *Crisis at Central High: Little Rock, 1957–58* (1980). For other works on the civil rights movement, see the literature on this topic cited for Chapter 32.

On McCarthyism and its origins, see the works cited for Chapter 30.

To the books on the Cold War cited in Chapter 30, add for the Eisenhower years the president's memoirs, *Mandate for Change* and *Waging Peace;* N. Graebner, *The New Isolationism* (1956); A. Wolfers (ed.), *Alliance Policy in the Cold War* (1959); E. Stillman and W. Pfaff, *The New Politics* (1961); R. A. Divine, *Eisenhower and the Cold War* (1981); H. A. Kissinger, *Nuclear Weapons and Foreign Policy* (1957) and *The Necessity for Choice* (1961); and H. Kahn, *On Thermonuclear War* (1960), an early think-tank product on the "unthinkable" balance of terror. On the nuclear-arms race and efforts to control it, see H. York, *The Advisors* (1976); R. A. Aliano, *American Defense Policy from Eisenhower to Kennedy* (1975); R. A. Divine, *Blowing in the Wind* (1978); and M. Mandelbaum, *The Nuclear Question: The United States and Nuclear Weapons 1946–76* (1980). On Dulles, see H. J. Morgenthau, "John Foster Dulles," in N. Graebner (ed.), *An Uncertain Tradition* (1961); R. Goold-Adams, *John F. Dulles* (1962); M. A. Guhin, *John Foster Dulles* (1972); and T. Hoopes, *The Devil and John Foster Dulles* (1973). On Middle Eastern issues, see N. Safran, *The United States and Israel* (1963); H. Finer, *Dulles over Suez* (1964); H. Thomas, *Suez* (1967); and R. E. Neustadt, *Alliance Politics* (1970).

T. Draper, *Castro's Revolution* (1962), R. Ruiz, *Cuba: The Making of a Revolution;* and R. F. Smith, *The United States and Cuba* (1961) are useful introductions. H. Thomas, *Cuba* (1971), is a massive study. See also the contrasting views of two American ambassadors to Cuba, E. Smith, *The Fourth Floor* (1962), and P. W. Bonsal, *Cuba, Castro, and the United States* (1971). The literature on American policy after the Cuban revolution is cited in the Kennedy section, to follow. On the Guatemalan intervention of 1954, see S. Schlesinger and S. Kinzer, *Bitter Fruit* (1982), and R. H. Immerman, *The CIA in Guatemala: The Foreign Policy of Intervention* (1982), and the literature on the CIA cited for Chapter 33.

The place to begin any examination of Vietnam is F. Fitzgerald, *Fire in the Lake: The Vietnamese and the Americans in Vietnam* (1972). J. Buttinger, *Vietnam: A Political History* (1970), and E. Hammer, *The Struggle for Indochina 1940–1955* (1966), provide background, along with B. Fall, *The Two Viet-Nams* (1967) and *Vietnam Witness 1953–1966* (1966). See also R. Shaplen, *The Lost Revolution: The U.S. in Vietnam 1946–1966* (1966) and *Time Out of Hand: Revolution and Reaction in Southeast Asia* (1969). On the deepening American military involvement, see the literature on Kennedy and the pertinent readings suggested for Chapter 32.

The 1960 campaign is covered in T. H. White, *The Making of the President* (1960). The Kennedy presidency as viewed by members of the White House staff may be found in A. M. Schlesinger, Jr., *A Thousand Days* (1965), and T. C. Sorenson, *Kennedy* (1965). For more critical assessments, see T. Wicker, *Kennedy without Tears* (1964); H. Fairlie, *The Kennedy Promise* (1973); and H. S. Parmet, *Jack: The Struggles of John F. Kennedy* (1980) and *JFK: The Presidency of John F. Kennedy* (1983).

Economic policy in the 1960s is examined in J. Galbraith, *The New Industrial State* (1967); W. W. Heller, *New Dimensions of Political Economy* (1966); S. E. Harris, *Economics of the Kennedy Years* (1964); and the editors of *Fortune* magazine, *America in the Sixties: The Economy and the Society* (1960). The question of poverty in an affluent society was newly opened by M. Harrington, *The Other America* (1962). H. Miller, *Rich Man, Poor Man* (1964), is a commentary on Harrington's thesis. See also G. Myrdal, *Challenge to Affluence* (1963); R. L. Heilbroner, *The Limits of American Capitalism;* and O. Lewis, *La Vida: A Puerto Rican Family in the Culture of Poverty—San Juan and New York* (1966).

R. Hilsman, *To Move a Nation* (1967), is a firsthand report on Kennedy's foreign policy. For a critical assessment, see R. Walton, *Cold War and Counter-Revolution* (1972). On the Bay of Pigs, see T. Szulc and K. E. Meyer, *The Cuban Invasion: The Chronicle of a Disaster* (1962). On the Cuban missile crisis, see E. Abel, *The Missile Crisis* (1966); R. A. Divine (ed.), *The Cuban Missile Crisis* (1971); R. F. Kennedy, *Thirteen Days,* a memoir and a recent reassessment, J. G. Blight and D. A. Welch, *On the Brink: Americans and Soviets Reexamine the Cuban Missile Crisis* (1988). The ultimate failure of the Alliance for Progress is analyzed in J. Levinson and J. de Onis, *The Alliance That Lost Its Way* (1970). On Kennedy and Vietnam, see D. Halberstam, *The Best and the Brightest* (1972), and the literature cited for Chapter 32.

On Kennedy's assassination, see *A Concise Compendium of the Warren Commission Report* (1964); E. J. Epstein, *Inquest* (1966); W. Manchester, *Death of a President* (1967); and P. Scott and others, *Dallas and Beyond* (1976).

CHAPTER 32

CRUMBLING CONSENSUS

On *Air Force One,* which was bringing the body of John F. Kennedy back to Washington, D.C., the most dramatic presidential succession in American history took place. Jacqueline Kennedy, her clothing stained with the blood of her husband, looked on as the oath of office was administered on November 22, 1963, to the new president, Lyndon B. Johnson. Even as Americans recovered from the shock of presidential assassination, they would learn to live with new violence, turbulence, and uncertainty in the next decade.

The deepening war abroad and civil strife at home shattered whatever remained of the consensus and complacency of the fifties. There were moments when the very survival of American society seemed threatened—not, as in the previous decade, from nuclear holocaust or Communists, but from America's own disenchanted people.

The kinds of investigatory commissions established in the sixties said a great deal about what absorbed the American people. The concerns and revelations were far different from those of the fifties, when Americans had focused on the past political "sins" of well-placed government officials. The Warren Commission examined the circumstances surrounding Kennedy's

assassination. The Kerner Commission, appointed by President Johnson on July 27, 1967, investigated widespread racial violence. It concluded that the basic cause was the white racism that pervaded American society. The National Commission on the Causes and Prevention of Violence examined still other civil disorders, including the violence at the Democratic party's national nominating convention of 1968. It reported that "in numbers of political assassinations, riots, politically relevant armed group attacks, and demonstrations," the United States was among "the half-dozen most tumultuous nations in the world."

Major investigations of campus disorders. drugs, and pornography were also undertaken. And America's sudden awakening to the contamination of the environment would produce a huge investigatory literature that warned of cosmic disaster.

The American experience in the sixties has been compared to weird pieces of science fiction or to comic-book fantasy. The scenario features assassinations, cities burned out by their own people, street warfare, masked soldiers in fogs of tear gas, massed youth sprawling over the countryside at rock festivals, campus buildings under siege, cult murders, terrorist bomb factories, and courtroom shoot-outs. The sixties, journalist Gary Wills recalled, sometimes conveyed the feeling of being locked up with a madman whose power made no sense.

The crises of the decade were made to order for the mass media. Government officials, politicians, professors, and priests competed with athletes, hippies, Yippies, and revolutionaries for machine-made national images. Television, often feared as an instrument of centralized government information control, became a major instrument of popular education and expression. More effectively than any other medium, television brought all of life into focused image, turning all kinds of people into media performers. Combat teams and tormented villagers in Vietnam, starving children in Biafra, moonbound astronauts, striking Mexican American grape workers, the welfare poor in New York City hotels, protest marchers, courtroom characters, celebrities from the world of sport and entertainment—all entered the living rooms of America.

Throughout the upheavals of the sixties, the war in Vietnam persisted and widened. Except for the Civil War, no previous conflict had so divided and alienated American society. With each passing month, with each new casualty list, with every promise of success, the divisiveness and disenchantment grew.

Perhaps no political rally or protest march had as much impact on the American people as one issue of *Life,* that of June 27, 1969, in which twelve pages were given over to photographs of the 242 Americans who had been killed in action the week of May 28 to June 3. Not an exceptional week, said *Life,* but the "average for any seven-day period during this stage of the war." To look at these men, some of them in uniform, some wearing the caps and gowns of their high school graduation, was to be impressed not only with their youth, but with how few of them resembled the students whose protests dominated the media. The war was largely being fought by young people—white and black—from the working class, for whom draft deferments and counseling were not so easily within reach.

The war was brought home to Americans in still another way. In April 1971 a military court sentenced First Lieutenant William Calley to life imprisonment for murdering twenty-two Vietnamese civilians at My Lai village in 1968. This trial dramatized for the American people—as no previous event had done—the question of national complicity in the Vietnam holocaust. As more evidence came to light of other massacres, of saturation bombing, of forced evacuation of villages in "free-fire" zones, the line between legitimate and illegitimate warfare, if such distinctions made any sense, virtually disappeared. Who were the criminals—the soldiers carrying out orders, or the men who gave them? The court-martial failed to resolve that question.

To some critics, it was Lyndon Johnson's war. But that would be a gross distortion of the historical record. The war was not the exclusive responsibility of any one president. Although Congress had not declared war, it had given the president— by overwhelming majorities—the power and the hardware required to wage war. The deepening involvement in Vietnam proved to be a tragic inheritance for LBJ, who had envisioned a Great Society that would unify the nation and inspire the world. Vietnam determined otherwise. By 1968, President Johnson himself had concluded that the only way to unify the nation was to end the war and his own political career.

THE GREAT SOCIETY

Few American presidents had entered the White House with a longer career in politics than Lyndon Johnson. Although he retained the top Kennedy men in his cabinet, notably Rusk and McNamara, the contrast between his personality and political style and those of Kennedy could hardly have been more striking. Johnson's wealth had been self-made, not inherited. He had none of Kennedy's charisma or urbanity and few of his cultural pretensions. He was as skeptical of intellectuals as they were of him. ("I don't believe that I'll ever get credit for anything I do in foreign affairs, no matter how successful it is, because I didn't go to Harvard.")

But LBJ knew how to get things done. He was a shrewd manipulator, and he had already demonstrated in his long years as Senate minority and then majority leader an uncanny mastery of political techniques. (One aide called him "a Machiavelli in a Stetson.") He invited and praised "consensus," while making certain his position prevailed.

LBJ's vision of the Great Society, though absorbing much of Kennedy's New Frontier, was more heavily influenced by his admiration for the New Deal. The ambitious domestic program he proposed was aimed at improving the quality of American life, maximizing opportunities for those who had been denied access to the "affluent society." Like FDR, he felt the need to secure Americans from the fear of hunger, unemployment, and old age. Unlike FDR, he felt the need to attack the special problems plaguing black Americans. Although Johnson's civil rights record in the Senate had been spotty, he seemed ready to extend his commitment to social justice to black people. The racial strife and agitation Johnson inherited as president also provided a stimulus for action exceeding that of any previous occupant of the White House.

Not all the Great Society measures proved workable. Some were too hastily drawn, and others suffered from lack of funding. But the commitment of the federal government to the concept of the welfare state seemed unquestioned. And it was this aspect of the Great Society that would arouse the most controversy and backlash in the seventies and eighties. For Johnson, the more immediate problem was how to wage a war on poverty while expanding the war in Vietnam. The cost of pursuing both wars at once proved too much. In the clash of priorities, the Great Society and the people of Vietnam were the principal victims.

The Transition Years

No sooner had Johnson become president than he proposed to Congress, as an appropriate memorial to Kennedy, that it act on a long-delayed prosperity tax cut and a civil rights bill. The tax-reform bill helped a sagging economy. The Civil Rights Act of 1964, the most sweeping such legislation in American history, enlarged *federal* power to protect voting rights, to provide access for all races to public facilities, to speed up school desegregation, and to ensure equal job opportunities in business and unions.

At the same time, Johnson set the stage for his Great Society program. In his first State of the Union message, in January 1964, he told Congress: "Unfortunately, many Americans live on the outskirts of hope, some because of their poverty and some because of their color, and all too many because of both." To raise the hopes of such people, he proposed a "war on poverty in America." This war Congress also endorsed, in August 1964, when it appropriated almost $950 million for ten separate antipoverty programs to be supervised by the new Office of Economic Opportunity. Key features included (1) a Job Corps, which would train underprivileged youth for the labor market; (2) work-training programs that would employ them; (3) a domestic peace corps (officially, Volunteers in Service to America, or VISTA), in which the privileged would be enlisted on behalf of the poor; and (4) Community Action programs, which would involve the poor themselves in the administration and planning of the "war."

The philosophy underpinning the War on Poverty was that the federal government could democratize the economic society without restructuring it. The government needed only to remove the institutional obstacles that denied deprived groups the opportunity to advance themselves economically. "There were times in those days," recalled LBJ's press secretary, Bill Moyers, "when he thought the poor are poor because the economy is mismanaged against them, but most of the time he thought the problems could be solved if the poor were managed better—train them for some better jobs, help them to see a doctor, move them to a better place." That was the premise on which the Great Society operated.

Encouraged by his legislative triumphs, Johnson eagerly anticipated the presidential election of 1964. What he wanted was a massive triumph at the polls that would make him president in his own right. He was not disappointed. The Republicans proved accommodating in this respect by providing Johnson with an ideal target. Determined to offer the American electorate "a choice, not an echo," they nominated Senator Barry Goldwater of Arizona, star of the strong conservative wing of the party. Although segregationist governor George C. Wallace of Alabama also entered the race by running in a number of Democratic primaries, Goldwater's nomination had deprived him of conservative support. At the Democratic convention, Johnson easily won the nomination; after a spirited contest for LBJ's nod, Senator Hubert H. Humphrey of Minnesota, identified with the liberal wing of the party, won the vice-presidential spot.

Goldwater stood for dismantling the welfare state, and many Americans suspected that the social security system would be among the victims. Nor did he help his candidacy when he suggested that NATO commanders be permitted to employ tactical nuclear weapons in a crisis. During the campaign, new uncertainties in world affairs made such statements seem particularly irresponsible. Nikita Khrushchev had lost power in the USSR, and China had exploded an atomic bomb.

Whereas Goldwater evoked visions of atomic confrontation, Johnson appeared to be a man of peace and moderation. "We don't want our American boys to do the fighting for Asian boys," he declared on September 25. "We don't want to get involved . . . and get tied down in a land war in Asia."

With 61 percent of the popular vote, Johnson surpassed even FDR's record in 1936. It was the sweeping mandate he had sought, and he intended to make the most of it. Even while preparing to escalate American military involvement in Vietnam, Johnson assured the American people: "This nation is mighty enough—its society is healthy enough—its people are strong enough—to pursue our goals in the rest of the world while still building a great society here at home."

Great Society Legislation

The Great Society was the central theme of LBJ's first message to the Eighty-ninth Congress, in January 1965. When that Congress finished its business in the fall of 1966, it had approved nearly every one of the Great Society measures the president had proposed—what Johnson later called "the greatest outpouring of creative legislation in the history of the nation."

The first measure, adopted in April 1965, was the Elementary and Secondary Education Act, which made available for the first time massive amounts of federal aid ($1.3 billion) to school districts. As part of Johnson's continuing commitment to the War on Poverty, Title 1 of the Education Act gave local school districts money to set up compensatory education programs for low-income students. The act also offered incentives for desegregation. As a condition for federal aid, the United States Office of Education now demanded proof that desegregation both for students and for teachers had been undertaken in good faith by the beginning of the 1966–1967 school term. Despite vigorous opposition to these new "guidelines," significant increases were reported in the number of blacks going to school with whites.

A second far-reaching measure was the adoption of the medicare amendments to the Social Security Act, which the president approved on July 30, 1965. The aged had won a significant victory over the relentless lobbying of the American Medical Association. Medicare provided hospital insurance and certain posthospital care for virtually all Americans sixty-five and older. It also made available inexpensive medical insurance covering doctor bills, diagnostic procedures, and other medical services and supplies.

In addition, the Eighty-ninth Congress ended the discriminatory national-origins quota system in immigration; provided special assistance for improvement of conditions in the depressed states of the Appalachian region; enacted programs promoting the purification of smog-laden air and the restoration of polluted waterways; created the National Foundation of the Arts and Humanities in order to encourage cultural and artistic development; and passed a Truth in Lending Act, designed to give consumers greater protection in credit transactions.

Recognizing the critical problems of urban Americans, Congress agreed to a rent-supplement program for low-income families and established the Department of Housing and Urban Development (HUD). Johnson appointed Robert C. Weaver to head the new agency, making him the nation's first black cabinet member. Massive new appropriations were made for older Great Society programs, including the War on Poverty, the regeneration of the cities, and the space program. By mid-1966, the United States was looking to the moon to the tune of over $5 billion annually. This sum in the federal budget was exceeded only by expenditures for national defense and fixed commitments such as interest payments and disbursements for social security.

The Great Society programs, much like the programs adopted in the name of national defense and space exploration, combined impressive successes with costly failures. In the rush to meet urgent needs, some of the programs suffered from poor planning and management. Although many of the programs had been designed to assist low-income Americans, the ways in which they were administered often limited their impact on the segments of that group most in need of help. And as with many of the New Deal programs, the benefits of Great Society programs were often reaped by those groups best organized to influence the distribution of funds.

The Great Society, however, did bring hope and help to millions of Americans. It enabled more than 11 million students to receive loans for a college education. Project Head Start, though underfunded, helped to prepare some 8 million low-income preschoolers for grade school, and the Upward Bound program granted comparable assistance to high school students from low-income families who aspired to a college education. The War on Poverty gave poor people medical care through medicaid, fed millions through such programs as food stamps, welfare, and school lunches, and provided legal counseling for people who could not otherwise afford it. Some 2 million senior citizens were raised above the poverty level by amendments to the Social Security Act that set minimum-payment requirements. The antipoverty programs also created 2 million government jobs, with blacks filling 850,000 of them. And the Community Action programs established under the War on Poverty trained tens of thousands of poor people in the arts of politics and management; a number of these people would ultimately run for public office. Many of these programs were deemed sufficiently successful to be permitted to survive into the 1990s.

But the Great Society, like the New Frontier, raised the expectations of many Americans with-

WORDS AND NAMES IN AMERICAN HISTORY

The original meaning of the word *grapevine* was self-evident. But for reasons not clear, about the middle of the nineteenth century it began to take on a completely different meaning, often in the combined form *grapevine telegraph* (the latter word itself being an invention of the 1840s). The *grapevine* came to mean a somewhat mysterious but very effective network of oral communication, an informal network that often conveyed scandalous, secret, or dangerous information. It came to be particularly associated with black people. Such networks did exist on and among slave plantations. After the Civil War, with so many blacks still unable to read or write, there remained a strong need for such channels. Blacks themselves embraced the term. As one popular black song of the 1960s went, "I heard it through the grapevine."

out necessarily fulfilling them. It created among many whites the perception that the social programs established in the name of the War on Poverty were draining public funds without producing visible results. Despite the enormous increase in public assistance, all too little had changed. Unlike the costly failures in the defense and space programs, the failures in the Great Society suggested to many Americans misguided extravagance and the need to reconsider the entire commitment to expensive social programs. That sentiment would mount steadily in the 1970s, as the economy weakened, and would culminate in the victory of Ronald Reagan in the election of 1980. "In the sixties," the newly elected president declared, "we waged a war on poverty, and poverty won." But in saying this Reagan failed to consider that the War on Poverty had lasted only four years—hardly sufficient time to reconstruct a flawed economic society—and was insufficiently funded to tackle the deep-seated programs afflicting America's poor.

When the Eighty-ninth Congress adjourned in October 1966, the American economy had enjoyed six solid years of extraordinary expansion. But some people had prospered far more than others. Social dissatisfaction deepened. Life on many family farms remained dreary; city dwellers were exposed to unprecedented violence and fear. Black Americans still found it hard to get jobs or to share in the affluence so visible around them. They were constantly exposed to success, and yet denied it. And so frustration mounted, especially among the young. "The way these kids see it," one black remarked, "equality is like Whitey holds you by the belt at the starting line until everyone else is halfway around the track, then gives you a big slap on the rump and says, 'Go baby, you're equal.' Takes an unusual man to win a race like that. It's easier to shoot the starter."

The Black Revolution

While the "We Shall Overcome" spirit generated by the March on Washington still prevailed, the struggle to achieve racial justice in the South continued to attract national attention. During the Freedom Summer of 1964, thousands of young blacks and white students converged on Mississippi to register its nearly one million black residents. By the end of the summer, three youths—two whites and one black—had been murdered by terrorists in Neshoba County. Numerous civil rights workers had been beaten,

more than a thousand had been arrested, and scores of churches and homes had been burned or bombed.

As the white youths returned to their homes and campuses in the North, growing rifts were revealed within the civil rights movement. Many of these stemmed from black fears of white domination and a growing determination among blacks to plot their own strategies and make their own decisions. Beyond this urge to be independent of their white allies, there persisted the more complex and age-old problems of white patronization.

Stokely Carmichael, a young black civil rights worker and leader in the Student Nonviolent Coordinating Committee (SNCC), tried to explain some of the dimensions of the problem:

Too many young middle-class Americans, like some sort of Pepsi generation, want . . . to come alive through the black community. They say things without realizing what they're saying. You know—"Yeah, man, I really dig that." . . . They use words out of context. They want to be accepted right away, without being accepted for their work. They want to be accepted as a Negro, not as an individual. "Look, I'm not like the other whites you know, I dig you." The white boy putting on a show was resented. As much as it would be resented if I put on a show to show how white I was—how much I had absorbed of the culture.

Before the civil rights coalition disintegrated altogether, it achieved its most dramatic hour in early 1965. The failure of certain southern states to enforce the voting provisions of the Civil Rights Act of 1964 had brought a new wave of black demonstrations, particularly in the town of Selma, Alabama. On February 1, 1965, Martin Luther King, Jr., and 770 other blacks were arrested. Early in March, Alabama state troopers and auxiliaries, using tear gas and whips, frustrated an attempted civil rights march from Selma to Montgomery, the state capital. Only after President Johnson federalized the Alabama National Guard and ordered it to protect the marchers (Governor Wallace having refused to do so) did the procession of some 25,000 blacks and sympathetic whites from all over the country begin. The night the march ended, one participant—a white woman from Detroit—was killed by Klan gunfire. Earlier, a Boston minister was slain. Their deaths enlarged the decade's toll of political activists.

With President Johnson himself now declaring that "we shall overcome," Congress responded by passing the Voting Rights Act of 1965. This measure suspended literacy tests and other devices still used to confine voting to whites. It

THE INHERITANCE

"I wondered what it was like to live. . . . Countless nights I cried myself to sleep. Sometimes I could look at my mother and I could feel the pains her body was undergoing because of the hard work done each day to make ends meet. . . . Sometimes mother would see the tears falling from my eyes. . . . When she asked me what was wrong I told her that something stuck in my eyes or a bug was in them. I must have asked God why a thousand times but I never got an answer. Was nine of us kids in the family and we all had to work. I stayed out of school a lot of days because I couldn't let my mother go to the cotton field and try to support all of us. I picked cotton and pecans for two cents a pound. I went to the fields six in the morning and worked until seven in the afternoon. When it came time to weigh up, my heart, body and bones would be aching, burning and trembling. I stood there and looked the white men right in their eyes while they cheated me, other members of my family, and the rest of the Negroes that were working. There were times when I wanted to speak, but my fearful mother would always tell me to keep silent. The sun was awful hot and the days were long. . . . The cost of survival was high. Why I paid it I'll never know."

The author of this account was Charles Wingfield, a member of the Student Nonviolent Coordinating Committee. As a sixteen-year-old honor student, Wingfield had placed a petition on the wall of his all-black school in Lee County, Georgia, calling for improved equipment for the school. He was expelled for his action. Parents voted to boycott the school and some 1000 students (out of an enrollment of 1300) refused to attend classes. But Wingfield was never readmitted.

Source: Howard Zinn, SNCC: *The New Abolitionists* (Boston: Beacon Press, 1964), pp. 136–37. Photograph by Danny Lyon, Magnum Photos.

empowered "federal examiners" to register qualified voters. The act also directed the attorney general to start suits against the surviving poll taxes in *state* elections. (The Twenty-fourth Amendment to the Constitution, ratified in January 1964, had abolished the poll tax in federal elections.) On March 17, 1966, the last of the poll taxes was killed by a decision of the Supreme Court. By then a new drive to register the two million eligible blacks in eleven southern states was under way, and many black candidates appeared on the ballots within a short time.

Although the Voting Rights Act of 1965 enhanced black political power in the South, this significant triumph did little to address the racial conflict growing throughout the country. Public-opinion polls only confirmed black suspicions that white racial attitudes had remained essentially the same. Most whites still preferred to live in exclusively white neighborhoods, feared or shunned social contact with blacks, and agreed that blacks were moving "too fast" to improve their position in American society.

The white image of black people, *Newsweek* magazine observed in late 1963, "is an implausible and contradictory caricature, half Stepin Fetchit—lazy, unwashed, shiftless, unambitious, slow-moving—half Sportin' Life—cunning, lewd, flashy, strong, fearless, immoral, and vicious."[*]

Other parts of the country seemed no more ready than the South for genuine integration. Although many whites had sympathized with black efforts to register voters and desegregate public facilities in the South, they had far less feeling for the grievances that were mounting in the urban North. Discrimination in employment, housing, and schooling persisted, even as more blacks poured into the cities and more whites poured into the suburbs. When Martin Luther King, Jr., attacking the problems of urban blacks, staged massive demonstrations in Chicago in 1967 to mobilize support for a national open-housing bill, he met resistance similar to that he had confronted in the South. "I have never seen such hate," he declared, "not in Mississippi, or Alabama, as I see here in Chicago." When his strategy failed and challenges to his leadership grew, King found himself addressing a hostile black audience in Chicago. He thought he knew why:

For 12 years I, and others like me, had held out radiant promises of progress. I had preached to them about my dream. I had lectured to them about the not too distant day when they would have freedom, "all, here and now." I had urged them to have faith in America and in white society. Their hopes had soared. . . . They were now hostile because they were watching the dream that they had so readily accepted turn into a nightmare.

The frustrations finally exploded. Between 1964 and 1967, more than a hundred riots shattered the peace of urban America. Few were planned. Indeed, it was the spontaneous quality of the uprisings that revealed the very depths of black disillusion and despair—the need to expose the deprivation of black ghetto dwellers and the complicity of white businessmen, shop owners, and police in maintaining the ghettos. "It may be that looting, rioting and burning," one observer remarked, "are really nothing more than a radical form of urban renewal, a response not only to the frustrations of the ghetto but to the collapse of all ordinary modes of change. As if a body, despairing of the indifference of doctors, sought to rip a cancer out of itself."

The first of the major riots broke out in the Watts ghetto of Los Angeles—98 percent black—in mid-August 1965. Thirty-five persons died, and property damage exceeded $100 million. When black leaders, including Martin Luther King, Jr., came to Watts to prevent further bloodshed, they were met with indifference or hostility. Later in 1965 and in 1966, similar rioting occurred in Harlem in New York City and in Chicago, San Francisco, and other cities. In the summer of 1967, racial rioting struck no fewer than sixty-seven cities across the nation.

In Newark, New Jersey, where black unemployment rates ran spectacularly high and housing shortages were among the most acute in the country, the riots of July 12–17 took twenty-five lives. Rioting a week later in Detroit took forty-three lives; more than four thousand fires pushed property losses above even those in Watts. The violence in Detroit defeated all pacification efforts until for the first time since the 1943 Detroit riots, federal troops were called in by a governor to restore order. Army tanks on Detroit streets illustrated newspapers around the world.

Meanwhile, black efforts to implement the Voting Rights Act of 1965 had brought new violence in the South, the worst of it in Mississippi. James Meredith, a black student whose admission to the University of Mississippi in 1962 had led to such fighting and harassment that he

Washington, D.C. riot. *(Burt Glinn, Magnum Photos)*

The most pervasive of these was the concept of *black power,* by which black people would assume control of their own communities, lives, and destinies, establish their own economic institutions, and end the "colonialism" that had tied them to white institutions. Politically, explained Stokely Carmichael, black power envisioned black people uniting "to elect representatives and *to force those representatives to speak to their needs.*" Economically, black power demanded that the money spent by black people remain in and be shared by the black communities.

The assumptions underlying the concept of black power had been forcefully explained by Malcolm X, the Black Muslim leader. His father, the Reverend Earl Little, a Baptist minister in Omaha, Nebraska, had been a devout follower of Marcus Garvey, whose campaign for racial dignity, community control, and the redemption of Africa had won the allegiance of many blacks in the twenties. The violence and humiliation that the Reverend Little's family suffered from "the good Christian white people" in the urban North deepened his son's alienation.

At the age of twenty-one, when he was convicted of theft and sentenced to prison, Malcolm X found himself in a subculture of prostitutes, pimps, hustlers, numbers runners, and narcotics dealers. "I was a true hustler—uneducated, unskilled at anything honorable, and I considered myself nervy and cunning enough to live by my wits, exploiting any prey that presented itself. I would risk just about anything."

In the religion of Islam, and in Elijah Muhammad's Black Muslim movement, Malcolm X found a path from the ghetto experience he recounts so vividly in his autobiography. "Yes, I'm an extremist," he conceded. "The black race here in North America is in extremely bad condition. You show me a black man who isn't an extremist and I'll show you one who needs psychiatric attention." On February 21, 1965, while he was speaking at the Audubon Ballroom in upper Manhattan, Malcolm X was assassinated, apparently as a result of strife arising within the black nationalist movement after Malcolm formed his own Organization of Afro-American Unity.

The violent death of Malcolm X only compounded the frustration and alienation that had overtaken so many blacks. "More than any other person," black writer Julius Lester said of him, "Malcolm X was responsible for the new militancy that entered The Movement in 1965. Malcolm X said aloud those things Negroes had been afraid to

soon withdrew, returned to the state on June 5, 1966, for a 220-mile pilgrimage from the Tennessee border to the capital at Jackson. His object was to demonstrate to the 450,000 unregistered Mississippi adult blacks that they need no longer fear murder for attempting to sign up and cast their ballots. Only a day later, Meredith was struck three times by a shotgun blast from a white assailant while on the pilgrimage route.

Although black leaders, including King and Carmichael, promptly resumed the pilgrimage to Jackson, further violence en route intensified the ongoing fragmentation within the civil rights movement. Even as King reaffirmed his faith in nonviolence and integration, others suggested that they be abandoned as the movement's primary tactic and goal. The persistence of white hostility and the betrayal of expectations encouraged new movements, strategies, and ideologies.

Malcolm X: "The day of nonviolent resistance is over. If they have the Ku Klux Klan nonviolent, then I'll be nonviolent. . . . But as long as you've got somebody else not being nonviolent, I don't want anybody coming to me talking any nonviolent talk." *(UPI/Bettmann Newsphotos)*

say to each other. . . . He was not concerned with stirring the moral conscience of America, because he knew—America had no moral conscience."*

In still another violent setback, the civil rights movement lost its apostle of nonviolence. On April 4, 1968, Martin Luther King, Jr., was assassinated in Memphis, Tennessee, where he had come to support a strike of the city's (mostly black) garbage men. He was shot while standing outside his motel room, speaking to some of his co-workers. The assassin, James Earl Ray, an escapee from the Missouri state penitentiary, was later caught and convicted. Although King had been the apostle of nonviolence, his assassination set off a new wave of rioting across the country. This time, the explosion centered in Washington, D.C. TV screens showed the spectacle of the Capitol lit up by the nearby fires while federal troops and troop carriers patrolled the streets.

The persistence of racial violence dramatized the limited significance of civil rights legislation

---

*From *Revolutionary Notes* by Julius Lester; published by the Richard W. Baron Publishing Co.

in the day-to-day lives of most black people. Economic differences between black and white Americans loomed larger than ever. Yet there were some significant breakthroughs. Middle-class blacks got substantial benefits from the black revolution. Certain fields of employment were opened to them. Blacks were more conspicuous now in business and the professions, on the TV screen, in sports and entertainment, and on college campuses. The 1970 census revealed that the proportion of black families whose annual incomes exceeded $10,000 had increased from 11 percent to 28 percent during the sixties.

This decade, then, was significant for black people in a number of ways, perhaps most spectacularly in enhanced racial consciousness and self-pride. Recognizing the immense problems that remained, Martin Luther King, Jr., had sounded a note of optimism: "Lord, we ain't what we oughta be. We ain't what we wanna be. We ain't what we gonna be. But thank God, we ain't what we was."

La Raza

Since the mid-nineteenth century, Mexican Americans had found themselves dispossessed of their lands, stereotyped, segregated, harassed, and deported at the whim of law officers. By World War II, their numbers had sharply increased, usually in response to demands for cheap labor. Federal legislation permitted the importation of *braceros* (temporary farm workers), and many other Mexicans (disparaged as "wetbacks") entered the country illegally, often swimming across the Rio Grande. From 1910 to 1920, some 800,000 Mexicans entered the United States; during the 1920s, even as Congress restricted immigration from Europe and Asia, some 1.5 million more Mexicans arrived. An unorganized labor reserve, politically powerless, badly housed, the victims of discrimination, they were concentrated in the Southwest. Many of them lived in *barrios*, or "Mex-towns," in the cities.

Attempts by Mexican Americans to organize within their communities in order to advance their position and combat discrimination encountered Anglo-American suspicion and opposition almost from the start. Strikes waged in the Imperial Valley in California in the 1920s and 1930s were crushed, the leaders often deported. Rising tensions between Mexican Americans and the dominant Anglo population erupted in 1943 in Los Angeles in the "zoot suit riots." With the police often looking on, servicemen and civilians attacked Mexican youths who were wearing zoot suits—jackets with long coattails and wide shoulders and loose black trousers with pegged ankles and a high waistline. This distinctive clothing imparted a sense of pride and identity to Mexican youths. But Anglo-Americans perceived the suits as the emblem of dangerous hoodlums. Responding to the riots, the Los Angeles City Council took the shortsighted step of making it a misdemeanor to wear a zoot suit. The conditions underlying the tensions remained, to resurface in the 1950s in "Operation Wetback": federal officers moved against illegal immigrants from Mexico, deporting Mexican Americans who could not immediately prove United States citizenship.

The civil rights movement had its impact on the Mexican American as well as the black community. Immigration from Mexico after World War II exceeded that of any other group, and in the 1960s and 1970s the nearly 5 million "Spanish-surnamed" Americans (as the Census Bureau defined them) manifested a new sense of ethnic dignity. Newly organized groups in the community pressed upon their people the need to rediscover their Mexican roots, to take pride in their culture and traditions, and to assert the power of their growing numbers. Although *Chicano* (a form of *Mexicano*) had once designated Mexican refugees in the United States, it now included all Mexican Americans, particularly those committed to the cause of *la raza* (literally "the race," but more broadly the entire Spanish-speaking community).

Chicanos expressed themselves politically in a variety of ways. In New Mexico, Reies Lopez Tijerina headed the Alianza, a nationalist movement that proposed sweeping land reforms, including a restoration of lands guaranteed large numbers of Mexicans in 1848 under the Treaty of Guadalupe Hidalgo. Eventually military force was required to contain Tijerina's movement. In Colorado, Rodolfo ("Corky") Gonzales, a former prize-fighter and War on Poverty official, inaugurated a Crusade for Justice. Still others, chosing to confront the political powerlessness of Mexican Americans, organized a political party, La Raza Unida, which ran candidates for public office in Texas, Colorado, and California. In the spring of 1968, some 15,000 high school students in East Los Angeles staged strikes ("blowouts") demanding teachers and curricula that were more sensitive to Mexican American history and traditions and an end to punishments for speaking Spanish.

Few events dramatized the Mexican American quest for social and economic justice more than Cesar Chavez's battle in California to organize a farm laborers' union. The seasonal nature of agricultural labor, requiring farm laborers to move from crop to crop, and the vigorous opposition of well-organized growers and corporate farmers had foiled previous organizing efforts. The farm-labor system, as a consequence, had rested essentially on an endless supply of cheap, docile, nonunion field labor. But in 1965, grape pickers in California struck for higher wages, improved working conditions, and union recognition. Soon the grape strike (*la huelga*) and a national consumer boycott of nonunion grapes had become a rallying point of Chicano protest.

Born in Yuma, Arizona, Chavez went to California in the 1940s. Like many of those he sought to organize, he had spent his youth in farm-labor camps, left school at the seventh grade, experienced discrimination, and was a devout Roman Catholic. Like Martin Luther King, Jr., he made his religion a weapon for social justice and pledged his movement to nonviolent resistance. To dramatize that commitment, Chavez in 1968 went on a twenty-five-day fast that gained nation-wide attention. "Our lives are really all that belong to us," he explained. "Only by giving our lives do we find life. I am convinced that the truest act of courage, the strongest act of manliness, is to sacrifice ourselves for others in a totally nonviolent struggle for justice." Through his National Farm Workers Association, founded in 1962, Chavez hoped not only to raise the living standards of Mexican Americans but to establish a precedent that would affect more than 4 million farm workers—brown, black, and white—who lacked job security and economic power. The grape pickers' strike, and in particular the national boycott of nonunion grapes, finally broke the resistance of the grape growers, leading in 1970 to a historic pact that brought union recognition to large numbers of farm workers.

By the end of the 1970s, Chavez's efforts had aroused considerable support and controversy. Most important, his union had secured higher wages and better working conditions for thousands of farm laborers, it had forced modern industrial labor patterns on a reluctant and backward agricultural industry, and it had broadened *la causa* to include social justice for all Mexican Americans. Even while the farm workers were engaged in their struggle, Mexican Americans organized around their new ethnic consciousness, established Chicano studies programs at numerous colleges and schools, broadened their efforts

Cesar Chavez, speaking in support of the boycott of nonunion grape growers: "God knows that we are not beasts of burden, we are not agricultural implements or rented slaves, we are men." *(UPI/ Bettmann Newsphotos)*

to improve the quality of life of barrio dwellers, and made some significant political gains, electing several mayors and U.S. representatives and increasing their numbers on court benches, city councils, and boards of education.

But the Chicano movement, though it enjoyed some impressive successes, suffered the fate of a number of similar movements in the 1970s. Disagreements over the direction and tactics of the movement resulted in increasing fragmentation and declining influence. By 1975, the movement was in disarray. Just as the black revolution had helped middle-class blacks, the upheaval in the *barrios* had benefited middle-class Mexican Americans and increased their numbers. But new problems emerged and old problems persisted among the large mass of Mexican Americans in the 1970s and 1980s, most of them members of the urban or rural working class: underemployment, an alarming dropout rate among schoolchildren, and a persistent racism often fed by the assumption that most Mexican Americans were illegal immigrants. The urgency to confront these problems would increase in the 1980s and 1990s,

when Hispanic Americans (including Mexican Americans) would become the nation's fastest-growing ethnic group.

Native Americans

After decades of neglect and indifference, the federal government took a new look at Indian affairs in the 1930s. Under men such as John Collier, a social reformer who had worked for ten years with the American Indian Defense Association, the Office of Indian Affairs succeeded under the Indian Reorganization Act of 1934 in restoring tribal landholding, self-government, and incentive. Indians were permitted to practice their own religions, educational facilities were improved, and cultural programs were encouraged. The government had not abandoned the objective of assimilating Indians into white society, but it appeared to be willing to permit them to have a greater say in the speed and conditions of such assimilation.

Meanwhile, improvements in public health and

New Deal relief policies helped to turn the "vanishing Americans" into one of the fastest-growing groups in the United States. Their number, including that of Eskimos, rose to over 800,000 by 1970—an increase of more than half a million in eighty years. Still another positive development was the establishment in 1946 of the Indian Claims Commission, which would seek to compensate tribes for lands taken unlawfully.

Indian troubles, however, were far from over. During World War II, about 25,000 Indians served in the armed forces. The experience increased their awareness and resentment of the discrimination they suffered. Wartime employment outside the reservations led many Indians to remain in the cities, and in some cases to adopt white culture. To speed this kind of assimilation among all Indians, westerners in Congress took the lead in trying to get "the government out of the Indian business."

At their urging, Congress adopted two unfortunate measures in 1953 that set back Indian–white relations. One, a joint resolution, set forth the intent, once and for all, to end federal responsibility for the surviving tribes. The second, a step in this direction, gave the states authority over criminal and civil issues on the reservations. The sudden ending of certain reservations threw the Indians on them into turmoil. The tribes suffered immense losses in jointly held property and business enterprises; individual Indians lost homes, public services, and security, and many were thrown on welfare. Finally, in September 1958, Secretary of the Interior Fred A. Seaton ordered that no tribe be terminated without its consent. By this time, however, Indians had no way of knowing what to expect from the federal government.

The Great Society programs of the 1960s tried to restore purpose and incentive to Indian lives by redirecting federal policy toward such matters as health, education, housing, and vocational training. More important, the Indians themselves showed a growing ethnic consciousness. Indian groups and leaders in the 1970s sought to awaken their people to a new sense of dignity and cultural pride. The television and motion-picture screens began to reflect a more balanced view of Indian–

To call attention to their cause, American Indians briefly occupied Alcatraz Island in 1969 and (below) took over Wounded Knee, South Dakota, in 1973. "We have everything at stake," one of the Alcatraz demonstrators remarked. "Not just on Alcatraz, but everyplace else, the Indian is in his last stand for cultural survival." *(UPI/Bettman Newsphotos)*

white relations, as did historians in their efforts to counter distorted, European-biased versions of the Indian past. "The whites told only one side," Yellow Wolf of the Nez Percé Indians once complained. "Told it to please themselves. Told much that is not true. Only his own best deeds, only the worst deeds of the Indians has the white man told." But the 1970s gave clear indication that this complaint was finally being listened to.

Even so, years of repression and neglect could not be wiped away simply by corrections in historical accounts. Problems persisted. In the 1970s, Indians still had one of the highest infant-mortality rates in the country; their life expectancy of forty-four years was far below the national average; disease continued to take a great toll. Average family income was well below that of other groups, and the unemployment rate on some reservations was as high as 50 percent.

To draw attention to these problems, Indian militants, many of them belonging to the American Indian Movement (AIM), challenged the paternalistic policies of the federal government. The Bureau of Indian Affairs, in their view was a highly inefficient, white-dominated bureaucracy; in its 150 years it had "stultified our ambitions, corrupted our society, and caused creeping paralysis to set in—economically and socially." In 1973, the militants dramatized their grievances by occupying the BIA office in Washington, D.C., and seizing Wounded Knee, South Dakota, where over three hundred Lakota Sioux Indians had been massacred in 1890. Some years earlier, in 1969, Indians had invaded Alcatraz Island, near San Francisco, and asked that it be converted to an Indian cultural center.

None of these actions proved to be anything more than symbolic reminders that native Americans, like their black and Chicano contemporaries, were no longer content to remain passive spectators; they demanded a voice in the decisions affecting their lives. But the interest and organizational activity aroused in the 1960s tended to diminish in the following decades. Meanwhile, poverty, unemployment, and federal indifference persisted and the Indian population grew. The census of 1980 recorded some 1.3 million American Indians. About 25 percent lived on reservations, and nearly half of these below the poverty level. By this time, Indians had begun to make headway with a new strategy—a legal offensive designed to recover or obtain compensation for lands illegally seized during the rapid and often violent westward expansion of the United States in the nineteenth century.

LBJ AND THE WORLD

The trouble with foreigners, Lyndon Johnson once said, "is that they're not like folks you were reared with." One trouble with Lyndon Johnson's foreign policy was his urge to make the world more congenial to Americans by making all people similar to ourselves. It was the familiar assumption, made most explicit by Woodrow Wilson, that American society could serve as a model and inspiration for all of humankind. Wilson envisioned that day when the Stars and Stripes "shall be the flag not only of America but of humanity." It was in that spirit that a United States senator once declared, "With God's help we will lift Shanghai up and up, ever up, until it is just like Kansas City."

The Mekong River in Vietnam impressed Lyndon Johnson only as a larger Pedernales in his Texas home county. He saw its development with Texas knowhow and technology as the best insurance for the continued Americanization of this ancient Asian land. "I want to leave the footprints of America there," the president said of Vietnam. "I want them to say, 'This is what the Americans left—schools and hospitals and dams. . . .' We can turn the Mekong Delta into a Tennessee Valley."

Johnson told the American people, as if they needed reassurance, that "our cause has been the cause of all mankind." He repeated with approval Wilson's pronouncement that the United States was determined to make the world safe for democracy. Like his predecessors, LBJ formulated his policies from the same set of assumptions about what was thought to be a worldwide Communist conspiracy. "If we don't stop the Reds in South Vietnam," he instructed one senator, "tomorrow they will be in Hawaii, and next week they will be in San Francisco."

Publication by the *New York Times* in mid-1971 of the secret Pentagon Papers, an "objective and encyclopedic" study of the Vietnam War ordered by Secretary of Defense McNamara, documented how successive American presidents had acted on that same premise in extending the American commitment in Vietnam. The policies of American decision makers were based as well on the supposedly unchanging nature of world communism and on the assumption that any nationalist revolution containing a Communist element posed a threat to American security. That Vietnam represented no departure in American foreign policy was revealed much closer to home—in Latin America.

Intervention in the Dominican Republic

Despite their professions of support for self-determination, neither Kennedy nor Johnson thought it inconsistent to differentiate between Communist take-overs and right-wing military coups. The United States seemed determined to crush the former, as in Cuba (1961), while tolerating if not encouraging the latter, as in Guatemala (1954) and Brazil (1964). The first major test of LBJ's Latin American policy came in the Dominican Republic in April 1965.

Four years earlier, three decades of brutal rule by Rafael Trujillo had ended when he was shot down on a lonely country road by one of his henchmen. The dispatch of American warships and 1200 marines forestalled a coup by the slain dictator's relatives. The next year, in the first free election since Trujillo's take-over, the poet Juan Bosch won the presidency. The Kennedy administration made much of this democratic development. But Bosch was soon overthrown by a military coup (supported by businessmen and landholders who resented his reforms) without United States opposition. Kennedy, however, wanted a civil regime, so one was quickly set up under Donald Reid Cabral.

The new regime, tainted by the American role in its establishment, soon lost popular support. On April 24, 1965, pro-Bosch forces unseated the Reid Cabral regime. They were promptly confronted by military forces backed by the U.S., and a civil war began. On April 28, LBJ disclosed the landing of 400 marines in Santo Domingo to protect American lives. A high-ranking navy officer said they were also "to see that no Communist government is established." By May 5, when a truce was worked out, the American force had exceeded 20,000 men, a number many thought incredible. "This was a democratic revolution smashed by the leading democracy of the world," Bosch observed.

LBJ thought otherwise, and he went on nationwide TV to share his Castroite panic with the public. "What began as a popular democratic revolution," he said, "moved into the hands of a band of Communist conspirators. . . . The American nation cannot, must not, will not, permit the establishment of another Communist government in the Western Hemisphere."

The administration soon backed away from these assertions and worked out a compromise settlement that included the participation of Bosch men in a new government. These steps only muddied the image of American foreign policy making shared by many members of Congress, other Americans, and people throughout Latin America. The whole episode enlarged the credibility gap already evident in White House reporting on the Vietnam War.

The Middle East: Seeds of Future Conflict

The United States's position appeared to be stronger in the Middle East. But America's moral commitment to Israel and its simultaneous dependence on Arab oil suggested how difficult that position could suddenly become. In May 1967, complying with the demand of Nasser of Egypt, United Nations troops were withdrawn after keeping Egypt and Israel apart for ten years. The Egyptian leader immediately called for a "holy war" against the Jewish state. Israel, however, beat him to the punch with an overpowering assault in the Six-Day War, June 5–10. The extent of the defeat humiliated Egypt and the USSR as well, for it was Soviet aid that had encouraged Nasser's militancy.

But Israel's victory only fueled the already volatile tensions and fostered a bigger arms buildup. After the war, moreover, Israel cited its own security as justification for keeping some of the territory it had occupied: the Sinai Peninsula, the Golan Heights, the Gaza Strip, and the West Bank of the Jordan River. In November 1967 the UN Security Council called upon Israel to withdraw its forces from the occupied territories, while urging all states in the region to acknowledge each other's sovereignty and independence. The result was a stalemate that defied solution.

Israel continued to ignore the plight of the thousands of Palestinian refugees who had been made homeless by previous conflicts and whose mounting discontent would soon manifest itself in organized resistance movements. The Arab states cynically exploited the Palestinians as part of their overall plan to destroy Israel. With the vast oil resources at their disposal, the Arabs appeared to have time on their side. By the mid-1970s, when that oil became a potent political and economic weapon, the United States, like much of the world, would be forced to reassess its Middle East policies.

While the United States was preoccupied with Vietnam and with rebellion at home, the USSR not only regained its standing in the Middle East but enlarged its influence in the entire Mediterranean region. Nearer home, the Soviet Union, like the United States, continued to insist on orthodoxy. This time, in August 1968, the victim was Czechoslovakia.

With a show of force even greater than that used in Hungary twelve years before, the Soviets ruthlessly crushed the Alexander Dubcek regime and the libertarian and democratic spirit it had fostered. The manner in which Soviet leaders justified the intervention should have been all too familiar to American policy makers—to preserve Czechoslovakia from the forces of "world imperialism" and "counterrevolution."

The United States was concerned with the same forces in Southeast Asia, and it would manifest that concern in a variety of ways. To ensure that Communists would not come to power in Indonesia, the largest country in Southeast Asia, the United States played a significant role in one of the worst massacres of the twentieth century. The CIA had systematically compiled the names of Communist operatives in Indonesia, ranging from the national leadership to village cadres, and in 1966 it turned over lists containing some 5000 names to the Indonesian army. In the purge that followed, the army hunted down and killed an estimated 250,000 to 500,000 Indonesians. The objective was achieved quickly and efficiently. The Partai Komunis Indonesia (PKI), the third largest Communist party in the world, was eliminated, and Suharto, the army commander, became president.

The United States met with far less success in its effort to thwart the Communist challenge in a less well known region of Southeast Asia, Vietnam. That failure would haunt American policy makers, Democratic and Republican, for nearly a decade.

The Lengthening Shadow of Vietnam

Few wars in history have been marked by the array of inconsistent official pronouncements that accompanied the American war in Vietnam. Except for the growing casualty lists, nothing contributed more to public discontent over the war than the mistrust created by confusion, secrecy, and deceit. Even Congress was deliberately misled or kept ignorant by the executive department, largely for self-serving rather than security reasons.

No incidents in the war were more clouded by contradictory explanations and the classification of essential documents than the events in the Tonkin Gulf, off North Vietnam, on August 2 and 4, 1964. Compounding the confusion was the United States' preoccupation at this time with the presidential campaign between Goldwater and Johnson. Early in July 1964, in response to saber rattling by a new Saigon regime, UN Secretary General U Thant declared that "the only sensible alternative is the political and diplomatic method of negotiations." He proposed a reconvening of the Geneva Conference for this purpose. But the Johnson administration's response left little room for compromise. The president himself stated: "We do not believe in conferences to ratify terror." The next day he announced a 30 percent increase in the American "military mission" to Vietnam, from 16,000 to 21,000 persons.

On August 2, North Vietnamese PT boats attacked the U.S. destroyer *Maddox* in Tonkin Gulf, and were driven off with the help of carrier-based fighter planes. The *Maddox* suffered neither damage nor casualties. The United States asserted that the attack was unprovoked; the *Maddox* was "on routine patrol in international waters." But on July 30 and 31 Hanoi had already filed a formal protest with the International Control Commission set up under the Geneva agreements. It declared that Saigon vessels had raided North Vietnamese fishing boats and that, under cover of protection by an American destroyer, had bombarded two North Vietnamese islands. The *Maddox* was attacked, Hanoi held, to stop such activities.

Secretary McNamara denied American complicity: "Our Navy played absolutely no part in, was not associated with, was not aware of, any South Vietnamese actions, if there were any." Four years later, McNamara admitted before a congressional hearing what the Pentagon Papers also confirmed—that North Vietnamese islands had been bombarded and that the United States and South Vietnam had made joint raids against North Vietnam. It was also made clear that the bombardment was part of a secret United States policy adopted in early 1964 to exert "new and significant pressures on North Vietnam." The point was to force North Vietnam to commit acts that would gain congressional authorization for whatever else "is necessary with respect to Vietnam."

This policy was stiffened after the attack on the *Maddox*. The president directed the navy to assign a second destroyer to join *Maddox*'s patrol and to order both vessels, together with the necessary air power, to repel any further assaults. Two days later, on August 4, the Defense Department announced that North Vietnam had at-

Infantryman in Vietnam. *(Donald McCullin, Magnum Photos)*

tacked both the *Maddox* and its companion, sixty-five miles offshore in the gulf, and that the attackers had been driven off with the loss of at least two boats. North Vietnam denied that any such attack had taken place. (Congress did not learn until several years later that evidence of such an attack was, at best, inconclusive.)

That very night, allowing no time for investigation and without consulting Congress, the president went on television to announce that in response to "repeated acts of violence against the armed forces of the United States," American planes were now engaged in action "against gunboats and certain facilities in Vietnam." He called his response "limited and fitting. We Americans know, although others appear to forget, the risks of spreading conflict. We seek no wider war." Yet he must have realized that this attack on North Vietnam was more than an escalation of a war officially described as one for the defense of the Saigon government against South Vietnamese guerrilla groups. Just prior to his telecast the president informed legislative leaders that he would send Congress a retroactive joint resolution the next day, to be adopted "before dark" and without amendment.

This resolution the administration promptly and persistently interpreted as a "functional equivalent" of a formal declaration of war in Southeast Asia. Restating the United States version of the events of August 2 and 4, the Tonkin Gulf Resolution of August 7, 1964, declared:

The Congress approves and supports the determination of the President, as Commander in Chief, to take all necessary measures to repel any armed attack against the forces of the United States and to prevent further aggression.

Rushed into session in a crisis mood, the House adopted the resolution without a dissenting vote. The Senate debated the measure for two days, but only because Wayne Morse of Oregon had threatened a filibuster. Only two senators—Morse and Ernest Gruening of Alaska—stood opposed to a measure granting the president almost unlimited power. Both, to their credit, saw through the smoke screens of at least two administrations. Gruening called the resolution "a predated declaration of war." Morse thought it a subversion of the Constitution and "a historic mistake."

But the Cold War mentality overrode reason on that day, and the president's assurances got the support of several senators who would later emerge as critics of the war. It was none other than J. William Fulbright, chairman of the For-

eign Relations Committee, who managed the resolution through the Senate. Among those who voted with him were Eugene McCarthy of Minnesota and George McGovern of South Dakota.

Armed with the resolution, Johnson rapidly escalated the war. The bombing of North Vietnam in August 1964 appears to have been as much a political as a military adventure. Regular missions of this sort did not begin until February 1965. During the preceding presidential election, Johnson had refused to endorse Goldwater's call for the bombing of North Vietnam. "We're not going north and drop bombs at this stage of the game," LBJ responded. "I want to think about the consequences of getting American boys into a war with 700 million Chinese."

With the election won and the new administration seated, McGeorge Bundy, now one of Johnson's hard-line advisers, returned from a visit to Saigon convinced of the need to buck up the South Vietnamese. The fear of Chinese intervention, however, still restrained the president. Even after February 1965, reporter Tom Wicker recalled, the missions went on "hesitantly and reluctantly" for six weeks.

During the spring of 1965, the administration developed a program for the systematic bombing of North Vietnam. The more intensive bombing, however, only reinforced North Vietnam's determination to resist. Even the CIA doubted the wisdom of the new strategy. With every new Vietcong provocation, however, Johnson stepped up the raids. And Congress, by huge majorities, voted the necessary hardware. When pressed to estimate how long the war might take, LBJ confidently replied that the continued bombing would force Hanoi and the Vietcong to their knees within six months.

In June 1965 American ground troops engaged the Vietcong in direct fighting for the first time in what were described as search-and-destroy missions. By the end of the year, American forces in Vietnam had exceeded 200,000. The South Vietnamese also promised to step up their efforts after Air Vice-Marshal Nguyen Cao Ky took over as premier of the eighth South Vietnamese government since Diem. Dissent in the United States began to mount, especially on college campuses. In October 1965, the first public burning of a draft card took place. The next month, some 30,000 people participated in a March on Washington for Peace in Vietnam. Yet the continuing escalation of military appropriations by Congress suggested that most Americans still shared the president's confidence and determination. "America wins the wars that she undertakes," LBJ had made clear in 1965.

By the end of 1966, American forces in Vietnam had reached 380,000. In April, their casualties exceeded those of the South Vietnamese for the first time; 4800 American soldiers were killed in action that year. Meanwhile, American hardware commitments now probably exceeded those of any other war in history. "What kind of a war are we fighting anyway?" asked an American soldier in his Vietnam diary in 1967. "They say we've got more fire-power out here than they had in both World War I and II. Yet these damn kids in black pajamas continue to hold out. I can't understand it. Each one of them must have 40 lives."

Perhaps part of the answer lay in the estimate that the search-and-destroy missions destroyed six civilians for every one Vietcong. Also, widespread chemical warfare and other new weaponry, whose use was largely concealed from Americans at home, contributed heavily to the devastation of South Vietnam while contributing little to the "pacification" of the Vietcong.

In a struggle that had developed into a war of body counts, *pacification* had come largely to mean extermination. Vietnamese civilians, North and South, were almost routinely included in the slaughter so that a better showing could be made. "Your Secretary of Defense loves statistics," a Vietnamese general remarked. "We Vietnamese can give him all he wants. If you want them to go up, they go up. If you want them to go down, they go down." The counts grew as suspect as all other aspects of this tragedy. Yet another source of revulsion was the means of killing, which brought anxiety over the possibility of war crimes.

In May 1967, Secretary McNamara himself recoiled from what was happening: "The picture of the world's greatest superpower killing or seriously injuring 1,000 noncombatants a week, while trying to pound a tiny backward nation into submission on an issue whose merits are hotly disputed, is not a pretty one." McNamara noted that the bomb tonnage dropped every week on North Vietnam had exceeded that of all the bombings of Germany in World War II.

By the end of 1967 United States troop strength in Vietnam was approaching 475,000—about 1500 more than the peak strength of American forces in the Korean War. Casualties rose proportionately. In May, total American casualties exceeded 10,000. The futility of bombing North Vietnam, and that strategy's immense political cost at home and abroad, was now being acknowl-

edged openly. McNamara admitted it publicly in August 1967, three months before his departure from the cabinet.

Despite growing dissent within his administration, LBJ persisted. Although the president defended the right of dissent, declaring that protest was "the life breath of democracy—even when it blows heavy," he had the FBI and CIA keep him posted on the dissenters. The once gregarious president was increasingly more guarded about his movements and exposure to the public; he even declined to attend his party's national convention in August 1968.

North Vietnam's Tet (New Year's) offensive against Saigon and other South Vietnamese cities in February 1968 demonstrated that Ho, despite the bombing, could launch massive assaults that would catch hardened United States field commanders by surprise. It also revealed that the USSR would not leave North Vietnam to confront American military technology merely with captured or stolen American weapons. In the Tet offensive, Hanoi used Soviet jet planes and tanks for the first time.

Although American and South Vietnamese troops recaptured several of the population centers lost in the Tet offensive, the cost was immense, and confidence in ultimate victory was seriously undermined. The ancient imperial city of Hue, where pitched battles had been fought, lay in ruins. Of still another Vietnamese town, an American officer observed: "It became necessary to destroy the town to save it." United States forces soared to 543,000 in April 1968, while combat deaths reached 22,951. The new campaign being planned by American field officers bore the ominous title of Operation Complete Victory.

Worldwide pressure for peace had grown very heavy by this time. Television filled America's living rooms with firsthand, all too realistic reports from Vietnam of American troops on search-and-destroy missions setting fire to peasant huts. The doubts raised by such sights were deepened by the weekly announcements of the American death toll. Riots and demonstrations on college campuses attested to the antiwar sentiment there, even among usually conservative and nonpolitical students. The flow of draft resisters to Canada had reached ten thousand.

The strength of the peace movement became evident in the showing of one of its leading congressional advocates, Senator Eugene J. McCarthy of Minnesota, in the Democratic presidential primary in New Hampshire on March 12,

WINNING THE VIETNAM WAR

In *Dispatches,* news correspondent Michael Herr wrote some of the most devastating personal accounts of the Vietnam War.

I knew one 4th Division Lurp [long-range reconnaisance patroller] who took his pills by the fistful, downs from the left pocket of his tiger suit and ups from the right, one to cut the trail for him and the other to send him down it. He told me that they cooled things out just right for him, that he could see that old jungle at night like he was looking at it through a starlight scope. "They sure give you the range," he said.

This was his third tour. In 1965 he'd been the only survivor in a platoon of the Cav wiped out going into the Ia Drang Valley. In '66 he'd come back with the Special Forces and one morning after an ambush he'd hidden under the bodies of his team while the VC walked around them with knives, making sure. They stripped the bodies of their gear, the berets too, and finally went away, laughing. After that, there was nothing left for him in the war except the Lurps. "I just can't hack it back in the World," he said. He told me that after he'd come back home the last time he would sit in his room all day, and sometimes he'd stick a hunting rifle out the window, leading people and cars as they passed his house until the only feeling he was aware of was all up in the tip of that one finger. "It used to put my folks real uptight," he said. . . .

But what a story he told me, as one-pointed and resonant as any war story I ever heard. It took me a year to understand it.

"Patrol went up the mountain. One man came back. He died before he could tell us what happened."

I waited for the rest, but it seemed not to be that kind of story; when I asked him what had happened he just looked like he felt sorry for me . . . .

Source: Michael Herr, *Dispatches* (New York: Knopf, 1977), pp. 5–6. Copyright 1968, 1969, 1977 by Michael Herr. Reprinted by permission of Alfred A. Knopf, Inc. Photograph by Donald McCullin, Magnum Photos.

1968. Although he had been given little chance against LBJ, McCarthy shocked the administration by taking 42 percent of the votes to the president's 49 percent. On March 31, Johnson said on nationwide TV: "We are prepared to move immediately toward peace through negotiations. So tonight, in the hope that this action will lead to early talks, I am taking the first step to deescalate the conflict."

This step was to halt all air and naval bombardment of North Vietnam, except in the area just north of the demilitarized zone where the enemy arms buildup was heaviest. Even more dramatic was the president's gesture toward unifying the country; he announced that he would not seek reelection.

The North Vietnamese responded quickly. On April 3, Ho Chi Minh's government declared its readiness to talk about peace, and one month later

preliminary talks began in Paris. But even as Johnson restricted the bombings, he increased the troop level in Vietnam to 543,000. On June 4 the United States command in Vietnam announced that American battle deaths in the first 6 months of 1968 exceeded all of those in 1967. By June 23, reckoning from December 22, 1961, the date of the first death of an American serviceman in Vietnam, the war there had become the longest in American history. The direct cost of the war had soared to an acknowledged $25 billion a year, and there were unacknowledged costs in the form of weapons development and other programs associated with the conflict.

Little progress was reported from Paris until shortly before the United States presidential elections. Then, following favorable information from the French capital, Johnson announced: "I have now ordered that all air, naval, and artillery

Instant justice during the Tet offensive of 1968: a Vietcong carrying a pistol was captured near Quang Pagoda and taken to the police chief, General Nguyen Ngoc Loan, who shot him on the spot. *(AP/Wide World Photos)*

bombardment of North Vietnam cease." The president looked forward to the meeting scheduled at the Paris peace talks on November 6, the day after the elections, for the sweet fruits of his decree.

But conflicts over the roles to be played by South Vietnam and its official enemy, the Vietcong, at the Paris talks ended his hopes. LBJ left the White House with the war still unresolved. Not only his

Thousands of antiwar demonstrators converged on the 1968 Democratic National Convention in Chicago, which turned into one of the bloodiest and most widely publicized confrontations between America's youth and the police. *(Roger Malloch, Magnum Photos)*

political career but his vision of the Great Society had become a casualty of the war and of the mounting strife at home.

The "Silent Majority" on Trial: The Election of 1968

The presidential election of 1968 may be said to have begun with the decision to bomb North Vietnam in February 1965. The ranks of doves swelled not only among McCarthy's colleagues in the Senate, but among the youth of the nation as well. McCarthy's performance in the New Hampshire primary showed that he had grown strong enough to split the party. When Senator Robert F. Kennedy of New York decided a few days later to enter the campaign, it seemed that the opposition to the administration would also be split. Johnson's withdrawal two weeks later deepened the conflict between his would-be Democratic successors.

The Kennedy mantle and mystique drew millions of American young people, black and white. On June 5, however, the very night of his victory in the California primary, Robert Kennedy was shot by Sirhan Sirhan, a young Arab nationalist resentful of Kennedy's support for Israel. Coming only two months after King's murder, the Kennedy assassination shocked the nation and changed the political scene.

The Democratic nomination was now a virtual certainty for Hubert H. Humphrey, Johnson's vice-president and a firm supporter of the war. He did not enter any primaries, but his quest for delegates did not end until the first ballot at the Democratic convention in Chicago, August 26–29. Although he easily won the nomination, the narrow victory of the plank on Vietnam revealed deep rifts in the party. What happened outside the convention center exposed even sharper divisions in the nation.

The International Amphitheater, where official sessions of the Democratic convention were held, took on the appearance of a fortress under siege. It was ringed with barbed wire, broken only by checkpoints for entering delegates, reporters, and guests. Several blocks around the amphitheater and around major downtown hotels swarmed with police, federal agents, and more than five thousand National Guardsmen called in to keep away antiwar demonstrators. The almost inevitable confrontation between the security forces and the demonstrators led to "unrestrained and indiscrim-inate police violence"—that is, to a "police riot"—an investigative report subsequently charged.

Amid pandemonium inside and outside the convention hall—all of it visible to millions on TV—Humphrey accepted the Democratic nomination. The next day he announced, and the convention confirmed, his choice for vice-president, Senator Edmund S. Muskie of Maine.

The Republican convention, comparatively peaceful, featured the remarkable political comeback of Richard M. Nixon. Despite his defeat in the California gubernatorial election of 1962, he had remained active in Republican politics and was now given a second chance at the presidency. The Republican platform warned that "lawlessness is crumbling the foundations of American society," and the campaign itself stressed the need for "law and order." In his acceptance speech, Nixon welcomed as the core of his constituency the "silent majority" of "forgotten Americans"—"the non-shouters, the non-demonstrators, that are not racist or sick, that are not guilty of the crime that plagues the land."

He selected as his running mate Governor Spiro T. Agnew of Maryland. The choice of Agnew, a southern candidate, could only strengthen the Republicans' "southern strategy," already manifest in a promise Nixon made to southern delegations the day before the convention balloting: if elected, he said, his administration would not "ram anything down your throats." He disliked federal intervention in local school-board affairs. He opposed school busing. He would appoint "strict Constitutionalists" to the Supreme Court.

Nixon's stand may have taken some of the wind out of the sails of a third candidate for president, George C. Wallace, the Alabama segregationist thought by many to be strong enough to deprive both regular-party candidates of an electoral majority. Wallace delighted audiences by his assaults on "scummy anarchists," "pseudointellectuals," federal meddlers, and those who coddled criminals. But he found it difficult to outdo the determination of Nixon and Agnew to bring "law and order" to the country.

With exceptional support from the old Democratic coalition of urban liberals, organized labor, and minority groups, Humphrey made a remarkably strong finish in the big industrial states. Nixon carried by small majorities the critical states of Ohio, Illinois, New Jersey, and California. Humphrey won in Michigan and Texas, as well as New York and Pennsylvania. Wallace's

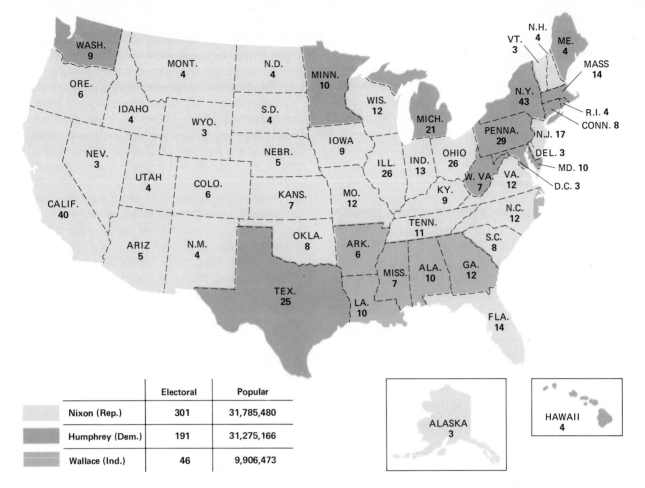

	Electoral	Popular
Nixon (Rep.)	301	31,785,480
Humphrey (Dem.)	191	31,275,166
Wallace (Ind.)	46	9,906,473

The Election of 1968

poor southern showing outside the few Deep South states he was certain to carry also helped Nixon gain a clear electoral majority.

Like Eisenhower in 1956, however, he failed to carry enough legislative candidates with him to change the Democratic majorities in the House and Senate. Nixon also failed to gain a popular majority. His margin over Humphrey, a mere 510,000 out of 73.2 million votes cast, gave him only 43.4 percent of the popular vote, the lowest for a successful candidate since Wilson in 1912. Humphrey gained 42.7 percent of the popular vote; Wallace, 13.5 percent.

The new president clearly embodied the sentiments of tens of millions of Americans, angry over the threats to their personal safety, frightened by the racial violence, and frustrated by a costly and futile war. In Richard Nixon and Spiro Agnew, they found forceful spokesmen to articulate their grievances, fears, and hopes. Few could have envisioned the fate that awaited these two apostles of law and order. For the tens of thousands of young political activists who had enlisted in McCarthy's "crusade" to bring the war to an end,

the disillusion was bound to be severe. The violence at the Chicago convention, the nomination of Humphrey, and the election of Nixon and Agnew reinforced for many of them the conviction that they had become strangers in their own land.

THE DISSENTING GENERATION

F. Scott Fitzgerald once said of his generation, which came of age in the 1920s, that it had found all gods dead, all wars fought in vain, and all faiths in humanity shaken. The generation of the 1960s, often described in similar terms, was thus not as unique as it preferred to believe. Even the relatively apathetic and silent generation of the 1950s had managed to produce the "rebel without a cause." When asked in the film The Wild One (1954) what he was rebelling against, the character portrayed by Marlon Brando replied "Whadda ya got?"

In the sixties, there was no end to the causes around which young people rallied. They ranged from the war in Vietnam, which they wanted to stop, to a corrupt and hypocritical adult society, which they expected to remake in their own image. What most of these "rebels" had in common was the middle-class inheritance they longed to renounce. But their staying power proved brief; the dominant society succeeded in absorbing both rebels and rebellion.

Sources of Disillusionment

For those who had experienced the Great Depression and World War II, the relative stability of the fifties had been welcome, along with the affluence many of them managed to acquire. If they cherished their security and the comfortable homes they purchased in suburbia, if they took pride in what they were able to pass on to their children in the way of educational and economic opportunities, they did so reminding themselves of their hardships in the thirties, their wartime sacrifices, and the other struggles they had endured to make all this possible. If they chose not to be skeptical of their major institutions and of the Protestant ethic of hard work, it was because these had served them well.

The generation of white middle-class youth that came of age in the sixties—products of the postwar baby boom—had good reason, then, to feel secure and hopeful about the society they entered. Neither their families nor their teachers suggested anything else. This was the first generation to have been raised in the age of television. By the time they were fourteen, according to one estimate, they had already seen 300,000 commercials; by the time they were eighteen, they had already compiled 17,000 hours of television viewing. If they took their values and attitudes from the TV screen, they found little reason to question the dominant institutions of American society. If they responded to politics, it was to the youthful appeal of John F. Kennedy and his call for young Americans to make a commitment to the New Frontier. Some enlisted in the Peace Corps; others were drawn into the civil rights struggle and helped to register black voters in the South.

But the idealism and hope with which many young Americans entered the sixties began to come apart after the assassination of President Kennedy and the Freedom Summer of 1964. The vision of a more humane society gave way to a nightmare of violence—not the manufactured variety they had become accustomed to on TV, but real violence: the assassinations of Robert F. Kennedy, Martin Luther King, Jr., and Malcolm X; the beatings and murder of civil rights demonstrators; police violence in the ghettos; and the massive and organized violence the United States was inflicting on the people of Vietnam.

What middle-class youth began to perceive was the enormous contradiction between the ideals and virtues they had been taught by family, school, and television on the one hand, and the spectacle of racism and poverty and the brutality of the war in Vietnam on the other. The universities many of them were attending were so impersonal and bureaucratized as to be unable to see their own deep complicity in the war abroad and racism at home.

The awakening came to different people at different times. Many of them enlisted in The Movement (as it came to be called) only after observing firsthand the attempts to suppress it. When the radical Students for a Democratic Society (SDS) drew up their manifesto (the Port Huron Statement), the signers agreed that the civil rights struggle, more than any other cause, had brought most of them "from silence to activism."

The presidential election of 1964 had no sooner ended than the Free Speech Movement (FSM) on the Berkeley campus of the University of California revealed the degree to which many middle-class youths were prepared to reject the apathy and indifference of their predecessors. What began as a protest over restrictions on campus political expression evolved into a movement that directly challenged the dominant values and assumptions of American society. Its purpose was to compel that society to recognize the depths of its hypocrisy.

As eight hundred students were about to stage a nonviolent sit-in at the Berkeley administration building, FSM leader Mario Savio, a veteran of the Freedom Summer earlier that year, told a massive rally outside:

There is a time when the operations of the machine become so odious, make you so sick at heart, that you can't take part, you can't even tacitly take part. And you've got to put your bodies on the gears and upon the wheels, upon the levers, upon all the apparatus, and you've got to make it stop. And you've got to indicate to the people who run it, to the people who own it, that unless you're free the machine will be prevented from working at all.

The effects of student activism would soon be felt on campuses across the country—and with ever greater intensity as American involvement in Vietnam deepened and as frustration and tension mounted at home.

The Free Speech Movement at the University of California, Berkeley, received massive support on campus and soon spread to other universities. *(Joe Wakabayashi)*

The Counterculture

The sixties witnessed the emergence of a youth culture (some called it a counterculture) characterized by distinct forms of expression and consciousness, including new styles of dress, social behavior, and music. Few exerted any greater influence on these styles than the Beatles, an English rock group that first visited the United States in 1963. The contagion of the Beatles and innumerable other groups and individual artists proved impossible to contain. The music suggested attitudes toward life and society far different from those the adult generation had been accustomed to hearing. There was an intensity to the music, moreover, that was inseparable from the message conveyed. In form, content, and volume, the new music heralded a liberation from traditional restraints and conventions.

For many young people, self-expression lay not in politics, but in the adoption of a radical lifestyle, a redefinition of sexual mores, and the use of hallucinatory drugs. They substituted the "be-in" and the "love-in" for the protest meeting and preached an ideology of anti-ideology. Few protest marches or political rallies attracted as many young people as the countless rock festivals. The

most spectacular and exhilarating of the latter took place in the summer of 1969 at Woodstock, New York, where some 400,000 came together. Two years earlier, the Love Summer of 1967 had attracted thousands of "flower children" (named after their habit of handing flowers to policemen and "straights") to San Francisco, turning the city's Haight-Ashbury district into a hippy mecca.

The young political activists who made up The Movement—many of whom found the drug culture counterproductive—were confident of their ability to turn both the Vietnam war and the nation around. Equally optimistic, Charles A. Reich forecast in 1970 in his much-discussed *The Greening of America* that the "corporate state" would soon destroy itself; the emerging youth culture would then ensure the end of established attitudes toward business, politics, leisure, and daily life. But none of these prophecies would be realized, at least not by this generation.

With relative ease, American society curbed and absorbed the radical impulses of the sixties, political and cultural. The counterculture proved short-lived. Many of its creative qualities, fads, and fashions—the hairstyles, the clothes, the dancing, the music, the language, even the "pot" parties—were incorporated into the larger cul-

Rock music is a necessary element of contemporary society. It is functional. It is healthy and valid artistically. It is also educational (how to ask a girl for a date, what love is like). It has all the answers to what your mother and father won't tell you. It is also a big business. This is a brief history of rock and its relationship to our society. . . .

Part One: The 50s

1. Who remembers beer? White port and lemon juice? For 10 points, what was the name of the guy in your school who used to buy your juice for parties? . . .

2. Who remembers making out and getting hot? For 10 points, how old were you when it happened? . . .

3. Who remembers duck tails, peggers, leather jackets, bunny shoes, brogans, tight sweaters, teardrops, full skirts, and a million starchy petticoats, Sir Guy shirts and khakis? For 10 points, how much did you pay for your St. Christopher medallion? . . .

4. Who remembers gang fights, tire chains, boys with razor blades in the toes of their wedgies, girls with razor blades in their hair, blood and sickening crunch? For 10 points, tell why the cops were afraid of your gang.

Part Two: The 60s

5. Who remembers speed? Smoke? Acid? Transcendental meditation? For 10 points, name your connection or guru. . . .

6. Who remembers getting stoned and having an orgy? For 10 points, how old were you when you learned you were incapable of relating to others in a tender, personal way and finally discovered you had become asexual? . . .

7. Who remembers electric hair, bell bottoms, plastic jackets, sandals, high boots, bulky knit sweaters, Guccis, miniskirts, De Voss shirts and velvet pants? For 10 points, look around the house, find your beads and bells, and recite Hare Krishna without laughing. . . .

8. Who remembers demonstrations, truncheons, Mace, police dogs, the Pentagon, Century City, blood and sickening crunch? For 10 points, tell why you were afraid to cut your hair, infiltrate the establishment, and do it the easy way. . . .

Our present state of sociosexual enlightenment is, to a certain extent, attributable to the evolution of rock and vice versa. . . .

Source: Frank Zappa, "The Oracle Has It All Psyched Out," *Life*, June 28, 1968. Photograph of Bob Dylan by John Launois, Black Star; photograph of Jimi Hendrix by Jim Cummins, Camera 5, Inc.

ture, which compromised, if it did not distort altogether, the initial spirit and ideals. Even *Time* magazine could publish a cover story recommending to its mass readership the Beatles' new album *Sgt. Pepper's Lonely Hearts Club Band*, calling it "a guaranteed package of psychic shivers" certain to turn "parents, professors, even business executives" into ardent Beatle fans.

Even as police battled and arrested thousands of antiwar demonstrators, Columbia Records appealed to its youthful purchasers in 1969 with the slogan "The Man can't bust your music." Finally, *Rolling Stone* magazine, founded in 1967 as an irreverent tabloid devoted to rock culture, took out a full-page ad in the *New York Times* in an effort to expand its readership: "If you are a corporate executive trying to understand what is happening to youth today, you cannot afford to be without *Rolling Stone*."

Elinor Langer, who had once shared the optimism of her generation, later reflected on how short-lived it proved to be:

AMERICAN SOCIETY IN THE TWENTIETH CENTURY:
THE YOUTH CULTURE

Youth: The Gang. *(Bruce Davidson, Magnum Photos)*

Roy Lichtenstein's *Hopeless* (1963). *(Launois Covello, Black Star)*

Color guard, Pittsburgh, Pennsylvania. *(I. Masser, Black Star)*

The rock concert near Woodstock, New York, in the summer of 1969 attracted more than 400,000 youths. *(Dan McCoy, Black Star)*

Performing at Woodstock. *(Dan McCoy, Black Star)*

Janis Joplin, the rock goddess of the sixties. *(Dan McCoy, Black Star)*

Youth: The Gang. *(Bruce Davidson, Magnum Photos)*

Two youths at the Woodstock concert. *(Dan McCoy, Black Star)*

END OF AN ERA

If John Lennon of the Beatles had once epitomized the exuberance and optimism of the sixties, in 1970 he was expressing feelings far more in tune with the new decade:

I don't believe in Magic
I don't believe in I-Ching
I don't believe in the Bible
I don't believe in Hitler
I don't believe in Jesus
I don't believe in Kennedy
I don't believe in Mantra
I don't believe in Gita
I don't believe in Yoga
I don't believe in Kings
I don't believe in Elvis
I don't believe in Zimmerman
I don't believe in Beatles
I just believe in me,
Yoko and me
And that's reality.
The dream is over

What can I say?
The dream is over
Yesterday
I was the dreamweaver
But now I'm reborn
I was the walrus
But now I'm John
And so dear friends
You just have to carry on
The dream is over.

For Lennon, that decade ended in tragedy. On December 8, 1980, he was murdered outside his New York apartment—a victim of the senseless violence that characterized life in urban America. To the generation that had grown up with Lennon's music, his death, more than any other single event, marked the end of an era.

Youth culture was a great romance; music, energy, drugs, a cultural disguise. But it was part of our revolutionary fantasy: we were guerrillas among the people, "fish in the sea." Patton's nephew attended the premier of Patton *with long hair and we saw militarism crumbling. We forgot that America could support any life style, as long as it used money as its medium of exchange.*

The political side of The Movement succumbed to slogans, communication by invective, and sectarianism. "Our creative political potential," said one dismayed activist, "has degenerated into a short-sighted repetition of demonstrations. . . . The 'politics of apocalypse' became the 'politics of despair.'" Meanwhile, an intensive survey of the younger generation undertaken by *Fortune* in 1968—the year of the worst student riots— revealed that some 60 percent still stood on "the practical side of the line." They were preparing themselves for power and affluence, and were committed to careers in big business or big government or in adjunct professions.

The dominant society demonstrated immense staying power. Its threats and warnings and its strategies for repression produced no permanent

"armies of the night," no guerrillas in the hills. Sporadic riots, street warfare, bombings, murders of and by police did not make a revolution. The Movement failed to make any inroads into the working class, which had had to send its sons into the war. Nor had liberating lifestyles or innovative musical expression lessened the inequalities in the ghettos and the barrios. With Richard Nixon's decisive victory over George McGovern in the 1972 presidential election, the familiar feeling of powerlessness, apathy, and cynicism once again gripped the college campuses. "Everything we thought was wrong is still wrong," Elinor Langer wrote, "but we are without the institutions, the influence, or the understanding to change it."

In 1963 Bob Dylan sang of far-reaching changes "blowing in the wind," changes that would presumably radicalize and humanize the dominant society. Some years later, he sang: "Although the masters make the rules/For the wise men and the fools/I've got nothin' Ma, nothin' to live up to." The generation of the sixties ended in Watergate, economic recession, and the triumph of a new politics.

SUMMARY

The 1960s were a decade of crises and war; they were also a decade of widespread social changes.

Lyndon Johnson, who had become president amid the national shock of Kennedy's assassination, set in

motion two major domestic programs—the Great Society and the War on Poverty. The commitment of the federal government to the concept of the welfare state seemed unquestioned. Among Johnson's Great Society measures were the Civil Rights Act of 1964, the most sweeping such legislation in American history; a tax-reform bill; and the establishment of the Office of Economic Opportunity to supervise ten separate antipoverty programs.

In the election of 1964, Johnson won a sweeping victory over the conservative Republican Barry Goldwater. Beginning in January 1965, the Eighty-ninth Congress approved nearly all the Great Society measures the president proposed: the Elementary and Secondary Education Act (April 1965); the medicare amendments to the Social Security Act (July 1965); special assistance for Appalachia; the end of the immigration quota system; antipollution legislation; the Truth in Lending Act; the National Foundation for the Arts and Humanities; and a new cabinet department, that of Housing and Urban Development.

But the Great Society, like the New Frontier, raised the expectations of many Americans without necessarily fulfilling them. Frustration mounted for blacks who found it hard to share in the affluence so visible around them. The civil rights movement reached a peak in early 1965 with the dramatic march in Alabama. Congress responded to the violence there with the Voting Rights Act of 1965, a significant triumph for southern blacks.

In the North, however, discrimination in employment, housing, and schooling persisted. Whites poured out into suburbs as blacks poured into the cities. The frustrations of urban blacks finally exploded in a series of riots from 1964 through 1967. Watts, Newark, and Detroit were the scenes of major violence. There were also confrontations in the South. New black movements, more militant and separatist, developed. On April 4, 1968, the apostle of nonviolence, Martin Luther King, Jr., was assassinated.

Black activism spurred activism on the part of other minorities. Cesar Chavez battled in California to organize a farm laborers' union; others organized Mexican Americans around the cause of la raza—racial and ethnic pride. Native Americans brought their cause to the public consciousness with demonstrations at Alcatraz and Wounded Knee. The decade brought enhanced racial consciousness and self-pride to minority groups, and some real gains in education, jobs, and political power.

In international affairs, the United States found itself in more and more difficulty. It intervened in the Dominican Republic in 1965 to prevent the establishment of a Communist government. At the end, there were twenty thousand American troops in that small country, and the United States had again smashed a nationalist movement that seemed to have popular support.

The Middle East remained explosive. As soon as UN troops were withdrawn in May 1967, Egypt and Israel went to war again. In an overpowering assault, Israel humiliated Egypt in the Six-Day War. It then kept some of the territory it had occupied—the Sinai Peninsula, the Golan Heights, the Gaza Strip, and the West Bank. The result was an angry stalemate that defied solution, and the reassertion of Soviet influence in the Middle East and the entire Mediterranean region.

While Johnson was fighting a war on poverty at home, he was waging a full-scale war on communism in Vietnam. For the United States, Vietnam overshadowed everything else. Deepening involvement, as well as confusion, secrecy, and deceit, created mistrust and discontent at home. Events in the Tonkin Gulf in August 1964 led to the president's demand for, and congressional approval of, a resolution that gave him almost sole authority to wage war in Southeast Asia as he saw fit. The war escalated and by February 1965, the bombing of North Vietnam had become a systematic policy. On the ground, search-and-destroy missions brought American troops in direct contact with the Vietcong. Both activities only stiffened resistance in North Vietnam.

In October 1965, the first public burning of a draft card took place in the United States. By the end of 1966, there were 380,000 troops in Vietnam; by the end of 1967, troop strength exceeded that at the peak of the Korean War. Casualties mounted accordingly. By the end of 1967, administration officials were openly admitting the futility of United States policies. The Vietnamese success in the Tet offensive of early 1968 brought heavy pressure, both domestic and worldwide, to end the war. There were riots and demonstrations on American campuses, and more draft resisters fled to Canada.

In March 1968, LBJ announced an end to the air and naval bombardment of North Vietnam; he also announced that he would not seek reelection. Talks began in Paris in April. But the number of American troops in Vietnam continued to rise, and by June the war had become the longest in American history.

LBJ left office with the war still unresolved, and with both his career and the Great Society as additional casualties. The election of 1968 was itself a period of tragedy and violence. Robert Kennedy was assassinated in June in California, only two months after Martin Luther King, Jr., had been killed. The Democratic convention in Chicago was the scene of a police riot as police clashed with antiwar demonstrators. Hubert Humphrey, Johnson's vice-president and a firm supporter of the war, lost to Richard Nixon and Spiro Agnew, who campaigned for "law and order" and the rights of the "silent majority."

These events had been accompanied by a vast youth movement of dissent and protest, and by the growth of a counterculture whose values were far different from those of the Establishment. It was characterized by distinct forms of expression and consciousness, including new styles of dress, social behavior, and music.

The Movement and the counterculture constituted a revolt by white middle-class youth disillusioned with the world of their parents, and it focused on the confusions and contradictions of the visible tragedy of Vietnam. But they were quickly invaded by exploiters. The drug culture had tragic results for many young Americans, and political activism turned into slogans, communication by invective, sectarianism, and terrorism. In the end, The Movement's staying power proved brief; the dominant society succeeded in absorbing both rebels and rebellion.

TIME LINE

1963   First visit of the Beatles to the United
       States

1964   War on Poverty program begins
       Twenty-fourth Amendment (poll tax)
       ratified
       Civil Rights Act
       Freedom Summer in Mississippi
       Gulf of Tonkin Resolution
       Johnson elected president
       Free Speech Movement at Berkeley

1965   War in Vietnam escalates; 200,000
       U.S. troops by December
       Demonstrations protest Vietnam War
       Selma to Montgomery civil rights
       march
       Voting Rights Act
       Race riot in Watts
       Malcolm X assassinated
       United Farm Workers' grape strike
       begins
       U.S. intervenes in Dominican
       Republic
       Elementary and Secondary Education
       Act
       Medicare
       National Foundation of the Arts and
       Humanities
       Department of Housing and Urban
       Development (HUD) created

1966   War in Vietnam escalates; 380,000
       U.S. troops by December

       Meredith march, Mississippi
       Black power movement emerges

1967   U.S. troops in Vietnam reach 475,000,
       casualties exceed 10,000
       Race riots in Newark, Detroit, and
       other cities
       Love Summer, San Francisco
       Sgt. Pepper's Lonely Hearts Club Band
       released
       Six-day War in Middle East

1968   Martin Luther King, Jr. assassinated
       North Vietnam's Tet (New Year's)
       offensive; U.S. troops reach 543,000
       Soviets crush dissident regime in
       Czechoslovakia
       Robert F. Kennedy assassinated
       Antiwar demonstrations escalate
       Race riots in American cities
       Chicago Democratic Convention riots
       American Indian Movement (AIM)
       founded
       Vietnam peace talks open in Paris
       Richard Nixon elected president

1969   American Indians occupy Alcatraz
       Island
       Woodstock rock festival

1971   Pentagon Papers published

1973   American Indians seize Wounded
       Knee, South Dakota

Suggested Readings

To get close to the sixties, one might start by listening to the Beatles, *Sgt. Pepper's Lonely Hearts Club Band* (1967); The Rolling Stones, *Aftermath* (1966); Bob Dylan, *Blonde on Blonde* (1966); Jefferson Airplane, *Surrealistic Pillow* (1967); Jimi Hendrix, *Electric Lady Land* (1968); and *Woodstock* (1970). One might also glance over M. Goodman (ed.), *The Movement toward a New America: The Beginnings of a Long Revolution* (1970); Time-Life, *This Fabulous Century: 1960–1970* (1970); and E. Quinn and P. J. Dolan (eds.), *The Sense of the 60's* (1968). Much of the feeling of this decade is conveyed by P. Joseph (ed.), *Good Times: An Oral History of America in the Nineteen Sixties* (1974); T. Wolfe, *The Kandy-Kolored Tangerine-Flake Streamline Baby* (1965) and *The Electric Kool Aid Acid Test* (1968); and several collections of photographs: C. Harbutt and L. Jones, *America in Crisis* (1969); B. J.

Fernandez, *In Opposition: Images of Dissent in the Sixties* (1968); Student Nonviolent Coordinating Committee, *The Movement* (1964); Rolling Stone, *Festival! The Book of American Music Celebrations* (1970); and B. Owens, *Suburbia* (1973). Some of the best social commentary and cultural history of the decade will be found in the issues of *Rolling Stone*. The most perceptive history is G. Hodgson, *America in Our Time* (1976). See also W. L. O'Neill, *Coming Apart* (1971); M. Viorst, *America in the 1960's* (1980); and A. J. Matusow, *The Unraveling of America: A History of Liberalism in the 1960s* (1984).

The many commission reports provide a guide to the anxieties of the sixties: Warren Commission (1964); National Advisory (Kerner) Commission on Civil Disorders (1968); (Scranton) Commission on Campus Unrest (1970); H. D. Graham and T. R. Gurr, *Violence in*

America: A Report to the National Commission on the Causes and Prevention of Violence (1969); J. H. Skolnick, The Politics of Protest (1969); and D. Walker, Rights in Conflict: The Violent Confrontation of Demonstrators and Police in the Parks and Streets of Chicago during the Week of the Democratic National Convention of 1968 (1968).

On the pervasive role of the media, see D. M. White and R. Averson (eds.), Sight, Sound and Society (1969); A. Sarris, The American Cinema (1968); M. McLuhan, The Medium is the Massage (1967); and E. Barnouw, The Image Empire (1970) and Tube of Plenty (1975). T. Gitlin, The Whole World is Watching: The Mass Media in the Making and Unmaking of the New Left (1980), examines the ways in which the media influenced perceptions of radical groups.

C. Lasch, The Agony of the American Left (1969), and I. Unger, The Movement (1974), are critical assessments of the New Left. On the youth culture and protest, see K. Keniston, The Uncommitted (1965), Young Radicals (1968), and Youth and Dissent (1971); and J. Newfield, A Prophetic Minority (1966). The nature of the commitment will be found in P. Jacobs and S. Landau (eds.), The New Radicals (1966); C. Oglesby (ed.), The Left Reader (1969); M. V. Miller and S. Gilmore (eds.), Revolution at Berkeley (1965); S. M. Lipset and S. S. Wolin (eds.), The Berkeley Student Revolt (1965); and S. M. Lipset and P. G. Altbach (eds.), Students in Revolt (1969). On the SDS, see J. Miller, "Democracy is in the Streets": From Port Huron to the Siege of Chicago (1987). The most important recent assessment of the radical upheavals of the era, partly autobiographical, is T. Gitlin, The Sixties: Years of Hope, Days of Rage (1987). See also T. Hayden, Reunion: A Memoir (1988). On film, Mark Kitchel's Berkeley in the Sixties (1990) is available from California Newsreel, 149 9th St/420, San Francisco, CA 94103.

M. Dickstein, Gates of Eden (1977), is a cultural history, largely devoted to developments on the East Coast. The best studies of the music culture are C. Gillett, The Sound of the City: The Rise of Rock and Roll (1970), and G. Marcus, Mystery Train: Images of America in Rock 'N' Roll Music (1976; rev. ed., 1990). On the counterculture, J. Didion, Slouching towards Bethlehem (1968) and The White Album (1979), are impressionistic works. See also T. Roszak, The Making of a Counter Culture (1969); H. Hopkins (ed.), The Hippie Papers (1968); Rolling Stone, The Age of Paranoia: How the Sixties Ended (1972); and H. Thompson, Hell's Angels: A Strange and Terrible Saga (1967) and Fear and Loathing in Las Vegas: A Savage Journey to the Heart of the American Dream (1971).

On Lyndon B. Johnson, a place to start is the president's own memoir, The Vantage Point (1971). Two perspectives by insiders are G. E. Reedy, Lyndon Johnson: A Memoir (1982), and E. F. Goldman, The Tragedy of Lyndon Johnson (1969). See also T. Wicker, JFK and LBJ (1968); D. Kearns, Lyndon Johnson and the American Dream (1976); and M. Miller, Lyndon:

An Oral Biography (1980). An exhaustive and highly critical examination, not yet concluded, is R. A. Caro, The Years of Lyndon Johnson: The Path to Power (1982) and Means of Ascent (1990).

The brief ascendancy of Great Society thinking, its limitations, and its decline are explored in M. E. Gettleman and D. Mermelstein, The Great Society Reader (1967). Government planning is examined in O. Graham, Toward a Planned Society: From Roosevelt to Nixon (1976), and M. Gelfand, A Nation of Cities (1976). J. C. Donovan, The Politics of Poverty (1967), dissects Johnson's War on Poverty. See also F. Piven and R. Cloward, Regulating the Poor: The Function of Public Welfare (1971). The emerging issue of ecology is studied in P. R. Ehrlich and A. H. Ehrlich, Population, Resources, Environment (1970); P. Shepherd and D. McKinley (eds.), The Subversive Science: Essays toward an Ecology of Man (1969); W. Anderson, A Place of Power: The American Episode in Human Evolution (1976); J. Petulla, American Environmental History (1977); and the pioneering work of Rachel Carson, Silent Spring (1962).

The literature on the black revolution is immense. A. Meier, E. Rudwick, and F. L. Broderick (eds.), Black Protest Thought in the Twentieth Century (1971), is a collection of contemporary documents. Powerful statements of the period reflect the changes in black ideology and tactics: M. L. King, Jr., Stride toward Freedom (1958) and Why We Can't Wait (1964); R. F. Williams, Negroes with Guns (1962); J. Baldwin, The Fire Next Time (1963); The Autobiography of Malcolm X (1964) and Malcolm X Speaks (1965); L. Jones, Home: Social Essays (1966); S. Carmichael and C. V. Hamilton, Black Power: The Politics of Liberation in America (1967); E. Cleaver, Soul on Ice (1968); J. Lester, Look Out Whitey! Black Power's Gon' Get Your Mama! (1968); and a moving and insightful autobiography by an activist, A. Moody, Coming of Age in Mississippi (1968). Two suggestive works on black ideology are H. Cruse, The Crisis of the Negro Intellectual (1967) and Rebellion or Revolution (1968). The most sweeping, absorbing, and authoritative account of the civil rights movement is T. Branch, Parting the Waters: America in the King Years, 1954–63 (1988). It should be supplemented by the television series, Eyes on the Prize, available on 14 video cassettes from PBS Video. See also R. Weisbrot, Freedom Bound: A History of America's Civil Rights Movement (1989); H. Sitkoff, The Struggle for Black Equality 1954–1980 (1980); A. Meier and E. Rudwick, Along the Color Line (1976) and CORE 1942–1968 (1973); H. Zinn, SNCC: The New Abolitionists (1964); W. H. Chafe, Civilities and Civil Rights: Greensboro, North Carolina, and the Black Struggle for Freedom (1979); D. Garrow, Protest at Selma (1978); and C. Carson, In Struggle: SNCC and the Black Awakening of the 1960s (1981) and D. McAdam, Freedom Summer (1988). For a retrospective view, see J. Farmer, Lay Bare the Heart: An Autobiography of the Civil Rights Movement (1985) and R. D. Abernathy, And The Walls Came Tumbling Down: An

Autobiography (1989). On Martin Luther King, Jr., see T. Branch, *Parting the Waters* (1988), D. L. Lewis, *King* (1970), and D. J. Garrow, *Bearing the Cross: Martin Luther King, Jr., and the Southern Christian Leadership Conference* (1986). H. Raines, *My Soul Is Rested* (1977), is an excellent oral history of the movement. J. H. Bracey, Jr., A. Meier, and E. Rudwick (eds.), *Black Nationalism in America* (1970), is a collection of documents. See also E. U. Essien-Udom, *Black Nationalism* (1962); C. E. Lincoln, *The Black Muslims in America* (1961); and the works of Malcolm X cited above. On racial violence, see R. Conot, *Rivers of Blood, Years of Darkness* (1967), for the Watts riot, and J. Hersey, *The Algiers Motel Incident* (1968), for the Detroit riot. Two valuable anthologies of black literature are A. Chapman (ed.), *New Black Voices* (1972), and L. Jones and L. Neal (eds.), *Black Fire* (1968). See also R. Ellison's powerful novel *Invisible Man* (1952) and his essays, *Shadow and Act* (1964) and *Going to the Territory* (1986). On black America in the 1970s, a powerful oral history is J. L. Gwaltney, *Drylongso* (1980).

There is a growing literature on the Mexican American. A good place to start is C. McWilliams, *North from Mexico* (1948). This may be updated with M. S. Meier and F. Rivera, *The Chicanos* (1972); S. Steiner, *La Raza* (1970); W. Moquin (ed.), *A Documentary History of the Mexican-Americans* (1971); A. Mirande and E. Enriquez, *La Chicana: The Mexican-American Woman* (1980); and R. Acuna, *Occupied America: A History of Chicanos* (2nd ed., 1980); D. Montejano, *Anglos and Mexicans in the Making of Texas, 1836–1986* (1987); and C. Munoz, Jr., *Youth, Identity, Power: The Chicano Movement* (1989). On Cesar Chavez and the farm workers' movement, see J. London and H. Anderson, *So Shall Ye Reap* (1970); P. Matthiessen, *Sal Si Puedes* (1969); R. B. Taylor, *Chavez and the Farm Workers* (1975); and J. E. Levy, *Cesar Chavez: Autobiography of La Causa* (1975).

The foreign policy of the Johnson presidency is critically examined in P. Geyelin, *Lyndon B. Johnson and the World* (1966); T. Draper, *Abuse of Power* (1967); J. W. Fulbright, *The Arrogance of Power* (1967); and I. F. Stone, *Time of Torment* (1967). For a vigorous defense, see W. W. Rostow, *The Diffusion of Power* (1972). On the intervention in the Dominican Republic, see T. Draper, *The Dominican Revolt* (1968), and A. F. Lowenthal, *The Dominican Intervention* (1972). The relationship between militarism and economic life is assessed in J. L. Clayton (ed.), *The Economic Impact of the Cold War* (1970).

The most compelling account of the War in Vietnam is M. Herr, *Dispatches* (1977), a savage, impressionistic memoir by a reporter. N. Sheehan, *A Bright Shining Lie: John Paul Vann and America in Vietnam* (1988) is a brilliant exploration of the conflict, focusing on an Army careerist who entered the war in 1962 as one of the earliest American military "advisers." The war is vividly depicted in the documentary film, *Hearts and Minds* (1975) and in the photography of D. D. Duncan,

War Without Heroes (1972). For the views of the participants, two useful anthologies, H. Maurer, *Strange Ground: Americans in Vietnam, 1945–1975: An Oral History* (1989) and J. V. B. and J. Dann (eds.), *In The Field of Fire* (1987), may be supplemented by R. Kovic, *Born on the Fourth of July* (1976), the autobiography of a former Marine sergeant wounded in Vietnam, and P. Caputo, *A Rumor of War* (1977). R. Stone, *Dog Soldiers* (1975), is a novel that explores parallels between the war and the home front. The literature on Vietnam implicates not one but several administrations. *The Pentagon Papers* (1971) is an indispensable source. The best introduction to American involvement is G. C. Herring, *America's Longest War* (rev. ed., 1986). See also, in addition to the works cited in previous chapters, S. Karnow, *Vietnam* (1983); M. G. Raskin and B. Fall (eds.), *The Vietnam Reader* (1965); G. Kolko, *Anatomy of a War: Vietnam, the United States, and the Modern Historical Experience* (1985); G. D. Moss, *Vietnam: An American Ordeal* (1990); M. E. Gettleman and others (eds.), *Vietnam and America: A Documented History* (1985); J. P. Kimball (ed.), *To Reason Why: The Debate About the Causes of U.S. Involvement in the Vietnam War* (1990); and W. Brown, *The Last Chopper: The Denouement of the American Role in Vietnam 1963–1975* (1976). The deepening involvement of the United States during the Kennedy, Johnson, and Nixon administrations is also examined in F. Fitzgerald, *Fire in the Lake* (1972); D. Halberstam, *The Making of a Quagmire* (1965) and *The Best and the Brightest* (1972); R. Shaplen, *The Road from War: Vietnam 1965–1971* (1971); and J. C. Goulden, *Truth Is the First Casualty: The Gulf of Tonkin Affair—Illusion and Reality* (1969).

Guenter Lewy, *America in Vietnam* (1978), is a defense of American behavior. For the view of "insiders," see C. L. Cooper, *The Lost Crusade: America in Vietnam* (1970); T. Hoopes, *The Limits of Intervention* (1969); M. Taylor, *Swords and Ploughshares* (1972); and Rostow, *The Diffusion of Power*. On the tragic consequences of American involvement, see especially F. Harvey, *Air War—Vietnam* (1967); C. Mydans and S. Mydans, *The Violent Peace* (1968); R. Hammer, *One Morning in the War: The Tragedy at Son My* (1971); S. Hersh, *My Lai 4: A Report on the Massacre and Its Aftermath* (1970) and *Cover Up* (1972) and J. Schell, *The Real War: The Classic Reporting on the Vietnam War* (1987). On dissent, the classic account is N. Mailer, *The Armies of the Night* (1968). See also D. Wakefield, *Supernation at Peace and War* (1968), and A. Kendrick, *The Wound Within* (1974). For personal accounts of the war, see the literature cited for Chapter 33.

Two contrasting views of the 1968 election are T. H. White, *The Making of the President 1968* (1969), and L. Chester, G. Hodgson, and B. Page, *An American Melodrama* (1969). See also N. Mailer, *Miami and the Siege of Chicago* (1968); J. McGinniss, *The Selling of the President 1968* (1969); and R. M. Scammon and B. J. Wattenberg, *The Real Majority* (1970).

THE POLITICS OF RIGHTEOUSNESS: NIXON AND CARTER

Toward the end of his administration, President Jimmy Carter thought it necessary to convene a domestic summit conference on the state of the nation. For six days in July 1979, he conferred at his Camp David retreat with cabinet members, political and civic leaders, bankers, clergymen, corporation executives, university professors and presidents, trade unionists, and economists. He also ventured into several nearby communities to talk with middle-class families about what troubled them. It was an unprecedented attempt by a president to assess his own leadership and the national mood.

The concerns that prompted such an assessment were clear enough—an energy and environmental crisis, inflation and unemployment, economic stagnation and an eroding standard of living, a hostile and revolutionary world, and public opinion polls that revealed a loss of confidence in the ability of the president to meet these challenges.

These concerns had dominated most of the decade. Some ten years earlier, Richard M. Nixon, in his inaugural address, had

acknowledged the deepening mood of desperation in the United States. He described a nation "rich in goods, but ragged in spirit; reaching with magnificent precision for the moon, but falling into raucous discord on earth. . . . We are torn by division, wanting unity. We see around us empty lives, wanting fulfillment." He then invoked the familiar political promise to unite the nation and rally it around the proper goals: "To a crisis of the spirit, we need an answer of the spirit."

Nixon's attempt to unite the American people and regenerate them spiritually ended in abuses of public power unprecedented in the history of the nation. His successors—Jerry Ford and Jimmy Carter—restored honesty and integrity to the presidency.

But Americans remained deeply troubled by problems that seemed to defy solution. Raised on the gospel of progress, few wanted to be told that there were limits to the nation's capacities, powers, and natural resources; that they must lower their expectations and aspirations; that they would need to exercise self-discipline and be prepared to make sacrifices. Nor did Americans accommodate easily to recession, inflation, and unemployment, polluted air and water, deteriorating neighborhood services and rising crime rates, new tax burdens, and the declining quality of public education.

Feeling helpless to control their lives and destinies, Americans turned to various remedies, not all of them political. The 1970s came to be called the Me Decade, and best-seller lists were dominated by books on the pleasures of self-improvement and self-awareness, books on how to make oneself more powerful and wealthy, and books on how to refurbish one's body and psyche. Spectator sports reached new heights of popularity, as did individualized forms of recreation such as jogging. Many Americans satisfied their emotional and spiritual hunger by becoming "born-again" or by embracing one of the new religious cults.

In the same decade, many women experienced a self-awareness that went beyond psychological fulfillment. Inspired by the civil rights movement of the previous decade, they sought to free themselves from demeaning cultural stereotypes, job and wage discrimination, and sexual harassment. Women made impressive gains in professions and occupations once the exclusive domain of men, and they achieved reforms in abortion laws. But the women's rights movement faced strong resistance as well, both from women themselves and from the many men who were hostile to changes in traditional female roles.

Watergate, Vietnam, and the Iranian hostage crisis cast their shadows over much of the seventies. Lacking any real parallel in the past, they proved to be bitter and emotionally draining experiences, perceived by most people as part of a collective failure. Even as Americans sought ways to improve themselves individually, they needed reassurance about the nation's moral fiber, power, virility, and destiny. Presidents Nixon, Ford, and Carter failed to provide those reassurances. That failure would be effectively exploited in 1980 by Ronald Reagan.

RICHARD NIXON IN POWER

The cut of Richard Nixon's clothes defined the image he wanted to convey: they were neat and well tailored, with the creases in place and the tie properly knotted. The American flag he wore in his lapel exalted his patriotism. He surrounded himself with aides who shared the qualities he most admired. They were tough-minded, clean-cut, ambitious, hardworking. If at times they appeared to be cold and devoid of imagination or vision, they more than compensated for these flaws with unswerving loyalty and a grasp of what had to be done. "I'll approve of whatever will work," White House chief of staff H. R. Haldeman promised, "and [I] am concerned with results— not methods." That promise set the tone for the Nixon presidency.

Nixon had always prided himself on his ability to know what people wanted. He claimed to understand the sources of their fears and frustrations. He felt in touch with the prevailing mood. The America that had elected him, as Nixon viewed that "silent majority," had grown weary of mounting welfare rolls crammed with chiselers,

federal intervention in state and community affairs, soft and overindulgent judges, and moral permissiveness. "As long as Richard Nixon is President," Vice-President Agnew promised, "Main Street is not going to turn into Smut Alley." The quietness in Washington promised a welcome release of tensions, gratifying not only to the silent majority but to others as well.

Retreat from Liberalism

The reluctance of the Nixon administration to press school desegregation in the face of local resistance reflected the president's sense of the national mood. In October 1970, the U.S. Commission on Civil Rights reported that "a major breakdown" in the enforcement of civil rights legislation had occurred, for which the federal government bore principal responsibility. The president was undisturbed by this finding. He knew his constituents well, and he no doubt knew of the public opinion polls that showed some 78 percent of the people opposed to the idea of busing schoolchildren to effect racial integration. Most of these people, including many Democrats who had not voted for him, applauded the president's recommendation that school-busing orders by federal courts be set aside until an alternative solution could be found.

This was an issue by no means confined to the South; it aroused strong emotions and resistance elsewhere in the nation. By the mid-1970s, the South had, in fact, achieved more racial integration than the North, and the most violent confrontations over busing were taking place in Boston. The "neighborhood school" acquired a halo that made it a convenient rallying point for those who wished to hold on to past racial patterns.

Vacancies on the Supreme Court gave the president the opportunity to redeem his campaign promise to appoint "strict-constructionist" justices and to satisfy the southern constituency that had made his election possible. Nixon's selection of Warren E. Burger of Minnesota to replace Earl Warren as chief justice was confirmed by the Senate in June 1969. But the president's move to name a southerner to the Court led to confrontation with the Senate. The dispute had less to do with the regional background of the nominees than with Nixon's selection of mediocrities with highly questionable records.

The Senate rejected Clement F. Haynesworth, Jr., of South Carolina largely for his carelessness in conflict-of-interest cases. Shocked by this setback, Nixon next chose G. Harrold Carswell of Florida. Carswell too proved vulnerable, for his racial record as well as for his professional competence. Nor did a Republican senator help Carswell's cause when he observed "that even if he were mediocre, there are a lot of mediocre judges and people and lawyers. Aren't they entitled to a little representation and a little chance? We can't have all Brandeises and Cardozos and Frankfurters and stuff like that. I doubt we can. I doubt we want to."

When the Senate rejected Carswell as unfit, Nixon nominated Harry A. Blackmun of Minnesota, whom the Senate unanimously confirmed. When a new vacancy occurred, the president appointed a southerner, Lewis F. Powell of Virginia, a competent, conservative jurist; the Senate likewise had no difficulty in approving this nomination.

Economic Game Plans

The president's proposal for *revenue sharing* between federal and state governments became the avowed keystone of his domestic program. With some 10 million Americans on welfare rolls in 1969, Nixon hoped to clean up the "welfare mess" by shifting the burden of payments from the states to the federal government. At the same time, he startled some of his more conservative backers by recommending that the welfare system be replaced with a family-assistance program. This program would include a guaranteed minimum income of $1600 a year for a family of four; food stamps would add another $820 to this sum. The amount was hardly sufficient, but the establishment of such a principle would be significant. The measure, however, died in Congress.

Depending on which economist or government expert made the assessment, recession or depression had overtaken the American economy by mid-1970. To check the inflationary spiral, President Nixon sought tighter money policies and a reduction in federal spending. But prices continued to rise. At the same time, unemployment, especially among the underprivileged and the young, added significantly to the cost of welfare. The overexpanded war industries were hard hit by the declining American involvement in Vietnam. Educated, middle-income technicians and engineers suddenly found themselves out of work and competing for jobs in a glutted market.

Since 1893, the United States had enjoyed a favorable balance of trade with foreign nations. But in 1971 the money paid out for international debts exceeded the money taken in by overseas sales. This added still another dimension to domestic economic difficulties.

In his game plan for reversing the inflationary surge, Nixon rejected as "unworkable" Democratic proposals for wage and price controls. But as the maneuvering for the 1972 elections intensified, Nixon ordered a ninety-day wage–price freeze. Once the freeze ended, a pay board and a price commission would have the authority to rule on wage and price increases. To regain American markets abroad, the president also declared virtual economic warfare on other industrial nations. His strategy here included taking the dollar off the gold standard, hoping that devaluation would cut the cost of American exports in terms of foreign currencies.

The business community gave the president's New Economic Policy a resounding vote of confidence. But labor leaders, distressed by the omission of a profit freeze, militantly opposed the wage freeze. For the tens of millions of unemployed, there was little relief or hope in the new policy. Joblessness among black youth, for example, soared over 40 percent in the summer of 1971. Structural unemployment, once limited to a few declining industries, such as coal mining in Appalachia and textile manufacture in New England, had by now spread to most central cities. Its predominantly racial character had made it a social as well as an economic issue.

Even as hard times settled on the nation, the American people enjoyed the dividends of a long-term government investment in space conquest. Only six months after entering the White House, President Nixon could boast of a masterful achievement by the United States—the first successful manned space mission to the moon.

Apollo 11 was launched on July 16, 1969. Four days later, its lunar module came down on a rock-strewn plain on the moon's Sea of Tranquility. When Neil Armstrong set foot on the moon's surface, he declared: "That's one small step for a man, one giant leap for mankind." While astronaut Michael Collins remained at the control of *Apollo* in lunar orbit, astronauts Armstrong and Edwin E. Aldrin, Jr., planted the American flag on the moon, installed a scientific station that would operate long after their departure, and collected samples of soil and rock. They then returned to *Apollo* and flew home to Earth, where they were greeted as heroes.

The Apollo 11 mission demonstrated the superiority of American technology and boosted the prestige of the United States in the world. But the persistent war in Vietnam continued to undermine that prestige while making greater demands on the technology and on American labor.

THE PRESIDENT AT WAR

Foreign affairs became the principal concern of Nixon's first administration. During the 1968 campaign, he ventured the opinion that the nation "could run itself domestically without a President. All you want is a competent Cabinet to run the country at home. You need a President for foreign policy; no Secretary of State is really important. The President makes foreign policy."

In foreign affairs, Henry A. Kissinger and his White House staff of 110 overshadowed not only Secretary of State William P. Rogers and the 11,000 State Department employees, but the Department of Defense and the National Security Council as well. Both as special assistant for national security affairs and later as secretary of state, Kissinger preferred secret diplomacy.

The foreign policy constructed by Nixon and Kissinger recognized that the Communist world was no longer unified. The growing tension between the Soviet Union and China underscored that recognition. Even as the United States pressed the war in Vietnam, it sought improved relations with both major Communist powers based on mutual acceptance of the prevailing balance of power. "It will be a safer world and a better world," said Nixon, "if we have a strong, healthy United States, Europe, Soviet Union, China, Japan—each balancing the other, not playing one against the other, an even balance."

At the same time, he made clear the willingness of the United States to "participate in the defense and development of allies and friends." But he preferred, he said, to leave the "basic responsibility" to those allies and friends, particularly when it came to military action. In Southeast Asia, however, that policy proved unworkable. Success eluded the United States—with tragic consequences.

Initiatives for Peace

Although Nixon entered the White House with the reputation of a hardened Cold Warrior, he took the initiative to thaw the Cold War and establish a stable world order based on détente with the Soviet Union and the People's Republic of China. In August 1971 he announced that he had accepted an invitation from Premier Chou En-lai to visit China. None of his initiatives revealed the president's turnabout more dramatically and elicited such excitement and anticipation.

The peace mission, as Nixon called it, came in February 1972 and resulted in mutual expressions of good will and agreements to settle differences peacefully and to expand trade and cultural relations. What few Democratic presidents might have risked, Nixon had achieved.

Committed to a strong defense establishment, Nixon moved cautiously in the sensitive area of disarmament. With the United States and the Soviet Union spending $130 billion annually for defense, the need for some kind of mutual limit on the balance of terror had long seemed desirable. Nixon agreed to enter strategic arms limitation (SALT) talks. To ensure the strongest possible bargaining position, however, he urged upon Congress a missile program designed to enlarge the already great strategic capacity of the United States.

Several months after his successful China mission, Nixon capped his détente diplomacy

Astronaut Buzz Aldrin, photographed on the moon by his *Apollo 11* partner, Commander Neil Armstrong. *(UPI/Bettman Newsphotos)*

with a trip to Moscow. On May 26, 1972, the president and Soviet premier Leonid Brezhnev agreed to limit the number of their countries' defensive missile sites and strategic offensive missiles.

The Middle East remained a source of tension. Lacking adequate guarantees of its security, Israel defied the 1967 United Nations resolution that called upon it to withdraw from territories occupied in the Six-Day War. The United States backed Israel with military aid and political support, while the Soviet Union helped arm Egypt and Syria. The continuing plight of Palestinian refugees and the demand for an independent Palestinian state complicated Kissinger's efforts to arrange a peace settlement among Egypt, Syria, and Israel.

In October 1973, hostilities again broke out as Egypt and Syria attacked Israel on the Jewish holy day of Yom Kippur. Both sides suffered heavy casualties, but Israel soon demonstrated its military superiority. The United Nations Security Council adopted a resolution that called for a cease-fire and peace negotiations based on its 1967 resolution. At the same time, the oil embargo imposed by the Arab nations impressed the entire world with the potential power of a unified bloc of oil-exporting nations. It raised havoc with available domestic supplies, sent gasoline prices skyrocketing, and made suddenly urgent the long-debated energy question.

But even as the Nixon administration tried to stabilize the Middle East and effect détente with the Soviets and Chinese, it needed to confront the continuing war in Southeast Asia.

Toward Vietnamization

Despite the Paris peace talks, the Vietnam War showed no signs of subsiding. As vice-president under Eisenhower, Nixon had urged military intervention to bolster the French position in Indochina. Subsequently he had supported the policies of Kennedy and Johnson, differing with them only in his willingness to maximize the military thrust. Sensing widespread war weariness, however, Nixon pledged during the 1968 election campaign to end the conflict on "honorable terms" and bring home the American prisoners of war.

At the time Nixon became president, United States troop strength in Vietnam had reached a peak of 542,500. The number of Americans killed in action was about to exceed the 33,639 killed in the Korean War. More bomb tonnage had been dropped on Vietnam than had been expended by the Allies on all of Europe during World War II. Moreover, the United States was spending more than $25 billion a year on what had become the most unpopular war in the nation's history.

The president relied considerably on the negotiating talents of Henry Kissinger, who had declared before joining the Nixon administration: "We fought a military war, our opponents fought a political one. We sought physical attrition; our opponents aimed for our psychological exhaustion. In the process we lost sight of one of the cardinal maxims of guerrilla war: the guerrilla wins if he does not lose. The conventional army loses if it does not win."

In June 1969, President Nixon announced his program for the Vietnamization of the war. By the end of August, he would bring home 25,000 American combat troops, who would be replaced by South Vietnamese contingents. The idea was simple: the United States would maintain military

Members of a South Vietnamese family struggle to escape from an aerial bombardment of their village. *(Kyoichi Sawada, UPI)*

pressure in the air; the South Vietnamese would assume the bulk of the casualties and fighting on the ground. There was nothing particularly new about Vietnamization; both Kennedy and Johnson had talked about the Vietnamese doing their own fighting. But it had not worked. How could a hopelessly corrupt and inefficient South Vietnamese government function without large-scale American assistance?

The War at Home

Having established his Vietnamization program, Nixon proceeded to step it up. But neither the pace of American withdrawal nor the progress of the war satisfied anyone. On October 15, 1969, hundreds of thousands across the country, most of them students and other young people, observed Vietnam Moratorium Day; it was the largest public protest since the war began. The most impressive of the antiwar demonstrations took place one month later in Washington, D.C., where more than 250,000 gathered. Outside the gates of the White House, some 40,000 participated in a March against Death, each holding a card with the name of an American killed in Vietnam.

The demonstrations had no apparent effect on the president. As if to underscore that fact, the White House announced that during the march, Nixon had been watching a football game on television. Convinced that the "great silent majority" stood behind him, the president lashed back at his critics: "North Vietnam cannot defeat or humiliate the United States. Only Americans can do that." He explained that the alternatives in Vietnam were to admit defeat and order an immediate and humiliating withdrawal, or to press the Vietnamization program and secure an honorable peace. When the choice was put that way, most Americans—some 77 percent, according to a Gallup poll—backed the president.

Nixon's response to war critics climaxed administration efforts to win public support. On Law Day, May 1, 1969, Attorney General John Mitchell warned that "the time has come for an end to patience" in dealing with student war dissenters. Vice-President Agnew charged that the disturbances had been instigated and manipulated by "an effete corps of impudent snobs who characterize themselves as intellectuals." Pleased with the response to this verbal offensive, Agnew became even bolder and attacked the media, singling out the "unelected elite" of "anchormen, commentators and executive producers," who "settle upon the 20 minutes or so of film and commentary that is to reach the public."

How Many My Lais?

The administration had good reason to be concerned with the television and press coverage of the war. The daily barrage of pictures and words constantly reminded the American public of the brutality and apparent futility of the conflict. Early in 1970, for example, the full details were revealed of an American attack in March 1968 on My Lai, a Vietnamese hamlet. Led by Lieutenant William L. Calley, Jr., a company of United States soldiers had massacred at least 175 and perhaps more than 500 Vietnamese, mostly old men, women, youths, and infants. The Army's official inquiry found the troops guilty of "individual and group acts of murder, rape, sodomy, maiming and assault on noncombatants and the mistreatment and killing of detainees."

The operation appeared to have been based on false intelligence reports and the difficulty of identifying Vietcong sympathizers. Women and children had been known to fire at unsuspecting American soldiers. "People were talking about killing everything that moved," one soldier remarked. "Everyone knew what we were going to do."

This was obviously not the kind of war Americans had been accustomed to fighting. Over nationwide television, a soldier described how they had entered the village: "We didn't see any VC. People began coming out of their hootches, and the guys shot them down and then burned the hootches or burned the hootches and shot the people when they came out. Sometimes they would round up a bunch and shoot them together. It went on like this all day." The lone American casualty had deliberately shot himself in the foot to avoid participating in the slaughter.

These startling revelations confirmed what many Americans had already suspected: the war had deteriorated into the kind of bloodbath the United States had initially intervened to prevent. Although wartime atrocities were hardly unique, the degree of American complicity in them disturbed a nation accustomed to seeing itself as civilized and decent. The conviction of Calley raised questions that were equally disturbing: Who bore ultimate responsibility? And was My Lai an isolated incident?

At his own trial, Calley's commander declared: "Every unit of brigade size had its My Lai hidden someplace." Moreover, the United States had long followed a policy of destroying hamlets suspected of harboring Vietcong guerrillas. Lieutenant Calley's platoon had simply performed that task with the thoroughness characteristic of the more impersonal aerial bombardment.

From "War by Tantrum" to "Peace with Honor"

On April 20, 1970, President Nixon announced that Vietnamization and the phased withdrawal of American troops were proceeding successfully. Within ten days, however, he ordered United States troops into neighboring Cambodia to clear out "enemy sanctuaries." Unknown to Congress or the American people, United States planes had already been bombarding Cambodia for over a year. The administration denied that the invasion was an undeclared war on an independent nation. It was not even an invasion, said the White House, but an "incursion" (a brief raid). By June 29, all American forces had been withdrawn, their objective presumably gained.

The casualties of the expanded war spread to the very heartland of America. College students responded to Nixon's latest move with massive protests that exceeded anything yet seen. Some schools were forced to close altogether, and disruptions hit colleges barely affected by previous protests. At Kent State University in Ohio, National Guardsmen called out during campus demonstrations fired into a crowd of students, killing four and wounding nine. Although Nixon deplored the incident, he reminded Americans "that when dissent turns to violence, it invites tragedy."

If the demonstrations were confined largely to campuses, the war weariness was not. Among American troops in Vietnam, it had begun to show itself in declining morale, insubordination, and increased use of narcotics. To fight this kind of war, some soldiers argued, it helped to be "stoned." In Congress, meanwhile, Republican senator Mark Hatfield of Oregon and Democratic senator George McGovern of South Dakota proposed to amend pending legislation so that all United States troops would be removed from Vietnam by the end of 1971. Although the Senate defeated the measure fifty-five to thirty-nine, the vote revealed growing skepticism and impatience in a body that had until now supported the policies of three administrations in Vietnam.

To speed up Vietnamization, President Nixon resumed full-scale bombing of North Vietnam in November 1970. Although the attacks were called "protective retaliation strikes," they amounted to the most massive aerial bombardment in history.

In February 1971, South Vietnamese forces invaded Laos in still another "incursion" designed to ferret out enemy forces and reduce the flow of supplies from North Vietnam into the South. Despite heavy American bombing support, however, the South Vietnamese were routed by Communist counterattacks. That debacle did little to advance the cause of Vietnamization.

In March 1972, Vietnamization suffered a serious setback when North Vietnamese and Vietcong forces launched a major offensive in the South. Nixon responded with saturation air raids on the North as well as an air and sea blockade. This action revived antiwar protest at home, but the White House reported mail favoring the president's policy by a five-to-one ratio. Not until much later was it learned that the Committee to Re-Elect the President had spent a good deal of money on bogus telegrams supporting Nixon.

Not long after Kissinger assured the world that agreement was near, the Paris negotiations again broke down. The president, reinforced by the large popular mandate he had received in the recent election, ordered B-52 bombers over Hanoi and other major northern cities in mid-December 1972. The assaults were massive, thorough, and round-the-clock. Neither hospitals and schools nor residential areas were spared. It had come to be, as one columnist put it, war by tantrum. Vietnamese casualties mounted, as did the number of American planes shot down and prisoners taken.

With both sides pressing for a settlement, intensive negotiations between Kissinger and Le Duc Tho of North Vietnam finally produced a cease-fire in late January 1973. United States troops would be withdrawn while North Vietnam was releasing American prisoners of war. "Peace with honor," the jubilant and relieved president announced, had finally been achieved. What remained questionable was the enormous price the United States had paid in waging the war and how long the peace could last.

With the Vietnam experience in mind, Congress moved to limit the power of the president to wage war without congressional approval. The War Powers Act provided that if the president should send troops to a foreign country, he must fully explain the action to Congress within forty-eight hours. Moreover, he was obliged to halt the operation within sixty days unless Congress thought otherwise. President Nixon angrily vetoed the measure, but the House and the Senate overrode the veto on November 7, 1973.

Earlier, in August, Congress had voted to deny the president the use of federal funds for military action in Cambodia, which the United States had continued to bomb in support of the war against Communist insurgents. In a "compromise," Nixon promised to stop the bombing on August 15, thereby ending United States military action in Southeast Asia.

The Election of 1972

While the war in Vietnam still raged, the Democratic convention of 1972 had nominated Senator George McGovern of South Dakota, an avowed antiwar candidate. That convention was unique in the history of the party. Changes in delegate selection had resulted in far greater representation of minority groups, women, and young people than in any previous party convention. The party's old guard, many deprived of their traditional seats as delegates, could only look on in dismay. The expanded role of young people reflected not only their stake in the Vietnam War, but also the Twenty-sixth Amendment to the Constitution (ratified on June 30, 1971), which lowered the voting age to eighteen.

If McGovern lacked the political savvy of the professional politician, he possessed an antiwar record and a commitment to social reform that attracted the party's new constituency. But his

Kent State University, May 4, 1970, after campus demonstrations against Nixon's expansion of the war into Cambodia were broken up by the Ohio National Guard. *(UPI/Bettmann Newsphotos)*

Reacting to student antiwar demonstrations, construction workers in New York City marched in support of the American war effort in Vietnam. *(UPI/Bettmann Newsphotos)*

nomination badly split the party, and the Republicans exploited domestic fears of radicalism. As *Time* magazine put it, Richard Nixon had decided to run against the sixties—"against radicalism, excess, permissiveness." McGovern was portrayed as an irresponsible leftist, committed to social reforms that would bankrupt the nation, to disarmament proposals that would endanger national security, and to an antiwar position that would result in a dishonorable peace. The contrast between the two candidates could not have been greater; the electorate had a uniquely clear-cut choice to make.

With so much at stake, the Committee to Re-Elect the President took nothing for granted, sparing neither funds nor constitutional and legal scruples. John Mitchell left his post as attorney general to take over command of the campaign. In his mind, the reelection of the president was nothing less than a matter of national survival. Endowed with a lavish campaign treasury (enriched by illegal corporate contributions), the committee was not above falsifying documents, forging letters, burglarizing confidential files, and gathering information on the private lives of opponents.

Its tactics were not altered by the assassination attempt on Governor George Wallace of Alabama, even though he was no longer a threat as a competing spokesman for conservative principles. The attack, which left Wallace permanently paralyzed, also ended his career as a national political figure.

The incumbent president rested on his record: the China mission, détente with the Soviet Union, and a Vietnamization program that had reduced the number of American casualties. McGovern campaigned on the peace issue. Just before the election, however, Kissinger said, "Peace is at hand," and the president assured the people it would be an honorable peace. McGovern called the Nixon administration "the most corrupt in history," but most Americans did not believe him. With 61 percent of the popular vote, Nixon won the victory he had coveted.

Shortly after Nixon's second inaugural, the Vietnam War ended in an uncertain truce. The president turned to mounting domestic problems. After his decision in early 1973 to substitute voluntary restraints for price and wage controls, the cost of living soared to new heights. In keeping with his political philosophy, Nixon tried to reduce federal spending, and the cuts came, predictably, at the expense of social programs. Even when Congress appropriated funds for such programs, the president often refused to spend the money, thereby redefining the constitutional relationship of Congress to the presidency.

Although Nixon had won a resounding mandate, he secluded himself from Congress and the public. Press conferences were infrequent. Despite his pledge to return "power to the people," the White House bureaucracy seemed more unapproachable than ever. The palace guard was headed by two men: John D. Ehrlichman, domestic-affairs adviser, and H. R. (Bob) Haldeman, White House chief of staff. They operated as the president's shield, controlled access to him, and placed loyalty to him above the law itself. With so much power in the hands of so few, abuses were no doubt inevitable. Few people thought them possible, and fewer still suspected their extent.

ABUSE OF POWER

From the beginning of the Nixon administration, the war in Vietnam and its escalation had sharply divided the American people. On college campuses and in the streets, antiwar demonstrations had grown more militant, as had the efforts to control them. Confronted with massive protests and disruptions, the Nixon administration came to view the opposition as a collection of conspirators made up of the president's traditional foes: liberals, intellectuals, and reporters. In mid-1970, the president endorsed a secret plan of intelligence operations so far-reaching and so clearly above the law that FBI director J. Edgar Hoover interceded to have it revoked. Nevertheless, a mood had been established in the White House that encouraged and justified, in the name of national security, clandestine activities infringing on the fundamental liberties of American citizens. *Time* magazine called it "a siege mentality."

The appropriate epitaph of the Nixon presidency was sounded quite inadvertently by John N. Mitchell, the president's former law partner and campaign manager and an avid champion of rigorous law enforcement. Shortly before assuming his post as attorney general, Mitchell suggested: "Watch what we do, not what we say." Less than halfway through Nixon's second term, what the American people saw and heard left them incredulous and dismayed.

Mitchell himself, among others, stood indicted on charges of conspiracy, obstruction of justice, and perjury. Through a series of events known collectively as Watergate, the public would be given an intimate glimpse of what went on in the privacy of the president's Oval Office. That was more than enough to destroy President Nixon's credibility, strip his administration of any moral authority, and pave the way for his downfall.

Break-in and Cover-up

On June 17, 1972, Frank Wills, a security guard at the elegant Watergate hotel-apartment-office complex in Washington, D.C., phoned the police to report suspicious activity. When the police arrived, they found five gloved men equipped with sophisticated electronic-surveillance devices and burglary tools in the headquarters of the Democratic party. Two of the suspects turned out to be employed by the Committee to Re-Elect the President (CREEP, as it would be called): James W. McCord, Jr., the committee's security officer and a former CIA wiretap expert, and G. Gordon Liddy, the committee's lawyer, a former FBI agent and White House consultant. Still another suspect, E. Howard Hunt, Jr., had been a former CIA agent and White House aide.

During the presidential campaign, the Democrats tried to make the most of the Watergate incident, but most Americans preferred to believe the official denials and explanations. Attorney General Mitchell said he had been "surprised and dismayed" by the Watergate burglary. President Nixon affirmed on August 29 "that no one in the White House staff, no one in this administration presently employed, was involved in this very bizarre incident."

The president knew better. He decided, as the nation would learn only later, to tell a calculated lie. New revelations would force him to repeat that lie on numerous occasions. The Watergate break-in proved to be part of a massive, deliberate, and illegally financed operation to sabotage the opposition's campaign and ensure the reelection of Richard Nixon. Only a few persons in the White House knew all the details of the operation. The arrest of the Watergate burglars prompted those officials to immediately cover their tracks by destroying relevant evidence, paying hush money to the defendants, and lying to the grand jury of the District of Columbia.

The burglary itself infuriated the president. But a full probe of the affair, he realized, might reveal too much about White House intelligence operations and implicate several of his closest advisers, including John Mitchell. Less than a week after the break-in, President Nixon agreed to the first stage of a cover-up. Using the pretext of national security, he instructed the CIA to intercede with the FBI to stop any further investigation of Watergate. By June 23, 1972, President Nixon had become a coconspirator in the criminal obstruction of justice.

When a grand jury indicted the Watergate Seven, Nixon was relieved, believing the case would proceed no further. The cover-up appeared to be working smoothly. But then came the trial, and by March 22, 1973, Nixon was no longer so certain. On that day, the president summoned John Mitchell, H. R. Haldeman, John Ehrlichman, and John Dean (his chief legal counsel) to the Oval Office. "I don't give a shit what happens," he told them. "I want you all to stonewall it, let them plead the Fifth Amendment, cover up or anything else if it'll save it—save the plan. That's the whole point."

What suddenly confronted the president in March 1973 was a bewildering range of options, all of them fraught with danger. He could reveal the full particulars of White House involvement, and thereby open "a can of worms." He could offer up some sacrifices, even Mitchell, without implicating himself. He could maintain the deception. The president opted for the continued cover-up, even if that required blackmail money to maintain the silence of the Watergate defendants. To reveal the truth was to invite certain trouble. "There is a certain domino situation here," Dean warned Nixon. "If some things start going, a lot of other things are going to start going. . . ."

Revelations and Purges

The trial of the Watergate burglars opened in early 1973. It proved to be brief. Five of the defendants pleaded guilty to wiretapping, burglary, and attempted bugging; two others—McCord and Liddy—were convicted by a jury. If the White House had had its way, the entire Watergate affair would have ended at that point. But before imposing sentences, John J. Sirica, the presiding judge, read the court a letter from McCord charging that highly placed White House advisers had known in advance of the break-in and that perjury had been committed during the trial.

The cover-up appeared to be coming apart. McCord revealed everything he knew to a grand

---

IN THE OVAL OFFICE

On September 15, 1972, President Nixon congratulated his chief legal counsel, John W. Dean, for his adroitness in handling the Watergate scandal, "putting your fingers in the dikes every time that leaks have sprung here and sprung there." As if the president had learned nothing from his recent experience, he then proceeded to discuss with Dean the need to move against their political enemies. His overwhelming electoral victory in November reinforced such designs.

PRESIDENT: I think we are going to fix the son-of-a-bitch. Believe me. We are going to. We've got to, because he's a bad man.

DEAN: Absolutely . . . one of the things I've tried to do, is just keep notes on a lot of the people who are emerging as,

PRESIDENT: That's right.

DEAN: as less than our friends.

PRESIDENT: Great.

DEAN: Because this is going to be over some day and they're—We shouldn't forget the way some of them have treated us.

PRESIDENT: I want the most, I want the most

comprehensive notes on all of those that have tried to do us in. Because they didn't have to do it.

DEAN: That's right.

PRESIDENT: They didn't have to do it. I mean, if the thing had been a clo—uh, they had a very close election, everybody on the other side would understand this game. But now they are doing this quite deliberately and they are asking for it and they are going to get it. And this, this—We, we have not used the power in this first four years, as you know.

DEAN: That's right.

PRESIDENT: We have never used it. We haven't used the Bureau [FBI] and we haven't used the Justice Department, but things are going to change now. And they're going to change, and, and they're going to get it right—

DEAN: That's an exciting prospect.

PRESIDENT: It's got to be done. It's the only thing to do.

HALDEMAN: We've got to.

Source: Transcripts of Eight Recorded Presidential Conversations: Hearings before the Committee on the Judiciary, House of Representatives, 93rd Cong. 2nd Sess., 1974.

jury, implicating others who in turn would soon be called to testify. With federal prosecutors closing in on his principal aides, the president publicly announced on April 17 that he had ordered "intensive new inquiries" into the Watergate case and that no one in his administration would be immune from prosecution. The president indicated too that not until March 21 had he learned of any attempts to cover up the scandal. Again, the president had taken refuge in a lie.

The public statement appeared to satisfy no one. And with John Dean now talking to federal prosecutors, the "scenarios" previously worked out had to be scrapped. On April 30, the president went on nationwide television—the first of several such appearances relating to Watergate—to affirm his innocence and his determination to bring the guilty to justice and "maintain the integrity of the White House." More dramatically, he announced the resignations of his key advisers and legal counsel—Haldeman, Ehrlichman, and Dean. He would, at the same time, replace Attorney General Richard Kleindienst with Elliot Richardson and authorize Richardson to appoint a special prosecutor to investigate Watergate.

Even as Nixon announced the departure of Haldeman and Ehrlichman, he praised them to the American people as "two of the finest public servants it has been my privilege to know." Such praise, coupled with forced resignations, obviously raised more questions than it answered.

The Ellsberg Case

The tentacles of Watergate reached out in unexpected directions. In June 1971, Daniel Ellsberg, a Defense Department analyst, had released to the press the classified Pentagon Papers, which documented the origins of United States involvement in Vietnam. Although they revealed the policies of previous presidents, the disclosures embarrassed the Nixon administration by showing that there were potentially dangerous leaks within the government. The Supreme Court denied the administration's attempt to block publication of the papers. But the government did indict Ellsberg for theft, conspiracy, and espionage.

At the same time, the president authorized the formation within the White House of a special investigation unit known as the Plumbers. While the Ellsberg trial was pending, the Plumbers broke into the office of Ellsberg's psychiatrist to search for material that would "nail the guy cold." Upon learning of the break-in and illegal

government wiretaps, the presiding judge at the Ellsberg trial dismissed the case. By this time, several other pertinent facts had come to light: (1) two Watergate conspirators had also been involved in the burglary of Ellsberg's psychiatrist's office; (2) White House aide John Ehrlichman had approved the covert operation, and had instructed the CIA deputy director to provide any necessary technical assistance; (3) while the trial was in progress, Ehrlichman had sounded out the presiding judge on becoming the new director of the FBI.

On May 22, 1973, President Nixon publicly acknowledged that he had authorized wiretapping in the interest of national security, had established a White House intelligence unit under the supervision of Ehrlichman, and had instructed it to "find out all it could about Mr. Ellsberg's associates and his motives." He had not, however, condoned "any illegal means," though he understood "how highly motivated individuals could have felt justified in engaging" in such activities. Turning to Watergate, Nixon declared that he had never had any "intent" or "wish" to impede an investigation of the break-in, nor had he tried to use the CIA for that purpose.

Crisis of Credibility

The summer of 1973 proved to be a turning point. On May 17, 1973, the Senate Watergate Committee (as it came to be called), headed by Senator Sam J. Ervin, Jr., of North Carolina, began public hearings. Millions of television viewers across the country witnessed a mountain of testimony revealing an ugly record of deception and political sabotage carried out by the highest echelons of the White House. Several witnesses, most spectacularly John Dean, implicated themselves, top White House aides, and the president.

The hearings outdid any of the soap operas their television coverage had displaced. During that summer the American people learned for the first time of hush money paid to the Watergate defendants, top-level discussions of executive clemency, destruction of evidence, complicity of top aides in the cover-up, and the way the break-in fitted into a pattern of political subversion. Nixon aides, moreover, had tried unsuccessfully to use the Internal Revenue Service and the threat of tax audits to harass individuals thought to be hostile to the president.

With each new revelation, the credibility crisis escalated and the president's support eroded. The question was no longer whether a conspiracy had existed, but how far it extended and how many in the White House it involved. On August 15, the president reaffirmed his innocence to a nation-wide television audience. Although he accepted "full responsibility" for the actions of his subordinates, he claimed to have been grossly misinformed by them. "Not only was I unaware of any cover-up, I was unaware there was anything to cover up."

The Undoing of Spiro Agnew

The Watergate scandal had in no way implicated Vice-President Agnew, who had been second only to Nixon in his moral preachments on law and order and in his attacks on "permissiveness" in the courts and the "coddling" of criminals. But even as Agnew expressed "total confidence in the President's integrity," serious questions were raised about his own. He found himself under investigation for bribery, extortion, conspiracy, and tax evasion. Finally he was charged with extorting bribes from contractors, first while a Maryland county official and then as governor, in exchange for influencing the awarding of government contracts.

Agnew protested his innocence. But with evidence of criminal conspiracy and graft mounting, the vice-president opted on October 10, 1973, to secure immunity from further criminal prosecution and thereby escape a prison term. After bargaining with the Justice Department, he pleaded no contest to lesser charges of tax fraud and resigned as vice-president. The court fined him $10,000 and placed him on three years' probation. At the same time, the Justice Department released an exhaustive summary of his illegal activities. It marked the first time a vice-

president had been forced from office as a convicted criminal.

To succeed Agnew, Nixon selected Gerald R. Ford, a veteran Michigan congressman and the House minority leader. Almost immediately, Ford toured the country in defense of Nixon, seeking to restore confidence in the president's leadership.

The Saturday Night Massacre

Despite the Senate hearings, the extent of President Nixon's involvement in the Watergate cover-up remained debatable. Dean had implicated him, but Ehrlichman and Haldeman had backed up the president's contention that he knew nothing until March 21, 1973. Faced with such contradictory testimony, how would the truth ever be known? The answer came most unexpectedly. During the Senate inquiry, a former White House operations aide revealed that the president had installed secret recording devices in his office that automatically taped telephone calls and office conversations. Obviously, the Senate committee was anxious to hear those tapes, as was Archibald Cox, whom Attorney General Richardson had appointed as the special prosecutor in charge of the Watergate case. The tapes were essential to Cox's investigation, and he demanded access to them. The president, however, refused to turn them over, claiming the tapes were confidential and protected by executive privilege.

When Cox persisted, the president reached the end of his patience. Although he had no wish "to intrude upon the independence of the special prosecutor," Nixon ordered Cox to make no further attempts to secure records of presidential conversations. On October 20, Cox refused to accept the order and prepared to take the matter to the courts. The president, in turn, ordered Attor-

---

NAMES AND WORDS IN AMERICAN HISTORY

Today the words *haze* and *hazing* can refer to the weather or to procedures for initiating people into a group such as a college fraternity. When referring to the weather, *haze* suggests a quality of light and a smoky or dusty-looking fog that obscures long-distance viewing. Originally the term was nautical, referring to poor but not bad visibility accompanying calm seas. Aboard sailing ships, these conditions often led to spare time and thus the opportunity for more experienced members of the crew to initiate new hands into proper onboard behavior. As a young

man from Boston wrote about his first sea voyage (around Cape Horn to California), "Every shifting of the studding-sails was only to 'haze' the crew." He added that " 'haze' is a word of frequent use on board ship, and never, I believe, used elsewhere. It . . . means to punish by hard work." The selection is from Richard Henry Dana's *Two Years before the Mast,* published in 1840. Hazing on college campuses has sometimes gotten drastically out of hand, but few people today, including students and deans, are aware of the maritime origins of the term.

ney General Richardson to fire Cox. Richardson refused, as did the deputy attorney general, and both men resigned their positions. Finally, on Saturday night, the solicitor general carried out the president's order.

The public reacted with outrage. Leading newspapers demanded the president's resignation, and for the first time in more than a century the House Judiciary Committee launched an inquiry to determine if there were adequate grounds for impeachment. If only to weather this fire storm, Nixon agreed to turn over the subpoenaed tapes to Judge Sirica and to appoint a new special prosecutor and provide him with whatever materials he needed.

Toward Impeachment

Despite Nixon's attempts to mobilize public support, the scandal gained momentum and reached closer to the president himself. In March 1974, a grand jury indicted three of Nixon's most intimate associates—Haldeman, Ehrlichman, and Mitchell—and four other White House aides on charges of conspiracy, obstruction of justice, and perjury. Although it was not yet publicly known, the grand jury also named an "unindicted coconspirator"— President Nixon. (The new special prosecutor, Leon Jaworski, had told the grand jury that the indictment of a president was most likely unconstitutional.)

Meanwhile, new charges were brought against the president, including illegal income tax deductions and the expenditure of public funds to improve his Florida and California estates. Nixon appeared to be under siege. At one point, the American people were presented with the sad spectacle of their president assuring them in a televised press conference, "I am not a crook."

On April 30, 1974, Nixon took his case to the people in still another television address. With pressure mounting on him to provide additional tapes, he declared his intention to make public 1254 pages of transcribed tape recordings containing "all the relevant" White House conversations about Watergate. This dramatic action, he assumed, would finally resolve the controversy. There was nothing else to disclose, Nixon insisted, and he was certain that the contents of the released tapes, although at times embarrassing, would reveal his innocence.

Rather than calm the storm, the edited transcripts of White House conversations eroded the

Appearing on nationwide television to resign his position, Nixon declared, "In all the decisions I have made in my public life, I have always tried to do what was best for the Nation." *(UPI/Bettman Newsphotos)*

president's support still further. Whatever the context in which they were read, they did nothing to instill confidence in the president's leadership or truthfulness. The transcripts, moreover, contained sufficient ambiguities and contradictions to raise more questions than they answered. The president had not, as he had assured the public, revealed all the relevant information. In refusing to turn over additional tapes to the House Judiciary Committee and Special Prosecutor Jaworski, Nixon argued that to do so would only "prolong the impeachment inquiry without yielding significant additional evidence." The president knew that this was not true.

While the Supreme Court readied its judgment on Nixon's refusal to provide additional materials, the House Judiciary Committee proceeded with its impeachment investigation. On July 30, 1974, after months of private and public hearings, the committee, with the support of several of its Republican members, adopted three articles of impeachment. The president was accused of obstructing justice, violating his oath of office, abusing his presidential powers, subverting the constitutional rights of citizens, and willfully disobeying lawful subpoenas for White House records and tapes. It appeared almost certain that the House would sustain the committee's recommendations, impeach the president, and thereby set the stage for a trial in the Senate.

The Downfall

The climax was sudden and spectacular. By August 1, 1974, Nixon's credibility was nil, his state of mind suspect. He had virtually sealed himself off from the outside world. Adding to his troubles, the Supreme Court on July 24 had unanimously ruled that executive privilege could not be invoked to withhold evidence needed for a criminal trial and had ordered Nixon to turn over the additional subpoenaed tapes to the special prosecutor. On August 5, the president agreed to release the new material, which revealed beyond any question his direct involvement in the cover-up and in a criminal obstruction of justice. Nixon conceded that he had withheld relevant evidence from the House Judiciary Committee as well as from his own lawyers, and that the newly released tapes were "at variance with certain of my previous statements."

With these final revelations of criminal wrongdoing, the Nixon presidency lay in shambles. Even his supporters on the House Judiciary Committee, confronted now with evidence of statutory crime, reversed their positions and made the vote recommending impeachment unanimous. Republican leaders in the House and Senate advised the president that he would be impeached and convicted. Rather than face this prospect, Richard Nixon went on television on August 8 to announce his resignation. He was the first president in American history to do so.

Less than two years after he won reelection by as huge a margin as any in the nation's history, Nixon departed from the White House in defeat and humiliation, still facing the prospect of criminal prosecution. In his final message to the people, Nixon admitted to no serious wrongdoing, only to exercising poor judgment, and he showed no remorse. He had acted, he insisted, "in what I believed at the time to be in the best interests of the nation."

The Legacy of Watergate

While Nixon was en route to his San Clemente, California, estate, Gerald Ford took the oath of office. "Our long national nightmare is over," he declared. Nearly one month later, President Ford moved to heal the nation's wounds and to avoid the spectacle of a former president under criminal indictment. On September 8, he granted Nixon "full, free, and absolute pardon . . . for all offenses against the United States which he . . . has committed or may have committed or taken part in" during his presidency.

Rather than end the nightmare, the pardon raised questions about a double standard of justice; the president had been permitted to stand above the law while those who carried out his orders were punished. President Ford's action only confirmed, said a United States senator, "what too many Americans already believe: that there is one set of laws for the rich and powerful, another set for everyone else." The pardon raised questions about "permissiveness" and "coddling" that Nixon himself had pressed on so many occasions. And it revived controversy over the government's refusal to grant similar amnesty to deserters and draft evaders during the Vietnam War.

Nixon's aides fared badly. On New Year's Day 1975, the jury returned its verdict in the Watergate conspiracy trial. Mitchell, Ehrlichman, and Haldeman were found guilty of conspiracy, obstruction of justice, and false testimony. Each was then sentenced to a prison term of from two and a half to eight years. Ehrlichman had previously been convicted for his part in the Ellsberg break-in.

By early 1975, nearly forty officials of the Nixon administration, including the vice-president, four cabinet officials, and top White House aides, had been named in criminal indictments. The criminal charges against Nixon's men in the White House presented a sorry record: obstruction of justice, fraud, extortion, burglary, perjury, illegal campaign activities, violation of campaign funding laws, illegal wiretapping, eavesdropping, destruction of evidence, and conspiracy to commit illegal acts. Along with the ending of the Vietnam War and détente with Red China and the Soviet Union, they would constitute the mixed legacy of the Nixon presidency.

Throughout his long political career, Richard Nixon had found it difficult to tolerate criticism or to admit defeat. His hatred of the media was matched only by the contempt he felt for many of his political enemies. Eventually, these obsessions consumed him and encouraged him to stand above the law and to violate his public trust. With the pardon and the convictions, the Watergate case came to an end. The lessons of Watergate, however, would persist, if only to remind the nation of the dangers of unbridled executive power and the possibilities for political abuses in the name of national security.

In the Name of National Security

Information made public during the Ford administration focused public attention on the two agencies entrusted with foreign and domestic surveillance—the Central Intelligence Agency and the Federal Bureau of Investigation. How obsession with internal security could result in gross violations of the constitutional rights of citizens was revealed in 1974 by the attorney general. Between 1956 and 1971, he reported, the FBI under J. Edgar Hoover had not only gathered data on suspect political groups but had tried to disrupt their activities.

The CIA as well had exceeded its legal mandate. In 1975 it was revealed that this agency had participated in various questionable operations. It had spent, for example, $8 million to assist the opponents of Salvador Allende, a Marxist who had come to power in Chile in a democratic election. (A rightist military coup toppled his government in 1973.) Although the National Security Act of 1947 had confined the CIA's espionage activities to foreign operations, the agency had conducted domestic surveillance. It had planted undercover agents in antiwar organizations, intercepted mail, engaged in illegal wiretaps and break-ins, and compiled intelligence files on some ten thousand American citizens, including members of Congress, antiwar critics, and civil rights leaders. Most of these operations took place during Johnson's administration and were based on his belief that hostile foreign governments might be actively supporting dissidents in the United States.

The American people were assured that such abuses of power would no longer be tolerated. The delicate balance between internal security and the constitutional rights of citizens, however, posed formidable questions for future generations of Americans.

THE FORD PRESIDENCY

The new president was personable, hardworking, and honest. To most Americans, these were attractive qualities after their recent political ex-

perience. On no issue—domestic or foreign—were there discernible differences between Ford and Nixon. Since 1949, when Ford was elected to the House, he had reflected the views of his conservative Michigan constituency. As House minority leader, he had won the respect of Democrats and Republicans, largely because of his amiability and even temper. He also possessed a candor and openness that reflected the confidence with which he voiced the views of Middle America: "It's the quality of the ordinary, the straight, the square that accounts for the great stability and success of our nation. It's a quality to be proud of."

Middle America in Power

After the exhausting Watergate ordeal, the good feelings that characterized the opening weeks of the Ford administration came as a relief. Ford's selection of Governor Nelson Rockefeller of New York as vice-president pleased Republican moderates. His regular consultations with Congress provided a welcome contrast with the infrequent appearances of his predecessor. His leniency program for Vietnam draft evaders and deserters reflected the national mood of reconciliation. But the Nixon pardon abruptly ended the political honeymoon, and the growing economic crisis provoked confrontations between Ford and a Democrat-controlled Congress.

Upon assuming office, Ford had declared war on inflation, calling it public enemy number one. The administration relied largely on fiscal restraint and tight monetary policies. By early 1975, however, the United States faced the grim prospect of the worst economic slump since the Great Depression and the highest percentage of joblessness in the work force since 1941. Although the inflation rate was reduced in the following year, unemployment and the high cost of living remained acute problems that neither the Democratic Congress nor the Republican president did much about.

Vietnam: End of an Era

The withdrawal of United States troops in early 1973 did not bring peace to Vietnam. The fighting continued, with both sides violating the truce. South Vietnam remained dependent on United States support—$3.8 billion in 1973 alone, almost all of it for military aid. The end came quickly and unexpectedly. In March 1975, President Nguyen Van Thieu of South Vietnam ordered his forces to abandon several outlying northern provinces (nearly one-fourth of the country) that had come under Communist attack. This "strategic withdrawal" turned into a headlong retreat. Within weeks, Communist troops were in the outskirts of Saigon, Thieu had fled the country along with thousands of refugees, the South Vietnamese army had lost its will to resist, and Congress refused to invest any additional funds. In late April, Saigon and the government fell.

The chaotic exodus from Saigon—the American ambassador escaped from the embassy roof by helicopter—gave evidence of the total collapse of a government having no basis of popular support. After thirty years of war and more than a decade of American military involvement, peace had finally come to Vietnam. At the same time, Cambodia fell under Communist control and Laos came under predominantly Communist influence.

With the fall of Indochina, an era in American history ended. Four American presidents had presided over United States intervention, some 56,000 Americans had died, more than 300,000 had been wounded, and $150 billion had been spent. In World War II, 50 percent of the casualties were civilians; in the Vietnam War, 90 percent. To Eisenhower, the future of Vietnam had assumed "a most terrible significance"; to Kennedy, Vietnam represented "the cornerstone of the Free World in Southeast Asia"; to Johnson, it was a question of confronting the Communists in Vietnam or having to face them in Hawaii or San Francisco; and to Nixon, Vietnam would be recorded in history as "one of America's finest hours." But in the end, the war's greatest significance was that it taught the United States a difficult lesson about the limits of its power.

The Bicentennial Election: 1976

On the occasion of America's two hundredth birthday, the nation's voters would be given the opportunity to decide who should lead them into the third century. Memories of Vietnam, Watergate, and the Nixon pardon reinforced popular suspicions of those in power. As the incumbent, Gerald Ford should have had no difficulty in securing the Republican nomination. But he had to mobilize all his political resources to defeat challenger Ronald Reagan, a former Hollywood actor and governor of California who had emerged as the spokesman of the Republican right wing.

Even as Ford nosed out Reagan for the nomination, with the support of the party's professional politicians, Reagan tightened his hold at the party's grass-roots level.

Among the many Democratic contenders, James (Jimmy) E. Carter, Jr., former governor of Georgia, was the least known. In the primaries, this Annapolis graduate, nuclear engineer, successful agrarian businessman, and born-again Southern Baptist deacon exploited the public's discontent with professional politicians and bureaucrats and their same old programs. The American people, Carter insisted, were searching for "new voices, new ideas, new leaders," and he managed to turn into a virtue his position as an outsider. "I have been accused of being an outsider," Carter asserted. "I plead guilty. Unfortunately, the vast majority of Americans are also outsiders. We are not going to get changes by simply shifting around the same groups of insiders, the same tired old rhetoric, the same unkept promises."

The strategy worked. Bolstered by his primary victories, Carter won the nomination at the Democratic convention and named as his running mate Walter F. Mondale, an able and liberal senator from Minnesota and a protégé of Hubert Humphrey. In the campaign, Ford defended his record of restoring honesty, integrity, and stability to government, and he promised more of the same. Carter appealed to liberal Democrats with pledges of full employment and social legislation. At the same time, he appeased moderates and conservatives by promising to eliminate bureaucratic waste in government and to balance the budget. To the American people, he promised moral leadership—decency, truthfulness, fairness, and compassion.

Despite Carter's sizable lead in the early polls, the election itself was close: 40.8 million votes for Carter to 39.1 million votes for Ford (a plurality that exceeded the winning margins of Kennedy in 1960 and Nixon in 1968), and an edge in the electoral college of 297 to 240. For the first time in forty-four years, an incumbent president had been defeated. And for the first time since before the Civil War, the nation had turned to the Deep South for a president.

To win, Carter had needed to revive the New Deal coalition of urban blacks, Catholics, Jews, and blue-collar workers, along with the South. He did so, but the old coalition had been very weak; only blacks rallied around Carter in substantial numbers (about 87 percent). Without them he would have lost. Only 53 percent of the people of voting age had chosen to vote. What remained uncertain was whether the results were a personal triumph and mandate for Carter the outsider, or a rejection of Ford as the candidate of a political party still under the shadow of Watergate.

THE CRISIS OF THE AMERICAN SPIRIT: JIMMY CARTER

In his election campaign, Carter had successfully exploited the outsider theme. But once elected, he needed to surmount persistent doubts about his capacity to govern. The issues he confronted were as formidable as those faced by any recent president, and the American people looked to Carter to make good on his promise to be a "strong, independent and aggressive President."

Four years later, those issues were still largely unresolved, and many Americans had come to view Carter as weak, indecisive, and ineffectual. "The insiders have had their chances," He had declared in 1976, "and they have not delivered. Their time has run out." His Republican opponent in 1980 would campaign on essentially the same theme.

The Outsider in Power

President Carter inaugurated his administration with a dramatic move. Ford had hoped to end the Watergate era with his pardon of Nixon. Carter wanted to end the Vietnam era by offering full pardons to civilian Vietnam War draft resisters. By issuing pardons, he insisted, he was not justifying their actions but merely granting forgiveness. It was less than the antiwar activists had demanded, and more than some Americans thought they deserved.

In the conduct of foreign policy, an area in which Carter seemed least experienced, the president had a record of impressive successes and unexpected failures. He strengthened relations with the People's Republic of China. Over strong opposition, he managed to win the Senate's ratification in 1978 of a treaty that would gradually yield to Panama control of the Panama Canal (not until the year 2000 would the United States relinquish full control of the waterway). In Africa, the United States improved its standing by supporting black majority rule in Rhodesia (Zimbabwe) and Southwest Africa (Namibia).

Even more spectacularly, Carter initiated a flexible American response to the ongoing Middle East crisis and, in a personal triumph, brought together the leaders of Egypt and Israel at Camp David in 1978 and helped them work out the framework for a peace agreement. Any permanent settlement, however, depended on resolution of the still critical issue of the Palestinian refugees and their claims to nationhood.

Early in his presidency, Carter moved to make respect for human rights a cornerstone of American foreign policy. This endeavor brought him difficulties, some of them of his own making. He singled out for condemnation Soviet treatment of dissidents and apartheid in South Africa, and he chastised several Latin American nations and South Korea for their repressive policies. But the president found it necessary to reconcile his strong convictions about human rights with pledges of support for repressive anti-Communist regimes that were thought essential to national security. He praised the shah of Iran, for example, and approved a multibillion-dollar arms sale to this "island of stability." That support soon plunged Carter into a crisis that defied any quick resolution and rapidly eroded popular support for his presidency.

Since the shah's return to power in 1953 (with the assistance of the United States), Iran had been a valuable ally against communism in the Middle East. While providing a steady flow of arms to back up the regime, successive American administrations had tended to ignore the domestic discontent with the shah's policies. In 1979, a revolution deposed the shah and sent him into exile. Seeking to eliminate all traces of the shah's Westernizing influence, Iranians embraced religious despotism under a Muslim spiritual leader, the Ayatollah Ruhollah Khomeini. At the same time, Iranians vented their anger on the United States for its support of the shah.

When Carter agreed to permit the exiled shah to enter the United States for medical treatment, mobs in Tehran attacked the American embassy and held the Americans there as hostages. Iran demanded as a condition for their release that the shah be returned for trial. Meanwhile, the Muslim nationalism unleashed by the revolution in Iran was making itself felt elsewhere in the Middle East, threatening to bring chaos to a region that supplied more than half the world's imported oil.

The shah died in exile in Egypt, but Iran continued to hold the American hostages, now demanding the return of the shah's wealth and the release of Iranian funds Carter had frozen in retaliation for that nation's actions. The president sent a military force to rescue the hostages, but

President and Mrs. Carter walk in the inaugural parade. *(UPI/Bettmann Newsphotos)*

On the first day of the occupation of the U.S. embassy in Tehran, the blindfolded American hostages were paraded before the mob by their captors. To many Americans, the prolonged captivity of the hostages was a national humiliation that revealed their country as a helpless giant. *(UPI/Bettmann Archive)*

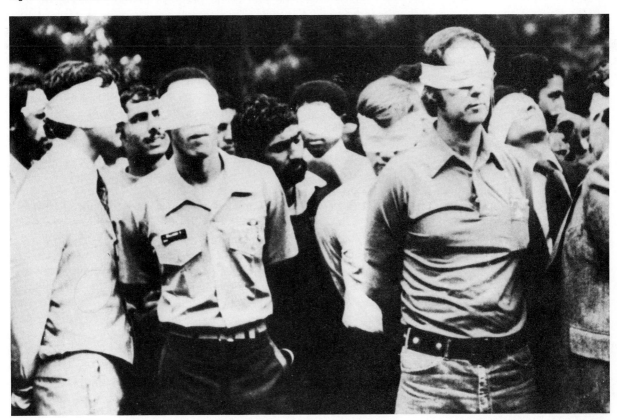

the mission failed. By the time the hostages were finally released in January 1981, after more than a year in captivity, they had come to symbolize to Americans the impotence of the United States abroad—an issue the Republican candidate in 1980 successfully exploited.

Even as President Carter grappled with the Iranian issue, he was plunged into a new crisis in Soviet-American relations. From the outset of his presidency, his criticism of the Soviet Union for its persecution of dissidents had cooled relations between the two countries. Nevertheless, after lengthy negotiations that had begun during the Ford presidency, Carter concluded the SALT II treaty, which imposed restrictions on strategic nuclear weapons. But the treaty floundered in the Senate, where some critics charged that America's military defenses had been compromised.

When Soviet troops moved into Afghanistan in December 1979 to bolster the Communist regime there, Carter reacted with outrage. He withdrew SALT II from the Senate (where its chances for passage were slim anyway), imposed a partial grain embargo on the Soviet Union, called for a boycott of the 1980 Olympic Games in Moscow, reduced cultural and technological exchanges with the Soviets, and asked Congress to authorize the registration of young Americans for a military draft.

The Soviet Union maintained that its presence in Afghanistan had been made necessary by anti-Communist rebels aided by hostile regimes, particularly China and Pakistan. The United States, along with a majority in the United Nations, condemned the move as outright aggression. With the avowed purpose of preventing "any outside force" from gaining control of the Persian Gulf region, Carter declared the region "vital" to American interests and sent in a naval force.

The crises in Iran and Afghanistan resulted in a rapid change in the foreign and military priorities of the Carter administration. Tension developed within the administration between Secretary of State Cyrus R. Vance, an experienced diplomat who favored arms control and improved relations with the Third World, and Zbigniew Brezezinski, national security adviser and a specialist in Soviet affairs, who advocated a harder line toward the Soviets. When Vance resigned over Carter's military mission to rescue the hostages in Iran, Brezezinski's hold on foreign policy tightened. To Carter's critics, however, the tension was reflected in the failure of the administration to articulate a clear and consistent foreign policy.

The Misery Index

The most conspicuous failure of the Carter presidency was its inability to stop the inflationary spiral that threatened the American people. His efforts to stimulate the economy and reduce unemployment were no more successful than his attempts to balance the budget and combat inflation. He rejected wage and price controls in favor of voluntary guidelines, a wage-and-price bureaucracy that would formulate and oversee the guidelines, and credit controls.

In the 1976 campaign, Carter had compiled a "misery index" by adding the levels of unemployment and inflation, and he had used it effectively against his opponent. Four years later, the misery index stood even higher—a point Ronald Reagan stressed. To increase employment, the president proposed various programs, including job training, public-service jobs, and tax incentives to private employers. But these proposals either ran aground in Congress or proved too feeble for Carter to make good on his promise to reduce an unemployment level he had found unacceptable.

Nor did Carter persuade Congress to accept his watered-down national health-insurance program or his proposed reform of a tax system he had called "a disgrace to the human race." Although he had made progress in reorganizing the civil service, he was only partly successful in reducing the "bureaucratic mess" in Washington. Critics mocked his reform efforts by noting the addition of two new cabinet-level departments, Energy and Education. Carter had vowed to make the conservation of energy a top priority, calling it "the moral equivalent of war." But his energy program was less ambitious than such rhetoric suggested; interest groups lobbied against various provisions, and Congress dismantled much of it. The United States was able to reduce its oil imports, but Americans paid higher prices for gasoline, and the decisions of the oil-producing nations remained the critical factor in determining those prices.

The achievements of the administration—in foreign policy, in energy conservation, in environmental protection, and in the unprecedented numbers of qualified minorities and women appointed to judgeships and government positions—were not enough to make up for the most conspicuous domestic and foreign failures. What ultimately undid Carter's presidency was his failure to inspire confidence. Whether any president could have dealt successfully with the do-

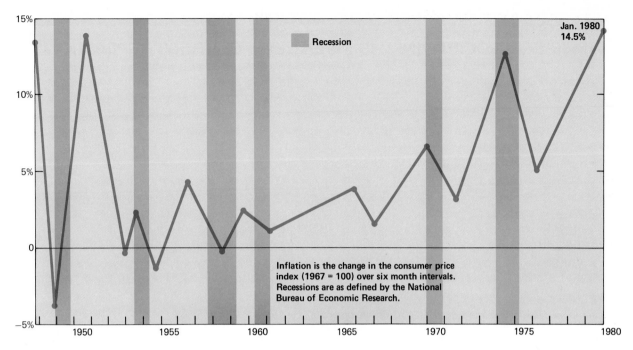

The misery index: Inflation and recession.

15%

10%

5%

0

-5%

1950   1955   1960   1965   1970   1975   1980

Recession

Jan. 1980
14.5%

Inflation is the change in the consumer price
index (1967 = 100) over six month intervals.
Recessions are as defined by the National
Bureau of Economic Research.

mestic and foreign crises of his administration
was less important than the public's perception
that he could not. President Carter, moreover,
never developed a style that convinced Americans
he could translate his high-minded rhetoric into a
clearly formulated program. In the end, the very
slogans he had used so successfully to win the
presidency were used to replace him in office.

THE REEMERGENCE OF THE WOMEN'S MOVEMENT

The women's rights and feminist movements had
declined after ratification of the Nineteenth
Amendment in 1920. But they reemerged in the
1960s and came of age during the 1970s. There
was little question that one of the major inspirations for this reemergence was the civil rights
movement, which had focused the nation's attention on issues of injustice, inequality, and second-
class citizenship. By the mid-1960s, many other
minority groups were modeling their protests after
the civil rights movement—not only ethnic and
racial minorities but prisoners, mental patients,
the physically disabled, and homosexuals.
Women, too, entered the fray, with far-reaching
consequences. Armed with the insights of enhanced self-awareness, women questioned the

constraints of traditional motherhood and marriage and produced a variety of organizations and
programs aimed at equalizing their place in
society and in the work force.

The Feminine Mystique

The publication in 1963 of Betty Friedan's *The
Feminine Mystique* sounded the clarion call of the
modern women's movement. Utilizing a variety of
case studies, Friedan articulated the frustrations
and disaffection, the boredom, anguish, and depression of American women who had lost their
identities in their suburban homes and their
traditional roles and ways of life. These women,
she charged, had been victimized by a "feminine
mystique," according to which women achieved
happiness only as wives and mothers. Advertisers,
prominent psychiatrists, the women's magazines,
and the media ratified the joys and rewards of
domesticity, assuring women of eternal happiness
in their "voluntary servitude." On television, "Father Knows Best," among other popular serials,
brought the dubious lesson of its title to millions of
American homes.

The feminine mystique, Friedan charged, had
produced a paradox in the lives of many women.
Society provided them a husband, a home, and a

George Tooker, *Landscape with Figures* (1963). *(Private collection)*

George Tooker, *The Subway* (1950). Egg tempera on composition board. 18 x 36 inches. *(Collection of Whitney Museum of American Art. Juliana Force Purchase. Acq. # 50.23)*

George Tooker, *Government Bureau* (1956). Egg on gesso panel. 19⅝ x 29⅝ inches. *(Metropolitan Museum of Art, George A. Hearn Fund, 1956) (56.78)*

George Tooker, *The Waiting Room II*, 1982. *(Marisa Del Re Gallery)*

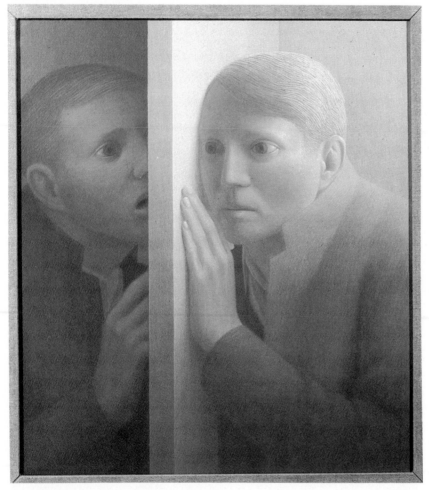

George Tooker, *Voice I*, 1963.
(Marisa Del Re Gallery)

family, and yet they remained dissatisfied with their lives. Each suburban wife, Friedan wrote, struggled alone with this paradox. "As she made the beds, shopped for groceries, matched slip-cover material, ate peanut butter sandwiches with her children, chauffeured Cub Scouts and Brownies, lay beside her husband at night—she was afraid to ask even of herself the silent question—'Is this all?' "

The Feminine Mystique, which sold more than a million copies, prompted many women in the 1960s and 1970s to perceive their lives in strikingly new ways. They experienced not only a transformation in their consciousness but a willingness to act on their enhanced self-awareness. Some women had begun to question their position in society through their experiences in the civil rights and antiwar movements. Participating in movements committed to democratizing American society, these women activists found themselves shunted into traditional roles and peripheral or subordinate positions. They formed a kind of ladies' auxiliary, serving chiefly as typists, cooks, and sexual companions but denied an equal voice or any voice at all in policy making. "The position of women in our movement," civil rights leader Stokely Carmichael once remarked, "should be prone."

Dissatisfied with their lack of progress in achieving equality, Friedan and other activists founded the National Organization for Women in 1966. Over the next decade, NOW grew rapidly in membership, drawing most of its support from well-educated professional women. Committed to political action, NOW proposed to work through the legislatures, Congress, the courts, and local and state organizations to gain opportunity in education, employment, and politics.

But by the late 1960s the heart and soul of the women's movement consisted in large part of young veterans of the civil rights, peace, and student movements meeting informally in small groups to discuss their lives. By sharing their problems, experiences, and feelings, these women would heighten their awareness of the restrictive roles and relationships that had molded their identities. Most important, they would come to understand that what they had perceived as individual problems, experiences, and feelings were in fact common to many women. These consciousness-raising groups, in the estimation of one feminist leader, by "simply bringing women together in a situation of structured interaction," proved to be as pivotal in the history of the women's movement as the factory was for the worker, the church for the Southern civil rights

---

THE TRAPPED HOUSEWIFE

In Betty Friedan's *The Feminine Mystique,* two women testify to the feelings of desperation that helped to inspire the feminist movement of the seventies and eighties. The first woman is a mother of four who left college at the age of nineteen to get married. The second woman, who has a Ph.D. in anthropology, is a Nebraska housewife with three children.

I've tried everything women are supposed to do—hobbies, gardening, pickling, canning, being very social with my neighbors, joining committees, running PTA teas. I can do it all, and I like it, but it doesn't leave you anything to think about—any feeling of who you are. I never had any career ambitions. All I wanted was to get married and have four children. I love the kids and Bob and my home. There's no problem you can even put a name to. But I'm desperate. I begin to feel I have no personality. I'm a server of food and putter-on of pants and a bedmaker, somebody who can be called on when you want something. But who am I?

A film made of any typical morning in my house would look like an old Marx Brothers' comedy. I wash the dishes, rush the older children off to school,

dash out in the yard to cultivate the chrysanthemums, run back in to make a phone call about a committee meeting, help the youngest child build a blockhouse, spend fifteen minutes skimming the newspapers so I can be well-informed, then scamper down to the washing machines where my thrice-weekly laundry includes enough clothes to keep a primitive village going for an entire year. By noon I'm ready for a padded cell. Very little of what I've done has been really necessary or important. Outside pressures lash me through the day. Yet I look upon myself as one of the more relaxed housewives in the neighborhood. Many of my friends are even more frantic. In the past sixty years we have come full circle and the American housewife is once again trapped in a squirrel cage. If the cage is now a modern plate-glass-and-broadloom ranch house or a convenient modern apartment, the situation is no less painful than when her grandmother sat over an embroidery hoop in her gilt-and-plush parlor and muttered angrily about women's rights.

Source: Betty Friedan, *The Feminine Mystique,* pp. 21 and 28. Copyright © 1974, 1963 by Betty Friedan. Published by W. W. Norton & Company, Inc. Reprinted by permission of the publisher.

movement, and the campus for the student. At the same time, a group of young feminist scholars, some of them active participants in the consciousness-raising groups, not only made respectable the study of American women but began to explore in their teaching, writing, and research the long history of the problems and relationships that Friedan had identified in her book.

Organization and Agitation

On August 26, 1970—the fiftieth anniversary of the ratification of the Nineteenth Amendment—a Women's Strike for Equality captured national attention. The nationwide demonstrations, which included a march of fifty thousand women up New York's Fifth Avenue, heralded a decade in which women organized and agitated in a variety of ways to improve the quality of their lives and to end their subservience to men and male values. Their activities ranged from picketing the Miss America contest to staging sit-ins in male sanctuaries that excluded women.

The goals of the women's movement, though wide-ranging, centered in the elimination of legal inequities and economic disparities. To improve the position of women in the workplace, the movement pressed for the same privileges afforded men, including equal pay for equal work. To increase women's access to the workplace, the movement demanded equal employment and educational opportunities and federal support for child-care centers. To gain control over their own bodies, women demanded reproductive freedom—the right to decide for themselves when to bear children and whether or not to terminate a pregnancy. The more radical feminists, while supporting these demands, entertained a more revolutionary visions—a far-reaching redefinition of sexual roles, relationships, and responsibilities that would free both men and women from traditional stereotypes and expectations.

The vast majority of American women did not belong to any of the women's rights organizations, nor did they necessarily subscribe to all the demands of the women's movement. But the influence of the movement in the 1970s could not be measured by the precise number of women activists. For many American women, serious questions about their families, their homes, child rearing, jobs, and sexual roles had been raised for the first time—questions that could no longer be answered in traditional ways. Innovations that

may initially have seemed trivial became almost conventional, including usages intended to free the English language from a male bias. The term *Ms.*, for example—a blend of *Mrs.* and *Miss*— came to be widely accepted as a title of respect that did not reveal marital status—much as *Mr.* had always been used. Far more controversial questions emerged as well, ranging from drafting women and using them in combat to repealing protective labor legislation and the right to an abortion. Such issues would divide Americans not simply by gender but often along class lines as well.

Indifferent in previous years, the federal government assumed an increasingly active role in the area of women's rights. In 1961, John F. Kennedy appointed a national Commission on the Status of Women, chaired by Eleanor Roosevelt, and gave it a sweeping mandate to study education, private and federal employment, family law, and the roles of women in the home and community. The investigators documented the second-class status of American women and urged the removal of obstacles to their advancement. Acting on one of their recommendations, President Kennedy issued an order in 1962 requiring federal employees to be hired and promoted without regard to sex. Two years later, discrimination in employment because of sex, race, color, religion, or national origin was made illegal by Title VII of the Civil Rights Act. In 1972, in still another pivotal action, Title IX of the Education Amendments made it illegal in most cases for federally assisted educational programs to discriminate on account of sex. And in 1978 Congress prohibited employers from firing a woman solely because she was pregnant.

But the effort to establish a national system of child-care centers—a principal objective of the women's movement—encountered heavy opposition. In 1971 Congress enacted a massive day-care program designed to make child-care facilities available to every working mother in the country, but President Nixon vetoed the measure. The family was "the keystone of our civilization," the president insisted, and the day-care program would enlist "the vast moral authority" of the federal government in support of "communal approaches to child-rearing." Institutional child care, he argued, threatened to "diminish both parental authority and parental involvement with children, particularly in the decisive early years when social attitudes and conscience and religious and moral principles are first inculcated."

The Equal Rights Amendment

Although the women's movement embraced a number of goals, it would focus much of its energy in the 1970s on a proposed Equal Rights Amendment to the Constitution: "Equality of rights under the law shall not be denied or abridged by any state on account of sex." Although the measure seemed modest, what it came to symbolize is what mattered most to its proponents—and to those who opposed it. The ERA, like the women's movement itself, had inspired hopes (and fears) of a revolutionary shift in the definition of woman as a person. It challenged the assumption of Progressive reformers that women needed special protection in the workplace as well as the traditional notion that a woman's principal role was as a housewife and mother. Passed by Congress overwhelmingly in 1972, the amendment was ratified by thirty-three states within two years; only five more states were needed for ratification, but there the campaign stalled.

From the outset, the women's movement faced internal debates over strategies and objectives, some of them reminiscent of the battles fought at the turn of the century between suffragists and more radical feminists. Some of the splits were along lines of class and race; working-class women felt little if any affinity with this largely white, middle-class movement of educated and professional women. To leave the house or another job to pursue a profession, for example, was never a realistic alternative for most women. For the growing proportion of women living in poverty, moreover, the ERA would provide little if any direct assistance, such as placing nourishment on the table; survival had a much higher priority than sexual freedom and constitutional guarantees of equal rights.

But the principal opponents of the women's movement were women and men who thought it imperiled traditional family values. With the strong support of conservative organizations, a coalition emerged in opposition to the feminist program. Made up largely of rural, small-town, and suburban Americans, Republicans and southern Democrats, and Christian fundamentalists, it singled out the Equal Rights Amendment as a symbol of a new definition of womanhood. According to these opponents, the ERA would undermine the woman's role as mother and wife and legitimate the idea that women could find fulfillment only in their own achievements. What was at stake, they warned, was the very survival of the traditional family and women's proper role in society. In their efforts to sway public opinion, they charged that the ERA would legalize homosexual marriages, unisex toilets, and combat duty for women, as well as expand rights to abortion. The amendment actually required none of these measures, but opponents argued, with apparent effectiveness, that it made such consequences likely.

The Supreme Court and Women

Even as women and men debated the merits of the ERA, women achieved greater economic and educational equality. The number of women attending law schools and medical schools increased, as did the number entering the professions and business. In a series of decisions, the Supreme Court used the equal-protection language of the Fourteen Amendment to strike down statutory sex bias across the country. (In doing so, the Court may have weakened the case for the ERA, making it seem less critical.) The Court also intervened in the sensitive area of birth control, finding in *Griswold v. State of Connecticut* (1965) that a Connecticut law banning contraceptives was unconstitutional because it violated the right to privacy.

In its most far-reaching decision of all affecting women, the Supreme Court addressed the conflict between the expanded view of women's rights and the restrictions placed on abortion. In *Roe v. Wade* (1973) the Court, by a seven-to-two majority, struck down state laws that made abortion a crime. The Court ruled that such laws violated a woman's right to privacy, and that women have a constitutionally protected right to abortion in the early stages of pregnancy. Only in the last three months of pregnancy could a state bar abortion. Otherwise, the state's power to regulate abortion was confined to requiring that the abortion be performed by a physician licensed by the state.

After 1973, then, abortions were available on demand. The number of legal abortions increased dramatically—from more than 200,000 in 1970 to 747,000 in 1973 to more than 1,000,000 in 1975. Public health officials reported an equally dramatic decrease in the number of mothers who suffered death or injuries from illegal abortions. Every year, in the 1970s and 1980s, an estimated 54 percent of American women, or some 6 million, conceived; about 3.3 million of the pregnancies were unplanned. In 1990, an estimated 1.5 million women chose an abortion. The majority were in their teens or early twenties; 82 percent were unmarried; nearly all were either working or attending school; some two-thirds had family incomes under $25,000 a year; and two-thirds were white (although abortion rates were higher for black and Hispanic women).

Ten years after it was passed by Congress, the Equal Rights Amendment to the Constitution died, falling three states short of the thirty-eight needed for ratification. By this time, the battleground over equal rights was already shifting—to the woman's right to control her body. And in the 1980s, in the Reagan era, the demands of women activists encountered even stiffer resistance, conflicting as they often did with a political rhetoric that reasserted the primacy of the home, the family, and traditional American values.

SUMMARY

Richard Nixon began his presidency in 1968 with a clear program and a clear mandate from a "silent majority" of Americans to retreat from the liberalism of the New Deal, the Fair Deal, the New Frontier, and the Great Society. For Nixon, this meant slowing down desegregation and appointing conservatives to Supreme Court vacancies. His economic game plan offered revenue sharing, tight-money policies, and a reduction in federal spending. But prices and unemployment continued to rise. And although the triumph of the moon landing on July 16, 1969, raised America's prestige, Vietnam continued to undermine it.

Foreign affairs became the major concern of the first Nixon administration, and a balance of power a major goal, with military action left to the discretion of allies and friends. The administration did succeed in effecting détente with the Soviet Union and China, and made an effort to stabilize the Middle East. But Vietnam was different: more troops, more bombs, Vietnamization—nothing seemed to work.

At home, protest against the war mounted on and off the campuses, fueled by revelations of American atrocities. In 1969 Nixon secretly ordered the bombing of Cambodia, and in 1970 the U.S. resumed full-scale bombing of North Vietnam. But neither the bombings nor "incursions" into Laos helped, and the South Vietnamese subsequently suffered a series of major defeats. A cease-fire was negotiated in January 1973—but still the war continued, in Vietnam and in Cambodia.

The election of 1972 brought Nixon back to office on a victorious tide. But the illegal activities of CREEP, the Committee to Re-Elect the President, soon erupted into what became known as the Watergate scandal. Before it was over, more than forty highly placed Nixon administration officials had been indicted, including the president's closest aides and the attorney general, and the president himself had been implicated in the lies, crimes, and systematic deception. Faced with impeachment, Nixon resigned in disgrace in the summer of 1974. His presidency was a shambles, and the American people's faith in government had been profoundly shaken. The previous year, Nixon's vice-president, Spiro Agnew, had also been forced to resign, to escape a prison term for tax fraud, bribery, extortion, and conspiracy.

Gerald Ford took office on August 9, 1974, and served out the remaining two years of Nixon's second term. He brought refreshing personal qualities to the office and tried to restore good feelings by such acts as leniency programs for Vietnam draft evaders and deserters. But his pardon of Nixon, along with the growing economic crisis and confrontation with the Democrat-controlled Congress, ended the political honeymoon.

In Vietnam, where the fighting had continued after the American troop withdrawal of early 1973, the South Vietnamese were close to collapse by early 1975. Saigon fell in April. At the same time, Cambodia and Laos came under Communist influence. The policy of four American presidents had failed, and the United States had learned a difficult lesson about the limits of its power.

In the bicentennial election of 1976, Americans turned to a political outsider, Jimmy Carter, and rejected Ford. But Carter's promises to "clean up the mess in Washington" and to balance the budget were not kept. Nor was his promise to provide moral leadership.

Economic and social problems worsened. Carter's success in the Middle East in 1978 was more than offset by what Americans saw as a humiliating failure in Iran, where Americans citizens were kept hostage for more than a year. By 1980 he seemed indecisive and ineffectual; Americans rejected his bid for reelection by turning to the Republicans and to Ronald Reagan, spokesman of that party's right wing.

Reagan ran on a conservative platform of tax cuts, a balanced budget, increased defense spending, and opposition to abortion and the ERA. His victory, along with the defeat of a number of liberal Democratic incumbents in the Senate by conservative Republicans, made the election of 1980 an impressive triumph for conservative principles and a sharp retreat from the New Deal tradition.

Inspired by the civil rights revolution of the 1960s, the women's rights movement reemerged in that decade and came of age in the 1970s, reflecting a new awareness by many women of their second-class status in American society. Betty Friedan's *The Feminine Mystique,* published in 1963, gave further impetus to the movement. In this best-selling book Friedan argued that women who gave their lives to their children and husbands sacrificed their own identity and opportunities. Acting on this awareness, she and like-minded women produced a variety of organizations and programs, most prominently the National Organization for Women. Founded in 1966, NOW aimed at eliminating legal inequities and economic disparities.

Although the women's movement embraced a number of goals, it came to focus on a proposed Equal Rights Amendment to the Constitution: "Equality of rights under the law shall not be denied or abridged by any state on account of sex." Passed by Congress, it failed to obtain the number of states necessary for ratification. In the meantime, women made progress in the work force, particularly in the professions and in business, and achieved reforms in abortion laws. Federal legislation in the 1970s sought to prohibit sexual discrimination in employment and in federally assisted educational programs. In the landmark decision of *Roe v. Wade* (1973), the Supreme Court affirmed the constitutional right of women to have an abortion and struck down state laws that interfered with that right.

The women's movement faced strong resistance, which reflected divisions among women as well as the hostility of many men to perceived threats to the family, the home, and traditional American values. Using the same organizational skills they had employed in defeating the Equal Rights Amendment, "pro-life" and "pro-family" forces mobilized to prohibit abortions.

TIME LINE

1963	Betty Friedan, *The Feminine Mystique*
1966	National Organization for Women (NOW) founded
1969	Warren E. Berger replaces Earl Warren as Chief Justice
	Apollo 11 moon landing
	Nixon announces Vietnamization program
	Vietnam Moratorium Day: largest public anti-war protests
	SALT talks begin
1970	Details of My Lai massacre (1968) revealed
	U.S. invades Cambodia
	Kent State shootings
	Women's Strike for Equality
1971	Twenty-Sixth Amendment (lowering voting age to 18) ratified
1972	Nixon visits China and the Soviet Union
	SALT I treaty on nuclear arms
	Congress approves Equal Rights Amendment
	Watergate break-in
	Nixon becomes a co-conspirator in obstruction of justice
	Nixon re-elected
	U.S. aerial bombardments of Hanoi and North Vietnam

1973	Cease-fire in Vietnam; U.S. troops withdrawn
	War Powers Act
	Arab-Israeli War
	Arab oil embargo
	Roe v. *Wade*
	Trials of the Watergate burglars
	Senate Watergate Committee hearings
	Agnew resigns; Gerald R. Ford becomes vice-president
	Grand Jury indicts Nixon's aides; convicted (1975)
	House Judiciary Committee votes to impeach Nixon
	Nixon resigns; Gerald Ford becomes president
	Ford pardons Nixon
1975	South Vietnam falls to Communists
1976	Jimmy Carter elected president
1978	Panama Canal treaties ratified
	Israeli-Egyptian peace agreement at Camp David
1979	Shah of Iran deposed; Khomeini comes to power
	Iranian hostage crisis begins
	Soviets invade Afghanistan
1980	U.S. boycotts Olympic Games in Moscow
1982	Equal Rights Amendment fails

Suggested Readings

The best introduction to America in the seventies is P. J. Dolan and E. Quinn (eds.), *The Sense of the 70s* (1978). But no student should venture into this decade without consulting the probing and often devastating cartoons of G. B. Trudeau, many of them collected in *The Doonesbury Chronicles* (1975). C. Lasch, *The Culture of Narcissism: American Life in an Age of Diminishing Expectations* (1979), explores changing attitudes. M. Rossman, a sixties activist, looks at the new religion of the counterculture—the human potential movement—in *New Age Blues: On the Politics of Consciousness* (1979).

The expectations of a modern president and the failure to meet them are analyzed in G. Hodgson, *All Things to All Men: The False Promise of the Modern Presidency* (1980). Indispensable sources for the study of Richard Nixon are his own memoirs: *Six Crises* (1962), *RN: The Memoirs of Richard Nixon* (1978); and *The Real War* (1980). Garry Wills, *Nixon Agonistes: The Crisis of the Self-Made Man* (1970), is a critical analysis that helps to make comprehensible the final debacle. See also S. E. Ambrose, *Nixon: The Education of a Politician 1913–1962* (1987) and *The Triumph of a Politician, 1962–1972* (1989), and R. Morris, *Richard Milhous Nixon: The Rise of an American Politician* (1989). Nixon's economic policies are analyzed in L. Silk, *Nixonomics* (1972). On the 1972 campaign, T. H. White, *The Making of the President 1972* (1972), and H. S. Thompson, *Fear and Loathing: On the Campaign Trail '72* (1973), offer sharply contrasting views. In *Common Ground: A Turbulent Decade in the Lives of Three American Families* (1985), J. A. Lukas tells of the court-ordered desegregation of Boston's public schools.

On Nixon and foreign policy, see H. Brandon, *The Retreat of American Power* (1972), and T. Szulc, *The Illusion of Peace* (1978). On China policy, see R. G. Sutter, *China-Watch: Toward Sino-American Reconciliation* (1978). On the Middle East, see W. C. Eveland, *Ropes of Sand: America's Failure in the Middle East* (1980); W. B. Quandt, *Decade of Decision: American Policy toward the Arab–Israel Conflict, 1967–1976* (1977); E. R. F. Sheehan, *The Arabs, Israelis and Kissinger* (1976); and B. Rubin, *Paved with Good Intentions: The American Experience and Iran* (1980). M. Kalb and B. Kalb, *Kissinger* (1974), is a sympathetic treatment. For a more critical view, see S. M. Hersh, *The Price of Power: Kissinger in the Nixon White House* (1983). Kissinger justifies his foreign-policy decisions in *White House Years* (1979) and *Years of Upheaval* (1982). The most devastating indictment of those decisions is W. Shawcross, *Sideshow: Kissinger, Nixon, and the Destruction of Cambodia* (1979).

On Nixon and Vietnam, see the literature cited for Chapter 32.

The crimes of the Nixon presidency may be viewed in the context of C. Vann Woodward (ed.), *Responses of the Presidents to Charges of Misconduct* (1974), in which sixteen historians examine executive miscon-duct since 1789. For background, see also A. Schlesinger, Jr., *The Imperial Presidency* (1973), and the works on Nixon cited previously. The Watergate scandal and the fall of Nixon produced a large number of personal and journalistic accounts. But the best place to start remains the voluminous government documents: the Senate Watergate hearings, the Nixon-edited White House tapes, and the House Judiciary Committee report and hearings. See especially *Impeachment of Richard M. Nixon* (93rd Cong., 2nd Sess., House Calendar No. 426, Report of the Committee on the Judiciary, 1974), and *Transcripts of Eight Recorded Presidential Conversations* (93rd Cong., 2nd Sess., Hearings before the Committee on the Judiciary, 1974). C. Bernstein and B. Woodward, two *Washington Post* reporters who helped to break the Watergate story, report their experiences in *All the President's Men* (1974) and the president's fall in *The Final Days* (1976). The undoing of the presidency is described in B. Sussman, *The Great Cover-Up: Nixon and the Scandal of Watergate* (1974); The Washington Post, *The Fall of a President* (1974); T. H. White, *Breach of Faith: The Fall of Richard Nixon* (1975); J. A. Lukas, *Nightmare: The Underside of the Nixon Years* (1976); and J. Schell, *The Time of Illusion* (1976) and *Observing the Nixon Years* (1989). For a scholarly assessment, see S. I. Kutler, *The Wars of Watergate* (1990).

Nixon defends his presidency in *RN: The Memoirs of Richard Nixon*. Memoirs of the conspirators include H. R. Haldeman, *The Ends of Power* (1978); J. W. Dean, *Blind Ambition: The White House Years* (1976); J. S. Magruder, *An American Life: One Man's Road to Watergate* (1974); and E. H. Hunt, *Undercover: Memoirs of an American Secret Agent* (1974). M. H. Stans, chief fund-raiser for Nixon's reelection, tells his version in *The Terrors of Justice: The Untold Side of Watergate* (1979). For the prosecution, see J. J. Sirica, *To Set the Record Straight: The Break-In, the Tapes, the Conspirators, the Pardon* (1979); S. Dash, *Chief Counsel: Inside the Ervin Committee* (1976); and L. Jaworski, *The Right and the Power: The Prosecution of Watergate* (1976).

The domestic activities of the CIA are revealed in *Report to the President by the Commission on CIA Activities within the United States* (1975). The role of the CIA at home and abroad is examined in D. Wise and T. B. Ross, *The Invisible Government* (1964); V. Marchetti and J. D. Marks, *The CIA and the Cult of Intelligence* (1974); J. J. Berman and M. H. Halperin (eds.), *The Abuses of the Intelligence Agencies* (1975); and T. Powers, *The Man Who Kept the Secrets: Richard Helms and the CIA* (1979). See also three memoirs by former agents: P. Agee, *Inside the Company: CIA Diary* (1975); F. Snepp, *Decent Interval* (1977); and J. Stockwell, *In Search of Enemies* (1979).

Ford's recollections of his presidential years may be found in *A Time to Heal: The Autobiography of Gerald R. Ford* (1979). Accounts by former aides include J. F.

terHorst, *Gerald Ford and the Future of the Presidency* (1974); R. Nessen, *It Sure Looks Different from the Inside* (1978); and J. J. Casserly, *The Ford White House* (1977). On Jimmy Carter, the best work is W. L. Miller, *Yankee from Georgia: The Emergence of Jimmy Carter* (1978). See also B. Glad, *Jimmy Carter: In Search of the Great White House* (1980), and the impressionistic account by J. Wooten, *Dasher: The Roots and the Rising of Jimmy Carter* (1978).

On the modern women's movement, B. Friedan, *The Feminine Mystique* (1963), is the place to begin. Among useful anthologies are R. Morgan (ed.), *Sisterhood Is Powerful* (1970); J. Sochen (ed.), *The New Feminism in Twentieth-Century America* (1971); A. F. Scott (ed.), *The American Woman: Who Was She?* (1971); G. Lerner (ed.), *Black Women in White America* (1972) and *The Female Experience: An American Documentary* (1977); L. K. Kerber and J. De Hart-Mathews (eds.), *Women's America: Refocusing the Past* (2nd. ed., 1987); and J. E. Friedman and others (eds.), *Our American Sisters: Women in American Life and Thought* (1987). W. H. Chafe, *The American Woman 1920–1970* (1972) is an insightful historical study. S. Evans, *Personal Politics: The Roots of Women's Liberation in the Civil Rights Movement and the New Left* (1979) is an illuminating personal chronicle. See also K. Millett, *Sexual Politics* (1970); J. Hole and E. Levine, *Rebirth of Feminism* (1971); J. Freeman, *The Politics of Women's Liberation* (1975); G. G. Yates, *What Women Want: The Ideas of the Movement* (1975); B. Friedan, *The Second Stage* (1981); B. S. Deckard, *The Women's Movement* (rev. ed., 1983); J. Mansbridge, *How We Lost the ERA* (1986); M. F. Berry, *Why ERA Failed* (1986); M. Faux, *Roe v. Wade* (1988); K. Luker, *Abortion and the Politics of Motherhood* (1984); and S. M. Bianchi, *American Women in Transition* (1987). Additional historical assessments of women in American life, many of them applicable to the 1960s, 1970s, and 1980s are cited in the literature for Chapter 25. On the family, see C. Lasch, *Haven in a Heartless World: The Family Besieged* (1977) and K. Keniston, *All Our Children: The American Family Under Pressure* (1977).

CHAPTER 34

TOWARD A NEW CENTURY: AMERICA IN THE '80S AND '90S

To much of the world, the idea that a Hollywood actor would become president of the United States must have seemed characteristically American. To much of the American electorate, the candidacy of Ronald Reagan afforded them the opportunity to recover their past—a time of heroic endings and heroic lives, when the nation's military and industrial supremacy had been unquestioned. In electing Ronald Reagan to the presidency, the American people, according to pollsters, had chosen the individual they deemed most likely to "make America feel good about itself again."

No doubt Reagan's film career, though unspectacular (he made some fifty grade B movies over a twenty-year period), helped make him familiar to several generations of Americans. But his considerable appeal also derived from his affability and his skill in exploiting the frustrations, fears, and hopes of the large majority. Between his film and political careers, Reagan was a successful salesman. Working for the General Electric Company between 1954 and 1962, he spoke to employees at plants across the country.

He also addressed chambers of commerce, trade associations, and civic clubs. His impressive political debut, a television speech on behalf of Barry Goldwater's presidential candidacy in 1964, raised his stature in the Republican party. Two years later he was elected governor of California, and in 1980 he was the Republican presidential candidate.

Whatever Reagan's audience, the message remained the same: the perils of government control and regulation. He was critical of much of the social legislation of the twentieth century, from the progressive income tax to social security to the Tennessee Valley Authority. But despite his strong ideas about limited government, he did not appear to most Americans as a hard-core ideologue. When he ran for president, moreover, he moderated a number of his political positions.

More effectively than any of his immediate predecessors, Reagan was able to communicate his ideas to the American people. His vision of America evoked a nostalgic view of the country, based on his own idealized midwestern boyhood in Dixon, Illinois. "There was the life," he wrote in his autobiography, "that has shaped my body and mind for all the years

Dennis Brack/Black Star.

to come." He promised the American people an America like that of his youth, rooted in the small-town, rural values he claimed to have learned: patriotism, self-help, hard work, morality, and belief in God, family, and the flag. To Reagan, America was a land of unlimited opportunity, made up of enterprising people who had seized upon chances and made the most of them. His own life resembled in many ways that of the classic Horatio Alger hero, who demonstrates the necessary spunk, grit, and ability to take advantage of every break that comes his way.

In the year of his election to the presidency, Reagan insisted he was "saying the same things I've been saying for twenty-five years on the mashed-potato circuit." With far greater skill than his Democratic opponent, the former actor talked to Americans about their lives and future prospects. He spoke in a language they readily understood. And not only did he make his ideas and programs sound like plain common sense, he made them seem attainable. That proved to be good enough for eight years in the White House, sufficient time for Reagan to inaugurate if not to realize the political and moral revolution he so fervently embraced.

In the election of 1988, Reagan talked of the presidential contest between Michael Dukakis and George Bush as a referendum on his presidency. "I feel a little like I'm on the ballot myself," he said. Bush did not hesitate to capitalize on the themes and successes of the previous eight years, and it would be left to him to carry forward the banner of Reaganism and conservatism. But he would need to do so in a rapidly changing world. Within a year of Bush's inauguration, events over which he commanded little influence overwhelmed his presidency: the apparent end of the Cold War and—one of the principal legacies of the Cold War and the Reagan presidency—a budget deficit that had reached staggering figures.

With the dramatic changes in the Soviet Union and Eastern Europe, the Cold War appeared to be at an end. For the United States, after some forty years of policies and spending predicated on that war, the transition to new ways of thinking and acting would dominate the 1990s.

The United States emerged from the Cold War the most powerful military power in the world. But it had paid a heavy price for that supremacy. The world's leading creditor nation in 1981 had become the world's largest debtor ten years later. In that same decade, the size of the federal deficit reached a level unprecedented in American history. The extraordinary opportunities opened up by the end of the Cold War, along with new and persistent challenges at home—rising poverty rates, homelessness, the AIDS epidemic, the drug problem, the deterioration of the nation's public schools, the battle over abortion, the absorption of the new immigrants, and the consequences of racism—suggested that in the last decade of the twentieth century the American people would need to reconsider both their domestic priorities and their place in a changing world.

REAGANISM TRIUMPHANT: NEW DEPARTURES

More fundamentally than any president since Franklin Delano Roosevelt, Ronald Reagan altered the nation's social and economic policy. For some fifty years, the nation had come to accept the idea that the welfare of Americans was a public issue. The New Deal operated under the assumption that the federal government had a responsi-bility to deal with poverty, unemployment, and inequality. Under subsequent presidents, Democratic and Republican alike, the exercise of that responsibility required considerable federal activity and spending. Truman's Fair Deal, Kennedy's New Frontier, and Johnson's Great Society inspired new and expanded programs that provided a broad range of health, education, and welfare services aimed at removing inequities in society and assisting low-income families. The Eisenhower and Nixon administrations, though professing more conservative principles, consolidated rather than curtailed federal activity in these areas.

But in the 1970s and 1980s, and especially in the eight years of the Reagan presidency, liberal federal activism faced a more skeptical and hostile audience in Congress and the White House. The role of the federal government would be redefined in accordance with a new set of priorities and some very different assumptions, the most important of which President Reagan proclaimed in his inaugural address: "Government is not the solution to our problem. Government is the problem."

The new president came to power on a wave of disillusion with the government's incapability at home and its apparent impotence abroad. In proclaiming that the federal government itself was the root of the problem at home and in promising to "get government off the backs of the people," he signaled a departure for the American people—a sharp retreat from the New Deal tradition. In proclaiming the Soviet Union to be "the focus of evil in the modern world," he signaled a more aggressive policy abroad, including the return to a Cold War rhetoric that divided the world into irreconcilable camps of good and evil.

The Election of 1980

Encouraged by the rapid decline in President Carter's popularity, the Republicans entered the 1980 election brimming with confidence. This time there was no mistaking the clear choice of the party's rank and file—Ronald Reagan. The Republican convention was dominated by the party's right wing, which pushed through a platform promising tax cuts, a balanced budget, increased defense spending, constitutional amendments banning nontherapeutic abortions and reinstating school prayer, the appointment of judges who opposed abortion, and opposition to the Equal Rights Amendment. As vice-president, Reagan chose George Bush of Texas, a former congressman and CIA director who had made an impressive run in the primaries.

The Democrats, rejecting a bid by Senator Edward Kennedy, renominated Carter and Mondale. But a mood of fatalism dominated the convention, and Kennedy's challenge in the primaries had already split the party. Nor was the Democratic cause aided by the independent candidacy of John Anderson, a moderate Republican and former Illinois congressman who felt the need to offer an alternative to Carter and Reagan. Although Anderson's political record was much closer to Reagan's philosophy than to Carter's, he managed to win the votes of many Democrats and self-styled liberals as well as some Republicans. But his candidacy did not affect the outcome of the election, nor did it promise a change in the nation's traditional two-party system.

In the campaign, Reagan successfully exploited domestic economic distress and international instability. He proclaimed his belief in reducing government interference in the lives of Americans while increasing the nation's military arsenal. He capitalized on the apparent disenchantment with the social ferment of the sixties, making clear his own perception of that decade: expensive and unproductive welfare systems, misguided civil rights programs, excessive environmental protection, an increasingly bloated federal bureaucracy, a morally bankrupt Supreme Court, and a post-Vietnam inertia that had reduced the nation's military defenses and jeopardized its position as a leader of the "free world."

To broaden his appeal, Reagan moderated his previous hostility to the more popular social programs, such as social security. And even as he called the Vietnam War a "noble crusade," he tried to assure voters that he would not lead the country into needless foreign conflicts. In speaking to unemployed workers and to union audiences, he capitalized on dissatisfaction with inflation and promised to put people back to work. To a middle class weary of government programs and the taxes needed to pay for them, he promised a sharp reduction in federal spending (except for defense) and tax relief. To Americans concerned with the humiliations the United States had suffered in Vietnam and Iran, he promised to restore the nation's power and credibility.

When Reagan told the viewers of his televised debate with Carter, "Ask yourself, are you better off than you were four years ago?" he scored a decisive point over his opponent. "The election," said Carter's political pollster, "ended up becoming exactly the referendum on unhappiness we had been trying to avoid." Not only had the Democrats underestimated Reagan's appeal, but President Carter's efforts to exploit Reagan's right-wing background had misfired badly. The confidence Carter seemed unable to inspire Reagan managed to capture with his folksy and nostalgic rhetoric about restoring the values of his youth and making Americans once again feel proud of their country.

Reagan won over the nation's increasingly white, middle-class voting population, and he effectively buried the old New Deal coalition, even in the South; only black voters remained loyal to the Democratic party. The election results, while an overwhelming triumph for Reagan, also revealed a new low in voter turnout, with only 52 percent of the eligible voters choosing to participate. The new president entered the White House having received a "landslide" of only 26 percent of the electorate.

Although Reagan's election had been expected, the success of the Republicans in securing control of the Senate for the first time in twenty-six years had not. The ideological makeup of the new crop of senators suggested that the election had been an impressive triumph for conservative principles. But with the House still Democratic, the president would face a divided Congress in his efforts to reorder federal priorities. The bipartisan coalition he managed to mobilize for that purpose confirmed Reagan's ability to make the most of his popularity with the electorate.

Less than four months after his inauguration, President Reagan was shot in the chest by a deranged assassin. With his characteristic good humor and self-deprecating manner, Reagan joked with the doctors and nurses who rushed him to surgery. "I forgot to duck," he quipped to his wife from the hospital bed. The way he handled the affair, along with his rapid recovery, further enhanced his popularity and reinforced the popular mandate he had been given by the American electorate. The assassination attempt, which permanently debilitated Reagan's press secretary, raised once again questions about the need for gun control. But the president resisted such pressures and maintained his opposition to any legislation designed to restrict the availability of guns to the American public.

The Domestic Program: Reaganomics

Reagan chose a cabinet and White House staff dominated by businessmen who shared his political philosophy and priorities. Although he often professed an admiration for Franklin Delano Roosevelt ("I was an enthusiastic New Deal Democrat," he wrote in his autobiography), he took his cues as president from the example of Calvin Coolidge, whom he admired for his success in reducing taxes and government expenditures. Those same ends would constitute the cornerstone of Reagan's domestic program. "Now you

hear a lot of jokes about Silent Cal Coolidge," Reagan remarked, "but I think the joke is on the people that make jokes, because if you look at his record, he cut the taxes four times. We had probably the greatest growth and prosperity that we've ever known. And I have taken heed of that because if he did nothing, maybe that's the answer [for] the federal government."

In confronting "the worst economic mess since the Great Depression," Reagan placed his confidence in orthodox conservative ideology and in supply-side economics. Previous administrations had favored the economic theories of John Maynard Keynes, the British economist, which called for stimulation of the economy at times of high unemployment and economic hard times, and for increases in government expenditures that would stimulate consumption and investment. Reagan, on the other hand, called for tight money, deep federal budget cuts, and incentives for business investment, such as tax breaks.

Reagan proposed to cut income taxes across the board. In 1981, he persuaded Congress to go along with his plan for a three-year reduction in both individual and corporate taxes. The principal benefits were reaped by wealthy individuals and corporations. But "Reaganomics" assumed that the tax cuts would revive a stagnant economy, that the beneficiaries would use their windfalls to improve industrial productivity. Sharp reductions in government spending along with the taxes collected after the economic revival would make up for the prospective deficits and enable the president to proceed with his military buildup. By 1984, Reagan promised, the federal budget would balance government revenues and expenditures. That promise was not kept; on the contrary, the tax reductions helped produce record federal deficits.

The Domestic Program: Reordering Priorities

In campaigning for the presidency, Reagan appealed, as had many previous candidates, to the Populist tradition. But he managed to turn the traditional Populist anger at big business against big government. And no sooner did he become president than Reagan proceeded to implement his promise to redefine the role of the federal government in American life. Because of his commitment to an overpowering defense, the budgets he sent to Congress called mostly for cutbacks in social programs. Reagan hoped to slow the growth of those programs, and eliminate some of them altogether. The objective, he declared, was to "trim the fat" from the federal budget and to eliminate services and benefits for those who should be able to make it on their own.

Reagan promised to retain services and benefits (the "safety net") for what he called the "truly needy," defining that group more narrowly than his predecessors in the White House. The president succeeded in dismantling the antipoverty programs of previous administrations, eliminating or sharply cutting back on various services. He obtained most of the cuts he sought in the welfare and food-stamp programs, both to restrict eligibility and to reduce benefits. Public pressure forced him to retreat on his plans for reductions in social security benefits, and public assistance was largely maintained for the elderly and those who were unable to work because of disability or other circumstances. With the social security system approaching bankruptcy, Reagan appointed a bipartisan commission to place it on a sounder financial footing. And with the cost of health care rapidly mounting, Congress agreed to substantial changes in medicare, the health program created in 1965 for the elderly and disabled.

Reagan proved adept in persuading Congress to accede to his principal proposals. In enhancing the nation's military arsenal—at a cost of some $2 trillion—he got virtually everything he demanded; including appropriations for the costly MX intercontinental missile (renamed the "peacemaker"). Although questions remained about the value and feasibility of that weapon, Secretary of Defense Caspar Weinberger told congress it was essential as a bargaining chip in arms talks with the Soviet Union. Congress went along as well with Reagan's efforts to revise the domestic agenda of previous administrations. In the Democrat-controlled House, a sufficient number of conservative southern Democrats voted with the Republicans to override liberal opposition to Reagan's deep cuts in social programs. In some cases Congress made more modest cuts than Reagan proposed, as in federal support for the arts and humanities, subsidized-housing programs, child nutrition, and student loans. Although the president sought "significant reductions in funding" for almost all education programs, Congress consistently provided more money than Reagan wanted. With a presidential commission warning that "a rising tide of mediocrity" threatened American education, Reagan summoned schools "back to basics," proposed merit pay for teachers, and urged principals to crack down on disciplinary

problems. But he continued to resist additional federal funding.

Although Reagan believed the nation had a God-given responsibility to preserve its natural resources, he reversed the momentum of previous administrations toward more stringent environmental protection. The administration eased the impact of antipollution laws on industry and permitted more private development of resources on public lands. Environmentalists active in both parties saw to it that Congress gave the president less than he wanted, but Reagan's appointments weakened the administration of environmental and resource laws.

James G. Watt, secretary of the interior, encountered early opposition. Environmental groups and their allies in Congress perceived him as anxious to shift the emphasis of his office from protection of public lands and resources toward their exploitation by private interests. He would be forced to resign under public pressure. In 1983, the director of the Environmental Protection Agency also resigned, along with other top agency officials, amid charges that they had been lax in enforcing hazardous-waste laws, had made deals with polluters, and had manipulated toxic-cleanup grants for political purposes.

If Reagan proved less than resolute in monitoring the disposition of the public lands, he moved with dispatch in 1981 to inflict a major defeat on organized labor. Ignoring a law that forbade them to strike, the nation's air traffic controllers walked off their jobs to press their demands. (The union had been one of the few to endorse Reagan in the recent election.) Reagan ordered the controllers back to work, but they refused, thinking the airlines could not function without them. The president responded by discharging the more than 1100 controllers and establishing programs to train replacements. When the strike collapsed, the president refused to rehire any of the strikers. The union never recovered, nor did organized labor.

During the remaining years of the Reagan presidency, organized labor played a diminishing role in American life. By 1987, real average hourly and weekly wages for American workers had reached their lowest levels in twenty-five years— a 10 percent decrease since 1972. In the 1980s, an estimated 12 million Americans lost their jobs as a result of plant closings and layoffs. For those laid off, the prospects were not encouraging—only a 62 percent chance of finding another job within a year. Nor were the new jobs created in the 1980s nearly as rewarding as the traditional jobs in

Workers at a Honda plant. *(Andrew Sacks/Black Star)*

manufacturing: nearly half of them paid less than $7400 a year (35 percent less than the poverty-line income for a family of four). The number of people having to work in jobs paying the minimum wage of $3.35 an hour ($6968 a year) grew from 5.1 million in 1981 to 7.8 million in 1987.

Consistent with his philosophy of limited government, Reagan had wanted to reduce the federal role in agriculture, particularly the costly program of price supports. But depressed export markets and bumper crops created massive surpluses, and many farmers faced economic disaster. The administration intervened with new programs to pay farmers to not plant excess crops. Price supports in 1983 exceeded those in any previous year, and farm foreclosures were higher than at any time since the Great Depression. Two years after Reagan's reelection, half the farmers in the country were in debt. Congress came to the rescue, as it had so often, by passing the Food Security Act of 1985. The bill cut farm price supports in an effort to recapture foreign markets for American growers. To make up the difference, the government increased subsidy payments to farmers. The act accomplished its objectives—

increased farm exports and income—but at a considerable cost to taxpayers. Federal expenditures for farm programs totaled $26 billion in 1986—more than all the income earned by farmers in 1982 and twice what they made in 1983. The effect of Reagan's farm policies was to increase productivity and preserve the most substantial and profitable commercial farms and corporations (those with sales of more than $500,000 a year), at the expense of tens of thousands of small landholders and family farmers, who were put out of business and forced to move to the cities.

Reagan had promised to get government "off the backs" of the American people, and his administration succeeded in obtaining substantial government deregulation. Those areas of American life most directly affected included the airlines, financial institutions, the trucking industry, and environmental protection. The results of deregulation occasioned considerable debate. To its supporters, it remained one of the principal achievements of the Reagan administration in limiting the role and power of government bureaucrats. But critics would claim that the Amer-

ON ACHIEVING THE AMERICAN DREAM

Most of us talk about the American Dream, but few of us can define it. *The Wall Street Journal* set out to do just that recently in a survey conducted by the Roper Organization, and some of its findings are surprising. While a lot of Americans define the American Dream as getting rich, a much larger share define it as having freedom of choice, owning a home, and getting a good education. Roper interviewed more than 1,500 Americans, and most of those polled—96 percent—include "freedom of choice in how to live one's life" as part of the Dream. Ninety-three percent of Americans include being "financially secure enough to have ample time for leisure pursuits" as part of the Dream. Ninety-one percent say it's the ability to start their own businesses. Only 80 percent believe that becoming wealthy defines the American Dream.

While some people scoff at the American Dream, fully 86 percent of Americans still believe in it. But is it still reachable? Almost half of those polled—45 percent—say the Dream is harder to reach now than it once was. Another 23 percent say it's easier to achieve, and 32 percent say it's as easy as it has always been.

Only 5 percent of Americans say they have achieved the American Dream. Three percent say they've just begun the journey, while the rest say they are partway there. The largest group—25 percent of those polled—say they are halfway to the Dream.

You would expect that the affluent are more likely to say they're living the American Dream than those who aren't so well off. But this isn't the case. While 5 percent of people with incomes of less than $15,000 a year believe they've attained the Dream, only 6 percent of those with incomes of more than $50,000 a year say they have.

How much does the Dream cost? For most Americans, about $50,000 a year. A median income of $50,000 would enable most men and women to live the American Dream. But the cost of the American Dream increases with household income, starting at $50,000 a year for those with annual household incomes less than $15,000 and rising to $100,000 for those with incomes of $50,000 and up.

Source: Reprinted with permission. © *American Demographics,* April 1987, Ithaca, NY.

---

ican people were paying an unacceptable price in terms of unsafe airlines, insolvent savings-and-loan banks, and increased environmental hazards.

Through much of Reagan's first term, economic revival remained an unfulfilled promise. The policy of reviving the economy through substantial tax cuts could not be easily reconciled with the Federal Reserve Board's attempt to check inflation through credit restraints. By early 1982, the United States was experiencing the highest levels of unemployment since the Great Depression. The basic industries, such as steel and automobiles, were especially hard hit, and this accelerated a decline that had begun much earlier. Many businesses went bankrupt, unemployment exceeded 10 percent of the work force (some 12 million workers were without jobs by the end of 1982), and interest rates for borrowed money remained discouragingly high.

By late 1983, however, the economy had improved sufficiently for Reagan to claim victory for his economic theories. Inflation had been checked (with the help of declining oil prices), interest rates had come down significantly, and factory production and employment had increased. The renewed vigor of the economy, which persisted into Reagan's second term, surprised forecasters and did much to enhance the president's popularity.

Not all Americans, however, benefited from the economic revival. The unemployment rate for blacks remained twice that for whites. Disparities between the incomes of poorer families and those of more affluent families grew markedly. The national poverty rate rose to 15.2 percent in 1983 from 13 percent in 1980; the number of poor people grew by 6 million, to a total of 35.3 million. (A family of four was classified as poor if it had a cash income of less than $10,178 in 1983.) Nearly 36 percent of all blacks lived in poverty in 1983, the highest rate since the Census Bureau began collecting data on black poverty in 1966.

The substantial increase in military spending and the consequent growth of the federal deficit to unprecedented levels also raised serious questions about the future of the economy. But for the overwhelming majority of the American electorate in 1984, Reagan's vision of a revived America—economically and militarily—seemed at hand.

Civil Rights

For some twenty years, the federal government had played an active role in expanding and enforcing programs designed to ensure the civil rights of black Americans. The Reagan presidency reflected growing doubts about the wisdom and effectiveness of some of these programs, particularly those aimed at eliminating discrimination in employment through affirmative or preferential hiring and at eliminating school segregation through busing. Despite the president's avowed support for civil rights, his administration reversed a bipartisan consensus and significantly restricted the range of remedies available to government to eliminate racial discrimination and to guarantee equal chances at jobs and promotions to blacks and women.

Federal agencies charged with enforcing civil rights found themselves frustrated by diminished appropriations or revised guidelines. The policy embraced by the Reagan administration required people alleging discrimination in employment, for example, to prove that it was intentional. This negated broad-based affirmative-action programs designed to reverse the effects of *past* discrimination. In a major victory for the administration, the Supreme Court ruled that judges could not alter the rules of a valid seniority system to prevent the layoff of recently hired blacks.

Once the watchdog over Democratic and Republican administrations' compliance with civil rights laws, the Civil Rights Commission came to be dominated by members who shared President Reagan's view of limited government and opposition to school busing and affirmative action. On some issues, the president bowed to public or congressional pressure to moderate his civil rights positions. Despite his initial resistance, for example, he ultimately signed a bill, passed overwhelmingly by Congress, to extend and strengthen the Voting Rights Act of 1965. Reagan showed similar flexibility in yielding to bipartisan support for establishing a national holiday on the anniversary of Martin Luther King's birth.

The civil rights arena had shifted in the 1970s to the North and to the question of how to achieve genuine racial integration in the public schools. The controversy rose out of the Supreme Court's argument in its 1954 decision that segregated education was inherently unequal because it perpetuated a caste system based on race. Since integration in most major cities was confined to the city limits, especially in the North, school systems remained in large measure segregated. Faced with this paradox, the courts held that combining urban school districts with those in the suburbs and if necessary busing pupils across municipal boundaries was a legitimate way to achieve a racially integrated system. Since nearly half of all schoolchildren in the nation already traveled to school by bus each day, desegregation

by busing appeared to require no radical departure from custom.

But the prospect of busing children to achieve racial integration produced considerable panic and hysteria in much of urban America, as did various proposals to reorganize school districts for the same purpose. The controversy intensified in the 1970s, with growing political repercussions. The Reagan administration no doubt reflected strong popular feelings when it authorized the Justice Department and law enforcement officials to assist communities and individuals seeking "relief" from desegregation and busing orders.

At the same time, the Reagan administration argued—unsuccessfully—in 1982 that the Internal Revenue Service did not have the authority to deny tax-exempt status to private educational institutions that practiced racial discrimination. After the Supreme Court forced the Justice Department by a vote of eight to one to back down on that decision, the administration renewed its efforts to obtain tax credits that would help parents offset tuition costs at private and parochial schools and colleges, even though this might have the effect of subsidizing "white flight" from the public schools. Congress, however, refused to approve the necessary legislation.

By the 1980s, more children in northern cities attended racially segregated schools than at the time of the Supreme Court decision in *Brown v. Board of Education*. In 1954, only one of the twenty largest cities in the country (Washington, D.C.) had a white minority in its public schools; twenty-five years later, whites were a minority in the schools of eighteen of the twenty largest cities. By 1980, nearly three-quarters of the black children in the nation's twenty-six largest cities attended schools with 90 to 100 percent black enrollment. White hostility to desegregation, in both the North and the South, underscored the depth and complexity of racial attitudes in the nation.

FOREIGN POLICY: PEACE THROUGH STRENGTH

Like the heroes he admired in Hollywood films, Ronald Reagan wanted to make Uncle Sam respected and feared once again in the world community. He appealed to that traditional sense of the United States as a moral frontier with a special, unique destiny—a "city upon the hill" that would inspire the world.

I've always believed that this land was placed here between the two great oceans by some divine plan. It was placed there to be found by a special kind of people. We built a new breed of human, called an American. We can meet our destiny, and that destiny is to build a land here that will be for all mankind a shining city on a hill.

The humiliations in Vietnam and Iran Reagan viewed as debilitating experiences for the American people. Respect would come, he believed, only from military strength and preparedness, and his determination to raise the level of military spending rested firmly on that belief. Once the nation had renewed its military power, it would be in a position to pursue a foreign policy that would make it once again the leader of the "free world."

Farewell to Détente

Upon becoming president Reagan chose as secretary of state Alexander Haig, a former Nixon aide and NATO commander. Haig seemed ideally suited for a commitment to a tougher foreign policy. "There are things worse than war," he told a Senate committee, and he vowed that the United States would not enter any war it was not prepared to win. That was the kind of language the president wanted to hear, and Reagan himself provided much of the inflated rhetoric for the departure in American foreign policy.

The inauguration had hardly ended before Reagan unleashed the kind of verbal attack on the Soviet Union that had not been heard since the 1950s. In his first press conference, he said the Russians could not be trusted because "they reserve unto themselves the right to commit any crime, to lie, to cheat" in order to achieve world domination. The Soviet Union, Reagan insisted, "underlies all the unrest" in the world. And he underscored the differences between the two great superpowers: "They don't subscribe to our sense of morality because they don't believe in any of the good things; they don't believe in an afterlife. They don't believe in a God or a religion, and . . . the only morality they recognize, therefore, is what will advance the cause of socialism." In a speech in Orlando, Florida, in 1983 to fundamentalist preachers, Reagan excoriated the Soviet Union as "an evil empire" and called upon his audience to enlist in a new crusade: "There is sin and evil in the world and we are enjoined by Scriptures and the Lord Jesus to oppose it with all our might."

Midway through Reagan's first term, Haig's feud with White House staff members resulted in his resignation under pressure. To replace him, Reagan turned to George Shultz, a former Nixon cabinet member who was regarded as a team player. But the change brought no lessening of the growing tension in Soviet-American relations. The assumption persisted that the Soviet Union was at the head of a monstrous international conspiracy bent on world conquest and the destruction of the American way of life. To confront and contain Soviet power and international communism became once again the guiding principle of American foreign policy.

Persuaded that the Soviets understood only force, Reagan proceeded with a massive military buildup. He did agree to resume arms-control talks with the Soviets, focused on mutual and balanced reductions in nuclear arsenals. But no agreement could be reached by the end of 1983, the date on which the United States had promised to deploy intermediate-range Pershing 2 and cruise missiles in Western Europe that could reach targets hundreds of miles inside the Soviet Union within a matter of minutes. The United States and NATO contended that the deployment was a necessary response to the Soviet modernization of its missiles aimed at Western Europe. The Soviet Union claimed that a balance of destructive weapons already existed and that deployment of the new missiles destabilized that balance.

The Reagan administration linked any reduction in Cold War tensions to a demonstrated improvement in Soviet behavior. The Soviet Union argued that its behavior in international affairs reflected a concern over threats to its own national security. Such a concern kept Soviet armed forces in Afghanistan in a frustrating and costly effort to bolster the Communist government there. Of equal concern to the Soviets was the emergence in Poland of an independent trade union movement (Solidarity). That Polish authorities were forced to recognize Solidarity as a legitimate trade union was in itself an impressive triumph in a Communist nation. But when Solidarity then insisted on still more fundamental reforms—an implied challenge to Communist hegemony in Poland and Eastern Europe—officials in both Warsaw and Moscow knew that a confrontation was unavoidable.

In the winter of 1981, the Polish government imposed martial law and dissolved Solidarity. The United States denounced the action as Soviet-inspired and imposed sanctions on both Poland and the Soviet Union. Eight years later, reflecting new leadership in the Soviet Union and a new toleration of dissent in Eastern Europe, a Polish court reinstated Solidarity as a legal trade-union organization. Within a year, Solidarity would move into political power—only one of the sweeping changes that would end forty-five years of Communist rule in Eastern Europe.

Mounting tensions and distrust between the United States and the Soviet Union had a tragic consequence on September 1, 1983, when a Soviet fighter plane shot down a South Korean airliner that had strayed off course into militarily sensitive Soviet territory. All 269 passengers aboard, including a number of Americans, were killed, and the world expressed profound shock. Reagan condemned it as an "act of barbarism." The Soviet Union defended the action, claiming the Korean airliner was on a spying mission or had been mistaken for one of the American spy aircraft that flew the same course. Subsequent investigation suggested that Soviet personnel had not known it was a commercial plane before ordering the attack. Ultimate responsibility, however, lay in the tensions that had provoked such an unwarranted response.

International Tensions, Old and New

In the Middle East, the Reagan administration pursued a foreign policy that differed in few respects from that of its predecessors. The United States sought a strong Israel aligned with "moderate" Arab states that would serve to discourage Soviet intrusion into the region and keep Western oil supplies flowing from the Persian Gulf. But policy makers in Washington never seemed to grasp the dimensions and complexity of the various religious, ethnic, and revolutionary movements that make up this volatile area. The position of the Palestinians, including the 1.2 million in Israeli-occupied Gaza and the West Bank, continued to deteriorate, and Israelis continued to construct Jewish settlements in the occupied territories.

In June 1982 Israel invaded Lebanon, ostensibly to secure its northern border from raids and shellings. But the major objectives appeared to be the destruction of the military strength of the Palestine Liberation Organization (PLO) and the restructuring of Lebanon. Israeli troops reached Beirut, inflicting heavy losses on the civilian population and forcing the evacuation from Lebanon of the bulk of the PLO armed forces. Public opinion in Israel was divided over the wisdom of the invasion, and many in Israel and elsewhere expressed revulsion over the consequences of an intensified civil war in Lebanon. In Muslim West Beirut, for example, Lebanese Christian militiamen supported and armed by Israel took charge of the Sabra and Shatila refugee camps, which housed the families of the evacuated Palestinian fighting men. As the Israelis stood by, Christian gunmen rampaged through the two camps, executing hundreds of defenseless Palestinians.

The United States, England, Italy, and France agreed to dispatch peacekeeping troops to Lebanon to replace the Israelis and to bolster the new Christian-led Lebanese government. But these troops soon became embroiled in the civil war among Muslims and Christians. The loss of American lives, including some 241 marines and sailors in a suicide truck bombing of the barracks headquarters, finally shocked Americans into action. In Congress, questions were raised about the wisdom of an operation designed to prop up a Christian-led government in a predominantly Muslim country. But President Reagan, using language that evoked memories of Vietnam, defended the American presence in Lebanon as "central to our credibility on a global scale" and necessary "to stop the cancerous spread of Soviet influence." In February 1984, however, the president reversed himself. Bowing to public concern, he reluctantly withdrew the marines.

Consistent with the administration's view of the Soviet Union as an expansionist power, the United States insisted on the need to combat Communist influence wherever it appeared and no matter what form it assumed. In a shift from the position of the Carter administration, Reagan's policy makers made it clear that the United States would be more flexible in the future in applying human-rights standards to friendly (anti-Communist) governments. But congressional and public pressures and pragmatic foreign-policy considerations forced some stiffening of this position.

The administration followed its immediate predecessors in pursuing friendly relations with Communist China, although Reagan had once insisted on support of the Nationalist Chinese on Taiwan as a major tenet of the conservative creed. The same pragmatism in 1986 forced Reagan to abandon his friend and ally, Ferdinand Marcos, the president and strong man of the Philippines, after he was deposed in a popular and peaceful uprising. The United States also bowed to pressure and became more critical of the minority white regime in South Africa. That government, underpinned by Western capital, used the practice of segregation (apartheid), disfranchisement, and brutal police tactics to repress the 23 million blacks who formed the overwhelming majority of the population. When Reagan came into the presidency, he pledged a policy of "constructive engagement" in South Africa, by which the United States would use quiet diplomacy and pressure to force changes in apartheid. When those pressures failed to produce any results, sentiment increased for more forceful measures, and in 1986 Congress approved economic sanctions against South Africa, overriding President Reagan's veto.

In Central America, the Reagan administration stood firm in its determination to contain and root out Communist influence. El Salvador had become a battleground between leftist guerrillas and a repressive military regime. The danger of a guerrilla victory took precedence over invasions of human rights and right-wing terrorism, and the Reagan administration gave its full support to the beleaguered anti-Communist regime. In May 1984 a United States–inspired election produced a new government under José Napoleon Duarte. But the problems of reform and internal rebellion remained unresolved, and Duarte and his successor were unable to halt the activities of right-wing death squads.

Of much greater concern to the Reagan administration, a leftist government had come to power in Nicaragua in 1979. Revolutionaries won their war against Anastasio Somoza, long an ally of the United States and the head of the family that had run the country for some forty-five years. The rebels, called Sandinistas, modeled themselves after Augusto Cesar Sandino, a Nicaraguan nationalist leader who had fought American marines in the early 1930s. The triumph of the Sandinistas, the revolutionary ideas they expounded, their growing ties with Castro's Cuba, and the suspicion that they actively assisted the rebels in El Salvador were deemed sufficient reasons for the United States to grant covert military support to Nicaraguan rebels (contras), many of them former Somoza supporters, seeking to overthrow the Sandinista government.

The president went so far as to proclaim the contras "the moral equivalent of our Founding Fathers," despite their record of attacking civilians indiscriminately, torturing and mutilating prisoners, and terrorizing the countryside. The controversy over support of the contras divided the United States, with opinion polls indicating public opposition and anxiety over the possible involvement of American troops. In Congress, the Nicaraguan issue generated an ongoing debate. Democrats and Republicans alike expressed concern over a Communist sanctuary in Central America. But disagreement prevailed over the advisability of United States intervention in the area, and serious questions were raised about the democratic commitments of the contra forces. Violations of human rights by the Nicaraguan government seemed no more flagrant than violations by the contras, which proved far more costly in lives and property. Congress vacillated, providing military assistance to the *contras*, then barring such assistance but sustaining the contra forces through nonlethal aid and pressing both sides for a negotiated settlement.

Although President Reagan raised his anti-Communist rhetoric to new heights, the actions he pursued never quite matched the harsh words. In Nicaragua, he resorted to covert activities rather than risk the direct intervention of American troops; in Lebanon he recalled the marines rather than risk the consequences of a stepped-up military role. Closer to home, however, Reagan found a way to demonstrate his firmness in foreign policy without paying a high cost or taking a large risk. On October 25, 1983, he ordered the invasion of the small island of Grenada in the eastern Caribbean. The administration claimed its purpose was to protect Americans on the island, to restore democratic institutions, to forestall a "Cuban occupation," and to remove "a brutal group of leftist thugs." Critics found little evidence of a major Communist threat in Grenada, but the move was popular with most Americans, and the casualties were minimal.

That the Grenada victory coincided with improved economic conditions in the United States and the patriotic frenzy that dominated the 1984 Olympic Games in Los Angeles boded well for Reagan's reelection campaign. It was less a political campaign on issues than a demonstration of Reagan's continued ability to project a favorable image for most Americans.

REAGAN'S "POLITICAL REVOLUTION": THE SECOND TERM

Although the president often evoked the past to serve his vision of America, the Reagan administration marked a fundamental break with the past. It sought to rewrite the national agenda, to reverse previous economic and social policy. Not only did it envision dismantling all but the most basic elements of the New Deal and Great Society social programs, but it proposed to make their restoration politically and financially impractical.

After four years in the White House, Reagan could boast to the Republican nominating convention in 1984 that he had achieved many of his goals. He had reduced the growth of the federal government. He had reduced interest rates and inflation. He had reduced taxes, thereby providing incentives for individuals and business. And, he concluded, "we said we would once again be respected throughout the world, and we are. We said we would restore our ability to protect our freedom on land, sea and in the air, and we have." He promised the delegates four more years of the same policy, striving to realize that "dream of an America that would be 'a shining city on a hill.' "

Reagan's Referendum: The Election of 1984

The election of 1984 was significant in several respects. The Democratic party became the first major party to nominate a woman, Representative Geraldine Ferraro of New York, for vice-president. In the Democratic primaries, moreover, the Reverend Jesse Jackson, a former co-worker of Martin Luther King and a black civil rights activist, became the first black candidate to win substantial support in a bid for the presidential nomination of a major party. Second, Ronald Reagan scored a landslide victory, winning forty-nine states and further fragmenting the old New Deal coalition. Walter Mondale, the Democratic candidate and former senator and vice-president, managed to win only his home state of Minnesota and the District of Columbia. Third, the census of 1980 confirmed the substantial movement of Americans from the Northeast to the Sunbelt states of the South and West, where conservative political principles and suspicion of federal power had long been entrenched; the latter states gave Reagan his most substantial majorities.

In the campaign Reagan defended his administration's record while Mondale tried unsuccessfully to exploit the huge deficit and show how the president's policies had hurt working people, farmers, and blacks. Reagan benefited from the remarkable economic recovery, including significantly reduced inflation and lower unemployment.

More effectively than his opponent, Reagan conveyed to Americans a sense of the direction in which he wanted to take the country. He emphasized individual and national self-reliance, a deregulated market, and slimmed-down and decentralized government. It was a simple and consistent message that spoke in broad terms of values rather than issues, and it succeeded spectacularly. Both Reagan and Mondale thought the election provided the American people with a clear ideological choice. But it appeared to be largely a contest of personalities and a referendum on Reagan's leadership, and on these grounds the incumbent held a clear advantage.

The presence of a woman on the Democratic ticket made no apparent difference in the outcome. Along with Ferraro, all the women Senate hopefuls and challengers for House seats were defeated. Reagan won 61 percent of the men's vote and 57 percent of the women's vote. The only group he lost overwhelmingly was the black electorate, of which some 90 percent voted for Mondale. Hispanics voted 65 to 33 percent for Mondale. But whites voted 66 to 34 percent for Reagan. As if to remind the president that the election was not necessarily a triumph for his conservative ideology, voters returned a Democratic House of Representatives.

Perhaps a more sobering election statistic was the number of Americans who found no compelling reason to exercise their right to vote. Despite the apparent popularity of Reagan, some 47 percent of the voting-age population failed to vote at all. The economic class to which potential voters belonged appeared to make a critical difference. Only 46 percent of eligible voters with a family income below $10,000 went to the polls, compared with 74 percent of those with incomes of $35,000 or more.

Farewell to the New Deal

In his State of the Union address at the start of his second term, Ronald Reagan reiterated an essential theme of his administration: keeping the United States militarily strong and prepared was the principal responsibility of the federal government. To that end, the president proposed a nearly 12 percent increase in military spending. Under the proposed buildup, military outlays would account for twenty-eight cents of every federal dollar spent in 1987. Consistent with the president's priorities, the new budget once again cut deeply into social programs, eliminating some of them altogether. Congress, on the other hand,

Ronald Reagan scored a landslide victory in the election of 1984, winning forty-nine states. *(Terry Arthur, The White House)*

preferred a more evenhanded approach, in which military and social programs would share the cuts necessary to reduce the deficit.

The new budget required the executive and legislative branches to operate under some new constraints. To meet growing concern over the huge federal deficit, Congress had passed a far-reaching and controversial deficit-reduction act (named after the co-sponsors, Senators Phil Gramm of Texas, Warren Rudman of New Hampshire, and Ernest Hollings of South Carolina) in 1984. The act would force a $36 billion reduction in the deficit in each of five fiscal years ending in 1991, ostensibly achieving a balanced budget by then. If the president and Congress failed to make such cuts in the conventional manner, the president would be required to impose the necessary reductions by cutting military as well as nonmilitary spending. The act aroused considerable controversy. Congress also needed to consider public opinion. Although Reagan remained immensely popular, polls showed that sizable majorities thought the government should spend more, not less, on aid to the poor and the environment; only 17 percent of the public favored increased military outlays.

With impressive bipartisan support, Congress completed a fundamental revision of the nation's tax system. The Income Tax Act of 1986 reduced the top levy on personal incomes from 50 percent to 28 percent and the tax on corporate profits from 46 percent to 34 percent. This far-reaching piece of legislation also attempted to eliminate tax shelters and special credits previously used by corporations and individuals to lower their tax bills. In addition, it exempted from federal income taxes some 6 million low-income Americans. With its two fixed rates (15 percent on taxable incomes below $17,850 for individuals and $29,750 for families; 28 percent on incomes above those amounts), the new act significantly altered the old assumption that those receiving a higher income should pay a progressively larger percentage of that income in taxes.

President Reagan hailed the measure as the kind of tax revision he had long favored; indeed, his resentment toward income taxes dated back to his high-earning years as a Hollywood actor. The tax policies of the Reagan presidency accelerated the realignment of wealth in the United States. The substantial tax cuts of 1981 and 1986 meant that the top personal income tax dropped from 70 percent to 28 percent. The prime beneficiaries were the wealthiest 5 percent of Americans. Although critics would pounce on Reagan's tax policy as evidence of his partiality toward the wealthy, the tax reductions could not have been enacted without the support and votes of congressional Democrats.

The domestic objectives Reagan had pursued in his first four years remained very much in place during the second term. The long-range effects of Reagan's "political revolution" seemed no longer in doubt. In his eight years in office, Reagan fundamentally altered the shape and role of government in American life, producing substantial changes in federal spending and in the substance and purposes of domestic programs. He succeeded, moreover, in altering the terms of the debate concerning the role of government and federal spending. The focus was no longer on which social programs to strengthen or expand, but on the size of the cuts and on which programs deserved to be scrapped altogether. The focus was no longer on expanding and enforcing civil rights rules, but rather on limiting their application and in some instances abandoning them.

In slowing the growth of federal programs, the Reagan administration reshaped the national agenda and reversed a trend in the role of government that Democratic and Republican presidents had previously accepted. Still, the federal budget accounted for more of the national wealth than it did on the day Reagan took office, mostly because of the enormous increases in military spending, interest costs on the federal debt, and the growth built into the largest automatic benefit programs, such as social security and medicare. The president who had vowed to balance the budget presided instead over the largest budget deficits in history (Reagan's final budget proposal projected a deficit of $92.5 billion) and an almost equally spectacular increase in the foreign debt. For the first time since World War I, the United States in 1986 owed foreigners more than they owed it.

The Moral Revolution

When Reagan became president, he promised a moral as well as a political revolution. But revelations of corruption and greed in high places undermined his pledge "to clean up the mess in Washington." Few administrations, Democratic or Republican, had not been tainted by officials charged with unethical conduct. But the Reagan administration proved especially vulnerable to conflicts of interest and financial scandals, perhaps reflecting the large number of businessmen in administrative posts.

During Reagan's first term, six high-ranking officials were indicted on criminal charges and twenty-five were discharged, resigned their posts, or had their nominations withdrawn under fire. By the end of Reagan's presidency, the number of officials who had come under criminal indictments or suspicion of corruption had climbed to well over a hundred. The revelations of illegal activity emanating from the Iran-contra scandal brought still more indictments against Reagan officials, including two national security advisers.

Reagan also came to office with a specific moral agenda reflecting his strong conservative and evangelical support. That agenda did not fare as well as his promised military buildup and reduction of social programs. Some obvious paradoxes confronted the president. He needed to reconcile his strong moral convictions regarding abortion and school prayer, for example, with his pledge "to get the government off the backs of the people." To implement some of the moral reforms he desired, such as constitutional amendments to outlaw abortion and to permit organized state-sponsored prayer in public schools, would be to increase government intervention in the day-to-day lives of Americans—the very trend he had promised to halt. None of the proposals came close to congressional passage.

But President Reagan laid the groundwork for ultimate implementation of his moral agenda in the appointments he made to the nation's courts. The most enduring legacy of Reagan's "political revolution" would no doubt be the transformation of the judiciary. The 378 appointments he made constituted a majority of the 752 judges in the lower federal courts. His appointments to the Supreme Court were no less critical. The most spectacular of his nominations was that of Sandra Day O'Connor to the Supreme Court—the first woman to serve in that position.

That O'Connor should also have had impeccable conservative credentials was consistent with Reagan's determination to have the nation's courts reflect his political and social philosophy. To replace Chief Justice Warren E. Burger, who resigned in 1986, Reagan chose the most conservative associate justice, William H. Rehnquist. To fill that vacancy, Reagan turned to still another staunch conservative, Antonin Scalia. But Reagan's effort to continue this trend with Robert H. Bork produced a bitter debate. Critics charged that Bork, based on his judicial record and speeches and writings, would reverse Supreme Court precedents in such critical areas as civil rights, women's issues, and privacy. The Senate rejected the Bork nomination (by the largest vote in history against a nominee for the Supreme Court), relegating the would-be justice to the lecture and writing circuit, where he blamed his defeat on a conspiracy of "left-liberal" pressure groups and "nihilists." Meanwhile, Reagan settled for Anthony M. Kennedy, a less controversial but no less conservative nominee, and the Senate this time gave its assent.

Although Reagan lost the Bork fight, he nevertheless changed fundamentally the composition and ideology of the federal judiciary system. For the first time in a generation, a conservative majority was in a position to establish a new direction in such critical areas as civil rights, criminal law, sex discrimination, and abortion. On government affirmative-action programs, the Court rejected several initiatives aimed at uprooting discrimination in employment and made it more difficult for plaintiffs to win job-discrimination suits. In equally far-reaching decisions, the Court gave states more freedom to restrict abortions and narrowed the rights of criminal defendants. The Court remained narrowly split, usually handing down decisions by five-to-four votes, but the Reagan appointments made the difference.

FOREIGN POLICY: NEW CHALLENGES AND OPPORTUNITIES

Since World War II, the United States had acquired, through treaties or political agreements, military commitments to some sixty countries. With one-third of the armed forces deployed abroad, the United States was particularly vulnerable to political upheavals, revolutionary uprisings, nationalistic outbreaks, and regional conflicts in various parts of the world. President Reagan, like his predecessors, faced an assortment of challenges. But he also enjoyed some unique opportunities to reduce international tensions and wind down the Cold War.

The Varied Meanings of Terrorism: The Middle East and Central America

Much of Reagan's second term was focused on how to respond to the rise in terrorist attacks and kidnappings aimed at Americans abroad, most of which stemmed from the ongoing tensions in the Middle East. Expressions of outrage were increasingly considered insufficient. In 1986 the United States chose armed retaliation by bombing military and intelligence bases in Libya, the country Reagan considered most responsible for encouraging terrorism. Such retaliation, however, usually claimed as its victims, as it did in Libya, innocent civilians rather than the alleged perpetrators of the acts being avenged.

The 1980s war between Iran and Iraq led to attacks on the ships of nations dependent on Middle East oil who used the critical sea lanes of the Persian Gulf. When President Reagan finally ordered American warships to ensure the safety of such ships, most Americans appeared to support him. But questions were raised nevertheless, in and out of Congress, about the need to limit America's role as the world's policeman. Those questions took on a new urgency when American armed presence in the Persian Gulf resulted in a tragedy of mistaken identity. On July 3, 1988, a United States missile cruiser, thinking it was protecting itself from a hostile aircraft, mistakenly shot down an Iranian airliner, killing 290 civilians. A military investigation subsequently concluded that the action had resulted from crew error arising from the psychological stress of being in combat for the first time. The tragedy prompted obvious comparisons to the earlier Soviet downing of a South Korean airliner, also because of mistaken identity. President Reagan had condemned that attack as "an act of barbarism, born of a society which wantonly disregards individual rights and the value of human life." Reacting to the disaster over the Persian Gulf, the president called it a "terrible human tragedy" but an "understandable accident."

The problem of combating terrorism in the world was complicated by varying perceptions of what constituted terrorism. President Reagan, for example, referred to the contra rebels in Nicaragua as freedom fighters, whereas the Sandinistas regarded them as little more than terrorists because of their indiscriminate attacks on Nicaraguan farm cooperatives and civilians. Supporters of the Palestine Liberation Organization hailed its soldiers as freedom fighters and deplored the "terrorist" behavior of Israeli troops in the occupied West Bank, while the United States and Israel refused to negotiate with the PLO on the grounds that it was a terrorist organization.

By the end of the Reagan presidency, the problems posed by these distinctions had mounted rapidly. In November 1987, the Palestine National Council proclaimed an independent nation in the West Bank and Gaza Strip, and by December Israeli forces were involved in an ongoing and costly battle to suppress an uprising of Palestinians, popularly known as the *intifada*. Most of the rebels were young and were armed with little more than rocks in their fight for freedom.

Closer to home, the Reagan administration remained deeply committed to the overthrow of the Sandinista government in Nicaragua. That commitment resulted in the most far-reaching scandal affecting the Reagan presidency—what came to be known as the Iran-contra affair, a complicated arrangement involving both the Middle East and Nicaragua. In 1986 President Reagan authorized the sale of arms to Iran (with whom the United States had no diplomatic relations) in exchange for Iran's influence in obtaining the release of four American hostages held by factions in Lebanon sympathetic to the Ayatollah Khomeini. The profits from the arms sales would be used to fund the contras in Nicaragua, although Congress had barred such assistance. To circumvent that ban, top administration officials and the Central Intelligence Agency also applied pressure on several friendly countries to provide aid to the contras.

In nationally televised hearings, Congress explored the involvement of federal officials and an assortment of outsiders in the scandal. Subsequent investigations by a special government prosecutor provided additional details of the illegal operations and of the attempted cover-up. Several administration aides were forced out of their posts, and some of these would be indicted for violations of federal law. Robert C. McFarlane, the president's former national security adviser, pleaded guilty to withholding information from Congress about the Reagan administration's secret efforts to assist the contras. John M. Poindexter, one of Reagan's closest aides and also a former national security adviser, was sentenced to prison for committing five felonies, including conspiracy to deceive Congress and lying to Congress. Oliver L. North, a former marine lieutenant colonel who served as a staff member on the National Security Council, was convicted of aiding and abetting the obstruction of Congress, destroying confidential documents, and accepting an illegal gift. In videotaped testimony at the Poindexter trial, Reagan said he had granted authority to supervise arms sales and contra-aid efforts, but he could recall few details of the operations and insisted he had never counseled disobedience of the law.

The Iran-contra scandal diminished President Reagan's popularity. Throughout his presidency,

Marine Lieutenant Colonel Oliver North before the House Foreign Affairs Committee. *(UPI/Bettmann Newsphotos)*

however, Reagan showed a remarkable capacity to bounce back from political embarrassments. The "teflon presidency," as some journalists labeled it, seldom had to bear responsibility for actions that went amiss. The president demonstrated a similar capacity for exploiting such fortuitous developments as the triumph of a new leadership in the Soviet Union.

Gorbachev and the Cold War

In March 1985, Mikhail S. Gorbachev became the new premier of the Soviet Union. Almost immediately, he signaled a sharp departure from his predecessors—in his moderation and flexibility, in his sensitivity to world opinion, in his unprecedented toleration of dissent and improvements in human rights, and in his determination to ease the economic burden on his people by spending less on military needs, ending the unpopular and costly war in Afghanistan, and reaching an accommodation with the United States.

That accommodation would not be quickly or easily reached. Nothing came of the initial summit conference between Reagan and Gorbachev in November 1985, but the two leaders appeared to get along, and that in itself eased tensions. Relations between the two countries remained highly volatile, however, alternating between expressions of willingness to cooperate and harsh rhetoric. Much of the debate over arms control revolved around President Reagan's decision to embrace the costly and still unproved Strategic Defense Initiative (popularly called Star Wars). This highly complex military system in space would, if successful, establish an impenetrable defensive shield against ballistic missiles. The Soviets denounced the proposed militarization of space and the decision by the administration in 1986 to halt its voluntary compliance with the SALT II agreement limiting nuclear weaponry (never ratified by the Senate).

But Gorbachev had his own compelling reasons to hasten an agreement with the United States. His attempt at domestic revitalization—*glasnost* (openness) and *perestroika* (restructuring)—required more flexibility in dealing with the world and an end to the costly arms race. With world opinion favorably inclined toward Gorbachev's bold new proposals in arms reductions, moreover, the United States needed to reassess previous assumptions about the "evil empire." Renewed negotiations and several meetings between Reagan and Gorbachev in 1987 produced a far-reaching treaty banning intermediate-range nuclear missiles—the first arms-control agreement since 1972. The result of six years of negotiation, the pact called for the destruction of 1752 Soviet and 859 American missiles and established on-site verification procedures.

In 1988, in an address to the United Nations, Gorbachev proposed sizable cuts in Soviet military forces in the hope that the United States would consider comparable reductions. The United States reacted favorably, and both sides indicated a desire to move toward additional agreements—cultural and military—that would bring the two nations closer together. The visit of Gorbachev to the United States and the visit of Reagan to the Soviet Union further cemented Soviet-American relations in ways that few might have predicted at the outset of the Reagan presidency.

Reagan's Farewell

In his farewell address, Ronald Reagan talked of the achievements of his presidency. He voiced particular pride in the nation's economic recovery and "the recovery of our morale" as a world power. "We meant to change a nation," he declared, "and instead we changed a world." After eight years in the White House, he still preferred to think of himself as a "citizen politician" who as president had tried to reduce the size and influence of the federal government. "I think we have stopped a lot of what needed stopping," he boasted.

Unlike some of his predecessors, Reagan chose not to subject his presidency to critical analysis. He said nothing of the loss of American lives in Beirut or of the Americans still held hostage in the Middle East. He did deplore the size of the federal deficit but he refused to accept responsibility. He made no mention of the growing problems of homelessness and poverty. For all his talk of a "safety net," far more families in the United States lived below the poverty line in 1988 than in 1980, including nearly one in four children. The Reagan presidency had significantly altered the economic landscape of America, widening considerably the gap between the nation's rich and poor.

In foreign affairs, the president could rightfully take pride in the arms-control agreement, a new relationship with the Soviet Union, and a truce between Iran and Iraq that eased tensions in the Persian Gulf. But violence persisted in the Middle East, and the Palestinian uprising in the Israeli-occupied West Bank and Gaza Strip posed new challenges to American policy in that region. In

Central America, the Reagan administration had failed to topple the Nicaraguan government, and civil war continued to rage in El Salvador. Consistent with the positive, optimistic tone of his farewell address, however, the same president who had talked only eight years earlier of an "evil empire" boasted of having established "a satisfying new closeness" with the Soviet Union. He praised Gorbachev, distinguishing him from previous Soviet leaders. "I think he knows some of the things wrong with his society and is trying to fix them."

The Reagan Referendum: The Election of 1988

The presidential election of 1988 pitted Vice-President George Bush against Michael Dukakis, governor of Massachusetts. In the primaries, Bush easily outdistanced his rivals, while Dukakis faced his most significant challenge in the Reverend Jesse Jackson, who continued to command overwhelming black support. If nothing else, Jackson infused the campaign with his personality and oratory, at the same time forcing a more spirited debate among the Democratic candidates and pushing them toward more liberal positions.

Dukakis, however, won the nomination decisively. Vague about his political positions, he insisted that the real issue was competence, not ideology. Bush effectively exploited the economic recovery of the Reagan years—the decline in unemployment, inflation, and interest rates—and the improved relations with the Soviet Union. He also opted for the emotional issues that had worked so well for Reagan in 1984—crime, drugs, gun control, abortion, military superiority, and patriotism. The Bush campaign made an issue of Governor Dukakis's alleged leniency toward criminals, focusing on the case of a black prisoner who had raped a white woman while on leave from a Massachusetts prison. In a television blitzkrieg, commercials featured the black convict and also depicted prisoners, many of them black or Hispanic, passing through revolving prison doors.

The election results left no doubt about whose message had reached the American public. Although commanding less than Reagan's over-

George Bush, Ronald Reagan, and Mikhail Gorbachev, December 7, 1988, New York City. *(David Valdez/The White House)*

whelming majorities, Bush easily defeated Dukakis. The voter turnout in 1988 was the lowest since Calvin Coolidge defeated John W. Davis in 1924, perhaps reflecting the inability of the candidates in either election to arouse much enthusiasm in the American electorate. Of the 182,628,000 Americans of voting age, only 91,584,820 voted in 1988. The percentage of Americans casting their ballots had declined from 62.8 percent in 1960 to 52.6 percent in 1980 to 50.1 percent in 1988.

Electoral contests by the 1980s had become costly extravaganzas, with political hopefuls of both parties expending large sums on consultants and television time. In 1986, for example, the average cost of running for the House of Representatives was $286,000; the figure for the Senate was $2,681,639.

In assessing the results of the election, the Democrats needed to consider the continuing flight of white voters, who made up more than 80 percent of the electorate, to the Republican party. Since 1948, in fact, Lyndon Johnson (in 1964) was the only Democratic presidential nominee to carry white voters. Dukakis got 40 percent of that vote in 1988.

THE AMERICAN WOMAN IN THE 1980S AND 1990S

When *Time* magazine devoted a special issue to American women, in the wake of the defeat of the Equal Rights Amendment in 1982, it chose to subtitle its report "The Climb to Equality." The contributing editor who wrote the report explained, "The past decade has been a major step forward for women, but it is only one step in a long march." As the United States entered the last decade of the twentieth century, the women's rights movement had not yet achieved its objectives, indeed had suffered some serious setbacks. But comparisons with previous decades nevertheless revealed some dramatic advances, most of them widely accepted across the country.

Strides toward Equality

By the 1990s, women had made considerable progress in striking down discrimination based on sex, whether in higher education, the workplace, or the English language. In many fields, they were pursuing careers that had once been virtu-

ally closed to women. The nation had placed a woman on its space shuttles. A major political party had nominated a woman for vice-president. There had been an extraordinary increase in the number of women in public office, ranging from governors to legislators to judges, and a woman had been elevated for the first time to the Supreme Court. The significance of Sandra Day O'Connor's appointment lay partially in its irony. It was hailed by some as a triumph of the women's rights movement, although President Reagan had evinced little sympathy for that movement. But the appointment underscored the need to measure gains not simply by counting the number of women in professional schools but by looking at the kinds of opportunities available to them upon graduation. When Justice O'Connor had graduated from law school in 1952, the only job she had been offered by a major West Coast law firm was that of legal secretary.

Between 1950 and 1990, the number of women who worked outside the home climbed each year. The number of one-earner households declined rapidly, from over 50 percent to less than 25 percent; the percentage of women aged twenty-five to thirty-four who worked outside the home doubled, from 35 percent in 1950 to over 70 percent in 1990; and for the first time the number of children with mothers who worked exceeded the number of children with mothers at home. In 1950, 12 percent of all women with children under the age of six were in the labor force; in 1990, 57 percent of all such mothers worked outside the home. By 1990, more than 56 million American women worked, making up 45 percent of the work force, compared with 38 percent in 1970. By the year 2000, women are expected to represent almost half the labor force.

As late as 1968, women had lagged seriously behind men in educational attainments. But by 1990 that gap, whether measured by high school graduation or by a college degree, had almost closed. And women had made impressive inroads into fields once virtually closed to them: law, medicine, engineering, and business. By 1990, one out of five of the nation's doctors and lawyers was a woman; in 1970, women had accounted for only 7 percent of the nation's doctors and 3 percent of the lawyers. And by 1990, almost half of all accountants and bus drivers were women. But even as women moved into hitherto male-dominated careers and occupations, disparities continued in the pay they received for performing comparable work. Women who worked full-time earned, on the average, seventy cents for every dollar a man earned (the ratio was improving: it had been sixty-two cents in the late 1960s).

The extensive changes in the place of women in American society could not be measured entirely by statistics. More elusive, not subject to quantification, were changes in the consciousness and expectations of women. As late as the 1960s, women had needed to consider the feasibility of having a family and at the same time sustaining a career. Thirty years later, more American women acted on the assumption that they could do both.

The prominence of women in the workplace altered but by no means eliminated the cultural stereotypes that exploited woman's traditional roles. Even as advertisers and women's magazines had once ratified the bliss and rewards of domesticity, they now gave voice to the New Woman of the 1980s and 1990s, who managed to balance challenging careers with domestic responsibilities and personal appearance. Advertisers of beauty aids, for example, now played on the theme "She's busy yet she's beautiful." Even more revealing, an actress, wife, and mother declared in an advertisement, "I'm often tired but I never show it."

The Controversy over Abortion

If the Equal Rights Amendment dominated the politics of the 1970s, the issue of abortion generated the deepest controversy in the 1980s and 1990s, spilling over into national, state, and local politics. More than any other issue, legal abortion came to preoccupy the women's rights movement. In demanding unrestricted abortion, activists rejected the traditional restraints placed upon women and attacked sexual double standards — the publicizing of unwanted pregnancies, for example, to deter and punish female sexual activity. The "pro-choice" activists included women who deemed the right to abortion on demand symbolic of their expectation of social and economic equality, and there were many as well who remembered vividly the often barbarous nature of illegal or self-inflicted abortions.

The same concerns that had mobilized women and men to oppose the Equal Rights Amendment were expressed with even greater vehemence and conviction in the opposition to abortions. Not only did abortions undermine moral values, opponents argued, they murdered the unborn. The "pro-life" movement emerged in the wake of the Supreme Court decision in Roe v. Wade. Although they had

a varied constituency, as did the "pro-choice" movement, the pro-lifers drew much of their support from moral conservatives and from women and men who not only equated abortions with murder but who viewed them as an affront to the sacredness of motherhood. The pro-life forces portrayed themselves as the defenders of the home and the family; they perceived the pro-choice movement, along with the gay rights movement, as imperiling not only the home, the family, and traditional values but the American Dream itself.

After the Supreme Court decision, birth control and abortion services were more widely available. But as the abortion issue polarized the nation, the tactics used by pro-life activists became more militant: fire bombs destroyed a number of medical offices and abortion clinics, and "rescue" squads blocked the entrances to the clinics, harassing patients and providers before being forcibly removed and arrested. Many antiabortion advocates deplored these tactics, preferring to focus on the arts of political persuasion. The issue assumed increasing political importance in 1977, when Congress curtailed federal funding of abortions. (The Supreme Court refused in 1980 to overturn that action, holding that government had no obligation to provide abortions to the poor, even for compelling medical reasons.) Both Presidents Reagan and Bush vigorously opposed abortion and promised to appoint conservatives to the courts who would be in sympathy with their philosophies.

With the composition of the Supreme Court having changed dramatically since 1973, the issue of abortion rights was bound to reemerge. On July 3, 1989, the Court, in Webster v. Reproductive Health Services, by a five-to-four vote, gave states the right to impose new restrictions on abortion. Although the Court stopped short of overturning the landmark Roe v. Wade decision, it upheld a Missouri law that restricted when and where a woman could terminate a pregnancy. The Court, in the words of one dissenting justice, had opened the door to "more and more restrictive" state regulations that would impede the "meaningful exercise" of Roe v. Wade. Clearly, a majority of the Court no longer considered abortion to be a constitutional right.

Far from ending the battles over judicial intrusion on abortion issues, the Court's decision shifted the battleground from the courts to the state and federal legislatures. Those issues promised to become among the most divisive in recent American political history.

Advances and Reversals

Despite the rapid advances made by women, the issues raised by the women's rights movement over the past three decades had by no means been resolved by the 1990s. Questions continued to be raised about the weakening fabric of the American family and about the ways women could best reconcile the competing demands of work and family. Such issues as day-care centers, pregnancy leaves, and equal rights in the workplace, along with abortion, came to be increasingly prominent in the political arena, figuring critically in national and state elections and often cutting across party lines. The Supreme Court's retreat on the abortion issue, along with the more militant and obstructionist tactics used by antiabortion forces, posed a formidable challenge to the women's rights activists. So did the lower earning power of women.

As the United States entered the last decade of the twentieth century, the problem of female poverty was reaching crisis proportions. Three out of five adults officially designated as living below the poverty line were women; indeed, about half of the poor families in America were maintained by women with no husband present. In 1988, 24 percent of the nation's 63 million children lived with only one parent—double the percentage in 1970. The burden of poverty fell disproportionately on minority women and their children: two-thirds of the children in black and Hispanic female-headed households were poor.

From the outset of his presidency, Reagan had opposed the Equal Rights Amendment to the Constitution. His administration reflected the conservative view of the family as the keystone of American civilization. It opposed programs that would diminish parental authority, and it resolutely condemned abortion. But although the president talked about preserving the sanctity of the American family, social programs that functioned primarily to sustain the families of poor and working women—such as Aid to Families with Dependent Children, Head Start, child nutrition, food stamps, and child care—fared badly during his administration.

Celebrating the triumphs of American women in the twentieth century, a cigarette company advertised itself under the motto "You've come a long way, baby." But emblematic of the many problems yet unresolved, a woman activist responded with a different assessment—"I haven't come a long way, and I'm not a baby." What seemed certain was that issues affecting American women, at home and in the workplace, would remain very much in the political and legislative arena in the 1990s.

THE BUSH PRESIDENCY

When Ronald Reagan became president, he had replaced the portrait of Thomas Jefferson in the White House with a portrait of Calvin Coolidge, expressing his admiration for Coolidge's ability to cut taxes and federal budgets. When George Bush became president, he replaced Coolidge's portrait with one of Theodore Roosevelt. The change suggested Bush's commitment to patrician reform, preservation of the environment, a vigorous foreign policy, a strong military, and greater personal involvement than his predecessor in the duties of the presidency.

Within a year of Bush's inauguration, dramatic events in Eastern Europe had signaled a possible end to the Cold War. Even as Americans welcomed those developments, they needed to consider their far reaching implications for the nation.

Domestic Priorities

Once he had secured the presidency, George Bush downplayed the bitter campaign and returned to his often repeated theme of a "kinder, gentler nation." He noted that despite his differences with Dukakis, they shared "a common interest in building a better America." Little more was heard about Massachusetts's prison-furlough system. "The American people," Bush remarked in his postelection press conference, "are wonderful when it comes to understanding when a campaign ends and the work of business begins."

In his inaugural address, Bush sought to underscore a new spirit of reconciliation by promising that the Bush years would be "the Age of the Offered Hand." But the president made few attempts to distance himself from the Reagan program or legacy. Only in confronting the growing deficit crisis did he threaten to break with that legacy and with his own campaign vow to not raise taxes: "The Congress will push me to raise taxes, and I'll say no, and they'll push, and I'll say no, and they'll push again, and I'll say to them, 'Read my lips; no new taxes.' " But within two years, while negotiating with Congress over a budget deficit estimated to be as high as $200

The floor of the New York Stock Exchange during the October 1987 crash. *(Joseph Rodriguez/Black Star)*

billion, the president conceded the need for a "tax revenue increase," along with cuts in both domestic and military spending.

On environmental questions, Bush also seemed willing to depart from Reagan, particularly in offshore-leasing policies. The Reagan administration had sought to make the entire 1.4-million-acre outer continental shelf available to the oil industry for offshore oil and gas drilling. President Bush, seeking to break a long deadlock with Congress over this question, sharply reduced the offshore acreage available to the industry for at least the next decade.

In establishing domestic priorities, Bush needed to consider a crisis of staggering proportions in the financial industry. The problem had its origins in the deregulation of that industry and in the actions of both Democrats and Republicans in Congress. Before 1982, savings-and-loan associations were required to place nearly all their loans in home mortgages, a relatively secure and stable class of assets. But in 1982, savings-and-loan institutions were granted far greater freedom in how they invested their funds, and many utilized that freedom recklessly and lost badly.

Since the federal government guaranteed deposits of up to $100,000 at banks and savings-and-loan institutions, it could not escape the consequences of the enormous losses sustained by those institutions. Already faced with a huge federal deficit, Congress needed to confront its obligations to stabilize the financial industry and to back up the losses of depositors. Few anticipated the full extent of the disaster. In 1989, Congress passed a bill calling for $166 billion over the next ten years to cover the savings-and-loan industry's losses; taxpayers would bear 75 percent of the cost. "The scandal," wrote economist John Kenneth Galbraith, "will stand as one of the most appalling such events in our civil history, and undoubtedly as the most expensive." By mid-1990 the ultimate cost of the bailout—from $325 to $500 billion—had risen far above earlier estimates.

No doubt the magnitude of the financial crisis and the cost of the bailout helped to persuade President Bush to renege on his pledge to seek no tax increases during his presidency. Meanwhile, the unwinding of the Cold War and the changes in Eastern Europe and the Soviet Union presented new opportunities to reorder priorities. In June 1990, responding to the reduced East–West tensions and the pressure from the budget deficit, Bush's secretary of defense sent to Congress a plan to cut the armed forces by 25 percent over the next five years, a plan that would reduce military spending by 10 percent. The call by congressional leaders for substantially larger cuts and the debate over whether to use the savings (popularly called a "peace dividend") to reduce the deficit or to spend them on urgent domestic problems would dominate the political agenda in Washington, D.C.

In establishing domestic priorities, the Bush administration needed to consider two additional problems—drugs and AIDS. Both had continued to mount in urgency and in the devastation they produced, and both were uphill struggles, de-

manding a far greater commitment in resources and federal action than had been expended by previous administrations.

Combating Illegal Drugs

The drug problem assumed a high priority in the Bush administration. The consumption of cocaine, for example, had leaped from 18 tons in 1976 to almost 100 tons in 1986. Once used almost exclusively in elite circles, the drug became increasingly available to the poor in the form of crack. In asking for a "national mobilization" against drugs, President Reagan had called drug pushers and users "as dangerous to our national security as any terrorist or foreign dictatorship." Bush, early in his administration, addressed the growing urgency of the problem, singling out drugs as "the gravest domestic threat facing our nation." To reduce cocaine and heroin abuse, he vowed to eliminate drug use at home and drug sources here and abroad. In declaring war on drugs, Bush announced a national strategy, ap-

Graffiti in New York City, 1986. *(UN/P. Sudhakaran)*

pointed a national drug policy coordinator to head up the attack, and proposed to spend $7.8 billion to reduce the demand for and the supply of illegal substances. Most of the funds would be expended on drug surveillance and additional prisons and law enforcement; the monies devoted to drug treatment were less than some critics had wanted.

The difficulty in waging a war on drugs was compounded by different opinions as to why people turned to drugs. William Bennett, the new drug czar, attributed drug use to the breakdown of law and order, the family, and the school. Others emphasized the ways in which drugs enabled the poor and downtrodden to escape, if only momentarily, their daily plight. "Up with hope, down with dope," declared black leader Jesse Jackson in his appeal to get at the economic roots of drug abuse. But the problem was not as simple as either Bennett or Jackson suggested. To confront the drug crisis required dealing both with millions of untreated drug addicts and millions of drug entrepreneurs. And all too many Americans chose to take refuge not in illegal drugs but in alcohol and nicotine, which killed approximately 150 Americans for every one who died from the effects of prohibited drugs. For all the focus on cocaine abuse, alcoholics still outnumbered cocaine users by more than two to one.

Combating AIDS

An unknown disease before 1981, AIDS—acquired immune deficiency syndrome—quickly assumed epidemic proportions. Deadly and thus far incurable, AIDS lays waste to the immune system, exposing patients to a debilitating succession of infections. As more came to be known about the disease, it appeared to be concentrated in the United States among homosexual and bisexual men and intravenous drug abusers. The proportion of heterosexual cases, however, was increasing, especially in Africa and Haiti, where it was thought to be transmitted principally through heterosexual intercourse.

By 1990, at least 600,000 Americans had become infected with the virus, more than 136,000 were sick, and some 83,000 had died. In the 1980s as many as 300,000 people had died from AIDS in 153 countries. The World Health Organization predicted that the case total could reach as many as 6 million by the year 2000.

Billions of dollars were poured into research aimed at finding a cure. Federal action and appropriations, however, lagged far behind the rapid spread of the disease, reflecting in part the initial apathy of the Reagan administration and the concerns of conservative politicians about homosexuality. Disagreements persisted, moreover, over whether and how to educate Americans, particularly young people, about safe sex. The Bush administration took a more aggressive stance than its predecessor, recommending the expenditure of $2.6 billion annually to combat the disease, but the amount was denounced by critics as belated and insufficient.

FAREWELL TO THE COLD WAR

Upon assuming the presidency, George Bush made no significant departure from the foreign policy laid down during the Reagan administration. The new president called for continued anti-Communist vigilance in Central America, even as he supported the reduction in tensions with the Soviet Union and welcomed the changes in Eastern Europe. Whatever the differences separating the United States and the Soviet Union—as, for example, over the future of a united Germany—Bush and Gorbachev sought in their meetings a common ground on which to build a better understanding.

Central America: Panama, Nicaragua, and El Salvador

If the Cold War appeared to be waning elsewhere, it remained very much alive in Central America. Fidel Castro maintained his dominance in Cuba, despite the continuing American economic boycott. The Sandinistas governed in Nicaragua, and the contras continued to inflict heavy casualties in their ongoing warfare in the countryside. Communist rebels continued to make war on the American-backed government in El Salvador, and in Panama General Manuel Antonio Noriega had become an unacceptable embarrassment to the same nation responsible for his rapid rise to power—the United States.

The political ascendancy of Noriega was intimately tied to American policy in the region. In the 1950s, he had been recruited by the Central Intelligence Agency as an informer; the relationship grew as Noriega rose through the ranks of Panamanian military intelligence and in 1983 took over as commander of the armed forces. As long as Noriega remained a valuable intelligence "asset," supplying information about Castro and the Sandinistas, even offering to assassinate Sandinista leaders, the United States chose to overlook recurring allegations of his deep involvement in corruption and drug trafficking. But Noriega proved to be an untrustworthy ally, sharing intelligence data and playing both sides for political gain. Beginning in 1981, he had run Panama with a repressive hand and heightened his anti-American rhetoric. Finally he had annulled the results of an election unfavorable to him. The Reagan administration imposed economic sanctions, and in 1988 federal grand juries in Florida indicted Noriega on drug-trafficking and racketeering charges.

When Bush came to power, he looked for ways to terminate Noriega's political career, finally settling on a time-honored hemispheric remedy. To restore "peace and democracy" to Panama and to bring Noriega to the United States to stand trial on drug charges, he sent in 24,000 troops on December 20, 1989—the largest American military operation in nearly twenty years. Twenty-three American soldiers were killed, and at least 539 Panamanians lost their lives, many of them civilians. Noriega was apprehended and brought in manacles to Miami to stand trial on the drug-trafficking indictments secured two years earlier.

Bush termed the successful Panama invasion Operation Just Cause. Congress gave it overwhelming rhetorical support, and opinion polls revealed strong public support. But the Organization of American States (OAS) condemned the invasion by a vote of twenty to one (the United States was the sole dissenter) and, along with the United Nations General Assembly, affirmed the right of the Panamanian people to "self-determination without outside interference."

After President Reagan had announced a trade embargo against Nicaragua in 1985, the United States had waged economic warfare in the hope of ending Sandinista rule. At the same time, beginning with covert aid in 1982, the United States had supported contra forces seeking to overthrow the Nicaragua government. While Congress wavered between military and "nonlethal" aid or no aid at all, the Reagan administration had sought other ways to bolster the contras, including assistance that contravened the United States Congress.

Panama invasion, December 1989. *(Christopher Morris/Black Star)*

Peace came to Nicaragua as the result of a proposal made by President Oscar Arias of Costa Rica. Greeted with skepticism and resistance by the Reagan administration, the plan was approved in February 1989 by the Central American presidents, including Daniel Ortega. It called for the demobilization of the contras and for free elections in Nicaragua in early 1990.

On February 25, 1990, a war-weary and economically devastated Nicaragua went to the polls. An American-supported and -financed coalition headed by Violeta Barrios de Chamorro, the widow of an anti-Somoza newspaper publisher slain in 1978, defeated Ortega for the presidency and won a majority of seats in the National Assembly. Her victory was hailed in the United States by the very officials who had scorned the peace plan that made the vote possible. Contra supporters cheered the results as a vindication of the Reagan administration's Nicaraguan policy. But critics of that policy disagreed. The elections, they argued, simply demonstrated that a superpower could apply sufficient military and economic pressure to bring a small, impoverished country to its knees. Nicaraguans appear to have voted for economic aid, relief from military conscription and the internal tensions of a society at war, and an end to the ten-year American-financed contra war, which had taken the lives of thirty thousand Nicaraguans and shattered the nation's economy.

With the end of contra warfare and the United States embargo, Nicaragua moved toward national reconciliation and economic recovery. The contras were demobilized, Chamorro retained the Sandinista commander of the armed forces and promised to respect the land reforms initiated by the Sandinista government, and the Sandinistas, with some 40 percent of the popular vote, remained the most powerful single political force in Nicaragua.

Free elections in Nicaragua and the ouster of Noriega in Panama had not ended armed confrontation in America's "backyard." For twenty-five years, people who had attempted to exercise their rights in El Salvador had been subject to assassination by that country's army. In 1980, Archbishop Oscar Arnulfo Romero pleaded with the United States to cut off aid to the Salvadoran army, which he found to be impervious to reform, but Romero himself was gunned down by the very forces he denounced. After investing ten years and $4 billion to increase civilian power and restrain violent extremists in El Salvador, the United States had achieved a tenuous stalemate.

The army still held dominant power, and the government persisted in its crackdowns on universities, unions, cooperatives, and the Catholic church on the grounds that they aided the rebel cause. Throughout the 1980s, human rights observers painted a dreary picture of army-directed death squads gunning down the most vocal advocates of reconciliation. In one decade, the civil war had claimed the lives of 70,000, and about one-tenth of the population had been uprooted.

The New Europe

If the forces of social change encountered continuing resistance in Central America, they had been unleashed in unprecedented ways in Eastern Europe. The rise to power of Mikhail Gorbachev in the Soviet Union had opened a new era in American-Soviet relations. Both at home and abroad, Gorbachev displayed a strikingly different kind of leadership, challenging his adversaries to think and to act in ways that broke sharply with the past. In the Soviet Union, the new openness and toleration of dissent and debate affected various areas of life—from the textbook version of history taught in the schools to experiments in democracy, including contested elections. But Gorbachev's failure to revive the stagnant economy and growing shortages of consumer goods undercut his support at home, even as ethnic violence and restive republics such as Lithuania, Estonia, and Latvia threatened to fragment the USSR.

Neither the United States nor perhaps Gorbachev anticipated the rapid dissolution of the Communist regimes in Eastern Europe. The most startling development was not so much the popular uprisings but the refusal of Gorbachev's Soviet Union to intervene militarily to suppress them. On the contrary, to the amazement and applause of much of the world, Gorbachev welcomed the transformations. In an extraordinary display of courage and commitment, almost entirely nonviolent, the peoples of Eastern Europe—Czechoslovakians, Poles, Hungarians, Bulgarians, Rumanians, and East Germans—asserted their right to self-determination, democratic elections, and free expression, ending some forty-five years of uncontested Communist supremacy.

In Poland, the momentum begun earlier in the decade continued, and in April 1989 the once harassed and outlawed Solidarity movement entered Parliament as the first freely elected opposition party in a Communist country. In still another dramatic development, the wall constructed in 1961 to separate East from West Berlin came down in 1989, and East Germany moved toward unification with West Germany. In 1989, within a month after police in Prague had cracked down on student demonstrators, a democratic movement established the first noncommunist government in Czechoslovakia since before the Communist coup in 1948. The new government, which was instituted without a shot being fired, was headed by Vaclav Havel, a dissident playwright who had spent years in prison. Hungary, too, took the democratic path, established a multiparty system, and acclaimed as heroes those who had struggled against Soviet tanks in 1956. By mid-1990, elections had been held in East Germany, Hungary, Rumania, Czechoslovakia, and Bulgaria, giving millions of people their first chance in more than four decades to freely choose their leaders.

Even as the reunification of East and West Germany continued apace, the question of how a united Germany would fit into the European community was yet to be resolved. The United States and NATO talked about transforming that predominantly military alliance into a predominantly political organization; at the same time, they insisted that a united Germany remain in NATO. But as Gorbachev reminded President Bush when they met in Washington in June 1990, more than 20 million Soviet citizens had perished in World War II; he could not accept an arrangement in Europe that in any way renewed the threat of a militarized and unified Germany. Faced with the collapse of the Communist regimes in Eastern Europe, however, and with critical challenges at home, Gorbachev was not in the strongest bargaining position.

For almost forty-five years, the Cold War and the perceived need to contain an expansive Soviet communism had been the organizing principle of American foreign policy. But within a few years, international relationships had been rapidly rearranged. The United States and the Soviet Union had once thought of themselves as destiny's elect, and both Reagan and Bush continued to proclaim that theme. But each superpower in the 1990s also needed to reconsider its global commitments and the possible irrelevance of its example.

While the United States and the Soviet Union moved to resolve their differences, the betrayed aspirations of masses of people still made for a turbulent and revolutionary world. The Mideast was no closer to peace, and the attempts to suppress the *intifada* in the territories occupied by Israel had largely failed. South Africa was edging toward a more democratic society. Nelson Mandela of the once-outlawed African National Congress had been released after twenty-seven years of imprisonment, and he made a triumphal tour of Europe and the United States in 1990. But apartheid persisted, and the majority black population remained voteless. For a time, China appeared to be moving toward greater toleration of dissent and debate, but authorities quickly and ruthlessly put an end to such aspirations on June 4, 1989, when they ordered troops to attack hundreds of mostly young demonstrators in Tiananmen Square in Beijing. The square had become a symbol of the new democratic spirit in China. The continuing crackdown on dissidents dampened relations between the United States and China.

Although trouble spots persisted, the importance of military strength and superiority appeared to be diminishing in a rapidly changing world. Neither the Soviet Union nor the United States was in a position to spend as lavishly as it had in the past on its military establishment. The Soviet economy was deteriorating, and the United States had become a debtor nation dependent on the willingness of others to provide the funds necessary to finance its budget deficit. The principal challenge to the United States was no longer communist ideology or expansion but European and Japanese financial and economic power. Since the mid-1970s, the competitive position of many American industries had been eroding, and by 1990 Japan had become the world's most successful trading nation, the world's greatest exporter of capital, and the financier of the United States budget deficit.

The Bush administration had its hands full seeking to keep stride with the extraordinary developments abroad. These had forced upon the administration a new way of thinking not only about the Soviet Union (what President Bush termed "beyond containment") but about national security and American priorities and purposes. By the time Bush and Gorbachev met in June 1990, much of the passion of the Cold War era had dissipated; they concluded their meeting with warm talk of friendship and cooperation. That same month, the NATO and Warsaw Pact nations agreed collectively that the Cold War had ended and that neither side posed a threat to the other. How to replace confrontation with cooperation and how to stabilize the altered European landscape and contain the old hostilities and ethnic conflicts would now dominate East–West relations. If nothing else, a respite from Cold War tensions might provide the opportunity to confront long neglected and urgent global economic and ecological concerns.

THE AMERICAN DREAM IN THE 1980S AND 1990S

The American people celebrated the two hundredth birthday of their constitution in 1987 and the bicentennial of George Washington's inauguration in 1989. From the White House, President Reagan in the 1980s and President Bush in the 1990s exuded optimism about the vitality and enduring qualities of the American Dream. Evoking memories of an America that had conquered many frontiers over the past two centuries, Reagan articulated a confidence that the same spirit would triumph in the future.

I'm talking about the very essence of what it is to be an American. We are different. We have always been different. If we all feel that way the world will once again look on in awe at us, astonished by the miracles of education and freedom, amazed by our rebirth of confidence and hope and progress, and when they are amazed and when it happens we'll be able to say to the world, "Well, what did you expect? After all, we're Americans."

That was the kind of confidence Reagan succeeded in conveying, and impressive numbers of Americans embraced his reaffirmation of the American Dream. The return of "good times" in the 1980s embellished the lives of many American families. But it left relatively untouched minorities and many of the nation's farmers and industrial workers. Studies revealed that the average family was better off financially in 1988 than in 1980. But the same studies revealed growing disparities in the incomes of rich and poor Americans and larger numbers of American families falling below the poverty line.

For black Americans, some of the gains of the civil rights movement were eroding, along with their standard of living. The number of black poor far exceeded those who managed to attain middle-class standing, and the economic gap between blacks and whites continued to widen. For urban whites, black and white, public schools deteriorated, as did public services and personal security. And with jobs still at a premium, the nation experienced difficulties absorbing the vast numbers of new refugees flocking to its shores. Finally, large numbers of farmers remained in deep trouble, desperately trying to hold on to their lands.

In the American myth of success, any person could make it to the top on the basis of hard work and ambition. But in the 1980s many blue-collar workers and middle-class Americans found it increasingly difficult to make ends meet because of the combined burden of federal and state income taxes and the soaring costs of housing, health care, and education. For many Americans in the last quarter of the twentieth century, the principal concern remained not so much lifting themselves up the economic ladder as trying to keep from falling lower. If they worked, they often did so at jobs that permitted them no opportunity for self-expression and little chance for advancement. In an interview conducted by Studs Terkel in 1974, Mike Lefevre, a steelworker, articulated feelings, frustrations, and aspirations about life and work that retained considerable force twenty years later, as Americans neared the twenty-first century:

I'm a dying breed. A laborer. Strictly muscle work . . . pick it up, put it down, pick it up, put it down. We handle between forty and fifty thousand pounds of steel a day. . . . It's hard to take pride in a bridge you're never gonna cross, in a door you're never gonna open. You're mass producing things and you never see the end result of it. . . . It isn't that the average working guy is dumb. He's tired, that's all. . . . At seven it starts. My arms get tired about the first half-hour. After that, they don't get tired any more until maybe the last half-hour at the end of the day. I work from seven to three thirty. My arms are tired at seven thirty and they're tired at three o'clock. I hope to God I never get broke in, because I always want my arms to be tired at seven thirty and three o'clock. 'Cause that's when I know that there's a beginning and there's an end. That I'm not brainwashed. In between, I don't even try to think. It's not just the work. Somebody built the pyramids. Somebody's going to build something. Pyramids, Empire State Building—these things just don't happen. There's hard work behind it. I would like to see a building, say, the Empire State, I would like to see on one side of it a foot-wide strip from top to bottom with the name of every bricklayer, the name of every electrician, with all the names. So when a guy walked by, he could take his son and say, "See, that's me over there on the forty-fifth floor. I put the steel beam in." Picasso can point to a painting. What can I point to? A writer can point to a book. Everybody should have something to point to. . . .

Yes, I want my signature on 'em, too. Sometimes, out of pure meanness, when I make something, I put a little dent in it. I like to do something to make it really unique . . . just so I can say I did it. . . . I'd like to make my imprint. . . .

This is gonna sound square, but my kid is my imprint. He's my freedom. . . . You know what I mean? This is why I work. Every time I see a young guy walk by with

THE 1980S: THE "LITE" DECADE

It used to take so much time—days, sometimes weeks—to read a classic. Moby Dick, alone, runs 710 pages. Today, thanks to a small publishing house called Workman, it takes a minute. Through abridging, reabridging and editing out "rambling soliloquies," Workman boasts that it has "cut down the literary canon to a lean pistol," producing an audiocassette tape that offers listeners "Ten Classics in Ten Minutes."

The result is light literature, the latest demonstration that in the 1980s light beer is not the only thing that is less filling. What started out as a way to justify drinking three beers instead of two—the creation of a light beer with a third fewer calories—has become part of a broader phenomenon in which less is valued above more. This is the Light Decade, or as some would have it, Lite.

Sociologists say that "lite," which started as a marketing term used to denote dietetic foods, has become a metaphor for what Americans are seeking in disparate parts of their lives. In their relationships, for example, they have turned away from soul-searching and stress of emotional commitment; at the movies, they would rather watch an invincible hero, like Rambo or the Karate Kid, who never lets the audience down.

"The notion of the word 'lite' tends to follow what seems to be a trend in American culture," said Ray B. Brown, chairman of the department of popular culture at Bowling Green State University in Ohio. "That is for everybody to be utterly selfish about themselves, for people to want easy cures, easy riches, easy jobs and easy wealth."

The Light Decade is a time when men and women can "fall in love without paying the price," as a

Honda Civic advertisement promises. They can undergo psychoanalysis in one sitting, because today's psychotherapy skips the formative years, namely childhood. For health care, busy executives can turn to a so-called Doc in a Box, a storefront medical clinic with extended hours, higher prices and no appointment, no referral—no medical history necessary.

There is light culture (books on tape), light shopping (buying clothes by video), light politics (candidates who run on image, not issues), light responsibility (the lowest voter participation rates of any democracy) and light music (Lite FM, where the heavy bass line has been removed so that the sound does not jar or stir listeners). And of course, there is light food, with which people can cut calories without changing their diets by using products like Jell-O Light, Cornitos Light Corn Chips, Heinz Lite Ketchup and Glace Lite, which, its manufacturer, Sweet Victory, says "gives you all the rich, delicious pleasures of 300-calorie premium ice cream" at 100 calories a scoop.

Food, notably dietetic food, is where the Light Decade started. It is also the clearest example of how the philosophy has caught on. "Lite," or "light," foods are now "one of the fastest growing segments of the American food industry," according to a recent Federal Food and Drug Administration report. . . .

Bernard Phillips, a sociologist at Boston University, calls the Light decade a "smorgasbord" approach to life, where people convince themselves that they can have the best of all worlds, immediately, by having a lightened version of everything. . . .

Source: William R. Greer, "In the 'Lite' Decade, Less Has Become More," *New York Times*, August 13, 1986.

---

a shirt and tie and dressed up real sharp, I'm lookin' at my kid, you know? That's it.

More than two hundred years after the birth of the nation, the American Dream persisted. George Bush, like Ronald Reagan, vowed to make that dream a reality in the lives of all Americans. But so had every American president in the twentieth century. Record federal deficits, the decline of the family farm, the widening gap between the wealthy and the poor, a growing underclass of interior exiles, the deterioration of the inner cities and the public schools, and the devastating consequences of crime, drugs, and the AIDS epidemic threatened to undermine much of the optimism articulated by political leaders. The American Dream was still attainable, but by fewer Americans. In the 1950s and 1960s, for example, workers could look forward to earning one-third more than their fathers; in the 1980s they earned

15 percent less than their fathers. The loss had its impact in a number of areas. In the 1980s, and for the first time since World War II, the percentage of American families owning their own homes fell.

Inequalities of Wealth

In his book *The Emerging Republican Majority*, published in 1960, political analyst Kevin Phillips correctly predicted the coming conservative era in American national politics, and in 1968 he served as a consultant in the successful Republican presidential campaign. In *The Politics of Rich and Poor*, published in 1990, Phillips assessed the growing disparity in the distribution of income in American society. Much like the late nineteenth century, at the very peak of the Gilded Age, the 1980s were "the triumph of upper America—an ostentatious celebration of wealth, the political ascendancy of the rich and a glorification of capitalism, free markets and finance. Not only did the concentration of wealth quietly intensify, but the sums involved took a megaleap." The American millionaire, Phillips noted, had become so common that there were some 1.5 million of them by 1989, along with at least 50 billionaires.

Between 1981 and 1989, a significant shift in the distribution of wealth occurred. The net worth of the Forbes 400 richest Americans nearly tripled; the share of national income going to the wealthiest 1 percent rose from 8.1 percent in 1981 to 14.7 percent in 1986. Underscoring the widening gap between the nation's rich and poor, the more than 40 million Americans in the bottom fifth of income distribution suffered a 1 percent decline in income adjusted for inflation and family size from 1973 to 1979, but a 10 percent decline from 1979 to 1987. By contrast, the adjusted income of Americans in the top fifth rose by 7 percent from 1973 to 1979, and by a staggering 16 percent from 1979 to 1987. In 1980, corporate chief executive officers made roughly forty times the income of average factory workers; by 1989, they were making ninety-three times as much.

While the rich and the upper-middle class gained, the average blue-collar wage and after-tax median family income declined. Many in the lower ranks of society failed to share in the "good times" of the eighties, and the burden fell disproportionately on female, black, Hispanic, and young Americans. From 1979 to 1987 the number of single-parent families living below the poverty level ($11,611 for a family of four) rose by 46 percent, and nearly one in four children under six years of age in the United States was poor.

Disparities in wealth helped to produce still another growing problem in American society in the 1980s, a phenomenon thought to have nearly disappeared in the 1970s—homelessness. In 1990, there were more homeless Americans than at any time since the Great Depression, and 700,000 of them were children. The source of the problem for most of the homeless was easy enough to trace—the absence of decent, affordable housing. Housing prices had more than doubled since 1975, and rents had increased at equally rapid rates, driving many families into the streets. In 1988 the National Education Association reported that 2.5 million people were being displaced from their homes every year because of soaring rents, revitalization or gentrification projects, and economic development plans. Federal housing programs might have been

expected to alleviate the problem. But after 1980 those programs were cut by more than 75 percent; federal support for low-income housing dropped from $30 billion in 1980 to $7.5 billion in 1988. Under Presidents Ford and Carter, 500,000 subsidized private housing units were constructed; by Reagan's second term, the number had dropped to 25,000.

The New Immigrants

Whatever the persistent inequalities in American life, the United States remained for hundreds of thousands of new arrivals the promised land. Many came seeking political asylum and freedom from oppression. Still others, many of them from lands of poverty, came in search of freedom from hunger and ignorance, the opportunity to better their lives economically, and a chance to educate their children.

After 1968 immigration quotas permitted a maximum of 170,000 immigrants to enter annually from countries outside the Western Hemisphere (with a 20,000 ceiling for any one country) and a maximum of 120,000 immigrants annually from countries within the Western Hemisphere on a first-come, first-served basis. Selected categories ("immediate relatives" of U.S. citizens or "special immigrants" designated by Congress) were granted entry as nonquota immigrants. In 1965 Congress liberalized immigration policy, abandoning the national-origins quotas in favor of a new system of quotas based on skills, refugee status, and family reunification. A maximum of 170,000 immigrants would be admitted from the Eastern Hemisphere (no more than 20,000 from any one country) and 120,000 from the Western Hemisphere. Parents, spouses and unmarried children of U.S. citizens were exempted from all quotas.

Legal immigration averaged 433,600 a year in the 1970s and increased to 566,600 in the first five years of the 1980s. The political upheavals and economic turmoil in Asia and South America produced large numbers of emigrants to the United States. In the closing years of the 1970s and the early years of the 1980s, fully three-quarters of the legal immigrants came from Asia and the Americas. More than 1.7 million Indochinese refugees fled their countries (Vietnam, Laos, and Cambodia), many of them migrating to the United States, still others to Western Europe, Canada, and Australia. The refugee status accorded Cubans and Haitians also produced large numbers of immigrants from those nations. By the mid-1980s, as Western Europe began to place more restrictions on immigration, the United States was accepting twice as many foreigners as the rest of the world's nations combined.

From Little Havana in Miami to Koreatown in Los Angeles, from the Central American communities in San Francisco to the enlarged Russian-Jewish community in New York, the new immigrants were changing the face of America. This new wave did not fit the traditional view of immigrants as young, working-age men who left their homelands in search of economic opportunities. A Labor Department study in 1985 revealed that women and children accounted for two-thirds of the legal immigrants to the United States.

The new immigrants, like the old, were not universally welcomed. Traditional fears of newcomers, stemming from job competition and the strain on community services, fed suspicions over the principal sources of immigration and concern over the substantial number of illegal immigrants entering the country each year, most of them crossing the border separating the United States and Mexico.

The nation's fastest-growing minority was, in fact, the Hispanic American. The number of Hispanic Americans increased 30 percent in the 1980s (five times as fast as the rest of the population), to 19 million, accounting for nearly 8 percent of the nation's population. More than half (63 percent) of the Hispanic population traced their roots back to Mexico. People of Puerto Rican origin were the next largest group, some 12 percent. The subgroups that experienced the most rapid increase traced their origin to Cuba and Central or South America; many of them had migrated as a result of political upheavals. By the year 2000 Hispanic Americans were expected to reach 30 million, or some 15 percent of the nation's population.

People of Mexican origin, the largest single group, were concentrated in the Southwest and California; most of the Puerto Ricans resided in the Northeast, some 700,000 Cubans were concentrated in Florida, and the growing numbers of immigrants from places such as El Salvador, Nicaragua, Haiti, the Dominican Republic, Ecuador, and Colombia were more evenly scattered over the United States.

With massive numbers of Mexicans entering the United States, the question of how to enforce restrictions on immigration took on added urgency. In 1964, when Mexicans were permitted to enter as agricultural laborers under the *bracero* program, the Immigration and Naturalization Service picked up only 45,000 undocumented Mexicans along the Southwest border. But that number soared after the program was terminated the next year. By 1971, federal authorities had apprehended hundreds of thousands of illegal aliens; in 1986 alone, officers seized some 1.7 million Mexicans seeking to cross the 1960-mile border separating Mexico and the United States.

The Immigration Reform and Control Act of 1986 tried to allay concerns about the large number of undocumented workers entering the United States. The law enabled illegal aliens who had entered the United States before 1982 to apply for amnesty; after 18 months, they would be eligible to become permanent residents—and ultimately United States citizens. At the same time, the law imposed penalties on employers who knowingly hired illegal immigrants. Although many aliens did apply for amnesty, the law was greeted with considerable suspicion; large numbers of illegal aliens, in fact, refused to apply, fearing the government would use the information gathered from their applications to deport them. The flow of illegal immigrants persisted, most of them motivated by the same considerations that had brought tens of millions to the United States over its 200-year history—the chance to make the American Dream a reality in their own lives.

Toward the Year 2001

The United States in the 1990s celebrated the five hundredth anniversary of Christopher Columbus's voyages of discovery—one of a series of voyages by which people from the western part of the Old World became familiar with Indian America. It seemed like an appropriate occasion for Americans to reflect over their rapid and remarkable growth and the degree to which the United States continued to inspire emulation and immigration.

The first national census in 1790 had counted 3,929,214 Americans (including 697,681 slaves). Some 200 years later, the population was expected to reach over 250 million, nearly doubling the number of Americans in the last half century (131 million in 1940). For the first time, in 1980, the center of population—located off the Maryland shore in Chesapeake Bay in the 1790 census—had moved west of the Mississippi, near De Soto, Missouri. With the continuing flight from the farms to the cities, density had increased

THE NEW GENERATION

Every generation has a way of categorizing and stereotyping its predecessors, sometimes drowning them in nostalgia, sometimes criticizing their excesses and exaggerating their follies. In the 1980s, commentators took note of a generation of young Americans significantly different from their predecessors, contrasting the more conservative, career-oriented academic utilitarians of the eighties with the more liberal, rebellious, and free-thinking college students of the sixties. Himself a member of the sixties generation, Garry Trudeau, the political cartoonist responsible for the popular *Doonesbury* series, addressed the graduating class at the College of William and Mary in Williamsburg, Virginia, in June 1982.

It is no wonder that you've given up on the culture. With no credible ego models, what's left but to flock to your bookstores and buy handbooks on living preppies, dead cats, inert cubes, living cats and dead preppies—the subjects of the five bestselling titles on American campuses last year? These are books for minds at rest. They are also the books favored by the rest of the nation, which suggests that the post-Vietnam fatigue syndrome has us all in its grip. Your values and interests are no worse or better than those that are filtering down from the larger society that nurtured you. If you have not given your elders any clear sense of who you are, perhaps it is because you are just like your elders. Your priorities do not turn out to be all that different from those of your parents.

considerably. Compared to the 23 percent of Americans living on farms in 1940, only 2 percent did so in 1990. The number of babies born every year in the United States was edging toward 4 million in 1990, a level not reached since the baby boom of the 1950s and which demographers had thought unlikely to be reached again until well into the twenty-first century. At the same time, Americans sixty-five years and over had increased their proportion of the total population to nearly 12 percent—the highest proportion in this age group in the nation's history.

The United States in the closing years of the twentieth century confronted some enormous challenges. Once the uncontested leader in a number of different areas, the United States retained its military supremacy. But it was also the world's largest debtor. It led all other major industrial countries in the gap dividing the upper fifth of the population from the lower fifth and in the percentage of children living in poverty. It ranked fourteenth out of sixteen industrial countries in expenditures on elementary and secondary education. It ranked nineteenth in the world in its infant mortality rate. And the homicide rate among young men (from fifteen to twenty-four years old) was four to seventy-three times the rate of other industrialized nations.

The United States remained, however, a nation with enormous resources, a large and capable labor force, and a democratic political tradition that had withstood many assaults, both from abroad and from within. Characteristically, American political leaders—Democrats and Republicans alike—continued to express confidence in the ability of the United States to overcome every obstacle, to explore and conquer new frontiers. Whatever the urgent problems demanding their attention, most Americans embraced a gospel of progress that envisioned the future as a more bountiful and better version of the present. That gospel continued each year to attract tens of thousands of new Americans.

The challenges were clear enough. Looking to the twenty-first century, Americans needed to assess their nation's use and abuse of its power, wealth, and resources. For some forty-five years, that assessment had been conditioned in large part by the fear of Soviet aggression and an obsession with national security that had few if any parallels in the American past. "Every age and generation," Thomas Paine wrote some 200 years ago, "must be as free to act for itself, *in all cases*, as the ages and generations which preceded it." Freed from a frustrating, debilitating Cold War, the generation of Americans coming of age at the close of the twentieth century would hopefully be able to face the future in an altogether different spirit. The challenges they faced demanded no less than a full commitment.

SUMMARY

Ronald Reagan in the 1980s became the first president since Franklin Delano Roosevelt to alter the nation's social and economic policy and redefine the presidency in fundamental ways. His two terms in the White House became an exercise in the politics of nostalgia—the hearkening back to "good old days" that featured a much more invisible and unobtrusive federal government. The tone of this presidency was set in his first inaugural address: "Government is not the solution to our problem. Government is the problem." And his landslide reelection in 1984 seemed to set the seal on a new direction for the federal government.

In reordering the nation's priorities, Reagan placed special emphasis on strengthening its military capability. He expected supply-side economics to cure the nation's economic ills. Through tax cuts and an easing of federal regulations, individuals and corporations would be in-duced to invest and stimulate economic growth. Reduced spending on social programs would help pay for the increased military budget and soften the impact of the tax cut.

The economy did revive by late 1983, but not before unemployment had reached the highest levels since the Great Depression. And there were still unprecedented federal budget deficits, which reflected the imbalance between cuts in domestic spending and massive increases in military spending. Nevertheless, the renewed vigor of the economy, which persisted through Reagan's second term, did much to enhance the president's popularity.

TIME LINE

1979	Sandinistas come to power in Nicaragua
1980	Ronald Reagan elected president
1981	Congress approves tax reduction Air controllers strike Solidarity movement in Poland Sandra Day O'Connor becomes first woman Supreme Court justice
1982	Highest unemployment levels since Great Depression Israel invades Lebanon Massacres in Sabra and Shatila Palestinian refugee camps U.S. sends troops to Lebanon Covert aid to *Contras* in Nicaragua begins
1983	Economy recovers Strategic Defense Initiative ("Star Wars") announced U.S. deploys cruise missiles in Western Europe Soviet Union downs South Korean airliner over Soviet territory U.S. invades Grenada
1984	U.S. troops withdrawn from Lebanon Gramm-Rudman Deficit Reduction Act Democrats nominate a woman for vice-president Reagan re-elected
1985	Gorbachev comes to power in Soviet Union First Gorbachev-Reagan meeting U.S. imposes economic embargo against Nicaragua Food Security Act
1986	Iran-Contra scandal breaks

Income Tax Act
Fall of Marcos in Philippines
U.S. bombers attack Libya
Congress approves economic sanctions against South Africa
U.S. becomes a debtor nation
Immigration Reform and Control Act

1987 Palestinian uprising (*Intifada*) begins
U.S. and U.S.S.R. negotiate arms control agreement

1988 U.S. downs Iranian airliner in Persian Gulf
George Bush elected president

1989 *Webster* v. *Reproductive Health Services*
Congress agrees to bail out savings and loan industry
Bush declares war on drugs
U.S. invades Panama
Uprisings in Eastern Europe
Oliver North convicted in Iran-Contra scandal
Central American presidents agree to Arias peace plan

1990 Elections in Nicaragua; Sandinistas defeated
Gorbachev and Bush meet in Washington
NATO and Warsaw Pact proclaim the end of the Cold War
Bush agrees to consider tax increase
AIDS epidemic escalates
John Poindexter convicted in Iran-Contra scandal
Mandela released from prison in South Africa; tours United States

Reagan's foreign policy was directed at containing Soviet influence and revolutionary upheavals perceived as endangering America's national interests. Soviet-American relations plummeted to a new low, exacerbated by Reagan's rhetoric, the deployment of new missiles in Western Europe, and Soviet actions in Afghanistan and Poland. To check Communist influence, the United States also became involved in civil conflicts in the Middle East and Central America.

After punishing failure in the election of 1980, the American electorate rewarded success in 1984. Reagan's landslide (he carried forty-nine states) further fragmented the old New Deal coalition. The Democrats' choice of a woman, Geraldine Ferraro of New York, as the vice-presidential candidate, seemed to make no difference in the outcome.

In Reagan's second term, the long-range effects of his "political revolution" became clearer. His administration had fundamentally altered the shape and role of government in American life, producing substantial changes in federal spending and in the substance and purposes of domestic programs. Reagan had also changed the terms of the debate on the role of government and federal spending. Perhaps the most enduring Reagan legacy, based on the number of appointments he made, was a fundamental change in the composition, direction, and ideology of the federal judiciary system, including the Supreme Court.

A new leader in the Soviet Union—Mikhail Gorbachev—and his new style of leadership produced a sharp turn in Soviet-American relations. Although Reagan still embraced the costly and unproved Strategic Defense Initiative (Star Wars), he was forced to revise his assumptions about the "evil empire" and agree to a far-reaching treaty with the Soviet Union banning intermediate-range missiles. The Soviet withdrawal from Afghanistan, along with a new openness (glasnost) in the USSR and an exchange of visits by Reagan and Gorbachev, produced a promising thaw in Cold War tensions and rhetoric.

George Bush exploited Reagan's successes and some highly emotional issues to defeat Governor Michael Dukakis in the election of 1988. Like Reagan, Bush projected a mood of optimism and confidence. But numerous problems remained unresolved, among them record deficits and trade imbalances, homelessness, poverty, racism, drugs, crime, and the AIDS epidemic. Conflicts in the Middle East, Central America, and Africa also demanded his attention, along with the need to respond to new Soviet proposals for a reduction in military forces and the extraordinary political changes in Eastern Europe.

Suggested Readings

The best source for Ronald Reagan is his autobiography, *Where's the Rest of Me?* (1965). The best critical assessment, with the emphasis on his pre-presidential years, is G. Wills, *Reagan's America: Innocents at Home* (1987). See also R. Dallek, *Ronald Reagan: The Politics of Symbolism* (1984); P. D. Erickson, *Reagan Speaks: The Making of an American Myth* (1985); W. Greider, *The Education of David Stockman and Other Americans* (1982); and H. Smith, *The Power Game* (1988). The Reagan presidency has also produced a large number of "insider" memoirs, among them D. Stockman, *The Triumph of Politics* (1986); L. Speakes, *Speaking Out: The Reagan Presidency from Inside the White House* (1988); M. Anderson, *Revolution* (1988); M. K. Deaver, *Behind the Scenes* (1989); D. T. Regan, *For the Record* (1988); and P. Noonan, *What I Saw At the Revolution: A Political Life in the Reagan Era* (1990). An indispensable study of the Reagan presidency as public relations is M. Hertsgaard, *On Bended Knee: The Press and the Reagan Presidency* (1988). On the "contra-gate" scandal, see J. Mayer and D. McManus, *Landslide: The Unmaking of the President, 1984-1988* (1988); W. S. Cohen and G. J. Mitchell, *Men of Zeal: A Candid Inside Story of the Iran-Contra Hearings* (1988); and B. Bradlee, Jr., *Guts and Glory: The Rise and Fall of Oliver North* (1988). Often more incisive and biting than any historical critique of the era is G. B. Trudeau, *Doonesbury Dossier: The Reagan Years* (1984).

On the conservative resurgence in American political and intellectual life, see A. Crawford, *Thunder on the Right: The "New Right" and the Politics of Resentment* (1980), and P. Steinfels, *The Neoconservatives: The Men Who Are Changing America's Politics* (1979).

The legacy of the Reagan era is the subject of K. Phillips's devastating examination, *The Politics of Rich and Poor: Wealth and the American Electorate in the Reagan Aftermath* (1990). Compare this work with G. Gilder, *Wealth and Poverty* (1981), which argued that injecting the poor with doses of the entrepreneurial spirit would eradicate poverty. On the American dream in the 1970s and 1980s, see S. Terkel, *Working: People Talk About What They Do All Day and How They Feel About What They Do* (1974) and *American Dreams: Lost and Found* (1980), both works of oral history, and B. Ehrenreich, *Fear of Falling: The Inner Life of the Middle Class* (1989) and *The Worst Years of Our Lives: Irreverent Notes from a Decade of Greed* (1990). On the working class, see also R. Sennett and J. Cobb, *The Hidden Injuries of Class* (1972); L. K. Howe (ed.), *The White Majority* (1970) and *Pink Collar Workers: Inside the World of Women's Work* (1977); S. Feldstein and L. Costello (eds.), *The Ordeal of Assimilation: A Documentary History of the White Working Class* (1974); and S. Aronowitz, *False Promises: The Shaping of American Working Class Consciousness* (1973). On class, race, and ethnicity in modern American society, see R. Polenberg, *One Nation Divisible* (1980).

On American women in the 1980s, see the literature cited in Chapter 33.

APPENDIX

The Declaration of Independence

When in the course of human events it becomes necessary for one people to dissolve the political bands which have connected them with another and to assume, among the powers of the earth, the separate and equal station to which the laws of nature and of nature's God entitle them, a decent respect to the opinions of mankind requires that they should declare the causes which impel them to the separation.

We hold these truths to be self-evident, that all men are created equal; that they are endowed by their Creator with certain unalienable rights; that among these are life, liberty, and the pursuit of happiness. That, to secure these rights, governments are instituted among men, deriving their just powers from the consent of the governed; that, whenever any form of government becomes destructive of these ends, it is the right of the people to alter or to abolish it, and to institute a new government, laying its foundation on such principles, and organizing its powers in such form, as to them shall seem most likely to effect their safety and happiness. Prudence, indeed, will dictate that governments long established should not be changed for light and transient causes; and, accordingly, all experience hath shown that mankind are more disposed to suffer, while evils are sufferable, than to right themselves by abolishing the forms to which they are accustomed. But when a long train of abuses and usurpations, pursuing invariably the same object, evinces a design to reduce them under absolute despotism, it is their right, it is their duty, to throw off such government and to provide new guards for their future security. Such has been the patient sufferance of these colonies, and such is now the necessity which constrains them to alter their former systems of government. The history of the present King of Great Britain is a history of repeated injuries and usurpations, all having, in direct object, the establishment of an absolute tyranny over these States. To prove this, let facts be submitted to a candid world:

He has refused his assent to laws the most wholesome and necessary for the public good.

He has forbidden his governors to pass laws of immediate and pressing importance, unless suspended in their operation till his assent should be obtained; and, when so suspended, he has utterly neglected to attend to them.

He has refused to pass other laws for the accommodation of large districts of people, unless those people would relinquish the right of representation in the legislature; a right inestimable to them and formidable to tyrants only.

He has called together legislative bodies at places unusual, uncomfortable, and distant from the depository of their public records, for the sole purpose of fatiguing them into compliance with his measures.

He has dissolved representative houses, repeatedly for opposing, with manly firmness, his invasions on the rights of the people.

He has refused, for a long time after such dissolutions, to cause others to be elected; whereby the legislative powers, incapable of annihilation, have returned to the people at large for their exercise; the state remaining, in the meantime, exposed to all the danger of invasion from without and convulsions within.

He has endeavored to prevent the population of these States; for that purpose, obstructing the laws for naturalization of foreigners, refusing to pass others to encourage their migration hither, and raising the conditions of new appropriations of lands.

He has obstructed the administration of justice by refusing his assent to laws for establishing judiciary powers.

He has made judges dependent on his will alone for the tenure of their offices and the amount and payment of their salaries.

He has erected a multitude of new offices and sent hither swarms of officers to harass our people and eat out their substance.

He has kept among us, in time of peace, standing armies, without the consent of our legislatures.

He has affected to render the military independent of, and superior to, the civil power.

He has combined with others to subject us to a jurisdiction foreign to our Constitution and unacknowledged by our laws, giving his assent to their acts of pretended legislation—

For quartering large bodies of armed troops among us;

For protecting them by a mock trial from punishment for any murders which they should commit on the inhabitants of these States;

For cutting off our trade with all parts of the world;

For imposing taxes on us without our consent;

For depriving us, in many cases, of the benefit of trial by jury;

For transporting us beyond seas to be tried for pretended offences;

For abolishing the free system of English laws in a neighboring province, establishing therein an arbitrary government, and enlarging its boundaries, so as to render it at once an example and fit instrument for introducing the same absolute rule into these colonies;

For taking away our charters, abolishing our most valuable laws, and altering, fundamentally, the powers of our governments;

For suspending our own legislatures and declaring themselves invested with power to legislate for us in all cases whatsoever.

He has abdicated government here by declaring us out of his protection and waging war against us.

He has plundered our seas, ravaged our coasts, burnt our towns, and destroyed the lives of our people.

He is, at this time, transporting large armies of foreign mercenaries to complete the works of death, desolation, and tyranny already begun with circumstances of cruelty and perfidy scarcely paralleled in the most barbarous ages, and totally unworthy the head of a civilized nation.

He has constrained our fellow citizens, taken captive on the high seas, to bear arms against their country, to become the executioners of their friends and brethren, or to fall themselves by their hands.

He has excited domestic insurrections amongst us and has endeavored to bring on the inhabitants of our frontiers, the merciless Indian savages, whose known rule of warfare is an undistinguished destruction of all ages, sexes, and conditions.

In every stage of these oppressions, we have petitioned for redress in the most humble terms; our repeated petitions have been answered only by repeated injury. A prince whose character is thus marked by every act which may define a tyrant is unfit to be the ruler of a free people.

Nor have we been wanting in attention to our British brethren. We have warned them, from time to time, of attempts made by their legislature to extend an unwarrantable jurisdiction over us. We have reminded them of the circumstances of our emigration and settlement here. We have appealed to their native justice and magnanimity, and we have conjured them, by the ties of our common kindred, to disavow these usurpations, which would inevitably interrupt our connections and correspondence. They, too, have been deaf to the voice of justice and consanguinity. We must, therefore, acquiesce in the necessity which denounces our separation, and hold them, as we hold the rest of mankind, enemies in war, in peace, friends.

We, therefore, the representatives of the United States of America, in general Congress assembled, appealing to the Supreme Judge of the world for the rectitude of our intentions, do, in the name and by the authority of the good people of these colonies, solemnly publish and declare, that these united colonies are, and of right ought to be, free and independent states: that they are absolved from all allegiance to the British Crown, and that all political connection between them and the state of Great Britain is, and ought to be, totally dissolved; and that, as free and independent states, they have full power to levy war, conclude peace, contract alliances, establish commerce, and to do all other acts and things which independent states may of right do. And, for the support of this declaration, with a firm reliance on the protection of Divine Providence, we mutually pledge to each other our lives, our fortunes, and our sacred honor.

The Constitution of the United States of America

We the people of the United States, in order to form a more perfect union, establish justice, insure domestic tranquillity, provide for the common defense, promote the general welfare, and secure the blessings of liberty to ourselves and our posterity, do ordain and establish this Constitution for the United States of America.

Article I

SECTION 1. All legislative powers herein granted shall be vested in a Congress of the United States, which shall consist of a Senate and House of Representatives.

SECTION 2. 1. The House of Representatives shall be composed of members chosen every second year by the people of the several States, and the electors in each State shall have the qualifications requisite for electors of the most numerous branch of the State legislature.

2. No person shall be a representative who shall not have attained to the age of twenty-five years, and been seven years a citizen of the United States, and who shall not, when elected, be an inhabitant of that State in which he shall be chosen.

3. Representatives and direct taxes[1] shall be apportioned among the several States which may be included within this Union, according to their respective numbers, which shall be determined by adding to the whole number of free persons, including those bound to service for a term of years, and excluding Indians not taxed, three fifths of all other persons.[2] The actual enumeration shall be made within three years after the first meeting of the Congress of the United States, and within every subsequent term of ten years, in such manner as they shall by law direct. The number of representatives shall not exceed one for every thirty thousand, but each State shall have at least one representative; and until such enumeration shall be made, the State of New Hampshire shall be entitled to choose three, Massachusetts eight, Rhode Island and Providence Plantations one, Connecticut five, New York six, New Jersey four, Pennsylvania eight, Delaware one, Maryland six, Virginia ten, North Carolina five, South Carolina five, and Georgia three.

4. When vacancies happen in the representation from any State, the executive authority thereof shall issue writs of election to fill such vacancies.

5. The House of Representatives shall choose their speaker and other officers; and shall have the sole power of impeachment.

SECTION 3. 1. The Senate of the United States shall be composed of two senators from each State, chosen by the legislature thereof,[3] for six years; and each senator shall have one vote.

2. Immediately after they shall be assembled in consequence of the first election, they shall be divided as equally as may be into three classes. The seats of the senators of the first class shall be vacated at the expiration of the second year, of the second class at the expiration of the fourth year, and of the third class at the expiration of the sixth year, so that one third may be chosen every second year; and if vacancies happen by resignation, or otherwise, during the recess of the legislature of any State, the executive thereof may make temporary appointments until the next meeting of the legislature, which shall then fill such vacancies.[4]

3. No person shall be a senator who shall not have attained to the age of thirty years, and been nine years a citizen of the United States, and who shall not, when elected, be an inhabitant of that State for which he shall be chosen.

4. The Vice President of the United States shall be President of the Senate, but shall have no vote, unless they be equally divided.

5. The Senate shall choose their other officers, and also a president pro tempore, in the absence of the Vice President, or when he shall exercise the office of the President of the United States.

---

[1] See the Sixteenth Amendment.
[2] See the Fourteenth Amendment.

[3] See the Seventeenth Amendment.
[4] See the Seventeenth Amendment.

6. The Senate shall have the sole power to try all impeachments. When sitting for that purpose, they shall be on oath or affirmation. When the President of the United States is tried, the chief justice shall preside: and no person shall be convicted without the concurrence of two thirds of the members present.

7. Judgment in cases of impeachment shall not extend further than to removal from office, and disqualification to hold and enjoy any office of honor, trust or profit under the United States: but the party convicted shall nevertheless be liable and subject to indictment, trial, judgment and punishment, according to law.

SECTION 4. 1. The times, places, and manner of holding elections for senators and representatives, shall be prescribed in each State by the legislature thereof; but the Congress may at any time by law make or alter such regulations, except as to the places of choosing senators.

2. The Congress shall assemble at least once in every year, and such meeting shall be on the first Monday in December, unless they shall by law appoint a different day.

SECTION 5. 1. Each House shall be the judge of the elections, returns and qualifications of its own members, and a majority of each shall constitute a quorum to do business; but a smaller number may adjourn from day to day, and may be authorized to compel the attendance of absent members, in such manner, and under such penalties as each House may provide.

2. Each House may determine the rules of its proceedings, punish its members for disorderly behavior, and, with the concurrence of two thirds, expel a member.

3. Each House shall keep a journal of its proceedings, and from time to time publish the same, excepting such parts as may in their judgment require secrecy; and the yeas and nays of the members of either House on any question shall, at the desire of one fifth of those present, be entered on the journal.

4. Neither House, during the session of Congress, shall, without the consent of the other, adjourn for more than three days, nor to any other place than that in which the two Houses shall be sitting.

SECTION 6. 1. The senators and representatives shall receive a compensation for their services, to be ascertained by law, and paid out of the Treasury of the United States. They shall in all cases, except treason, felony, and breach of the peace, be privileged from arrest during their attendance at the session of their respective Houses, and in going to and returning from the same; and for any speech or debate in either House, they shall not be questioned in any other place.

2. No senator or representative shall, during the time for which he was elected, be appointed to any civil office under the authority of the United States, which shall have been created, or the emoluments whereof shall have been increased, during such time; and no person holding any office under the United States shall be a member of either House during his continuance in office.

SECTION 7. 1. All bills for raising revenue shall originate in the House of Representatives; but the Senate may propose or concur with amendments as on other bills.

2. Every bill which shall have passed the House of Representatives and the Senate, shall, before it become a law, be presented to the President of the United States; If he approves he shall sign it, but if not he shall return it, with his objections, to that House in which it shall have originated, who shall enter the objections at large on their journal, and proceed to reconsider it. If after such reconsideration two thirds of that House shall agree to pass the bill, it shall be sent, together with the objections, to the other House, by which it shall likewise be reconsidered, and if approved by two thirds of that House, it shall become a law. But in all such cases the votes of both Houses shall be determined by yeas and nays, and the names of the persons voting for and against the bill shall be entered on the journal of each House respectively. If any bill shall not be returned by the President within ten days (Sundays excepted) after it shall have been presented to him, the same shall be a law, in like manner as if he had signed it, unless the Congress by their adjournment prevent its return, in which case it shall not be a law.

3. Every order, resolution, or vote to which the concurrence of the Senate and the House of Representatives may be necessary (except on a question of adjournment) shall be presented to the President of the United States; and before the same shall take effect, shall be approved by him, or being disapproved by him, shall be repassed by two thirds of the Senate and House of Representatives, according to the rules and limitations prescribed in the case of a bill.

SECTION 8. The Congress shall have the power

1. To lay and collect taxes, duties, imposts, and excises, to pay the debts and provide for the common defense and general welfare of the United States; but all duties, imposts, and excises shall be uniform throughout the United States;

2. To borrow money on the credit of the United States;

3. To regulate commerce with foreign nations, and among the several States, and with the Indian tribes;

4. To establish a uniform rule of naturalization, and uniform laws on the subject of bankruptcies throughout the United States;

5. To coin money, regulate the value thereof, and of foreign coin, and fix the standard of weights and measures;

6. To provide for the punishment of counterfeiting the securities and current coin of the United States;

7. To establish post offices and post roads;

8. To promote the progress of science and useful arts, by securing for limited times to authors and inventors the exclusive right to their respective writings and discoveries;

9. To constitute tribunals inferior to the Supreme Court;

10. To define and punish piracies and felonies committed on the high seas, and offenses against the law of nations;

11. To declare war, grant letters of marque and reprisal, and make rules concerning captures on land and water;

12. To raise and support armies, but no appropriation of money to that use shall be for a longer term than two years;

13. To provide and maintain a navy;

14. To make rules for the government and regulation of the land and naval forces;

15. To provide for calling forth the militia to execute the laws of the Union, suppress insurrections and repel invasions;

16. To provide for organizing, arming, and disciplining the militia, and for governing such part of them as may be employed in the service of the United States, reserving to the States respectively, the appointment of the officers, and the authority of training the militia according to the discipline prescribed by Congress;

17. To exercise exclusive legislation in all cases whatsoever, over such district (not exceeding ten miles square) as may, by cession of particular States, and the acceptance of Congress, become the seat of the government of the United States, and to exercise like authority over all places purchased by the consent of the legislature of the State in which the same shall be, for the erection of forts, magazines, arsenals, dockyards, and other needful buildings; and

18. To make all laws which shall be necessary and proper for carrying into execution the foregoing powers, and all other powers vested by this Constitution in the government of the United States, or any department or officer thereof.

SECTION 9. 1. The migration or importation of such persons as any of the States now existing shall think proper to admit, shall not be prohibited by the Congress prior to the year one thousand eight hundred and eight, but a tax or duty may be imposed on such importation, not exceeding ten dollars for each person.

2. The privilege of the writ of habeas corpus shall not be suspended, unless when in cases of rebellion or invasion the public safety may require it.

3. No bill of attainder or ex post facto law shall be passed.

4. No capitation, or other direct, tax shall be laid, unless in proportion to the census or enumeration hereinbefore directed to be taken.[5]

---

[5] See the Sixteenth Amendment.

5. No tax or duty shall be laid on articles exported from any State.

6. No preference shall be given by any regulation of commerce or revenue to the ports of one State over those of another: nor shall vessels bound to, or from, one State be obliged to enter, clear, or pay duties in another.

7. No money shall be drawn from the treasury, but in consequence of appropriations made by law; and a regular statement and account of the receipts and expenditures of all public money shall be published from time to time.

8. No title of nobility shall be granted by the United States: and no person holding any office of profit or trust under them, shall, without the consent of the Congress, accept of any present, emolument, office, or title, of any kind whatever, from any king, prince, or foreign State.

SECTION 10. 1. No State shall enter into any treaty, alliance, or confederation; grant letters of marque and reprisal; coin money; emit bills of credit; make any thing but gold and silver coin a tender in payment of debts; pass any bill of attainder, ex post facto law, or law impairing the obligation of contracts, or grant any title of nobility.

2. No State shall, without the consent of the Congress, lay any imposts or duties on imports or exports, except what may be absolutely necessary for executing its inspection laws: and the net produce of all duties and imposts laid by any State on imports or exports, shall be for the use of the treasury of the United States; and all such laws shall be subject to the revision and control of the Congress.

3. No State shall, without the consent of the Congress, lay any duty of tonnage, keep troops, or ships of war in time of peace, enter into any agreement or compact with another State, or with a foreign power, or engage in war, unless actually invaded, or in such imminent danger as will not admit of delay.

Article II

SECTION 1. 1. The executive power shall be vested in a President of the United States of America. He shall hold his office during the term of four years, and, together with the Vice President, chosen for the same term, be elected, as follows:

2. Each State shall appoint, in such manner as the legislature thereof may direct, a number of electors, equal to the whole number of senators and representatives to which the State may be entitled in the Congress: but no senator or representative, or person holding any office of trust or profit under the United States, shall be appointed an elector.

The electors shall meet in their respective States, and vote by ballot for two persons, of whom one at least shall not be an inhabitant of the same State with themselves. And they shall make a list of all the persons voted for, and of the number of votes for each; which list they shall sign and certify, and transmit sealed to the seat of the government of the United States, directed to the president of the Senate. The president of the Senate shall, in the presence of the Senate and House of Representatives, open all the certificates, and the votes shall then be counted. The person having the greatest number of votes shall be the President, if such number be a majority of the whole number of electors appointed; and if there be more than one who have such majority, and have an equal number of votes, then the House of Representatives shall immediately choose by ballot one of them for President; and if no person have a majority, then from the five highest on the list the said House shall in like manner choose the President. But in choosing the President, the votes shall be taken by States, the representation from each State having one vote; a quorum for this purpose shall consist of a member or members from two thirds of the States, and a majority of all the States shall be necessary to a choice. In every case after the choice of the President, the person having the greatest number of votes of the electors shall be the Vice President. But if there should remain two or more who have equal votes, the Senate shall chose from them by ballot the Vice President.[6]

—————
[6] Superseded by the Twelfth Amendment.

3. The Congress may determine the time of choosing the electors, and the day on which they shall give their votes; which day shall be the same throughout the United States.

4. No person except a natural born citizen, or a citizen of the United States, at the time of the adoption of this Constitution, shall be eligible to the office of President; neither shall any person be eligible to the office who shall not have attained to the age of thirty-five years, and been fourteen years a resident within the United States.

5. In case of the removal of the President from office, or of his death, resignation, or inability to discharge the powers and duties of the said office, the same shall devolve on the Vice President, and the Congress may by law provide for the case of removal, death, resignation or inability, both of the President and Vice President, declaring what officer shall then act as President, and such officer shall act accordingly until the disability be removed, or a President shall be elected.

6. The President shall, at stated times, receive for his services a compensation which shall neither be increased nor diminished during the period for which he shall have been elected, and he shall not receive within that period any other emolument from the United States, or any of them.

7. Before he enter on the execution of his office, he shall take the following oath or affirmation:—"I do solemnly swear (or affirm) that I will faithfully execute the office of President of the United States, and will to the best of my ability, preserve, protect and defend the Constitution of the United States."

SECTION 2. 1. The President shall be commander in chief of the army and navy of the United States, and of the militia of the several States, when called into the actual service of the United States; he may require the opinion in writing, of the principal officer in each of the executive departments, upon any subject relating to the duties of their respective offices, and he shall have power to grant reprieves and pardons for offenses against the United States, except in cases of impeachment.

2. He shall have power, by and with the advice and consent of the Senate, to make treaties, provided two thirds of the senators present concur; and he shall nominate, and by and with the advice and consent of the Senate, shall appoint ambassadors, other public ministers and consuls, judges of the Supreme Court, and all other officers of the United States, whose appointments are not herein otherwise provided for, and which shall be established by law; but the Congress may by law vest the appointment of such inferior officers, as they think proper, in the President alone, in the courts of laws, or in the heads of departments.

3. The President shall have power to fill up all vacancies that may happen during the recess of the Senate, by granting commissions which shall expire at the end of their next session.

SECTION 3. He shall from time to time give to the Congress information of the state of the Union, and recommend to their consideration such measures as he shall judge necessary and expedient; he may, on extraordinary occasions, convene both Houses, or either of them, and in case of disagreement between them with respect to the time of adjournment, he may adjourn them to such time as he shall think proper; he shall receive ambassadors and other public ministers; he shall take care that the laws be faithfully executed, and shall commission all the officers of the United States.

SECTION 4. The President, Vice President, and all civil officers of the United States, shall be removed from office on impeachment for, and conviction of, treason, bribery, or other high crimes and misdemeanors.

Article III

SECTION 1. The judicial power of the United States shall be vested in one Supreme Court, and in such inferior courts as the Congress may from time to time ordain and establish. The judges, both of the Supreme and inferior courts, shall hold their offices during good behavior, and shall, at stated times, receive for their services, a compensation, which shall not be diminished during their continuance in office.

SECTION 2. 1. The judicial power shall extend to all cases, in law and equity, arising under this Constitution, the laws of the United States, and treaties made, or which shall be made, under their authority;—to all cases affecting ambassadors, other public ministers and consuls;—to all cases of admiralty and maritime jurisdiction;—to controversies to which the United States shall be a party;[7]—to controversies between two or more States;—between a State and citizens of another State;—between citizens of different States;—between citizens of the same State claiming lands under grants of different States, and between a State, or the citizens thereof, and foreign States, citizens or subjects.

2. In all cases affecting ambassadors, other public ministers and consuls, and those in which a State shall be party, the Supreme Court shall have original jurisdiction. In all the other cases before mentioned, the Supreme Court shall have appellate jurisdiction, both as to law and fact, with such exceptions, and under such regulations as the Congress shall make.

3. The trial of all crimes, except in cases of impeachment, shall be by jury; and such trial shall be held in the State where the said crimes shall have been committed; but when not committed within any State, the trial shall be at such place or places as the Congress may by law have directed.

SECTION 3. 1. Treason against the United States shall consist only in levying war against them, or in adhering to their enemies, giving them aid and comfort. No person shall be convicted of treason unless on the testimony of two witnesses to the same overt act, or on confession in open court.

2. The Congress shall have power to declare the punishment of treason, but no attainder of treason shall work corruption of blood, or forfeiture except during the life of the person attainted.

Article IV

SECTION 1. Full faith and credit shall be given in each State to the public acts, records, and judicial proceedings of every other State. And the Congress may by general laws prescribe the manner in which such acts, records and proceedings shall be proved, and the effect thereof.

SECTION 2. 1. The citizens of each State shall be entitled to all privileges and immunities of citizens in the several States.[8]

2. A person charged in any State with treason, felony, or other crime, who shall flee from justice, and be found in another State, shall on demand of the executive authority of the State from which he fled, be delivered up to be removed to the State having jurisdiction of the crime.

3. No person held to service or labor in one State under the laws thereof, escaping into another, shall, in consequence of any law or regulation therein, be discharged from such service or labor, but shall be delivered up on claim of the party to whom such service or labor may be due.[9]

SECTION 3. 1. New States may be admitted by the Congress into this Union; but no new State shall be formed or erected within the jurisdiction of any other State; nor any State be formed by the junction of two or more States, or parts of States, without the consent of the legislatures of the States concerned as well as of the Congress.

2. The Congress shall have power to dispose of and make all needful rules and regulations respecting the territory or other property belonging to the United States; and nothing in this Constitution shall be so construed as to prejudice any claims of the United States, or of any particular State.

SECTION 4. The United States shall guarantee to every State in this Union a republican form of government, and shall protect each of them against invasion; and on application of the legislature, or of the executive (when the legislature cannot be convened) against domestic violence.

Article V

The Congress, whenever two thirds of both Houses shall deem it necesary, shall propose amendments to this Constitution, or, on the application of the legislatures of two thirds of the several States, shall call a convention for proposing amendments, which in either case, shall be valid to all intents and purposes, as part of this Constitution, when ratified by the legislatures of three fourths of the several States, or by conventions in three fourths thereof, as the one or the other mode of ratification may be proposed by the Congress; Provided that no amendment which may be made prior to the year one thousand eight hundred and eight shall in any manner affect the first and fourth clauses in the ninth section of the first article; and that no State, without its consent, shall be deprived of its equal suffrage in the Senate.

Article VI

1. All debts contracted and engagements entered into, before the adoption of this Constitution, shall be as valid against the United States under this Constitution, as under the Confederation.[10]

2. This Constitution, and the laws of the United States which shall be made in pursuance thereof; and all treaties made, or which shall be made, under the authority of the United States, shall be the supreme law of the land; and the judges in every State shall be bound thereby, any thing in the Constitution or laws of any State to the contrary notwithstanding.

3. The senators and representatives before mentioned, and the members of the several State legislatures, and all executive and judicial officers, both of the United States and of the several States, shall be bound by oath or affirmation to support this Constitution; but no religious test shall ever be required as a qualification to any office or public trust under the United States.

Article VII

The ratification of the conventions of nine States shall be sufficient for the establishment of this Constitution between the States so ratifying the same.

Done in Convention by the unanimous consent of the States present the seventeenth day of September in the year of our Lord one thousand seven hundred and eighty-seven, and of the independence of the United States of America the twelfth. In witness whereof we have hereunto subscribed our names.

[Names omitted]

* * *

Articles in addition to, and amendment of, the Constitution of the United States of America, proposed by Congress, and ratified by the legislatures of the several States, pursuant to the fifth article of the original Constitution.

Amendment I [First ten amendments ratified December 15, 1791]

Congress shall make no law respecting an establishment of religion, or prohibiting the free exercise thereof; or abridging the freedom of speech, or of the press; or the right of the people peaceably to assemble, and to petition the government for a redress of grievances.

Amendment II

A well regulated militia, being necessary to the security of a free State, the right of the people to keep and bear arms, shall not be infringed.

---

[7] See the Eleventh Amendment.
[8] See the Fourteenth Amendment, Sec. 1.
[9] See the Thirteenth Amendment.

---

[10] See the Fourteenth Amendment, Sec. 4.

Amendment III

No soldier shall, in time of peace be quartered in any house, without the consent of the owner, nor in time of war, but in a manner to be prescribed by law.

Amendment IV

The right of the people to be secure in their persons, houses, papers, and effects, against unreasonable searches and seizures, shall not be violated, and no warrants shall issue, but upon probable cause, supported by oath or affirmation, and particularly describing the place to be searched, and the persons or things to be seized.

Amendment V

No person shall be held to answer for a capital or otherwise infamous crime, unless on a presentment or indictment of a grand jury, except in cases arising in the land or naval forces, or in the militia, when in actual service in time of war or public danger; nor shall any person be subject for the same offense to be twice put in jeopardy of life or limb; nor shall be compelled in any criminal case to be a witness against himself, nor be deprived of life, liberty, or property, without due process of law; nor shall private property be taken for public use, without just compensation.

Amendment VI

In all criminal prosecutions, the accused shall enjoy the right to a speedy and public trial, by an impartial jury of the State and district wherein the crime shall have been committed, which district shall have been previously ascertained by law, and to be informed of the nature and cause of the accusation; to be confronted with the witnesses against him; to have compulsory process for obtaining witnesses in his favor, and to have the assistance of counsel for his defense.

Amendment VII

In suits at common law, where the value in controversy shall exceed twenty dollars, the right of trial by jury shall be preserved, and no fact tried by a jury shall be otherwise reexamined in any court of the United States, than according to the rules of the common law.

Amendment VIII

Excessive bail shall not be required, nor excessive fines imposed, nor cruel and unusual punishments inflicted.

Amendment IX

The enumeration in the Constitution of certain rights shall not be construed to deny or disparage others retained by the people.

Amendment X

The powers not delegated to the United States by the Constitution, nor prohibited by it to the States, are reserved to the States respectively, or to the people.

Amendment XI [January 8, 1798]

The judicial power of the United States shall not be construed to extend to any suit in law or equity, commenced or prosecuted against one of the United States by citizens of another State, or by citizens or subjects of any foreign State.

Amendment XII [September 25, 1804]

The electors shall meet in their respective States, and vote by ballot for President and Vice President, one of whom, at least, shall not be an inhabitant of the same State with themselves; they shall name in their ballots the person voted for as President, and in distinct ballots, the person voted for as Vice President, and they shall make distinct lists of all persons voted for as President and of all persons voted for as Vice President, and of the number of votes for each, which lists they shall sign and certify, and transmit sealed to the seat of the government of the United States, directed to the President of the Senate;— The President of the Senate shall, in the presence of the Senate and House of Representatives, open all the certificates and the votes shall then be counted;—The person having the greatest number of votes for President, shall be the President, if such number be a majority of the whole number of electors appointed; and if no person have such majority, then from the persons having the highest numbers not exceeding three on the list of those voted for as President, the House of Representatives shall choose immediately, by ballot, the President. But in choosing the President, the votes shall be taken by States, the representation from each State having one vote; a quorum for this purpose shall consist of a member or members from two thirds of the States, and a majority of all the States shall be necessary to a choice. And if the House of Representatives shall not choose a President whenever the right of choice shall devolve upon them, before the fourth day of March next following, then the Vice President shall act as President, as in the case of the death or other constitutional disability of the President. The person having the greatest number of votes as Vice President shall be the Vice President, if such number be a majority of the whole number of electors appointed, and if no person have a majority, then from the two highest numbers on the list, the Senate shall choose the Vice President; a quorum for the purpose shall consist of two thirds of the whole number of Senators, and a majority of the whole number shall be necessary to a choice. But no person constitutionally ineligible to the office of President shall be eligible to that of Vice President of the United States.

Amendment XIII [December 18, 1865]

SECTION 1. Neither slavery nor involuntary servitude, except as a punishment for crime whereof the party shall have been duly convicted, shall exist within the United States, or any place subject to their jurisdiction.

SECTION 2. Congress shall have power to enforce this article by appropriate legislation.

Amendment XIV [July 28, 1868]

SECTION 1. All persons born or naturalized in the United States, and subject to the jurisdiction thereof, are citizens of the United States and of the State wherein they reside. No State shall make or enforce any law which shall abridge the privileges or immunities of citizens of the United States; nor shall any State deprive any person of life, liberty, or property, without due process of law; nor deny to any person within its jurisdiction the equal protection of the laws.

SECTION 2. Representatives shall be apportioned among the several States according to their respective numbers, counting the whole number of persons in each State, excluding Indians not taxed. But when the right to vote at any election for the choice of electors for President and Vice President of the United States, representatives in Congress, the executive and judicial officers of a State, or the members of the legislature thereof, is denied to any of the male inhabitants of such State, being twenty-one years of age, and citizens of the United States, or in any way abridged, except for participating in rebellion, or other crime, the basis of representation therein shall be reduced in the proportion which the number of such male citizens shall bear to the whole number of male citizens twenty-one years of age in such State.

SECTION 3.   No person shall be a senator or representative in Congress, or elector of President and Vice President, or hold any office, civil or military, under the United States, or under any State, who having previously taken an oath, as a member of Congress, or as an officer of the United States, or as a member of any State legislature, or as an executive or judicial officer of any State, to support the Constitution of the United States, shall have engaged in insurrection or rebellion against the same, or given aid or comfort to the enemies thereof. But Congress may by a vote of two thirds of each House, remove such disability.

SECTION 4.   The validity of the public debt of the United States, authorized by law, including debts incurred for payment of pensions and bounties for services in suppressing insurrection or rebellion, shall not be questioned. But neither the United States nor any State shall assume or pay any debt or obligation incurred in aid of insurrection or rebellion against the United States, or any claim for the loss or emancipation of any slave; but all such debts, obligations, and claims shall be held illegal and void.

SECTION 5.   The Congress shall have the power to enforce, by appropriate legislation, the provisions of this article.

Amendment XV [March 30, 1870]

SECTION 1.   The right of citizens of the United States to vote shall not be denied or abridged by the United States or by any State on account of race, color, or previous condition of servitude.

SECTION 2.   The Congress shall have power to enforce this article by appropriate legislation.

Amendment XVI [February 25, 1913]

The Congress shall have power to lay and collect taxes on incomes, from whatever source derived, without apportionment among the several States, and without regard to any census or enumeration.

Amendment XVII [May 31, 1913]

The Senate of the United States shall be composed of two senators from each State, elected by the people thereof, for six years; and each senator shall have one vote. The electors in each State shall have the qualifications requisite for electors of the most numerous branch of the State legislature.

When vacancies happen in the representation of any State in the Senate, the executive authority of such State shall issue writs of election to fill such vacancies: *Provided*, That the legislature of any State may empower the executive thereof to make temporary appointments until the people fill the vacancies by election as the legislature may direct.

This amendment shall not be so construed as to affect the election or term of any senator chosen before it becomes valid as part of the Constitution.

Amendment XVIII[11] [January 29, 1919]

After one year from the ratification of this article, the manufacture, sale, or transportation of intoxicating liquors within, the importation thereof into, or the exportation thereof from the United States and all territory subject to the jurisdiction thereof for beverage purposes is thereby prohibited.

---

[11] Repealed by the Twenty-first Amendment.

The Congress and the several States shall have concurrent power to enforce this article by appropriate legislation.

This article shall be inoperative unless it shall have been ratified as an amendment to the Constitution by the legislatures of the several States, as provided in the Constitution, within seven years from the date of the submission hereof to the States by Congress.

Amendment XIX [August 26, 1920]

The right of citizens of the United States to vote shall not be denied or abridged by the United States or by any State on account of sex.

Congress shall have the power to enforce this article by appropriate legislation.

Amendment XX [January 23, 1933]

SECTION 1.   The terms of the President and Vice President shall end at noon on the 20th day of January and the terms of Senators and Representatives at noon on the 3d day of January, of the years in which such terms would have ended if this article had not been ratified; and the terms of their successors shall then begin.

SECTION 2.   The Congress shall assemble at least once in every year, and such meeting shall begin at noon on the 3d day of January, unless they shall by law appoint a different day.

SECTION 3.   If, at the time fixed for the beginning of the term of President, the President-elect shall have died, the Vice President-elect shall become President. If a President shall not have been chosen before the time fixed for the beginning of his term, or if the President-elect shall have failed to qualify, then the Vice President-elect shall act as President until a President shall have qualified; and the Congress may by law provide for the case wherein neither a President-elect nor a Vice President-elect shall have qualified, declaring who shall then act as President, or the manner in which one who is to act shall be selected, and such person shall act accordingly until a President or Vice President shall have qualified.

SECTION 4.   The Congress may by law provide for the case of the death of any of the persons from whom the House of Representatives may choose a President whenever the right of choice shall have devolved upon them, and for the case of the death of any of the persons from whom the Senate may choose a Vice President whenever the right of choice shall have devolved upon them.

SECTION 5.   Sections 1 and 2 shall take effect on the 15th day of October following the ratification of this article.

SECTION 6.   This article shall be inoperative unless it shall have been ratified as an amendment to the Constitution by the legislatures of three-fourths of the several States within seven years from the date of its submission.

Amendment XXI [December 5, 1933]

SECTION 1.   The Eighteenth Article of amendment to the Constitution of the United States is hereby repealed.

SECTION 2.   The transportation or importation into any State, Territory, or possession of the United States for delivery or use therein of intoxicating liquors in violation of the laws thereof, is hereby prohibited.

SECTION 3.   This article shall be inoperative unless it shall have been ratified as an amendment to the Constitution by conventions in the several States, as provided in the Consititution, within seven years from the date of the submission thereof to the States by the Congress.

Amendment XXII [March 1, 1951]

No person shall be elected to the office of the President more than twice, and no person who has held the office of President, or acted as President, for more than two years of a term to which some other person was elected President shall be elected to the office of the President more than once.

But this article shall not apply to any person holding the office of President when this article was proposed by the Congress, and shall not prevent any person who may be holding the office of President, or acting as President, during the term within which this article becomes operative from holding the office of President or acting as President during the remainder of such term.

This article shall be inoperative unless it shall have been ratified as an amendment to the Constitution by the legislatures of three-fourths of the several States within seven years from the date of its submission to the States by the Congress.

Amendment XXIII [March 29, 1961]

SECTION 1.   The District constituting the seat of Government of the United States shall appoint in such manner as the Congress may direct.

A number of electors of President and Vice President equal to the whole number of Senators and Representatives in Congress to which the District would be entitled if it were a State, but in no event more than the least populous State; they shall be in addition to those appointed by the States, but they shall be considered, for the purposes of the election of President and Vice President, to be electors appointed by a State; and they shall meet in the District and perform such duties as provided by the twelfth article of amendment.

SECTION 2.   The Congress shall have power to enforce this article by appropriate legislation.

Amendment XXIV [January 23, 1964]

SECTION 1.   The right of citizens of the United States to vote in any primary or other election for President or Vice President, for electors for President or Vice President, or for Senator or Representative in Congress, shall not be denied or abridged by the United States or any State by reason of failure to pay any poll tax or other tax.

SECTION 2.   The Congress shall have power to enforce this article by appropriate legislation.

Amendment XXV [February 10, 1967]

SECTION 1.   In case of the removal of the President from office or of his death or resignation, the Vice President shall become President.

SECTION 2.   Whenever there is a vacancy in the office of the Vice President, the President shall nominate a Vice President who shall take office upon confirmation by a majority of both Houses of Congress.

SECTION 3.   Whenever the President transmits to the President pro tempore of the Senate and the Speaker of the House of Representatives his written declaration that he is unable to discharge the powers and duties of his office, and until he transmits to them a written declaration to the contrary, such powers and duties shall be discharged by the Vice President as Acting President.

SECTION 4.   Whenever the Vice President and a majority of either the principal officers of the executive departments or of such other body as Congress may by law provide, transmit to the President pro tempore of the Senate and the Speaker of the House of Representatives their written declaration that the President is unable to discharge the powers and duties of his office, the Vice President shall immediately assume the powers and duties of the office as Acting President.

Thereafter, when the President transmits to the President pro tempore of the Senate and the Speaker of the House of Representatives his written declaration that no inability exists, he shall resume the powers and duties of his office unless the Vice President and a majority of either the principal officers of the executive departments or of such other body as Congress may by law provide, transmit within four days to the President pro tempore of the Senate and the Speaker of the House of Representatives their written declaration that the President is unable to discharge the powers and duties of his office. Thereupon Congress shall decide the issue, assembling within forty-eight hours for that purpose if not in session. If the Congress, within twenty-one days after receipt of the latter written declaration, or, if Congress is not in session, within twenty-one days after Congress is required to assemble, determines by two-thirds vote of both Houses that the President is unable to discharge the powers and duties of his office, the Vice President shall continue to discharge the same as Acting President; otherwise, the President shall resume the powers and duties of his office.

Amendment XXVI [June 30, 1971]

SECTION 1.   The right of citizens of the United States who are eighteen years of age or older to vote shall not be denied or abridged by the United States or by any State on account of age.

SECTION 2.   The Congress shall have power to enforce this article by appropriate legislation.

YEAR	NUMBER OF STATES	CANDIDATES	PARTY	POPULAR VOTE*	ELECTORAL VOTE†	PERCENTAGE OF POPULAR VOTE
1789	11	GEORGE WASHINGTON	No party designations		69	
		John Adams			34	
		Other Candidates			35	
1792	15	GEORGE WASHINGTON	No party designations		132	
		John Adams			77	
		George Clinton			50	
		Other Candidates			5	
1796	16	JOHN ADAMS	Federalist		71	
		Thomas Jefferson	Democratic-Republican		68	
		Thomas Pinckney	Federalist		59	
		Aaron Burr	Democratic-Republican		30	
		Other Candidates			48	
1800	16	THOMAS JEFFERSON	Democratic-Republican		73	
		Aaron Burr	Democratic-Republican		73	
		John Adams	Federalist		65	
		Charles C. Pinckney	Federalist		64	
		John Jay	Federalist		1	
1804	17	THOMAS JEFFERSON	Democratic-Republican		162	
		Charles C. Pinckney	Federalist		14	
1808	17	JAMES MADISON	Democratic-Republican		122	
		Charles C. Pinckney	Federalist		47	
		George Clinton	Democratic-Republican		6	
1812	18	JAMES MADISON	Democratic-Republican		128	
		DeWitt Clinton	Federalist		89	
1816	19	JAMES MONROE	Democratic-Republican		183	
		Rufus King	Federalist		34	
1820	24	JAMES MONROE	Democratic-Republican		231	
		John Quincy Adams	Independent Republican		1	
1824	24	JOHN QUINCY ADAMS		108,740	84	30.5
		Andrew Jackson		153,544	99	43.1
		William H. Crawford		46,618	41	13.1
		Henry Clay		47,136	37	13.2
1828	24	ANDREW JACKSON	Democrat	647,286	178	56.0
		John Quincy Adams	National Republican	508,064	83	44.0
1832	24	ANDREW JACKSON	Democrat	687,502	219	55.0
		Henry Clay	National Republican	530,189	49	42.4
		William Wirt	Anti-Masonic	33,108	7	2.6
		John Floyd	National Republican		11	
1836	26	MARTIN VAN BUREN	Democrat	765,483	170	50.9
		William H. Harrison	Whig		73	
		Hugh L. White	Whig	739,795	26	49.1
		Daniel Webster	Whig		14	
		W. P. Mangum	Whig		11	
1840	26	WILLIAM H. HARRISON	Whig	1,274,624	234	53.1
		Martin Van Buren	Democrat	1,127,781	60	46.9
1844	26	JAMES K. POLK	Democrat	1,338,464	170	49.6
		Henry Clay	Whig	1,300,097	105	48.1
		James G. Birney	Liberty	62,300		2.3
1848	30	ZACHARY TAYLOR	Whig	1,360,967	163	47.4
		Lewis Cass	Democrat	1,222,342	127	42.5
		Martin Van Buren	Free Soil	291,263		10.1
1852	31	FRANKLIN PIERCE	Democrat	1,601,117	254	50.9
		Winfield Scott	Whig	1,385,453	42	44.1
		John P. Hale	Free Soil	155,825		5.0
1856	31	JAMES BUCHANAN	Democrat	1,832,955	174	45.3
		John C. Frémont	Republican	1,339,932	114	33.1
		Millard Fillmore	American	871,731	8	21.6

* Percentage of popular vote given for any election year may not total 100 percent because candidates receiving less than 1 percent of the popular vote have been omitted.
† Prior to the passage of the Twelfth Amendment in 1904, the electoral college voted for two presidential candidates; the runner-up became Vice-President. Data from *Historical Statistics of the United States, Colonial Times to 1957* (1961), pp. 682–683, and *The World Almanac*.

YEAR	NUMBER OF STATES	CANDIDATES	PARTY	POPULAR VOTE	ELECTORAL VOTE	PERCENTAGE OF POPULAR VOTE
1860	33	ABRAHAM LINCOLN	Republican	1,865,593	180	39.8
		Stephen A. Douglas	Democrat	1,382,713	12	29.5
		John C. Breckinridge	Democrat	848,356	72	18.1
		John Bell	Constitutional Union	592,906	39	12.6
1864	36	ABRAHAM LINCOLN	Republican	2,206,938	212	55.0
		George B. McClellan	Democrat	1,803,787	21	45.0
1868	37	ULYSSES S. GRANT	Republican	3,013,421	214	52.7
		Horatio Seymour	Democrat	2,706,829	80	47.3
1872	37	ULYSSES S. GRANT	Republican	3,596,745	286	55.6
		Horace Greeley	Democrat	2,843,446	*	43.9
1876	38	RUTHERFORD B. HAYES	Republican	4,036,572	185	48.0
		Samuel J. Tilden	Democrat	4,284,020	184	51.0
1880	38	JAMES A. GARFIELD	Republican	4,453,295	214	48.5
		Winfield S. Hancock	Democrat	4,414,082	155	48.1
		James B. Weaver	Greenback-Labor	308,578		3.4
1884	38	GROVER CLEVELAND	Democrat	4,879,507	219	48.5
		James G. Blaine	Republican	4,850,293	182	48.2
		Benjamin F. Butler	Greenback-Labor	175,370		1.8
		John P. St. John	Prohibition	150,369		1.5
1888	38	BENJAMIN HARRISON	Republican	5,447,129	233	47.9
		Grover Cleveland	Democrat	5,537,857	168	48.6
		Clinton B. Fisk	Prohibition	249,506		2.2
		Anson J. Streeter	Union Labor	146,935		1.3
1892	44	GROVER CLEVELAND	Democrat	5,555,426	277	46.1
		Benjamin Harrison	Republican	5,182,690	145	43.0
		James B. Weaver	People's	1,029,846	22	8.5
		John Bidwell	Prohibition	264,133		2.2
1896	45	WILLIAM MCKINLEY	Republican	7,102,246	271	51.1
		William J. Bryan	Democrat	6,492,559	176	47.7
1900	45	WILLIAM MCKINLEY	Republican	7,218,491	292	51.7
		William J. Bryan	Democrat; Populist	6,356,734	155	45.5
		John C. Woolley	Prohibition	208,914		1.5
1904	45	THEODORE ROOSEVELT	Republican	7,628,461	336	57.4
		Alton B. Parker	Democrat	5,084,223	140	37.6
		Eugene V. Debs	Socialist	402,283		3.0
		Silas C. Swallow	Prohibition	258,536		1.9
1908	46	WILLIAM H. TAFT	Republican	7,675,320	321	51.6
		William J. Bryan	Democrat	6,412,294	162	43.1
		Eugene V. Debs	Socialist	420,793		2.8
		Eugene W. Chafin	Prohibition	253,840		1.7
1912	48	WOODROW WILSON	Democrat	6,296,547	435	41.9
		Theodore Roosevelt	Progressive	4,118,571	88	27.4
		William H. Taft	Republican	3,486,720	8	23.2
		Eugene V. Debs	Socialist	900,672		6.0
		Eugene W. Chafin	Prohibition	206,275		1.4
1916	48	WOODROW WILSON	Democrat	9,127,695	277	49.4
		Charles E. Hughes	Republican	8,533,507	254	46.2
		A. L. Benson	Socialist	585,113		3.2
		J. Frank Hanly	Prohibition	220,506		1.2
1920	48	WARREN G. HARDING	Republican	16,143,407	404	60.4
		James M. Cox	Democrat	9,130,328	127	34.2
		Eugene V. Debs	Socialist	919,799		3.4
		P. P. Christensen	Farmer-Labor	265,411		1.0
1924	48	CALVIN COOLIDGE	Republican	15,718,211	382	54.0
		John W. Davis	Democrat	8,385,283	136	28.8
		Robert M. La Follette	Progressive	4,831,289	13	16.6
1928	48	HERBERT C. HOOVER	Republican	21,391,993	444	58.2
		Alfred E. Smith	Democrat	15,016,169	87	40.9

* Because of the death of Greeley, Democratic electors scattered their votes.

YEAR	NUMBER OF STATES	CANDIDATES	PARTY	POPULAR VOTE	ELECTORAL VOTE	PERCENTAGE OF POPULAR VOTE
1932	48	FRANKLIN D. ROOSEVELT	Democrat	22,809,638	472	57.4
		Herbert C. Hoover	Republican	15,758,901	59	39.7
		Norman Thomas	Socialist	881,951		2.2
1936	48	FRANKLIN D. ROOSEVELT	Democrat	27,752,869	523	60.8
		Alfred M. Landon	Republican	16,674,665	8	36.5
		William Lemke	Union	882,479		1.9
1940	48	FRANKLIN D. ROOSEVELT	Democrat	27,307,819	449	54.8
		Wendell L. Willkie	Republican	22,321,018	82	44.8
1944	48	FRANKLIN D. ROOSEVELT	Democrat	25,606,585	432	53.5
		Thomas E. Dewey	Republican	22,014,745	99	46.0
1948	48	HARRY S. TRUMAN	Democrat	24,105,812	303	49.5
		Thomas E. Dewey	Republican	21,970,065	189	45.1
		J. Strom Thurmond	States' Rights	1,169,063	39	2.4
		Henry A. Wallace	Progressive	1,157,172		2.4
1952	48	DWIGHT D. EISENHOWER	Republican	33,936,234	442	55.1
		Adlai E. Stevenson	Democrat	27,314,992	89	44.4
1956	48	DWIGHT D. EISENHOWER	Republican	35,590,472	457†	57.6
		Adlai E. Stevenson	Democrat	26,022,752	73	42.1
1960	50	JOHN F. KENNEDY	Democrat	34,227,096	303‡	49.9
		Richard M. Nixon	Republican	34,108,546	219	49.6
1964	50	LYNDON B. JOHNSON	Democrat	42,676,220	486	61.3
		Barry M. Goldwater	Republican	26,860,314	52	38.5
1968	50	RICHARD M. NIXON	Republican	31,785,480	301	43.4
		Hubert H. Humphrey	Democrat	31,275,165	191	42.7
		George C. Wallace	American Independent	9,906,473	46	13.5
1972	50	RICHARD M. NIXON*	Republican	47,165,234	520	60.6
		George S. McGovern	Democrat	29,168,110	17	37.5
1976	50	JIMMY CARTER	Democrat	40,828,929	297	50.1
		Gerald R. Ford	Republican	39,148,940	240	47.9
		Eugene McCarthy	Independent	739,256		
1980	50	RONALD REAGAN	Republican	43,201,220	489	50.9
		Jimmy Carter	Democrat	34,913,332	49	41.2
		John B. Anderson	Independent	5,581,379		
1984	50	RONALD REAGAN	Republican	53,428,357	525	59.0
		Walter F. Mondale	Democrat	36,930,923	13	41.0
1988	50	GEORGE BUSH	Republican	48,901,046	426	53.4
		Michael Dukakis	Democrat	41,809,030	111	45.6

† Walter B. Jones received 1 electoral vote. ‡Harry F. Byrd received 15 electoral votes.
* Resigned August 9, 1974: Vice President Gerald R. Ford became President.

INDEX

Reference to pages on which an illustration or map about the topic appears are shown in *italic*.

Creek Indians, 420
Creel, George, 612-13
"Crime of '73," 476
Crisis (journal), 597
Crittenden Resolution (1861), 391
Crocker, Charles, 444
Croker, Richard, 507, 508
Croly, David, 389
Croly, Herbert, 571
"Cross of Gold" speech, 489-91
"Cross Road Blues," 598
Crow Indians, 420
Cruise missiles, 871
Crusade in Europe (Eisenhower), 767
Cuba, 548, 563
    Bay of Pigs, 786
    Castro and, 779-80, 786-87
    immigrants from, 893
    Missile Crisis, 786-87
    Roosevelt's policies toward, 699
    Spanish-American War and, 552-54
    under US military governorship
      (1898-1902), 557-58
Culture
    of dissent, 637-44
      disillusion and disenchantment,
        638-42
      Harlem renaissance, 642-44
      prelude to, 637-38
    drug, 819
    in the Gilded Age, 520-24, 536-40. *See
      also* Thought in the Gilded Age
cummings, e.e., 639
Cumming v. *County Board of Educa-
    tion*, 414
Currency, 492
Currency Act (1900), 491
Current, electrical, 447-48
Curtis, Cyrus H.K., 513
Curtis, George W., 474
Curtis, S.R., 423
Custer, George A., 423, *423*, 424
Cutthroat competition, 446
Czechoslovakia, 619, 719, 741, 810, 889
Czolgosz, Leon, 569

D

Dai, Bao, 774, 776
Dakota country, 419
Dana, Richard Henry, 843
Daniels, Jonathan, *706*, 707, 710
Darlan, Jena, 715
Darrow, Clarence, 636
Darwin, Charles, 440-41, 522-24
Daugherty, Harry M., 649-50
Davis, David, 408
Davis, Jefferson, 390
Davis, John W., 651, 881
Dawes Act (1887), 425-26
Dayton flood (1913), 575
D-Day (1944), 716, 717-21, *717*
Deadline, origin of word, 530
Deadwood Gulch, 427-28
Dean, John, 841, 842, 843
Debs, Eugene, 461, *461*, 492, 571, 583,
    599, 612, 614, 621, 649
Debt, foreign, 876
Declaration of Independence, 897-98
Defense industries, mobilization for
    World War II and, 710-11

Defense Plant Corporation, 710, 737
Deficit, budget, 846, 876, 883-84
De Forest, Lee, 648
De Gaulle, Charles, 715, 717, 779
Delarge, Robert C., *400*
DeLeon, Daniel, 462
De Mille, Cecil B., 647
Demobilization after World War II, 734
Democratic National Convention
    (1968), *815*, 816
Democratic party. *See also* Elections,
    presidential; Politics
    in Gilded Age, 470-74
    Mississippi Plan and, 404
    New Deal and, 686, 687
    progressivism and, 582-84
Demography, 893-94
Demonstrations
    antiwar, 812, 813, *815*, 836, 837
    black, 800
    in Chicago (1967), 802
Denby, Edwin, 650
Dennis, Eugene, 750
Depression(s), 448
    of 1870s, 407, 514, 515
    of 1880s, 411
    of 1890s, 475, 482
    of mid-1870s, 407
Deregulation under Reagan, 866-69,
    884-85
Desegregation, 770-72
    in armed services, 738
    in education, 770-72, 798-99, 870
Desert Land Act (1877), 432
De-Stalinization, 779
Détente diplomacy, 834-35, 871-82
Detroit, Michigan
    race riots of 1943, 710
    riots of 1965, 802
Dewey, George, 552, 554
Dewey, John, 525, *526*
Dewey, Thomas E., 704, 713, 738, 739,
    754
DeWitt, J.L., 708, 709
Díaz, Porfirio, 563
Díaz regime (1877-1911) in Mexico,
    698-99
Dickinson, Emily, 533
Diem, Ngo Dinh, 776, 787, 788
Dienbienphu, siege of (1954), 774, 775
Dietrich, Senator, 557
Dillon, C. Douglas, 782
DiMaggio, Joe, *653*
Dime novels, 537
Dingley tariff (1897), 491
Diplomacy. *See also* Foreign policy
    by alliance, 776-77
    conference, 716-17
    détente, 834-35, 871-82
    Dollar, 561, 563
    of flexible response, 786-90
    power and, 550-51
    by rhetoric, 773
    Western Hemispheric, 551
Direct current, 447
Direct primary, 575
Disarmament, post-World War I,
    696-97
Discrimination
    racial, 710, 870. *See also* Blacks
    sex, 856, 881
Disfranchisement of blacks, 412-14,
    415, 594

Disillusionment
    in 1960s, 818-19
    after World War I, 638-42
Dispatches (Herr), 814
Dissent
    culture of (post-World War I), 637-44
      disillusion and disenchantment,
        638-42
      Harlem renaissance, 642-44
      prelude to, 637-38
    in 1950s, 766
    in the 1960s, 812, 813, 817-25
      counterculture of, 819-25
      sources of disillusionment, 818-19
    over Vietnam War, 812, 813, 836, 837
Divorce rate, 585, 626
Dix, Dorothy, 626
Dixiecrats, 738-39
Dixon, Thomas, 595
Dodge City, Kansas, 430-31
Doheny, Edward F., 650
Dole, Sanford B., 549
Dollar Diplomacy, 561, 563
Domestic programs. *See* Economy; Leg-
    islation; *specific programs*
Domestic service, 454, 456, 499, 511-12
Dominican Republic, 562-63, 809
Domino theory, 774, 788
Doolittle, James H., 721
Dos Passos, John, 637, 647
Douglass, Frederick, 405, 460
Draft, 702, 704, 710
Draft resisters, 848
Drake, Edwin L., 445
Dreiser, Theodore, 535-36
Dresden, Germany, 696
Dressler, Marie, 647
Drew, Daniel, 442, 515
Drug culture of 1960s, 819
Drugs, illegal, 885-86
Dry farming, 434
Duarte, José Napoleon, 873
Dubcek, Alexander, 810
Du Bois, W.E.B., 403, 405, 529, 530,
    596-98, *596*, 599, 642, 644, 686,
    708
Dukakis, Michael, 864, 880-81, *880*, 883
Dulles, Allen, 786
Dulles, John Foster, 767, 772, 773, 776-
    77, 778
Dumbarton Oaks conference (1944),
    730
Dumbbell tenement, 511
Dunne, Finley Peter, 481, 573
DuPont company, 657
Durant, William C., 657
Durr, Virginia, 689
Dylan, Bob, 825
Dynamic Sociology (Ward), 523

E

East, railroads' battle for, 442-43
Eastern Europe, 872, 883, 885, 888
East Germany, revolt of 1953, 773
Eastman, Crystal, 594
Eaton, Horace M., 457
Eckford, Elizabeth, *771*
*Economic Interpretation of the Consti-
    tution, An* (Beard), 526
Economics
    of dependency, 409-12

Grimke, Francis J., 599
Grissom, Virgil I., 790
Griswold, John, 454
Griswold v. *State of Connecticut*, 857
Gruening, Ernest, 812
Guadalcanal, 722
Guadalupe Hidalgo, Treaty of (1848), 805
Guam, 555
Guantanamo Bay, 558, 699
Guaranteed minimum income, 833
Guatemala, 773-74, 786, 787
Guggenheim family, 429
Guiteau, Charles, 477
Gun control, 866

H

Haagland, Joel Ammanuel (alias Joe Hill), 462, 463
Habeas corpus, Lincoln's suspension of, 396
Hagerty, Thomas J., 462
Haig, Alexander, 871-82
Haight-Ashbury, 819
Haiti, 563
Halberstam, David, 782
Haldeman, H.R. (Bob), 832, 840, 841, 842, 843, 844, 845
Half-Breeds, 407, 471
Halsey, William F. (Bull), 708
Hammer v. *Dagenhart*, 576
Hampton, Wade, 409
Hampton's (magazine), 573
Hancock, Winfield Scott, 476-77
Handy, W.C., 647
Hanna, Mark, 477, 489, 490, 491, 578
Hanoi, 774
Harburg, E.Y., 672
Harding, Warren G., 621, 626-27, *631*, 640, 649-50, 651, 697
Hard Times (Terkel), 675, 689
Harlem renaissance, 642-44
Harlem riot (1935), 685
Harper's Weekly, 507, 513
Harriman, Edward H., 444-45
Harris, Joel Chandler, 533
Harris, Townsend, 548
Harrison, Benjamin, 480-81, 482, 551
Harrison, William Henry, 549
Harte, Bret, 533
Harvard University, 531
Harvey, William H., 489
Hatfield, Mark, 837
Havel, Vaclav, 889
Hawaii, 548, 549, 558-59
Hawley-Smoot tariff (1930), 651, 665
Hawthorne, Nathaniel, 533
Hay, John, 559-60, 561
Hayes, Rutherford B., 407-9, 458, 474-76
Haymarket Square riot (1886), 460
Haynesworth, Clement F., 833
Hay-Pauncefote Treaty (1901), 561
Hays, Will H., 647
Haywood, William (Big Bill), 462, *462*
Hazard of New Fortunes, A (Howells), 534
Haze and hazing, use of terms, 843
Head Start, 883
Hearst, William Randolph, 513, 552, *553*

Heavy industry, 445-48, 657
Hecker, Isaac T., 516
Hegel, G.W.F., 525
Heifetz, Jascha, 647
Heline, Oscar, 670
Heller, Joseph, 797
Heller, Walter C., 782
"Hell Hound on My Trail," 598
Hemingway, Ernest, 638-39
Henderson, Leon, 711
Hepburn Act (1906), 580
Hepburn v. *Griswold*, 475
Herr, Michael, 814
Hickok, Wild Bill, 430-31
Higher education, 530-31
Higher Learning in America, The (Veblen), 531
Hill, James J., 444-45
Hill, Joe (Joel Ammanuel Haagland), 462, 463
Hirohito, Emperor, 723
Hiroshima, Japan, 696, 723
Hispanic Americans, 893
Hiss, Alger, 750-52, *752*
History, 526-27
Hitler, Adolf, 618, 695, 696, 700, 704, 716, 717, 718. *See also* World War II
    invasion of Europe, 703
    invasion of Soviet Union, 705
    rise to power, 702-3
    Spanish civil war and, 700, 701
    suicide of, 720
Hoar, E.R., 548
Ho Chi Minh, 774, 775, 816
Ho Chi Minh Trail, 787
Holding companies, 481, 683
Holland, 545
Hollings, Ernest, 875
Hollywood, California, 647, 750, *751*
Holmes, Oliver Wendell, Jr., 482, 504, 526, 585, 628, 636-37, 750
Homelessness, 892
Home Owners Loan Corporation, 688
Homestead Act (1862), 431, 432
Homesteading, 431, *433*
Homestead strike (1892), 460, 482
Home to Harlem (McKay), 642, 643
Homicide rate, 894
Honduras, 563
Hong Kong, 559
Hoover, Herbert, 611, 626, 635, 649, 658, 663, 664, 665-66, 667, 697
Hoover, J. Edgar, 749, 769, 840, 846
"Hoovervilles," 663
Hopeless (Lichtenstein), 822
Hopi Indians, 420
Hopkins, Harry, 667, 689, 705
Hopkins, Mark, 444
Hornet (aircraft carrier), 721
Horsecar, 509
Hostages in Iran (1979-1981), 848-50, *849*
Houdini, Harry, 539
Hough, Frank O., *721*
House, Edward M., 608
House Judiciary Committee, 844, 845
House Un-American Activities Committee (HUAC), 750-52, 766
Housework, 456
Housing
    New Deal and, 688

post-World War II, 736
    prices of, 892
    urban, 510-11
Housing and Urban Development, Department of (HUD), 799
Howard, Oliver Otis, 391
Howard, Roy W., 683
Howe, Julia Ward, 585
Howells, William Dean, 534
Huerta, Victoriano, 563
Hughes, Charles Evans, 608-10, 649, 697
Hughes, Langston, *641*, 642-44
Hughes, Robert P., 557
Hull, Cordell, 667, 699, 706, 716
Hull House, 515
Human rights, 848
Humphrey, Hubert H., 738, 798, 816, 817, 847
Hungary, 719, 779, 889
Hunt, E. Howard, Jr., 840
Huntington, Collis, 444
Huntington, Collis P., 444, *470*
Hurley, Patrick J., 744, 745
Hurston, Zora Neale, 643
Hydrogen bomb, 765

I

Iceboxes, 448
Iceland, 704
Ickes, Harold L., 667, 674
Idaho, 419, 428
Idealism, German, 525
Ignorance, enforced, 529
Illiteracy, 527
Immigrants. *See also specific ethnic and racial groups*
    bossism and, 507
    "new," 505-6, 595, 892-93
    sources of (1900-1920), *499*
Immigration
    into cities, 499-506, *500-503*
    to the plains, 433-34
    race prejudice and, 506
    restrictions and quotas, 626, 630-31, 892
Immigration Reform and Control Act (1986), 893
Immigration Restriction Act (1921), 506, 630
Immigration Restriction League, 630
Impeachment of Nixon, mobilization for, 844-45
Imperialism, 546, 558-59, 564. *See also* Empire, American
Imperial Valley, California, 804
Inchon, Korea, 747
Income
    distribution of, in 1920s, 664
    guaranteed minimum, 833
Income tax, 492, 651, 713
    constitutionality of, 581
    Reagan cuts, 866
    Supreme Court decision on (1895), 488
Income Tax Act (1986), 875-76
Independents (Mugwumps), 471, 474, 478
Indian Affairs, Bureau of, 808
Indian Affairs, Office of, 806
Indian Bureau of the Department of the Interior, 421

MX intercontinental missiles, 867
Myers, Isaac, 459
My Lai massacre (1968), 796, 837
Myth, log cabin, 441

N

Nagasaki, 696, 723
Namibia, 848
Naples, capture of (1943), 716
Napoleon III of France, 546-47
Nasser, Gamal Abdel, 776, 777, 809
Nast, Thomas, 473, 479, 507, 508
Nation, Carry A., 577
National Association for the Advance-
    ment of Colored People (NAACP),
    597, 770, 772
National Association of Manufacturers,
    577
National Broadcasting Company (NBC),
    648
National Child Labor Committee, 576
National City Bank, 445
National Colored Labor Union, 459-60
National Commission on the Causes and
    Prevention of Violence, 795
National Consumers' League, 593
National debt during World War II, 713
National Farmers' Alliance, 484-85
National Farm Workers Association, 805
National Foundation of the Arts and Hu-
    manities, 799
National Grange, 628
National Guard, 669, 771, 816, 837
National Housing Act (1949), 740
National Industrial Recovery Act
    (NIRA), 668, 669
Nationalism (social theory), 523-24
Nationalist China, 744-45
Nationalist movements in 1950s, 773-76
National Labor Relations Board
    (NLRB), 684
National Labor Relation (Wagner) Act
    (1935), 683, 684, 688
National Labor Union, 458, 459
National League of Professional Baseball
    Clubs, 539-40
National Organization for Women
    (NOW), 855
National Origins Act (1924), 630
National Progressive Republic League,
    582
National Recovery Administration
    (NRA), 668-69
National security. See Security, search
    for
National Security Act (1947), 734, 846
National Security Council, 773
National unions, 458-59
National War Labor Board, 612
National Woman's Party, 587, 593
National Woman's Suffrage Association
    (NAWSA), 585, 587
National Youth Administration (NYA),
    674
Nation magazine, 595
Nation (newspaper), 556
Native Americans, Great Society and,
    806-8
Naturalism and naturalists, 535, 536
Navajo Indians, 420
Naval Advisory Board, 550

Naval War College, 550
Navy, U.S., 550
Nazis, 695, 696, 718, *719*, 732. *See also*
    Hitler, Adolf; World War II
Nebraska, 483
    range cattle industry in, 430
Neshoba County, Mississippi, 800
Neutrality, 606-7
    World War I and, 606-8
Neutrality Acts (1935), 700, 703, 705
Nevada, 419
    prospecting in, 428
Newark, New Jersey, riots in (1965),
    802
New Deal, 666-90, 736, 738, 768
    Agricultural Adjustment Administra-
        tion (AAA), 669-72, 685
    assessment of, 689-90
    bank crisis (1933) and, 667-68
    blacks and, 685-86
    Civilian Conservation Corps (CCC),
        674, 685
    climax of, 687-90
    critics and crusaders, 677-83
    departure from, 864-65
    farewell to, 874-76
    housing and labor standards in, 688
    money supply, experiments with, 668
    National Recovery Administration
        (NRA), 668-69
    Public Works Administration (PWA),
        674
    reforms of 1935, 683-84
    relief program, 672-76
    Roosevelt and, 666-76, 685-86
    Supreme Court on, 669, 671
    Tennessee Valley Authority (TVA),
        672
    Works Progress Administration
        (WPA), 674-76, 688
New Economic Policy, 833-34
New Freedom, 583-84
New Frontier, 766, 780, 782-86, 864
"New" immigrants, 505-6, 595
New Mexico, 419
New Nationalism, 571, 582
New Panama Canal Company, 561
New South, 409-15
Newspapers, city, 512-13
Newsweek magazine, 802
Newton, Isaac, 525
New York Central Railroad, 479
New York City
    growth of, 498, 499
    immigrants in, 504, 505-6
New York Customs House, 408
New York Herald-Tribune, 750
New York Journal, 513, 552
New York Stock Exchange, 448
    the crash (1929), 663, 664-66
New York Times, 458, 507, 513, 552,
    699, 808
New York Warehouse and Securities
    Company, 448
New York World, 552
New York World-Telegram, 669
New Zealand, 548, 776
Nez Percé, 424
Niagara movement, 596-97
Nicaragua, 698, 873, 886, 887-88
    Marines in, 563
    Reagan administration and, 698, 873,
        877, 878, 880, 887, 888

Nickelodeons, 645
Nigger Heaven (Van Vechten), 643
Nimitz, Chester, 722
Nine-Power Pact, 697
Nineteenth Amendment, 851
Nisei, 708
Nixon, Richard M., 778, 790, 831, 832-
    46, 847
    Checkers speech, 759
    on child-care centers, 856
    downfall of, 845
    economic game plan, 833-34
    election of 1952, 754, 759
    election of 1960, 780-81
    election of 1968, 816-17
    election of 1972, 825, 838-40
    HUAC and, 750, 751, 752
    in People's Republic of China, 745,
        834
    retreat from liberalism under, 832-33
    as vice president, 774, 779, 835
    Vietnam War and, 834-38
    Watergate and abuse of power by,
        840-46
Nixon administration, 864
Noble Order of the Knights of Labor,
    458
Non-Partisan League, 686
Noriega, Manuel Antonio, 886-87
"Normalcy" in government, 649, 650-56
Normandy invasion (1944), 716, 717-18,
    717
Norris, Frank, 535
Norris, George W., 612, 672
Norris-La Guardia Act (1932), 461, 656
North, Oliver L., 878
North, the
    black revolution in, 802
    civil rights movement in 1960s in, 784
    racism in, 404
North African front in World War II,
    713, 715-16
North Atlantic Treaty (1949), 743
North Atlantic Treaty Organization
    (NATO), 742, 743, 776, 777
North Carolina, Populists in, 413
Northern Pacific Railroad, 424, 444
Northern Securities Company, 445, 579
North Vietnam, bombing of, 812, 813,
    814, 837-38. *See also* Vietnam
    War
Notes, Federal Reserve, 584
Novels, dime, 537
Nuclear arms race, 765
Nuclear energy, 731
Nuclear missiles, ban on intermediate-
    range, 879
Nuclear testing treaty (1963), 787
Nuremberg trials (1945-1946), 732

O

Oberlin College, 531
Occupations, service and white-collar,
    499
Ochs, Adolph S., 513
O'Connor, Sandra Day, 876, 881
Octopus, The (Norris), 535
Office, mechanization of, 447
Offshore-leasing policies, 884
"Ohio gang," 649-50
Ohio Idea, 397